Costa Rica

written and researched by

Keith Drew and Jean McNeil

with additional contributions from

Steven Horak

www.roughguides.com

Falkirk Council
GM
Askews & Holts
917.286
£15.99

Contents

Adventure travel colour section following p.288

◀◀ Surfers at Santa Teresa ◀ Arenal Hanging Bridges

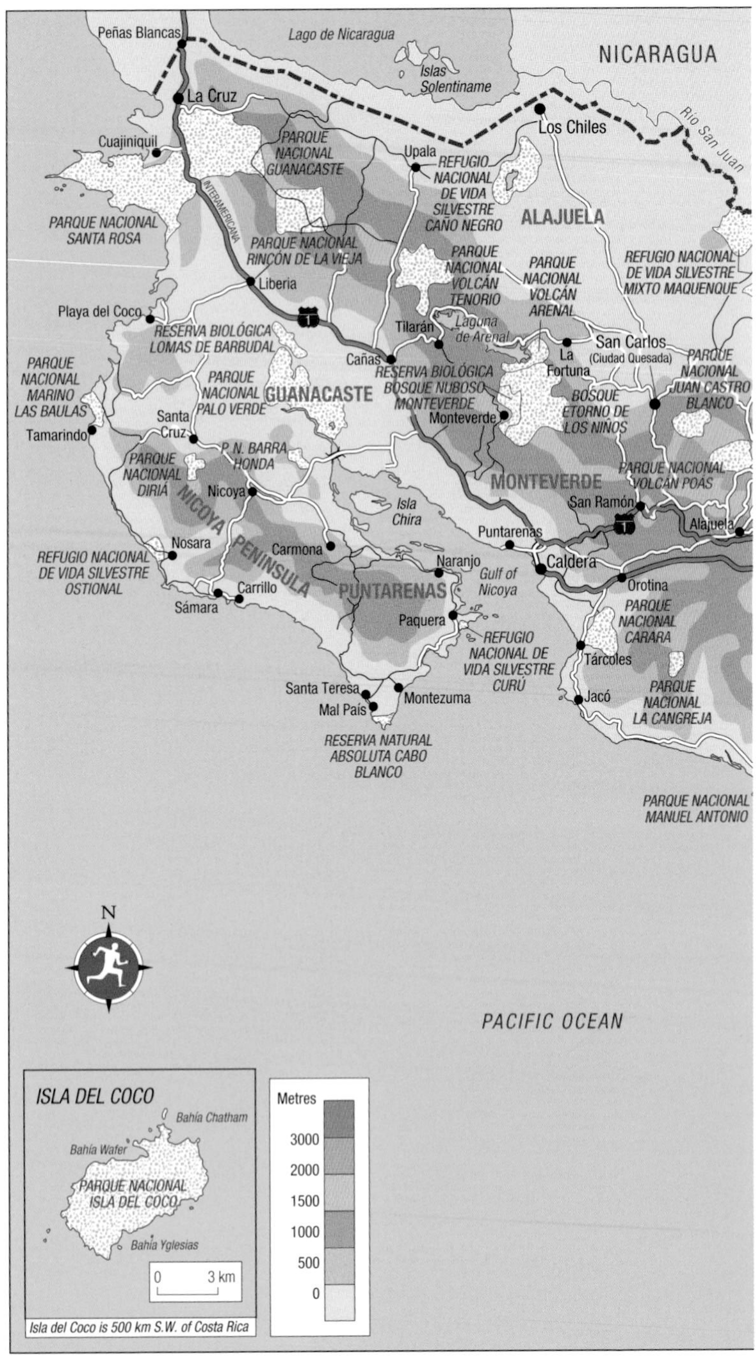

NICARAGUA
Lago de Nicaragua
Islas Solentiname
Peñas Blancas
La Cruz
Los Chiles
Río San Juan
Cuajiniquil
PARQUE NACIONAL GUANACASTE
Upala
REFUGIO NACIONAL DE VIDA SILVESTRE CAÑO NEGRO
ALAJUELA
PARQUE NACIONAL SANTA ROSA
INTERAMERICANA
PARQUE NACIONAL RINCÓN DE LA VIEJA
PARQUE NACIONAL VOLCÁN TENORIO
PARQUE NACIONAL VOLCÁN ARENAL
REFUGIO NACIONAL DE VIDA SILVESTRE MIXTO MAQUENQUE
Liberia
Playa del Coco
RESERVA BIOLÓGICA LOMAS DE BARBUDAL
Tilarán
Laguna de Arenal
San Carlos (Ciudad Quesada)
La Fortuna
PARQUE NACIONAL JUAN CASTRO BLANCO
Cañas
RESERVA BIOLÓGICA BOSQUE NUBOSO MONTEVERDE
PARQUE NACIONAL MARINO LAS BAULAS
PARQUE NACIONAL PALO VERDE
GUANACASTE
BOSQUE ETORNO DE LOS NIÑOS
Monteverde
Tamarindo
Santa Cruz
P. N. BARRA HONDA
PARQUE NACIONAL DIRIÁ
MONTEVERDE
PARQUE NACIONAL VOLCÁN POAS
Nicoya
NICOYA PENINSULA
Isla Chira
San Ramón
Alajuela
Puntarenas
Nosara
Carmona
Caldera
REFUGIO NACIONAL DE VIDA SILVESTRE OSTIONAL
Naranjo
Gulf of Nicoya
Orotina
Carrillo
Sámara
PUNTARENAS
Paquera
PARQUE NACIONAL CARARA
REFUGIO NACIONAL DE VIDA SILVESTRE CURÚ
Tárcoles
Santa Teresa
Mal País
Montezuma
Jacó
PARQUE NACIONAL LA CANGREJA
RESERVA NATURAL ABSOLUTA CABO BLANCO
PARQUE NACIONAL MANUEL ANTONIO
N
PACIFIC OCEAN
ISLA DEL COCO
Bahía Chatham
Bahía Wafer
PARQUE NACIONAL ISLA DEL COCO
Bahía Yglesias
0
3 km
Isla del Coco is 500 km S.W. of Costa Rica
Metres
3000
2000
1500
1000
500
0

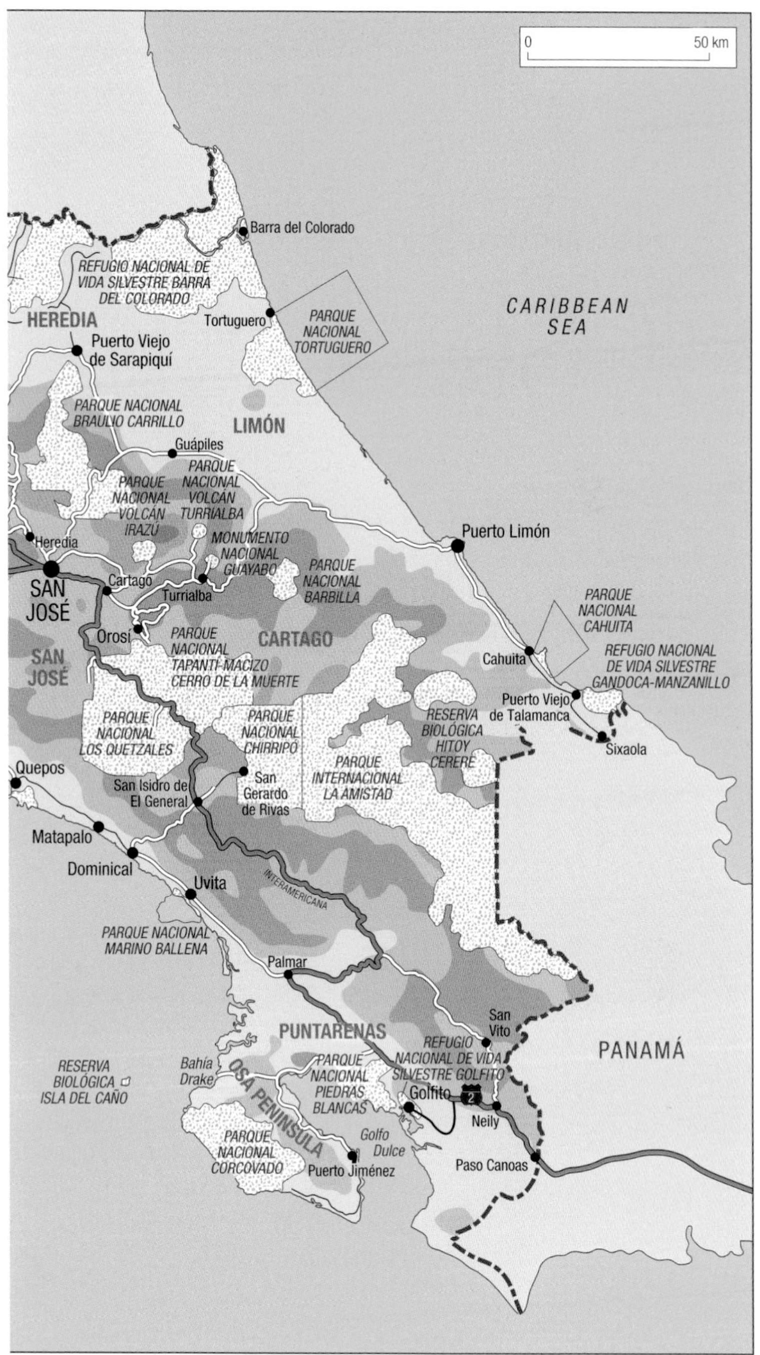

0
50 km
Barra del Colorado
REFUGIO NACIONAL DE VIDA SILVESTRE BARRA DEL COLORADO
HEREDIA
Tortuguero
PARQUE NACIONAL TORTUGUERO
CARIBBEAN SEA
Puerto Viejo de Sarapiquí
PARQUE NACIONAL BRAULIO CARRILLO
LIMÓN
Guápiles
PARQUE NACIONAL VOLCÁN TURRIALBA
PARQUE NACIONAL VOLCÁN IRAZÚ
Heredia
MONUMENTO NACIONAL GUAYABO
Puerto Limón
SAN JOSÉ
Cartago
Turrialba
PARQUE NACIONAL BARBILLA
PARQUE NACIONAL CAHUITA
Orosí
PARQUE NACIONAL TAPANTÍ-MACIZO CERRO DE LA MUERTE
CARTAGO
Cahuita
REFUGIO NACIONAL DE VIDA SILVESTRE GANDOCA-MANZANILLO
SAN JOSÉ
Puerto Viejo de Talamanca
RESERVA BIOLÓGICA HITOY CERERE
PARQUE NACIONAL LOS QUETZALES
PARQUE NACIONAL CHIRRIPÓ
Sixaola
PARQUE INTERNACIONAL LA AMISTAD
Quepos
San Isidro de El General
San Gerardo de Rivas
Matapalo
Dominical
Uvita
INTERAMERICANA
PARQUE NACIONAL MARINO BALLENA
Palmar
San Vito
PUNTARENAS
REFUGIO NACIONAL DE VIDA SILVESTRE GOLFITO
PANAMÁ
RESERVA BIOLÓGICA ISLA DEL CAÑO
Bahía Drake
OSA PENINSULA
PARQUE NACIONAL PIEDRAS BLANCAS
Golfito
2
Neily
PARQUE NACIONAL CORCOVADO
Golfo Dulce
Puerto Jiménez
Paso Canoas

Introduction to

Costa Rica

Hemmed in between the Pacific and Atlantic oceans near the narrowest point of the Central American isthmus, the tiny republic of Costa Rica is often pictured as an oasis of political stability in the midst of a turbulent region. This democratic and prosperous nation is also one of the most biodiverse areas on the planet, an ecological treasure-trove whose wide range of habitats – ranging from rainforests and beaches to volcanoes and mangrove swamps – support a fascinating variety of wildlife, much of it now protected by an enlightened national conservation system widely regarded as a model of its kind.

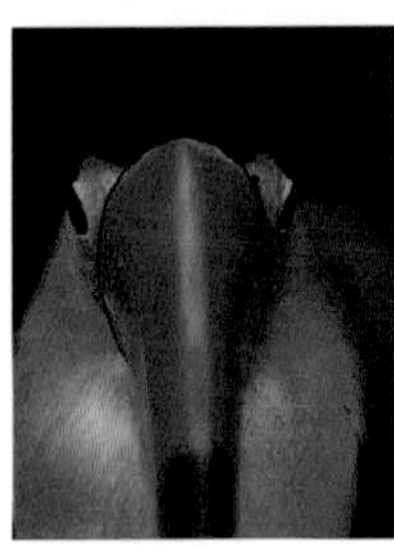

Though this idyllic image might not do justice to the full complexities of contemporary Costa Rican society, it's true that the country's long democratic tradition and complete absence of military forces (the army was abolished in 1948) stand in sharp contrast to the brutal internal conflicts that have ravaged its neighbours. This reputation for peacefulness has been an important factor in the spectacular growth of Costa Rica's tourist industry – some two million people visit the country annually, mainly from North America. Most of all, though, it's Costa Rica's outstanding natural beauty that has made it one of the world's prime **eco-tourism** destinations, with visitors flocking here to hike trails through ancient rainforest, climb active volcanoes or explore the Americas' last vestiges of high-altitude cloudforest, home to jaguar, tapir and resplendent quetzal.

▲ Xandari Resort & Spa

Admittedly, tourism has made Costa Rica less of an "authentic" experience than some travellers would like: some towns exist seemingly to provide visitors with a place to sleep and a tour to take, while previously remote spots are being bought up by foreign entrepreneurs. And as more hotels open, malls go up and visitors flock to resorts and national parks, there's no doubt that Costa Rica is experiencing a significant social change, while the darker side of outside involvement in the country – sex tourism, real-estate scams and conflicts between foreign property-owners and poorer locals – are all on the increase.

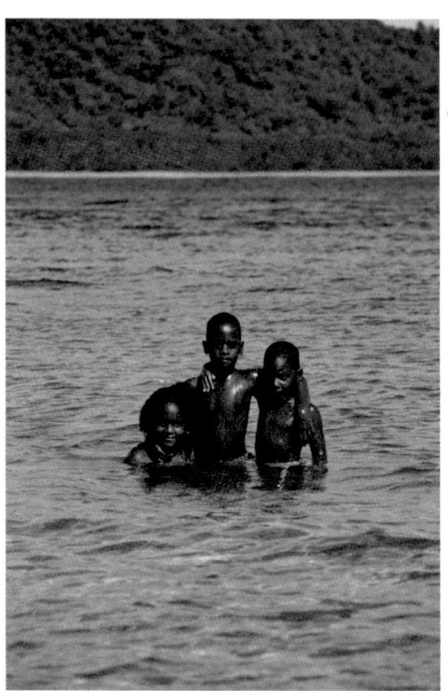

◀ Swimming on the Caribbean coast

Costa Rica's economy is the most diversified in Central America, and some argue that of all the regional nations, it has the least to gain from the Central American Free Trade Agreement (CAFTA), which it finally officially entered into in January 2009 – an

Fact file

• The Republic of Costa Rica lies on the Central American isthmus between the Atlantic and Pacific oceans, consisting of a mountainous backbone – rising to 3819m at the summit of Cerro Chirripó, its highest point – flanked by low-lying coastal strips. Though set in one of the most **geologically active** regions on Earth, Costa Rica has suffered less from **earthquakes** and **volcanic** eruptions than its northern neighbours – the worst incident in modern times was the earthquake that struck near Cartago in April 1910, killing 1750 people.

• The country's **population** is largely of Spanish extraction, though there's a substantial community of English-speaking Costa Ricans of African origin around the Caribbean coast, along with 65,000 or so indigenous peoples. Costa Rica is a young country: out of its population of 4.5 million, more than a quarter are aged under 15; men currently enjoy a life expectancy of 77, women of 81.

• Costa Rica's main **exports** are **coffee** and **bananas**, though in recent years income from these products has been overtaken by that from **tourism**. The country's recent prosperity has also been partly funded by massive borrowing – per capita, Costa Rica's levels of debt are among the highest in the world. Despite widespread poverty (around 21 percent of the population), the free and compulsory primary education system means that the country boasts a **literacy** rate of 95 percent, the best in Central America.

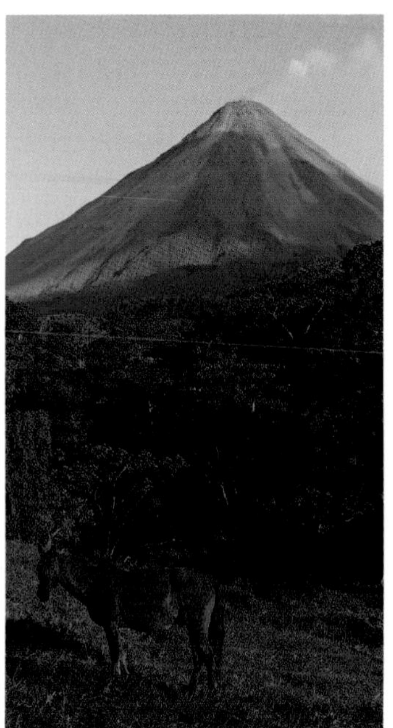

◀ Volcán Arenal

important step in its economic history, and in particular the history of its relationship with the US. Regional integration may mean prosperity, or job losses – only time will tell.

In any case, revenue from tourism is one of the reasons Costa Ricans – or Ticos, as they are generally known – now enjoy the highest rate of literacy, health care, education and life expectancy in the isthmus. That said, Costa Rica is certainly not the middle-class country that it's often portrayed to be – a significant percentage of people still live below the poverty line – and while it is modernizing fast, its character continues to be rooted in distinct local cultures, from the Afro-Caribbean province of Limón, with its Creole cuisine, games and patois, to the traditional *ladino* values embodied by the *sabanero* (cowboy) of Guanacaste. Above all, the country still has the highest rural population density in Latin America, and society continues to revolve around the twin axes of countryside and family: wherever you go, you're sure to be left with mental snapshots of rural life, whether it be horsemen trotting by on dirt roads, coffee-plantation day-labourers setting off to work in the dawn mists of the Highlands or avocado-pickers cycling home at sunset.

Where to go

Though everyone passes through it, hardly anyone falls in love with **San José**, Costa Rica's underrated capital. Often dismissed as an ugly urban sprawl, the city enjoys a dramatic setting amid jagged mountain peaks, plus some excellent cafés and restaurants, leafy parks, a lively university district and a good arts scene. The surrounding **Valle Central**, the country's agricultural heartland and coffee-growing region, is home to several of its finest volcanoes, including the steaming crater of Volcán Poás and the largely dormant Volcán Irazú, a strange lunar landscape high above the regional capital of Cartago.

While nowhere in the country is further than nine hours' drive from San José, the far north and the far south are less visited than other regions. The broad alluvial plains of the **Zona Norte** feature active Volcán Arenal, which spouts and spews within sight of the friendly tourist hangout of La Fortuna, and the wildlife-rich jungles of the Sarapiquí region, its dense rainforest harbouring monkeys, poison-dart frogs and countless species of bird, including the endangered great green

▲ Basilica de Nuestra Señora de Los Angeles, Cartago

macaw. Up by the border with Nicaragua, the seasonal wetlands of the Refugio Nacional de Vida Silvestre Caño Negro provide a haven for water birds, along with gangs of basking caiman.

Off-the-beaten-path travellers and serious hikers will be happiest in the rugged **Zona Sur**, home to Cerro Chirripó, the highest point in the country, and, further south on the outstretched feeler of the Osa Peninsula, Parque Nacional Corcovado, which protects the last significant area of tropical wet forest on the Pacific coast of the isthmus; Corcovado is probably the best

Biodiversity under protection

Despite its small size, Costa Rica possesses no less than five percent of the world's total **biodiversity**, in part due to its position as a transition zone between temperate North and tropical South America, and also thanks to its complex system of interlocking **micro-climates**, created by differences in topography and altitude. This biological abundance (which includes over 885 species of birds and a quarter of the world's known butterflies) is now safeguarded by one of the world's most enlightened and dedicated conservation programmes – about 25 percent of Costa Rica's land is protected, most of it through the country's extensive system of national parks and wildlife refuges.

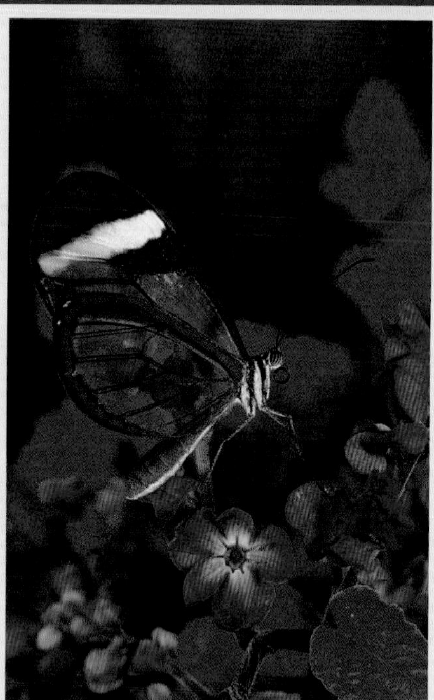

▲ Clearwing butterfly

Costa Rica's **national parks** range from the tropical jungle lowlands of Corcovado to the grassy volcanic uplands of Rincón de la Vieja, an impressive and varied range of terrain that has enhanced the country's popularity with eco-tourists. Outside the park system, however, land is assailed by **deforestation** – ironically, there are now no more significant patches of forest left anywhere in the country outside of protected areas.

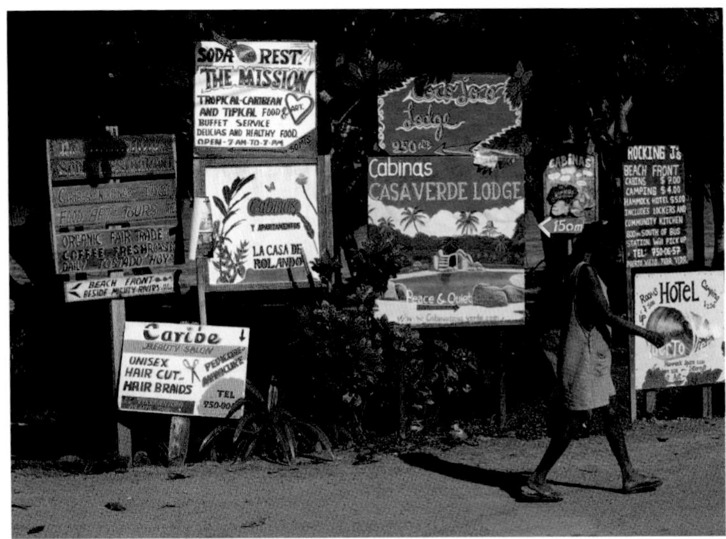

▲ Puerto Viejo de Talamanca

destination in the country for walkers – and also one of the few places where you have a fighting chance of seeing some of the more exotic wildlife for which Costa Rica is famed.

In the northwest, the cattle-ranching province of **Guanacaste** is often called "the home of Costa Rican folklore", and *sabanero* culture dominates here, with exuberant ragtag rodeos and large cattle haciendas occupying the hot, baked landscape that surrounds the attractive regional capital of Liberia. The province's beaches are some of the best – and, in parts, most developed – in the country, with Sámara and Nosara, on the Nicoya Peninsula, providing picture-postcard scenery without the crowds.

Limón Province, on the Caribbean coast, is the polar opposite to traditional *ladino* Guanacaste. It's home to the descendants of the Afro-Caribbeans who came to Costa Rica at the end of the nineteenth century to work on the San José–Limón railroad – their language (Creole English), Protestantism and the West Indian traditions remain relatively intact to this day. The reason most visitors venture here, however, is for Parque Nacional Tortuguero, and the three species of marine turtles that lay their eggs on its beaches each year.

Close to the **Pacific coast**, Monteverde has become the country's number-one tourist attraction, pulling in the visitors who flock here to walk through some of the most famous cloudforest in the Americas. Further down the coast is popular Parque Nacional Manuel Antonio, with its sublime ocean setting and tempting beaches, plus the equally pretty but more surf-oriented sands of Montezuma and Santa Teresa/Mal País, on the southern Nicoya Peninsula.

◀ White-faced Capuchin monkeys, Parque Nacional at Manuel Antionio

When to go

Although Costa Rica lies between eight and eleven degrees north of the equator, temperatures, governed by the vastly varying altitudes, are by no means universally high, and can plummet to below freezing at higher altitudes. Local microclimates predominate (see p.81 for a temperature and rainfall chart) and make weather unpredictable, though to an extent you can depend upon the **two-season rule**. In the dry season (roughly mid-Nov to April), most areas are just that: dry all day, with occasional blustery northern winds blowing in during January or February and cooling things off; otherwise you can depend on sunshine and warm temperatures. In the wet season (roughly May to mid-Nov), you'll have afternoon rains and sunny mornings. The rains are heaviest in September and October and, although they can be fierce, will impede you from travelling only in the more remote areas of the country – the Nicoya Peninsula especially – where dirt roads become impassable to all but the sturdiest 4WDs.

In recent years, Costa Rica has been booked solid during the peak season, the North American winter months, when bargains are few and far between. The crowds peter out after Easter, but return again to an extent in June and July. Travellers who prefer to play it by ear are much better off coming during the low or rainy season (euphemistically called the "green season"), when many hotels offer discounts. The months of November, April (after Easter) and May are the best times to visit, when the rains have either just started or just died off, and the country is refreshed, green and relatively untouristy.

things not to miss

It's not possible to see everything that Costa Rica has to offer in one trip – and we don't suggest you try. What follows is a selective and subjective taste of the country's highlights: outstanding national parks, spectacular wildlife, gorgeous beaches and thrilling outdoor activities. They're arranged in five colour-coded categories, so you can browse through to find the very best things to see, do, buy and experience. All highlights have a page reference to take you straight into the guide, where you can find out more.

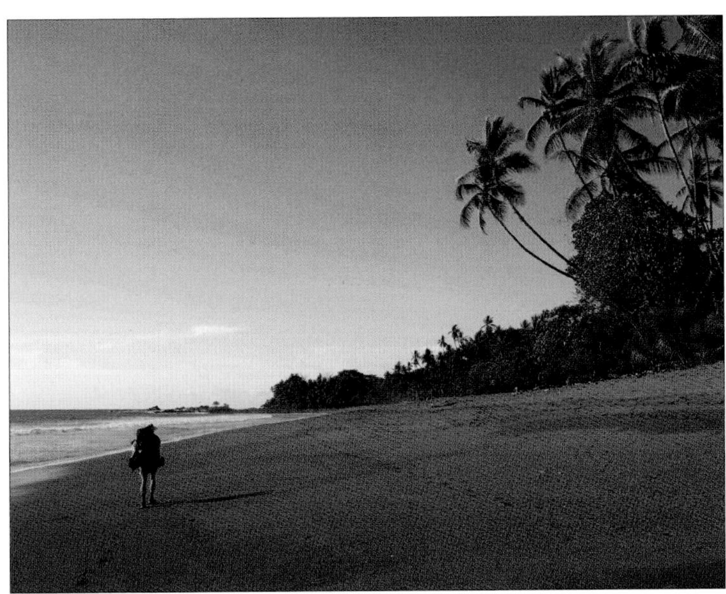

01 Trekking in Parque Nacional Corcovado Page **408** • This biologically rich coastal rainforest is one of Costa Rica's finest destinations for walking and wildlife-spotting.

02 Parque Nacional Santa Rosa Page **277** • This gorgeous park protects a rare stretch of dry tropical rainforest.

03 Turtle-watching Pages **187**, **290** & **309** • View some of the thousands of turtles – leatherbacks, hawksbill, olive ridleys and greens – that come ashore to lay their eggs each year, and, if you're lucky, glimpse the babies hatch and return to the sea.

04 Volcán Arenal Page **227** • One of the Western Hemisphere's most active volcanoes, Arenal's upper slopes are periodically doused in flows of red-hot lava.

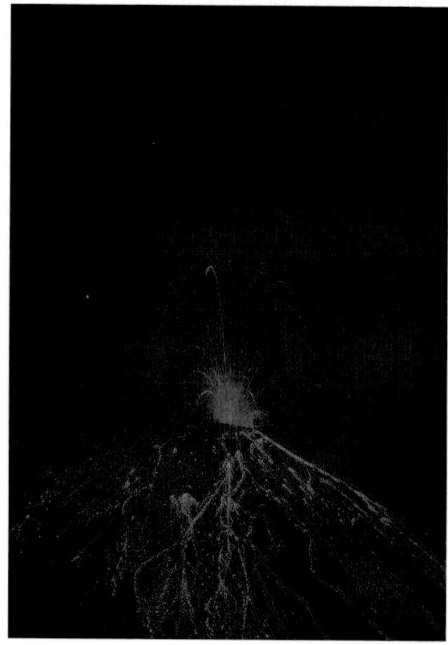

05 Reserva Rara Avis Page **247** • Costa Rica's premier eco-tourism destination flourishes with primitive ferns and has more kinds of plants, birds and butterflies than in all Europe.

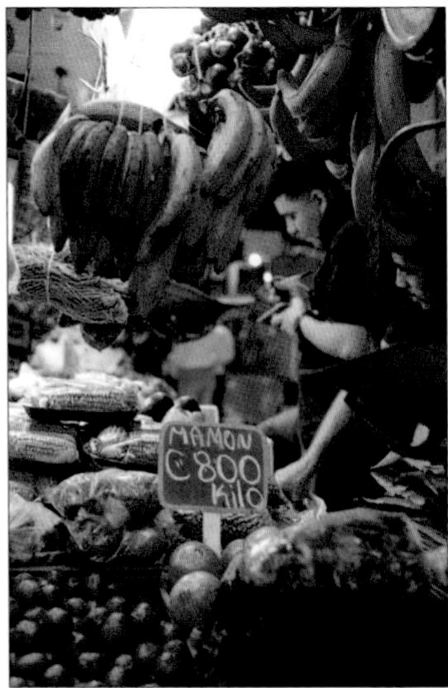

06 Fruit Pages **44** & **468** • Costa Rica's tropical fruit ranges from the ubiquitous banana, papaya and mango to the custard fruit *anona* and the spiny but sweet *mamones chinos*.

07 Museo de Oro Precolombino Page **100** • One of the country's best museums, with a dazzling display that features over two thousand pre-Columbian gold pieces.

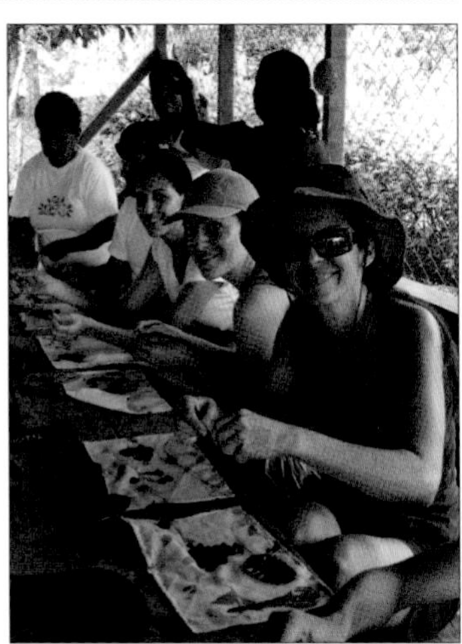

08 Community tourism Pages **234**, **336** & **205** • Learn how the Maleku use medicinal plants, shop for crafts at a women's cooperative in the Gulf of Nicoya, or take a walking tour with the Bribrí – just some of the ways of gaining a better insight into Costa Rica's remaining indigenous communities.

09 **Refugio Nacional de Vida Silvestre Caño Negro** Page **240** • Crammed with caiman and home to hundreds of species of birds, this isolated reserve near the Nicaraguan border is one of the most important wetlands in the world.

10 **Fishing** Page **68** • Anglers battle big fish in Costa Rica's coastal waters, teeming with swordfish, marlin, tarpon and snook.

11 **Volunteering** Page **71** • Give something back by working on an organic farm, counting jaguar populations or helping to regenerate cloudforest.

12 Teatro Nacional, San José Page **100** • Central America's grandest theatre, built in imitation of the Paris Opéra with money raised by a tax on coffee.

13 Parque Nacional Manuel Antonio Page **371** • This perennially popular park boasts white-sand beaches, tropical forests full of sloths and monkeys, and stunning coastal scenery peppered with striking rock formations.

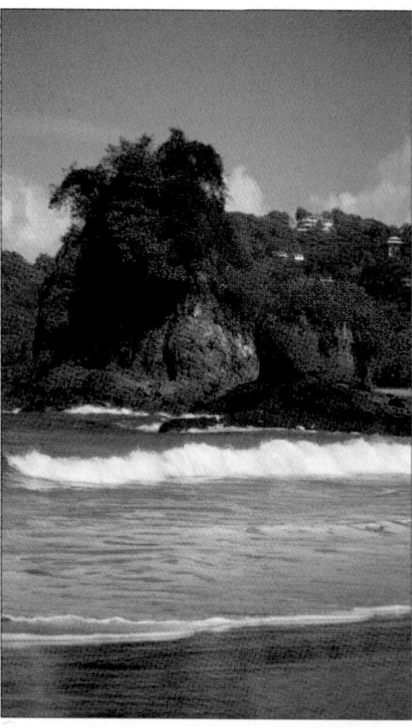

14 Stay at an eco-lodge Page **49** • From rustic simplicity to luxury in the jungle, Costa Rica has some of the best eco-lodges in the Americas, all offering a variety of ways to further immerse yourself in the natural world.

15 Birdwatching Page **68** • Costa Rica is the natural habitat of the most colourful birds in the Americas, including hummingbirds, scarlet macaws, toucans and the resplendent quetzal.

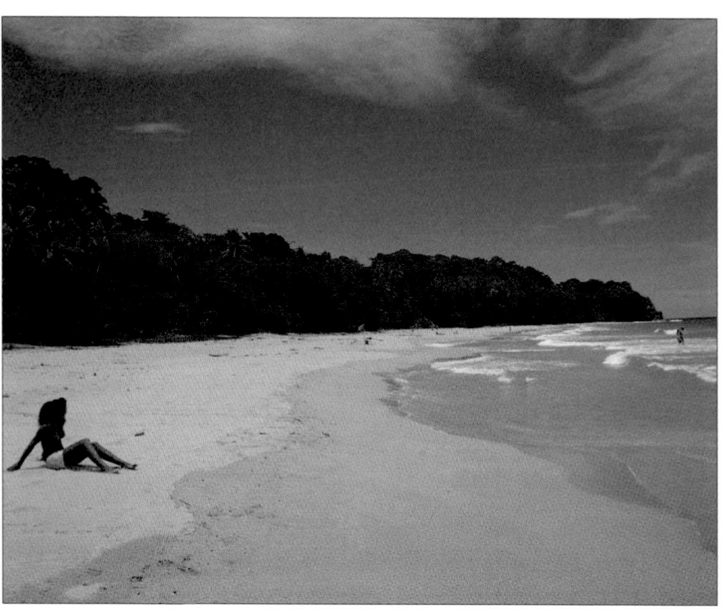

16 Playa Cocles Page **206** • One of the most appealing beaches on the entire Caribbean coast, with pristine tropical scenery, a soothing atmosphere and excellent accommodation.

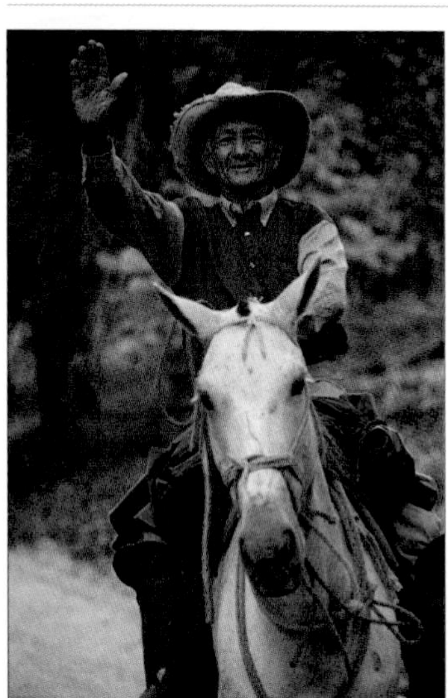

17 Cowboys Page **259** • Guanacaste is home to Costa Rica's cowboys, or *sabaneros* – iconic figures whose ranching skills and bullfighting prowess have become part of national legend.

18 White-water rafting Page **63** • White-water rafting is one of Costa Rica's most popular outdoor activities, with a range of rivers to suit all abilities.

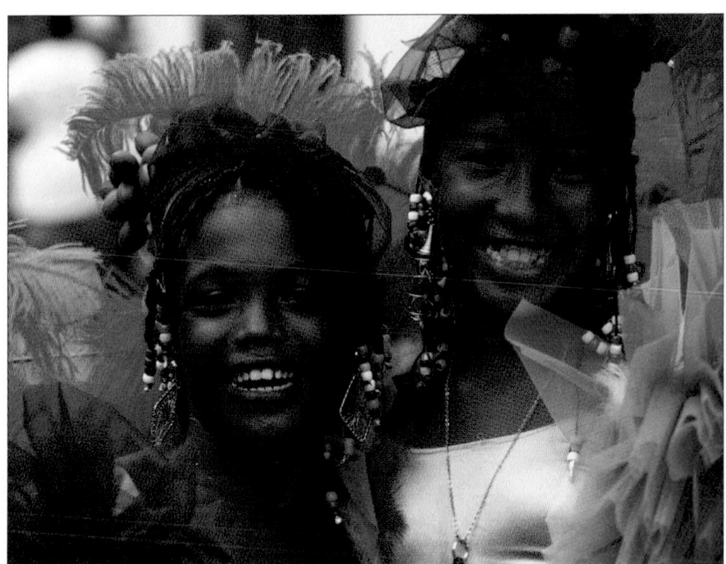

19 El Día de la Raza, Puerto Limón Page **178** • Young bloods and grandparents alike take to the streets during Costa Rica's raciest carnival.

20 Reserva Biológica Bosque Nuboso Monteverde Page **328** • Experience the bird's-eye view – and a touch of vertigo – from a suspended bridge in the lush Monteverde cloudforest.

21 Volcán Poás Page **140** • Poás is one of the world's more easily accessible active volcanoes, with a history of eruptions that goes back eleven million years.

22 Surfing Page **65** • With nearly 1300km of palm-fringed coastline, and a variety of beach breaks, reef breaks, long lefts and river mouths, Costa Rica has a wave for just about every surfer out there.

23 Coffee Page **52** • Sample a cup of Costa Rica's most famous export, and the foundation of the country's prosperity.

24 Parque Nacional Rincón de la Vieja Page **273** • Clouds of sulphurous smoke and steaming mudpots dot the desiccated slopes of Rincón de la Vieja volcano, one of the country's more thermally active areas.

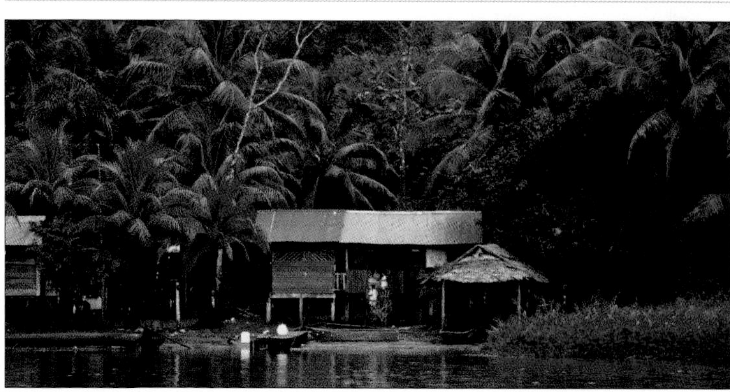

25 Exploring the Tortuguero Canal Page **182** • Ride the boat north from Puerto Limón along the Tortuguero Canal, past luxuriant vegetation and colourful wooden houses on stilts.

The wildlife of Costa Rica

This field guide helps you identify some of the more common and distinctive mammals, reptiles, amphibians and birds that you might spot in Costa Rica, together with their Spanish names. Photos show easily identified markings and features, while notes give clear pointers about the most likely kinds of habitat to see each species, their distribution and behaviour, and tips on spotting them. The abbreviations used below are PN Parque Nacional; RNA Reserva Natural Absoluta; EB Estación Biológica; RBBN Reserva Biológica Bosque Nuboso; RB Reserva Biológica; and RNdVS Refugio Nacional de Vida Silvestre. For further details on the country's wildlife, see p.438.

Mantled Howler Monkey

Alouatta palliata (Mono Congo or Mono Aullador)

❀ Primary and secondary wet and dry forest, up to 2500m, on both Pacific and Caribbean slope; most common species of monkey in Costa Rica; particularly PN Tortuguero.

Named for blond mantle on its neck; lives in troupes of around 10 to 15 (sometimes up to 45), led by a dominant male; endangered; eats flowers, fruit (figs are a favourite) and, uniquely for New World monkeys, leaves.

✓ Least active of Costa Rica's monkeys, covering less than 1km of ground a day; usually seen in upper canopy; easily located thanks to male's loud, rasping call, which can be heard several kilometres away.

Central American Spider Monkey

Ateles geoffroyi (Mono Colorado or Mono Araña)

❀ Dense primary wet and dry forest, up to 2800m, on both Pacific and Caribbean slope; endangered; particularly PN Guanacaste, PN Santa Rosa, PN Tortuguero, PN Santa Elena.

Ranges in troupes of up to 40, which separate during the day into smaller "communities"; agile, with very strong prehensile tail; eats fruit.

✓ Prefers mature, undisturbed forest; often seen using long arms to swing, gibbon-like, through upper canopy; wary of humans as traditionally hunted for meat (it's allegedly the region's best-tasting primate).

❀ HABITAT AND DISTRIBUTION   BEHAVIOUR   ✓ SIGHTING TIPS

White-Faced Capuchin Monkey

Cebus capucinus (Mono Carablanco)

❀ Primary and secondary wet and dry forest and mangroves, up to 3000m, on both Pacific and Caribbean slope; particularly PN Manuel Antonio and RNA Cabo Blanco.

Moves through canopy in troupes of up to 30; mainly eats fruit and insects, though males can be aggressively carnivorous; has developed ability to use tools.

✓ Despite name, has a pinkish face (fur surrounding this is white); in some areas is extremely habituated to humans and will even steal food from backpacks.

Central American Squirrel Monkey

Saimiri oerstedii (Mono Tití)

❀ Mostly secondary wet forest, up to 300m, in few pockets of southwest Pacific slope; endangered (less than 3000 individuals); particularly PN Manuel Antonio and PN Corcovado.

Ranges in large troupes (up to 70 individuals); hyperactive, due to high sugar content in diet.

✓ At 30cm is smallest of CR's monkeys; although uncommon, is easy to spot due to high-pitched chattering; subspecies found south of Río Grande de Térraba (ie PN Corcovado) is more colourful.

Hoffmann's Two-Toed Sloth

Choloepus hoffmanni (Perezoso de Dos Dedos)

❀ Common in primary and secondary wet forest, up to 3300m, on both Pacific and Caribbean slope, though prefers disturbed growth; particularly PN Tortuguero, RBBN Monteverde and EB La Selva.

Slow metabolism; can sleep for up to 20 hours a day, though more mobile than three-toed cousin; arboreal, save for weekly journey down to ground to defecate.

✓ Mostly nocturnal; common but difficult to spot – scan mid and upper branches of cecropia and guarumo trees, especially V-shaped intersections between branches.

Brown-Throated Three-Toed Sloth

Bradypus variegatus (Perezoso de Tres Dedos)

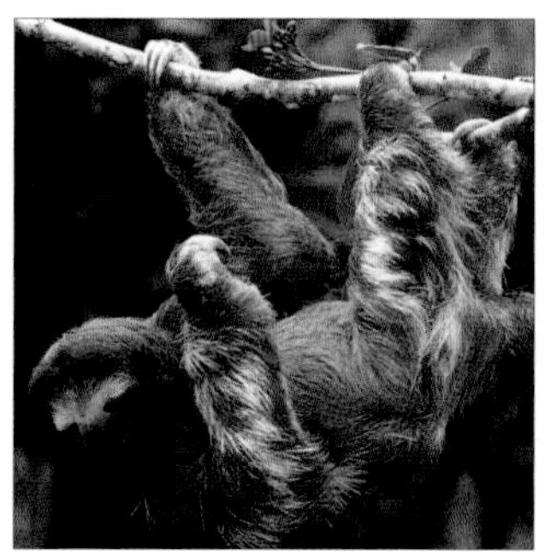

❀ Common in primary and secondary forest, up to 2400m, on both Pacific and Caribbean slope; prefers disturbed growth; particularly PN Manuel Antonio, PN Corcovado, PN Cahuita and PN Tortuguero.

Diurnal and nocturnal; arboreal, but descends on a weekly basis to defecate at ground level, where it can lose up to a third of its body weight.

✓ Apart from hands (both species have three toes on feet), is also differentiated from two-toed sloth by: greyer, wiry hair, with brown stripe on back; black eye masks; stubby tail (two-toed is tail-less).

❀ HABITAT AND DISTRIBUTION BEHAVIOUR ✓ SIGHTING TIPS

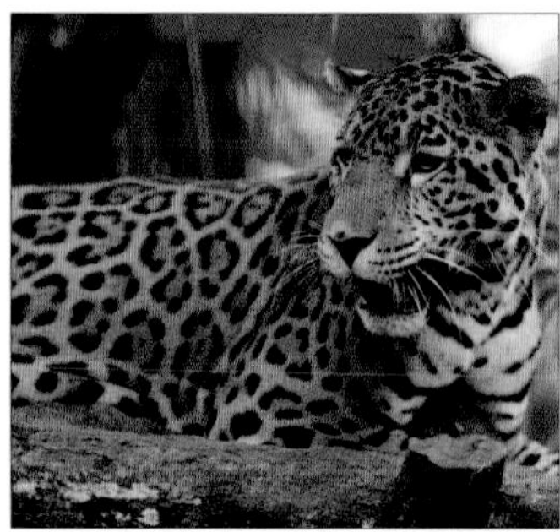

Jaguar

Felis onca (Tigre)

Range of habitats up to 3500m, though mostly primary lowland forest of biggest national parks and reserves; very rare.

Largest of CR's cats; diurnal and nocturnal; territorial, requiring up to 40,000 hectares of home range; will take whatever prey is most abundant, from sloths to turtles.

✓ May see tracks (jaguar's toe prints are rounder than puma's) on trails and beaches (during turtle-nesting season), though deep-forest hiking in PN Corcovado offers only real chance of sighting.

Ocelot

Felis pardadis (Manigordo)

Primary and secondary forest and open country, up to 3000m, on both Pacific and Caribbean slope; uncommon and rarely spotted, though sightings include PN Tortuguero and RB Tirimbina.

Mostly nocturnal, spending up to twelve hours roaming for a variety of prey, particularly rodents; threatened due to slow reproductive cycle.

✓ Closer roseate pattern helps distinguish it from smaller margay; forepaw print wider than hind paw, hence Spanish name ("Fat Hand").

Kinkajou

Potos flavus (Martilla)

Common in primary and secondary forests, up to 2200m, on both Pacific and Caribbean slope; particularly RBBN Monteverde and EB La Selva.

Mostly nocturnal; uses long, narrow tongue to eat fruit, nectar and insects; makes dens in hollow trees.

✓ Ranges in colour from russet orange to grey-brown depending on elevation; often seen hanging from branches by prehensile tail; eyes reflect orange in torch beam; slightly bigger than similar-looking olingo, which is absent from Pacific slope.

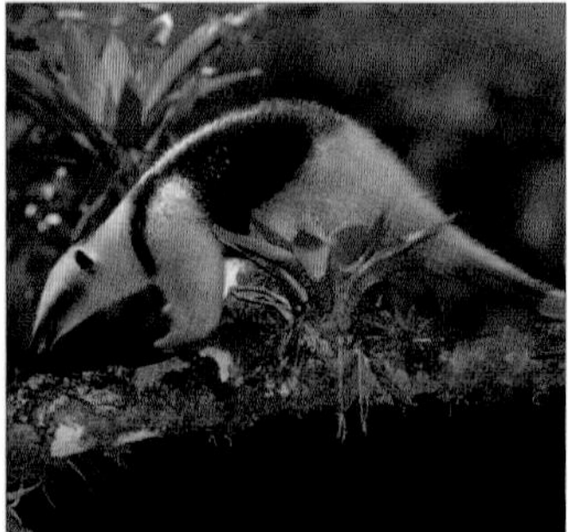

Northern Tamandua or Collared Anteater

Tamandua mexicana (Osa Hormiguero)

Primary and secondary forests and open country, up to 1500m; uncommon; particularly PN Rincón de la Vieja and Reserva Rara Avis.

Diurnal and nocturnal; terrestrial and arboreal; solitary; has no teeth, instead using sticky tongue to extract ants and termites from mounds; tail is as long as body.

✓ Leaves interlocking paw tracks; look for large gashes in ant and termite mounds – smaller scuffs are usually the work of other animals.

White-Nosed Coati

Nasua narica (Pizote)

Very common, in all habitats, up to 3500m, on both Pacific and Caribbean slope.

Diurnal; terrestrial and arboreal; omnivorous; has long muzzle and ringed tail, usually held vertically; travels in bands of up to 25.

✓ Habituation to humans and comparative abundance makes it easy to spot; sometimes seen in roadside bands (females only; males are solitary) or scavenging in national park car parks.

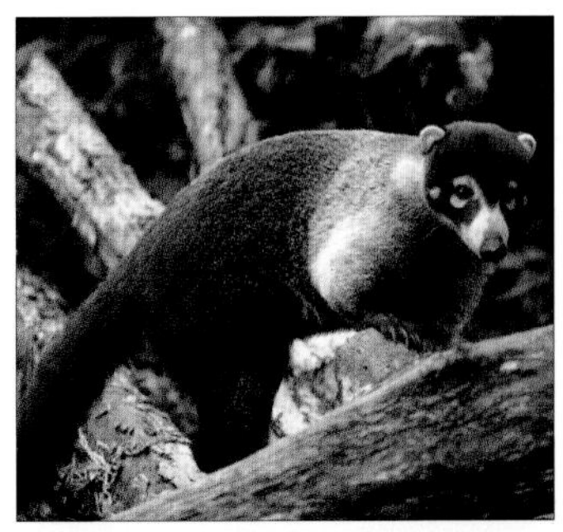

Central American Agouti

Dasyprocta punctata (Gautusa)

Common in primary and secondary forest, up to 2400m, on both Pacific and Caribbean slope; particularly PN Manuel Antonio and PN Carara.

Diurnal; terrestrial; monogamous pairs share territory, but spend most of their time alone; makes dens in hollow trees or log piles.

✓ Often seen on trails, or foraging on forest floor; will follow troupes of white-faced capuchin and spider monkeys, feeding on fallen tidbits.

Collared Peccary

Tayassu tajacu (Saíno)

Common in primary and dense secondary wet and dry forest, up to 3000m, on both Pacific and Caribbean slope; particularly PN Corcovado, PN Santa Rosa, PN Palo Verde and PN Braulio Carrillo.

Diurnal and nocturnal; travels in herds of up to 30; clacks teeth when aggravated; much less aggressive than the rarer white-lipped peccary.

✓ Mostly seen by water; herds leave conspicuous trail through undergrowth; Brazil-nut-shaped track (white-lipped peccary's resembles teardrop).

Baird's Tapir

Tapirus bairdii (Danta)

Dense primary forest and undisturbed open country, up to 4000m, on both Pacific and Caribbean slope; now restricted to protected areas.

Diurnal and nocturnal; terrestrial; solitary; adults have smooth reddish-brown fur, young have white streaks; eats mostly leaves and stems.

✓ Largest of CR's mammals, up to 2m long and weighing up to 250kg; country's only odd-toed ungulate; essentially restricted to PN Corcovado, though occasional sightings at Reserva Rara Avis – look in muddy areas around water.

HABITAT AND DISTRIBUTION  BEHAVIOUR ✓ SIGHTING TIPS

Leatherback Turtle
Dermochelys coriacea (Tortuga Baula)

Green Turtle
Chelonia mydas (Tortuga Verde)

Hawksbill Turtle
Caretta caretta (Tortuga Carey)

❀ Deep (leatherback, olive ridley) and shallow (all) ocean, and shallow bays, estuaries and lagoons.

Olive ridley is smallest of CR's sea turtles (70cm), leatherback is largest (180cm); leatherback, hawksbill and olive ridley are endangered; only come ashore to nest, laying eggs on same beach as they were born.

✓ Leatherback: soft, dark-grey ridged carapace; nests March–May at PN Tortuguero and RNdVS Gandoca-Manzanillo, Oct–Feb at PN Marino Las Baulas.

Green: dark-green to brown, heart-shaped shell; closer mosaic patterns on flippers than hawksbill; nests July–Oct, Atlantic green at PN Tortuguero, Pacific green at PN Santa Rosa and PN Manuel Antonio.

Hawksbill: heart-shaped shell has mottled tortoise-shell patterns; distinctive hooked "beak"; nests July–Oct at PN Tortuguero, PN Santa Rosa and PN Marino Ballena.

Olive ridley: olive, heart-shaped shell; Pacific coast only, nests July–Nov at PN Santa Rosa, PN Marino Ballena, RNdVS Ostional and Playa Hermosa.

Olive Ridley Turtle
Lepidocheylis olivacea (Tortuga lora)

American Crocodile
Crocodylus acutus (Cocodrilo)

❀ Lowland rivers, lagoons and estuaries, on both Pacific and Caribbean slope; particularly PN Carara, RNdVS Mixto Maquenque and RNdVS Gandoca-Manzanillo.

Unable to control body temperature, so often open-mouthed in attempt to cool down; males can grow up to 7m.

✓ Usually seen on riverbanks or in muddy shallows; longer, more pointed snout than caiman, with two projecting teeth, one on either side of lower jaw, which caiman lack.

Spectacled Caiman
Caiman crocodilus (Caimán or Guajipal)

❀ Lowland rivers, swamps and wetlands, on both Pacific and Caribbean slope; common locally; particularly PN Palo Verde and RNdVS Caño Negro.

Named for bony ridge in front of eyes; will eat other young caiman; parents guard nest made of twigs.

✓ Smaller and lighter in colour (tan or brown) than "flatter"-looking crocodile; in dry season, large numbers gather in diminishing pools of water with only eyes and snout visible.

Green Iguana

Iguana iguana (Iguana Verde)

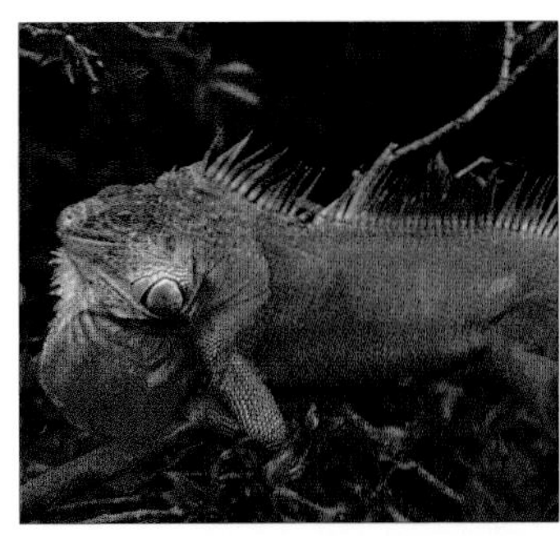

❀ Common in wet forest, rivers and wetlands, on both Pacific and Caribbean slope, up to 500m.

Largest lizard in Costa Rica, growing up to 2m; diurnal; mostly arboreal; often forms social groups; predominantly vegetarian; yellow or orange head indicates breeding male.

✓ Basks on high branches over water; distinguished from spiny-tailed iguana by comb-like yellow crest along spine, a large, circular scale below ear, and its hanging dewlap (throat sac).

Spiny-Tailed Iguana

Ctenosaura similis (Iguana Negra)

❀ Very common in wet and dry forest, along coastal plains and on beaches on Pacific slope, up to 750m.

More terrestrial than green iguana; extremely territorial; omnivorous; can tolerate high temperatures.

✓ Often seen in or by road, or at back of beaches; basks on logs on forest floor or in high branches; told apart from green iguana by bluish-grey colour, bands of spiny scales encircling tail, and black stripes extending to dorsal crest.

Emerald Basilisk Lizard

Basiliscus plumifrons (Basilisca Verde)

❀ Common around rivers, streams, lagoons and in wetlands, up to 775m, on Caribbean slope and southern Pacific; particularly PN Palo Verde and RNdVS Caño Negro.

Male has three crests along back, female has two; ability to "walk" on water (for up to 4.5m) earns it moniker of "Jesus Christ lizard".

✓ Regularly seen in damp leaf litter and on low-hanging branches; more colouful than brown (Pacific slope) and striped (Caribbean slope) basilisks.

Fer-de-Lance

Bothrops asper (Terciopelo)

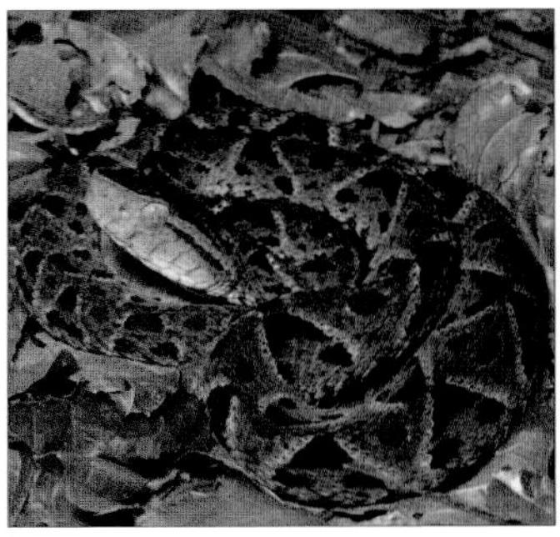

❀ Common and abundant in wet forest and agricultural areas, up to 1200m, of Caribbean slope and parts of Pacific (absent from Guanacaste's dry forest and Nicoya Peninsula).

Terrestrial, though juveniles also arboreal; scales sheen-like (hence Spanish name, meaning "velvet"); extremely dangerous (venom can kill within 2hr).

✓ Triangular head, with dark stripe running from behind eye; brown body marked with cream chevrons and dark triangles resembling "X"s (sometimes an hourglass); lurks in dense vegetation during day.

Central American Bushmaster

Lachesis stenophrys (Matabuey)

Not uncommon in primary wet forest, up to 1000m on Caribbean slope (black-headed bushmaster endemic to Osa Peninsula).

CR's largest venomous snake, growing over 3.5m; terrestrial; extremely dangerous, packing a highly potent bite (hence Spanish name, meaning "bull killer").

✓ Thick, triangular head, with broad, dark stripe behind eye; tan or reddish-brown, with dark triangles running down from ridge along back; shy, but when seen is often around base of large tree or fallen logs.

Red-Eyed Tree Frog

Agalychnis callidryas (Rana Calzonuda)

Very common and abundant in wet forest, swamps and small pools, up to 1000m, on both Pacific and Caribbean slope (absent from Guanacaste dry forest).

Nocturnal; arboreal; sticky pads on webbed orange feet help cling to leaf surface; male much smaller than female.

✓ Spotted on leaves around water; very active during wet season; breeding males call (a short chuck or chuck-chuck) on humid nights; on Caribbean variety, flanks and upper arms and legs are purple-blue, on Pacific variety are russet brown.

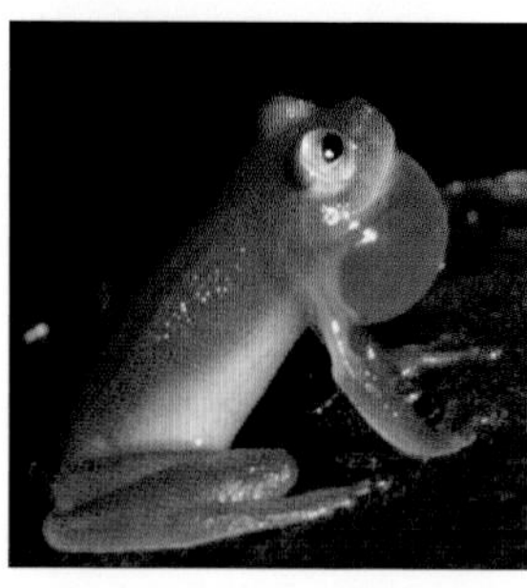

Fleischmann's Glass Frog

Hyalinobatrachium fleischmanni (Rana de Cristal)

Common and widespread in moist and wet forest, between 100m and 1700m, on both Pacific and Caribbean slope (absent from Guanacaste dry forest).

Mostly nocturnal; translucent, with some internal organs (and white bones) visible through skin; forward-facing eyes (tree frogs orientated to side).

✓ Found on leaves overhanging fast-flowing water; most active on rainy nights; male calls (whistle-like wheet) from underside of leaf.

Strawberry Poison-Dart Frog

Dendrobates pumilio (Rana Venenosa Roja y Azul)

Very common and abundant in wet forest, up to 800m, on Caribbean slope, particularly the Sarapiquí.

Small, around 2.5cm long; diurnal; mostly terrestrial; dark-blue hind legs give it nickname of "Blue Jeans"; female carries tadpole on back to small water pools that form in treetop plants.

✓ Easy to spot due to bright colour and comparatively loud buzz-buzz-buzz croak; often seen tiptoeing through leaf litter (especially after rain), though also scales trees in search of bromelia.

Magnificent Frigatebird

Fregata magnificens (Rabihorcado Magno)

Coastal waters and mangrove keys, nesting in low-level shrubs; very common along Pacific coast, less so on Caribbean.

Rarely dives underwater due to absorbent plumage; males inflate scarlet throat sac during courtship.

✓ Easily determined by sleek, V-shaped tail and large wingspan (up to 2m); often seen at harbours and docks, circling over fishing boats.

Boat-Billed Heron

Cochlearius cochlearius (Pico Cuchara)

Fairly common in wetlands, mangroves and coastal lowlands, on both Caribbean and Pacific slope.

Nocturnal feeder with keen eyesight; snaps keel-like beak if disturbed; call is a throaty croak.

✓ Unmistakeable thanks to eponymous wide grey beak; rests in trees near water during day.

Roseate Spoonbill

Platalea ajaja (Espatula Rosada)

Common in coastal waters and open wetland in Pacific lowlands, and in RNdVS Caño Negro.

Unique pink plumage (is only such-coloured bird in Costa Rica) attained through diet of crustaceans; feeds in groups in both fresh- and salt- water.

✓ Usually seen in shallow water, trawling for food with flattened, spatula-shaped bill.

Black Vulture

Coragyps atratus (Zopilote Negro)

Widespread below 2000m in open country, urban refuse, roadsides and degraded forest.

Extremely gregarious, roosting in large colonies, which sometimes include numbers of red-headed Turkey Vulture; generally silent.

✓ Most commonly sighted bird of prey in Costa Rica, usually seen soaring or picking at roadside carrion.

HABITAT AND DISTRIBUTION 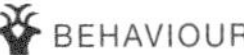 BEHAVIOUR  ✓ SIGHTING TIPS

Northern Jaçana

Jacana spinosa (Jacana Centroamericana)

❀ Common in all areas below 1500m, but mostly wetlands, ponds and rivers; particularly PN Palo Verde, RNdVS Caño Negro and waterways of PN Tortuguero.

Easily agitated; females mate with several males, who care for separate clutch of eggs.

✓ Usually seen in pairs; easily recognizable due to elongated toes that help it walk on floating vegetation; displays lemon-yellow underwings in flight.

Scarlet Macaw

Ara macao (Lapa roja)

❀ Confined to dense rainforest of PN Carara and Osa Peninsula, though numbers increasing in PN Palo Verde, PN Santa Rosa and RB Lomas Barbudal.

Large, growing over 85cm; endangered; raucous squawk heard only in flight; eats fruits and seeds.

✓ Prefers high canopy of forest fringes; easily distinguished from the rest of CR's predominantly green species; usually seen flying in pairs.

Violet Sabrewing

Campylopterus hemileucurs (Ala de Sable Voláceo)

❀ Common in wet forest, forest fringes and clearings in high elevations on both Pacific and Caribbean slope.

Largest of CR's hummers; despite size, is timid and easily scared off feeding sites by smaller birds; forms breeding leks.

✓ Prefers forest understorey; often seen hovering around heliconia and banana plants, and is a regular at nectar-feeders; due to wing size, you can actually hear them beating.

Green Hermit

Phaethornis guy (Ermitaño Verde)

❀ Common throughout Costa Rica in wet forest, plantations and gardens, up to 1750m.

Follows defined route when feeding, stopping at each flower as it goes; principal pollinator of many species of heliconia; forms breeding leks.

✓ Prefers forest understorey; highly curved reddish bill; male all glossy green, female has white underbody, both have black stripe through eye; produces squeaky chirps and loud wing snaps.

❀ HABITAT AND DISTRIBUTION BEHAVIOUR ✓ SIGHTING TIPS

Violaceous Trogon

Trogon violaceus (Trogón Violáceo)

❀ Common in low and middle elevation wet forest, particularly tall secondary growth, on both Pacific and Caribbean slope.

Usually solitary but sometimes in pairs; lays eggs in wasps' or ants' nest in upper canopy.

✓ Can be difficult to spot, as fairly inactive, often perched motionless in upper reaches of forest canopy; male has blue head and green back, female grey head and back.

Resplendent Quetzal

Pharomachrus mocinno (Quetzal)

❀ Fairly common in upper elevations of cloudforest and secondary wet forest, from 1300m to 3000; particularly PN Los Quetzales and RBBN Monteverde.

Largest of CR's trogons, measuring over a metre to tip of extravagant tail feathers; particularly fond of aguacates (small avocados); nests in rotten tree bough.

✓ Male unmistakeable, with noticeable helmet-like green crest, red chest and very long curving tail feathers; frequents mid to upper canopy.

Blue-Crowned Motmot

Momotus momota (Barranquero)

❀ Readily seen in gardens and forest fringes of Valle Central, but also in Pacific lowlands.

Solitary or in pairs; nests in burrows in ground-level banks; eats insects, small lizards and fruit.

✓ Distinctive pendulous tail ends in twin racket-shaped tips; often inactive, perched in lower canopy; soft woot-woot call gives it its name.

Chestnut-Mandibled Toucan

Ramphastos swainsonii (Dios Tedé)

❀ Fairly common in coastal lowlands, wet forest and clearings, up to 1200m on Caribbean slope and 1850m on Pacific.

Largest of CR's toucans; small flocks move through forest in short hops; named for brown colour in bill, differentiating it from more flamboyantly adorned keel-billed toucan (see p.6).

✓ Easier to see on Pacific slope; prefers upper canopy but sometimes seen in understorey; Spanish name derived from onomatopoeic call – keel-billed toucan's is more of a croak.

Great Kiskadee

Pitangus sulphuratus (Bientaveo Grande)

Common throughout Costa Rica in forest clearings and gardens.

Hunts on own or in pairs; opportunistic feeder, and has adapted well to urban environments; named for loud call: "Kis-Ka-Dee".

✓ Largest of CR's tyrant flycatchers, and distinguished from similar-looking boat-billed flycatcher by yellow crown, thin beak and brown back; regularly seen perching on telephone wires.

Three-Wattled Bellbird

Procnias tricarunculatus (Campenero Tricarunculado)

Endemic to Costa Rica, becoming increasingly less common in wet and humid forests; particularly PN Santa Elena.

Migrates between low-level elevations to Tilarán and Talamanca cordilleras to breed (March–June); large black mouth aids eating and territorial displays.

✓ Easily recognized by male's unique worm-like wattles that dangle from base of beak; found at highest point in canopy; metallic-sounding "boink" call can be heard up to 1km away.

Red-Capped Manakin

Pipra mentalis (Saltarin Cabecirrojo)

Common in primary rainforest on Caribbean and central and southern Pacific slope, up to 900m; particularly EB La Selva.

Famous for flamboyant leks, where males gather to woo females with elaborate courtship displays that resemble a speedy Moonwalk; female rears young alone; primarily a fruit-eater.

✓ Aside from eponymous "helmet", male also easily identified by bright yellow thighs; like most manakins, female is a dull green colour; mostly seen feeding or lekking in lower canopy; call is a high-pitched, lengthy spweeee.

Montezuma Oropendola

Psarocolius montezuma (Oropéndola de Moctezuma)

Very common in gardens, wet forests and forest fringes of Caribbean lowlands, less so higher up, and rarer on northwest Pacific slope.

Male larger and much heavier than female; noisy colonies (up to 170 birds) will monopolize a single tree, weaving long pendulous nests.

✓ Distinctive orange-and-black beak and pretty facial markings; long, warbling call ends with loud gurgle.

Basics

Basics

Getting there

Costa Rica has two international airports. Juan Santamaría (SJO), just outside San José, receives the majority of flights, while Daniel Oduber (LIR), near the northern city of Liberia, handles some flights from the US and Canada, plus the odd seasonal flight from the UK. Although there are a few direct flights from Europe, the vast majority of routes pass through the US, meaning that passengers have to comply with US entry requirements, even if merely transiting the country.

Airfares always depend on the **season**, with the highest being around July, August and December to mid-January; you'll get the best prices during the wet summer (May–Nov). Note, too, that although prices are steepest during the Christmas period (mid-Dec until the first week in Jan) when flying from the US, in Europe this can be the cheapest time to travel. Also, flying at weekends is usually more expensive; price ranges quoted below assume midweek travel.

From the US and Canada

Daily direct flights depart for San José from numerous cities in **the US**, including Miami (3hr), Dallas, Houston and Denver (3–4hr), New York (5hr) and Los Angeles (6hr). LACSA (the Costa Rican carrier that operates as a subsidiary of TACA) usually offers the cheapest fares **from Miami** and **Dallas** (starting at $300 in high season), while Continental's flights **from Houston** start at around $525; American Airlines and Continental both fly from many US cities to Dallas, Miami or Houston to connect with flights to Costa Rica. Frontier Airlines flies from Denver for around $540, while JetBlue and Spirit Airlines both run services from Florida (Orlando and Fort Lauderdale, respectively, around $330). The best fares **from New York** are on Continental and TACA via San Salvador (from $400); Continental also offers the cheapest fare **from Chicago** ($355), via New York. **From LA,** the best deals are on TACA (via San Salvador); flights start at $540.

There are no non-stop flights to San José **from Canada**. The cheapest fare **from Toronto** is on TACA's thrice-weekly service (Can$780; 6hr 45min), while American Airlines' daily flight costs the same but involves a plane change in New York or Miami. **From Montréal**, American Airlines is the best bet, with daily flights, also requiring a plane change in Miami (Can$785; 8hr 45min). The quickest and cheapest flight **from Vancouver** is on American, with a change of planes in Dallas (Can$885; 10hr). Good deals are occasionally offered by the charter operator Air Transat, which flies weekly from Toronto to San José in high season.

From the UK and Ireland

The only direct flight **from the UK** to Costa Rica is Thomson's weekly service from Gatwick to Liberia (Nov to mid-April), which is both the quickest (12hr) and cheapest (£450) way of getting there. Otherwise, Continental has flights from the UK via Newark and Houston, while American Airlines flies via JFK, Dallas or Miami, and United via New York or Houston: of the three, Continental generally has the lowest fares (from £545 in high season) and offers an excellent service, with swift connections. Iberia's flights via Madrid are one of the quicker routings, and avoid the US, but start at around £650. Indirect flights can still take as little as thirteen hours, including changes.

Note that if you leave Costa Rica by air, you'll need to pay a $26 **departure tax** at the airport (payable in dollars or colones, in cash or by credit card), which is not included in the price of your air ticket.

Six steps to a better kind of travel

At Rough Guides we are passionately committed to travel. We feel strongly that only through travelling do we truly come to understand the world we live in and the people we share it with – plus tourism has brought a great deal of **benefit** to developing economies around the world over the last few decades. But the extraordinary growth in tourism has also damaged some places irreparably, and of course **climate change** is exacerbated by most forms of transport, especially flying. This means that now more than ever it's important to **travel thoughtfully** and **responsibly**, with respect for the cultures you're visiting – not only to derive the most benefit from your trip but also to preserve the best bits of the planet for everyone to enjoy. At Rough Guides we feel there are six main areas in which you can make a difference:

- Consider what you're contributing to the **local economy**, and how much the services you use do the same, whether it's through employing local workers and guides or sourcing locally grown produce and local services.
- Consider the **environment** on holiday as well as at home. Water is scarce in many developing destinations, and the biodiversity of local flora and fauna can be adversely affected by tourism. Try to patronize businesses that take account of this.
- Travel with a purpose, not just to tick off experiences. Consider **spending longer** in a place, and getting to know it and its people.
- Give thought to how often you **fly**. Try to avoid short hops by air and more harmful night flights.
- Consider **alternatives to flying**, travelling instead by bus, train, boat and even by bike or on foot where possible.
- Make your trips "**climate neutral**" via a reputable carbon offset scheme. All Rough Guide flights are offset, and every year we donate money to a variety of charities devoted to combating the effects of climate change.

There are no direct flights **from Ireland** to Costa Rica. Your best option is to fly via the US or Madrid, where you can connect with flights to San José (see p.35). Delta has the widest range of flights from Dublin (and several from Shannon) to New York and Atlanta, from where you can get an onward flight to San José, though you'll probably have to change planes at least once more. Continental are the cheapest, with flights via New York starting at around €650.

From Australia, New Zealand and South Africa

There are no direct flights from Australia, New Zealand or South Africa to Costa Rica – the quickest and easiest option is to fly via the US. Note that it's best to book several weeks ahead.

From Australia, the cheapest fares **to San José** from Sydney are via Los Angeles and Mexico City with Delta-Aeromexico (from Aus$1950 in high season). American Airlines' fares to San José via LA are higher (Aus$2500). Fares from all eastern Australian cities are generally the same; fares from Perth and Darwin are about Aus$200 more.

From New Zealand, the best through-tickets **to San José** depart Auckland and travel via LA and Dallas on American Airlines (around NZ$3200 in high season); expect to pay an extra NZ$150 for flights from Christchurch and Wellington.

From **South Africa**, the least convoluted route to San José is with Delta from Johannesburg via Atlanta (ZAR12,800); you can fly from Cape Town to Jo'burg and then on to Atlanta and San José for ZAR15,700.

Overland to Costa Rica

Costa Rica's international bus company, Ticabus (ⓣ2221-0006, ⓦwww.ticabus.com), runs a good **overland bus** service between Mexico (Tapachula), Guatemala, El Salvador, Honduras, Nicaragua and

Costa Rica and south onto Panamá. The service is very popular, and you'll need to reserve your tickets up to a month in advance in the high season (up to three months in Dec).

Ticabus leaves **Tapachula** daily for San José at 7am, arriving in **Guatemala City** at noon and departing at 1pm; from here, it's a two-and-a-half-day trip, entailing nights (at your own expense) in San Salvador and Managua. A one-way fare is $84 ($73 from Guatemala City). From **Tegucigalpa** in Honduras, Ticabus leaves for San José ($40) daily at 9.15am, arriving (after an overnight stop in **Managua**, again at your own expense) at 4pm the following day. From **Managua** in Nicaragua, Ticabus departs daily for San José at 6am, 7am & noon (8–10hr; $23); alternatively, you can get a Nicaraguan SIRCA bus (daily 6am) or a more deluxe service run by Transnica (daily 5am, 7am & 1pm; 8hr). From **Panamá City**, a Ticabus leaves daily at 11pm, getting to San José at 2pm ($35).

The main northern **border crossing** with Nicaragua is at Peñas Blancas (see p.284) on the Interamericana. Further east, another crossing at Los Chiles (see p.239) involves a boat trip (and usually an overnight stop to catch it in the morning) to/from San Carlos on the shores of Lago Nicaragua, although a bridge is allegedly in the pipeline. The main route south to and from Panamá is again along the Interamericana, at Paso Canoas (see p.399). On the Caribbean coast, Sixaola is a smaller crossing, across one of the most decrepit bridges in the world, while in the southern highlands, two little-used routes link San Vito with the border towns of Río Sereno and Cañas Gordas.

Airlines, agents and operators

Airlines

Aeromexico ⓦ www.aeromexico.com
Air Canada ⓦ www.aircanada.com
Air Transat ⓦ www.airtransat.ca
American Airlines ⓦ www.aa.com
British Airways ⓦ www.ba.com
Continental Airlines ⓦ www.continental.com
Delta ⓦ www.delta.com
Frontier Airlines ⓦ www.frontierairlines.com
Grupo TACA ⓦ www.taca.com

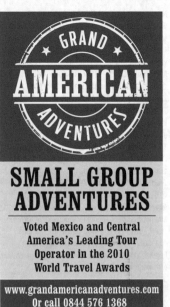

Iberia ⓦ www.iberia.com
Jet Blue ⓦ www.jetblue.com
Spirit Airlines ⓦ www.spirit.com
Thomson ⓦ flights.thomson.co.uk
United Airlines ⓦ www.unitedairlines.co.uk
US Airways ⓦ www.usairways.com
Virgin Atlantic ⓦ www.virgin-atlantic.com.

Travel agents

Anywhere Travel Australia ⓣ 02/9663 0411, ⓦ www.anywheretravel.com.au. Discount flight agent offering discounted flights, as well as accommodation, tours and car rental.

eBookers UK ⓣ 0203/320 3320, ⓦ www.ebookers.com. Low fares on an extensive range of scheduled flights.

Flightcentre US ⓣ 1-877/992-4732, Canada ⓣ 1-877/967-5302, UK ⓣ 0870/499 0040, Australia ⓣ 13 31 33, New Zealand ⓣ 0800/243 544, South Africa ⓣ 0860/400 727; ⓦ www.flightcentre.com. Rock-bottom fares worldwide.

Harvey World Travel New Zealand ⓣ 0800/758 787, ⓦ www.harveyworld.co.nz; South Africa ⓣ 0860/626 364, ⓦ www.harveyworld.co.za. Excellent deals on flights and holidays.

Journey Latin America UK ⓣ 020/8747 8315, ⓦ www.journeylatinamerica.co.uk. Latin American specialists, adept at arranging unusual itineraries at competitive fares. They also offer tours (see p.38).

North South Travel UK ⓣ01245/608 291, ⓦwww.northsouthtravel.co.uk. Friendly, competitive travel agency, offering discounted fares worldwide. Profits are used to support projects in the developing world, especially the promotion of sustainable tourism.

STA Travel US ⓣ1-800/781-4040, UK ⓣ0871/230 0040, Australia ⓣ1300/134 782, New Zealand ⓣ0800/474 400, South Africa ⓣ0861/781 781; ⓦwww.statravel.com. Worldwide specialists in low-cost independent travel; also student IDs, travel insurance, car rental, rail passes and more.

Tico Travel US ⓣ1-800/493-8426, ⓦwww.ticotravel.com. Costa Rican travel specialists who also offer discount airfares.

Trailfinders UK ⓣ020/7938 3939, Ireland ⓣ01/677 7888, Australia ⓣ02/9276 4200; ⓦwww.trailfinders.com. One of the best-informed and most efficient agents for independent travellers.

Travel Cuts US ⓣ1-800/592-2887, Canada ⓣ1-888/246-9762, ⓦwww.travelcuts.com. Popular, long-established student-travel organization, with worldwide offers.

Tour operators

See p.46 for a list of recommended tour operators in Costa Rica itself.

Adventure Associates Australia ⓣ02/8916 3000, ⓦadventureassociates.com. Escorted small-group tours from San José, including a seven-day boat and hiking tour through the rainforests of Parque Nacional Corcovado and Isla del Caño (Aus$2450). They also arrange independent trekking, mountain biking, white-water rafting, canal trips and sports-fishing, plus city stopovers and cruises in and around Costa Rica.

Adventures Abroad US ⓣ1-800/665-3998, ⓦwww.adventures-abroad.com. Adventure specialists, with one- to four-week trips throughout Costa Rica and other Central American countries.

Backroads US ⓣ1-800/462-2848, ⓦwww.backroads.com. Cycling, hiking and multi-sport tours designed for the young at heart, with the emphasis on going at your own pace. Accommodation ranges from deluxe campsites to luxury hotels. Also family-friendly options and singles trips.

Contours Australia ⓣ03/9328 8488, ⓦwww.contourstravel.com.au. Specialists in Latin America, with a decent range of trips across Costa Rica – their two-week Discover Costa Rica tour takes in Parque Nacional Tortuguero, Puerto Viejo de Talamanca, Volcán Arenal and Monteverde (Aus$1480).

Costa Rican Adventures US ⓣ1-800/551-7887, ⓦwww.costaricanadventures.com. Small-group and private trips, on "EcoVacations" or in "EcoClassrooms" with a company dedicated to creating a healthier and more sustainable Costa Rica through eco-centred travel.

Costa Rica Undiscovered US ⓣ202/518-6193, ⓦwww.costaricaundiscovered.com. A fully independent tour operator specializing in Costa Rican sustainable tourism, and following the code of ethics outlined by The Institute for Central American Studies' Department of Responsible Travel.

Exodus UK ⓣ0845/287 7421, ⓦwww.exodus.co.uk. Experienced adventure-tour operators offering a range of Central American itineraries, with a sixteen-day Discover Costa Rica tour including visits to Parque Nacional Tortuguero, Reserva Santa Elena and Parque Nacional Piedras Blancas (£2360).

GAP Adventures US & Canada ⓣ1-888/800-4100, UK ⓣ0844/272 0000, Ireland ⓣ207/243 9878, Australia ⓣ1300/79 66 18, NZ ⓣ0800/33 33 07; ⓦwww.gapadventures.com. Two-week trekking and public-transport trips along the coast, visiting Costa Rican rain- and cloudforests and national parks.

Geographic Expeditions US ⓣ1-800/777-8183, ⓦwww.geoex.com. Luxury adventure travel and cultural tours, including rainforest and river trips, plus customized itineraries (from $3995).

Global Exchange US ⓣ415/255-7296, ⓦwww.globalexchange.org. Human rights organization offering "Reality Tours" to meet local activists and participate in educational workshops. They run two trips a year to Costa Rica (one to the Caribbean coast, one to the northern Pacific) concentrating on eco-tourism and sustainability.

Journey Latin America UK ⓣ020/8747 8315, ⓦwww.journeylatinamerica.co.uk. Specialist in flights, packages and adventurous, tailor-made trips to Latin America, including a dozen or so tours of Costa Rica, from eight-day introductions to four-week language courses.

Journeys International US ⓣ1-800/255-8735, ⓦwww.journeys.travel. Prestigious, award-winning operator focusing on eco-tourism and small-group trips, including to national parks in Costa Rica.

Kumuka Expeditions US ⓣ1-800/517-0867, Canada ⓣ1-888/358-6852, UK ⓣ0800/068 885, Ireland ⓣ1800/946 843, Australia ⓣ1300/667 277, NZ ⓣ0800/44 04 99, South Africa ⓣ0800/991 503; ⓦwww.kumuka.com. Independent tour operator specializing in overland expeditions, as well as local and private transport tours.

Maxwell's Travel Ireland ⓣ01/679 5700. Very experienced Latin American specialist, and the Irish agent for many tour operators.

Nature Expeditions International US ⓣ1-800/869-0639, ⓦwww.naturexp.com. Small-group expeditions led by specialists in anthropology, biology and natural history; Costa Rican trips offer optional lectures on the environment, eco-tourism and local cultures.

Peregrine UK ⓣ0845/004 0673, ⓦwww.peregrineadventures.com. Experienced small-group adventure specialists offering a number of good-value tours, from nine to fourteen days (from £925).

Road Scholar US ⓣ1-800/454-5768, ⓦwww.roadscholar.org. Extensive network of educational and activity programmes, including photography trips, birdwatching tours and two-week educational trips studying environment and history. Participants must be over 55 (companions may be younger).

Sunvil Holidays UK ⓣ020/8758 4747, ⓦwww.sunvil.co.uk. Flexible fly-drive itineraries and tailor-made tours, specializing in luxury and wildlife-watching trips, with accommodation in a number of areas including Caño Negro and the Osa Peninsula.

USIT Northern Ireland ⓣ028/90 327111, Ireland ⓣ01/602 1904; ⓦwww.usitnow.com. Specialists in student, youth and independent travel – flights, study tours, TEFL, visas and more.

Wildlife Worldwide UK ⓣ0845/130 6982, ⓦwww.wildlifeworldwide.com. Tailor-made trips for wildlife and wilderness enthusiasts, visiting more off-the-beaten-track places such as Parque Nacional Braulio Carrillo and Refugio Nacional de Vida Silvestre Gandoca-Manzanillo.

Getting around

Costa Rica's public bus system is excellent, cheap and quite frequent, even in remote areas. Taxis regularly do long- as well as short-distance trips and are a fairly inexpensive alternative to the bus, at least if you're travelling in a group. Car rental is more common here than in the rest of Central America, but is fairly expensive and driving can be quite a hair-raising experience, with precipitous drops in the highlands and potholed roads just about everywhere else.

Domestic airlines are reasonably economical and can be quite a time-saver, especially since Costa Rica's difficult terrain makes driving distances longer than they appear on the map. A number of **tour operators** in San José organize individual itineraries and packages with transport included, well worth checking out before making any decisions about heading out on your own.

By bus

Travelling by **bus** is by far the cheapest way to get around Costa Rica. **San José** is the hub for virtually all bus services in the country; indeed, it's often impossible to travel from one place to another without backtracking to the capital. The most expensive journey in the country (from San José to Paso Canoas on the Panamanian border) costs $12.50, while fares in the mid- to long-distance range vary from $4 to $6. Some popular buses, like the service to Golfito, ought to be **booked in advance**, though you may be lucky enough to get on without a reservation. **Tickets** on most mid- to long-distance and popular routes are issued with a date and a seat number; you are expected to sit in the seat indicated. Make sure the date is correct; even if the mistake isn't yours, you cannot normally change your ticket or get a refund. Neither can you buy **return** bus tickets on Costa Rican buses, which can be quite inconvenient if you're heading to very popular destinations like Monteverde, Jacó or Manuel Antonio at busy times – you'll need to buy your return ticket as soon as you arrive to assure yourself a seat.

Bus **schedules** change with impressive frequency, so be sure to check in advance; you can download a comprehensive timetable at ⓦwww.visitcostarica.com/ict/paginas/LEYES/pdf/ItinerarioBuses_en.pdf or for updated information on schedules, check ⓦthebusschedule.com/EN/cr. For more details on bus companies and terminals, see p.118.

Distance chart (in km)

	Alajuela	Cahuita	Cartago	Dominical	Golfito	Guápiles	Heredia	Jacó	Liberia	Limón
Alajuela	-	192	40	179	331	64	12	100	200	148
Cahuita	192	-	195	334	486	128	175	287	392	44
Cartago	40	195	-	139	291	70	35	131	240	151
Dominical	179	334	139	-	152	219	174	118	309	290
Golfito	331	486	291	152	-	371	326	270	461	442
Guápiles	64	128	70	219	371	-	47	159	264	84
Heredia	12	175	35	174	326	47	-	112	205	131
Jacó	100	287	131	118	270	159	112	-	191	243
Liberia	200	392	240	309	461	264	205	191	-	348
Limón	148	44	151	290	442	84	131	243	348	-
Nicoya	185	377	225	295	442	249	197	161	83	333
Paso Canoas	337	492	291	162	54	379	332	284	471	448
Peñas Blancas	277	469	317	377	524	341	289	259	77	425
Puerto Jiménez	354	509	314	175	127	394	349	293	454	465
Puerto Viejo de Sarapiquí	79	168	119	241	393	57	67	179	272	124
Puerto Viejo de Talamanca	209	17	212	351	503	145	192	304	409	61
Puntarenas	98	290	138	187	339	162	103	75	132	246
Quepos	175	377	182	43	195	239	187	75	263	333
San Carlos	56	225	96	235	387	97	68	144	185	181
San Isidro de El General	153	308	111	28	180	180	146	251	351	264
San José	17	175	23	162	309	47	12	117	217	131
Tamarindo	257	449	297	357	524	321	269	239	69	405
Tilarán	174	366	214	274	421	236	186	156	70	322
Turrialba	85	150	45	187	336	70	80	176	285	106

Nicoya	Paso Canoas	Peñas Blancas	Puerto Jiménez	Puerto Viejo de Sarapiquí	Puerto Viejo de Talamanca	Puntarenas	Quepos	San Carlos	San Isidro de El General	San José	Tamarindo	Tilarán	Turrialba
185	337	277	354	79	209	98	175	56	153	17	257	174	85
377	492	469	509	168	17	290	377	225	308	175	449	366	150
225	291	317	314	119	212	138	182	96	111	23	297	214	45
295	162	377	175	241	351	187	43	235	28	162	357	274	187
442	54	524	127	393	503	339	195	387	180	309	524	421	336
249	379	341	394	57	145	162	239	97	180	47	321	236	70
197	332	289	349	67	192	103	187	68	146	12	269	186	80
161	284	259	293	179	304	75	75	144	251	117	239	156	176
83	471	77	454	272	409	132	263	185	351	217	69	70	285
333	448	425	465	124	61	246	333	181	264	131	405	322	106
-	452	160	465	264	394	118	242	210	336	202	72	95	272
452	-	534	159	399	509	355	209	393	186	320	534	431	342
160	534	-	547	383	486	210	334	223	428	304	146	173	355
465	159	547	-	416	526	362	218	410	203	332	527	444	359
264	399	383	416	-	185	170	254	57	201	67	336	253	164
394	509	486	526	185	-	307	394	242	325	192	466	383	167
118	355	210	362	170	307	-	150	108	249	115	190	107	183
242	209	334	218	254	394	150	-	119	326	192	314	231	227
210	393	223	410	57	242	108	119	-	209	73	272	115	141
336	186	428	203	201	325	249	326	209	-	134	408	325	156
202	320	304	332	67	192	115	192	73	134	-	274	191	68
72	534	146	527	336	466	190	314	272	408	274	-	139	335
95	431	173	444	253	383	107	231	115	325	191	139	-	252
272	342	355	359	164	167	183	227	141	156	68	335	252	-

Finding your way around Costa Rican towns

In Costa Rica, there is only one vision of urban planning: the **grid system**. However, there are a number of peculiarities that are essential to get to grips with if you want to find your way around with ease. The following rules apply to all cities except Limón:

Typically, you'll see **addresses** written as follows: *Bar Esmeralda*, Av 2, C 5/7 (abbreviated from Avenida 2, calles 5/7). This means that *Bar Esmeralda* is on Av 2, between Calle 5 and Calle 7. *Bar Lotto*, C 5, Av 2, on the other hand, is on the corner of Calle 5 and Avenida 2. Apartado (Aptdo) means "postbox", and bis means, technically, "encore": if you see "Av 6 bis" in an address, for example, it refers to another Avendia 6, right next to the original one.

Many **directions**, in both written and verbal form, are given in terms of metres rather than blocks. In general, one block is equivalent to 100m. Thus "de la Escuela Presidente Vargas, 125 metros al sur, cincuenta metros al oeste", translates as "from the Presidente Vargas School, 125 metres south [one block and a quarter] and 50 metres west [half a block]". More confusingly, verbal directions are commonly given in relation to **landmarks** that everyone – except the visitor – knows and recognizes. Even more frustratingly, some of these landmarks may not even exist any longer. This is something to get the hang of fast: taxi drivers will often look completely bewildered if given street directions, but as soon you come up with a landmark (the town church, the *parque central*, a *Pops Heladería*), the proverbial light bulb goes on.

The majority of the country's buses are in fairly good shape, although most lack air conditioning and there's very little room for luggage, or long legs. Most comfortable are the **Ticabuses** – modern air-conditioned vehicles with good seats, adequate baggage space and very courteous drivers – that run from San José to Panamá and Managua, and on to Tegucigalpa, San Salvador, Guatemala City and Tapachula in Mexico (see p.36). Most buses in Costa Rica have buzzers or bells to signal to the driver that you want to get off, though you may still find a few people using the old system of whistling, or shouting "*¡parada!*" ("stop!") – despite signs requesting otherwise. The atmosphere in Costa Rican buses is generally friendly, and if the driver starts to drive away while you're halfway out the back door trying to get off, your fellow passengers will erupt in spontaneous help. Though there are no **toilets** on the buses, drivers make (admittedly infrequent) stops on longer runs. Often, there'll be a lunch or dinner stop at a roadside restaurant or service station; failing that, there is always a bevy of hardy food and drinks sellers who leap onto the bus proffering their wares.

In recent years, travellers have begun to make much more use of the network of air-conditioned **minibuses** that connect most of Costa Rica's main tourist destinations. While these cost more than five times as much as the public buses, they are significantly faster, more comfortable and will pick up and drop off at hotels. The main operator is **Interbus** (Ⓣ2283-5573, Ⓦwww.interbusonline.com), with comprehensive routes across the country; they charge $25–60 for a mid- to long-range journey. The similar but slightly more expensive **Gray Line** (Ⓣ2220-2126, Ⓦwww.graylinecostarica.com) runs direct services between many tourist spots; fares range from $35 to $75 one-way.

By car

Although there's little traffic outside the Valle Central, the common perception of **driving** in Costa Rica is of endless dodging around cows and potholes, while big trucks nudge your rear bumper in an effort to get you to go faster around that next blind bend. The reality is somewhat different. While many minor roads are indeed badly potholed and unsurfaced, driving is relatively easy, and with your own vehicle you can see the

Some useful road-sign meanings

No Hay Paso No Entry
Ceda El Paso Give Way
Una Via One Way
Despacio Slow
Peigroso Danger
Carretera En Mal Estado Road In Bad Condition
Hombres Trabajando En La Via Men Working In The Road
Salida De Camiones Truck Exit

country at your own pace without having to adhere to bus or plane schedules – road signage, however, is poor, particularly in the Valle Central, so a good map is essential (see p.77).

Citizens of the US, Canada and the UK need only a **valid driver's licence** to drive a car in Costa Rica (for up to three months). Technically, residents of Australia, New Zealand and South Africa should get an **international drivers licence** (available from the relevant national automobile associations), although in practice both police and rental agencies readily accept domestic licences from these countries.

The **speed limit** on highways is either 75kph or 90kph and is marked on the road surface or on signs; it reduces to 40kph elsewhere and 25kph in built-up areas. New laws introduced in March 2010 have clamped down on motoring offences, with greatly increased **fines** (*multas*) for jumping a red light, talking on a mobile phone and driving without a seatbelt – all of which can incur fines of up to $425. Reckless driving and speeding are the worst offences; speed traps are fairly common, and if you're caught speeding you may have to pay a fine up to $575. If a motorist – especially a trucker – in the oncoming direction flashes his headlights at you, you can be almost certain that traffic cops with speed-trapping radar are up ahead. Although traffic cops routinely accept bribes to tear up tickets, it's a very serious offence and should not be attempted under any circumstances.

Petrol is positively cheap by European standards: about $1.15 per litre or $4.30 per gallon (fuel prices are regulated by the government, so you'll pay the same at all petrol stations). Most cars take regular; all petrol stations (*bomboneras* or *gasolineras*) are serviced.

Parking is relatively easy given the lack of traffic, though in most towns in the Valle Central you'll need to either use a *parqueo*, a secure car park lot (around $2 per hour), or, if parking on the street during the day, buy a dated permit (from around ¢75), available at local shops.

If you're unlucky enough to have an **accident** in Costa Rica, don't attempt to move the car until the traffic police (Ⓣ2222-9330 or 2222-9245) arrive: call the National Insurance Institute (Ⓣ2287-6000, Ⓦwww.ins-cr.com), who will send an inspector to check the vehicles involved to assess who caused the accident – vital if you're using a rental car.

Car rental

Car rental in Costa Rica is expensive. Expect to pay about $235 per week ($375 with full insurance) for a regular vehicle, and up to $495 for an intermediate 4WD ($635 with full insurance); extras such as additional driver, child seats, mobile phone and cool box will push the price up further (though note that Vamos Rent A Car include these as standard; see p.44). Rental days are calculated on a 24-hour basis: thus, if you pick up your car on a Tuesday at 3pm for a week, you have to return it before that time the following Tuesday.

The **minimum age** for rental is usually 25, and you'll need a credit card, either Mastercard or Visa, which has sufficient credit for the entire cost of the rental. There are rental offices in all the major tourist spots, and you can arrange to pick up your car in another part of Costa Rica and drop it off at the airport when you leave – this normally entails a charge of $30 or more, though it may be waived if you're taking the vehicle for more than a few days. It's worth knowing that most tour operators in Costa Rica can

Car safety in Costa Rica

Although the majority of the country's roads are fairly light on traffic, the **road accident** rate is phenomenal – and rising. Though Ticos blame bad road conditions, the real cause is more often poor driving – you're advised to drive extremely defensively. Sections of washed out, unmarked or unlit road add to the hazards, as do big trans-isthmus trucks. Another hazard is **car crime** – break-ins are an unfortunately regular occurrence – and **scams**, such as thieves puncturing your tyres and then robbing you after stopping to "help".

- Keep your doors locked and windows shut, especially in San José.
- If someone suspicious approaches your vehicle at a red light or stop sign, blow your horn.
- Do not pull over for flashing headlights – note that an emergency or police vehicle has red or blue flashing headlights.
- If you get lost, find a public place, like a service station, to consult your map or ask for directions.
- If someone tells you something is wrong with your vehicle, do not stop immediately. Drive to the nearest service station or other well-lit public area.
- Keep valuables in the trunk or out of sight, and your car locked at all times.
- Do not park at remote trailheads – leave your car at the nearest manned ranger station.
- Avoid driving at night, when wild animals are more active.
- Be aware of steep roadside gullies used to channel rainwater runoff when turning or reversing.
- Do not pick up hitchhikers.
- In case of emergency, call 911.

arrange car hire more cheaply than the major overseas operators; local rental companies also provide a better deal.

If you're planning to visit the Nicoya Peninsula, Santa Elena and Monteverde or other remote spots, it's definitely worth paying the extra money for a **4WD**; indeed, in some areas of the country during the rainy season (May–Nov), it's a necessity. Whilst a 4WD doesn't grant you immunity to the laws of physics, it does provide greater traction in the wet and higher clearance for rough roads and river crossings. Furthermore, in smaller vehicles, punctures are a depressingly regular experience, and although getting them repaired is a matter of a couple of minutes' hammering at the rim at the local garage, it's not the best way to spend a holiday.

Most **car rental companies** in Costa Rica are located in San José and at or around the international airports near Alajuela and Liberia (note that airport rentals incur an additional twelve percent charge); you can also rent cars in various towns around the country. Prices vary considerably from agency to agency (Vamos and Adobe are particularly recommended), but renting outside San José is generally a bit more expensive. During peak season (especially Christmas, but any time from December to March), it's wise to reserve a car before you arrive.

Car rental companies around San José

In all the following, where two numbers are given, the first is the company's downtown office, the second, the airport office.

Adobe Av 12, C 28 ⓣ2258-4242, ⓣ2442-2422, ⓦwww.adobecar.com.

Alamo Paseo Colón ⓣ2442-7733, ⓣ2441-1260, ⓦwww.alamocostarica.com.

Budget Paseo Colón, C 30 ⓣ2255-4240, ⓣ440-4412, ⓦwww.budget.co.cr.

Hertz Paseo Colón, C 38 ⓣ2221-1818, ⓦwww.hertz.com.

National C 40, Av 3/5 ⓣ2242-7878, ⓦwww.natcar.com.

Payless C10, Av 13/15, Barrio México ⓣ2257-0026, ⓣ2441-9366, ⓦwww.payless.com.

Vamos Rent A Car C 4 Plaza Aeropuerto ⓣ2432-5258, ⓦwww.vamos4x4.com.

Car rental essentials

You have to exercise caution when **renting a car** in Costa Rica. While the agencies listed opposite are all recommended for their service, it is not uncommon for rental companies to claim for "damage" they insist you inflicted on the vehicle, and you may wish to rent a car through a Costa Rican ICT-accredited **travel agent** (see p.46), which could work out cheaper than renting on your own and will help guard against false claims of damage and other accusations.

Make sure to **check the car** carefully before you sign off the damage sheet. Check the oil, brake fluid, fuel gauge (to make sure it's full) and that there is a spare tyre with good air pressure and a jack. Look up the Spanish for "scratches" (*rayas*) and other relevant terminology first, so you can at least scrutinize the rental company's assessment. Keep a copy of this document on you.

Take the full **insurance** (around $20 per day), not just the basic CDW; because of the country's high accident rate, you need to be covered for damage to the vehicle, yourself and any third party and public property.

By motorcycle

A **motorcycle** is one of the best ways to discover the diversity of Costa Rica. However, one should have a decent amount of biking experience and will need a valid motorcycle licence or endorsement, in order to rent a bike. Smaller motorcycles for day-trips (125–155cc) can be rented in some beach towns (ie Jaco and Tamarindo), with daily rates around $80.

Those who want to tour the country can rent larger motorcycles or book **guided tours** out of San José. Once outside the metropolitan area, an endless number of curvy back-roads and scenic gravel trails await. While the notorious road conditions of Costa Rica can be tiring in a car, they are usually great fun on a dual-sport motorcycle (Enduro motorcycle) with its large suspension.

Motorcycle rental companies in San José

Costa Rica Motorcycle Tours ⓣ2289-5552, ⓦwww.costaricamotorcycles.com. Harley Davidson rental from $150 a day.

Maria Alexandra Tours ⓣ2225-6000, ⓦwww.costaricamotorcycletours.com. Rental and tours on KTM and Aprilia.

Wild Rider Motorcycles ⓣ2258-4604 or 8844-6568, ⓦwww.wild-rider.com. Very helpful German-run motorcycle rental and tours, dual-sport bikes 250–650cc, as well as regular vehicles for about thirty percent less than the major agencies.

By bicycle

Costa Rica's terrain makes for easy **cycling** compared with neighbouring countries and, as there's a good range of places to stay and eat, you don't need to carry the extra weight of a tent, sleeping bag and stove. Always bring warm clothes and a cycling jacket, however, wherever you are. As for **equipment**, rear panniers and a small handlebar bag (for maps and camera) should be enough. Bring a puncture repair kit, even if your tyres are supposedly unbustable. You'll need a bike with a triple front gear – this gives you 15 to 21 gears, and you will really need the low ones. Make sure, too, that you carry and drink lots of water – five to eight litres a day in the lowlands.

There is very little **traffic** outside the Valle Central, and despite their tactics with other cars (and pedestrians), Costa Rican drivers are some of the most courteous in Central America to cyclists. That said, however, bus and truck drivers do tend to forget about you as soon as they pass, sometimes forcing you off the road. **Roads** are generally good for cyclists, who can dodge the potholes and wandering cattle more easily than drivers. Bear in mind that if you cycle up to Monteverde, one of the most popular routes in the country, you're in for a slow trip: besides being steep, there's not much traction on the loose gravel roads. Although road signs will tell you that cycling on the Interamericana (Panamerican Highway, or

Hwy-1) is not permitted, you will quickly see that people do so anyway.

San José's best **cycle shop** is Ciclo Los Ases, 50m east of the Gimnasio Nacional, Av 10, C 38/40 (ⓣ2255-6256, ⓦwww.ciclolosasescr.com). They have all the parts you might need, can fix your bike and may even be able to give you a bicycle carton for the plane.

By plane

Costa Rica's two **domestic air carriers**, Sansa and NatureAir, offer reasonably economical flights between San José and many beach destinations and provincial towns. Both fly small twin-propeller aircraft, and service more or less the same destinations. These flights can be very handy, saving many hours of bus travel better spent on the beach.

Of the two, **NatureAir** (ⓣ2299-6000, ⓦwww.natureair.com), which flies from Tobías Bolaños Airport in Pavas, 7km northwest of San José, is generally more reliable and has more frequent services on some runs. **Sansa** (ⓣ2290-4100, ⓦwww.flysansa.com) flies from Juan Santamaría airport, 17km northwest of San José, and is cheaper but less dependable. On both airlines, make your reservations as far as possible in advance, and even then be advised that a booking means almost nothing until the seat is actually paid for. Reconfirm your flight in advance of the day of departure and again on the day of travel, if possible, as schedules can change at short notice. Note that the airports at Quepos and Tambor (both $2) and Arenal ($7) charge **departure/arrival taxes**.

If you're planning to cover a lot of ground in a limited amount of time, the Nature **Air Pass** ($499/799 for 2/4 weeks) gives you unrestricted use of all their services bar the route to Bocas del Toro (available for an additional $100). For a rundown of Sansa and NatureAir **schedules**, along with their addresses and phone numbers, see p.120.

While fares will be at least double that of Sansa and NatureAir, **air-charter taxis** (journeys cost from $895 for a seven-person flight from San José to Quepos) can prove a reasonably cheap way to get to the beaches and more remote areas if several people split the expense. Most charter planes operate from Tobías Bolaños Airport.

Tour operators

There are scores of **tour operators** in Costa Rica, some very good, some not so – bear in mind that although you may save a few dollars by going with the cheapest agency, you could end up on a badly organized tour with poor accommodation and underqualified guides. Go with a reputable tour operator (such as those listed below, and in the relevant sections of each chapter) and not with one of the freelance "guides" who may approach you on the street. The following is not a comprehensive list, but all those that we've listed are experienced and recommended, offering a good range of services and tours. They're all licensed (and regulated) by the ICT.

Tour operators in San José

ACTUAR 100m east of the Ministario de Trabajo, Barrio Tournón ⓣ2248-9470, ⓦwww.actuarcostarica.com. The Costa Rican Association of Community-based Rural Tourism, whose highly rewarding trips give a real insight into cooperatives, locally owned coffee farms and indigenous reserves among other grassroot organizations.

Camino Travel C 1, Av 0/1 ⓣ2234-2530, ⓦwww.caminotravel.com. A young, enthusiastic staff with high standards (and a mainly European clientele) offers upmarket and independent travel, including individual tours with quality accommodation. They can also help with bus and transport information and car rental.

Costa Rica Expeditions C Central, Av 3 ⓣ2257-0766, ⓦwww.costaricaexpeditions.com. The longest-established and most experienced of the major tour operators, with superior accommodation in Tortuguero, Monteverde and (currently being refurbished) Corcovado, a superlative staff of guides and tremendous resources. You can drop into the busy downtown office and talk to a consultant about individual tours.

Ecole Travel Bo. Escalante, Del Centro Cultural Costarricense Norteamericano ⓣ2234-1669, ⓦwww.ecoletravel.com. Small agency, popular with backpackers, offering well-priced tours to Tortuguero (2/3 days; from $185) and the Osa Peninsula (3 days; from $365). They also run trips with the Bribri.

Expediciones Tropicales Av 11/13, C 3 bis ⓣ2257-4171, ⓦwww.costaricainfo.com.

Well-regarded agency with knowledgeable guides who run popular combination day-tours of Volcán Poás and nearby sights ($92; 10hr), as well as a host of other trips from San José at competitive prices.

Horizontes Nature Tours C 28, Av 1/3 ⓣ2222-2022, ⓦwww.horizontes.com. Highly regarded agency concentrating on rainforest walking and hiking, volcanoes and birdwatching, all with an emphasis on natural and cultural history.

OTEC Viajes C 3, Av 1/3 ⓣ2523-0500, ⓦwww.otecviajes.com (Spanish only). This large agency – particularly focused on student travel – specializes in adventure tours including fishing, trekking, surfing and mountain biking, plus hotel reservations and car rentals.

Serendipity Adventures Apdo 90-7150 Turrialba ⓣ2558-1000, ⓦwww.serendipityadventures.com. This superior travel agency offers individual custom-made tours for self-formed groups with a sense of adventure, mostly to undiscovered parts of Costa Rica. They're experts in canyoning and rappelling, and are the only operators in Costa Rica to offer hot-air balloon trips.

Simbiosis Tours Apdo 6939-1000, San José ⓣ2290-8646, ⓦwww.simbiosistours.com. Tour company offering community-based rural tourism programmes alongside various day-trips and activities; some of their excellent hiking trips are held in conjunction with local cooperative, and involve staying in community lodges.

Specops ⓣ443/889-9648, ⓦwww.specops.com. Adventure education group, comprising US Special Forces veterans and expert Costa Rican guides, which specializes in white-knuckle thrills and jungle-survival courses.

Accommodation

Most towns in Costa Rica have a wide range of places to stay, and even the smallest settlements usually have basic lodgings. Prices are higher than you'd pay in other Central American countries, but they're by no means exorbitant, and certainly not when compared with the US or Western Europe. Budget accommodation runs the gamut from the extremely basic, where $20 will get you little more than a room and a bed, to reasonably well-equipped accommodation with a clean, comfortable en-suite room, a fan and possibly even a TV for around $30 a night. In the middle and upper price range, facilities and services are generally of a very good standard throughout the country. When considering the cost, remember that not all hotels list the hotel tax in the published price, which is thirteen percent.

The larger places to stay in Costa Rica are usually called **hotels**. **Posadas**, **hostals**, **hospedajes** and **pensiones** are smaller, though *posadas* can sometimes be quite swanky, especially in rural areas. **Casas** tend to be private guesthouses or B&Bs, while **albergues** are the equivalent of lodges. **Cabinas** are common in Costa Rica,

Accommodation price codes

All the accommodation in this book has been graded using the following **price codes**. The prices quoted are for the **least expensive double room in high season**, and do not include the thirteen percent national tax that is automatically added onto hotel bills. Unless otherwise stated, breakfast is included in the price.

- ❶ $19 and under
- ❷ $20–29
- ❸ $30–39
- ❹ $40–54
- ❺ $55–74
- ❻ $75–99
- ❼ $100–149
- ❽ $150–199
- ❾ $200 and over

Staying with a Costa Rican family

There's no better way to experience life off the tourist trail and to practise your Spanish than **staying with a Tico family**. Usually enjoyable, sometimes transformative, this can be a fantastic experience, and at the very least is sure to provide genuine contact with Costa Ricans.

Most **homestay programmes** are organized by the country's various **language schools** and cater mainly to students. However, some schools may be willing to put you in contact with a family even if you are not a student at the school in question. The **Ilisa Language School** (Ⓣ2280-0700, Ⓦwww.ilisa.com), one of San José's largest, is particularly helpful in this regard. Stays can last from one week to several months, and many travellers use the family home as a base while touring the country. You'll have your own key, but in most cases it would be frowned upon if you brought someone home for the night. The one rule that always applies is that guests and hosts communicate in Spanish. Costs, which include meals and laundry, average about $840 a month.

For a **non-study-based option**, try **Bells' Home Hospitality** (Ⓣ2225-4752, Ⓦwww.homestay-thebells.org), run by a long-time resident of Costa Rica, Vernon Bell, and his wife Marcela, who arrange for individuals, couples and families to stay in private rooms in a family home, with private or shared bath; singles cost $30, doubles $50. Breakfast is included in the price, with evening meals available for an additional $9. Another recommended organization is **Monteverde Homestays** (Ⓣ2645-6627, Ⓦwww.monteverdehomestay.com), which offers accommodation in a range of family homes near the Santa Elena and Monteverde reserves for $25 per night including breakfast.

Other points of contact for homestays as well as longer-term **apartment rentals and houseshares** include adverts in the *Tico Times* (although homestays and flats listed here tend to be expensive), the (Spanish) classifieds in *La Nación* and the notice boards of hostels and guesthouses.

particularly in coastal areas: they're usually either a string of motel-style rooms in an annexe away from the main building or, more often, separate self-contained units. Usually – although not always – they tend toward the basic, and are most often frequented by budget travellers. More upmarket versions may be called "villas" or "chalets". Anything called a **motel** – as in most of Latin America – is unlikely to be used for sleeping.

Few hotels except those at the upper end of the price range have double beds, and it's more common to find two or three single beds. **Single travellers** will generally be charged the single rate even if they're occupying a double room, though this is sometimes not the case in popular beach towns and at peak seasons.

Incidentally, wherever you're staying, don't expect to get much reading done in the evenings – light bulbs are very wan, even in good hotels. Also bear in mind that in Costa Rican hotels, the term "**hot water**" can be misleading. Showers are often equipped with squat plastic nozzles (water heaters), inside which is an electric element that heats the water to a warm, rather than hot, temperature. Some of the nozzles have a button that actually turns on the element. Under no circumstances should you touch this button or get anywhere near the nozzle when wet – these contraptions may not be quite as bad as their tongue-in-cheek name of "suicide showers" suggests, but there's still a distinct possibility you could get a nasty shock. The trick to getting fairly hot water is not to turn on the pressure too high. Keep a little coming through to heat the water more efficiently.

Reservations

Costa Rica's hotels tend to be chock-full in high season (Nov–April), especially at Christmas, New Year and Easter, so **reserve well ahead**, particularly for youth hostels and good-value hotels in popular spots. Many hotels, even budget ones, are online, so the easiest and surest way to reserve in advance is with a credit card by email. Once on the ground in Costa Rica, phone or email again to reconfirm your reservation. Some establishments will ask you to reserve and pay in advance – the more popular hotels and lodges require you to do this as far as thirty days ahead, often by money transfer.

If you prefer to be a little more spontaneous, travelling in the low season, from roughly after Easter to mid-November, can be easier, when you can safely wait until you arrive in the country to make reservations. During these months, it's even possible to show up at hotels on spec – there will probably be space, and possibly even a low-season discount of as much as thirty to fifty percent.

Pensiones and hotels

When travelling, most Costa Ricans and nationals of other Central American countries stick to the lower end of the market and patronize traditional **pensiones** (a fast-dying breed in Costa Rica, especially in San José) or established Costa Rican-owned hotels. If you do likewise, you may well get a better price than at the tourist or foreign-owned hotels, although this is not a hard-and-fast rule. Though standards are generally high, you should expect to get what you pay for – usually clean but dim, spartan rooms with cold-water showers. If you think you might have a choice or want to shop around, it's perfectly acceptable to ask to see the room first.

The majority of accommodation catering to foreigners is in the **middle range**, and as such is reasonably priced – although still more expensive than similar accommodation in other Central American countries. Hotels at the lower end of this price category will often offer very good value, giving you private bath with hot water, perhaps towels, and maybe even air conditioning (which, it has to be said, is not really necessary in most places; a ceiling fan generally does fine). At the upper end of this price range, a few extras, like TV, may be thrown in.

Top 5 eco-lodges

As the original eco-tourist destination, Costa Rica has some of the best **eco-lodges** in the Americas, and there can be few more gratifying ways to spend your holiday than by lushing it up in a luxury lodge in the middle of the rainforest, safe in the knowledge that you're having no negative impact on your surroundings and that your money is going to a good cause or causes. See p.453 for more on what defines eco-tourism and an eco-lodge.

Finca Rosa Blanca Coffee Plantation & Inn ⓣ2269-9392, ⓦwww.fincarosablanca.com Gorgeous, idyosyncratically designed rooms and suites on an organic coffee plantation in the Valle Central. Solar heating and recycling (including a vermiculture compost) are just some of their sustainable practices. See p.145.

Lapa Ríos ⓣ506/2735-5130, ⓦwww.laparios.com. Upmarket lodge built using renewable resources on the diversity-rich Osa Peninsula. Protects its own thousand-acre conservancy, invests heavily in the local community and is completely locally staffed. See p.408.

Rancho Margot ⓣ2479-7259 or 8302-7318, ⓦwww.ranchomargot.org. Self-sufficient organic farm and wildlife rescue centre with a range of accommodation to suit all budgets – join in with milking the cows or help in the herb garden. See p.229.

Reserva Rara Avis ⓣ2764-1111, ⓦwww.rara-avis.com. Remote rainforest lodge that doubles as a research station, set in thick primary forest that's home to a variety of unique flora and thrilling fauna. See p.247.

El Silencio Lodge & Spa ⓣ2761-0301, ⓦwww.elsilenciolodge.com. Inviting hillside cabins overlooking swathes of cloudforest (much of it the lodge's private reserve). Carbon-offsetting initiatives and waste-management programmes, plus most of the staff, including the management, is local; profits go towards primary school projects. See p.137.

Resorts, lodges and B&Bs

There are many **resorts** scattered throughout Costa Rica, ranging from swanky hotels in popular places like Manuel Antonio to lush **rainforest eco-lodges** in areas of outstanding natural beauty – the sort of hideaways that have their own jacuzzis, swimming pools, spas, gourmet restaurants and private stretches of jungle. These rank among the finest – and most expensive – places to stay in the country (see box, p.49 for a few of our favourites), though prices can fall dramatically out of season, when you might be able to get yourself a night or two of luxury for as little as $150.

A new breed of **B&Bs** (often owned by expats) has sprung up in recent years, similar to their North American or UK counterparts, offering rooms in homes or converted homes with a "family atmosphere", insightful local advice and a full breakfast. As well as those listed in the Guide, you can search online for Costa Rican B&Bs at ⓦwww.bedandbreakfast.com/costa-rica.html.

Camping

Though **camping** is fairly widespread in Costa Rica, gone are the days when you could pitch your tent on just about any beach or field. With the influx of visitors, local residents (especially in small beachside communities) have grown tired of campers leaving rubbish on the beach – you'll have a far better relationship with them if you ask politely whether it's OK to camp first.

In beach towns, you'll usually find at least one well-equipped **private campsite**, with good facilities including lavatories, drinking water and cooking grills; staff may also offer to guard your clothes and tent while you're at the beach. You may also find hotels, usually at the lower end of the price scale, where you can pitch your tent on the grounds and use the showers and washrooms for a fee. Though not all **national parks** have campsites, the ones that do usually offer high standards and at least basic facilities, with lavatories, water and cooking grills – all for around $2 per person per day. In some national parks, you can bunk down at the **ranger station** if you call well in advance; for more details, see p.59.

There are three general **rules of camping** in Costa Rica: first, never leave your tent (or anything of value inside it) unattended, or it may not be there when you get back. Second, never leave your tent open except to get in and out, unless you fancy sharing your sleeping quarters with snakes, insects, coati or toads. Finally, take your refuse with you when you leave.

Youth hostels

Costa Rica has over two hundred **hostels** and **backpackers'**, offering dorm beds for as little as $5 a night; most have a range of double, triple and family rooms, and many offer additional services including internet access (often for free), laundry and luggage storage. Bed linen, towels and soap are generally included in the price. There are

What to bring when camping in Costa Rica

- Tent
- Backpack
- Lightweight (summer) sleeping bag, except for climbing Chirripó, where you may need a three-season bag
- Rain gear
- Mosquito net
- Maps
- Torch
- Knife
- Matches, in a waterproof box
- Firelighter
- Compass
- Insect repellent
- Water bottles
- Toilet paper
- Hat
- Sunglasses
- Sunblock
- Plastic bags (for wet clothes/refuse)

only four official **youth hostels** affiliated with Hostelling International – *Jardines Arenal* in La Fortuna, *Vista Serena Hostel* in Manuel Antonio (see p.368) and *Hostel Casa Yoses* and *Mi Casa Hostel* in San José – which cost around $11–14 per night. As with all accommodation in Costa Rica, bookings should ideally be made several months in advance if you're visiting in high season.

Youth hostel associations

In the US and Canada

Hostelling International USA ⓣ301/495-1240, ⓦwww.hiusa.org.

Hostelling International Canada ⓣ1-800/663-5777 or 613/237-7884, ⓦwww.hihostels.ca.

In the UK and Ireland

Irish Youth Hostel Association ⓣ01/830 4555, ⓦwww.anoige.ie.

Youth Hostel Association (YHA) ⓣ0800/019 1700, ⓦwww.yha.org.uk.

In Australia and New Zealand

YHA Australia ⓣ02/9565 1699, ⓦwww.yha.com.au.

YHA New Zealand ⓣ0800/278 299, ⓦwww.yha.co.nz.

Food and drink

Costa Rican food – called comida típica ("native" or "local" food) by Ticos – is best described as unpretentious. Simple it may be, but tasty nonetheless, especially when it comes to the interesting regional variations found along the Caribbean coast, with its Creole-influenced cooking, and in Guanacaste, where there are vestiges of the ancient indigenous peoples' use of maize. For more on the cuisine of these areas, see the relevant chapters in the Guide.

Típico dishes you'll find all over Costa Rica include rice and some kind of meat or fish, often served as part of a special plate with coleslaw salad, in which case it's called a **casado** (literally, "married person"). The ubiquitous **gallo pinto** ("painted rooster"), often described as the national dish of Costa Rica, is a breakfast combination of red and white beans with rice, sometimes served with *huevos revueltos* (scrambled eggs). The heavy concentration on starch and protein reveals the rural origins of Costa Rican food: *gallo pinto* is food for people who are going out to work it off.

Of the dishes found on menus all over the country, particularly recommended are **ceviche** (raw fish "marinated" in lime juice with coriander and peppers), **pargo** (red snapper), **corvina** (sea bass) and any of the ice creams and **desserts**, though these can be too sickly for many tastes. The fresh **fruit** is especially good, either eaten by itself or drunk in *refrescos* (see p.52). Papayas, pineapple and bananas are all cheap and plentiful, along with some less familiar fruits like *mamones chinos* (a kind of lychee), *anona* (custard fruit), *pejibaye* (peach-palm fruit) and *marañón*, whose seed is the cashew nut. Look out, too, for fresh strawberries around Volcán Poás and sweet, fleshy *guanábana* along the Caribbean coast.

See p.468 for a Spanish/English glossary of food and drink terms.

Eating out

Eating out in Costa Rica will cost more than you might think, and has become even more expensive over the past few years. Main dishes can easily cost over $10, and then there are those sneaky **extra charges**: the

Coffee in Costa Rica

There are two types of coffee available in Costa Rica: **export quality** (*grano d'oro*, literally the "golden bean"), typically packaged by either Café Britt or Café Rey and served in good hotels and restaurants; and the **lower-grade blend**, usually sold for the home market. Costa Rica's export-grade coffee is known the world over for its mellowness and smoothness. The stuff produced for the domestic market, however, is another matter entirely; some of it is even pre-sweetened, so if you ask for it with sugar (*con azúcar*), you'll get a saccharine shock.

All coffee in Costa Rica is Arabica; it's illegal to grow anything else. Among the best brews you'll find are **La Carpintera**, a smooth, rich, hard bean grown on Cerro de la Carpintera in the Valle Central, and **Zurqui**, the oldest cultivated bean in the country, grown for 150 years on the flanks of Volcán Barva. Strong, but with a silky, gentle taste, **Café el Gran Vito**, grown by Italian immigrants near San Vito in the extreme south of the country, is an unusual grade of export bean, harder to find than those grown in the Valle Central.

Several small coffee producers run **tours** of their plantations, allowing you to see the coffee-cultivating process up close and to try their home-grown roasts on site. For places that offer coffee tours in the Valle Central, home to five of the country's eight regional varieties, see box on p.126; for places around Monteverde, see box on p.326.

service charge (10 percent) and the sales tax (13 percent), which bring the meal to a total of 23 percent more than the menu price. Add this all up, and dinner for two can easily come to $25 for a single course and a couple of beers. **Tipping** (see p.80) is not necessary, however. Costa Rica's best restaurants are on the outskirts of San José, and in popular tourist destinations such as Tamarindo, Manuel Antonio and around La Fortuna, where demand has created some excellent gourmet options.

The cheapest places to dine in Costa Rica – and where most workers eat lunch, their main meal – are the ubiquitous **sodas**, halfway between the North American diner and the British greasy café. *Sodas* offer filling set *platos del día* (daily specials) and *casados* for about $4; most do not add sales tax. You usually have to go to the cash register to get your bill. *Sodas* also often have takeaway windows where you can pick up snacks such as the delicious little fingers of fried dough and sugar called *churros*. Many *sodas* are vegetarian, and in general **vegetarians** do quite well in Costa Rica. Most menus will have a vegetable option, and asking for dishes to be served without meat is perfectly acceptable.

Because Costa Ricans start the day early, they are less likely to hang about late in restaurants in the evening, and establishments are usually empty or **closed** by 9.30 or 10pm. Non-smoking sections are uncommon, to say the least, except in the most expensive establishments, but in general Ticos don't smoke much in restaurants.

Drinking

Costa Rica is famous for its **coffee**, and it's usual to end a meal with a small cup, traditionally served in a pitcher with heated milk on the side. Most of the best blends are exported, so premium coffee is generally only served in high-end restaurants and sold in shops.

Always popular are **refrescos**, cool drinks made with milk (*leche*) or water (*agua*), fruit and ice, all whipped up in a blender. You can buy them at stalls or in cartons, though the latter tend to be sugary. You'll find **herb teas** throughout the country; those served in the Caribbean province of Limón are especially good. In Guanacaste, you can sample the distinctive **corn-based drinks** *horchata* and *pinolillo*, made with milk and sugar and with a grainy consistency.

Costa Rica has several local brands of **lager**, a godsend in the steamy tropics. Most popular is Imperial, with its characteristic eagle logo, but Bavaria Gold is the best of the bunch, with a cleaner taste and more complex flavour; they also produce a decent dark beer. Of the local low-alcohol beers, Bavaria Light is the best tasting.

Wine, once a rare commodity, has become far more common in mid- and top-range restaurants, where you'll often find good Chilean and Argentinian varieties on offer, as well as (for a premium) Spanish brands. **Spirits** tend to be associated with serious drinking, usually by men in bars, and are rarely consumed by local women in public. There is an indigenous hard-liquor drink, **guaro**, of which Cacique is the most popular brand; it's a bit rough, but good with lime sodas or in a cocktail. For an after-dinner tipple, try Café Rica, a creamy **liqueur** made with the local coffee.

Bars

Costa Rica has a variety of **places to drink**, from shady macho domains to pretty beachside bars, with some particularly cosmopolitan nightspots in San José. The capital is also the place to find the country's last remaining **boca bars**, atmospheric places that serve *bocas* (tasty little tapas-like snacks) with drinks; though historically these were free, nowadays even in the most traditional places you'll probably have to pay for them (for more on San José's *boca* bars, see p.113). In even the smallest town with any foreign population – either expat or tourist – you'll notice a sharp split between the places frequented by locals and those that cater to foreigners. Gringo grottoes abound, especially in beach towns, and tend to have a wide bar stock, at least compared to the limited *guaro*-and-beer menu of the local bars. In many places, especially port cities like Limón, Puntarenas and Golfito, there is the usual contingent of rough-and-ready bars where testosterone-fuelled men go to drink gallons and fight; it's usually pretty obvious which ones they are – they advertise their seediness with a giant Imperial placard parked right in front of the door so you can't see what's going on inside.

Most bars typically **open** in the morning, any time between 8.30 and 11am, and **close** at around 11pm or midnight. **Sunday** night is usually dead: many bars don't open at all and others close early, around 10pm. Though Friday and Saturday nights are the busiest, the **best nights** to go out are often week nights (particularly Thursdays), when you can enjoy live music, happy hours and other specials. **Karaoke** is incredibly popular, and if you spend much time in bars, you'll soon pick out the well-loved Tico classics. The **drinking age** in Costa Rica is 18, and many bars will only admit those with ID (*cédula*); a photocopy of your passport page is acceptable.

Health

Health-wise, travelling in Costa Rica is generally very safe. Food tends to be hygienically prepared, so bugs and upsets are normally limited to the usual "traveller's tummy". Water supplies in most places are clean and bacteria-free, and outbreaks of serious infectious diseases such as cholera are rare.

In general, as in the rest of Latin America, it tends to be local people, often poor or without proper sanitation or access to health-care, who contract infectious diseases. Although Costa Rica's **healthcare** is of a high standard, the facilities at its major public hospitals (thirty of which are affiliated to CAJA, the country's social healthcare system) vary widely, and while some, such as the Hospital Nacional de Niños in San

José (see p.70), are very good, you are advised to use private hospitals and clinics where possible – and get extensive health insurance before you travel. The capital's two excellent **private hospitals** (CIMA San José and Clinica Biblica; see p.117) are equipped to handle medical, surgical and maternity cases, and have 24 hour emergency rooms; the latter also has a good pediatric unit.

Inoculations

No compulsory **inoculations** are required before you enter Costa Rica unless you're travelling from a country that has Yellow Fever, such as Colombia, in which case you must be able to produce a current inoculation certificate. You may, however, want to make sure that your polio, typhoid, diphtheria and hepatitis A and B jabs are up to date, though none of the diseases is a major risk. Rabies, a potentially fatal illness, should be taken very seriously if you're going to be spending a significant amount of time in the countryside. There is a vaccine comprising a course of three injections that has to be started at least a month before departure and which is effective for two years – though it's expensive and serves only to shorten the course of treatment you need. If you're not vaccinated, stay away from dogs, monkeys and any other potentially biting or scratching animals. If you do get scratched or bitten, wash the wound at once, with alcohol or iodine if possible, and seek medical help immediately.

The sun

Costa Rica is just eight to eleven degrees north of the Equator, which means a blazing-hot sun directly overhead. To guard against **sunburn** take at least factor-15 sunscreen (start on factor-30) and a good hat, and wear both even on slightly overcast days, especially in coastal areas. Even in places at higher altitudes where it doesn't feel excessively hot, such as San José and the surrounding Valle Central, you should protect yourself. **Dehydration** is another possible problem, so keep your fluid level up, and take rehydration salts (Gastrolyte is readily available) if necessary. **Diarrhoea** can be brought on by too much sun and heat sickness, and it's a good idea to bring an over-the-counter remedy such as Imodium from home – it should only be taken for short periods, however, and only when really necessary (such as travelling for long periods on a bus) as extensive use leads to constipation and only serves to keep whatever is making you ill inside you.

Drinking water

The only areas of Costa Rica where it's best not to drink the tap water (or ice

A traveller's first-aid kit

Among the items you might want to carry with you, especially if you're planning to go hiking, are:

- Antiseptic cream
- Plasters/Band-Aids
- Imodium for emergency diarrhoea treatment
- Paracetamol/aspirin
- Rehydration sachets
- Calamine lotion
- Hypodermic needles and sterilized skin wipes
- Iodine soap for washing cuts (guards against humidity-encouraged infections)
- Insect repellent
- Sulphur powder (fights the sand fleas/chiggers that are ubiquitous in some of Costa Rica's beach areas)

Note that most of Costa Rica's major towns have well-stocked **pharmacies** (*farmacias* or *boticas*) where trained pharmacists are licensed to dispense a wide range of drugs (essentially anything other than antibiotics or psychotropic drugs, for which you'll need a prescription).

cubes, or drinks made with tap water) are the port cities of **Limón** and **Puntarenas**. Bottled water is available in these towns; drink from these and stick with known brands, even if they are more expensive. Though you'll be safe drinking tap water elsewhere in the country, it is possible to pick up **giardia**, a bacterium that causes stomach upset and diarrhoea, by drinking out of streams and rivers – campers should stock up on water supplies from the national parks waterspouts, where it's been treated for drinking.

The time-honoured method of **boiling** will effectively sterilize water, although it will not remove unpleasant tastes. A minimum boiling time of five minutes (longer at higher altitudes) is sufficient to kill micro-organisms. Boiling water is not always convenient, however, as it is time-consuming and requires supplies of fuel or a travel kettle and power source. **Chemical sterilization** can be carried out using either chlorine or iodine tablets or (better) a tincture of iodine liquid; add a couple of drops to one litre of water and leave to stand for twenty minutes. **Pregnant women** or people with **thyroid problems** should consult their doctor before using iodine sterilizing tablets or iodine-based purifiers. Inexpensive iodine removal filters are recommended if treated water is being used continuously for more than a month or if it is being given to babies.

Malaria and dengue fever

Although some sources of information – including perhaps your GP – will tell you that you don't need to worry about **malaria** in Costa Rica, there is a small risk if you're travelling to the southern **Caribbean coast**, especially Puerto Limón and south towards Cahuita and Puerto Viejo de Talamanca. Around five hundred cases of malaria are reported annually, with about half of these being tourists, though numbers have dropped in recent years. If you want to make absolutely sure of not contracting the illness, and intend to travel extensively anywhere along the southern Caribbean, you should take a course of prophylactics (usually chloroquine rather than mefloquine), available from your doctor or clinic.

Dengue fever is perhaps more of a concern, although by no means a major one: some 20,000 cases were reported in an outbreak in late 2010 that affected San José and parts of the Valle Central, Guanacaste and the Pacific coast, in particularly the Osa Peninsula. Otherwise, most cases occur during the rainy season when the mosquito population is at its height. The symptoms are similar to malaria, but with extreme aches and pains in the bones and joints, along with fever and dizziness. On rare occasions, the illness may develop potentially fatal complications, though this usually only affects people who have caught the disease more than once. The only cure for dengue fever is rest and painkillers, and, as with malaria, the best course of action is prevention: to avoid getting bitten by mosquitoes, cover up with long sleeves and long trousers, use insect repellents (containing DEET) on exposed skin and, where necessary, sleep under a mosquito net.

Snakes

Snakes abound in Costa Rica, but the risk of being bitten is incredibly small – there has been no instance of a tourist receiving a fatal bite in recent years. Most of the victims of Costa Rica's more venomous snakes are field labourers who do not have time or the resources to get to a hospital (there are around five such deaths each year). Just in case, however, travellers hiking off the beaten track may want to take specific **antivenins** plus sterile hypodermic needles; if you're worried, you can buy antivenin at the Instituto Clodomiro Picado, the University of Costa Rica's snake farm in Coronado, outside San José (Ⓣ2229-0344, Ⓦicp.ucr.ac.cr), where herpetologists (people who study snakes) are glad to talk to visitors about precautions.

If you have no antivenin and are unlucky enough to get bitten, do not try to catch or kill the specimen for identification, as you only risk getting bitten again. Clean the wound with soap and water (do not try to suck out the venom), immobilize the bitten limb (do not apply a tourniquet) and get the victim to the nearest hospital as soon as possible.

In general, **prevention** is better than cure. As a rule of thumb, you should approach rainforest cover and grassy uplands – the kind of terrain you find in Guanacaste and the Nicoya Peninsula – with caution. Always watch where you put your feet and, if you need to hold something to keep your balance, make sure the "vine" you're grabbing isn't, in fact, a surprised snake. Be particularly wary at dawn or dusk – before 5.30am or after 6pm – though note that many snakes start moving as early as 4.30pm, particularly in dense cloud-forest cover. In addition, be careful in "sunspots", places in thick rainforest where the sun penetrates through to the ground or to a tree; snakes like to hang out here, absorbing the warmth. Above all, though, don't be too alarmed: thousands of tourists troop through Costa Rica's rainforests and grasslands each year without encountering a single snake.

HIV and AIDS

HIV and **AIDS** (in Spanish, SIDA) is present in the country (an estimated 9600 adults in Costa Rica are living with HIV), but isn't prevalent. That said, the same common-sense rules apply here as all over the world: sex without a condom, especially in some of the popular beach towns, is a serious health risk. **Condoms** sold in Costa Rica are not of the quality you find at home; it's best to bring them with you. Though hospitals and clinics use sterilized equipment, you may want to bring sealed hypodermic syringes anyway.

Medical website resources

Ⓦwww.cdc.gov/travel The US government's official site for travel health.

Ⓦwww.fitfortravel.nhs.uk The official site of the NHS, with information and advice on recommended inoculations, malaria risk and the general health situation in listed countries.

Ⓦwww.istm.org The website of the International Society for Travel Medicine, with a full list of clinics specializing in international travel health. Publishes outbreak warnings, suggested inoculations, precautions and other background information for travellers.

Ⓦwww.tmvc.com.au Contains a list of all Travellers Medical and Vaccination Centres throughout Australia, New Zealand and South Africa, plus general information on travel health.

Ⓦwww.tripprep.com Travel Health Online provides an online-only comprehensive database of necessary vaccinations for most countries, as well as destination and information on travel medical providers.

The media

Though the Costa Rican media generally pumps out relatively anodyne and conservative coverage of local and regional issues (shadowing the antics of the president and the political elite with dogged tenacity), it's possible to find good investigative journalism, particularly in the daily La Nación. There are also a number of interesting local radio stations, though TV coverage leaves a lot to be desired.

Newspapers

In San José, all **domestic newspapers** are sold on the street by vendors. Elsewhere, you can find them in newsagents and *pulperías* (general stores). All are tabloid format, with colourful, eye-catching layout and presentation.

Though the Costa Rican press is free, it does indulge in a certain follow-the-leader journalism. Leader of the pack is the daily **La Nación** (Ⓦwww.nacion.com), voice of the (right-of-centre) establishment and owned by the country's biggest media consortium; other highbrow dailies and television channels more or less parrot its line. Historically, *La Nación* has featured some good investigative reporting, as in the Banco Anglo corruption scandal and Costa Rica's continuing drug-trafficking problems. It also comes with a useful daily pull-out arts section, **Viva**, with listings of what's on in San José, and the classifieds are handy for almost anything, including long-term accommodation.

Also quite serious is **La República** (Ⓦwww.larepublica.net), even if they do have a tendency to slap a football photo on the front page no matter what's happening in the world. **Al Día** (Ⓦwww.aldia.cr) is the populist "body count" paper, which will give you a feel for the kind of newspaper read by most Costa Ricans. Alternative voices include **El Heraldo** (Ⓦwww.elheraldo.net), a small but high-quality daily, and **La Prensa Libre** (Ⓦwww.prensalibre.cr), the very good left-leaning evening paper. The weekly **Semanario Universidad** (Ⓦwww.semanario.ucr.ac.cr), the voice of the University of Costa Rica, certainly goes out on more of a limb than the big dailies, with particularly good coverage of the arts and the current political scene; you can find it on or around campus in San José's university district of San Pedro, and also in libraries.

Local English-language papers include the venerable and serious **Tico Times** (Ⓦwww.ticotimes.net), which comes out on Fridays and is a good source of information for travellers; the ads regularly feature hotel and restaurant discounts, as do the various other glossies produced by the tourist board. As for the **foreign press**, you can pick up recent copies of the *New York Times*, *International Herald Tribune*, *USA Today*, *Miami Herald*, *Newsweek*, *Time* and sometimes the *Financial Times* in the souvenir shop beside the *Gran Hotel Costa Rica* in downtown San José and at the La Casa de Revistas on the southwest corner of Parque Morazán. Of the San José bookstores, Librerías Lehmann at Av Central, C 1/3 and Librería Universal keep good stocks of mainstream and non-mainstream foreign magazines; the Mark Twain Library at the Centro Cultural Costarricense-Norteamericano (see p.117) also receives English-language publications.

Radio

There are lots of **commercial radio stations** in Costa Rica, all pumping out techno and house, along with a bit of salsa, annoying commercials and the odd bout of government-sponsored pseudo propaganda promoting the general wonder that is Costa Rica. Some of the more interesting **local radio stations** have only a limited airtime, such as Radio Emperador (107.1FM), Radio Costa Rica (930AM) and Radio Alajuela (1280AM), which features Costa Rican singers, along with some talk spots, from 8.30pm to midnight. A fascinating programme is *El Club del Taxista Costarricense* – the "Costa Rican Taxi Driver's Club" – broadcast by Radio Columbia (780AM) from 9 to 10.30am. This social and political talk show, nearing its 40th year, was initially directed only at taxi drivers, but its populist appeal has led to it being adopted by the general population. Radio Dos (99.5FM) has an English-language morning show, *Good Morning Costa Rica*, which runs from 6 to 9am.

Television

Most Costa Rican households have a **television**, beaming out a range of wonderfully awful Mexican or Venezuelan *telenovelas* (soap operas) and some not-so-bad domestic news programmes. On the downside, Costa Rica is also the graveyard for 1970s American TV, the place where *The Dukes of Hazzard* and other such delights, dubbed into Spanish, come back to haunt you.

Canal 7, owned by Teletica, is the main national station, particularly strong in local and regional news. Other than its news show, **Telenoticias**, Costa Rica has few home-grown products, and Canal 7's programming comprises a mix of bought-in shows from Spanish-speaking countries plus a few from the US. Repretel's **Canal 6** is the main competitor, very similar in content, while **Canal 19** mostly shows US programmes and movies dubbed into Spanish. The **Mexican cable channels** are good for news, and even have reports from Europe. Many places also subscribe to CNN and other cable channels, such as HBO, Cinemax and Sony Entertainment, which show wall-to-wall reruns of hit comedy shows and films.

Holidays and festivals

Though you shouldn't expect the kind of colour and verve that you'll find in fiestas in Mexico or Guatemala, Costa Rica has its fair share of lively holidays and festivals, or feriados, when all banks, post offices, museums and government offices close. In particular, don't try to travel anywhere during Semana Santa, Holy (Easter) Week: the whole country shuts down from Holy Thursday until after Easter Monday, and buses don't run. Likewise, the week from Christmas to New Year is invariably a time of traffic nightmares, overcrowded beach towns and suspended transport services.

Provincial holidays, such as Independence Day in Guanacaste (July 25) and the Limón carnival (the week preceding Oct 12) affect local services only, but nonetheless the shutdown is drastic: don't bet on cashing travellers' cheques or mailing letters if you're in these areas at party time.

January 1 New Year's Day. Celebrated with a big dance in San José's Parque Central.

January Fiesta de Palmares. Two weeks of dancing, music and horse parades in the small town of Palmares.

February Puntarenas Carnival. A week of parades, music and fireworks at the end of the month.

February/March Monteverde Music Fest. National and international musicians gather in the cloudforest town for a month of song and dance.

March 19 El Día de San José (St Joseph's Day). The patron saint of the San José Province is celebrated with fairs, parades and church services.

Ash Wednesday Countrywide processions; in Guanacaste, they're marked by horse, cow and bull parades, with bullfights (in which the bull is not harmed) in Liberia.

Holy Week (Semana Santa) Dates vary annually, but businesses will often close for the entire week preceding Easter weekend.

April International Arts festival. San José plays host to two weeks of theatre shows, concerts, dance performances and art exhibitions.

April 11 El Día de Juan Santamaría. Public holiday to commemorate the national hero who fought at the Battle of Rivas against the American adventurer William Walker in 1856.

May 1 El Día del Trabajo (Labour Day). The president delivers her annual "state of the nation" address while everyone else heads to the beach.

May 29 Corpus Christi Day.

June 29 St Peter's and St Paul's Day.

July Virgin del Mar (Virgin of the Sea). Elaborately decorated boats fill the Gulf of Nicoya on the Saturday nearest to the 16th, celebrating the patron saint of Puntarenas.

July 25 El Día de Guanacaste (Guanacaste Province only). Celebrations mark the annexation of Guanacaste from Nicaragua in 1824.

August 2 El Día de La Negrita (Virgin of Los Angeles Day). Worshippers make a pilgrimage to the basilica in Cartago to venerate the miraculous Black Virgin of Los Angeles (La Negrita), the patron saint of Costa Rica.

August 15 Assumption Day and Mother's Day.

September 15 Independence Day, with big patriotic parades celebrating Costa Rica's independence from Spain in 1821. The highlight is a student relay race across the entire Central American isthmus, carrying a "freedom torch" from Guatemala to Cartago (the original capital of Costa Rica).

October 12 El Día de la Raza (Columbus Day; Limón Province only). Centred on the carnival, which takes place in the week prior to October 12.

November 2 All Souls' Day. Families visit cemeteries to pay their respects to their ancestors.

Christmas Week The week before Christmas is celebrated in San José with fireworks, bullfights and funfairs.

December 25 Christmas Day. Family-oriented celebrations with trips to the beach and much consumption of apples and grapes.

December 27 San José Carnival. Huge parade with colourful floats and plenty of music.

National parks and reserves

Costa Rica protects a quarter of its total territory under the aegis of a carefully structured system of national parks, wildlife refuges and biological reserves – in all, there are currently more than 185 designated protected areas. Gradually established over the last 35 years, the role of these parks in conserving the country's rich fauna and flora is generally lauded.

In total, the parks and reserves harbour approximately five percent of the world's total **wildlife species** and **life zones**, among them rainforests, cloudforests, paramo (high-altitude moorlands), swamps, lagoons, marshes and mangroves, and the last remaining patches of tropical dry forest in the isthmus. Also protected are areas of historical significance, including a very few pre-Columbian settlements, and places considered to be of immense scenic beauty – valleys, waterfalls, dry lowlands and beaches. Costa Rica has also taken measures to safeguard beaches where marine turtles lay their eggs, as well as a number of active volcanoes. For a **history** of the park system in Costa Rica, see p.449.

Definitions

A **national park** (*parque nacional*) is typically a large chunk of relatively untouched wilderness – usually more than 2500 acres – dedicated to preserving features of outstanding ecological, environmental or scenic interest. These are generally the most established of the protected areas, typically offering walking, hiking or snorkelling opportunities. Though habitation, construction of hotels and hunting of animals is prohibited in all national parks, "buffer zones" are increasingly being designated around them, where people are permitted to engage in a limited amount of agriculture and hunting. In most cases, park boundaries are surveyed but not demarcated – rangers and locals know what land is within the park and what is not – so don't expect fences or signs to tell you where you are.

Although it also protects valuable ecosystems and conserves areas for scientific research, a **biological reserve** (*reserva biológica*) generally has less of scenic or recreational interest than a national park, though hunting and fishing are usually still prohibited. A **national wildlife refuge** (*refugio nacional de vida silvestre* or *refugio nacional de fauna silvestre*) is designated to protect the habitat of wildlife species. It will not be at all obviously demarcated, with few, if any, services, rangers or trails, and, the Refugio Nacional de Vida Silvestre Caño Negro notwithstanding, is generally little visited by tourists. An "**absolute**" **reserve** (*reserva absoluta*) is purely dedicated to scientific research, with no public entry permitted – the one exception being the Reserva Natural Absoluta Cabo Blanco, on the tip of the southern Nicoya Peninsula, which was Costa Rica's first piece of nationally protected land and grants visitors similar access to a national wildlife refuge or national park.

There are also a number of **privately owned reserves**, chief among them community-initiated projects such as the now famous reserves at Monteverde and nearby Santa Elena. While the money you pay to enter these does not go directly to the government, they are almost always not-for-profit places; the vast majority are conscientiously managed and have links with national and international conservation organizations. For more on how national parks and protected areas link up in Costa Rica's conservation strategy, see p.449.

Visiting the parks

Despite their role in attracting tourists to the country, national parks – and the national park system in general – are underfunded, and facilities at some of the more remote and less visited parks (such as Juan Castro

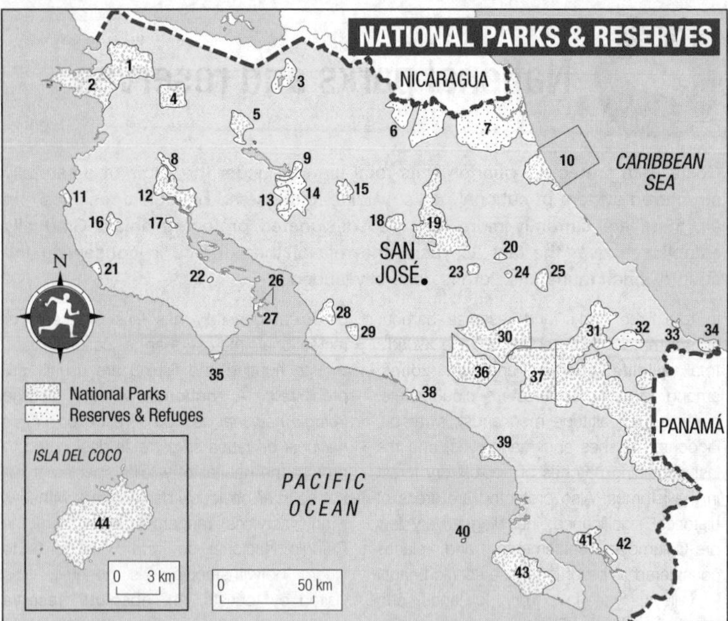

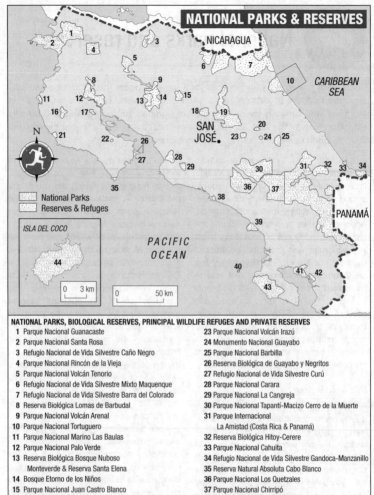

NATIONAL PARKS, BIOLOGICAL RESERVES, PRINCIPAL WILDLIFE REFUGES AND PRIVATE RESERVES

1 Parque Nacional Guanacaste
2 Parque Nacional Santa Rosa
3 Refugio Nacional de Vida Silvestre Caño Negro
4 Parque Nacional Rincón de la Vieja
5 Parque Nacional Volcán Tenorio
6 Refugio Nacional de Vida Silvestre Mixto Maquenque
7 Refugio Nacional de Vida Silvestre Barra del Colorado
8 Reserva Biológica Lomas de Barbudal
9 Parque Nacional Volcán Arenal
10 Parque Nacional Tortuguero
11 Parque Nacional Marino Las Baulas
12 Parque Nacional Palo Verde
13 Reserva Biológica Bosque Nuboso Monteverde & Reserva Santa Elena
14 Bosque Etorno de los Niños
15 Parque Nacional Juan Castro Blanco
16 Parque Nacional Diriá
17 Parque Nacional Barra Honda
18 Parque Nacional Volcán Poás
19 Parque Nacional Braulio Carrillo
20 Parque Nacional Volcán Turrialba
21 Refugio Nacional de Vida Silvestre Ostional
22 Refugio Nacional de Vida Silvestre Reserva Karen Mogensen
23 Parque Nacional Volcán Irazú
24 Monumento Nacional Guayabo
25 Parque Nacional Barbilla
26 Reserva Biológica de Guayabo y Negritos
27 Refugio Nacional de Vida Silvestre Curú
28 Parque Nacional Carara
29 Parque Nacional La Cangreja
30 Parque Nacional Tapantí-Macizo Cerro de la Muerte
31 Parque Internacional La Amistad (Costa Rica & Panamá)
32 Reserva Biológica Hitoy-Cerere
33 Parque Nacional Cahuita
34 Refugio Nacional de Vida Silvestre Gandoca-Manzanillo
35 Reserva Natural Absoluta Cabo Blanco
36 Parque Nacional Los Quetzales
37 Parque Nacional Chirripó
38 Parque Nacional Manuel Antonio
39 Parque Nacional Marino Ballena
40 Reserva Biológica Isla del Caño
41 Parque Nacional Piedras Blancas
42 Refugio Nacional de Vida Silvestre Golfito
43 Parque Nacional Corcovado
44 Parque Nacional Isla del Coco

Blanco, Volcán Turrialba and La Cangreja) can be surprisingly threadbare or even non-existent. Most parks, however, have an entrance **puesto**, or ranger station, often little more than a small hut where you pay your fee (usually around $10) and pick up a general map. Typically, the main ranger stations – from where the internal administration of the park is carried out, and where the rangers (or *guardaparques*) sleep, eat and hang out – are some way from the entrance *puesto*; it's a good idea to pay these a visit, as you can talk to the *guardaparques* (if your Spanish is good)

National parks at a glance

National Park	Location	Topography	Wildlife	Activities
La Amistad*	border with Panamá	rainforest	mammals, birds	hiking
Ballena**	192km SW of San José	marine coral	mammals, marine life	diving, snorkelling
Barbilla	101km E of San José	rainforest	birds, mammals	hiking
Barra Honda	330km W of San José	subterranean caves	bats, reptiles, birds	caving
Las Baulas**	301km NW of San José	beach, marine	turtles	turtle-watching
Braulio Carrillo	20km N of San José	cloudforest, rainforest	birds, reptiles, mammals	hiking, birdwatching
Cahuita	195km SE of San José	marine, beaches	marine life, reptiles, mammals	swimming, walking, snorkelling
La Cangreja	87km SW of San José	rainforest	birds, mammals	hiking
Carara	90km W of San José	rainforest, tropical dry forest	birds, mammals, reptiles	birdwatching, hiking
Chirripó	151km SW of San José	mountain peaks, paramo	mammals, birds (incl. quetzal)	hiking, climbing
Corcovado	380km SW of San José	rainforest	mammals, amphibians, reptiles	hiking
Diriá	287km W of San José	tropical dry forest	mammals, birds	hiking
Guanacaste	250km NW of San José	rainforest, tropical dry forest	butterflies, moths, birds, mammals	hiking
Guayabo***	84km E of San José	rainforest	mammals, birds	archeology, history, walking
Isla del Coco	500km offshore	volcanic, rainforest	marine life	diving
Juan Castro Blanco	64km NW of San José	rainforest	birds, mammals	hiking
Manuel Antonio	132km S of San José	rainforest, mangroves, beaches	mammals, marine life, reptiles	hiking, swimming
Palo Verde	240km NW of San José	seasonal wetlands, savanna	birds, mammals	birdwatching, hiking
Piedras Blancas	321km SW of San José	rainforest, beach	birds, mammals, marine life	hiking, swimming
Los Quetzales	75km S of San José	cloudforest	mammals, birds (incl. quetzal)	birdwatching, hiking
Rincón de la Vieja	253km NW of San José	rainforest, savanna	birds	hiking, volcano-watching
Santa Rosa	261km NW of San José	tropical dry forest	mammals, turtles	hiking, history, turtle-watching
Tapantí-Macizo Cerro de la Muerte	40km SW of San José	primary montane forests	mammals, birds	hiking
Tortuguero	254km NE of San José	rainforest, beach	turtles, mammals, birds	turtle-watching
Volcán Arenal	136km NW of San José	volcanic	birds, mammals	volcano-watching, hiking
Volcán Irazú	54km E of San José	volcanic	birds	volcano-watching
Volcán Poás	56km N of San José	volcanic, dwarf cloudforest	mammals, birds	volcano-watching
Volcán Tenorio	160km NW of San José	volcanic	birds	volcano-watching, hiking
Volcán Turrialba	64km E of San José	volcanic	birds	volcano-watching, hiking

*** Parque Nacional Internacional ** Parque Nacional Marino *** Monumento Nacional**

about local terrain and conditions, enquire about drinking water and use the bathroom. In some parks, such as Corcovado, you can sleep in or camp near the main stations, which usually provide basic but adequate accommodation, be it on a campsite or a bunk, in a friendly atmosphere.

In general, the **guardaparques** are extremely knowledgeable and informative and are happy to tell you about their encounters with fearsome bushmasters or placid tapirs. Independent travellers and hikers might want to ask about the possibility of joining them on patrol during the day (you'll probably have to speak some Spanish), while the more adventurous can volunteer to help out at remote ranger stations (see p.72 for more); you have to be pretty brave to do this, as you are expected to do everything that a ranger does, which includes patrolling the park (often at night) against poachers.

Outside the most visited parks – Volcán Poás, Volcán Irazú, Santa Rosa and Manuel Antonio – **opening hours** are erratic. Many places are open daily, from around 8am to 4pm, though there are exceptions, while other parks may open a little earlier in the morning. Unless you're planning on camping or staying overnight, there's almost no point in arriving at a national park in the afternoon. In all cases, especially the volcanoes, you should aim to arrive as early in the morning as possible to make the most of the day and, in particular, the weather (especially in the wet season); early morning is also the best time to spot the wildlife that the parks protect. You'll usually find a *guardaparque* somewhere, even if he or she is not at the ranger station – if you hang around for a while and call "¡*Upe*!" (what people say when entering houses and farms in the countryside), someone will usually appear.

Costa Rica's protected areas are overseen by the Sistema Nacional de Areas de Conservación (National System of Conservation Areas), or **SINAC** (Ⓣ2256-0917, Ⓦwww.sinac.go.cr), which operates within MINAE and can provide information on individual parks, transport and camping facilities. The only central office where you can make reservations and buy **permits**, where required, is the **Fundación de Parques Nacionales** (Av 15, C 25, Barrio Escalante, San José, Ⓣ2257-2239, Ⓔfpncr@ice.co.cr), who will contact those parks for which you sometimes need reservations, chiefly Santa Rosa, Corcovado and Chirripó (see the individual accounts in the Guide for more details); other parks can be visited on spec.

Outdoor activities

Costa Rica is famous for year-round adventure tourism and its variety of adrenaline-fuelled outdoor activities, with numerous well-organized packages and guided outings (see p.46 for details of tour operators). For further information on sporting activities, pick up the bi-monthly Costa Rica Outdoors magazine or visit Ⓦwww.costaricaoutdoors.com – they specialize in fishing, but cover other sports, too.

Hiking

Almost everyone who comes to Costa Rica does some sort of **hiking** or **walking**, whether it be through the rainforest, on grassy uplands or drylands, or ambling along beaches and well-maintained national park trails. From lowland tropical forest to the heights of Mount Chirripó, there are opportunities for walking in all kinds of terrain, often for considerable distances.

Make sure you **bring** sturdy shoes or hiking boots and a hat, sunblock and lightweight

Top 5 hikes

Costa Rica's national parks and wildlife refuges are home to some truly spectacular **trails**, enabling you to hike deep into verdant rainforest, past bubbling mud pools or along surf-lashed beaches. Below are a few of our favourites.

Cerro Chirripó A long, cold and sometimes wet slog up and across alpine-esque moorland rewards you with (on a clear day) superb views from Costa Rica's highest point. See p.386.

Estación Biológica Pocosol Arguably the most adventurous trek in the country, the two-day hike from Monteverde to this research station on the edge of the Bosque Eterno de los Niños traverses unmarked trails and is accompanied by armed rangers. See p.326.

Sendero Laguna Meándrica Perhaps the finest birding trail of any national park (and that's saying something), this 4.3km round-trip in the western half of Parque Nacional Carara leads through transitionary terrain to a croc-filled lake that's home to myriad birdlife. See p.353.

Sendero Los Patos–Sirena Tough 20km trek through the dense rainforest cover of Parque Nacional Corcovado, offering experienced hikers the chance to spot some of Costa Rica's more elusive large mammals, including tapirs and collared peccaries. See p.411.

Sendero Las Pailas A terrific 6km circuit, taking in the best of Parque Nacional Rincón de la Vieja: sulphur pools, geothermal "stoves" and thermal mud pots, all within the shadow of a smoking volcano. See p.275.

rain gear. It helps to have binoculars, too, even if you don't consider yourself an avid birder or animal-spotter; it's amazing what they pick up that the naked eye misses. In certain areas, like Parque Nacional Corcovado – where you'll be doing more walking than you've ever done before, unless you're in the Marines – most people also bring a tent. In the high paramo of Chirripó, you'll need to bring at least a sleeping bag.

There are a number of things you have to be careful of when hiking in Costa Rica. The chief danger is **dehydration**: always carry lots of water with you, preferably bottled, or a canteen, and bring a hat and sunscreen to protect yourself against sunstroke (and use both, even if it's cloudy).

Each year many hikers **get lost**, although they're nearly almost always found before it's too late. If you're venturing into a remote and unfamiliar area, bring a map and compass and make sure you know how to use both. To lessen anxiety if you do get lost, make sure you have matches, a torch and, if you are at a fairly high altitude, warm clothing. It gets cold at night above 1500m, and it would be ironic (and put quite a damper on your holiday) to end up with hypothermia in the tropics.

White-water rafting

After hiking and walking, **white-water rafting** is probably the single most popular activity in Costa Rica. Some of the best rapids and rivers to be found south of the Colorado are here, and there's a growing mini-industry of rafting outfitters, most of them in San José, Turrialba or La Virgen.

White-water rafting entails getting in a rubber dinghy with about eight other people (including a guide) and paddling, at first very leisurely, down a river, before negotiating exhilarating rapids of varying difficulty. Overall it's very safe, and the ample life jackets and helmets help. **Wildlife** you are likely to see from the boat includes crocodiles, caiman, lizards, parrots, toucans, herons, kingfishers and iguanas. Most trips last a day, though some companies run overnight or multi-day excursions; **costs** range between $75 and $115 for a day, including transport, equipment and lunch. Dress to get wet, with a bathing suit, shorts and surfer sandals or gym shoes.

Rafters classify their rivers from Class I (easiest) to Class V (pretty hard – don't venture onto one of these until you know what you're doing). The **most difficult** rivers in Costa Rica are the Class III–IV+ Pacuaré and Reventazón (both reached from Turrialba; see p.162), Río Naranjo (near Quepos; see p.364) and Río Toro, and the Class V Upper Balsa (the last two both accessed from La Fortuna; see p.221). The **moderately easy** Río Sarapiquí (see p.252) is a Class II river with some Class III rapids, and a fearsome Class IV upper section; the Río Savegre, near Quepos (see p.364) runs Class II–III rapids. The gentlest of all is the Río Corobicí (see p.261) a lazy ride along Class I flat water.

White-water rafting outfitters

Aguas Bravas ⓣ2292-2072, ⓦwww.aguas-bravas.co.cr. One of the largest rafting specialists in the country, operating on the Toro, Balsa and Peñas Blancas rivers, near La Fortuna; the Puerto Viejo and Sarapiquí, near La Virgen; and the Chirripó, closer to San José.

Aventuras Naturales ⓣ2225-3939, ⓦwww.adventurecostarica.com. Focuses on running the Sarapiquí and the Pacuaré rivers – its two- and three-day trips on the latter include an overnight stay at the sumptuous *Pacuaré Jungle Lodge*.

Costa Rica Expeditions ⓣ2257-0766, ⓦwww.costaricaexpeditions.com. This long-established operator (see p.46 for more) has been rafting for over twenty years, with a good selection of day-trips and longer excursions, mostly on the Pacuaré; their "Connoisseur" trips include a riverbank gourmet lunch.

Exploradores Outdoors ⓣ2222-6262, ⓦwww.exploradoresoutdoors.com. Specializes in Costa Rica's more extreme white water, including the notorious Pascua section of the Río Reventazón. Their multi-day adventure that combines the Reventazon with the Río Pacuaré is rafting at its best: 54km of river running, taking in more than eighty rapids en route.

Ríos Tropicales ⓣ2233-6455, ⓦwww.riostropicales.com. One of the larger outfitters, with challenging one- to four-day trips on the Reventazón and Pacuaré, plus one- or two-day rides on the Savegre and the Sarapiquí – a good choice for experienced rafters.

Kayaking

More than twenty rivers in Costa Rica offer good **kayaking** opportunities, especially the Sarapiquí, Reventazón, Pacuaré and Corobicí. The small town of in the Zona Norte, is a good base for customized kayaking tours, with a number of specialist operators or lodges that rent boats, equipment and guides (see p.252). The "Week of Rivers" trip run by Costa Rica Rios (US & Canada ⓣ1-888/434-0776, UK ⓣ0800/612 8718, ⓦwww.costaricarios.com) takes in four of the country's best kayaking rivers and includes three days on the Pacuaré.

Sea kayaking has become increasingly popular in recent years. This is an activity for experienced kayakers only, and should never be attempted without a guide – the number of rivers, rapids and streams pouring from the mountains into the oceans on both coasts can make currents treacherous, and kayaking dangerous without proper supervision. One of the best operators is Seascape Kayak Tours (ⓣ8314-8605, ⓦwww.seascapekayaktours.com), who run recommended trips around the Refugio Nacional de Vida Silvestre Curú on the southern Nicoya Peninsula (see p.341).

Canopy tours, hanging bridges and aerial trams

The **canopy tour** craze that started in Monteverde in the early 1990s has swept the country, and now pretty much any town worth its salt has a zip-line or two. The standard tour consists of whizzing from lofty platform to platform via traverse cables, and while you're moving too fast to see much wildlife, it's definitely a thrill. In recent years, Tarzan swings and Superman cables (which you ride horizontally, arms stretched out like the eponymous superhero) have upped the ante, and several places now let you zip-line at night. Monteverde (see box, p.323) and the area around Volcán Arenal (see box, p.220) have some of the best canopy tours in Costa Rica.

More sedate, and more worthwhile for wildlife-watching, are the **hanging bridges** complexes, where you can experience spectacular views – if not a touch of vertigo – as you walk across the wobbly structures over serious heights. Several bridges take you right alongside the canopy of tall trees, some of which have colonized the bridges, draping their woody lianas over the ramparts; most offer tours with a naturalist guide, which can be a great way of gaining a better insight into life in the treetops. Again, Monteverde and Volcán Arenal are recommended places to take a "sky walk".

For an even more relaxing meander through the canopy, you could try riding on an **aerial tram**, a gondola-like cable car that slowly circuits the upper reaches of the rainforest. Several places that operate canopy tours and hanging bridges also have aerial trams, though the most famous is the Rainforest Aerial Tram (now known as the Rainforest Adventures Costa Rica Atlantic), just outside Parque Nacional Braulio Carrillo (see p.149); there's also a Pacific branch, just north of Jacó (see p.360).

Swimming

Costa Rica has many lovely **beaches**, most of them on the Pacific coast. You do have to be careful swimming at many of them, however, as more than two hundred **drownings** occur each year – about four or five a week. Most are unnecessary, resulting from **riptides**, strong, swift-moving currents that go from the beach out to sea in a kind of funnel (see box below). It's also important to be aware of fairly heavy **swells**. These waves might not look that big from the beach but can have a mighty pull when you get near their break point. Many people are hurt coming out of the sea, backs to the waves, which then clobber them from behind – it's best to come out of the sea sideways, so that there is minimum body resistance to the water.

In addition to the above **precautions**, never swim alone, don't swim at beaches where turtles nest (this means, more often than not, sharks), never swim near river estuaries (pollution and riptides) and always ask locals about the general character of the beach before you swim.

Surfing

Surfing is very good on both of Costa Rica's coasts, although there are certain beaches that are suitable during only parts of the year. You can surf all year round on the **Pacific**: running north to south the most

Riptides

Riptides are always found on beaches with relatively heavy surf, and can also form near river estuaries; some are permanent, while some "migrate" up and down a beach. If caught in a rip tide – and you'll know when you're in one as they can move at an alarming rate of up to 10kph – you should follow some simple advice.

Don't panic While riptides may drag you out to sea a bit, they won't take you far beyond the breakers, where they lose their energy and dissipate. They also won't drag you under – that's an undertow – and there are far fewer of those on Costa Rica's beaches. Relax as much as possible panicking will exhaust you fast and cause you to take in water.

Don't swim against the current this is a pointless exercise. Instead, float, call for help and wait until the current dies down. Then swim back towards the beach at a 45-degree angle, not straight in; by swimming at an angle, you'll avoid getting caught in the current again.

Beaches with riptides

Some of the most popular and frequented **beaches** in Costa Rica are, ironically, also the worst for riptides. Take extra care when swimming at the following destinations:

Playa Avellanas (Guanacaste)
Playa Bonita (Limón)
Playa Cahuita the first 400m of beach (Limón)
Playa Doña Ana (Central Pacific)
Playa Espadilla Manuel Antonio (Central Pacific)
Playa Jacó (Central Pacific)
Playa Junquillal (Guanacaste)
Playa Tamarindo (Guanacaste)
Punta Uva (Limón)

popular beaches are Naranjo, Tamarindo, Boca de Barranca, Jacó, Hermosa, Quepos, Dominical and, in the extreme south near the Panamá border, Pavones. On the **Caribbean** coast, the best beaches are at Puerto Viejo de Talamanca and Punta Uva, further down the coast.

The **north Pacific Coast and Nicoya Peninsula** is the country's prime surfing area, with a wide variety of reef and beach breaks and lefts and rights of varying power and velocity. **Playa Potrero Grande** (also known as Ollie's Point and made famous in the surf flick *Endless Summer II*) is only accessible by boat from Playa del Coco and offers a very fast right point break. Within Parque Nacional Santa Rosa, **Playa Naranjo** (or Witch's Rock) gives one of the best breaks in the country and has the added attraction of good camping facilities, though you'll need your own 4WD to reach them.

Moving down to the long western back of the Nicoya Peninsula, **Playa Tamarindo** has three sites for surfing, though parts of the beach are plagued by rocks. While they don't offer a really demanding or wild ride, Tamarindo's waves are very popular due to the large number of hotels and restaurants in the town nearby. **Playa Langosta**, just south of Tamarindo, offers right and left beach breaks, a little more demanding than Tamarindo. **Playa Avellanas** has a good beach break, with very hollow rights and lefts, while the faster **Playa Negra** nearby has a right point break that is one of the best in the country. **Playa Nosara** offers a fairly gentle beach break, with rights and lefts, though things hot up a bit as you work your way towards the tip of the peninsula, where *playas* **Coyote**, **Manzanillo**, **Santa Teresa**, **Carmen**, **Mal País** and, on the east coast, **Monteurma**, have consistent breaks.

Near Puntarenas on the **Central Pacific Coast**, **Boca Barranca** is a river mouth break with a very long left, while **Puerto Caldera** also has a good left. **Playa Tivives** (beach break) and **Valor** (a rocky point break) have good lefts and rights, as does the point break at **Playa Escondida**. **Playa Jacó** is not always dependable for good beach breaks, and the surf is not too big, though it's within easy reach of **Roca Loca**, a rocky point break to the north, and, to the south, **Playa Hermosa**, a good spot for more experienced surfers, with a very strong beach break. The adjacent *playas* **Esterillos Este**, **Esterillos Oeste**, **Bejuco** and **Bocas Damas** offer similarly good beach breaks.

On the south Pacific coast, the river mouth at **Quepos** has a small left point break, while **Playa Espadilla** at Manuel Antonio is good when the wind is up, with beach breaks and left and right waves. Southwards, **Playa El Rey** offers left and right beach breaks, but you're best off continuing to **Dominical** and some really great surfing, with strong lefts and rights and beautiful surroundings. Down at the very south of the country, **Bahía Drake**, accessible only by boat, gets going on a big swell. A much more reliable wave hits the shore at **Playa Pavones**, one of the longest left points in the world, very fast and with a good formation; it's offset by the nearby right point break at **Matapalo**. Only hardcore surfers tend to tackle the remote reef break at **Punta Burica**.

The best surfing beaches on the **Caribbean coast** lie towards the south, from Cahuita to Manzanillo villages. **Playa Negra** at Cahuita has an excellent beach break, with the added bonus of year-round waves. **Puerto Viejo de Talamanca** is home to **La Salsa Brava**, one of the few legitimate "big waves" in Costa Rica, a very thick, tubular wave formed by deep water rocketing towards a shallow reef. Further south, **Manzanillo** has a very fast beach break in lovely surroundings.

Further north towards Puerto Limón are a couple of beaches that, while not in the class of Puerto Viejo, can offer experienced surfers a few good waves. **Westfalia**'s left and right beach breaks only really work on a small swell, while **Playa Bonita**, a few kilometres north of Limón, is known for its powerful and dangerous left; only people who really know what they are doing should try this. The right point break at **Portete** is easier to handle, though the left-breaking waves at **Isla Uvita**, just off the coast from Puerto Limón, are also considered tricky. The **north Caribbean coast** has a number of decent beach breaks, which you can reach along the canals north of Moin.

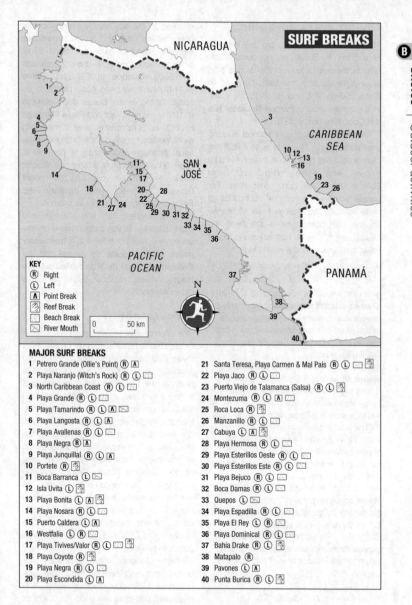

MAJOR SURF BREAKS

1 Petrero Grande (Ollie's Point) (R) [Point Break]
2 Playa Naranjo (Witch's Rock) (R) (L) [Beach Break]
3 North Caribbean Coast (R) (L) [Beach Break]
4 Playa Grande (R) (L) [Beach Break]
5 Playa Tamarindo (R) (L) [Point Break] [River Mouth]
6 Playa Langosta (R) (L) [Point Break]
7 Playa Avallenas (R) (L) [Beach Break]
8 Playa Negra (R) [Point Break]
9 Playa Junquillal (R) (L) [Point Break]
10 Portete (R) [Reef Break]
11 Boca Barranca (L) [River Mouth]
12 Isla Uvita (L) [Reef Break]
13 Playa Bonita (L) [Point Break] [Reef Break]
14 Playa Nosara (R) (L) [Beach Break]
15 Puerto Caldera (L) [Point Break]
16 Westfalia (L) (R) [Beach Break]
17 Playa Tivives/Valor (R) (L) [Beach Break] [Reef Break]
18 Playa Coyote (R) [Reef Break]
19 Playa Negra (R) (L) [Beach Break]
20 Playa Escondida (L) [Point Break]
21 Santa Teresa, Playa Carmen & Mal País (R) (L) [Beach Break] [Reef Break]
22 Playa Jaco (R) (L) [Beach Break]
23 Puerto Viejo de Talamanca (Salsa) (R) (L) [Reef Break]
24 Montezuma (R) (L) [Point Break] [Beach Break]
25 Roca Loca (R) [Reef Break]
26 Manzanillo (R) (L) [Beach Break]
27 Cabuya (L) [Point Break] [Reef Break]
28 Playa Hermosa (R) (L) [Beach Break]
29 Playa Esterillos Oeste (R) (L) [Beach Break]
30 Playa Esterillos Este (R) (L) [Beach Break]
31 Playa Bejuco (R) (L) [Beach Break]
32 Boca Damas (R) (L) [Beach Break]
33 Quepos (L) [River Mouth]
34 Playa Espadilla (R) (L) [Beach Break]
35 Playa El Rey (L) (R) [Beach Break]
36 Playa Dominical (R) (L) [Beach Break]
37 Bahía Drake (R) (L) [Reef Break]
38 Matapalo (R)
39 Pavones (L) [Point Break]
40 Punta Burica (R) (L) [Reef Break]

If you're interested in **learning to surf**, there are several surf camps and schools in Tamarindo, Santa Teresa/Mal País and Jacó (see p.292, p.347 & p.355 for details). You can check **tide times** online at Ⓦ www.ticotravel.com/surfing/tidetables.htm. Costa Rica is small enough that if things are quiet on one coast, it's fairly easy to pack up your kit and hit the other (shuttle buses will take your board for an additional $10 or so). Serious surfers spending some time in the country will find *The Surfer's Guide to Costa Rica* by Mike Parise an invaluable guide.

Diving and snorkelling

Though **diving** is less of a big deal in Costa Rica than in Belize or Honduras's Bay Islands, there are a few worthwhile dive sites around the country: the best, however, lie some 500km off Costa Rica's Pacific coast in the waters around **Parque Nacional Isla del Coco** (see box, p.337).

You can also theoretically **snorkel** all along the Pacific coast – Playa Flamingo in northern Guanacaste has clear waters though not a lot to see, while Playa Panamá and Bahía Ballena also have good snorkelling. For people who want to see an abundance of underwater life, the small **reef** near Manzanillo on the Caribbean coast is the best; the nearby reef at Cahuita has suffered in recent years from erosion and is now dying.

Dive outfitters

Aquamor Talamanca Adventures ⓣ2759-9012, ⓦwww.greencoast.com/aquamor2.htm. Excellent dive operation situated within the Refugio Nacional de Vida Silvestre Gandoca-Manzanillo. Employs local captains and works in alliance with the Talamanca Dolphin Foundation.

Bill Beard's Costa Rica ⓣ1-877/853-0538, ⓦwww.billbeards.com. Experienced operator running trips in the northern Guanacaste region, Parque Nacional Manuel Antonio and Bahía Drake, as well as liveaboards to Parque Nacional Isla del Cocos. PADI certification courses available.

Costa Rica Adventure Divers ⓣ2231-5806, ⓦwww.costaricadiving.com. Boat dives, dive courses and snorkelling around Bahía Drake and the pristine reef of nearby Isla del Caño.

Ocotal Beach Resort and Marina ⓣ2670-0321, ⓦwww.ocotaldiving.com. PADI certification courses and dive trips to Catalina and Murciélago islands; five- to eight-day packages also available.

Rich Coast Diving ⓣ2670-0176, ⓦwww.richcoastdiving.com. Snorkelling and scuba-diving trips in northern Guanacaste, plus PADI certification courses.

Fishing and sports-fishing

Costa Rica has hit the big time in the lucrative **sports-fishing** game. Both coasts are blessed with the kind of big fish serious anglers love – marlin, sailfish, tarpon and snook among them. Sports-fishing is just that: sport, with the vast majority of fish returned to the sea alive. Its most obvious characteristic, though, is its tremendous **expense**: day-trips start at around $400, while multi-day packages can cost upwards of $3500. **Quepos** (p.362) and **Golfito** (p.414) have long been good places to do some fishing, while **Barra del Colorado** (p.189) in the northeast and **Playa Flamingo** (p.288) in Guanacaste have turned into monothematic costly sports-fishing destinations. Although good fishing is possible all year round, the catch is seasonal (Pacific marlin, for example, can only be caught between Nov & April); **January** and **February** are the most popular months.

Casual anglers can find cheaper and more low-key fishing opportunities in the country's many trout-rich **freshwater rivers**, or in **Laguna de Arenal** and the **Refugio Nacional de Vida Silvestre Caño Negro**, where rainbow bass fishing is especially good.

Birdwatching

One oft-repeated statistic you'll hear about Costa Rica is that the country boasts more than 885 species of birds (including migratory ones), a higher number than all of North America. Consequently, the **birding** is hugely impressive, and it's likely that you'll spot hummingbirds, scarlet macaws, toucans, kingfishers and a variety of trogons (the best time to see migratory birds is the dry season). The resplendent quetzal, found in the higher elevations of Monteverde, Parque Nacional Braulio Carrillo and the Cordillera de Talamanca, is elusive, but can still be spotted – the tiny hamlet of San Gerardo de Dota (see p.381), close to Cerro de la Muerte, and the nearby Parque Nacional Los Quetzales, are by far the best places to see them.

Several **lodges** cater specifically for birders, including *Rancho Naturalista* (see p.161) and *Bosque de Paz* (see p.137) organizing day-trips and multi-day tours of various nearby habitats. See p.459 for recommended birdwatching **field guides**.

Specialist birdwatching operators

Birding on a Budget ⓣ2446-8452, ⓦwww.birdingonabudgetcr.com. Good-value birdwatching tours run by a conservationist couple with over thirty years' experience: day-trips to less-visited destinations such as Juan Castro Blanco and Braulio Carrillo national parks, plus week-long cross-country tours.

Costa Rica Gateway ⓣ2433-8278, ⓦwww.costaricagateway.com. Long-established operator running a dozen one- and two-week tours using birder-friendly lodges; can also help put together tailor-made trips including transport, accommodation and local guides.

Costa Rican Bird Route ⓣ8840-1267, ⓦwww.costaricanbirdroute.com. Network of eighteen private reserves and lodges in the Zona Norte, including *Selva Verde Lodge*, *Laguna del Lagarto* and the Estación Biológica La Selva (see below), which harbours over 500 of the country's bird species. Their four-day Great Green Macaw tour is the only multi-day trip in the country that focuses on observing, photographing and learning about this endangered species. See box on p.251 for more.

Organization of Tropical Studies ⓣ2524-0607, ⓦwww.ots.ac.cr. Fantastic twelve-day tour taking in the three research stations operated by the OTS (Las Cruces, La Selva and Palo Verde), and their varying habitats and species, with some of the best naturalist guides in the country. Also offers a day-long birdwatching course at the Estación Biológica La Selva – an excellent introduction to birdwatching in the tropics.

Mountain biking

Only certain places in Costa Rica lend themselves well to **mountain biking**. In general, the best areas for extensive biking are Parque Nacional Corcovado, the road from Montezuma to the Reserva Natural Absoluta Cabo Blanco on the southern Nicoya Peninsula and Parque Nacional Santa Rosa. The La Fortuna and Volcán Arenal area is also increasingly popular: you can bike to see the volcano (although not up it) and around the pretty Laguna de Arenal. Some tour operators also offer mountain biking as part of the transfer from La Fortuna to Monteverde.

There are plenty of bike **rental shops** throughout the country; you may also be able to rent one from local tour agencies. Prices range from $3 to $5 an hour or $10 to $20 for the day. See p.45 for more on independent cycling around Costa Rica.

Bike tours

Bike Arenal ⓣ2479-7150, ⓦwww.bikearenal.com. Exciting week-long rides through the Valle Central and Zona Norte and along the Pacific coast, with a paved-road option for the less adventurous. Their scenic one-day tour around Laguna de Arenal is the closest you can get to Volcán Arenal on two wheels.

Coast to Coast Adventures ⓣ2280-8054, ⓦwww.ctocadventures.com. Multi-activity operator with mountain-bike trips (from one to three days) in the Valle Orosí, from San José to Manuel Antonio and across the southern Nicoya Peninsula.

Serendipity Adventures ⓣ2558-1000, ⓦwww.serendipityadventures.com. Adventure specialists offering all-inclusive customized biking tours.

Horseriding

Almost everywhere you go in Costa Rica, with the exception of the waterlogged northern Limón Province, you should be able to hook up with a **horseriding tour**. Guanacaste is probably the best area in the country for riding, with a cluster of excellent haciendas (working cattle ranches) that also cater to tourists, offering bed, breakfast and horse hire.

Riding **on the beach** on the Nicoya Peninsula, especially in Montezuma in the south and Sámara on the west coast, is also very popular; however, there has been a history of mistreatment of horses in these places, so don't expect the animals here to be in great shape. If you see any extreme cases of mistreatment, complain to the local tourist information centre or local residents.

Horseriding tours

Desafío Tours La Fortuna ⓣ2479-9464, Santa Elena ⓣ2645-5874, ⓦwww.desafiocostarica.com & www.monteverdetours.com. Trips on well-cared-for horses around La Fortuna and Monteverde, and horseriding as part of the transfer between the two. They can also arrange bespoke horse tours across the country.

Mr Big J Cahuita ⓣ2755-0353. Friendly tour company that organizes rides through Parque Nacional Cahuita and along the lovely black-sand beach of Playa Negra.

Nature Lodge Finca Los Caballos ⓣ2642-0124, ⓦwww.naturelodge.net. Riding tours for guests only, with horses for all levels, and trips along beaches, to waterfalls and through rainforest.

Volcán Turrialba Lodge ⓣ2273-4335, ⓦwww.volcanturrialbalodge.com. Five-hour rides up to the volcano and through remote and spectacular cloudforest.

Travelling with children

A small, inherently peaceful country, with a friendly populace, a good healthcare system and a decent transport infrastructure, Costa Rica is arguably the most child-friendly destination in Central America. Add a bounty of exotic wildlife, countless beaches and enough outdoor activities to keep even the most adrenaline-fuelled teenager quiet for a week or two, and it's easy to see why the country is fast becoming one of the most popular destinations for families looking for a break with a bit more bite.

Like most other Latin countries, children are a fundamental part of society in Costa Rica, and you'll be made to feel more than welcome in **hotels and restaurants** and on guided tours and trips; indeed, in many restaurants, junior (especially if they're blond and blue-eyed) is likely to prove the star attraction. Very few hotels do not accept children (we've noted in the Guide those that don't), and you'll find that the comparatively early opening hours in restaurants actually favour the routines of younger families.

Costa Rica is also a very **safe** destination to travel around, with a long history of political stability and far less crime than in neighbouring countries. You don't need specific inoculations to visit (and malaria is only present in the southern Caribbean) and most tourist places have a high standard of food hygiene, so **health** problems are rarely an issue – though Costa Rica's position near the equator means that you should take the necessary precautions with the sun. In the unlikely scenario that you do require medical help, note that the (private) healthcare system in Costa Rica is excellent, with a couple of top-notch clinics in San José (see p.117), while the capital's Hospital Nacional de Niños at C 14, Av Central (☎2222-0122) has the best pediatric specialists in Central America. See p.53 for more on health (and keeping healthy) in Costa Rica.

Activities

Costa Rica's incredible **wildlife** will undoubtedly provide your children with the most abiding memories of their trip, and you'd struggle to spend a couple of weeks in the country and not see a blue morpho butterfly, a colourful keel-billed toucan or a sloth or howler monkey working their way through the rainforest canopy – the latter two are particularly prevalent in Tortuguero and Manuel Antonio national parks. Most parks have well-maintained **trails**, many of which are short circuits; travellers with very young children will find pushchair-friendly paths at Poás (see p.140) and Carara (see p.353) national parks and the Reserva Santa Elena (see p.331), while the main-crater viewpoint at Parque Nacional Volcán Irazú (see p.153) is also reachable with a buggy.

Butterfly farms are a big hit for younger children. It can sometimes seem that every small rural village has its own *finca de la mariposa*, but two of the best – and most interesting for the adults – are the La Gaucima Butterfly Farm just outside Alajuela, in the Valle Central (see p.133), and the Butterfly Conservancy at El Castillo, near La Fortuna (see p.229), the biggest in the country. Similarly, **frog gardens**, or *ranariums*, should also appeal thanks to the variety of croaking, whirring, garishly coloured species that are easily spotted hopping about; most major tourist centres, such as Monteverde, have a frog garden, while several private wildlife reserves run evening frog walks.

Costa Rica's two long coastlines are backed by some beautiful beaches, though **swimming** should be supervised at all times – the same waves that make the country so popular with surfers can be dangerous for children, while some of the best beaches are plagued by riptides (see box, p.65). Older children can rent **bodyboards and surfboards** in major surfing resorts such as Tamarindo and Santa Teresa/Mal País.

Taking a dip in an outdoor **hot spring** is a novel experience likely to be enjoyed by young children and teenagers alike. Most complexes have a variety of pools (of varying temperatures), many "fed" by waterfalls that you can perch under, and some have water slides as well; the springs around Volcán Arenal (see p.225) make great spots for a thermally heated soak. Given its constant activity, Arenal is also the best place for some serious **volcano viewing**, offering (weather permitting) memorable scenes of molten lava and hot rocks spilling down its flanks, especially from the (relative) safety of the *Arenal Observatory Lodge* (see p.228). Always heed local safety warnings, and follow the advice in the box on p.228.

The variety of outdoor activities available to teenagers is seemingly endless, and few will be able to resist hurtling through the treetops attached to cables on a **zip line**; **hanging bridges** (see p.64 for both) offer a more relaxing alternative to exploring the upper canopy. You can go **bungee-jumping** in the Valle Central (see p.149) and at Jacó on the Pacific coast (see p.360), and **caving** in Parque Nacional Barra Honda and Venado, near La Fortuna (see p.310 & p.234). Older teenagers can try their hand at **white-water rafting** by tackling the raging rapids of the Pacuaré and Reventázon rivers among others, though there are also "safari floats" on much calmer waters that will appeal to all the family; see p.63 for more.

Studying and volunteering

Costa Rica is a great place to broaden your mind, and an increasing number of visitors kick off their travels through the country with an immersive language course, or break up their vacation with a few days of volunteering, which can range from helping maintain trails in a cloudforest reserve to measuring turtles on the Pacific coast. There are also a great number of opportunities for travellers with more time and a scientific interest in the country's flora and fauna to enrol in a variety of research projects.

Study programmes and learning Spanish

There are over 125 **language schools** in Costa Rica, with San José and the Valle Central offering a wealth of Spanish courses. Though you can arrange a place through organizations based in your home country (see p.38), the best way to choose (at least in the low season, from May to November) is to visit a few, perhaps sit in on a class or two, and judge the school according to your own personality and needs; in the high season, many classes will have been booked in advance. Note that courses in Costa Rica generally cost more than in Mexico or Guatemala.

Some of the **language schools** listed here are Tico-run; some are branches of international (usually North American) education networks. Instructors are almost invariably Costa Ricans who speak some English. School notice boards are an excellent source of information and contact for travel opportunities, apartment shares and social activities. Most schools have a number of Costa Rican families on their books with whom they regularly place students for **homestays**. If you want **private tuition**, any of the places listed below can recommend a tutor – rates run from $16 to $23 per hour.

Language schools

Academia Latinoamericana de Español ⓣ2224-9917, ⓦwww.alespanish.com. Friendly school running small groups (up to 6) and intensive courses (20hr weekly; $170), with morning or afternoon schedules; homestay programmes (which include breakfast and dinner) cost a further $150 per week; all materials included.

Conversa ⓣ2203-2071, ⓦwww.conversa.com. Well-established institute whose classes have a minimum of four students (5hr 30min daily for a super-intensive course) with thorough teaching that puts the emphasis on grammar; stay either with a Tico family or at the centre's five-acre former dairy farm, 10km outside San José. Not cheap at $760–850 per week, though the price also includes Latin dance and cooking classes.

Costa Rica Spanish Institute (COSI) ⓣ2234-1001, ⓦwww.cosi.co.cr. Small classes in San Pedro, as well as a "beach and rainforest programme" in Parque Nacional Manuel Antonio. Homestays are arranged (or you can stay in an apartment or hotel), as are tours and cultural activities. Four-week (4hr per day) programme costs $1690 including homestay accommodation.

Costa Rican Language Academy ⓣ2280-1685, ⓦwww.learn-spanish.com. Small, friendly and Costa Rican-owned school, with a conversational approach to learning, based on current affairs. There are also Latin dance and cooking classes every afternoon, and trips to discos to practise the steps. Four-week (4hr per day) programme costs just $1499 including homestay accommodation.

Instituto Británico ⓣ2225-0256, ⓦwww.institutobritanico.co.cr. Lessons for all levels of proficiency, including tailor-made courses focusing on specific vocabulary (like business Spanish) and two-week "Fast Tack" Spanish ($650). Unlike most other schools, materials and airport pick-up are extra.

Instituto Para Estudiantes Extranjeros ⓣ2283-7731, ⓦwww.ipee.com. Small school that prides itself on a cosy atmosphere, total-immersion methodology and small groups (max six people). All ages and levels of Spanish are catered for, and courses run year-round, from one week to six months or more. Facilities include free internet, and they can also arrange field trips and excursions and homestays. Four-week (4hr per day) programme costs $1285 including homestay accommodation.

Montaña Linda Spanish School ⓣ2533-3640, ⓦwww.montanalinda.com. Popular school in the gorgeous Valle Orosí run by a friendly and knowledgeable team. Tuition is either one-to-one or in tiny classes (3hr per day) up to a maximum of three people, with the choice of grammar or conversation. Accommodation is provided in a nearby hostel, homestay or guesthouse (starting from $125 for five nights in the hostel), and a wide range of tours and sightseeing activities are available.

Universal de Idiomas ⓣ2223-9662, ⓦwww.universal-edu.com. Well-established school with programmes offering three to four hours of tuition daily. Tours can also be arranged. Four-week (4hr per day) programme costs $1310 including homestay accommodation.

Universidad Veritas ⓣ2283-4747, ⓦwww.uveritas.ac.cr. Intensive one- ($705), three- ($1970) and four-month ($2541) courses, with twenty hours' tuition weekly; accommodation (homestays or student residence) and materials cost extra.

Volunteer work and research projects

There's a considerable choice of **volunteer work** and **research projects** in Costa Rica – some include food and lodging, and many can be organized from overseas. You'll be required to spend at least a week working on a project (which includes monitoring sea turtles, helping conserve endangered parrots and working with rural communities), and sometimes up to three months, though the extra insight you'll gain – and, of course, the enormous sense of achievement – are ample rewards.

A good resource **in the US** for volunteer work programmes is *Transitions Abroad* (ⓣ1-802/442-4827, ⓦwww.transitionsabroad.com), a bimonthly magazine and website focusing on living and working overseas. Prospective **British** volunteers should contact the Costa Rican Embassy in London (see p.74). In **Australia**, details of current student exchanges and study programmes are available either from the Costa Rican consul (see p.74), or from the AFS in Sydney (ⓣ02/9215 0077, ⓦwww.afs.org.au); in **New Zealand** and South Africa, you should also contact the AFS, in Wellington (ⓣ04/494 6020, ⓦwww.afsnzl.org.nz) and Johannesburg (ⓣ011/447 2673 ⓦwww.afs.org.za), respectively.

Volunteer programmes

In addition to the programmes recommended below, many private reserves take volunteers direct, including the Reserva

Biológica Bosque Nuboso Monteverde and the Reserva Santa Elena (see box, p.332).

Amigos de las Aves ⓣ2441-2658, ⓦwww.hatchedtoflyfree.org. This organization works on breeding pairs of scarlet and great green macaws, with volunteers required for a minimum of two weeks (Breeding Centre; $23per day) or two months (Release Site; $10per day); rates include accommodation.

ASVO ⓣ2258-4430, ⓦwww.asvocr.org. Non-profit association enabling volunteers to work in national parks and wildlife refuges, local schools or communities, from monitoring turtle nests in the Refugio Nacional de Vida Silvestre Gandoca-Manzanilo to helping in a cheese factory in Zapotal.

Sea Turtle Conservancy ⓣ1-800/678-7853, ⓦwww.cccturtle.org. Volunteer research work on leatherback and green turtles at Parque Nacional Tortuguero.

Earthwatch In the US ⓣ1-800/776-0188, in the UK ⓣ01865/318838, in Australia ⓣ03/9682 6828; ⓦwww.earthwatch.org. Leatherback turtle study in Guanacaste, helping with a turtle hatchery and relocating threatened nests; monitoring the effect of climate change on Costa Rica's caterpillars; or helping coffee growers create more environmentally friendly farms.

Global Volunteers ⓣ1-800/487-1074, ⓦwww.globalvolunteers.org. Volunteer programme helping to construct a variety of buildings in Monteverde, including healthcare centres and school classrooms.

Monteverde Institute ⓣ2645-5053, ⓦwww.mvinstitute.org. Volunteer projects in the Monteverde cloudforest including teaching, fieldwork on trails and other conservation efforts.

Friends of the Osa ⓣ2735-5756, ⓦwww.osaconservation.org. Hands-on help at a sea-turtle project on the southern tip of the Osa Peninsula, measuring turtles, monitoring nesting sites and hatchlings, and patrolling the beach at night. Minimum one week.

Proyecto Campanario ⓣ2258-5778, ⓦwww.campanario.org. Research station and eco-tourist project on the Osa Peninsula, which sometimes offers free or discounted lodging and meals in exchange for a minimum of three months' work on and around the reserve.

Reserva Rara Avis ⓣ2764-1111, ⓦwww.rara-avis.com. This off-the-beaten-track research station and rainforest lodge in the Zona Norte regularly requires volunteers to help with guiding, research or conservation projects. Minimum three months.

Volunteers for Peace ⓣ1-802/540-3060, ⓦwww.vfp.org. Volunteer stints in Costa Rica, including sea-turtle projects, working at a wildlife rescue centre and helping out in the Reserva Santa Elena.

Travel essentials

Costs

Costa Rica is the most **expensive** country in Central America. Just about everything – from ice-cream cones and groceries to hotel rooms, meals and car rental – costs more than you might expect. Some prices, especially for upper-range accommodation, are comparable with those in the US, which never fails to astonish American travellers and those coming from the cheaper neighbouring countries. That said, you can, with a little foresight, travel fairly cheaply throughout the country.

The high cost of living is due in part to the **taxes**, which are levied in hotels (13 percent) and restaurants (23 percent), and also, more recently, to the International Monetary Fund, whose restructuring policies of balancing the country's payments deficit have raised prices. Even on a rock-bottom **budget**, you're looking at spending $25 a day for lodging, three meals and the odd bus ticket. Staying in mid-range accommodation, eating in nice restaurants and taking part in the odd activity could push you over $100 a day, while the sky's the limit at the upper end, where one night in a swanky hotel can cost over $400 in some places.

The good news is that **bus travel**, geared towards locals, is always cheap – about 25¢ to $1 for local buses, and around $6 for long-distance buses (3hr or more). For notes on **tipping** in Costa Rica, see p.80.

Dancing

Costa Ricans love to **dance**, and it's common to see children who have barely learned to stand up grooving and bopping, much encouraged by their parents. Consequently, there are many good discos, mainly in San José. Your popularity at discos or house parties will have something to do with how well you can dance; if you're really keen, you might want to take salsa and merengue lessons before you come. Fitting in at a disco is easier for women, who simply wait to be asked to dance. Men, however, are not only expected to go out and hunt down female dance partners, but also to lead, which means they actually have to know what they're doing. For a list of dance schools in San José, see p.112.

Electricity

The **electrical current** in Costa Rica is 110 volts – the same as Canada and the US – although plugs are two-pronged, without the round grounding prong.

Emergencies

The national **emergency number** is ⓣ911.

Entry requirements

Citizens of the US, Canada, the UK, Ireland, Australia, New Zealand, South Africa and most Western European countries can obtain a ninety-day entry stamp for Costa Rica without needing a **visa**. Whatever your nationality, you must in theory show your passport (with more than six months remaining), a valid onward (or return) air or bus ticket, a visa for your next country (if applicable) and proof of "sufficient funds" (around $1000), though if you arrive by air the last is rarely asked for. Most other nationalities need a visa (a thirty-day visa costs $20); always check first with a Costa Rican consulate concerning current regulations. The website ⓦwww.migracion.go.cr gives up-to-date requirements.

Your **entrance stamp** is very important: no matter where you arrive, make sure you get it. You have to carry your passport (or a photocopy) with you at all times in Costa Rica. If you are asked for it and cannot produce it, you may well be detained and fined.

The easiest way to **extend your entry permit** is to leave Costa Rica for 72 hours – to Panamá or Nicaragua, say – and then re-enter, fulfilling the same requirements as on your original trip. You should then be given another ninety-day (or thirty-day) stamp, although it is at the discretion of the immigration officer. If you prefer not to leave the country, you can apply for a permit or visa extension at the immigración near San José (see p.117), a time-consuming and often costly business. You'll need to bring all relevant documents – passport and four photographs, personal letter, onward air or bus ticket – as well as proof of funds ($200 in cash or travellers' cheques). If you do not have a ticket out of Costa Rica, you may have to buy one in order to get your extension. Bus tickets are more easily refunded than air tickets; some airlines refuse to cash in onward tickets unless you can produce or buy another one out of the country. Note that you will pay approximately ten percent tax on all air tickets bought in Costa Rica. If you **overstay your limit**, you'll need to go to the Departamento de Migración in San José with your passport and onward ticket and will be charged an overstayers' fee of $100 per month.

Costa Rican embassies and consulates abroad

Australia Consulate-General, De la Sala House, 11/30 Clarence St, Sydney, NSW 2000 ⓣ02/9261 1177.
Canada 325 Dalhousie St, Suite 407, Ottawa, Ontario, K1N 7G2 ⓣ613/562-2855, ⓦwww.costaricaembassy.com.
Ireland no representation; contact the UK embassy.
New Zealand no representation; contact the Australian consulate-general.
South Africa 56 Dennis, Blandford Ridge, Sandton, Johannesburg ⓣ117/053434.
UK Flat 1, 14 Lancaster Gate, London W2 3LH ⓣ020/7706 8844, ⓔcostaricanembassy@btconnect.com.
US 2112 S St NW, Washington, DC 20008 ⓣ202/328-6628, ⓦwww.costarica-embassy.org.

Gay and lesbian Costa Rica

Costa Rica has a good reputation among gay and lesbian travellers, and continues to be generally hassle-free for gay and lesbian visitors. The country has a large gay community by Central American standards, and to a smaller extent a sizeable lesbian one, too; it's pretty much confined to San José (which holds a **Gay Pride Festival** every June), though there is also a burgeoning scene in Manuel Antonio.

Although there have been some incidents of police harassing gays in bars, in general you will be met with respect, and there's no need to assume, as some do, that everyone is a raving hetero-Catholic poised to discriminate against homosexuals. Part of this **tolerance** is due to the subtle tradition in Costa Rican life and politics summed up in the Spanish expression "*quedar bien*", which translates roughly as "don't rock the boat" or "leave well alone". People don't ask you about your sexual orientation or make assumptions, but they don't necessarily expect you to talk about it unprompted, either.

Where once it was difficult to find an entrée into gay life (especially for women) without knowing local gays and lesbians, there are now several **points of contact** in Costa Rica for gay and lesbian travellers. On the web, try Purple Roofs Gay and Lesbian Travel directory (ⓦwww.purpleroofs.com/centralamerica/costarica/costaricaregion.html), which provides information about gay-friendly accommodation and nightlife, or Tiquicia Travel (ⓦwww.tiquiciatravel.net) and Costa Rica Gay Vacation (ⓦwww.costaricagayvacation.com), travel agents that specialize in gay and lesbian holidays to Costa Rica. For a more informal introduction to the scene in the country itself, head to *Déjà Vu*, a mainly gay disco in San José (see p.114 for this and other gay bars).

Information

The best source of information about Costa Rica is the **Instituto Costarricense de Turismo** (ICT), Apartado 777-1000, San José (ⓣ2299-5800, ⓦwww.visitcostarica.com); you can email them for information before your trip, though you'll probably only receive pretty but not particularly informative glossy pamphlets and brochures.

You're better off going in person to the ICT office, located in the unprepossessing bunker beneath the Plaza de la Cultura in central San José (see p.90), where the friendly, bilingual staff will do their best to answer your queries. On request, they'll give you a free city map plus a very useful comprehensive bus timetable (also available online) with recent additions and changes corrected on the spot. The office can also provide a list of museums and their opening hours, details of many San José restaurants and bars as well as a brochure produced by the Costa Rican Hotel Association with contact details for many of the country's hotels. The small ICT booths at the three main entry points to the country – in the Juan Santamaría International Airport, Peñas Blancas on the Nicaraguan border and Paso Canoas on the Panamanian border – can provide the map and hotel brochure but not the timetables. Outside the capital, there are eight regional ICT tourist offices offering information and advice; otherwise, you'll have to rely on locally run initiatives, often set up by a small business association or the chamber of commerce, or hotels and tourist agencies.

A number of Costa Rican **tour operators**, based in San José, can offer information and guidance when planning a trip around the country, though bear in mind that they may not be as objective as they could be; see p.46 for details.

Useful websites

In addition to the below, many of Costa Rica's newspapers, such as *La Nacíon* and *The Tico Times*, have online editions, which are good resources for current affairs, cultural events and the like (see p.56).

ⓦ**www.1costaricalink.com** Huge online tourist resource.

ⓦ**www.centralamerica.com** Costa Rica-based travel specialists, which also has information on other Central American countries.

ⓦ**www.costaricatourism.co.cr** Website of CANATUR, the Costa Rican National Tourism Chamber.

Ⓦ **www.costarica.com** Good, up-to-date information on the country's key attractions and wildlife, plus trip-planning advice.

Government websites

Australian Department of Foreign Affairs Ⓦ www.dfat.gov.au, www.smartraveller.gov.au
British Foreign and Commonwealth Office Ⓦ www.fco.gov.uk
Canadian Department of Foreign Affairs Ⓦ www.international.gc.ca
Irish Department of Foreign Affairs Ⓦ www.foreignaffairs.gov.ie
New Zealand Ministry of Foreign Affairs Ⓦ www.mft.govt.nz
South African Department of Foreign Affairs Ⓦ www.dfa.gov.za
US State Department Ⓦ www.travel.state.gov

Insurance

It's always a good idea to take out **insurance** before travelling. A typical policy usually provides cover for the loss of baggage, tickets and – up to a certain limit – cash or cheques, as well as cancellation or curtailment of your journey. It's particularly important to have one that includes **health cover**, too, since while private medical treatment in Costa Rica is likely to be cheaper than in your home country, it can still be expensive.

You can buy a policy from a specialist travel insurance company, or consider the deal we offer (see box below). When choosing a policy, always check whether **medical benefits** will be paid as treatment proceeds or only after you return home, and if there is a **24-hour medical emergency number**. When **securing baggage** cover, make sure that the per-article limit – typically under £500/$750 and sometimes as little as £250/$400 – will cover your most valuable possession. Most policies exclude so-called **dangerous sports** unless an extra premium is paid: in Costa Rica, this can mean scuba-diving, white-water rafting, surfing and windsurfing and trekking.

If you need **to make a claim**, you should keep receipts for medicines and medical treatment, and in the event you have anything stolen, you must obtain an official statement from the police: tell them *"He sido robado"* ("I've been robbed") and they'll provide you with the necessary paperwork.

Internet

Most hostels and hotels provide free internet access to their guests, and many places offer wi-fi. Should you need to get online while out and about, however, the majority of Costa Rican towns have at least one **internet café**, while popular tourist places usually have many more; charges are low, around $1 per hour in major towns and around $3 in more remote areas where they rely on (rather slow) satellite link-up.

Language

The language of Costa Rica is **Spanish**. Although tourists who stay in top-end hotels will find that "everyone speaks English" (a common myth perpetrated about Costa Rica), your time here will be far more meaningful if you arm yourself with at least a one-hundred-word Spanish vocabulary, or better still by enrolling in a language course at the start of your trip (see p.72). Communicating with *guardaparques* and people at bus stops, asking directions and ordering *bocas* – not to mention finding salsa partners – is greatly facilitated by speaking the language. For more on Costa Rican Spanish, see p.449.

Laundry

There are very few **launderettes** in Costa Rica, and they're practically all in San José (see p.117 for a list); in the main tourist towns, though, you'll usually be able to find someone running a small **laundry service**, charging by the kilo (around $1.50). Most hotels can do your laundry, although charges are generally outrageously high.

Mail

Even the smallest Costa Rican town has a **post office** (*correo*), but the most reliable place to mail overseas is from San José's lime-green Correo Central (main post office; see p.117). Airmail letters to the US and Canada cost 350 colones, and take one to two weeks to arrive; letters to Europe cost 395 colones and take two weeks or more; letters to Australasia and South Africa cost 495 colones and take three or four weeks.

Most post offices have a **poste restante** (*lista de correos*) – an efficient and safe way to receive letter mail, especially at the main office in San José. They will hold letters for up to four weeks for a small fee (though in smaller post offices you may not be charged at all). Bring a photocopy of your passport when picking up mail, and make sure that correspondents address letters to you under your name exactly as it appears on your passport.

One thing you can't fail to notice is the paucity of **mailboxes** in Costa Rica. In the capital, unless your hotel has regular mail pick-up, the only resort is to hike down to the Correo Central. In outlying or isolated areas of the country, you will have to rely on hotels or local businesses' private mailboxes. In most cases, especially in Limón Province, where mail is very slow, it's probably quicker to wait until you return to San José and mail correspondence from there. For opening hours of post offices, see p.78.

Although letters are handled fairly efficiently, **packages** are another thing altogether – the parcels service both coming and going gets snarled in paperwork and labyrinthine customs regulations, besides being very expensive and very slow. If you must send parcels, take them unsealed to the post office for inspection.

Maps

The **maps** dished out by Costa Rican embassies and the ICT are basic and somewhat out of date, so arm yourself with some general maps before you go. The best **road maps**, clearly showing all the major routes and national parks, are the *Costa Rica Road Map* (1:650,000; Berndtson & Berndtson; Ⓦwww.berndtson.com) and the annually updated *Costa Rica Waterproof Travel Map* (1:470,000; Toucan Maps; Ⓦwww.mapcr.com), which also has a very useful, highly detailed section of the Valle Central and San José, plus area maps of Monteverde, Volcán Arenal, Tamarindo and Manuel Antonio. Other maps with clearly marked contour details, petrol stations, national parks and roads include the waterpoof, rip-proof *Rough Guide Map Costa Rica and Panama* (1:550,000; Rough Guides; Ⓦwww.roughguides.com) and *Costa Rica* (1:650,000; Borch; Ⓦborch.com). Road and park markings are less distinct on Nelles Verlag's large *Central America Map* (1:900,000; Ⓦwww.nelles-verlag.de), but it's handy if you are travelling throughout the isthmus.

In Costa Rica, it's a good idea to go to one of San José's two big downtown bookstores, Librería Lehmann or Librería Universal (see p.116) and look through their stock of **maps,** which are contoured and show major topographical features such as river crossings and high-tide marks; you can buy them in individual sections. You can also go to the government maps bureau, the **Instituto Geográfico Nacional**, Av 20/22, C 9/11, San José, which sells more lavishly detailed colour maps of specific areas of the country; whilst out of date, the smaller-scale series (available in 133 sheets) is useful for serious hiking trips.

Considering it's such a popular hiking destination, there are surprisingly few good maps of Costa Rica's **national parks**. Those given out at ranger stations are very general; your best bet is to get hold of the book *National Parks of Costa Rica*, published by

SINAC and usually available in the major San José bookshops. Although rather cramped, not too detailed and of little practical use for walking the trails, these maps (of all the parks currently in existence) do at least show contours and give a general idea of the terrain, the animals you might see and the annual rainfall.

Money

The official currency of Costa Rica is the **colón** (plural colones), named after Colón (Columbus) himself. There are two types of **coins** in circulation: the old silver ones, which come in denominations of 5, 10 and 20, and newer gold coins, which come in denominations of 5, 10, 25, 50, 100 and 500. The silver and gold coins are completely interchangeable, with the exception of public payphones, which don't accept gold coins. **Notes** are available in 1000, 2000, 5000 and 10,000. You'll often hear colones colloquially referred to as "pesos"; in addition, the 1000 is sometimes called the "rojo" (red). The colón floats freely against the US dollar, which in practice has meant that it devalues by some ten percent per year; at the time of writing, it was around 515 colones to the $1. Obtaining colones outside Costa Rica is virtually impossible: wait until you arrive and get some at the airport or border posts. While the **US dollar** has long been the second currency of Costa Rica and is accepted almost everywhere (we quote dollar prices throughout the Guide), the vast majority of Costa Ricans get paid in colones, and buy and sell in colones, so it's still a good idea to get the hang of the currency.

Outside San José, there are effectively no official **bureaux de change** – the Juan Santamaría International Airport does have one, but service is very slow and rather surly. In general, legitimate money-changing entails going to a bank, a hotel (usually upper-range) or, in outlying areas of the country, to whoever will do it – a tour agency, the friend of the owner of your hotel who has a Chinese restaurant… That said, it's unlikely that you'll need to change US dollars into colones, but if you do, or if you are changing other currencies such as sterling or euros, you'll find that the efficient and air-conditioned private banks (such as Banco Popular and the Banco de San José) are much faster but charge scandalous commissions; the state banks such as the Banco Nacional don't charge such high commissions but are slow and bureaucratic.

When heading for the more remote areas, try to carry sufficient colones with you, especially in small denominations – you may have trouble changing a 5000 note in the middle of the Nicoya Peninsula, for example. Going around with stacks of mouldy-smelling colones may not seem safe, but you should be all right if you keep them in a money belt, and it will save hours of time waiting in line. Some banks may not accept bent, smudged or torn dollars. It's also worth noting that, due to an influx of counterfeit **$100 notes** a few years ago, some shops, and even banks, are unwilling to accept them; if you bring any into the country, make sure that they are in mint condition. For more on banking hours, see below.

Opening hours

Banks are generally open Monday to Friday 8 or 9am to 3.30 or 4pm; **post offices** Monday to Friday 8am to 4.30 or 5.30pm (sometimes with an hour's break between noon and 1pm), and Saturdays 8am to noon; government offices, Monday to Friday 8am to 5pm; and **shops** Monday to Friday 9am to 6 or 7pm, and often on Saturday mornings, as are a few banks. In rural areas, shops generally close for lunch. Practically the only places open on Sundays are **supermarkets**, which are generally open daily from 7 or 8am to 8pm, though sometimes they don't close until 9 or 10pm.

Phones

The **country code** for all of Costa Rica is ⓣ**506**. There are no area codes, and all phone numbers have eight digits: in March 2008, a "2" was added to the beginning of landline numbers, and an "8" to mobile numbers, though not all signs, brochures and business cards have been updated. Calls **within Costa Rica** are inexpensive and **calling long-distance** can work out very

Useful phone numbers

International information ⓣ124

International operator (for collect calls) ⓣ09 or 116

Calling home from abroad

Note that the initial zero is omitted from the area code when dialling the UK, Ireland, Australia and New Zealand from abroad.

Australia international access code + 61

Ireland international access code + 353

New Zealand international access code + 64

South Africa international access code + 27

UK international access code + 44

US and Canada international access code + 1

Calling-card access codes

AT&T ⓣ0800/011-4114

BT ⓣ0800/044-1044

Canada Direct ⓣ0800/015-1161

MCI ⓣ0800/012-2222

Sprint ⓣ0800/013-0123

For all other countries, look in the White Pages (the Costa Rican phone book).

reasonably if you ring directly through a public telephone network, and avoid calling from your hotel or other private business.

The easiest way to make an **international call** is to purchase a phonecard (*tarjeta telefónica*), available from most grocery stores, street kiosks and pharmacies. You'll need card number 199 (card number 197 is for domestic calls only), which comes in denominations of 3000 colones, $10 or $20; to use it, insert the card into a payphone, dial ⓣ199 and then press "2" for instructions in English. Holders of AT&T, MCI, Sprint, Canada Direct or BT calling-cards can also make calls from payphones; simply dial the relevant access code (see box above); charges will automatically be billed to your calling-card account. You can also **call collect** to virtually any foreign country from any phone or payphone in Costa Rica; simply dial ⓣ09 (or ⓣ116 to get an English-speaking operator, a more expensive option), then tell them the country code, area code and number; note that this method costs twice as much as dialling direct.

Another way of making calls is by purchasing a prepaid SIM card for your **mobile phone** at the ICE counter in the arrivals area at Juan Santamaría International Airport or from ICE offices around the country; cards come in denominations of 2500, 5000 and 10,000 colones (the more expensive, the better the rate per minute) and last for 30, 45 or 60 days, respectively. Your phone will need to work on the 1800mhz range (any quad band and most tri-band phones; there's an approved list on the ICE website ⓦwww.grupoice.com) and must be unlocked (check with your provider).

Photography

Film is extremely expensive in Costa Rica, so if you've got a conventional camera bring lots from home. Although the incredibly bright equatorial light means that 100ASA will do for most situations, remember that rainforest cover can be very dark, and if you want to take photographs at dusk you'll need 400ASA or even higher. San José is the main place in the country where you can process film.

Prostitution

Prostitution is legal in Costa Rica, and is particularly prevalent in San José and Jacó.

While there is streetwalking (largely confined to the streets of the capital, especially those in the red-light district immediately west and south of the Parque Central), many prostitutes work out of bars. Bars in San José's "Gringo Gulch" (more or less on C 7, Av Central/5) tend to cater to and attract more foreign customers than the bars in the red-light district, which are frequented by Ticos. Streetwalkers around C 12 look like women but are not – *travestís* are transsexual or transvestite prostitutes. In recent years, Costa Rica has gained a reputation as a destination for sex tourism (see p.455), and more specifically for child-sex tourism. The government is trying to combat this with a public information campaign and strict prison sentences for anyone caught having sex with a minor.

Shopping

Compared with many Latin American countries, Costa Rica does not have an impressive crafts or artisan tradition. However, there are some interesting souvenirs, such as carved wooden salad bowls, plates and trays. Wherever you go, you'll see hand-painted wooden **replica ox-carts**, originating from Sarchí in the Valle Central (see p.135) – perennial favourites, especially when made into drinks trolleys.

Reproductions of the **pre-Columbian pendants and earrings** displayed in San José's Museo Nacional, the Museo de Oro and the Museo de Jade are sold both on the street and in shops. Much of it isn't real gold, however, but gold-plated, which chips and peels: check before you buy.

Costa Rican **coffee** is one of the best gifts to take home. Make sure you buy export brands Café Britt or Café Rey – or better yet, home-grown roasts straight from the coffee plantation itself (see p.126 & p.326) – and not the lower-grade sweetened coffee sold locally. It's often cheaper to buy bags in the supermarket rather than in souvenir shops, and cheaper still to buy beans at San José's Mercado Central. If you want your coffee beans roasted to your own taste, go to the *Café Gourmet* in San José for excellent beans and grinds. For more on coffee, see p.52.

Indigenous crafts are available at places such as the Reserva Indígena Maleku (see p.205) and the Reserva Indígena Kéköldi (see p.336), but in the general absence of a real home-grown crafts or textile tradition, generic **Indonesian** dresses and clothing – batiked and colourful printed cloth – are widely sold in the beach communities of Montezuma, Cahuita, Tamarindo and Quepos. In some cases, this craze for all things Indo extends to slippers, silver and bamboo jewellery – and prices are reasonable.

If you have qualms about buying goods made from **tropical hardwoods**, ask the salesperson what kind of wood the object is made from, and avoid mahogany, laurel, purple heart and almond (which is illegal anyway). Other goods to avoid are coral, anything made from tortoise shells, and furs such as ocelot or jaguar.

Time

Costa Rica is in North America's **Central Standard time zone** (the same as Winnipeg, New Orleans and Mexico City) and six hours behind **GMT**.

Tipping

Unless **service** has been exceptional, you do not need to leave a tip in restaurants, where a ten percent service charge is automatically levied. **Taxi drivers** are not usually tipped, either. When it comes to **nature guides**, however, the rules become blurred. Many people – especially North Americans, who are more accustomed to tipping – routinely tip guides up to $10 per day. If you are utterly delighted with a guide, it seems fair to offer a tip, although be warned that some guides may be made uncomfortable by your offer – as far as many of them are concerned, it's their job.

Toilets

The only place you'll find so-called "public" conveniences – they're really reserved for customers – is in fast-food outlets in San José, petrol stations and roadside restaurants. When travelling in the outlying areas of the country, you may want to take a roll of **toilet paper** with you. Note that except in the poshest hotels – which have their own sewage system/septic tank – you should not put toilet paper down the toilet. Sewage systems are not built to deal with paper, and you'll only cause a blockage. There's always a receptacle provided for toilet paper.

Travellers with disabilities

While public transport isn't **wheelchair-accessible**, an increasing number of hotels are – we've noted where this is the case in our accommodation reviews. Travellers with disabilities will also find short but **accessible trails** at Poás (see p.140) and Carara (see p.353) national parks, and the Reserva Santa Elena (see p.331), while the main-crater viewpoint at Parque Nacional Volcán Irazú (see p.153) is also accessible to wheelchair users. A good starting point for your trip is the Instituto Internacional de Desarrollo Creativo (ⓣ2771-7482, ⓔchabote@racsa.co.cr), who can suggest places to visit.

Weather

Although small, Costa Rica encompasses a surprisingly wide range of altitudes, from sea level to Mount Chirripó, looming over the Zona Sur at 3819m. This varied topography results in a network of local **microclimates**, with pockets of humid rainforest, montane cloudforest and hot, tropical lowlands all lying within a few hours of each other. As a general rule, though, the Caribbean coast is the wettest (it can rain in Parque Nacional Tortuguero and Refugio Nacional de Vida Silvestre Barra del Colorado all year round), while Guanacaste is hotter and drier than the rest of the country.

Women travellers

Educated urban women play an active role in Costa Rica's public life and the workforce – indeed, in 2010, the country voted in its **first female president** (see p.434) – while woman in more traditional positions are generally accorded the respect due to their role as mothers and heads of families. Despite this, however, women may be subjected to a certain amount of machismo.

In general, people are friendly and helpful to solo **women travellers**, who get the *pobrecita* (poor little thing) vote, because they're *solita* (all alone), without family or man. Nonetheless, Costa Rican men may

Average temperature and rainfall

	Jan	Feb	Mar	Apr	May	Jun	Jul	Aug	Sep	Oct	Nov	Dec
Caribbean coast												
max (˚C)	27	28	29	30	31	31	31	31	31	30	28	27
min (˚C)	19	21	22	23	24	24	24	24	23	22	20	20
max (˚F)	80	81	84	86	88	88	88	88	88	88	82	80
min (˚F)	66	70	71	76	75	75	75	75	73	71	68	68
rainfall (mm)	137	61	38	56	109	196	163	170	244	305	226	185
San José												
max (˚C)	24	26	26	24	27	26	25	26	26	25	25	24
min (˚C)	14	14	15	17	17	17	17	16	16	16	16	14
max (˚F)	75	79	79	75	80	80	79	77	79	77	77	75
min (˚F)	57	57	59	62	82	62	62	61	61	61	61	57
rainfall (mm)	15	5	20	46	229	241	211	241	305	300	145	41
Pacific Coast												
max (˚C)	31	32	32	31	30	31	31	30	29	29	29	31
min (˚C)	22	22	22	23	23	23	23	23	23	23	23	23
max (˚F)	88	89	89	88	86	88	88	86	84	84	84	88
min (˚F)	71	71	71	73	73	73	73	73	73	73	73	73
rainfall (mm)	25	10	18	74	203	213	180	201	208	257	259	122

throw out unsolicited comments at women in the street: "*mi amor*", "*guapa*", "*machita*" ("blondie") and so on. If they don't feel like articulating a whole word, they may stare or hiss – there's a saying used by local women: "Costa Rica's full of snakes, and they're all men".

Blonde, fair-skinned women are in for quite a bit of this, whereas if you look remotely Latin you'll get less attention. This is not to say you'll be exempt from these so-called compliments, and even in groups, women are targets. Walk with a man, however, and the whole street theatre disappears as if by magic. The accepted wisdom is to pass right by and pretend nothing's happening. If you're staying in Costa Rica for any time, though, you may want to learn a few responses in Spanish; this won't gain you any respect – men will look at you and make *loca* (crazy) whirligig finger gestures at their temples – but it may make you feel better.

None of this is necessarily an expression of sexual interest: it has more to do with a man displaying his masculinity to his buddies than any desire to get to know you. **Sexual assault figures** in Costa Rica are low, you don't get groped and you rarely hear *piropos* outside of towns. But for some women, the machismo attitude can be endlessly tiring, and may even mar their stay in the country.

In recent years, there has been a spate of incidents allegedly involving Rohypnol, the so-called **date-rape drug** (legal and available over the counter in Costa Rica), whereby women have been invited for a drink by a man, or sent a drink from a man in a bar, which turns out to be spiked with the drug (often by the bartender, who's in on the game). In the worst cases, the women have woken up hours later having no recollection of the missing time, and believe they were raped. This is not to encourage paranoia, but the obvious thing to do is not accept opened drinks from men and be careful about accepting invitations to go to bars with unknown men. If you do, order a beer and ask to open the bottle yourself.

Guide

Guide

1 San José

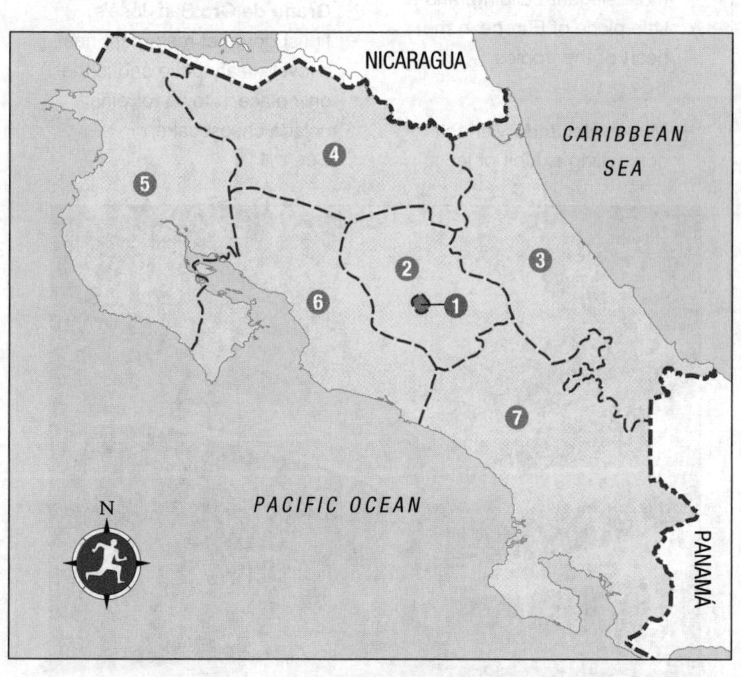

CHAPTER 1

Highlights

* **Mercado Central** Enormous, labyrinthine food market where crimson sides of beef and crispy *chicharrones* (deep-fried pork skins) share the aisles with teetering mounds of papaya and sacks of pungent coffee beans. **See p.99**

* **Teatro Nacional** San José's most elegant building, and a little piece of Europe in the heart of the tropics. **See p.100**

* **Museo del Jade** Visit this compelling exhibit of jade artefacts created by Costa Rica's indigenous peoples. **See p.102**

* **Parque la Sabana** Enjoy a serene respite from the city's congestion, where you can meander amid towering eucalyptus and visit the renovated Museo de Arte Costarricense. **See p.107**

* **Grano de Oro** San José's finest gourmet restaurant has a lovely, leafy patio and is the only place in town for piña colada cheesecake. **See p.111**

▲ The Teatro Nacional

1

San José

Sprawling smack in the middle of the fertile Valle Central, **SAN JOSÉ**, the only city of any size and administrative importance in Costa Rica, has a spectacular setting, ringed by the jagged silhouettes of soaring mountains – some of them volcanoes – on all sides. On a sunny morning, the sight of the blue-black peaks piercing the sky is undeniably beautiful. At night, from high up on one of these mountains, the valley floor twinkles like a million Chinese lanterns.

That's where the compliments largely end, however. Costa Ricans can be notoriously hard on the place, calling it, with a mixture of familiarity and contempt, "**Chepe**"– the diminutive of the name José – and writing it off as a maelstrom of stress junkies, rampant crime and other urban horrors. Travellers, meanwhile, tend to view it as an unavoidable stopover jarringly at odds with expectations and impressions of the rest of the country. The gridlocked **centre** is drab and hectic, with vendors of fruit, T-shirts and cigarettes jostling one another on street corners, and shoe stores seemingly crammed into every block. Though you can sometimes sense an underlying order behind the chaos, walking around town means, more often than not, keeping your eyes glued to the ground to avoid stepping in deep open drains or on one of the boxes of clucking chicks sold on so many street corners. **Street crime** is very real, and pedestrians adopt the defensive posture (bags clutched securely, knapsacks worn on the front, determined facial expression) that's commonplace in other big cities. All in all, walking in San José is often a stressful experience, which is a shame, because exploring on foot is really the best way to get around.

Despites its many ills, if you have the time it's worth getting to know Chepe a little better. San José has a sprinkling of excellent **museums** – some especially memorable for their bizarre locations – a couple of elegant buildings and landscaped parks. Cafés and art galleries line the streets, and as you wander amid the colonial-era wooden houses in the leafy barrios of **Amón** and **Otoya**, you could just as well be in an old European town.

Today, one in four Costa Ricans lives within the San José metropolitan area, and the capital suffers from pressure on land due to the population density of the Valle Central and to rural migration. Most Josefinos live in the **suburbs**, now awash with the mega-supermarkets and American-style malls that have colonized San José in the last few years, though some districts, like comfortable **Escazú** and hip **San Pedro** (home to the University of Costa Rica), still merit a visit in their own right.

Some history

San José was established in 1737 at the insistence of the Catholic church in order to give a focal point to the scattered populace living in the area. For the

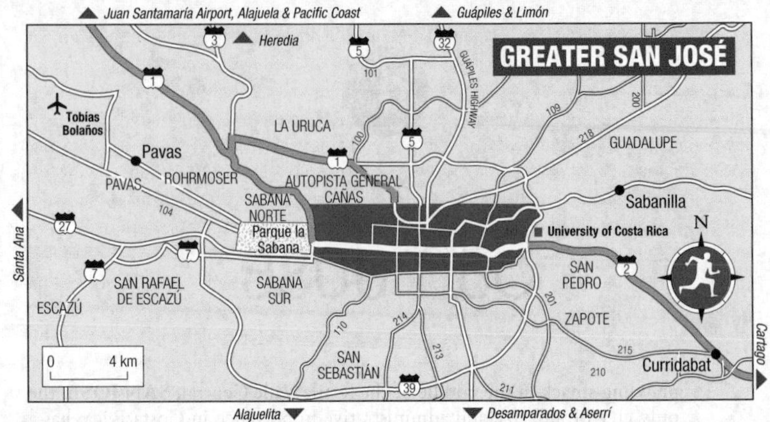

next forty years, **Villa Nueva de la Boca del Monte**, as it was cumbersomely called, remained a muddy village of a few squalid adobe houses, until coffee was first planted in the Valle Central in 1808 (see p.127), triggering the settlement's expansion.

The single most crucial event in determining the city's future importance, however, was Costa Rica's **declaration of independence** from the Spanish Crown in 1821. Following the declaration, Mexico's self-proclaimed "emperor", General Agustín de Iturbide, ordered Costa Rica's immediate annexation, a demand which caused a rift between the citizens of Heredia and Cartago, who supported the move, and those of Alajuela and San José, who saw it for what it was: a panicky imperialist attempt to stifle Latin America's burgeoning independence movements. A short **civil war** broke out, won in 1823 by the *independentistas*, who moved the capital from Cartago to San José in the same year.

Despite its status, San José remained a one-horse town until well into the nineteenth century. The framed sepia photographs in the venerable *Balcón de Europa* restaurant show wide dirt roads traversed by horse-drawn carts, with simple adobe buildings and a few spindly telegraph wires. Like the fictional town of Macondo in García Márquez's *One Hundred Years of Solitude*, this provincial backwater attracted piano-teaching European flotsam – usually young men looking to make their careers in the hinterland – who would wash up in the drawing rooms of the country's nascent bourgeoisie. Accounts written by early foreign tourists to San José give the impression of a tiny, stultifying backwater society: "The president of the republic has to sit with his followers on a wooden bench", they wrote, aghast, after attending a church service. In the city's houses they found dark-skinned young women, bound tight in white crinoline dresses, patiently conjugating French verbs, reflecting the degree to which Costa Rica's earliest cultural affiliations and aspirations lay with France. Even the mansions of former *finqueros* (coffee barons) in San José's Barrio Amón – especially the Alianza Francesa – resemble mansions in New Orleans or Port-au-Prince, with their delicate French ironwork, Moorish-influenced lattices, long, cool corridors of deep-blooded wood and brightly painted exteriors.

By the 1850s, fuelled largely by the tobacco boom, the city had acquired the trappings of bourgeois prosperity, with leafy parks, a few paved avenues and some fine examples of European-style architecture. Grand urban houses were built to accommodate the new class of burgeoning burghers, coffee middlemen and industrialists; these Europhile aspirations culminated in 1894 with the construction of the splendid **Teatro Nacional** – for which every molecule of material, as well as the finest craftsmen, were transported from Europe.

During the twentieth century, San José came to dominate nearly all aspects of Costa Rican life. As well as being the seat of government, since the 1970s it has become the Central American headquarters for many foreign non-governmental organizations which has considerably raised its international profile. Multinationals, industry and agribusiness have based their national and regional offices here, creating what at times seems to be a largely middle-class city, populated by an army of neatly suited, briefcase-toting office and embassy workers.

Arrival

Arrival in San José, whether by plane or bus, is straightforward; even if you don't speak Spanish, getting into town is a well-oiled procedure and there's less opportunistic theft than at most other Central and South American arrival points.

By air

Most international **flights** arrive at the modern new terminal at Juan Santamaría International Airport (ⓣ2443-2622), 17km northwest of San José and 3km southeast of Alajuela. The **ICT office** here (Mon–Fri 9am–5pm; ⓣ2443-1535) can supply maps and give advice on accommodation. There's also a **post office** (Mon–Fri 8am–5pm), an **ATM** machine (handily situated next to the departure tax desk), and a **bank**, downstairs on the departure level (Mon–Fri 6.30am–6pm, Sat & Sun 7am–1pm); colones are not necessary for taxis, but you'll need them for the bus. The departure tax is $26; it is best paid in cash as credit card transactions are treated as a cash advance.

The best way to get into central San José from the airport is by **taxi**, which takes about twenty to thirty minutes in light traffic and costs around $20. Official airport taxis are orange and line up outside the terminal. You'll have no problems getting a cab, as the drivers will stampede for your business while you're practically still in customs. Take a deep breath and make sure to agree on the fare before you get in the cab. Some taxi drivers take travellers who haven't made accommodation bookings to hotels where they get commission – these are often more expensive than you were bargaining for, so be firm about where you want to go. Taxi drivers accept dollars as well as colones, although they tend not to accept notes larger than $20.

The Alajuela–San José **bus** (every 10min between 4am & 11pm; every 30min at other times) stops right outside the airport's undercover car park. Though it's much cheaper than a taxi, there are no proper luggage racks inside and the buses are nearly always full – you can just about get away with it if you're carrying only a light backpack or small bag. Drivers will indicate which buses are on their way to San José (a thirty-minute journey) and which to Alajuela. The fare to San Jose is 500 colones (about $1) – payable in local currency; pay the driver. The bus drops passengers in town at Av 2, C 12/14 near the Hospital de San Juan de Dios, where there are plenty of taxis.

By bus

Most **international buses** from Nicaragua, Honduras, Guatemala and Panamá pull into the Tica Bus station, C 3 Av 26 (ⓣ2221-8954 or 2221-0006), several blocks south of the city centre. Coming from Managua on Transica, you'll arrive at the terminal at C 22, Av 3/5 (ⓣ2223-4242 ext 101); taxis can be flagged down on Avenida 3.

Safety in San José

Be particularly wary, even during the day, in the streets around La Coca-Cola bus terminal and Parque Central, Av 2. A few places have a bad reputation day and night, including Barrio México in the northwest of the city and the red-light districts of C 12, Av 8/10, and Av 4/6, C 4/12, just southwest of the centre. The **dangers** are mainly mugging, purse-snatching or jewellery-snatching rather than serious assault, and many people walk around without encountering any problems at all. However, taxis are cheap enough that it's probably not worth taking the risk.

Crossing streets

You have to be careful when crossing the street in San José, as drivers are very aggressive, and pedestrian fatalities are distressingly common (you'll see lots of stories about "*atropellados*" in the national newspaper). There are a few ground rules, however, that can help minimize your chances of ending up in hospital.

- If possible, always try to cross the street at an official crossing point alongside other pedestrians. Note that there are only a handful of pedestrian lights in the entire city.
- Traffic lights are not easy to spot (they're hung about 5m above your head), so watch the traffic and other pedestrians.
- Take particular care negotiating the city's very wide roadside storm drains.
- Run if it looks like the light is changing.
- Don't expect anyone to stop for you under any circumstances. You have to get out of their way, not vice versa.

The closest thing San José has to a main **domestic bus station** is **La Coca-Cola**, five blocks west of the Mercado Central at Av 1/3, C 16/18 (the main entrance is on C 16). Named after an old bottling plant, La Coca-Cola not only applies to the station proper – which is quite small and the arrival point for only a few buses, principally those from Jacó, Quepos and Dominical – but also the surrounding area, where many more buses pull in. Like many bus stations, La Coca-Cola is well on its way to being an irredeemable hellhole – noisy, hemmed in by small, confusing streets crammed with busy market traders, and invariably prowled by pickpockets. Lugging your bags and searching for your bus stop around here makes it very hard not to look like a confused gringo, thus increasing the chances that you'll become the target of opportunistic theft: best to arrive and leave in a taxi. Be especially careful of your belongings around the **Tilarán terminal** (C 12, Av 7/9; ⓣ2222-3854), which is also used by buses to Monteverde: people waiting here for the 6.30am bus to Monteverde seem to be particularly at risk of attempted theft.

For details on getting out of the city from La Coca-Cola, see "Travel details", pp.118–119.

Information

San José's **Instituto Costarricense de Turismo (ICT) office** (Mon–Fri 9am–5pm; ⓣ2291-5764 or 2299-5800 ext 408, ⓦwww.visitcostarica.com) is beneath the eastern edge of the Plaza de la Cultura, C 5, Av 0/2. It gives out free maps, hotel brochures and – most crucially – comprehensive booklets detailing the national bus schedule. Staff here also hand out the free monthly *Culture Calendar*, which details concerts and festivals throughout the country.

City transport

Once you've got used to the deep gutters and broken pavements, San José is easily negotiated **on foot**. Several blocks in the city centre around the Plaza de la Cultura have been completely pedestrianized. There is little need to take **buses** within the city centre, though the suburban buses are useful, particularly if you are heading out to Parque la Sabana, a thirty-minute walk west along Paseo Colón. Escazú is a twenty-minute ride to the west, and the University of Costa Rica and San Pedro are a ten-minute ride to the east.

Buses stop running between 10–11pm and **taxis** become the best way to get around. These days street crime is on the rise, and most Josefinos advise against walking alone after dark, women especially.

Buses

Fast, cheap and frequent **buses** connect the centre of the city with virtually all San José's neighbourhoods and suburbs, and generally run from 5am until 10–11pm everyday. Most buses to San Pedro, Tres Ríos and other points east leave from the stretch of Avenida Central between C 9 and C 15. You can pick up buses for Paseo Colón and Parque la Sabana (labelled "Sabana-Cementerio") at the bus shelters on Av 2, C 5/7. In an enlightened move, city authorities are hoping to move the bus stops out of the centre proper in order to cut traffic and pollution (most city buses belch depressingly black streams of diesel fumes from their exhaust pipes).

All buses have their routes clearly marked on their windshields, and usually the **fare** too. This is payable either to the driver or his helper when you board and is usually 200 colones, though the faster, more comfortable *busetas de lujo* (luxury buses) to the suburbs cost upwards of 250 colones. The traditional method of stopping the bus to get off is for men to whistle and women to call out "*¡Parada!*" (stop), but bus drivers have recently taken to putting up testy signs saying "*los monos gritan, los pájaros silvan, por favor toca el timbre*" ("monkeys yell, birds whistle, please use the bell").

Taxis

Taxis are cheap and plentiful, even at odd hours of the night and early morning. Licensed vehicles are red with a yellow triangle on the side, and have

Useful bus routes

The following is a rundown of the main inner-city routes, all of which stop along Avenida Central or Avenida 2 in the centre of town. If in doubt, ask "*¿dónde está la parada para...?*" ("Where is the stop for...?").

Sabana–Cementerio buses travel west along Paseo Colón to Parque la Sabana, and are ideal for going to any of the shops, theatres and restaurants clustered around Paseo Colón, the Museo de Arte Costarricense or Parque la Sabana.

Sabana–Estadio services run basically the same route, with a tour around Parque la Sabana. Good for the neighbourhoods of Sabana norte and Sabana sur.

Sabanilla–Bethania buses run east through Los Yoses and beyond to the quiet residential suburb of Sabanilla.

San Pedro (also **La U**) or **Tres Ríos** buses will also take you east through Los Yoses and on to the University of Costa Rica and the hip neighbourhood of San Pedro. Other buses serving San Pedro are: Vargas Araya, Santa Marta, Granadilla, Curridabat and Cedros.

San José's street system and addresses

San José, along with most Costa Rican towns of any size, is planned on a grid system. It's intersected east–west by **Avenida Central** (called Paseo Colón west of La Coca-Cola bus station) and north–south by **Calle Central**. From Avenida Central, parallel avenidas run to the north (odd numbers) and to the south (even numbers). From Calle Central, even-numbered calles run to the west and odd numbers to the east. Avenidas 8 and 9, therefore, are actually quite far apart. Similarly, calles 23 and 24 are at opposite ends of the city. When you see **bis** (literally "encore" – again) in an address it denotes a separate street, usually a dead end (*calle sin salida*), next to the avenida or calle to which it refers. Av 8 bis, for example, is between Av 8 and 10. "**0**" in addresses is shorthand for "Central": thus Av 0, C 11 is the same as Av Central, C 11.

Most times, locals – and especially taxi drivers – won't have a clue what you're talking about if you try to use street numbers to find an address. When possible, give directions in relation to local **landmarks**, buildings, businesses, parks or institutions. In addition, people use **metres** to signify distance: in local parlance 100 metres equals one city block. There are precious few street signs, so it's helpful to count streets as you go along so as not to miss your turn. Note that most roads are one-way, usually (but not always) the opposite direction to the previous road.

"SJP" ("San José Público") licence plates. A ride anywhere within the city costs $2–3, and around double that to get out to the suburbs. The starter fare – about $1 – is shown on the red digital read-out, and you should always make sure that the meter is on before you start (ask the driver to "*toca la maría, por favor*"). Some drivers may claim that the meter doesn't work – if this is the case, it's best either to agree on a fare before you start out or to find another taxi whose meter is working. Many drivers are honest – don't immediately assume everyone's trying to cheat you. After midnight, taxis from the El Pueblo centre charge forty percent extra. These are institutionalized higher fares, and you shouldn't attempt to negotiate. Tipping is not expected. There are several taxi companies in the city; two of the more reliable are Coopeirazu ⓣ2254-0533 and Coopetaxi ⓣ2235-9966.

By car and bike

There's no need to **rent a car** specifically for getting around San José – indeed, most Josefinos advise foreigners against driving in the city, at least until they're familiar with the aggressive local style of driving. In addition, most of the city's streets are one-way, though sometimes unmarked as such. Cars left on the street anywhere near the city centre are almost certain to be broken into or stolen. If you do rent a car, always use the secure **parqueos** (guarded car parks) that dot the city: most close at 8 or 8.30pm, although there are some 24-hour parks, including one on the corner of Av 0, C 19. Some hotels have on-site parking. If you have to leave your car on the street, most areas have a man whose job is to guard the cars – look for the fellow with the truncheon and expect to pay around 300 colones. If driving in the centre of the city, keep your windows rolled up and your doors locked so no one can reach in. For a list of car **rental companies**, see p.43.

It's generally not a good idea to **cycle** in San José. Diesel fumes, potholes and un-cycle-conscious drivers don't make for pleasant cycling, although riding in the suburbs or Parque la Sabana is easier and less hazardous to your health.

Accommodation

San José has plenty of quality hotel rooms, with reasonable prices in all categories. The budget-to-moderate sector has improved markedly with several guesthouses and family-run hotels. Rock-bottom hotels, however, still tend, with a few exceptions, to be depressing cells that make the city seem infinitely uglier than it is. San José has its fair share of international **hotel chains**, many of whose names (and generic facilities) – *Radisson*, *Holiday Inn* and *Best Western* – will be familiar to North Americans and Europeans. While some are comfortable and have excellent service, they don't offer much in the way of local colour. It's also worth noting that while these hotels employ Costa Ricans, most of their profits are repatriated to the company's home country.

If you are coming in **high season** (Dec–May), and especially over busy periods like Christmas and Easter, be prepared to reserve (and, in some cases, even pay) in advance. Room **rates** vary dramatically between high and low seasons – the prices we quote are for a double room in peak season, and you can expect to get substantial discounts at less busy times. Unless otherwise indicated, breakfast is usually not included.

Many of San José's rock-bottom hotels have cold-water showers only. Unless you're particularly hardy, you'll want some form of **heated water**, as San José can get chilly, especially from December to March. At the budget end of the spectrum, so-called "hot" water is actually often no more than a tepid trickle, produced by one of the eccentric electric contraptions you'll find fitted over showers throughout the country (see Basics, p.48) – it's still better than cold water, however.

Though staying in one of the budget hotels in the **city centre** is convenient, the downside is noise and, in many places, a lack of atmosphere. Not too far from downtown, in quieter areas such as **Paseo Colón**, **Los Yoses** and **Barrios Amón** and **Otoya**, is a group of more expensive hotels, many of them in old colonial homes.

To the west of the city is Escazú, the stomping ground of American expats, and popularly known as "Gringolandia". The vast majority of B&Bs here are owned by foreign nationals, with higher prices than elsewhere in town. Street names and addresses are particularly confusing in this area so get clear directions or arrange to be picked up. East of the city and closer to the centre is studenty San Pedro, with better connections to downtown and a more cosmopolitan atmosphere. It's a great place to stay, but unfortunately there are only a couple of hostels in the area.

Central San José

All the accommodation listed below is marked on the Central San José map on p.94.

Ara Macao Inn C 25 bis, Av 0/2, 50m south of *Pizza Hut* in Barrio California ⓣ2233-2742, ⓦwww.aramacaoinn.com. Small and pleasant B&B with twelve rooms (eight with kitchenettes for longer stays), just outside the city centre, but near the restaurants of Barrio California and Los Yoses. Rooms are airy and have private bath, cable TV and internet access. Singles are a good deal at $45. Breakfast included. ❺

Le Bergerac C 35, Av 0 ⓣ2234-7850, ⓦwww.bergerachotel.com. For luxury without the price tag, this elegant and relaxing top-end hotel is an excellent choice. The 26 spacious rooms all have cable TV and phone, internet access and some also have their own private gardens. The agreeable restaurant, next to an interior courtyard, serves local and North American fare, and there's a travel service that arranges tours. Continental breakfast included. ❻

Casa León Av 6 bis, C 13/15 ⓣ2221-91651, ⓦwww.hotelcasaleon.com. This Swiss-run small guesthouse has dorms ($15 per person in a three-bed room) and basic private rooms with a spotlessly clean shared bath and kitchen. There is laundry service and luggage storage. The house is a little hard to find; look for it next to the train tracks and tell your taxi driver it's in a *calle sin salida*. ❸

Casa Ridgway C 15, Av 6 bis between Av 6/8 ⓣ2233-2693, ⓦwww.amigosparalapaz.org/casaridgway. Near the Tica Bus stop, this homely Quaker guesthouse is a good budget choice with several clean, single-sex dorms ($15 per person), plus a few private singles ($22) and doubles

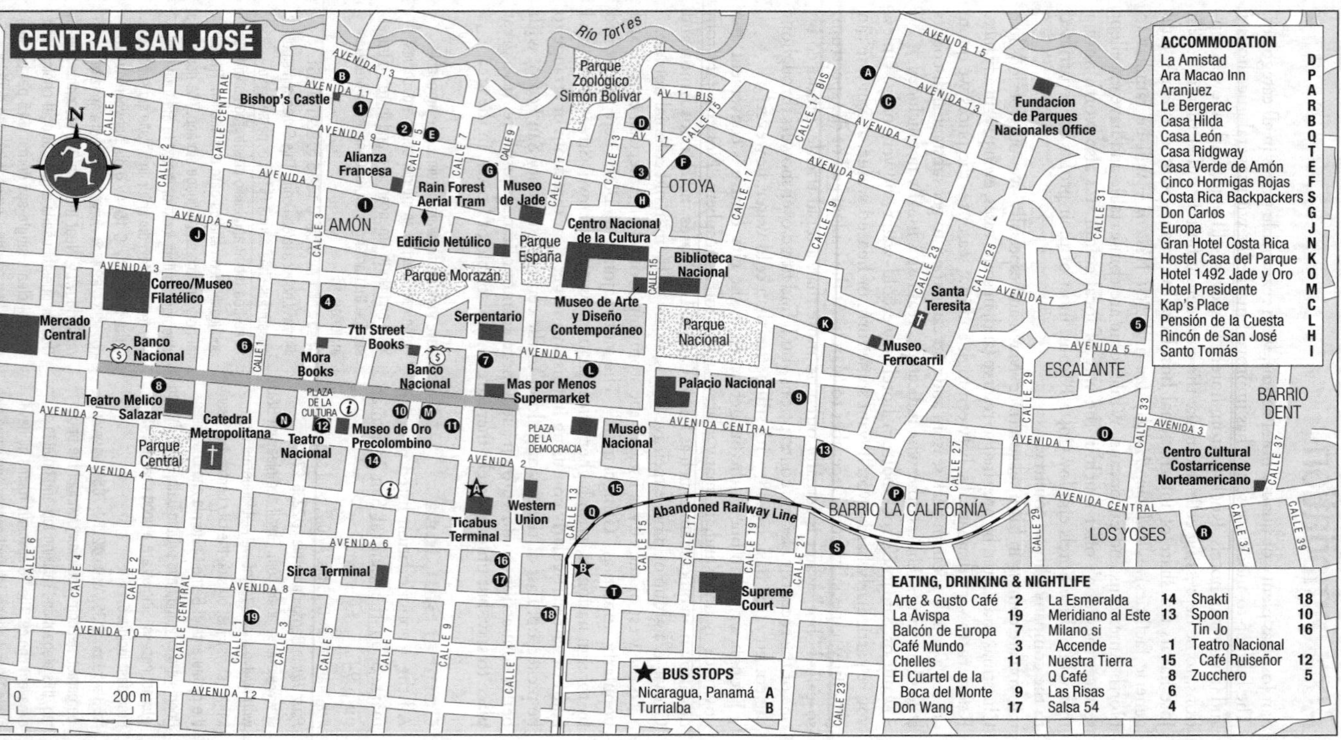
CENTRAL SAN JOSÉ
N
ACCOMMODATION
La Amistad D
Ara Macao Inn P
Aranjuez A
Le Bergerac R
Casa Hilda B
Casa León Q
Casa Ridgway T
Casa Verde de Amón E
Cinco Hormigas Rojas F
Costa Rica Backpackers S
Don Carlos G
Europa J
Gran Hotel Costa Rica N
Hostel Casa del Parque K
Hotel 1492 Jade y Oro O
Hotel Presidente M
Kap's Place C
Pensión de la Cuesta L
Rincón de San José H
Santo Tomás I
EATING, DRINKING & NIGHTLIFE
Arte & Gusto Café 2
La Avispa 19
Balcón de Europa 7
Café Mundo 3
Chelles 11
El Cuartel de la Boca del Monte 9
Don Wang 17
La Esmeralda 14
Meridiano al Este 13
Milano si Accende 1
Nuestra Tierra 15
Q Café 8
Las Risas 6
Salsa 54 4
Shakti 18
Spoon 10
Tin Jo 16
Teatro Nacional Café Ruiseñor 12
Zucchero 5
BUS STOPS
Nicaragua, Panamá A
Turrialba B
Río Torres
Parque Zoológico Simón Bolívar
Bishop's Castle
Alianza Francesa
Rain Forest Aerial Tram
Museo de Jade
AMÓN
OTOYA
Edificio Netúlico
Parque España
Centro Nacional de la Cultura
Biblioteca Nacional
Parque Morazán
Correo/Museo Filatélico
Mercado Central
Banco Nacional
7th Street Books
Mora Books
Serpentario
Museo de Arte y Diseño Contemporáneo
Parque Nacional
Santa Teresita
Museo Ferrocarril
Fundacion de Parques Nacionales Office
ESCALANTE
BARRIO DENT
Mas por Menos Supermarket
Palacio Nacional
PLAZA DE LA CULTURA
Teatro Melico Salazar
Catedral Metropolitana
Teatro Nacional
Museo de Oro Precolombino
Parque Central
PLAZA DE LA DEMOCRACIA
Museo Nacional
Ticabus Terminal
Western Union
Abandoned Railway Line
BARRIO LA CALIFORNÍA
Centro Cultural Costarricense Norteamericano
LOS YOSES
San Pedro
Sirca Terminal
Supreme Court
AVENIDA CENTRAL
CALLE CENTRAL
0 200 m

($34) with communal bathrooms. There's also a shared kitchen, laundry and luggage storage. Note that alcohol is banned and there's a "quiet time" after 10pm. Reserve ahead in high season, and try not to arrive after 8pm except by prior arrangement. ❸

Costa Rica Backpackers Av 6, C 21/23 ⓣ2221-6191,ⓦwww.costaricabackpackers.com. A great place to meet fellow travellers, this is one of the city's best budget guesthouses with both single- and mixed-sex dorms ($13 per person) plus a few private double rooms ($32). Facilities include a fully equipped kitchen, a garden with swimming pool, luggage storage, laundry service, a TV room, wi-fi and free parking. ❶

Europa C 0, Av 3/5 ⓣ2222-1222, ⓦwww.hotel europacr.com. Mid-range casino-hotel, San José's oldest, located in the heart of downtown, with a restaurant, bar, indoor pool, lots of bright communal areas and a 24-hour Egyptian-themed gaming room. Outside rooms tend to get street noise but more light while inside rooms are quieter but less airy. There's a helpful tour desk inside the hotel with good contacts throughout the country. ❻

Gran Hotel Costa Rica Av 0/2, C 3 ⓣ2221-4000, ⓦwww.granhotelcr.com. This elegant hotel has over 100 spotlessly clean but rather unimaginatively furnished rooms – some are enormous, some are small, but all have TV, phone, wi-fi and 24hr room service. The central location – overlooking the Plaza de la Cultura, and with a popular terrace café below – can be noisy, especially when the buskers are in full swing. Discounts are often available in low season. ❻

Hostel Casa del Parque C 19, Av 1/3 ⓣ22233-3437, ⓦwww.hostelcasadel parque.com. With a serene location adjacent to Parque Nacional, this small, family-run hostel is easily one of the city's better budget choices. The dorm rooms have six or eight beds and there's one double room – all are clean and comfortable. The friendly staff can book tours, the common areas are smarter than you'd expect for this category and there's free wi-fi throughout. Dorm ❶, double room ❸

Hotel 1492 Jade y Oro Av 1, C 31/33 ⓣ2256-5913 or 2225-3752, ⓦwww.hotel1492.com. On a quiet stretch of Av 1, this comfortable hotel has ten well-appointed rooms, some surrounding an elegant antique- and art-filled atrium and others adjoining a small tropical garden. All have private shower and TV. The friendly staff can arrange tours. ❺

Hotel Presidente Av 0, C 7 ⓣ2010-0000, ⓦwww.hotel-presidente.com. Plush, immaculate hotel smack in the middle of downtown. Over 90 rooms, each tastefully designed and well-appointed with cable TV, a/c, safe and wi-fi and some have a jacuzzi. There's a spa on site, as well as a gym, sports lounge and the excellent *News Café* (see p.109). Standard double room ❼, spa suites ❽

Pensión de la Cuesta Av 1, C 11/15 ⓣ2256-7946, ⓦwww.pensiondelacuesta.com. Tranquil rooms – though some are a bit gloomy – in a pink and blue colonial-style wooden house, with a plant-filled lounge area, gold masks on walls and decorated bedsteads. All rooms have shared bath, plus there's a communal kitchen, laundry service and luggage storage. Staff can arrange tours and car rental. Good deals for weekly stays. ❷

North of the centre: Barrios Amón, Otoya and Aranjuez

All the accommodation listed below is marked on the Central San José map opposite.

La Amistad Av 11, C 13 ⓣ2258-0021, ⓦwww .hotelamistad.com. Set in a large house in historic Barrio Otoya, this American-owned hotel has over 30 rooms all with cable TV, wi-fi, in-room safe, private bath and queen-sized beds; there are also six penthouse suites with a/c and two apartments ($86 for four people) with a/c. Serious breakfast buffet included. ❺

Aranjuez C 19, Av 11/13 ⓣ2256-1825, ⓦwww.hotelaranjuez.com. In quiet Barrio Aranjuez yet still close to the centre, the rooms of this hotel are in converted houses that have been joined with communal sitting areas. Relax in the pretty garden around the back, where organic waste from the hotel is used as fertilizer. They serve a good buffet breakfast and can arrange tours to *Laguna Lodge* in Tortuguero. Be sure to reserve ahead. The 36 rooms either have shared bath (❸) or private bath and TV (❹); all have wi-fi.

Casa Hilda Av 11, C 3 & 3 bis, house no. 353 ⓣ2221-0037, ⓔc1hilda@racsa.co.cr. Small and affordable hotel in an old-style wooden house on a quiet street near the city centre. The five rooms are basic but comfortable and have private bath with hot water and fans. Rooms with outside-facing windows are best; the others are a bit dark. There's also a patio garden and communal sitting areas with cable TV. Good single rates. ❸

Casa Verde de Amón Corner of C 7 & Av 9 ⓣ2223-0969, ⓔcasaverde@racsa.co.cr. Set in a historic late nineteenth-century mansion, this quiet, beautifully restored hotel is filled with antiques and oriental rugs. Well-furnished rooms and suites have wooden floors and fittings – and some even have Victorian bathtubs. Prices are very reasonable,

particularly in low season, and there are weekly discounts. Rooms ❺, suites ❼

Cinco Hormigas Rojas C 15, Av 9/11, 200m east of the back of the INS building and then 25m north ⓣ2255-3412, ⓦwww.cincohormigasrojas.com. The "five red ants" is a small hippie paradise in quiet Barrio Otoya, decorated with vibrant paintings by the friendly owner Mayra Güell. With its walled-in tropical garden that's home to several species of bird throughout the year, this is a fantastic spot to ease into San José. The six, bright rooms have names like "jungle window" and "bouncing lead" and share two bathrooms; all have wi-fi access. Breakfast included. No smoking. ❹

Don Carlos C 9, Av 7 & 9 ⓣ2221-6707, ⓦwww.doncarloshotel.com. An elegant landmark hotel, once the home of two presidential families, now filled with replicas of pre-Columbian art and a lovely kitsch breakfast terrace/cocktail lounge with a fountain and a pretty tiled mural of the city hand-painted by Costa Rican artist Mario Aroyabe. All rooms have cable TV and safe (some also have private patios) and there's wi-fi and a small pool, plus an excellent souvenir shop and travel agency. ❻

Kap's Place C 19, Av 11/13 ⓣ2221-1169, ⓦwww.kapsplace.com. One of the city's best mid-range choices, this family-friendly hotel is run by the unstintingly helpful Karla Arias who is a bottomless source of information on all things San José. There are several different types of accommodation; most of the 23 rooms have private baths and all are colourfully decorated. There's a fully equipped communal kitchen. Tours arranged on request. ❺

Rincón de San José Av 9, C 13/15 ⓣ2221-9702, ⓦwww.hotelrincondesanjose.com. This renovated Dutch-owned hotel in pretty Barrio Amón has 27 clean rooms (all with cable TV), wooden floors and piping-hot showers, plus the use of a computer and safe. Some rooms have wi-fi access. The excellent *Café Mundo* restaurant is just across the street. Breakfast included. ❺

Santo Tomás Av 7, C 3/5 ⓣ2255-0448, ⓦwww.hotelsantotomas.com. In quiet, elegant Barrio

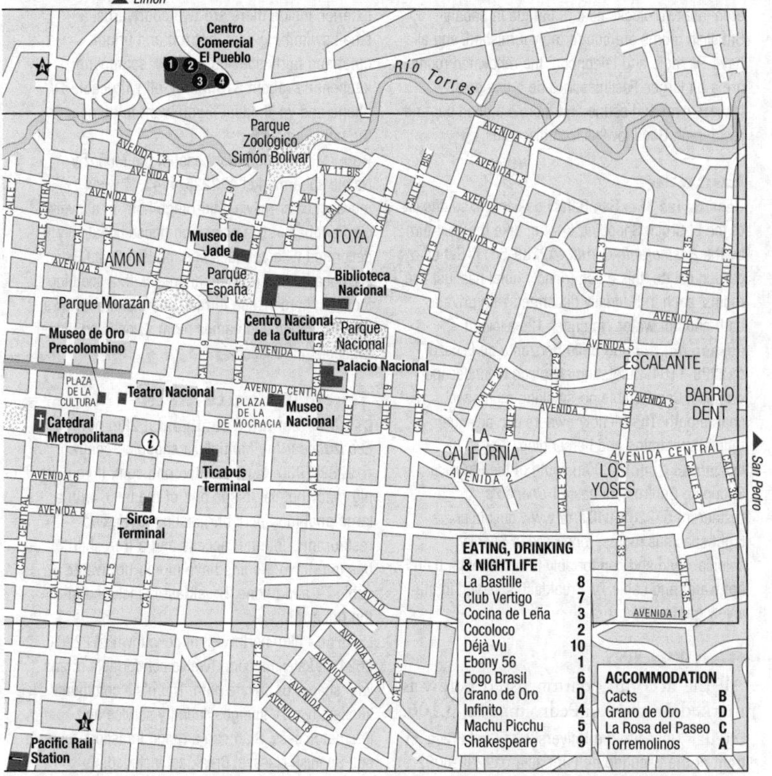

Amón, near downtown, this is one of San José's best boutique hotels. It occupies an old mansion awash in soft lighting and decorated with burnished wood and Persian rugs. Twenty rooms vary widely in size, character and price, though all have TV, telephone and internet access. There's a small swimming pool, hot tub, an excellent open-air restaurant and a travel service ❺

West of the centre

All the accommodation listed below is marked on the San José map above.

Cacts C 28/30, Av 3 bis ⓣ2221-6546 or 2928, ⓦwww.hotelcacts.com. *Cacts* has 25 rooms, all with ceiling fans and TV; all but four have private baths. A sunny roof terrace, tropical garden, swimming pool and jacuzzi add to its charm. Enjoy a complimentary breakfast buffet of fresh fruits and baked goods. The friendly owners run a travel agency and can book tours and reservations. ❹

Grano de Oro C 30, Av 2/4 ⓣ2255-3322 ⓦwww.hotelgranodeoro.com. Elegant converted mansion in a quiet area west of the centre, a block from Paseo Colón. The 40 well-appointed rooms and suites are furnished in faux-Victorian style, with wrought-iron beds and polished wooden floors. Several of the deluxe rooms have lovely private gardens and all rooms have cable TV, minibar, phone and wi-fi. A rooftop sun terrace equipped with twin hot tubs provides expansive views over the centre. The staff are exceedingly helpful, and an excellent breakfast is served in its gourmet restaurant (see p.111). ❼

La Rosa del Paseo Paseo Colón, C 28/30 ⓣ2257-3258, ⓦwww.rosadelpaseo.com. Converted late nineteenth-century house on busy Paseo Colón. Rooms have nice touches – sparkling bathrooms, wooden floors and Victorian fittings – and all come with private bath and cable TV. Breakfast included. ❻

Torremolinos C 40, Av 5 bis ⓣ2222-5266, ⓦwww.occidentalhotels.com. Part of the Occidental hotel chain and currently undergoing renovation, this well-maintained hotel is in a quiet area just two blocks east of Parque la Sabana. Smallish rooms are comfortably furnished, and all have TV, radio and telephone; the renovated rooms are a bit larger. Facilities include a tiny pool, jacuzzi, gym and sauna and there's a good bar and restaurant. Good low-season discounts. ❻

Escazú

Casa de las Tias San Rafael de Escazú, southeast of the El Cruce Shopping Centre; take the east turn by the *Restaurante Cerutti* ⓣ2289-5517. Set on a garden estate, this quiet, friendly hotel has just five rooms, each individually decorated with private bath and hot water. No under-12s allowed. ❻

Posada del Bosque Bello Horizonte de Escazú ⓣ2228-1164. Quiet, homely place in landscaped grounds. Comfortable no-smoking rooms with shared bath. The friendly owners can arrange tennis, swimming and horseriding. ❺

Posada El Quijote 800m south of the El Cruce Shopping Centre, just east of *Chango's* restaurant ⓣ2289-8401, ⓦwww.quijote.cr. Eight spacious rooms, renovated in Spanish colonial style and comfortably furnished with bath, hot water and cable TV. Breakfast is served in the lovely garden. ❻

San Pedro

All the accommodation listed below is marked on the San Pedro map on p.106.

D'Galah Opposite the University of Costa Rica, in front of the Facultad de Farmacia ⓣ2280-8092, ⓦwww.dgalah.com. Despite a characterless exterior, inside there are two courtyards, a small swimming pool, hot tub and bright, quiet and fairly spacious rooms, some with kitchenette (about $10 more), all with cable TV, phone and wi-fi. Ideal if you want to be near the university. ❺

Hotel Milvia 250m northeast of the Muñoz y Nanne supermarket ⓣ2225-4543, ⓦwww.novanet.co.cr/milvia. Mid-range hotel in a lovely old Caribbean-style plantation house beautifully decorated with antiques and modern Costa Rican art. Located in a residential area, with a soothing fountain, garden, sun terrace and mountain views, plus TV lounge and games room. Lunch and dinner available on request. ❺

The city outskirts

Camino Real Inter-Continental 2km north of Escazú, near the Multiplaza shopping centre ⓣ2289-7000, ⓦwww.interconti.com. If you like big fancy hotels, this is one of the best, with a large pool (and pool bar), sauna, gym, two restaurants, internet access and a free shuttle bus into town. Rooms have piping-hot water, cable TV and phone. Breakfast is included in the price. ❽

La Uruca 5km northwest of downtown ⓣ2290-2624, ⓦkalexma.com. Twelve comfortable rooms with shared or private bath. There's a communal kitchen, two TV lounges, laundry service and internet access. Staff can arrange transport, tours, and Spanish classes. Breakfast included. ❶ without bathroom, ❷ with bathroom.

The City

Few travellers come to San José for the sights, and going by first impressions it's easy to see why. San José certainly doesn't exude immediate appeal, with its nondescript buildings and aggressive street life full of umbrella-wielding pedestrians, narrow streets, noisy food stalls and homicidal drivers. Scratch the surface, though, and you'll find a civilized city, with museums and galleries and plenty of places to walk, meet people, enjoy a meal, and go dancing. It's also relatively manageable, with less of the chaos and crowds that plague most other Latin American cities. San José is a surprisingly green and open city: small, carefully landscaped parks and paved-over plazas punctuate the centre of town. All the attractions lie near each other, and you can cover everything of interest in a couple of days.

Of the city's museums, the major draws are the exemplary **Museo de Oro Precolombino,** featuring over 2000 pieces of pre-Columbian gold, and the **Museo del Jade**, the Americas' largest collection of the precious stone. Less visited, the **Museo Nacional** offers a brutally honest depiction of the country's colonization and some interesting archeological finds. The **Museo de Arte y Diseño Contemporáneo** displays some of the most striking contemporary works in the Americas.

The centre itself is subdivided into little neighbourhoods (*barrios*) that flow seamlessly in and out of one another. **Barrios Amón** and **Otoya**, in the north, are the prettiest, lined with the genteel mansions of former coffee barons. To the west are **La Californía** and **Los Yoses**, home to the *Toruma* youth hostel, most of the embassies and the Centro Cultural Costarricense Norteamericano. The esteemed University of Costa Rica rises amid the lively student bars and cafés of the **San Pedro** barrio, just east of the city centre.

Parque Central

At the heart of the city centre is **Parque Central**, Av 2, C 0/2, a landscaped square punctuated by tall royal palms and centred on a weird Gaudí-esque bandstand. Green parrots roost nightly in the palms; come twilight, their noisy chatter drowns out the constant rumble of traffic. Less frantic than many of the city's squares, it's a nice place to snack on the lychee-like *mamones chinos* or papayas sold by the nearby fruit vendors.

At the eastern edge of the Parque Central looms the huge columnar **Catedral Metropolitana** (Mon–Sat 6am–noon & 3–6pm, Sun 6am–9pm), nicely restored and well worth a peek inside for its colourful frescoes and gilded columns. On the square's northeastern corner, the Neoclassical **Teatro Melico Salazar** (free guided visits can be arranged by appointment on ⓣ2221-5172; see p.115) is one of Costa Rica's premier theatres, second only to the Teatro Nacional a few blocks further east. The barely contained hubbub of Calle 2 and its assorted electronics and shoe shops overtakes the park's northwestern corner.

Avenida Central

Two blocks north of Parque Central, the pedestrianized **Avenida Central** bisects the city from east to west. Despite the constant ebb and flow of people pressing onward, it's a pleasant and surprisingly welcoming stretch of street and makes for a good introduction to the city. Department stores dot the Avenida, including Universal, with a particularly good book department, the cavernous book-stationery shop Librería Lehmann (see p.116 for both) and, further down, a clutch of *sodas* and fast-food outlets.

Mercado Central and around

Just beyond the western end of Avenida Central's pedestrianized section on the corner of Calle 6, is the squat **Mercado Central** (Mon–Sat 8am–5pm). Though it's more orderly than the usual chickens-and-*campesinos* Latin American city markets, it's still quite an experience. Entering the labyrinthine market, you're assaulted by colourful arrangements of strange fruits and vegetables, dangling sides of beef and elaborate, silvery rows of fish. At certain times of the day (lunch and late afternoon, for example) the Mercado Central can resemble the Eighth Circle of Hell – choking with unfamiliar smells and an almighty crush of people – while at other times you'll be able to enjoy a relaxed wander through wide uncrowded alleys of rural commerce. It's certainly the best place in town to get a cheap bite to eat, and the view from a counter stool is fascinating, as traders and their customers jostle for regional produce from *chayotes* (a pear-shaped vegetable) and *mamones* (a lychee-type fruit) to *piñas* (pineapples) and *cas* (a sweet-sour pale fruit.) With a little Spanish, and a pinch of confidence, shopping for fruit and vegetables here can be miles cheaper than in the supermarket.

The streets surrounding the market, which can look quite seedy even during the day (in sharp contrast to the roads just one or two blocks east), are also full of noisy traders and determined shoppers. All this activity encourages **pickpockets**, and in this environment tourists stick out like sore thumbs. Carry only what you need and be on your guard.

Two blocks east and one block north of the Mercado Central, in the Correo Central, C 2, Av 1/3, the **Museo Filatélico y Numismatico** (Mon–Fri 8am–5pm; free) has an impressive collection of stamps and coins, though it is really only of interest to keen philatelists. Nearby, on Calle 2 and Avenida 3, the **Farmacia Fischel**, one of the oldest pharmacies in the city, has a good stock of both conventional and herbal remedies.

Plaza de la Cultura

Just east of the Parque Central, **Plaza de la Cultura** (Av Central, C 3/5) is one of the few places in San José where you can sit at a pleasant outdoor café – the *Café Parisienne*, under the arches of the *Gran Hotel Costa Rica* on the plaza's western edge – and watch the world go by to the accompaniment of buskers. The Neoclassical Teatro Nacional rises elegantly over the plaza's southern side while the (rather poorly signposted) joint-entrance to the city's underground tourist office and Museo de Oro Precolombino can be found on the plaza's eastern edge.

Museo de Oro Precolombino

The Plaza de la Cultura cleverly conceals one of San José's treasures, the Banco Central-owned **Museo de Oro Precolombino**, or Pre-Columbian Gold Museum (Tues–Sat 10am–4pm; $9; ⓣ2243-4202, ⓦwww.museosdelbancocentral.org). The bunker-like underground museum is unprepossessing but the gold on display is truly impressive – all the more extraordinary if you take into account the relative paucity of pre-Columbian artefacts in Costa Rica (compared with Mexico, say, or Guatemala). Most of the exquisitely delicate goldwork is by the **Diquis**, ancient inhabitants of southwestern Costa Rica.

The gold pieces are hung on transparent wires, giving the impression of floating in space, mysteriously suspended in their perspex cases. Most of the gold pieces are small and unbelievably detailed, with a preponderance of disturbing, evil-looking animals. Information panels (in English and Spanish) suggest that one of the chief functions of these portents of evil – frogs, snakes and insects – was to protect the bearer against illness. The Diquis believed that sickness was transmitted to people through spirits in animal form. The *ave de rapiña*, or bird of prey, seems to have had a particular religious relevance for the Diquis: hawks, owls and eagles, differing only fractionally in shape and size, are depicted everywhere. Watch out, too, for angry-looking arachnids, ready to bite or sting; jaguars and alligators carrying the pathetic dangling legs of human victims in their jaws; grinning bats with wings spread; turtles, crabs, frogs, iguanas and armadillos; and a few spiny lobsters. Museum displays highlight the historical and geographical context of Costa Rican gold. Maps pinpoint gold-production centres and there are models of gold-making settlements.

Sharing the building is the marginally interesting **Museo de Numismática** (free with admission to Gold Museum, and same opening hours) with a collection of Costa Rican coins. Look out for the old five-colón note, decorated with a delicate, brightly coloured panorama of Costa Rican society.

Teatro Nacional

Reputedly modelled on the Paris Opéra, San José's heavily colonnaded, grey-brown **Teatro Nacional** sits on the corner of Calle 5 and Avenida 2, tucked in behind the Plaza de la Cultura. The theatre's marbled stairways, gilt cherubs and red velvet carpets would look more at home in Europe than in Central America.

Costa Rican gold

Little, if anything, is known of the prehistory of the **Diquis**, who were responsible for most of the goldwork at the Museo de Oro Precolombino. However, the history of goldworking in the New World is fairly well documented. It was first recorded (around 2000 BC) in Peru, from where it spread northwards, reaching Mexico and the Central American isthmus by 700–900 AD. All the ancient American peoples favoured more or less the same methods and styles, using a gold-copper alloy (called *tumbaga*) and designs featuring extremely intricate shapings, with carefully rendered facial expressions and a preference for ingenious but rather diabolical-looking zoomorphic representations – growling peccaries, threatening birds of prey, and a two-headed figure, each mouth playing its own flute. The precise function of these intricately crafted creations is still the subject of some debate since many of the objects show no sign of having been worn (there are no grooves in the pendant links to indicate they were worn on chains). Archeologists believe they may have been intended for ceremonial burial and, indeed, some were even "killed" or ritually mutilated before being entombed. Others may have been worn as charms protecting the bearer against illness and evil spirits.

The Diquis would have obtained the gold by panning in rivers, and it is speculated that in Osa, at least, the rivers routinely washed up gold at their feet. Diquis *caciques* (chiefs) and other social elites used their gold in the same way it is used today – to advertise wealth and social prestige. Ornaments and insignias were often reserved for the use of a particular *cacique* and his family, and these special pieces were traded as truce offerings and political gifts between various rulers, maintaining contacts between the *caciques* of distant regions. Indeed, it was the removal of native distinctions of social rank following the Spanish Conquest of the country in the seventeenth century that heralded the almost immediate collapse of the Costa Rican gold-making industry.

Although the Diquis were the undisputed masters of design, archeological digs in the Reventazón Valley suggest that gold-working could also be found among the peoples of the Atlantic watershed zone. When Columbus first came ashore in 1502, he saw the local (Talamancan) peoples wearing gold mirror-pendants and headbands and rashly assumed he had struck it rich – hence the country's name. An early document of a subsequent expedition to the Caribbean coastal region of Costa Rica, now housed in archives in Cartago, contains the impressions of native wealth recorded by one gold-crazed Spaniard in Diego de Sojo's 1587 expedition: "The rivers abound with gold…and the Indians extract gold with calabashes in very large grains…from these same hills Captain Muñoz…took from the tombs of the dead… such a great quantity of gold as to swell two large chests of the kind in which shoes and nails for the cavalry are brought over from Castile."

You won't find such impressive elegance anywhere else between here and the Manaus Opera House in deepest Amazonia.

Teatro Nacional's story is an intriguing one, illuminating the industrious, no-nonsense attitude of the city's coffee bourgeoisie, who demonstrated the national pride and yearning for cultural achievement that came to characterize Costa Rican society in the twentieth century. In 1890, the world-famous prima donna Adelina Patti was making a tour through the Americas, but could not stop in Costa Rica as there was no appropriate theatre. Mortified, and determined to raise funds for the construction of a national theatre, the wealthy coffee farmers responded by levying a tax on every bag of coffee exported. Within a couple of years the coffers were full to bursting; European craftsmen and architects were employed, and by 1897 the building was ready for its inauguration, a stylish affair with singers from the Paris Opéra performing *Faust*.

The theatre itself is lavishly done in red plush, gold and marble, with richly detailed frescoes and statues personifying "Dance", "Music" and "Fame". The upstairs "salons" are decorated in mint and jade-green, trimmed with gold, and lined with heavy portraits of former bourgeoisie. In the main lobby, look for the mural depicting the coffee harvest (once featured on the five-colón note), a gentle reminder of the agricultural source of wealth that made this urban luxury possible. All in all, the building remains in remarkably good condition, despite the dual onslaught of the climate and a succession of earthquakes. The latest, in 1991, closed the place for two years – until recently, the huge marble staircases on either side of the entrance still had wooden supports strapped onto them like slings. Above all it is the details that leave a lasting impression: plump cherubim, elegantly numbered boxes fanning out in a wheel-spoke circle, heavy hardwood doors and intricate glasswork in the washrooms.

Even if you're not coming to see a performance (see p.115) you can wander around the post-Baroque splendour, though you'll be charged $7 for the privilege (guided tours offered). Just off the foyer is an elegant café serving good coffee, juices and European-style cakes.

Parque España and around

Lined with tall trees, the verdant **Parque España** (three blocks east and two blocks north of Plaza de la Cultura) is surrounded by several excellent museums. On the western corner, facing Avenida 5, stands the **Edificio Metálica** (Metal Building, also known as the "Escuela Metálica"), so-called because its exterior is made entirely out of metal plates shipped from France over a hundred years ago. Though the prospect sounds dour, the effect – especially the bright multicoloured courtyard as seen from the **Museo del Jade**, high above – is very pretty, if slightly military. Just west of Parque España lies **Parque Morazón**, more a concrete-paved square than a park proper. It's centred on the landmark grey-domed bandstand floridly known as the Templo de Música.

Museo del Jade

On the north side of the Parque España rises one of the few office towers in San José: the INS, or Institute of Social Security, building. The eleventh floor of this uninspiring edifice contains one of the city's finest museums, the **Marco Fidel Tristan Museo del Jade** (Jade Museum; Mon–Fri 8.30am–3pm; $8; ⓣ2287-6034), home to the world's largest collection of American jade.

As in China and the East, jade was much prized in ancient Costa Rica as a stone with religious or mystical significance, and for Neolithic civilizations it was an object of great power. It was and still is considered valuable because of its mineralogical rarity. Only slightly less hard than quartz, it's well known for its durability, and is a good material for weapons and cutting tools like axes and blades. As no quarries of the stone have been found in Costa Rica, the big mystery is how the pre-Columbian societies here got hold of so much of it. The reigning theories are that it came from Guatemala, where the Motagua Valley is home to one of the world's six known jade quarries, or that it was traded or sold down the isthmus by the Olmecs of Mexico. This would also explain the Maya insignia on some of the pieces – symbols that had no meaning for Costa Rica's pre-Columbian inhabitants.

The museum displays are ingenious, subtly back-lit to show off the multicoloured and multi-textured pieces to full effect. Jade exhibits an extraordinary range of nuanced colour, from a milky-white green and soft grey to a deep green; the latter was associated with agricultural fertility and particularly prized by the inhabitants of the Americas around 600 BC. No two pieces in the collection are alike in hue and opacity, though, as in the Museo de Oro, you'll see a lot of **axe-gods**: anthropomorphic bird-cum-human forms shaped like an axe and worn as a pendant, as well as a variety of ornate necklaces and fertility symbols.

Incidentally, the **view** from the museum windows is one of the best in the city, taking in the sweep of San José from the centre to the south and then west to the mountains.

Museo de Arte y Diseño Contemporáneo

Sprawling across the entire eastern border of the Parque España, the former National Liquor Factory, dating from 1887, today houses an arts complex that includes the Centro Nacional de la Cultura, Juventud y Deportes (Ministry of Culture, Youth and Sports), known as CENAC. Many Josefinos still refer to the buildings as the old *Liquoría*; indeed you can still see a massive old distilling machine in the grounds, complete with the nameplate of its Birmingham manufacturers. The main attraction here is the cutting-edge **Museo de Arte y Diseño Contemporáneo**, or Museum of Contemporary Art and Design (Tues–Sun 10am–5pm; $2.50; ⓣ2257-9370, ⓦwww.madc.ac.cr), entered from the corner of Calle 15 and Avenida 3. Opened in 1994 under the direction of dynamic artist Virginia Pérez-Ratton, it's a highly modern space, with a cosmopolitan, multimedia approach – there's an area specially designed for outdoor installations by up-and-coming Central American artists. The CENAC complex also houses two theatres, a dance studio (wander around during the day for glimpses of dancers and musicians rehearsing) and an amphitheatre.

Barrios Amón and Otoya

Weaving its way north up the hill from the Parque España, the historic **Barrio Amón** leads into another old barrio, **Otoya**. Lined with stately buildings and the former homes of the Costa Rican coffee gentry, these two neighbourhoods are among the most attractive in San José. After decades of neglect they are currently undergoing something of a rediscovery by hoteliers and café and restaurant owners. More than a hundred years old, Amón is home to fine examples of "neo-Victorian" tropical architecture, with low-slung wooden houses girthed by wide verandas and iron railings. Striking examples include the **Alianza Francesa** building (C 5 & Av 7), the turreted **Bishop's Castle** (Av 11 bis & C 3), and the grand old **Casa Verde de Amón** hotel (C 7 & Av 9; see p.95).

Parque Zoológico Simón Bolívar

Two blocks north of Parque España, in Barrio Otoya, at Av 11 and C 7/9, is the entrance to the **Parque Zoológico Simón Bolívar** (Tues–Fri 8am–4pm, Sat & Sun 9am–5pm; $2). There are plans to move it to a location outside San José sometime in the future, but until then the zoo, with its pitifully cramped conditions, should be avoided by animal lovers. Nevertheless, it continues to draw Tico families on Sundays and gaggles of schoolchildren on weekdays. If you do visit and want to do something about the facilities, the zoo operates an "adopt-an-animal" programme – ask at the entrance kiosk or the museum office.

El Pueblo and the Centro de la Ciencia y la Cultura

The cluster of shops, restaurants, bars and discos that make up the **Centro Comercial El Pueblo** – generally known simply as "El Pueblo" – lies about 200m north of the zoo across the Río Torres. For a tourist complex, El Pueblo is well designed and a sensible initiative that gives both tourists and Josefinos – who love it

– an attractive, atmospheric place to shop, eat, drink and dance, all within the same complex. El Pueblo's whitewashed adobe buildings with wooden staircases evoke a type of colonial architecture that has found it hard to survive in Costa Rica, due to the successive tremors of earthquakes. Walking to El Pueblo means running a gauntlet of pedestrian-unfriendly traffic, however, and most people take a taxi, which costs around $2.50 from the Plaza de la Cultura. The adjacent **Spirogyra Jardín de Mariposas** (daily 8am–4pm; $5) has a wide variety of butterflies fluttering about, with daily guided tours pointing out particularly unusual and pretty ones.

Near El Pueblo, at the end of Calle 4, is the **Centro Costarricense de la Ciencia y la Cultura** (Tues–Fri 8am–4.30pm, Sat & Sun 9.30am–5pm; $5). Located in a former prison, this complex devotes most of its space to the mildly interesting **Museo de los Niños** (Children's Museum; ⓣ2258-4929), where Costa Rican kids learn about their country's history, culture and science through interactive displays. The complex also houses the **Museo Histórico Penitenciario** (Penitentiary History Museum), with original prison cells restored to their nineteenth-century condition, and some rather anodyne accounts of the country's penal history.

The Parque Nacional and around

San José's **Parque Nacional**, one of the city's finest open spaces, marks the heart of downtown San José. Bordered by avenidas 1 and 3 and calles 15 and 19 and overlooked by rows of mop-headed palms and thick deciduous trees, it's popular among courting couples and older men discussing the state of the nation. After gaining notoriety as a hangout for muggers and prostitutes, it was equipped with tall lamps to add extra light – a tactic which has apparently succeeded in drawing the courting couples back to its nocturnal benches. Even so, it's still probably not a good idea to wander around here after dark.

Biblioteca Nacional and the Galería Nacional de Arte Contemporáneo

Immediately north of the park, the modernist **Biblioteca Nacional** is Costa Rica's largest and most useful library, at least for readers of Spanish (Mon–Fri 8.30am–4.30pm). Anyone can rifle through the newspaper collection to the right of the entrance on the ground floor. At the library's southwest corner, the **Galería Nacional de Arte Contemporáneo** (Mon–Sat 10am–1pm & 2–5pm; free) features small and often quirky displays of work by local artists.

Palacio Nacional and the Museo Ferrocarríl

You can hear government debates Costa Rican-style at the **Palacio Nacional**, home to Costa Rica's Legislative Assembly, just south of the park at the corner of Calle 15 and Avenida Central. The fun starts at 4pm, but check first if the Legislature is in session. East of the Palacio, at the top end of Avenida 3 between calles 21/23, the **Museo Ferrocarríl** (Railway Museum; Mon–Fri 9am–4pm; $1), was the terminus for the old "Jungle Train" (see p.428). Today it holds a largely photographic collection dedicated to the famed train that once ran from San José to Limón before being dealt two blows in quick succession: one by the April 1991 earthquake and another by the government, who made the decision not to finance its repair. It's worth a look if you're in the area, especially for railway enthusiasts, but doesn't merit a trip in its own right.

Plaza de la Democracía

A block southwest of the Parque Nacional sits the concrete **Plaza de la Democracía**, yet another of the city's soulless squares which is just one aesthetic notch up from a paved car park. Constructed in 1989 to mark President Oscar Arias' key involvement in the Central American Peace Plan, this expanse of terraced concrete slopes up towards a fountain. At its western end is a row of **artisans' stalls** selling hammocks, thick Ecuadorian sweaters, leather bracelets and jewellery. You can also buy Guatemalan textiles and decorative *molas* (patchwork textiles in vibrant colours) made by the Kuna people of Panamá, though at steeper prices than elsewhere in Central America. Other stalls sell T-shirts and wooden crafts and trinkets. The traders are friendly and won't pressure you; a bit of gentle bargaining is a must.

The Museo Nacional

The north end of the square is crowned by the impressive **Museo Nacional** (Tues–Sat 8.30am–4.30pm, Sun 9am–4.30pm; $6; ⓣ2257-1433, ⓦwww.museocostarica.go.cr), occupying the renovated former Bellavista Barracks. Bullet holes from the 1948 insurrection (see Contexts) can still be seen on the north side of the building's thick walls. More than a century old (and that *is* old for Costa Rica), the museum's collection, though rather haphazard, gives a fascinating introduction to the story of Costa Rica's **colonization**. A grisly series of drawings, deeply affecting in their simplicity, tells the story of the fate of Costa Rica's **indigenous** people at the hands of the Spanish settlers. Violence, it appears, was meted out in both directions, including beheadings, hangings, clubbings, shooting of priests and the pouring of liquid gold down throats. Infanticide and suicide as a means of resistance in the indigenous community are also mercilessly depicted. Displays explain (in both English and Spanish) how the arrival of the Spanish forever disturbed the balance of social and political power among the indigenous groups. There's also an explanation on the function of gold in the indigenous social hierarchy, with descriptions on which objects were used to identify warriors, chiefs and shamans.

The museum's **colonial-era** section is dominated by the massive but spartan furniture and cheesy Spanish religious iconography. Exhibits make clear how slowly culture and education advanced in Costa Rica, giving a sense of a country struggling to extricate itself from terrible cultural and social backwardness – in European terms – until well into the twenty-first century. In the same room are examples of **colonial art**, which replaced indigenous art forms with scores of lamentable gilt-and-pink Virgin Marys.

Other highlights include petroglyphs, pre-Columbian stonework, and wonderful anthropomorphic gold figures in the **Sala Arqueológica**. This is the single most important archeological exhibition in the country; the grinding tables and funerary offerings, in particular, show precise geometric patterns and incredible attention to detail, but the really astounding pieces are the "flying panel" **metates**, corn-grinding tables used by the Chorotega peoples of present-day Guanacaste, each with three legs and meticulously sculpted from a single piece of volcanic stone.

Los Yoses and La California

The neighbourhoods of **Los Yoses** and **La California,** facing one another from opposite sides of Avenida Central as it runs east from the Museo Nacional to San Pedro, are oases of calm just blocks from the city centre. Mainly residential, Los Yoses is home to foreign embassies and a few stylish hotels. The commercial La California runs into Barrio Escalante and Barrio Dent, two of San José's nicest residential districts. Walking through Barrio Escalante is the way to head east, and much more pleasant than bus-choked Avenida Central.

Centro Cultural Costarricense Norteamericano

Homesick North American tourists should head to the **Centro Cultural Costarricense Norteamericano**, 100m north of the Am-Pm supermarket on the corner of Avenida Central and Calle 37 in Barrio Dent (Mon–Fri 7am–7pm, Sat 9am–noon; ⓣ2207-7500, ⓦwww.cccncr.com). The library has English-language publications – the *Miami Herald*, *New York Times* and *USA Today* – as well as all the main Costa Rican dailies. There's also an art gallery, the Eugene O'Neill Theater, with jazz festivals and English-language theatre performances, a pleasant café and CNN beamed out on the communal TV.

Librería Internacional and the San Pedro Mall

About 300m northeast of the Centro Cultural is San José's best bookstore, **Librería Internacional** (Mon–Sat 9am–7pm; ⓣ2253-9553), with a well-stocked Latin American literature section, including Costa Rican authors, and a good selection of both fiction and nonfiction in English as well as maps and tourist guides. At the very end of Barrio Dent, where Avenida Central runs into the fountain-roundabout that separates San José proper from San Pedro, is the truly ugly but wildly popular **San Pedro Mall**. A ceramic-coloured multistorey building festooned with plants and simulated waterfalls, inside it's a jumble of American chain stores and fast-food outlets. If anything, it offers a glimpse into the dating rituals and shopping habits of upper-class Costa Rican teenagers.

San Pedro

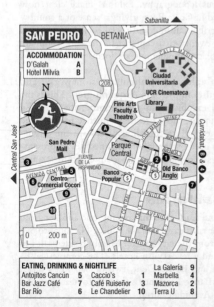

First impressions of **San Pedro** can be off-putting. Avenida Central (known here also as Paseo de los Estudiantes) appears to be little more than a strip of petrol stations, broken-up pavements and shopping malls. Walk just a block off the Paseo, however, and you'll find a lively university student quarter, plus a few elegant old residential houses. The area has traditionally been home to some of the city's best restaurants and nightlife, but an increasing proliferation of dark bars filled with shouting college students means that it's often not the most relaxing spot to be on a Friday or Saturday night, at least during term time.

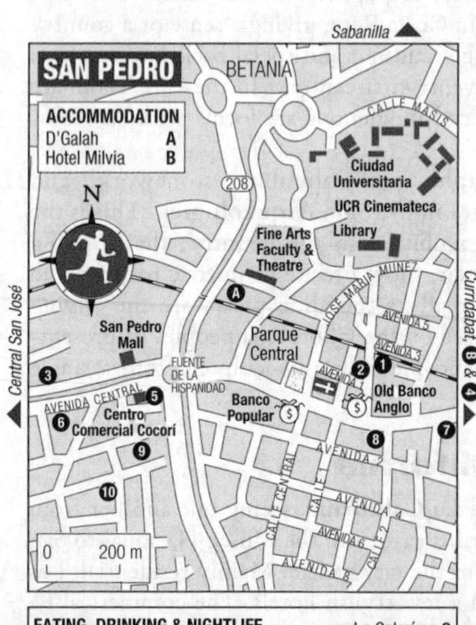

Theoretically it's possible to walk to the campus from Los Yoses, but this entails dealing with the huge, threatening Fuente de la Hispanidad roundabout. This is not recommended, as there are no provisions at all for pedestrians; it's much better to take any university-bound bus from Los Yoses. Buses to San Pedro from the centre of town stop opposite the small **Parque Central**, with its bubblegum-orange bandstand and monument to John F. Kennedy. Walking north from the park, through three blocks of solid *sodas*, bars and bookshops you come to the cool, leafy campus of the **University of Costa Rica**, one of the finest in Central America, and certainly the most prestigious educational institution in the country. Founded in 1940, the university has in the past been accused of being too rigidly academic and elitist, but the overall campus atmosphere is busy, egalitarian and stimulating.

The best places to hang out on **campus** and meet both young Josefinos and students from other countries are the frenzied and cheap cafeteria in the building immediately to the right of the library (there's also an excellent **bookstore** across from the back entrance of the cafeteria), the Comedor Universitario, or **dining hall**, and the Facultad de Bellas Artes, which has a wonderful open-air **theatre** used for frequent concerts. Notice boards around campus, particularly in front of the *Vida Estudiantíl* office (Student Life office, Building A, fourth floor), keep you up to date with what's going on; try also to get hold of a copy of *Semana Universitaria*, the campus newspaper, which is sold in most restaurants and bookshops in the area and lists upcoming events. The three or four blocks surrounding the university are lined with lively bars and restaurants, though in most of them you'll feel more comfortable if you're under thirty. For Spanish-speakers this is a great place to meet people, watch movies and browse around the several well-stocked bookstores. One of the best is Librería Macondo, 100m before you come to the university proper; look for the lime-green storefront.

Paseo Colón and Parque la Sabana

Clustered around the main entrance to La Coca-Cola, off Calle 16 near Avenida 1, shops selling women's underwear, cosmetics and luggage compete for space with a variety of cheap snack bars and drinks stalls. Two blocks south, however, the atmosphere changes, as Avenida Central turns into **Paseo Colón**, a wide boulevard of upmarket shops, restaurants and car dealerships. At the very end of the *paseo*, a solid expanse of green today known as **Parque la Sabana** was San José's airport until the 1940s, and is now home to the country's key art museum, the **Museo de Arte Costarricense**. To get to the park, take the Sabana Cementerio bus from Avenida 2, or walk (20–30min from downtown).

Concerted efforts to maintain its cleanliness, an ongoing project to introduce hundreds of trees native to Costa Rica and the reopening of the Museo de Arte Costarricense all provide the verdant Parque la Sabana with a sense of vitality. Its status as San Jose's finest green space was confirmed in May 2010, when the park was chosen as the site of the inauguration of Laura Chinchilla, the country's first female president.

Most people, though, come to the park to enjoy an afternoon stroll amid leafy trees shading a central lake and colourful modern sculptures scattered around. On Sunday afternoons, hordes of local families feed the resident geese and eat ice cream. It's also one of the best places in San José to **jog**. The cement track is usually full of serious runners in training, but if it gets too crowded you can also run quite safely throughout the park.

Museo de Arte Costarricense

The bright white Neocolonial edifice of the old air terminal at the eastern end of Parque la Sabana has been converted into the attractive **Museo de Arte Costarricense** (Tues–Fri 9am–5pm, Sat–Sun 10am–4pm; $5, $3 students, free Sun 10am–2pm; ⓣ2222-7155, ⓦwww.musarco.go.cr), with a fine collection of mainly twentieth-century Costa Rican paintings displayed in a handsome setting. Highlights of the permanent collection include the outstanding landscapes of **Teodorico Quirós**, with their Cézanne-inspired palettes of russets and burnt siennas, along with Enrique Echandi, Margarita Berthau, abstract painter Lola Fernández and a scattershot selection of foreign artists including Diego Rivera and Alexander Calder. The remarkable **Salon Dorado** upstairs features four full walls of bas-relief wooden carvings overlaid with sumptuous gold, portraying somewhat idealized scenes of Costa Rica's history since the Spanish arrived. On the western wall are imagined scenes from the lives of the indigenous peoples, followed on the north wall by Columbus's arrival, to which the indigenous peoples improbably respond by falling to their knees and praying solemnly. Other golden representations include the Costa Rican agrarian gods of horses, oxen and chickens, and an image of this very building when it was San José's airport, little biplanes buzzing around it like mosquitoes.

Museo de Ciencias Naturales La Salle

On the southwest corner of Sabana Park, across the road in the Ministry of Agriculture and Livestock complex, is the quirky natural science museum **Museo de Ciencias Naturales La Salle** (Mon–Fri 8am–4pm, Sun 9am–5pm; $2; ⓣ2232-1306). Walk in, and after about 400m you'll see the painted wall proclaiming the museum; the entrance is at the back. It's an offbeat collection, with displays ranging from pickled fish and snakes coiled in formaldehyde to some rather forlorn taxidermy exhibits – age and humidity have taken their toll. Highlights include the model of the huge **baula**, or leatherback turtle, the biggest reptile on earth, and the **dusky grouper** fish, a serious contender for first prize in the Ugliest Animal in the World contest. Tons of crumbly fossils and an enormous selection of pinned butterflies (twelve cases alone of titanium-bright Blue Morphos) finish off the collection. Live turtles, virtually motionless, doze in the courtyard garden. The Sabana–Estadio **bus** (see p.91) stops right outside the museum. Note, on your left as you go by on the way to the museum, the futuristic air-traffic-control-tower shape of the **Controlaría de la República**: this is the government's administrative headquarters.

Eating

For a Central American city of its size, San José has a surprising variety of **restaurants** – Italian, Thai and even macrobiotic – along with simple places that offer dishes beginning and ending with rice (rice-and-shrimp, rice-and-chicken, rice-and-meat). For excellent *típico* cooking, try the upmarket restaurants specializing in grills or barbecues (*churrascos*).

Many of the city's best restaurants are in the relatively wealthy and cosmopolitan neighbourhoods of **San Pedro**, along **Paseo Colón**, and in **Escazú**. Wherever you choose, eating out in San José can set your budget back on its haunches. **Prices** are generally steep, and the 23 percent tax on restaurant food (which includes a 10 percent "service charge") make it even pricier to eat out. The cheapest places are in the centre, especially the snack bars and **sodas**, where the restaurant tax doesn't apply. Sadly, however, the best of these are disappearing at an alarming rate because of competition from fast-food outlets. The *sodas* that remain generally open early, close late and are cheap and cheerful. A *plato del día* lunch in a *soda* will rarely set you back more than $5. They also have *empanadas* and sandwiches to take out – combine these with a stop at one of the fruit stalls on any street corner and you've got a quick, cheap lunch. The pieces of papaya and pineapple sold in neatly packaged plastic bags have been washed and peeled by the vendors and should be safe, but if in doubt, wash again. Snacks sold at the **Mercado Central** are as tasty as anywhere, and there's a good cluster of *sodas* hidden away in the Galería shopping arcade, Av 2, C 5/7.

Fast-food outlets in San José are proliferating so rapidly that at times it can look like a veritable jungle of *Pizza Huts*, *Taco Bells* and *KFCs*, not to mention

McDonald's. **Cafés** also abound; some, like *Giacomín*, have old-world European aspirations; others, such as *Spoon*, are resolutely Costa Rican, with Josefinos piling in to order birthday cakes or grab a **coffee**. Most cafés serve exclusively export Costa Rican coffee which has a mild, soft flavour: for more on coffee, see Basics, p.52. As is the case with shops and restaurants, some of the best cafés are in the **shopping malls** outside San José. **Bakeries** (*pastelería, repostería*) on every corner sell cakes, breads and pastries, most of them heavy with white refined flour. Worthwhile bakery chains include *Musmanni*, *Spoon*, *Schmidt* and *Giacomín*. The city's fantastic **ice cream** is another source of woe to dieters. Pops is the best of the major chains, with particularly good fruit flavours.

Working Josefinos eat their main meal between noon and 2pm, and at this time *sodas* especially get very busy. Many of the more upmarket restaurants close at 3pm and open again in the evening. In the listings below we have given a phone number only for places where you might need to **reserve** a table.

Cafés and bakeries

Café de Artistas 100m south of the Plaza in San Rafael de Escazú. Under new ownership, but still the home of the local artist community, discussing the city's latest cultural offerings over steaming cups of coffee, tasty flaky pastries and artful brunches too. Open Tues until Sat 7.30am–6.30pm and Sun 8.30am–2pm.

Café Parisienne *Gran Hotel Costa Rica*, Av 2, C 3/5. The closest thing in San José to a European street café, complete with wrought-iron chairs and trussed-up waiters. Laze away the afternoon over coffee and cake while taking in the tunes and antics of buskers and performers on Plaza de la Cultura. It's one of the few cafés that serves continental breakfast. Open 24hr.

Café Ruiseñor 250m west of the San Pedro Mall in Los Yoses ⓣ2225-2562. Upmarket café serving sandwiches and pastries on a pleasant outdoor terrace. The old-fashioned, European-style atmosphere and service are a treat, but you pay for it. Mon–Fri 7am–8pm, Sat 10am–6pm.

Giacomín Branches next to the Automercado in Los Yoses, in San Pedro, and in Escazú. Comfortable café for chocolate and cake lovers, with lots of seasonal cakes such as stollen and panettone. Mon–Sat 8.30am–noon, 2–6.30pm.

News Café Av 0, C 7/9 in the *Hotel Presidente* (see p.95). Refuel over a cup (or two) of Costa Rica's potent coffee at this midtown café. Find a comfortable perch on the balcony and people-watch to your heart's content. Inside, the walls are adorned with pictures that tell the story of Costa Rica's coffee-growing industry. Daily 6am–11pm.

Q Café Av 0, C 2. Sleek, upmarket café on Avenida Central that's a great spot to idle away a couple of hours, especially while sipping their signature espresso accented with slivers of chocolate or one of their several other house-blend coffee drinks. They also serve hamburgers and various pastries, though prices are high. Mon–Fri 8am–9pm, Sat & Sun 10am–8pm.

Spoon Av 0, C 5/7 and other branches throughout San José and the Valle Central. Popular chain packed with Josefinos ordering birthday cakes. The coffee, served with mix-it-yourself hot milk, is somewhat bitter, but the choice of cookies and cakes is endless. They serve full breakfasts and lunches, too and at good prices. Mon–Fri 8am–8pm, Sat 9am–8pm, Sun 10am–6pm.

Teatro Nacional Café Ruiseñor Av 2, C 3/5. Coffee, fruit drinks, sandwiches and fantastic cakes served amid a Neoclassical decor of marble, crystal and dark wood. Settle in at a table by the window and check out the goings-on in Plaza de la Cultura. Mon–Fri 9am–5pm, Sat 9am–4pm.

Zucchero C 33, Av 5, just north of Los Yoses. Excellent coffee and French-style pastries and cakes served up in quiet, residential Barrio Escalante. Mon–Sat 6am–10pm.

Sodas

Bologna Av 8, C 17. An Italian version of a traditional Costa Rican *soda*. Fill up on ciabattas and focaccias washed down with super-strong Italian coffee.

Castro Casa 279, Av 10, C 2/4. The 1970s fluorescent and vinyl decor and surrounding rough neighbourhood belie the treats inside. Definitely not on the tourist trail, this huge *soda* is where local families take their kids for a Sunday ice-cream treat (there's also a play area) and to sample the excellent fruit salads.

Chelles Av 0, C 9. Open 24 hours, this spartan bar, with bare fluorescent lighting and a TV blaring away in the corner, is a San José institution and a great place to sit and watch your fellow customers or the street action outside. Aproned waitresses serve up cold, cheap beer, snacks and *casados*.

Isabel C 19, Av 9. Permanently filled (or so it seems) with locals shooting the breeze, downing endless cups of coffee and munching on tortillas and *casados*. A street kiosk just outside sells snacks to those too busy to stop. Open Mon–Sat from 7am–10pm.

Manolo's Churrería Av 0, C 0/2. A 24-hour *soda* that's become an institution with Josefinos as a late-night hangout. It's not cheap, but it's safe after hours and the sinful pastries and hearty sandwiches hit the spot after a few too many *cervezas*. The downstairs café is less expensive and perfect for people-watching. Worth a stop alone for the sugar-laden *churros* which are easily the best to be found downtown.

El Parque C 2, Av 4/6. This 24-hour *soda* caters to everyone from businessmen grabbing a cup of coffee on their way to work and retail workers popping out for a quick lunchtime snack to late-night bar hoppers looking to eat themselves sober. Try the *pinto con huevo* (rice, beans and eggs), a bargain at just $1.

Tapia Southeast corner of Parque la Sabana. Huge place, open to the street with views (across the busy ring road) of Parque la Sabana. Especially handy for late-night snacks, with sandwiches and burgers for those weary of *casados*.

La Vasconia Av 1, C 3/5. Get off the tourist trail and dig into cheap breakfasts, ceviche and *empanadas* alongside Costa Rican workers at this casual *soda*. Adorning the walls are thousands of photos of the national football team (some dating back to 1905) and, there's karaoke nightly, for better or worse.

Vishnu Three branches at Av 1, C 1/3; Av 3, C1; Av 8, C 9/11. These cheery vegetarian *sodas* are an obligatory pit stop for healthy fare in San José. Enjoy delicious, reasonably priced *platos del día* with brown rice and also generous vegetable dishes and soups. The vegetarian club sandwich with chips will set you back a mere $3; fruit plates with yoghurt are around $1.50.

Restaurants

Central San José

All the listings below are marked on the Central San José map on p.94.

Arte & Gusto Café Av 9, C 5, Barrio Amón ⓣ2257-0153. Breezy, contemporary restaurant serving well-conceived salads, such as shrimp and octopus with couscous and mango and pineapple slices. Also offers baked goods and heavier meals.

Balcón de Europa C 9, Av 0/1 ⓣ2221-4841. The pasta and other Italian staples are nothing special at this city landmark, but the atmosphere is great. Sepia photos of San José's early days line the wood-panelled walls, along with treacly snippets of "wisdom". Monster cheeses dominate the dining room, as does the game strummer who serenades each table. Closed Sat.

Café Mundo Av 9, C 15, Barrio Otoya ⓣ2222-6190. One of the finest restaurants in San José, the Italian-influenced cuisine is a delight, served in a beautiful dark-wood dining room or, if the weather is nice, on a leafy terrace. The Caesar ($5) and niçoise ($10) salads are large but a bit overpriced. If you're on a budget, go for the pizza, or just come for a cappuccino ($2). At night the bar attracts a largely gay clientele. Closed Sat & Sun.

Don Wang C 11, Av 6/8 ⓣ2233-6484. If you have a craving for dim sum, this authentic Chinese restaurant, with tables set around a Koi pond, should be your first and only stop. Hot pots are a specialty and there are several vegetarian dishes on offer, all at reasonable prices.

Meridiano al Este Av 0, C 21 ⓣ2256-2705. Opposite the La California petrol station (but don't let that put you off), this reasonably priced restaurant draws a young, hip crowd with its quality international cuisine, including pastas, steaks, pizzas and tapas. Nightly entertainment features everything from live music by local bands to poetry recitals and comedy performances.

Nuestra Tierra Av 2, C 15 ⓣ2258-6500. Hugely popular in spite of its gimmicky feel, *Nuestra Tierra* offers reliable Tico fare and a dining experience that is anything but dull. Expect dancing singers, a lively atmosphere, hefty portions and a bill that is more than you might expect.

Shakti C 13, Av 8. The self-proclaimed "home of healthy food" offers filling *platos del día* of *sopa negra* or salad, hearty vegetarian *casado*, a *refresco* and tea or coffee, all for only $3. Tasty breakfast specials include granola, fruit juice and coffee or tea for just $2. It's popular for lunch, so go early or late for a seat. Open Mon–Fri lunch only.

Tin Jo C 11, Av 6/8 ⓣ2221-7605. Quiet, popular and fairly formal Asian restaurant with a choice of Chinese, Indian, Indonesian, Thai, Burmese or Japanese cuisine. The lemongrass soup, bean-thread noodle salad in lime juice and coconut milk curries are particularly recommended. Dinner with wine is around $40 for two; skip the alcohol, or go for lunch, and you'll get away with half that.

Centro Comercial El Pueblo

Cocina de Leña Centro Comercial El Pueblo ⓣ2255-1360. See map, pp.96–97. Some see this as an example of Tico food at its best, superb meals cooked in a wooden oven and served in faux-rustic surroundings. Others see it as a glorified *soda* selling overpriced staples to gullible tourists. The truth lies somewhere in between. The succulent chicken dishes are recommended and it's certainly handy if you're making a night of it among the bars and discos of El Pueblo. Dinner for two costs around $40.

West of the centre

All the listings below are marked on the San José map on p.96.

La Bastille Av 0, C 22 ⓣ2255-4994. Swanky restaurant-cum-art gallery with a dining room bedecked in garishly coloured modern art, including some strange Gaudí-esque chairs. Though the decor is strictly "love it or hate it", the French-Italian cuisine is some of the finest in the city – the ravioli is particularly recommended. Around $50 for two with wine.

Fogo Brasil 100m north of the Nissan dealership, La Sabana. A true carnivore's delight, this Brazilian steakhouse is a popular stopoff on the way to or from Juan Santamaría. The skewered red meat is adroitly cooked and doled out until you practically have to plead for mercy. Against all odds, there's a massive salad bar, too. It's pricey, though, and dinner for two could cost upwards of $100.

Grano de Oro C 30, Av 2/4 ⓣ2253-3322. Upmarket restaurant with beautiful hacienda-style decor and a changing menu. Breakfast (from 6am) includes fresh fruit, eggs benedict and banana macadamia pancakes. The salads are excellent – try the spinach, avocado and gorgonzola – while main courses feature Costa Rican takes on international staples, such as filet mignon stuffed with tropical fruits. Amazing desserts, including tiramisu and piña colada cheesecake. Book ahead and bring plenty of funds.

Machu Picchu C 32, Av 1 ⓣ2222-7384. Velvet llamas hang on the walls at this San José favourite, one of the top South American restaurants in town. The appetizers, including ceviche and Peruvian *bocas,* tend to be more interesting than the main dishes. Around $30 for two with beer or wine; the Pisco sour should not be missed. Closed Sun.

San Pedro and Los Yoses

All the listings below are marked on the San Pedro map on p.106.

Antojitos Cancún In the Centro Comercial Cocorí, 50m west of the Fuente de la Hispanidad roundabout, Los Yoses. Cheap, filling Mexican food, not wholly authentic, but good for late-night snacks and cheap all-you-can-eat buffets. Draught beer and an outside terrace where you can sit and watch the 4WDs whizz round the fountain. Mariachi Fri and Sat from 10pm.

Le Chandelier 100m west and 100m south of the ICE (Instituto Costarricense de Electricidad) building in Los Yoses ⓣ2225-3980. Exquisite French food prepared by the restaurant's Swiss owner. Try the lobster in pastry or the delicious trout with almonds. A homely decor of exposed ceiling beams and a crackling fireplace. Dinner for two costs about $35–45. Closed Sun.

La Galería 50m west of *Spoon*, behind the *Aparthotel Los Yoses* ⓣ2234-0850. Expensive restaurant that's popular with Josefinos on a special night out. A variety of European dishes in heavy sauces; cheese-lovers will swoon over the fondue. Classical music adds to the upscale atmosphere. Closed Sat & Sun.

Marbella In the Centro Commercial Calle Real, San Pedro ⓣ2224-9452. Spanish cuisine, including excellent veal dishes and delicious paella ($15 for two) with real rabbit (unusual in Costa Rica). Closed Sun evening & Mon.

Mazorca 200m east and 100m north of San Pedro Church; just east of the entrance to UCR. Inexpensive macrobiotic meals served amid a simple, homely decor. The tasty bread, soups, peanut-butter sandwiches and macrobiotic cakes are a welcome change from greasy *arroz con pollo.* Lunch is $5; takeaways are also available.

Escazú

La Cascada Behind the Centro Comercial Trejos Montalegre, Escazú ⓣ2228-0906. This difficult-to-find restaurant (there's no sign) with ho-hum decor is actually the best steakhouse in San José. Hugely popular, it's often full of Tico families, especially on Sun afternoon. The hunks of beef are fantastic, and the terrifically filling plates all come with rice and veggies.

Drinking and nightlife

San José pulsates with the country's most diverse nightlife, and is home to scores of **bars, clubs** and **live music** venues. Most young Josefinos, students and foreigners in the know stay away from the centre of town and head, instead, to Los Yoses or San Pedro. Avenida Central in **Los Yoses** is a well-known "yuppie trail" of bars, packed with middle- and upper-middle-class Ticos imbibing and conversing.

Note that prostitution (see p.79) is legal in Costa Rica and particularly prevalent in downtown San José. Many of the city centre "bars" are, in reality, little more

Salsa like a Josefino

One of the best ways to meet people and prepare yourself for San José nightlife is to take a few **salsa lessons** at one of the city's many *academias de baile*. You don't necessarily need a partner, and you can go with a friend or in a group. The tuition is serious, but the atmosphere is usually relaxed. The best classes in San José are at Bailes Latinos, in the Costa Rican Institute of Language and Latin Dance, Av 0, C 25/27 (Ⓣ2233-8938,); at Malecón, C 17/19, Av 2 (Ⓣ2222-3214); and at Merecumbé, which has various branches, the most central of which is in San Pedro (Ⓣ2224-3531).

than pick-up joints for professional prostitutes. The cluster of casinos and bars on Avenida Central between calles 5 and 11 fall mainly into this category. At any time of day or night (most are open 24 hours), these bars are full of scantily clad young ladies trying to attract the attention of glassy-eyed gringos and Europeans. They're best avoided unless you want to spend every few minutes explaining why you're not interested in doing a little "business".

San Pedro nightlife is geared more towards the university population, with a strip of studenty bars to the east of the UCR entrance. Those looking for local atmosphere should head to a **boca bar** (see box opposite) or seek out places to hear **peñas**, slow, acoustic folk songs from the Andean region that grew out of the revolutionary movements of the 1970s and 1980s.

Even if you don't dance, it's entertaining to watch the Ticos burn up the floor at one of the city's **discos**. Because locals are usually in couples or groups, the atmosphere at most places isn't a "scene". In general, the **dress code** is relaxed: most people wear smart jeans and men need not wear a jacket. **Cover charges** run up to about 1000 colones ($2), though the big mainstream discos at El Pueblo charge slightly more than places downtown.

Many bars don't offer **music** during the week, but change character drastically come Friday or Saturday, when you can hear jazz, blues, up-and-coming local bands, rock and roll, or South American folk music. That said, activity is not relentlessly weekend-oriented. It's possible, with a little searching, to hear good live music on a Wednesday, or find a packed disco floor on a Monday or Tuesday. People do stay out later on the weekends, but even so, with the exception of the studenty bars in San Pedro, most places close by 2 or 3am, and earlier on Sunday.

San José is one of the best places in Central (possibly Latin) America for **gay** nightlife. Establishments come and go – those in our listings are the best established places – and it helps if you have a local lesbian or gay contact to help you hunt down small local clubs.

For full details of **what's on**, check the *Cartelera* in the *Tiempo Libre* section of *La Nación*, which lists live music along with all sorts of other activities, from swimming classes to cultural discussions. Or for a more hip magazine, try *San José Volando* (Ⓦwww.sanjosevolando.com).

Bars and live music

Bar Jazz Café In San Pedro, near the Banco Popular Ⓣ2253-8933. The best bar in San José for live jazz, with an intimate atmosphere and consistently good groups. The cover charge varies from $5 to $10 (sometimes including a glass of wine) and is well worth it. Music starts after 10pm.

Bar México Barrio México, opposite the church. Strictly off the tourist trail, northwest of the city centre but well worth hunting out, this traditional bar serves tasty *bocas* to its largely working-class clientele. Full of atmosphere, it's a great place to mix with locals. Live Latin music on Wed. Mon–Fri 3pm–midnight, Sat 11am–midnight.

Bar Río Boulevard Los Yoses. Wildly popular Los Yoses sports bar with a large terrace. Inside, eight (count 'em) TV screens, each usually showing a different football match and in the back is a large

Boca bars

In Costa Rica, *bocas* (appetizers) are the tasty little snacks traditionally served free in bars. **Boca bars** are a largely urban tradition, and although you find them in other parts of the country, the really famous ones are all in San José. Because of mounting costs, however, and the erosion of local traditions, few places serve *bocas* gratis any more. Several bars have a *boca* menu, among them *El Cuartel de la Boca del Monte* (see below) near Los Yoses, but the authentic *boca* bars are concentrated in suburban working- or lower-middle-class residential neighbourhoods. They have a distinctive convivial atmosphere – friends and family spending the evening together – and are very busy most nights. Saturday is the hardest night to get a table; get there before 7.30pm. You'll be handed a menu of free *bocas* – one beer gets you one *boca*, so keep drinking and you can keep eating. The catch is that the beer costs about twice as much as elsewhere ($2 as opposed to $1) but even so, the little plates of food are generous enough to make this a bargain way to eat out. You'll do better if you speak Spanish, but you can get by with point-and-nod. Typical *bocas* include deep-fried plantains with black-bean paste, small plates of rice and meat, shish kebabs, tacos or *empanadas*; nothing fancy, but the perfect accompaniment to a cold beer.

One of the most authentic and well-known *boca* bar is the working-class, long-established *Bar México* (see opposite) in Barrio México – it's a pretty rough neighbourhood, so go by taxi. Alternatively, you'll find a varied clientele – but conspicuously few foreigners – at *Los Perales* and *El Sesteo* (both Mon–Sat 7pm–midnight) in the eastern suburb of Curridabat. They're about 100m from each other on the same street – hard to find on your own, but taxi drivers will know them.

dance area. Live music on Tues and the occasional weekend. The starchy fast-food menu is a good way to soak up the alcohol.

Caccio's 200m east and 25m north of San Pedro Church. A great spot to meet Ticos is this insanely popular student hangout where guys wearing baseball caps sing along loudly to outdated songs. Knock back cheap, cold beer while munching on pizza. Open till 2am. Closed Sun.

Chelles Av 0, C 9 ☎ 2221-1369. This simple, brightly lit, 24-hour bar, with football on TV and cheap beers and *bocas*, pulls in an eclectic crowd of weary businessmen and late-night revellers.

El Cuartel de la Boca del Monte Av 1, C 19/21 ☎ 2221-0327. Lively, long-established bar – with great lunch, dinner and *bocas* – that still packs in Josefinos, particularly on Mon and Wed when there's live music (Latin, rock and reggae) by up-and-coming bands. Open until 2am Wed–Sat.

La Esmeralda Av 2, C 5/7 ☎ 2221-0530. Colourful, landmark bar that doubles as the headquarters of the union of Mariachi bands, who whoosh by your table in a colourful swirl of sombreros and sequins before dashing off in a taxi to serenade elsewhere in San José. Closed Sun.

Meridiano al Este Av 0, C 21 ☎ 2256-2705. One of San José's better restaurants (see p.110) – and an outstanding venue for live music as well as poetry recitals and comedy. The programme changes often, but Sun nights usually feature the pick of San José's up-and-coming jazz and Latin performers.

Milano si Accende Av 11, C 3 bis. Self-consciously European bar with Italian food and oh-so comfortable sofas. On Mon, groove to European dance and electronica.

Raíces Av 2, C 45. Dedicated reggae bar with a booming sound system and hordes of dreadlocked Ticos packing the small dancefloor. Closed Mon & Tues.

Las Risas C 1, Av 0/1 ☎ 2223-2803. One of the best downtown bars, on three floors. A young crowd packs the small dancefloor at the popular top-floor disco. Bring ID – a copy of your passport will suffice – or the bouncers won't let you in. The cover charge of $2 will usually get you two drinks or a tequila. Sat is ladies' night.

Shakespeare Av 2, C 28 ☎ 2258-6787. Quiet, friendly bar. Popular for a quick drink before heading to a performance at the adjacent Sala Garbo cinema or Laurence Olivier theatre. Occasionally has live jazz.

Clubs

Club Vertigo Paseo Colón, C 36/38. When a big-named international DJ tours Central America, a date at *Club Vertigo* is pretty much a certainty. The lines are almost inevitably long – particularly on Sat night – and the dress code is somewhat strict for San José, but they're small prices to pay for a vibe that can't be matched elsewhere in town. The action is split between two rooms, and the music you'll hear in each differs nightly, with trance and house usually amping up the joint.

Cocoloco El Pueblo. Smart, well-dressed clientele, small dancefloors, and the usual Latin techno-pop/reggae/merengue mix.

Ebony 56 El Pueblo. One of the most popular among El Pueblo's glut of discos. Several large dancefloors play salsa and US and European dance music with the odd 1980s/1990s pop hit thrown in. Closed Sun.

Infinito El Pueblo. Similar to *Cocoloco*, with three dancefloors and booming salsa, US and European dance music, as well as 1970s romantic hits spun by excellent DJs. Attracts an older, smarter crowd. Closed Sun.

Salsa 54 C 3, Av 1/3 ⓣ2233-3814. Downtown alternative to the El Pueblo discos, this lively joint plays the favoured mix of Latin and American tunes but, as the name implies, also goes heavy on the salsa and merengue. The best place to dance in San José proper, attracting the most talented *salseros*.

Terra U San Pedro, one block east of San Pedro Church ⓣ2225-4261. With three open-air levels and a heaving dancefloor, this is one of San José's weekend hot spots. Latin and Jamaican dance hits predominate. Music videos (and occasional football match highlights) play on the TV.

Gay and lesbian nightlife

La Avispa C 1, Av 8/10 ⓣ2223-5343, ⓦwww.laavispa.co.cr. Landmark gay and lesbian disco-bar with a friendly atmosphere, "The Wasp" has three dancefloors and several pool tables housed in a distinct black and yellow building. The big nights are Sun & Tues, Thurs is karaoke, but it's closed Mon & Wed. There's a varying cover charge Fri to Sun, usually $5 or less.

Café Mundo Av 9, C 15, Barrio Otoya ⓣ2222-6190. In the restaurant (see p.110) of the same name, this low-key bar-restaurant attracts a mainly gay clientele.

Déjà Vu C 2, Av 14/16 ⓣ2236-3758. A mixed crowd – gay, lesbian and straight – come for the hot and happening atmosphere and music, mostly house and techno with some salsa and reggae. Two large dancefloors plus a quiet bar and a café. The neighbourhood is pretty scary, so best to take a taxi. Cover charge varies from $3 to $5, though drinks are cheap. Closed Sun & Mon.

The arts and entertainment

Bearing in mind the decreasing financial support from the national government, the quality of the arts in San José is very high. Josefinos especially like **theatre**, and there's a healthy range of venues for a city this size, staging a variety of inventive productions at affordable prices. If you speak even a little Spanish it's worth checking to see what's on.

Costa Rica's **National Dance Company** has an impressive repertoire of classical and modern productions, some by Central American choreographers, arranged specifically for the company – again, ticket costs are low. The city's premier venues are the Teatro Nacional and the Teatro Mélico Salazar; here you can see performances by the **National Symphony Orchestra** and **National Lyric Opera Company** (June–Aug), as well as visiting orchestras and singers, usually from Spain or other Spanish-speaking countries. The Teatro Mélico Salazar occasionally stages performances of traditional Costa Rican singing and dancing.

Going to the **cinema** in San José is a bargain ($3–5 a ticket), though many venues have decamped to the suburbs, particularly to shopping malls, such as the Cinemark in Escazú's Multiplaza, which you can only reach by car or taxi. There are still a few good downtown cinemas left, however, several of which retain some original features, along with plush, comfortable seats. Most cinemas show the latest American movies, which are almost always subtitled. The few that are dubbed will have the phrase "*hablado en Español*" in the newspaper listings or on the posters. For Spanish-language art movies, head to Sala Garbo.

For **details of all performances**, check the *Cartelera* section of the *Tiempo Libre* supplement in *La Nación* on Thursday and the listings in the *Tico Times*, which also distinguish between English- and Spanish-language films and productions.

Theatres

Bellas Artes Facultad de Bellas Artes University of Costa Rica, San Pedro ⓣ 2207-4095. Generally excellent and innovative student productions with new spins on classical and contemporary works.

Eugene O'Neill Centro Cultural Costarricense-Norteamericano, Los Yoses ⓣ 2207-7554. Works by modern playwrights in innovative independent productions.

Laurence Olivier In the Sala Garbo building, Av 2, C 28 ⓣ 2222-1034. Modern theatre specializing in contemporary productions, plus occasional jazz concerts and film festivals.

Mélico Salazar C Av 2 ⓣ 2221-5172, ⓦ www.teatromelico.go.cr. San José's "workhorse" theatre stages occasional performances of traditional Costa Rican song and dance.

Teatro Nacional C 5, Av 2 ⓣ 2221-3756. ⓦ www.teatronacional.go.cr. The city's premier theatre hosts opera, ballet and concerts, as well as drama.

Cinemas

Alianza Francesa Barrio Amón, Av 7, C 5 ⓣ 2222-2283. Occasional French-language films, usually dubbed or subtitled in Spanish.

Cine Omni C 3, Av 0/1 ⓣ 2221-7903. Downtown cinema showing US blockbusters.

Colón Paseo Colón, C 38/40 ⓣ 2221-4517. US mall-style cinema, with mainstream Hollywood films.

Facultad de Derecho Cinema Law School Cinema, University of Costa Rica, San Pedro ⓣ 2207-5322. Occasional European and arthouse films.

Multcines San Pedro In San Pedro Mall ⓣ 2280-9585. American-style multiplex with ten screens, full surround-sound and popcorn on tap.

Sala Garbo Av 2, C 28 ⓣ 2223-1960. Popular arthouse cinema showing independent films from around the world usually in the original language with Spanish subtitles.

Variedades C 5, Av 0/1 ⓣ 2222-6104. Old but well-preserved downtown movie house with Rococo-style decor showing good foreign and occasionally Spanish-language films.

Shopping and markets

San José's **souvenir and crafts shops** are well stocked and in general fairly pricey; it's best to buy from the larger shops run by government-regulated crafts cooperatives, from which more of the money filters down to the artisans. You'll see an abundance of pre-Columbian gold jewellery copies, Costa Rican liqueurs (Café Rica is the best known), T-shirts with jungle and animal scenes, weirdly realistic wooden snakes, leather rockers from the village of Sarchí (see p.135), walking sticks, simple leather bracelets, hammocks and a vast array of woodcarvings, from miniature everyday rural scenes to giant, colourfully hand-painted Sarchí ox-carts. Look out too for *molas*, handmade and appliquéd clothes, mostly shirts, occasionally from the Bahía Drake region of southwestern Costa Rica, but more usually made by the Kuna peoples of Panamá.

A good place to buy any of these handicrafts is at San José's **street craftmarket** in the Plaza de la Democracía (see p.104). Also on sale are regional leather and silver jewellery and a selection of crafts from other Latin American countries, including Ecuadorian sweaters. It's worth bargaining, although the goods are already a little cheaper than in shops.

Souvenirs and crafts

Atmósfera C 5, Av 1. Elegant gallery-like outlet selling jewellery, furniture and woodwork.

CANAPI C 11, Av 1. Big shop with a good stock of wooden bowls, walking sticks and boxes.

La Casona C 0, Av 0/1. Large two-floor marketplace with stalls selling the usual local stuff along with Guatemalan knapsacks and bedspreads. It's great for browsing, and the traders are friendly, but quality at some stalls is pretty poor, and there's not one good T-shirt in evidence.

Hotel Don Carlos C 9, Av 9. Good pre-Columbian artefacts and jewellery reproductions.

Mercado Central Av 0/1, C 6/8. *The* place to buy coffee beans, but make sure they're export quality – ask for Grano d'Oro ("Golden Bean").

Mercado de Artesanía Av 2 C 15 bis. A block from Parque Nacional, this orderly market sells souvenirs and crafts, featuring Sarchí ox-carts, and jewellery. Though you can find it cheaper elsewhere in the country, the quality is usually fairly good.

Plaza Esmeralda La Uruca, Pavas, about 5m northwest of city centre. Craft cooperative run by local artisans where you can watch cigars being rolled, necklaces being set and the ubiquitous Sarchí ox-carts being painted. Closed Sun.

Sol Maya Paseo Colón, C 18/20. Rather pricey indigenous and Guatemalan arts and crafts.

Tienda de la Naturaleza Curridabat Av 0, 1km east of San Pedro. The shop of the Fundación Neotrópica, this is a good place to buy the posters, T-shirts and other paraphernalia painted by English artist Deirdre Hyde that you see all over the country. She specializes in the landscapes of tropical America and the animals that live there, jaguars in particular.

Bookstores

7th Street Books C 7, Av 0/1 ☎2256-8251. Has both new and used books, including English literature, as well as a wide selection of books and maps on Costa Rica in English and Spanish.

Chispas C 7, Av 0/1 ☎2223-2240. Sells new and secondhand books, and has the best selection of English-language fiction in town. It also sells a good array of guidebooks and books about Costa Rica (in English and Spanish), plus the *New York Times*, *El País* and several English-language magazines.

Librería Lehmann Av 0, C 1/3 ☎2223-1212. Has a good selection of mass-market Spanish-language fiction and non fiction, as well as maps, children's books and a small (mainly secondhand) collection of English-language books.

Librería Internacional 300m west of *Taco Bell* in Barrio Dent (☎2253-9553) and in the Multiplaza Escazú (☎2298-1138). Has the best selection of international fiction; it also stocks travel books and Spanish-language fiction, as well as books in English and German.

Librería Universal Av 0, C/1 ☎2222-2222. Strong on Spanish fiction, books about Costa Rica (in Spanish), and country maps.

Librería y Bazar Guillen At La Coca-Cola bus terminal. A good place to browse for reading material before leaving on a trip.

Macondo Opposite the entrance to the library at the university campus in San Pedro. Probably the best bookshop in town for literature in Spanish, especially from Central America, as well as academic disciplines such as sociology and women's studies.

Mora Books Av 1, C 3/5, in the Omni building ☎2255-4136. A pleasant shop with a good selection of secondhand English-language books, CDs, guidebooks, magazines and comics.

Listings

Airline offices Alitalia, C 38, Av 3 (☎2295-6870); American, Paseo Colón, C 26/28 (☎2257-1266); Continental, C 19, Av 2 (☎2296-4911); Copa, C 1, Av 5 (☎2212-6640); Delta, at the airport (☎2257-8946); Iberia, C 40, Paseo Colón (☎2257-8266); Lacsa, C 1, Av 5 (☎2212-9383); LanChile, Sabana Oeste (☎2290-5222); Lufthansa, C 5, Av 7/9 (☎2243-1818); Mexicana, C 1, Av 2/4 (☎2295-6969); SAM, Av 5, C 1/3 (☎2233-3066); Sansa, Av 5, C 1/3 (☎2221-5774); TACA, C 1, Av 1/3 (☎2296-9353); United Airlines, Sabana Sur (☎2220-4844); Varig, Av 5, C 1/3 (☎2290-5222).

Banks State-owned banks in San José include the Banco de Costa Rica, Av 2, C 4/6 (Mon–Fri 9am–3pm; Visa only) and Banco Nacional, Av 0/1, C 2/4 (Mon–Fri 9am–3pm; Visa only). Private banks include Banco Mercantil, Av 3, C 0/2 (Mon–Fri 9am–3pm; Visa only); Banco Metropolitano, C 0, Av 2 (Mon–Fri 8.15am–4pm; Visa only); Banco Popular, C 1 Av 2/4 (Mon–Fri 8.30am–3.30pm, Sat 9am–1pm; Visa & MasterCard); and Banco de San José, C 0, Av 3/5 (Visa & MasterCard); BANEX, C 0, Av 1 (Mon–Fri 8am–5pm; Visa only). There's an American Express office at C Av 0/1 (Mon–Fri 8.30am–5pm; ☎2257-1792, www.americanexpress.com).

Car rental see p.43.

Embassies and consulates Argentina, 400m south of *McDonald's* in Curridabat (☎2234-6520 or 2234-6270); Belize, 400m east of the Iglesia Santa Teresita, Rohrmoser (☎2253-5598); Bolivia, in Rohrmoser (☎2232-9455); Brazil, Paseo Colón, C 20/22 (☎2223-1544); Canada, C 3, Av 1 (☎2296-4149); Chile, 50m east and 225m west of the Automercado, Los Yoses (☎2224-4243); Colombia, 175m west of *Taco Bell*, in Barrio Dent (☎2283-6861); Ecuador, 100m west and 100m south of the Centro Comercial Plaza Mayor, in Rohrmoser (☎2232-1503); El Salvador, Av 10, C 33/35, Los Yoses (☎2256-4047); Guatemala, 100m north and 50m east of *Pizza Hut*, in

Curridabat (☎2283-2557); Honduras, 300m east and 200m north of ITAN, in Los Yoses (☎2234-9502); México, Av 7, C 13/15 (☎2257-0633); Nicaragua, Av 0, C 25/27 (☎2222-2373 or 2233-8747); Panamá, C 38, Av 5/7 (☎2281-2442); Peru, 100m south and 50m west of the San José Indoor Club, in Curridabat (☎2225-1786); UK, 11th floor, Edificio Centro Colón, Paseo Colón, C 38/40 (☎2258-2025); US, opposite the Centro Comercial in Pavas – take the bus to Pavas from Av 1, C 18 (☎2220-3939); Venezuela, Av 2, C 37/39, Los Yoses (☎2225-5813 or 8810). There is no consular representative for Australia or New Zealand.

Hospitals The city's public (social security) hospital is San Juan de Dios, Paseo Colón, C 14/16 (☎2257-6282). Of the private hospitals, foreigners are most often referred to Clínica Biblica, Av 14, C 0/1 (☎2257-5252; emergency and after-hours number ☎2257-0466), where basic consultation and treatment (for example, a prescription for a course of antibiotics) starts at about $100. CIMA San José, 500m west of the tollbooths on the Prospero Fernández Freeway (☎2208-1000), is also a good private hospital. San José has many excellent medical specialists, too – your embassy will have a list.

Immigration Costa Rican *inmigración* (Mon–Fri 8am–4pm; ☎2220-0355) is on the airport highway opposite the Hospital México; take an Alajuela bus and get off at the stop underneath the overhead walkway. Get there early, if you want visa extensions or exit visas. Larger travel agencies, such as Tikal Tours can take care of the paperwork for you for a fee (roughly $10–25).

Internet access Most of the hotels and guesthouses in San José now offer internet access, often for free. You'll also find plenty of internet cafés in town. Expect to pay around 300 colones per half-hour (sometimes less). Many cafés also serve a range of drinks and snacks. Try *Café Digital*, Av 0, C 5/7, which also has a snack bar, a cigar shop and a balcony overlooking Av Central; *Neotopia Cyber Café*, Av 1, C11 or *Internet Café Costa Rica*, Av 0, C 0/2.

Laundry Burbujas, 50m west and 25m south of the Mas por Menos supermarket in San Pedro, has coin-operated machines and sells soap; Lava y Seca, 100m north of Mas por Menos, next to Autos San Pedro, in San Pedro, will do your laundry for you, as well as dry-cleaning. Other places include Lava Más, C 45, Av 8/10, next to *Spoon* in Los Yoses; Lavamatic Doña Anna, C 13, Av 16; and Sixaola (one of a chain), Av 2, C 7/9. Many hotels and guesthouses also offer a laundry service.

Libraries and cultural centres The Alianza Francesa, C 5, Av 7 (Mon–Fri 9am–noon & 3–7pm; ☎2222-2283) stocks some French publications; the Quaker-affiliated Friends' Peace Center, C 15, Av 6 bis (Mon–Fri 10am–3pm; ☎2221-8299) has English-language newspapers, plus weekly meetings and discussion groups. Other libraries/cultural centres include the Biblioteca Nacional, C 15, Av 3 (Mon–Sat 9am–5pm) and the Centro Cultural Costarricense-Norteamericano, 100m north of the Am-Pm supermarket in Barrio Dent (Mon–Fri 7am–7pm, Sat 9am–noon; ☎2207-7500, Ⓦwww.cccncr.com).

Pharmacies Clínica Biblica, Av 14, C 0/1 (open 24hr; ☎2257-5252); Farmacia del Este, on Av Central near Mas por Menos in San Pedro (open until 8pm); Farmacia Fischel, Av 3, C 2; there are many pharmacies in the blocks surrounding the Hospital Calderon Guardia, 100m northeast of the Biblioteca Nacional, in Barrio Otoya.

Post office The Correo Central, C 2, Av 1/3 (Mon–Fri 7am–5pm, Sat 7am–noon; ☎2258-8762) is two blocks east and one block north of the Mercado Central. They'll hold letters for up to four weeks (10 colones per letter; you'll need a passport to collect your post).

Sports The sports complex behind the Museo de Arte Costarricense on Parque la Sabana has a gym, Olympic-size pool and a recently refurbished running track. The park itself has tennis courts, and is as good a place as any for jogging, with changing facilities and showers. There are lots of runners about in the morning, though there have been reports of assaults on lone joggers in the evening and it's wise to stay away from the heavily wooded northeastern corner of the park. Parque de la Paz in the south of the city is also recommended for running and has a velodrome and a roller hockey rink; in San Pedro you can jog, swim and play basketball at the UCR campus. The Club Deportivo Cipresses (☎2253-0530), set in landscaped grounds 700m north of the La Galera petrol station in Curridabat offers a $7 day membership which gives access to weights, machines, pools and aerobics classes. The nearest public pool to San José is at Ojo de Agua, 17km northwest of town; you can get a bus there from Av 2, C 20/22 (15min). A very impressive rock-climbing facility is El Rocodromo (☎2846-6645) in the Mundo Aventura strip mall, 100m north, 25m west of Toyota, on Paseo Colón. For yoga aficionados, try Derya Yoga, 100m west of De Cable Tica on the Pavas road (☎2232-2468), which offers free first classes in the Ashtanga and Hatha styles.

Telephone offices Radiográfica, C 1, Av 5 (daily 7.30am–9pm; ☎2287-0087) is the state-run office where you can use directories, make overseas calls and send or receive faxes. Unfortunately, it charges a flat fee of $3 for the use of its phones on top of the price of the call.

Travel details

San José is the **transport hub** of Costa Rica. Most bus services, flights and car rental agencies are located here. Wherever you are in the country, you're technically never more than nine hours by highway from the capital, with the majority of destinations being much closer than that. Eventually, like it or not, all roads lead to San José.

Domestic buses

Thefts from the luggage compartments of long-distance **bus** services are becoming more common, especially on the Monteverde and Manuel Antonio routes. The accepted wisdom is, if possible, to take your luggage onto the bus with you. Even then, make sure all compartments are locked and that you have nothing valuable inside easily unzipped pockets. If you have to put your bags in the luggage hold, make sure only the driver or his helper

Bus companies in San José

A bewildering number of **bus companies** use San José as their hub. The following is a rundown of their head office addresses and/or phone numbers, and the abbreviations that we use in the listings below.

ATSC	Autotransportes San José-San Carlos	(☎2255-4318 or 2256-8914)
BL	Autotransportes Blanco-Lobo, C 12, Av 9	(☎2771-4744)
BM	Buses Metropoli	(☎2530-1064)
EA	Empresa Alfaro, C 14, Av 3/5	(☎2222-2666)
EG	Empresarios Guápileños	(☎2710-7780)
EM	Empresa Esquivel	(☎2666-1249)
EU	Empresarios Unidos	(☎2222-0064)
ME	Transportes MEPE, Av 11, C 0/1	(☎2257-8129)
MO	Transportes Delio Morales, C 16, Av 1/3	(☎2223-5567)
MRA	Microbuses Rapiditos Heredianos, C 1, Av 7/9	(☎2223-8392)
MU	MUSOC, C 16, Av 1/3	(☎2222-2422)
Nica	Nicabus	(☎2223-0293)
PA	Panaline	(☎2256-8721)
PU	Pulmitan, C 14, Av 1/3	(☎2222-1650)
SA	SACSA, C 5, Av 18	(☎2551-0232)
TB	Transportes Blanco, C 14, Av 9/11	(☎2257-4121)
TBO	Transportes Bocatoreños, C 14/16, Av 5	(☎2227-6900)
TC	Transportes Caribeños	(☎2221-2596)
Tica	Ticabus, C 9, Av 4/6	(☎2221-8954)
TIL	Transportes Tilarán, C 14, Av 9/11	(☎2222-3854)
TJ	Transportes Jacó	(☎2223-1109)
TRA	TRALAPA, C 20, Av 1/3	(☎2221-7202)
TRC	Tracopa-Alfaro, Av 18, C 2/4	(☎2221-4214)
TRN	Transnica	(☎2223-4242)
TRS	Transtusa, Av 6, C 13	(☎2556-4233)
TU	Tuasa, C 12, Av 2	(☎2442-9523)
Tuan	Tuan	(☎2441-3781)

handles them, and get a seat from where you can keep an eye on the luggage compartment during stops.

The buses listed below are **express services** from San José. Regional bus information is covered in the relevant accounts in the Guide. As schedules are prone to change, exact departure times are not given here, though some details are given under individual destinations elsewhere in the book. If you're going to be travelling by bus, your best bet is to get a complete timetable at the ICT office (see p.90) when you arrive. The initials below correspond to the bus company that serves the route; see opposite for telephone numbers. PN = Parque Nacional; RNdVS = Refugio Nacional de Vida Silvestre; MN = Monumento National.

Direct buses from San José

To Alajuela (and airport): TU; Av 2, C 12/14 (every 5min; 35min).
To PN Braulio Carrillo see **Guápiles**
To Cahuita: ME; C 0, Av 11/13 (4 daily; 4hr).
To RNdVS Caño Negro see **Los Chiles**
To Cartago: SA; C 5, Av 18/20 (every 5min; 45min).
To PN Chirripó see **San Isidro**
To PN Corcovado see **Puerto Jiménez**
To La Fortuna: ATS; C 16, Av 1/3 (12 daily; 4hr 30min).
To Golfito: TRC; C 14, Av 3/5 (2 daily; 8hr).
To Guápiles: EG; C 0, Av 11/13 (every 45min; 35min).
To MN Guayabo see **Turrialba**
To Heredia: TU/MRA; C 1, Av 7/9 & Av 2, C 12/14 (every 5min; 25min).
To La Selva/Selva Verde see **Puerto Viejo de Sarapiquí**
To Liberia: PU; C 14, Av 1 (17 daily; 4hr).
To Limón: TC; C 0, Av 11/13 (25 daily; 2hr 30min).
To Los Chiles: ATS; C 12, Av 7/9 (2 daily; 5hr).
To PN Manuel Antonio see **Quepos**
To Monteverde: TIL; C 12, Av 7/9 (2 daily; 3hr 30min).
To Nicoya: EA; C 16, Av 3/5 (8 daily; 6hr).
To Nosara: EA; C 14, Av 3/5 (1 daily; 6hr).
To Palmar: TRA; C 14, Av 5 (7 daily; 5hr).
To Playa Brasilito: TRA; C 20, Av 3/5 (2 daily; 6hr).
To Playa Coco: PU; C 24, Av 5/7 (3 daily; 5hr).
To Playa Flamingo: TRA; C 20, Av 3/5 (2 daily; 6hr).
To Playa Hermosa: EM; Av 5, C 20/22 (1 daily; 5hr).
To Playa Jacó: TJ; C 16, Av 1/3 (5 daily; 2hr 30min).
To Playa Junquillal: TRA; C 20, Av 3/51 (daily; 5hr).
To Playa Panamá: EM; Av 5, C 20/22 (1 daily; 5hr).
To Playa Potrero: TRA; C 20, Av 3 (2 daily; 6hr).
To Puerto Jiménez: TB; C 14, Av 9/11 (1 daily; 8hr).
To Puerto Viejo de Sarapiqui: ME; C 0, Av 15 (10 daily; 2hr).
To Puerto Viejo de Talamanca: ME; C 0, Av 13 (4 daily; 4hr 30min).
To Puntarenas: EU; C 16, Av 10/12 (15 daily; 2hr).
To Quepos: MO; C 16, Av 3/5 (4 daily; 3hr 30min).
To Sámara: EU; C 14, Av 3/5 (1 daily; 6hr).
To San Carlos (Ciudad Quesada): ATS; C 12, Av 7/9 (15 daily; 3hr).
To San Isidro de El General: MU; C 0, Av 22/24 (14 daily; 3hr).
To Santa Cruz: TRA; Av 3, C 18/20 (9 daily; 5hr).
To Sarchí: Tuan; Av 3, C 16/18 (30 daily; 1hr 30min).
To Tamarindo: EA; C 14, Av 5 (2 daily; 6hr).
To Turrialba: TRS; C 13, Av 6/8 (17 daily; 1hr 40min).
To Volcán Arenal see **La Fortuna**
To Volcán Irazú: BM; Av 2, C 1/3 (1 Sat & Sun; 2hr)
To Volcán Poás: TU; Av 2, C 12/14 (1 daily; 1hr 30min).

International buses from San José

The codes listed below correspond to the relevant bus company (see opposite). Advance purchase – at least a week in advance, particularly for Managua and Panamá City – is necessary for all routes.

To David: TRC, C 5, Av 18/20 (1 daily; 9hr).
To Guatemala City: Tica, Av 4, C 9/11 (3 daily; 60hr with overnight in Managua & El Salvador).
To Managua: Nica, C 0, Av 11 (1 daily; 11hr); Tica, Av 4, C 9/11 (4 daily; 11hr); TRN, C 22, Av 3/5 (4 daily; 11hr).
To Panamá City: PA, C 16, Av 3/5 (1 daily; 16hr); Tica, Av 4, C 9/11 (2 daily; 16hr).
To Changuinola, Panama: TBO, C 14/16, Av 5 (1 daily; 6hr).

Domestic flights

Domestic flights from San José are run by Sansa, the state airline, and NatureAir, a commercial company. Sansa flies from Juan Santamaría International airport, 17km northwest of the city. They change their schedules frequently, so it's best to phone ahead or double-confirm when booking. NatureAir, more reliable in terms of schedules, flies from

Pavas airport, 7km west of the city. Although the table gives as accurate a rundown of the routes as possible, flight durations are subject to change at the last minute. Both NatureAir and Sansa fly small propeller planes which are often grounded by inclement weather. Keep in mind that, in the event of a cancellation, both airlines offer credit rather than money back. Some of the routings, particularly those to the Nicoya Peninsula, tend to be roundabout, often with one or two stops. Note that advance purchase (14 days) is necessary to ensure yourself a seat during the high season, especially for Quepos, Sámara and Tamarindo. Both companies have offices and agents throughout the country in most of the destinations they serve, or you can book and pay for tickets at a travel agent. Sansa check-in is at their San José office one hour before departure; they run a free bus to get you to the airport, and in some cases offer free transfers to your hotel at the other end. Fares for both airlines generally range from $55 one-way to $110–130 return for most destinations.

Flights from San José

Sansa C 24, Paseo Colón/Av 1 (ⓣ2221-9414, reservations ⓣ2257-9444, ⓦwww.flysansa.com). To: Bahía Drake (1 daily; 50min); Golfito (3 daily; 1hr); Nosara (1 daily; 1hr); Palmar Sur (2 daily; 50min); Puerto Jiménez (4 daily; 50min); Quepos (8 daily; 30min); Sámara (1 daily; 1hr); Tamarindo (3 daily; 1hr); Tambor (2 daily; 20min); Tortuguero (1 daily Mon, Wed & Fri; 45min).

NatureAir Tobías Bolaños airport, Pavas (ⓣ2220-3054 or 2296-1102, ⓦwww.natureair.com). To: Bahía Drake (4 daily; 45min); Golfito (2 daily; 55min); Liberia (4 daily; 1hr 10min); Nosara (2 daily; 45min); Palmar Sur (1 daily; 1hr); Puerto Jiménez (5 daily; 50min); Quepos (4 daily; 25min); Tamarindo (4 daily; 55min); Tambor (3 daily; 25min); Tortuguero (1 daily; 30min).

2

The Valle Central and the highlands

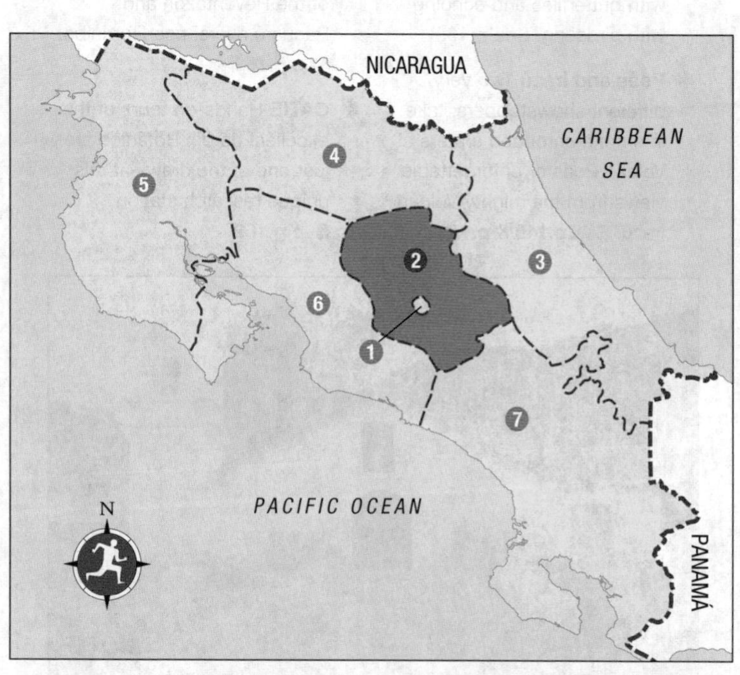

CHAPTER 2

Highlights

* **Coffee tours** Learn the finer points of coffee-tasting – and the whole coffee-making process – on an insightful plantation tour. **See p.126**
* **Villa Blanca Cloudforest Hotel & Nature Reserve** Relax by the fireplace in your luxury *casita* on the edge of the misty cloudforest alive with butterflies and echoing with birdsong. **See p.139**
* **Poás and Irazú** Two very different showstoppers: take in smoke-shrouded craters at Volcán Poás or unforgettable views from the mighty Volcán Irazú. **See p.140 & p.153**
* **Orosí** Soak in riverside hot springs or brush up on your Spanish in this beguiling village, that is home to Costa Rica's oldest working church, and is set amid the cool, coffee-studded hills of the Valle Orosí. **See p.154**
* **White-water rafting** Tackle the churning white waters of the Reventazón and Pacuaré rivers, near Turrialba. **See p.162**
* **CATIE** Hands-on tours of the excellent Jardín Botánico are just one of the draws at this unique research station. **See p.162**

▲ Orosí church

2

The Valle Central and the highlands

Costa Rica's **VALLE CENTRAL** ("Central Valley") and the surrounding **HIGHLANDS** form the cultural and geographical fulcrum of the country. Rising between 3000 and 4000m, this wide-hipped inter-mountain plateau – often referred to as the Meseta Central or "Central Tableland" – has a patchwork-quilt beauty, especially when lit by the early morning sun, with staggered green coffee terraces set in sharp contrast to the blue-black summits of the nearby mountains.

Many of these are **volcanoes** – the Valle Central is edged by a chain of volcanic peaks, running from Poás in the north to Turrialba in the east – and their volatile nature can sometimes give the region an air of unease. The sight of **Poás**, **Irazú** and **Turrialba** spewing and snorting, raining a light covering of fertile volcanic ash on the surrounding farmland, is a fairly common one, though seismic activity over the last couple of years has been a lot more significant: in January 2009, an earthquake devastated the area around Poás, and a year later Turrialba erupted for the first time in nearly 150 years, causing nearby villages to be evacuated.

Although occupying a relatively small area, the fertile Valle Central supports roughly two-thirds of Costa Rica's population, the majority of whom live in San José (covered in Chapter 1) or one of the provincial capitals of **Alajuela**, **Heredia** and **Cartago**. The tremendous pressure on land is noticeable even on short forays from San José: urban areas, suburbs and highway communities blend into each other, and in some places, every spare patch of soil sprouts coffee bushes, fruit trees or vegetables.

The Valle Central in a nutshell

One easy, albeit fairly whistle-stop way of visiting the Valle Central's major sights is on a **tour** from San José. All kinds of packages exist, but some of the most popular are organized by Expediciones Tropicales (☎2233-5151, ⓦwww.expedicionestropicales.com). Their full-day tour of the northern Valle Central visits Volcán Poás, the Doka coffee estate and the La Paz Waterfall Gardens ($89), while their jaunt around the southern highlights takes in Volcán Irazú, the botanical gardens at Lankester and the beautiful Valle Orosí ($74); prices include breakfast, lunch and guide. See p.46 for details of other tour operators.

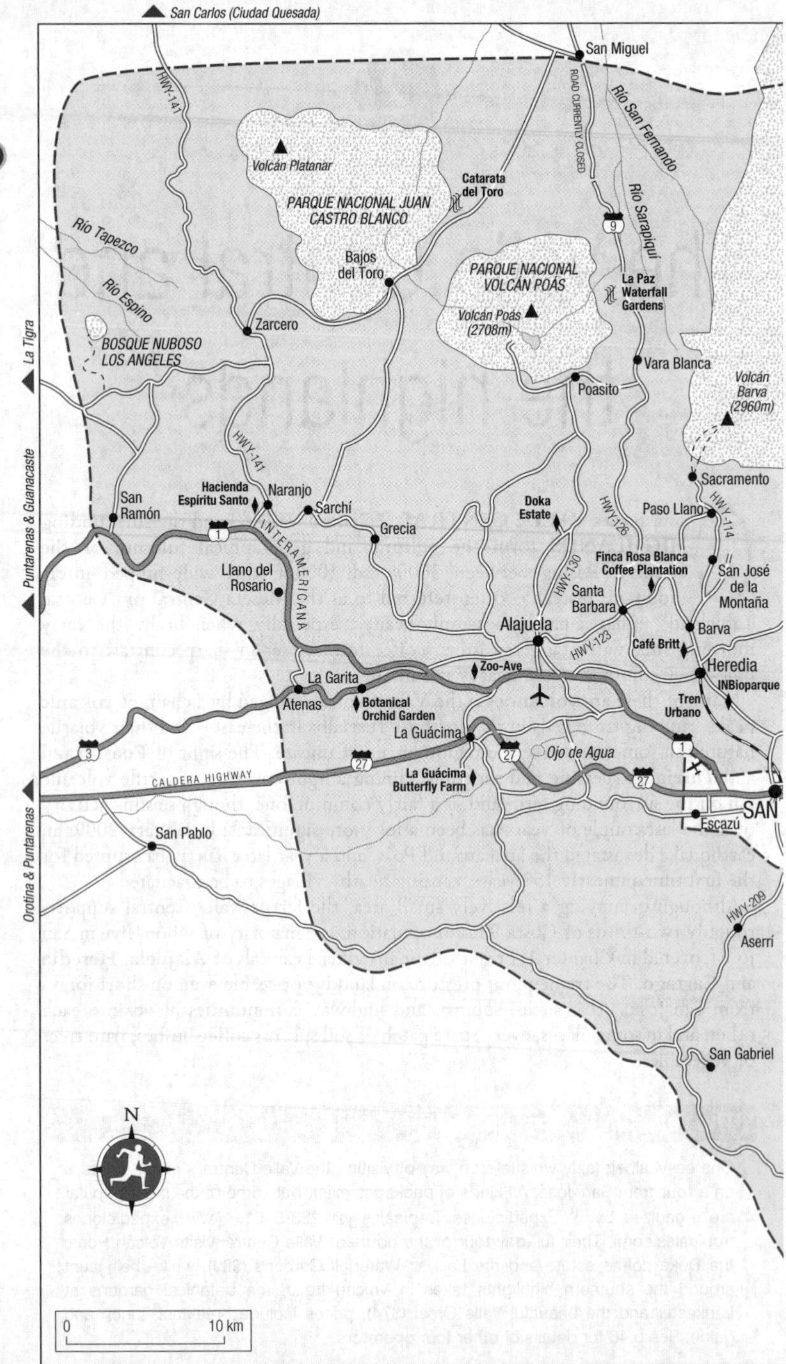
San Carlos (Ciudad Quesada)
San Miguel
HWY-141
ROAD CURRENTLY CLOSED
Río San Fernando
Volcán Platanar
Catarata del Toro
PARQUE NACIONAL JUAN CASTRO BLANCO
Río Sarapiquí
9
Río Tapezco
Bajos del Toro
PARQUE NACIONAL VOLCÁN POÁS
La Paz Waterfall Gardens
Río Espino
Volcán Poás (2708m)
Zarcero
La Tigra
BOSQUE NUBOSO LOS ANGELES
Vara Blanca
Poasito
Volcán Barva (2960m)
HWY-141
Sacramento
HWY-126
HWY-114
San Ramón
Hacienda Espíritu Santo
Naranjo
Sarchí
Doka Estate
Paso Llano
Puntarenas & Guanacaste
1
Grecia
INTERAMERICANA
Finca Rosa Blanca Coffee Plantation
Llano del Rosario
HWY-130
Santa Barbara
San José de la Montaña
Alajuela
Barva
HWY-123
Café Britt
Zoo-Ave
Heredia
La Garita
INBioparque
Atenas
Botanical Orchid Garden
Tren Urbano
3
La Guácima
27
Ojo de Agua
1
27
CALDERA HIGHWAY
La Guácima Butterfly Farm
27
SAN
Puntarenas
Escazú
San Pablo
HWY-209
Orotina & Puntarenas
Aserrí
San Gabriel
N
0
10 km

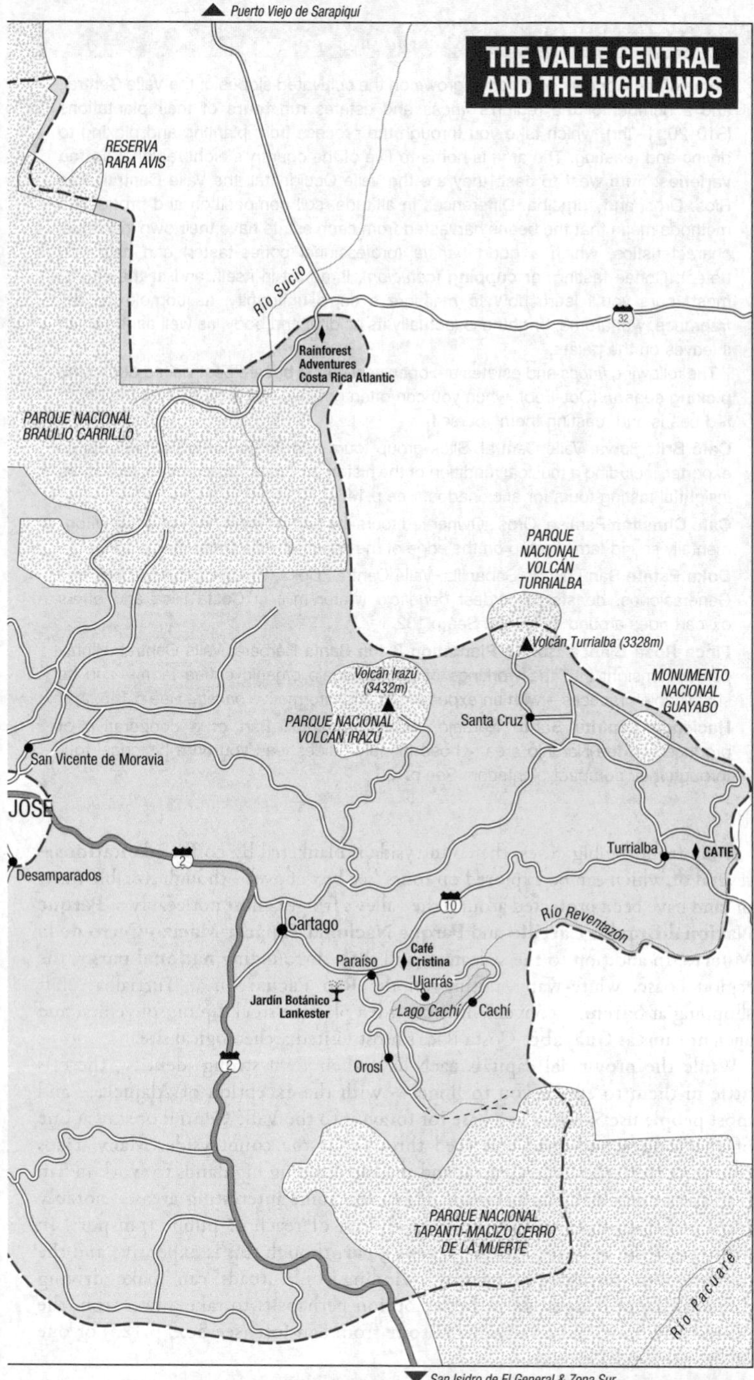
THE VALLE CENTRAL AND THE HIGHLANDS
Puerto Viejo de Sarapiquí
RESERVA RARA AVIS
Río Sucio
32
Siquerres & Puerto Limón
Rainforest Adventures Costa Rica Atlantic
PARQUE NACIONAL BRAULIO CARRILLO
PARQUE NACIONAL VOLCÁN TURRIALBA
Volcán Turrialba (3328m)
Volcán Irazú (3432m)
PARQUE NACIONAL VOLCÁN IRAZÚ
MONUMENTO NACIONAL GUAYABO
Santa Cruz
San Vicente de Moravia
JOSE
2
Desamparados
Turrialba
CATIE
10
Río Reventazón
Cartago
Café Cristina
Paraíso
Ujarrás
Jardín Botánico Lankester
Lago Cachí
Cachí
Orosí
2
PARQUE NACIONAL TAPANTÍ-MACIZO CERRO DE LA MUERTE
Río Pacuaré
San Isidro de El General & Zona Sur

Anyone for coffee?

Some of the world's finest coffee grows on the cultivated slopes of the Valle Central, and a number of the region's *fincas* and estates run **tours** of their plantations ($10–20; 1–2hr), which take you through the process from planting and picking to drying and roasting. The area is home to five of the country's eight regional **coffee varieties**: from west to east, they are the Valle Occidental, the Valle Central, Tres Ríos, Orosí and Turrialba. Differences in altitude, soil composition and production methods mean that the beans harvested from each estate have their own individual characteristics, which a good *barista* (professional coffee-taster) can help you detect. Coffee-tasting, or **cupping** (*catación*), is an art in itself, and at the end of most tours you'll learn how to measure a cup's uniformity, its complexity, dry fragrance, wet aroma, brightness (actually its acidity) and body, as well as the finish it leaves on the palate.

The following *fincas* and estates are open year-round but are best visited during the **picking season** (Oct–Feb), when you can often get involved in harvesting the bright red beans and roasting them yourself:

Café Britt Barva; Valle Central. Slick group tours from the country's largest coffee exporter, including a musical rendition of the history of Costa Rican coffee, plus more insightful tasting tours for aficionados. See p.146.

Café Christina Paraiso; Orosí. Owner-led tours (by appointment only) of this environmentally sound family setup on the edge of the beautiful Valle Orosí. See p.156.

Doka Estate San Luis de Sabanilla; Valle Central. Doka, which produces Café Tres Generaciones, boasts the oldest *beneficio* (water mill) in Costa Rica and offers ox-cart rides around its estate. See p.132.

Finca Rosa Blanca Coffee Plantation & Inn Santa Bárbara; Valle Central. Highly personal insight into the workings of a small-scale organic coffee farm – and its sustainable practices – with an experienced and informative *barista*. See p.146.

Hacienda Espíritu Santo Naranjo; Valle Occidental. Part of a cooperative of producers in the Naranjo area, whose friendly guides lead you on a historical tour through their compact plantation. See p.136.

Away from the big cities, the countryside is blanketed by **coffee plantations** – several of which can be explored on tours (see box above) – though sizeable tracts of land have been protected around the valley's fringes, most noticeably at **Parque Nacional Braulio Carrillo** and **Parque Nacional Tapantí-Macizo Cerro de la Muerte**. In addition to the volcanoes and their surrounding **national parks**, the region boasts white-water rafting on the **Río Pacuaré** near Turrialba; craft shopping at **Sarchí**, a convenient if crowded place to stock up on souvenirs; and ancient ruins at **Guayabo**, Costa Rica's most visited archeological site.

While the provincial capitals each have their own strong identity, there is little in them to entice you to linger – with the exception of Alajuela – and most people use San José as a base for forays into the Valle Central or stay at one of the **lodges and inns** scattered throughout the countryside. Many Ticos commute from the Valle Central and the surrounding highlands to work in San José via an efficient **bus** network. However, some interesting areas – notably Irazú and Tapantí – remain frustratingly out of reach of public transport. In many cases the only recourse is to **rent a car**, though this is expensive and the mountainous terrain and narrow, winding, unlit roads can make driving difficult, if not dangerous. A better option perhaps is to take a taxi from the nearest town, or join an organized **tour** from San José (see box, p.123) or one of the provincial capitals.

Some history

Little is known about the Valle Central's **indigenous** inhabitants, except that they lived in the valley for at least 12,000 years, cultivating corn and grouping themselves in small settlements like the one excavated at **Guayabo**, near Turrialba.

In 1560, the Spanish started to **colonize** the area, founding **Garcimuñoz**, in the west of the region, in 1561, and a further settlement at modern-day Cartago three years later. Though the first settlers found fertile land, the rich-pickings that they had expected didn't materialize: the region had few settlements and no roads (until 1824 there was only the Camino Real, a mule path to Nicaragua, and a thin ox-cart track to Puntarenas) and, crucially, far less **free labour** than they had hoped – the indigenous population proved largely unwilling to submit to Spanish rule, either to the system of slave labour, known as *encomienda*, or to the taxation forced upon them. Some tribes and leaders collaborated with the settlers, but in general they did what they could to resist the servitude the Spanish tried to impose, often fleeing to the jungles of Talamanca. Forced to till their own fields, many of the first settler families ended up living in as "primitive" a state as the peoples they had hoped to exploit. Indeed, money was so scarce that in 1709 the settlers adopted the cacao bean – the currency of the indigenous peoples – as a kind of barter currency, and it was used as such until the 1850s, when it was finally replaced by officially minted coins.

In 1808, Costa Rica's governor, Tomás de Acosta, brought **coffee** here from Jamaica; a highland plant, it flourished in the mineral-rich soil of the Valle Central. Legislators, keen to develop a cash crop, offered incentives to farmers – San José's town council gave free land and coffee seedlings to settlers, while families in Cartago were ordered to plant coffee bushes in their backyards. In 1832, there were enough beans available for export, and real wealth – at least for the exporters and coffee brokers – came in 1844, when the London market for Costa Rican coffee opened up. It was the country's main source of income until war and declining prices devastated the domestic market in the 1930s.

Heredia and Cartago provinces still earn much of their money from coffee, and today the Valle Central remains the most economically productive region in the country. **Fruit**, including mangoes and strawberries, is cultivated in Alajuela; **vegetables** thrive in the volcanic soil near Poás and Irazú; and on the slopes of Irazú and Barva, Holstein **cattle** provide much of the country's milk. Venture anywhere outside the urban areas and you will see evidence of the continued presence of the yeoman farmer, as small plots and family holdings survive despite the population pressure that continues to erode available farmland.

Alajuela and around

At first sight, it may be hard to distinguish **ALAJUELA** from San José, until the pleasant realization dawns that you can smell bougainvillea rather than petrol fumes as you walk down the street. Alajuela was founded in 1657 and remains a largely agricultural centre, with a **Saturday market** (6am–2.30pm) that draws hundreds of farmers who come to sell fruit, vegetables, dairy products and flowers.

Alajuela's most cherished historical figure is the drummer-boy-cum-martyr **Juan Santamaría**, hero of the 1856 Battle of Rivas (see p.280) and subject of his own **museum**, about the only formal attraction in town; he also has his own festival, the **Día de Juan Santamaría** (April 11, the anniversary of the great battle), when the townsfolk kick up their heels with bands, parades and fireworks.

Alajuela can be seen in half a day or so, but it makes a convenient base for visiting the surrounding sights (most of the Valle Central's main attractions lie within a

30km radius, and the city is considerably warmer than San José) or a useful place to stay if you've an early-morning flight to catch – the **airport** is just a five-minute bus ride away, compared to forty minutes or more from the capital.

Arrival and information

The majority of international **flights** arrive at Juan Santamaría International Airport, less than 3km from Alajuela; most hotels and hostels include airport pick-up, or you can catch a bus (signed, unsurprisingly, "Alajuela") into town.

Tuasa **buses** from San José (every 10min; 20min) and Heredia (every 15min; 45min) arrive at their station on Calle 8, four blocks west of the Parque Central; the Station Wagon Alajuela bus from San José drops you off on Avenida 4, 50m southwest of Parque Juan Santamaría, a few minutes' walk from the centre. If you're **driving** from San José, head in the direction of the airport on Hwy-1 (the Interamericana, or Autopista General Cañas); the turn-off to Alajuela is 17km northwest of San José – don't use the underpass or you'll end up at the airport.

The best source of **information** in town – other than your hotel or hostel – is Goodlight Books on Av 3, C 1/3 (see p.132), where staff can usually help with public transport questions and the like.

Accommodation

Due to its proximity to the airport, **accommodation** fills up quickly, and it's important to reserve ahead even in the rainy season; the finest options are actually just **outside town**, including the *Xandari Resort & Spa*, one of Costa Rica's loveliest hotels. Most places can organize **tours** of the surrounding attractions.

In town

Alajuela Backpackers Corner of Av 4 & C 4 ⓣ2441-7149, ⓦwww.alajuelabackpackers.com. Spotless, spacious dorms ($15) and en-suite doubles in a towering (for Alajuela) building opposite leafy Parque los Niños. Pull up a beanbag in the whitewashed TV room, with fifty-inch plasma screen. Free internet. Airport pick-up – but not breakfast – included. ❹

Charly's Place Hotel Av 5, C0/2 ⓣ2441-0115, ⓦwww.charlysplacehotel.com. This friendly hotel attracts a gringo crowd who often fill up the large clean rooms, some with private bath and hot running water. Hang out in the plant-festooned courtyard or in the decent TV lounge. Dorm beds are $15. ❸

Cortez Azul Av 5, C 2/4 ⓣ2443-6145, ⓔhotelcorteazul@gmail.com. Comfortable hostel (dorms $10) run by a welcoming local artist (whose works hang on the walls), with five rooms (some with private bath), communal kitchen looking onto a small garden, and laundry facilities. ❷

Moving on

The are frequent Tuasa **buses to San José** (every 10min) and **Heredia** (every 15min), with Station Wagon Alajuela buses also running to the capital: all leave from their respective terminals (see above). The daily bus to **Volcán Poás** (departs 9.15am; 1hr 30min) also uses the Tuasa terminal.

Local services leave from either the **Estacíon al Pacífico** on Av 2, C 8/10, or from one of the surrounding jumble of bus stops: there are regular departures for La Garita (for Zoo-Ave; 15min), Sabanilla (for Doka Estate; 40min), Atenas, Grecia, Sarchí and Naranjo (all about 1hr), and less so for La Guácima Abajo (for the Butterfly Farm; 40min).

Long-distance buses depart from **La Radial** station (officially known as Multi-centro La Estacíon), 75m south of the Shell station, on C 4, running to San Carlos (11 daily; 1hr 55min), La Fortuna/Volcán Arenal (3 daily; 3hr 25min), Monteverde (7am & 3pm; 4hr), Liberia (frequent; 4hr), Puntarenas (frequent; 2hr 10min) and Jacó (3 daily; 2hr 30min).

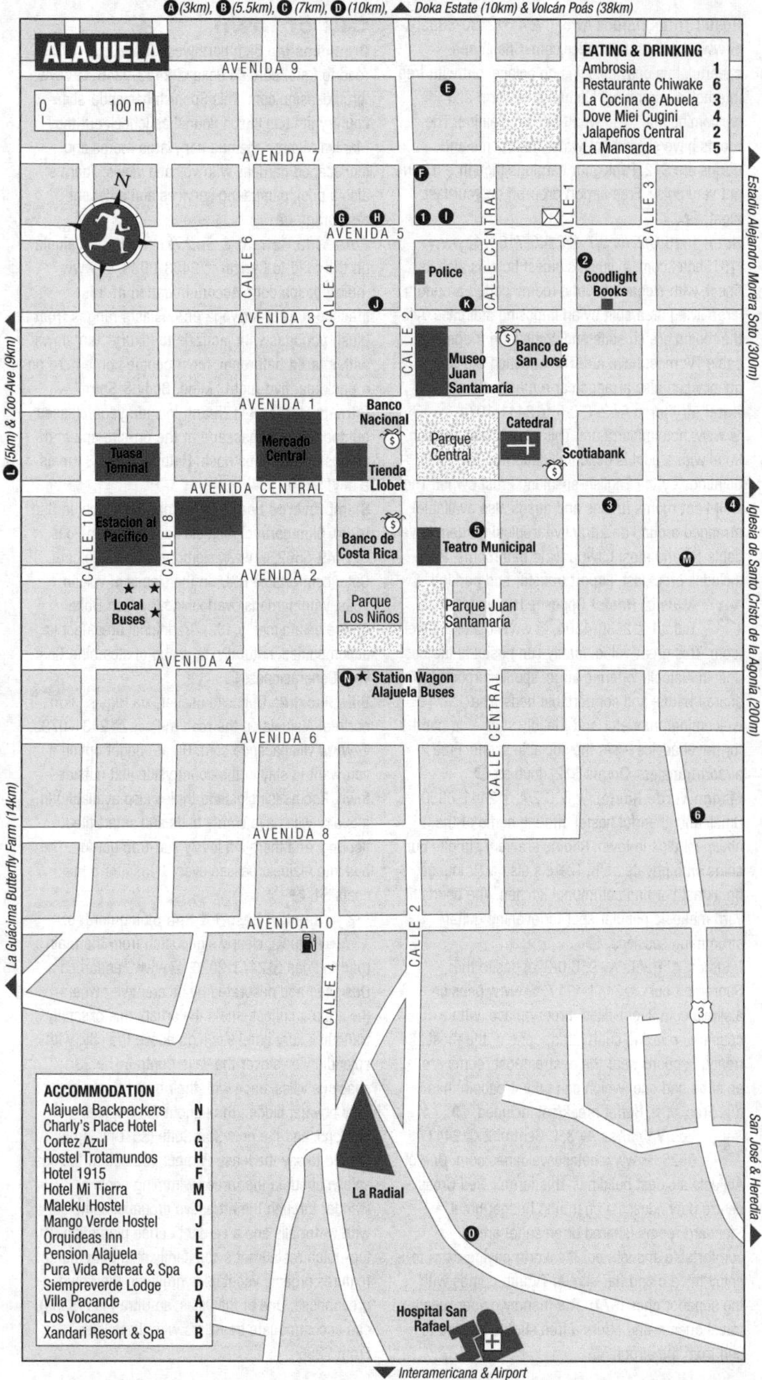
ALAJUELA
A (3km), B (5.5km), C (7km), D (10km), Doka Estate (10km) & Volcán Poás (38km)
0 100 m
N
EATING & DRINKING
Ambrosia 1
Restaurante Chiwake 6
La Cocina de Abuela 3
Dove Miei Cugini 4
Jalapeños Central 2
La Mansarda 5
ACCOMMODATION
Alajuela Backpackers N
Charly's Place Hotel I
Cortez Azul G
Hostel Trotamundos H
Hotel 1915 F
Hotel Mi Tierra M
Maleku Hostel O
Mango Verde Hostel J
Orquideas Inn L
Pension Alajuela E
Pura Vida Retreat & Spa C
Siempreverde Lodge D
Villa Pacande A
Los Volcanes K
Xandari Resort & Spa B
AVENIDA 9
AVENIDA 7
AVENIDA 5
AVENIDA 3
AVENIDA 1
AVENIDA CENTRAL
AVENIDA 2
AVENIDA 4
AVENIDA 6
AVENIDA 8
AVENIDA 10
CALLE 10
CALLE 8
CALLE 6
CALLE 4
CALLE 2
CALLE CENTRAL
CALLE 1
CALLE 3
Police
Goodlight Books
Banco de San José
Museo Juan Santamaría
Banco Nacional
Catedral
Parque Central
Scotiabank
Tuasa Teminal
Mercado Central
Tienda Llobet
Estacion al Pacifico
Banco de Costa Rica
Teatro Municipal
Local Buses
Parque Los Niños
Parque Juan Santamaría
Station Wagon Alajuela Buses
3
La Radial
Hospital San Rafael
L (5km) & Zoo-Ave (9km)
La Guácima Butterfly Farm (14km)
Estadio Alejandro Morera Soto (300m)
Iglesia de Santo Cristo de la Agonía (200m)
San José & Heredia
Interamericana & Airport

Hostel Trotamundos Av 5, C 2/4 ⓣ2430-5832, ⓦwww.hosteltrotamundos.com. Cheap and cheerful, this busy hostel is no palace, but with free internet, a communal kitchen and warm and welcoming staff, you won't be complaining. The rooms have shared hot-water bathrooms and dorms are $12. Pack your earplugs though – it can get very noisy. Free airport drop-off on your last night. ❸

Hotel 1915 C 2, Av 5/7 ⓣ2440-7163, ⓦwww.1915hotel.com. Alajuela's oldest hotel is also its finest, with elegantly subtle rooms dotted around a large living area split by an imposing staircase. All the rooms are en suite and come with fridge and cable TV; most have a/c. The attached Bio Tours agency can also arrange car rental and flights. ❺

Hotel Mi Tierra Av 2, C 3/5 ⓣ2441-1974, ⓦwww.hotelmitierra.net. This perennially popular hotel with a pool is beautifully adorned with paintings by the English-speaking artist owner. The well-kept rooms (triples and quads also available), arranged around an attractive tropical garden, have cable TV, and most have private bathrooms. Price includes breakfast, airport transfer and parking. ❸

Maleku Hostel Opposite Hospital San Rafael ⓣ2430-4304, ⓦwww.malekuhostel.com. This great-value, family-run hostel is the best deal in Alajuela, offering large, spotless rooms (all shared baths) and comfortable beds. The welcoming proprietor and friendly staff – on hand for travel advice – set the sociable scene. Free airport transfers. Dorms $12, doubles ❸

Mango Verde Hostel Av 3, C 2/4 ⓣ2441-6330. Small and cheerful hostel offering some of the cheapest digs in town. Rooms are very simple, but come with private bath. There's also a TV lounge, breakfast bar and communal kitchen. The poorly lit yard makes a popular spot for evening guitar-strumming sessions. ❷

Pension Alajuela Av 9, C 0/2, opposite the Supreme Court ⓣ2441-1717, ⓦwww.pensionalajuela.com. Light-filled, breezy place, with a couple of relaxing courtyards – one of the most tranquil options near the centre. Most rooms are en suite and one (which can take 4 people) has a/c. Free wi-fi. Buffet breakfast included. ❸

Los Volcanes Av 3, C Central/2 ⓣ2441-0525, ⓦwww.hotellosvolcanes.com. One of Alajuela's oldest buildings, this former Red Cross centre now houses a charming budget hotel. Standard rooms (shared or en suite) are comfortable enough, but it's worth paying extra to enjoy the a/c and flat-screen TV that comes with the superior ones ($74). The friendly owner runs a travel agency and offers a free shuttle service to and from the airport. ❹

Out of town

Orquideas Inn 5km northwest of Alajuela, on the road to San Pedro de Poás ⓣ2443-9346, ⓦwww.orquideasinn.com. This Spanish hacienda-style country inn has kitsch flourishes (check out the Marilyn Monroe-themed bar), large rooms and landscaped gardens with volcano views. There's also a pool, pampering services and a decent restaurant. ❻

Pura Vida Retreat & Spa 7km north of Alajuela on the road to Carizal ⓣ2483-0033, ⓦwww.puravidaspa.com. Accommodation at this lifestyle retreat for yoga enthusiasts ranges from plush pagodas with jacuzzis to luxury "tentalows" with shared bathroom. Most people come here on a package: five-night "Mind, Body & Spirit" retreats start at $1125 and include yoga classes, guided tours, a massage at the on-site spa and oodles of nutritious nosh. Rates include 3 meals a day. $250

Siempreverde Lodge 2km from the school in San Isidro, 8km north of Alajuela on the road to Poás ⓣ2449-5562, ⓦwww.siempreverdebandb.com. Cute, comfortable B&B on the slopes of Volcán Poás, with gardens overlooking the lush Doka Coffee estate (see p.132). Traditional breakfast is accompanied, naturally, by a cup of steaming Café Tres Generaciones. ❻

Villa Pacande Opposite Escuela de Hiquis, 3km north of Alajuela on the road to Poás ⓣ2431-0783, ⓦwww.villapacande.com. Great budget option if you want to stay in the countryside just outside town. Rooms (singles and triples also available) in this airy villa have comfy beds and smart tiled flooring, and there's a lovely sun-trap garden. The bus into Alajuela passes every 20min, or a taxi costs $4. ❹

Xandari Resort & Spa 5.5km north of Alajuela, clearly signposted from the main road to Poás ⓣ2443-2020, ⓦwww.xandari.com. Designed and decorated by its creative owners (he's the architect, she's the artist), this blissfully tranquil luxury hotel sits high above the city, with splendid views over the Valle Central. The 23 spacious villas, each with their own terrace, feel very private, hidden throughout the tropical gardens, and the new Star Suite ($510) is aptly named to say the least. Pamper yourself at the spa, splash about in the three swimming pools or wander through the attractive grounds, complete with waterfalls and a verdant coffee plantation. The top-notch restaurant's constantly changing menu features organic vegetables grown in their own greenhouse. One of the villas, an Ultra Plus ($355), can accommodate travellers with disabilities. From $255.

The Town

Alajuela's few attractions can be found near the peaceful **Parque Central** (officially called Plaza del General Tomás Guardia), which is shaded by giant mango trees and frequented by the usual assortment of bored retirees. Most impressive of the old colonial buildings that fringe the park is the sturdy whitewashed former jail that now houses the **Museo Juan Santamaría** (Tues–Sat 10am–5.30pm; free; Ⓦwww.museojuansantamaria.go.cr), entered through a pretty tiled courtyard garden lined with long wooden benches. The curiously monastic atmosphere of the rooms is almost more interesting than the small collection, which runs the gamut from mid-nineteenth-century maps of Costa Rica to crumbly portraits of figures involved in the battle of 1856. Temporary exhibitions showcase local crafts or modern art, while the auditorium hosts cultural lectures (in Spanish) on regional topics.

Flanking the eastern end of the square, the white-domed **Catedral de Alajuela** possesses no great architectural merit – not helped by the damage it received in a 1990 earthquake – though it does have pretty floor tiles, round stained-glass windows and a large cupola bizarrely decorated with *trompe l'oeil* balconies. One block south of the Parque Central, the small and empty **Parque Juan Santamaría** is saved from looking like a car park by a statue of the ubiquitous local hero.

Outside the centre, the town is leafy, quiet and residential, with occasional views of the blue mountain ridges and bright green carpet of the Valle Central. The **Iglesia de Santo Cristo de la Agonía**, five blocks east of the Parque Central, was constructed in 1935, but looks much older, with a Baroque exterior painted in two-tone cream. Head inside for a look at the lovely wooden, gilt-edged altar, with naive Latin American motifs and gilt-painted columns edging the bright tiled floor. Realist murals, apparently painted from life, show various stages in the development of Christianity in Costa Rica, depicting monsignors and indigenous people gathering with middle-class citizens to receive the Word.

Eating, drinking and nightlife

Alajuela has several decent **restaurants**, and you can dig into particularly tasty ceviche and *casados* at the friendly **Mercado Central** (daily 11am–10pm). **Nightlife**, however, is limited and most bars close around 11pm, when the action shifts to The Fiesta Casino, near the airport, with live music, restaurants and gambling galore.

The **Teatro Municipal de Alajuela**, on the northwest corner of Parque Juan Santamaría, is fast becoming the city's cultural hub and features regular concerts and theatrical events.

In a Liga their own

Football (*fútbol*) is big in Costa Rica, even more so since their near-qualification for the 2010 World Cup (they lost in a play-off to eventual semi-finalists Uruguay), and Alajuela is home to one of most historic teams in the country: **Liga Deportivo Alajuelense** (Ⓣ2443-1617, Ⓦwww.lda.cr), who ply their trade at the impressive 18,000-seater Estadio Alejandro Morera Soto, northeast of the centre on C 9, Av 9. One of the original founders of the national league in 1921, LDA have won the Primera División 24 times but have lost out in recent seasons to Deportivo Saprissa, their great rivals from San José – derbies between the two teams, known as the **Clasíco de Costa Rica**, can be fiery affairs, and are certainly worth catching if you can.

Matches are played on Sundays during the Winter (late July to late Dec) and Summer (mid-Jan to mid-May) championships; **tickets** start at just $6 and can be bought at the stadium, or in advance on Ⓣ2206-7770 or at Ⓦwww.specialticket.net/alajuela.

Ambrosia Av 5, C 2. Tiny café with an outdoor terrace; food from the Italian-influenced menu can be a bit patchy, so you're probably better off sticking to the gooey cakes. Mon–Sat 10.30am–6.30pm.

La Cocina de Abuela Av 0, C 1/3. "*Grandma's Kitchen*" runs a surf and turf-dominated menu, of which the hearty steak *churrascos* ($16) and pork stews best live up to the restaurant's name. Daily 11.30am–midnight.

Dove Miei Cugini Av 0, C 5. Literally "At My Cousin's", this family-run restaurant serves up mouthwatering Italian staples, including minestrone soup, pastas and, of course, pizza (takeaway available on ⓣ2240-6893). Wash it down with a beer or cocktail at the downstairs bar. Daily 5–10pm.

Jalapeños Central C 1, Av 1/3. Fajitas, burritos, nachos, quesadillas – this authentic little Tex-Mex has it all. The tasty fare ($6 lunch, $7.50 dinner; individual dishes from $4.50) is prepared with love and attitude by a Colombian-American. Closed Sun.

La Mansarda Second floor, C 0, Av 0/2. Popular restaurant boasting an extensive menu (in English and Spanish) of international and Tico classics (*casados* $5), best enjoyed with a glass of wine, and topped off with a cocktail at the bar (till 1am). Daily 10.30am–10pm.

Restaurante Chiwake Av 8, C 3. Excellent Peruvian restaurant, authentic down to its Inka Kolas and Pisco sours. Choose from half a dozen or so ceviches (from $5.50), or try one of the delicious chef specials, such as *aji de gallina*, shredded chicken in a smooth, spicy sauce ($7.50), or *jalea de mariscos*, an assortment of lightly breaded seafood ($9). Daily 11am–9pm.

Listings

Banks Banco Nacional, opposite the Parque Central; Banco de Costa Rica C 2, Av 0/2; Scotiabank, Av Central, C1. All have 24hr ATMs and change travellers' cheques.

Bookshop Goodlight Books Av 3 C 1/3 ⓦwww.goodlightbooks.com (daily 9am–6pm) carries an extensive selection of used English-language travel guides, maps and phrasebooks.

Car rental Most rental agencies in and around the airport will bring your car to your hotel in Alajuela; otherwise, try BioTours (through *Hotel 1925*), Joe's (through *Maleku Hostel*) or *Hotel Mi Tierra*; from around $300 per week.

Hospital San Rafael Av 12 ⓣ2436-1000.

Internet access Goodlight Books (see above).

Police Public ⓣ2440-8889/90, emergencies ⓣ911.

Post office C 1, Av 5 (Mon–Fri 8am–5.30pm, Sat 8am–noon).

Doka Estate

Set amid rolling coffee fields 10km north of Alajuela, signposted off the road to Volcán Poás, the **Doka Estate** (tours daily 9am, 10am, 11am, 1.30pm & 2.30pm, Mon–Fri also 3.30pm; 1hr, 2hr on Fri at 11am; $18, children $10; ⓣ2449-5152, ⓦwww.dokaestate.com) is one of the most historic coffee farms in the country. The Vargas family have been growing beans here for over seventy years – their *beneficio* (water mill) is the oldest in Costa Rica – and today produce a variety of roasts for Café Tres Generaciones. Enthusiastic guides cover the entire coffee-making process (the longer Friday morning tour also includes an ox-cart ride around the plantation), and finish with a free tasting – look out for their Peaberry Estate, a smooth medium roast containing the *caracolillo* bean, a mutation that gives the cup a sweeter flavour. You can also visit their new butterfly farm (included in the price), and grab lunch at the on-site restaurant (daily 11am–2pm; $9).

To get to Doka, take the **bus** from Alajuela to the nearby town of Sabanilla, from where a taxi to the estate costs $3; alternatively, a taxi direct from Alajuela will set you back about $20. The estate can also provide transportation from anywhere in the Valle Central (phone for details).

Doka has its own **café** a couple of kilometres beyond the turning off the main road to Poás, where you can sample the estate's various brews in an attractive setting (see p.142).

Zoo-Ave

The largest aviary in Central America, **Zoo-Ave** (daily 8.30am–5pm; $15, children $13; ⓣ2433-8989), 9km west of Alajuela, is just about the best place in the country – besides the wild – to see Costa Rica's fabulous **birds**. The exceptionally well-run rescue and rehabilitation centre has large, clean cages and carefully tended grounds. Many of the birds fly free, fluttering around in a flurry of raucous colours: look out for the kaleidoscopic scarlet macaws and wonderful blue parrots. Other birds include chestnut-mandibled toucans and resplendent quetzals – Zoo-Ave is one of the few places in the world where you can get up close to these mythical creatures – and you'll also see **primates**, from monkeys to marmosets, plus a variety of the country's resident **reptiles**, including crocodiles and iguanas.

The frequent La Garita **bus** from Alajuela passes right by Zoo-Ave (15min).

La Guácima Butterfly Farm

La Guácima Butterely Farm (daily 8.30am–5pm, tours at 8.45am, 11am, 1pm & 3pm; $15, children $7.50; ⓣ2438-0400, ⓦwww.butterflyfarm.co.cr), 14km southwest of Alajuela, breeds valuable pupae for export to zoos and botanical gardens all over the world. Informative two-hour tours begin with an audiovisual exhibit introducing the processes involved in commercial butterfly breeding, after which guides give a hands-on explanation of all aspects of butterfly life, including their cruelly short life spans, while flashes of bright colours (there are more than 45 species here) flutter prettily around the mesh-enclosed breeding area – look out in particular for the Blue Morpho, one of Costa Rica's most beautiful butterflies.

Mornings are the **best times to visit**, when the butterflies are more active and you can often watch them emerging from their chrysalides in the laboratory; note, too, that on export days (usually Mon, Tues & Thurs), you can also see the sorting and packing of pupae, ready to be shipped off across the globe.

Buses from San José to La Guácima (1hr) run hourly from C 8, Av 2/4, returning at 12.25pm, 3.25pm and 5.25pm. The **Alajuela** service, marked "La Guácima Abajo" (30min), leaves hourly from near the Estacíon al Pacífico (to hook up with the tours you'll need to catch the 8am, 10am, noon or 2pm services): ask the driver for "La Finca de Mariposas", and they will let you off at the gates. Return buses pass by on the hour. The farm runs a **pick-up service** from hotels in central San José ($35 including entrance, under-12s $15; reserve in advance) for all tours except the 1pm one. If **driving**, follow signs for Los Reyes Country Club; the farm is 500m after the club, on the left-hand side.

La Garita and Atenas

Famed for their wonderful weather, **LA GARITA**, 12km west of Alajuela, and **ATENAS**, a few kilometres further along Hwy-3, were deemed by *National Geographic* to have the best climate in the world; fruits, ornamental plants and flowers flourish here, as does maize, a fact most evident in the corn restaurants that line the road between the two (see p.134). The area sees less tourist traffic since the opening of the Caldera Highway in March 2010, which links San José to the Pacific and has superseded Hwy-3 as the quickest route to the coast, but has a few notable attractions.

Botanical Orchid Garden

A welcome recipient of the area's clement climate, the **Botanical Orchid Garden** (Tues–Sun 8.30am–4.30pm; $12, children $6; ⓣ2487-8095, ⓦwww.orchidgardencr.com), signed off Hwy-3 just beyond La Garita, is home to some 150 orchid species, half of them native. Walking trails (accessible to wheelchairs and buggies) lead through extensive gardens awash with colour (the blooms are at their peak from Jan–March); keep an eye out for the *guaria morada*, a delicate purple orchid that is Costa Rica's national flower.

Regular **buses** from Alajuela to Atenas (1hr) can drop you off on Hwy-3, from where it's an 800m walk up to the gardens.

Tropical Bungee and Costa Rica Bungee

At **Llano del Rosario**, a few kilometres north of La Garita on Hwy-1 (and also accessible on a back-road from Atenas), you can try Costa Rica's original **bungee jump**. Tropical Bungee ($65, free pick-up from San José at 8am & 1pm; ⓣ2248-2212, ⓦwww.bungee.co.cr) organizes leaps from the 70m-high bridge over the Río Colorado. Right next door, rival company Costa Rica Bungee ($65; free pick-up if you combine the jump with one of their other activities; ⓣ2494-5102 or 8355-7207, ⓦwww.bungeecostarica.com) offers jumps from the same bridge. If you require some Dutch courage before taking the leap, the large open-air *Bungee Bar* is right beside the bridge and does great cheap *bocas*, home-made pizza and hosts live music at weekends. Costa Rica Bungee also organizes canyoning adventures down the 60m-high waterfall at Las Cataratas de Los Chorros, a picturesque spot 5km south of Grecia ($65).

Practicalities

There are a several attractive **accommodation** options around Atenas, which can make pleasant first- or last-night stops – the airport is about 25 minutes away. Up a steep hill in Sabana Larga, 3km west of Atenas, the relaxing *Hotel B&B Vista Atenas* (ⓣ2446-4272, ⓦwww.vistaatenas.com; ❻) enjoys lovely views across the Valle Central, particularly from the pool terrace. The welcoming Belgian owner fosters a homely ambience – many of the guests in the *cabinas* and *casitas* (both $350 per week) are long-term, repeat visitors – and is gradually making her property eco-friendly, having installed a solar-powered hot-water system and now adding a freshwater well to the replanted grounds. Alternatively, in Rio Grande, 4km outside Atenas, airy *Orchid Tree* (ⓣ2477-2314, ⓦwww.orchidtreecostarica.com; ❺) has four tastefully furnished rooms, with a Balinese influence – like the open-sided living areas – and an inviting pool, set in lush tropical gardens.

Further north, 2km from Llano del Rosario, the luxury bungalows of the *Vista del Valle Plantation Inn* (ⓣ2451-1165, ⓦwww.vistadelvalle.com; ❽) are poised on the edge of a canyon above the gushing Río Grande. Accommodation ranges from thatched-roofed suites with canopy beds and outdoor showers to large villas with huge stone bathrooms you could get lost in; two cheaper rooms are also available in the main lodge ($100). The property has its own 90m-high waterfall, and there's also horseriding, hiking, pampering services and a swimming pool and jacuzzi to occupy your time. Breakfast is included at the smart restaurant, which has an emphasis on organic, locally sourced produce.

The most popular of the area's corn **restaurants** is the *Fiesta del Maíz* (Mon, Wed & Thurs 10am–8pm, Fri–Sun 7am–9pm), a buzzing fast-food-style *cantina* on the road to Atenas that draws swarms of Ticos for its tasty fare (around $5), nearly all of it made from the eponymous grain. Leaving Atenas and heading west on Hwy-3, it's worth pulling in to *La Casa del Café* (daily 7am–5.30pm), a popular pit stop on the (slower) road to the Pacific, for its tremendous views down a valley of folded hills, with birds of prey circling overhead; the *chuleta gallo* is good value at $3.50, or you could just settle for a mango *fresca*.

Sarchí and around

Touted as Costa Rica's centre for arts and crafts, **SARCHÍ**, 30km northwest of Alajuela, is famous for producing the brightly painted ox-carts, or *carretas*, that have become the country's national symbol. The setting is pretty enough, between precipitous verdant hills, but don't expect to see picturesque scenes of craftsmen sitting in small historic shops, sculpting marble or carving wood – Sarchí is an overly commercialized village, firmly on the tourist trail, and most of the factories are rather soulless showrooms. In a few of them, however, you can watch carts and furniture being painted and assembled, and at the very least, the ox-carts and rocking chairs are less expensive here than anywhere else in the country.

The Town

Straggling along the road for several kilometres, Sarchí is split by the Río Trojas into **Sarchí Sur**, essentially a collection of roadside workshops (*fábricas*) and furniture stores (*mublerias*), and **Sarchí Norte**, a residential area further up the hill. Besides the shops and factories, the town's only site of interest is Sarchí Norte's

The Carreta de Sarchí

The **Carreta de Sarchí** or Sarchí ox-cart was first produced by enterprising local families for the immigrant settlers who arrived at the beginning of the twentieth century to run the coffee plantations. The original designs featured simple geometric shapes, though the ox-carts sold today are kaleidoscopically painted square creations built to be hauled by a single ox or team of two oxen. Moorish in origin, the designs can be traced back to immigrants from the Spanish provinces of Andalucía and Granada. Full-scale carts ($1000-plus) are rarely sold, but many smaller-scale coffee table-sized replicas are made for tourists ($245–500), while dinky desktop versions can be picked up for under $5.

Fábricas de carretas

Cooperativa de Artesanas y Mublerías de Sarchí Sarchí Norte, on the right-hand side of the main road just after the petrol station (look for the large spinning ox-cart wheel out front) ⓣ2454-4050. While their prices are generally lower than the rest, they haven't skimped on the real deal; this is as good a place as any to browse for ox-carts, made by water-wheel-powered machines. They also stock traditional wooden handicrafts and furniture. Mon–Fri 8am–6pm, Sat & Sun 9am–6pm.

Fábrica de Carretas Joaquín Chaverrí Sarchí Sur, on the left-hand side of the main road as you enter the village ⓣ2454-4411, ⓦwww.sarchicostarica.net. Wander around the painting workshop and see dozens of ox-carts in progress at Sarchí's largest ox-cart factory, which has been in business since 1903. They'll arrange shipping and transport for souvenirs, and credit cards are accepted. Daily 8am–5.30pm.

Taller Eloy Alfaro Sarchí Norte, 125m up Calle 1 de Eva, one block east of the football field ⓣ2454-4131. Alfaro and his sons have been crafting *carretas* since 1923, and you can watch the younger generation still using age-old methods in their rickety wooden workshop, the last of its kind in Sarchí. Daily 6am–6pm.

pretty pink-and-white **church**; inside, its tiles are delicate pastel shades of pink and green. The **giant ox-cart** in the little park fronting the church is a record-breaking 14m long and weighs in at two tonnes; it was built in 2006 by Taller Eloy Alfaro, the only workshop in the country still making ox-carts the traditional way (see box, p.135).

Practicalities

Buses from **Alajuela** leave for Sarchí every half-hour (1hr 15min); buses back can be hailed on the main road from Sarchí Norte to Sarchí Sur. From **San José,** a daily express service (Mon–Fri 12.15pm, 5.30pm & 5.55pm, Sat noon; 1hr 30min) runs from La Coca-Cola; buses return via Alajuela. Alternatively, you can take the twice-hourly bus to Naranjo from La Coca-Cola, and switch there for a local service to Sarchí.

Tourist information is available from the internet café diagonally opposite Fábrica de Carretas Joaquín Caverri, on the right as you come into Sarchí Sur (Mon–Sat 8am–6pm, Sun 9am–noon). **Banco Nacional**, on the main road opposite the football field, changes dollars and travellers' cheques, as does a smaller branch in the Plaza de la Artesanía. The **post office** is 50m east of the football field (Mon–Fri 8am–5pm).

The best of Sarchí's few **hotels** is *Hotel Daniel Zamora* (Ⓣ2454-4596; ❸), on Calle 2, opposite the eastern end of the football field, with simple but clean rooms and hot water. If you want to stay well away from the consumer frenzy and cool off in a swimming pool to boot, the same owner runs the *Villa Sarchí Lodge* (Ⓣ2454-5000, Ⓔhotelvillasarchi@ice.co.cr; ❸), 1km northwest of the petrol station.

Las Carretas, the **restaurant** attached to the Fábrica de Carretas Joaquín Chaverri (daily 8am–5.30pm), refuels many a souvenir-shopper with its standard Tico dishes. *La Finca,* to the left of the Cooperativa de Artesanas souvenir shop as you face north, serves cheap but filling corn soup and grilled steak.

Grecia

The small town of **GRECIA**, some 12km southwest of Sarchí, is noticeable for its remarkable *fin-de-siècle* church. After their first church burned down, the prudent residents of Grecia decided to take no chances and built the second out of pounded sheets of metal, imported from Belgium. The white-trimmed rust-coloured result is surprisingly beautiful, with an altar that's a testament to Latin American Baroque froth, made entirely from intricate marble and rising up into the eaves of the church like a wedding cake. A couple of kilometres outside Grecia on the Alajuela road, **The World of Snakes** (daily 8am–4pm; $11, children $6; Ⓣ2494-3700, Ⓦwww.theworldofsnakes.com) is a small collection of fifty species of snakes from around the world housed in large glass boxes. The entrance fee includes a highly informative guided tour (in English or Spanish; 1hr), during which you learn all kinds of strange snake information, such as the fact that they are completely deaf, and that they frequently die of stress.

Half-hourly **buses** run to Grecia from Alajuela and San José (La Coca-Cola); both take around an hour.

Hacienda Espíritu Santo

The red berries lining the fields at **Hacienda Espíritu Santo** (tours 9am, 11am, 1pm & 3pm; 1hr 30min; $20; Ⓣ2450-3838, Ⓦwww.espiritusantocoffeetour.com), a co-op coffee plantation just outside the town of Naranjo, 5km northwest of Sarchí, end up in the bags of Café Bandola that you'll see in all the stores around here. Thanks to the local climate, the beans are of the Valle Occidental variety – something that is explored in greater depth on one of the hacienda's tours, which also cover the nursery, mill and roasting room, as well as a walk around the plantation itself. Tours end with that all-important tasting ($3 extra).

Local **buses** run from Sarchí to Naranjo every 25 minutes (20min); Espíritu Santo is a signposted 800m walk west from the Banco Nacional, opposite the Parque Central in the middle of town.

Parque Nacional Juan Castro Blanco and around

Harbouring the headwaters for five rivers, the 143-square-kilometre **PARQUE NACIONAL JUAN CASTRO BLANCO** is one of Costa Rica's least-explored national parks, partly due to its isolated location but mostly because of its seemingly permanent status as a national-park-in-waiting – scant marked trails and minimal tourist infrastructure in the surrounding villages has made it something of an off-the-beaten-path destination for **hikers** and **wildlife** enthusiasts. Created in 1992 to protect the Platanar and Porvenir volcanoes from logging, more than half the park consists of lush primary forest. Rare species of birds, such as resplendent quetzal and black guan, can be spotted here, while armadillo, tapir, red brocket deer and white-faced capuchin monkeys also roam the park.

The best way to visit the park is on a **tour** with Mapache Tours (Ⓣ2479-8333, Ⓦwww.mapachetours.com), who run full-day trips from La Fortuna ($80). If you want to visit independently, you'll need your own car – the recently improved road from Sarchí is the easiest approach, the rough roads from San Carlos or Zarcero the more spectacular, providing tremendous views as you zigzag down into **Bajos del Toro**, a cluster of corrugated houses 7km from the park entrance. If you need a **guide**, most of the hotels and restaurants in the village can hook you up with a knowledgeable local.

Beyond Bajos del Toro, the road climbs for another 6km before coming to the **Catarata del Toro** (daily 7am–5pm; $10, children $6; Ⓣ2761-0681, Ⓦwww.catarata-del-toro.com), a hugely impressive waterfall that plunges 100m into the caldera of an extinct volcano. Trails lead through primary forest to the base of the falls (500 steps back up) or around the crater rim; the more adventurous can rappel right alongside the thundering cascade ($60).

Accommodation

Accommodation can be found in Bajos del Toro, and in two private reserves just outside the village, which are destinations in their own right.

Bajos del Toro Hotel y Villas 300m south of the church Ⓣ2761-0284. Compact roadside hotel (though "road" is a bit of an exaggeration), where spotless en-suite rooms come with TV and balcony overlooking the bubbling Río Gaurion. ❹

Bosque de Paz 1.5km west of Bajos del Toro, on the road to Zarcero Ⓣ2234-6676, Ⓦwww.bosquedepaz.com. Top birwatching lodge, set in its own cloudforest reserve that features 22km of walking trails and is home to over 330 species of bird, including quetzal and three-wattled bellbird. Attractively rustic rooms, with wrought-iron beds, look out onto the surrounding forest. ❼

El Silencio Lodge & Spa Just south of Bajos del Toro, on the road to Sarchí Ⓣ2761-0301, Ⓦwww.elsilenciolodge.com. Nestled at the foot of a thick wall of cloudforest, the ultra-stylish rooms (two wheelchair-accessible) at this tranquil eco-retreat have bamboo-shrouded outdoor jacuzzis and wooden terraces that enjoy glorious jungle views. There are a bevy of treatments available at the therapeutically sited spa, and various guided hikes head off into the lodge's private reserve. Rates include three meals a day at the excellent restaurant. Profits help fund a local social programme. Two-night min stay. $480

Truchas Nene 400m south of the church ⓣ2761-1932. Amicable setup, with two comfortable *cabinas* featuring hot-water bathrooms, and a restaurant with trout-fishing ponds. Horseriding also available. ❹

San Ramón

At the far western edge of the Valle Central, the colonial town and agricultural centre of **SAN RAMÓN** sits amid verdant rolling hills surrounded by coffee plantations and sugar cane fields. As a crossroads town between San José and La Fortuna, Liberia and the Pacific coast, it receives plenty of tourist traffic, and its leafy Parque Central, home to the imposing Gothic-style **Iglesia de San Ramón** and a couple of museums, makes a decent destination while waiting for onward connections.

Known as the "City of Poets and Presidents", San Ramón has given birth to no less than five of Costa Rica's former leaders, most notably the visionary and social reformer José "Don Pepe" Figueres Ferrer, who famously abolished the military in 1948. His childhood home, opposite the northern side of the church, has been converted into the **Centro Cultural y Historíco José Figueres Ferrer** (Mon–Sat 10am–7pm, free; ⓣ2447-2178, ⓦwww.centrojosefigueres.org), a museum dedicated to his life and politics which also hosts rolling art and photographic exhibitions. Across the road, **Museo de San Ramón** (Mon–Fri 8am–5pm; free; ⓣ2437-9851) is strong on local history.

Practicalities

Buses arrive at and leave from C 16, Av 1/3, 150m west of the Mercado Central, with hourly services to Alajuela (45min) and San José (1hr). There are also services to San Carlos via Zarcero (8 daily; 1hr).

For some entertaining local **tourist information**, pop into the old-world cigar shop *La Casa de Los Hidalgo* (ⓣ2445-5463), one block south of the church, to chew the fat with María Isabelle Coste, its gregarious Cuban owner, and her chain-smoking husband Pablo Hidalgo; the pair are a wealth of local knowledge. There are a number of **banks** clustered just east of the church, including Banco Popular; Banco Nacional is one block south of the church and the **post office** a further two blocks west.

If you need to bunker down in San Ramón, *La Posada Hotel* (ⓣ2445-7359, ⓦwww.posadahotel.net; ❹–❺), four blocks north of the church, is by far the nicest option. Rooms have wide-screen TV, super-clean bathrooms and regal decorative flourishes such as ornate wooden bedheads; internet is included. For a good budget option, *La Cima Lodge* (ⓣ2445-9418; ❸) lies 3km east of town and has basic cabins scattered on a lovely hillside.

Aromas Café, 150m southwest of the *parque* (daily 8am–8pm), is a clean, airy **café** with a garden courtyard out back; fill up on chicken *empanadas* ($2.50) and the like or indulge in some coconut flan or lemon pie (around $2).

Reserva Bosque Nuboso Los Angeles

Roughly 20km northwest of San Ramón, the **RESERVA BOSQUE NUBOSO LOS ANGELES** (daily 8am–4pm; $20; ⓣ2461-0643) is a less crowded alternative to the larger and far more famous cloudforest at Monteverde. Climbing from 700m to nearly 1400m, Los Angeles' twenty square kilometres contain a number of habitats and microclimates, including dark, impenetrable cloudforest, often shrouded in light misty cloud and resounding with the calls of monkeys.

Entrance fees are paid at the office, some 500m from the reserve itself, where you can also hire a guide ($30) to accompany you on one of the two easy dirt-track **trails**: Sendero Anastacio Alfaro (2km; 50min) or the longer Sendero Alberto Brenes (4km; 2hr 30min). Both give a great introduction to the reserve's flora and fauna, and you'll stand a good chance of spotting coatis and racoons.

Additional **activities** include **horseriding** ($20 per hr) and a twice-daily **zip-line canopy tour** (9am & 1.30pm; $50).

Practicalities

To reach the reserve from San Ramón, take a right fork opposite the hospital towards La Fortuna and follow the road until you reach the hamlet of Los Angeles Norte, from where *Villa Blanca* (see below) and the reserve are well signed (note that the last 9km is down a bumpy potholed track). If you don't have your own transport, a taxi from San Ramón costs approximately $20.

You can **stay** near Los Angeles at the *Villa Blanca Cloudforest Hotel and Nature Reserve* (Ⓣ2461-0300, Ⓦwww.villablanca-costarica.com; ❽), whose 35 traditional en-suite *casitas*, complete with wood-burning stoves, are set in their own adjoining private reserve, **El Silencio de Los Angeles**. *Villa Blanca* once belonged to ex-president Rodrigo Carazo – the grounds contain a small chapel, La Mariana, built to celebrate his fiftieth wedding anniversary – but is more notable today for being the first hotel to host an **INBio Research Station**, here to investigate the reserve's staggering variety of moths (some 3000 species). You'll spot a fair few of them on the short trail that runs around the forest fringes, while the hotel runs various guided tours deeper into the reserve ($26; all 2hr). There's also an on-site spa, and a fine-dining restaurant, though its prices cater to a captive audience.

Zarcero

ZARCERO, 52km northwest of Alajuela on Hwy-141, sits at more than 1700m, almost at the highest point of this stretch of the Cordillera Central in an astounding landscape where precipitous inclines plunge into deep gorges, and contented Holstein cattle munch grass in the valleys. A pleasant mountain town, Zarcero's focal point is its Parque Central, dotted with a motley collection of fabulous, Doctor Seuss-like **topiary sculptures**: an elephant, a helicopter, a dinosaur, along with Gaudí-esque archways of scented hedges, all the work of Costa Rican landscape gardener Evangelisto Blanco.

Zarcero is also known for its organic produce as well as a fresh, white, relatively bland **cheese**, called *palmito* (heart-of-palm, which is what it looks like); you can buy it from any of the shops near the bus stop on the south side of the main square.

Practicalities

Buses leave from C 12, Av 7/9 in San José every 45 minutes and from La Coca-Cola at 9.15am, 12.20pm, 4.20pm and 5.20pm (both 1hr 30min), arriving in Zarcero on the northern side of the main square; they depart from the southwest corner, for San José (every 45min or so), San Ramón (every 2hr; 1hr) and San Carlos (every 30min–1hr; 1hr). Banco de Costa Rica on Zarcero's main street changes **travellers' cheques** and has an ATM.

The small, friendly *Hotel Don Beto* (Ⓣ2463-3137, Ⓔrickhoteldonbeto@hotmail.com; ❹) is on the northern corner of the Parque Central. You'll find only a few **places to eat**, most near the main square: *Restaurante El Higaron* and *Pizzeria Galería* both serve decent, inexpensive local food.

Parque Nacional Volcán Poás

PARQUE NACIONAL VOLCÁN POÁS (daily 8am–4pm; $10, $2 parking; Ⓣ2482-2165), 38km north of Alajuela, is home to one of the world's most accessible active volcanoes, with a history of eruptions that goes back eleven million years. Poás' last gigantic blowout was on January 25, 1910, when it dumped 640,000 tons of ash on the surrounding area, and from time to time you may find the volcano off-limits due to sulphurous gas emissions and other seismic activities – it was closed for a while following the **Chinchona Earthquake** in January 2009 (see box opposite). It's worth checking conditions with the park before you set off, but even if all's well, you'll still need to get to the volcano before the clouds roll in, which they invariably do at around 10am.

The park

Though measuring just 65 square kilometres, Poás packs a punch: it's a strange, otherworldly landscape, dotted with smoking fumaroles (steam vents) and tough ferns and trees valiantly surviving regular scaldings with sulphurous gases – the battle-scarred *sombrilla de pobre*, or poor man's umbrella, looks the most woebegone. The volcano itself has blasted out three craters in its lifetime, and due to the more-or-less constant activity, the appearance of the **main crater** changes regularly – it's currently 1500m wide and filled with milky turquoise water from which sulphurous gases waft and bubble (with a ph value of 0.8, this is reputably the most acidic lake on earth). Although it's an impressive sight, you only need about fifteen minutes' viewing and picture-snapping; otherwise, you can take one of the short trails that lead off the main route to the crater.

The park's **visitor centre** (daily 8.30am–3.15pm) shows film of the volcano – handy if the real thing is covered by cloud – and has a couple of displays explaining the science behind it; there's also a simple snack shop, but you're probably better off packing a picnic or grabbing lunch at one of the nearby restaurants (see opposite).

The trails

From the visitor centre, a few very well-maintained, short and unchallenging **trails** lead through a rare type of cloudforest called **dwarf** or **stunted cloudforest**, a combination of pine-needle-like ferns, miniature bonsai-type trees and bromeliad-encrusted ancient arboreal cover, all of which have been kept clipped by the

Watching wildlife at Volcán Poás

Birds ply this temperate forest, from the colourful but shy quetzal to the robin and several species of hummingbird, including the endemic **Poás volcano hummingbird**, distinguished by its iridescent rose-red throat. Although a number of large **mammals** live in the confines of the park, including wildcats such as the margay, you're unlikely to spot them around the crater; one animal you will come across, however, is the small, green-yellow **Poás squirrel**, unique to the region.

The Cinchona Earthquake

In the early afternoon of January 8, 2009, an **earthquake** measuring 6.2 on the Richter scale struck the area just west of Volcán Poás, leaving at least 34 people dead and making thousands homeless. The worst quake to hit Costa Rica in nearly 150 years, it destroyed the village of **Cinchona** and scythed through nearby **Vara Blanca**; **Poasito** and **Fraijanes** were also damaged, while landslides affected **Parque Nacional Volcán Poás** and buried parts of **La Paz Waterfall Gardens** (see p.142), stranding some 300 tourists in the process.

The area's return to normality has been slow. Aftershocks continued in the Valle Central throughout the year – more than 2000 **tremors** were registered along the Chinchona fault line in 2009 – and workers were still repairing damage to the region's roads and buildings more than a year on; at the time of writing, the road north to San Miguel remained closed. The national park and gardens have long since reopened, though, and from the dust, a new community, **Nueva Cinchona**, is rising – built in Cariblanco, 6km from the original, it will house 1200 of the survivors who lost their homes in the surrounding area.

cold weather (temperatures can drop to below freezing), continual cloud cover, and acid rain from the mouth of the volcano.

The **Crater Overlook Trail**, which winds around the main crater along a paved road, is only 750m long and is accessible to wheelchairs and pushchairs. A side trail (830m; 20–30min; last access 2.30pm) heads through the forest to the pretty, emerald **Lago Botos** that fills an extinct crater and is a lovely spot to picnic. Named for the pagoda-like tree commonly seen along its way, the **Escalonia Trail** (1km; 30min) starts at the picnic area (follow the signs), taking you through ground cover less stunted than that at the crater.

Getting to the park

Most visitors visit Poás on a pre-arranged **tour** from San José (around $45, including return transport and guide; see p.123 for details of tour operators) or Alajuela. Otherwise, a Tuasa **bus** leaves daily from Av 2, C12/14 in San José at 8.30am, travelling via their terminal in Alajuela (9.15am) and returning from the volcano at 2.30pm. If you want to reach Poás before the tour buses and, more importantly, dense cloud cover arrive, you'll need to either drive or take a **taxi** from Alajuela or San José.

Accommodation

No **camping** is allowed in the park, but if you want to get a really early start to beat the clouds, you'll find plenty of places to stay in the vicinity, including a couple of comfortable **mountain lodges** on working dairy farms (though you'll need a car to get to them) and other, simpler and cheaper *cabinas* lining the road leading up to the volcano and reached on the bus to Poás.

Lagunillas Lodge Signposted 2km south of the park, and down a very steep 1km rutted dirt track, accessible by 4WD only ☎8389-5842. Tico-family-owned, this high-altitude rustic lodge offers rooms and *cabinas* with hot water. The views are simply breathtaking and you can even catch your dinner (from $7.50) from the on-site trout pond. For added kicks, take a guided hike or horse trot through the surrounding forest. ❺

Poás Lodge 6km south of the park on the road from Alajuela ☎2482-1091, Ⓦwww.poaslodge.com. The friendly new (South African) owners have injected some much-needed life into this pleasant little spot on the road up to Poás. Its smart rooms, which include a six-bed dorm ($15) and a spacious family room (❺), seem to hang out over the valley; the restaurant (daily 8am–8pm) enjoys the same superb views and makes a great lunchtime stop for cheeseburgers and the like. Free shuttle to the park leaves daily at 8am. ❹

Poás Volcano Lodge 6km east of Poasito, which is 10km before the park, on the road from Alajuela; take a right towards Vara Blanca ⓣ2482-2194, ⓦwww.poasvolcanolodge.com. Set on a working dairy farm, this rustic lodge was severely damaged by the Cinchona Earthquake and was undergoing a stylish-looking renovation at the time of writing. The standard en-suite rooms are nice enough, but it's better to fork out for the junior suites ($110). Master suites with floor-to-ceiling windows ($250) are being built in the new main lodge, which features an attractive eating area with sunken fireplace. Walking trails run through the extensive grounds, and there's a basement games room with pool and ping-pong tables. The lodge is 5km from La Paz and offers discounted tickets to the gardens. ❻

Eating and drinking

There are some great places to stop for a bite **to eat** on the way to or from Poás, including some of the best *tipíco* cuisine in the area and an unexpectedly good gourmet French restaurant.

La Casa del Café de la Luis 10km north of Alajuela, on the road to Poás. Roadside outlet of the Doka Estate – and thereby serving some mighty smooth Café Tres Generaciones roasts – this lovely little café enjoys superb views of the surrounding coffee fields from its breezy balcony. Daily 7am–5pm.

Chubascos Fraijanes, 12km south of the park on the road from Alajuela ⓣ2482-2280, ⓦwww.restaurantechubascos.com. This extremely welcoming and relaxed restaurant, overlooking a large garden, draws crowds for its superlative local cuisine – the *gallotes*, huge tortillas heaped with various goodies (from $5) take some beating – and top-notch *casados* (from $4.50). The area around the volcano abounds with strawberry fields, and *Chubascos* makes one of the best strawberry *refrescos* in the country. Mon–Fri 10.30am–5pm, Sat 9.30am–9pm, Sun 9.30am–5.30pm.

Colbert Restaurant About 1km past the *Poás Volcano Lodge* (see above), in Vara Blanca ⓣ2482-2776, ⓦwww.colbert.co.cr. It can come as quite a surprise to stumble upon this smart French restaurant, perched on a hill at the eastern end of Vara Blanca, just beyond the petrol station – the menu includes such Gallic delights as rabbit fillet in Dijon mustard ($13) and seafood casserole à La Rochelle ($15), the chef's former haunt. Daily noon–9pm, closed Thurs.

Jaulares 15km north of Alajuela, on the road to Poás ⓣ2482-2155, ⓦwww.jaulares.com. Simple restaurant with *tipíco* dishes, using local produce cooked on a wood-burning stove (try the *sopa negra*; $3), and a generous buffet ($12). Live music Sat. Daily 7am–9pm, Fri & Sat till midnight, Sun till 8pm.

La Paz Waterfall Gardens

One of Costa Rica's most popular attractions, the **LA PAZ WATERFALL GARDENS** (daily 8am–5pm; $35, children $20; ⓣ2482-2720, ⓦwww.waterfallgardens.com), 15km east of Poás, bore the brunt of the Cinchona Earthquake (see box, p.141), with landslides washing out several of the trails and causing extensive damage to the grounds, closing the gardens for five months. The resulting renovations, however, have returned La Paz to its former glory, and enabled the owners to make a number of improvements and additions.

Self-guided tours meander through a pretty garden planted with native shrubs and flowers, taking in a butterfly observatory; orchid display; frog house; snake garden; hummingbird garden, home to 26 different species; and, the newest attraction, a **jungle cat** exhibit ($5 extra). The 35 felines here were brought to La Paz when the rescue centre housing them closed, and it is now home to five of Costa Rica's six cats (only the oncilla is absent); it's hoped that any future offspring will be released back into the wild.

Beyond the frog house, an immaculate series of riverside trails links five **waterfalls** on the Río La Paz, starting with Tempio and winding past Magia Blanca – the highest, which crashes deafeningly 40m down into swirling white water – before concluding at the top of the eponymous La Paz Waterfall, Costa Rica's most photographed cascade (it can also be seen from the public highway that runs over a large rickety bridge below); viewing platforms at various points along the way place you above and beneath the falls.

Practicalities

When the road to San Miguel reopens, **buses** heading to Puerto Viejo de Sarapiqui (via Heredia) from San José's Terminal del Caribe on Calle Central, Av 15, will pass by La Paz again; for the time being, though, you'll need to visit the gardens as part of an organized **tour** – Expediciones Tropicales (see p.123) includes La Paz as part of their combination tour. If you're **driving**, take a right at the junction in Poasito towards Vara Blanca and, on reaching the village, take a left at the petrol station and follow the well-marked signs for about 5km.

You can **stay** at the luxurious but expensive *Peace Lodge* (Ⓣ2482-2720, Ⓦwww.waterfallgardens.com; $275, breakfast not included), where the handsome rooms feature handmade canopy beds, stained-glass windows, private bathrooms, hot tubs and balconies overlooking the gardens (and up to Volcán Poás). Staying in the lodge entitles you to entry to the gardens outside the official opening hours, when you can explore its lush expanses away from the otherwise constant crowds.

If you're feeling hungry during your visit, pop into the decent **café** in the park reception area (set lunch $12), that serves typical Costa Rican cuisine with an upper level that overlooks the lovely gardens.

Heredia and around

Just 11km northeast of San José lies the lively city of **HEREDIA,** boosted by the student population of the Universidad Nacional (UNA), at the eastern end of town. The town centre is a little run-down, with the Parque Central flanked by tall palms and a few historical buildings. Although there's not a great deal to see in town, Heredia is a natural jumping-off point for excursions to **Volcán Barva**, and many tourists also come for the **Café Britt tour**, hosted by the nation's largest coffee exporter, about 3km north of the town centre.

As befits a university town, Heredia is also home to the excellent **Intercultura Spanish language school** (Ⓣ2260-8480, Ⓦwww.interculturacostarica.com), with rates from $285 a week ($425 including homestay).

Arrival and information

Heredia has no central bus terminal, but a variety of well-signed **bus stops** are scattered around town, with a heavy concentration around the Mercado Central. **Buses** from San José (every 5min; 30min) and Alajuela (every 15min; 45min), arrive in Heredia on Avenida 8, just east of the market: they leave from here too (same frequencies), as do buses for Santo Domingo (for INBioparque; every 10min; 15min). Frequent **local services** to Barva (for Café Britt and the Museo de Cultura Popular) and, much less so, Sacramento (for Volcán Barva; 3 daily; 1hr 45min) leave from stops along Avenida 8 and Calle 1. **Taxis** line up on the east side of the market, and on the southern side of the Parque Central.

The commuter train, the **Tren Urbano**, from San José's Estación del Atlántico arrives at the station in Heredia, on Av 10, C 0 (Mon–Fri every half-hour 6.20–8.50am & 4.30–8.20pm; 20min), returning every half-hour from 6 to 8.30am and from 4 to 8pm (20min).

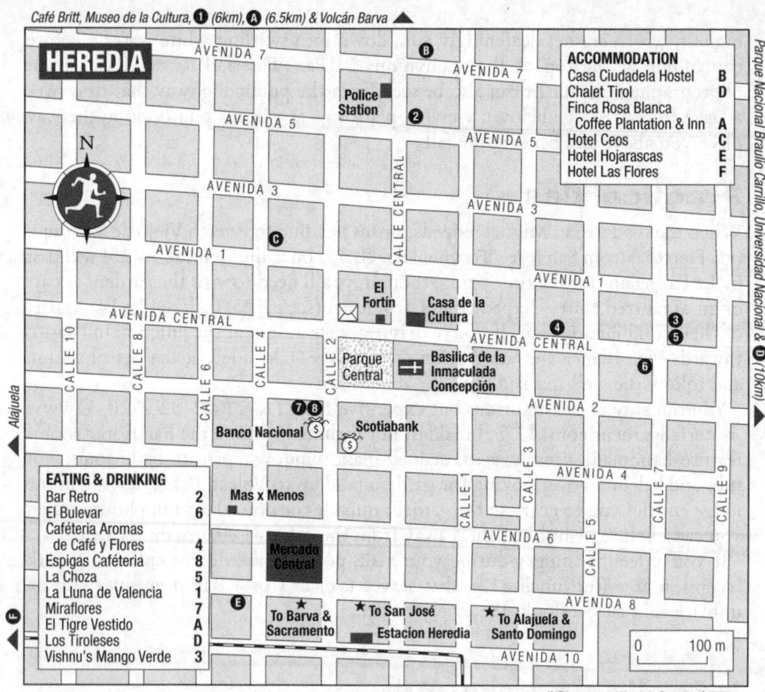

The Banco Nacional at C 2, Av 2/4 and Scotiabank at Av 4, C 0/2 both have **ATMs**, and change currency and travellers' cheques. The **post office** (Mon–Fri 8am–5.30pm, Sat 8am–noon) is on the northwest corner of the Parque Central.

Accommodation

While decent **accommodation** in downtown Heredia is pretty sparse, it's unlikely, in any case, that you'll need to stay in town; San José is within easy reach, and there are several country hotels nearby, including *Finca Rosa Blanca*, one of the finest in the country.

In town

Casa Ciudadela Hostel Av 7, C 0/1 ⓣ2263-5578, ⓦwww.casaciudadela.com. The nicest hostel in town is on a quiet residential street and has mixed and women-only dorms ($15) with brand-new mattresses. There's a spacious communal kitchen, complimentary breakfast, and a sweet little garden. ❹

Hotel Ceos Corner of Av 1 y C 4 ⓣ2262-2628, ⓦwww.hotelamericacr.com. Quiet hotel with spotless but no-frills en-suite rooms, some with balconies. For meals, try the hotel's decent seafood restaurant. ❸

Hotel Hojarascas Av 8, C 4/6, ⓣ2261-3649, ⓦwww.hotelhojarascas.com. The comfortable whitewashed rooms, offset by bright bed linen, are spotless, but it's the incredibly friendly owners who make the difference at this popular spot in the southwest part of town. It's quite a pricey option for Heredia, but you get what you pay for – which includes a delicious Continental buffet of fruits and freshly baked pastries plus free internet, airport pick-up/drop-off and luggage storage. ❺

Hotel Las Flores Av 12, C 12/14, ⓣ2261-8147, ⓦwww.hotel-lasflores.com. While it's a bit of hike or a short taxi ride from the centre, it's more than worth it for the bright, immaculate rooms with balconies and spotless hot-water bathrooms. ❷

Out of town

Chalet Tirol 10km north of Heredia, well signposted on the road to Los Angeles via San

Rafael ⓣ2267-6222, ⓦwww.hotelchaleteltirol.com. Sitting in a lovely pine forest on the edge of the Parque Nacional Braulio Carrillo, this incredibly kitsch hotel with ten alpine chalets was built to accommodate diners at *Los Tiroleses*, its renowned French restaurant (see p.146). The grounds contain a reproduction Tirol (traditional Austrian-style) village church for concerts and events. Guided walking tours also available. ❻–❼

Finca Rosa Blanca Coffee Plantation & Inn On the road between Barva and Santa Bárbara, 6.5km northwest of Heredia ⓣ2269-9392, ⓦwww.fincarosablanca.com. One of the top hotels in Costa Rica, this classy place roosts like a giant white bird above the surrounding coffee fields. The thirteen unique suites, four of which can be opened up to form two villas ($490), have been beautifully decorated with hand-painted murals, and feature bamboo-fibre linen, outdoor jacuzzis and the like. You can relax in the fairy-tale-like main lounge or take a dip in the gorgeous tiled pool, set among Higueron trees and seemingly dripping over the hillside. The restaurant is also one of the area's best (see p.146). The hotel runs a sustainability tour (*Finca Rosa Blanca* has flawless eco-credentials) and a recommended tour of its organic coffee fields (see p.146). From $290.

The Town

Heredia's quiet **Parque Central**, shaded by towering palm trees, marks the centre of town. Overlooking the Parque is the **Basílica de la Inmaculada Concepción**, whose unexciting squat design – "seismic Baroque" – has kept it standing through several earthquakes since 1797. North of the *parque*, the old colonial tower of **El Fortín**, "The Fortress" (no access), features odd gun slats that fan out and widen from the inside to the exterior, giving it a medieval look.

East of the tower on Avenida Central, the **Casa de la Cultura** (daily 8am–8pm), a colonial house with a large breezy veranda, formerly home to President Alfredo Gonzáles Flores (1913–17), displays local art, including sculpture and paintings by Heredia schoolchildren. The **Mercado Central** (daily 5am–6pm) is a clean, orderly place, its aisles lined with rows of fruits and veggies, dangling sausages and plump prawns.

Eating and drinking

With such a large student population, Heredia is crawling with excellent cafés, patisseries, ice-cream joints and vegetarian **restaurants**. The low-key **nightlife** is concentrated around the four blocks immediately to the west of the Universidad Nacional, in the east of Heredia.

In town

Bar Retro C 0, Av 5. Kick back with a beer in this popular bar – an overgrown shed of a place that is unnervingly close to the police station – while rocking out to the strains of Janis Joplin, The Doors and Led Zeppelin. Daily 1pm–midnight.

El Bulevar Av 0, C 7. The "in" place for Heredia's student population, this lively sports bar opens to the street so you can people-watch while downing inexpensive beer-and-*boca* specials. Daily 11am–1.30am.

Caféteria Aromas de Café y Flores Av 0, C 3/5. Next door to a florist, the walls of this spacious café are adorned with historical photographs of Heredia. The extensive menu includes all-day breakfast, sandwiches, fajitas, steaks and an assortment of cakes. Daily 8am–8pm, Sat & Sun till 6pm.

La Choza Av C, C7. This pumping bar is popular with students, who spill out onto the first- and second-floor plant-lined balconies.

Espigas Caféteria Southwest corner of Parque Central. You'll find all your hangover needs at this central café: cappuccino, sweet pastries and filling breakfasts ($6) should get your day off to a good start. Daily 7am–9.30pm.

Miraflores Av 2, C 2/4. Heredians dance salsa and merengue at this lively disco and bar, the longest-running in the country, that attracts a slightly older crowd. Daily 8pm–5.30am, Fri–Sun till 6am.

Vishnu's Mango Verde C 7, Av 0/1. One of a chain of vegetarian eateries, this rustic, plant-filled restaurant has a pretty back garden and serves good vegetarian food, including sandwiches made to order (from $3). Mon–Thurs 8am–6pm, Fri & Sat, Sun 9am–6pm.

Out of town

La Lluna de Valencia San Pedro de Barva, 6km northwest of Heredia ⓣ2269-6665, ⓦwww.lallunadevalencia.com. The gregarious owner Vincente works the tables at this top Spanish outpost on the road to Alajuela. Tapas (around $8) are decent, but the house speciality is, naturally, paella ($11), large and lip-smackingly tasty. Music (acoustic guitar sets, flamenco) at the weekends. Thurs 7–10pm, Fri & Sat noon–10pm, Sun noon–5pm.

El Tigre Vestido *Finca Rosa Blanca Coffee Plantation & Inn*, on the road between San Pedro de Barva and Santa Bárbara de Heredia ⓣ2269-9392, ⓦwww.finca-rblanca.co.cr. The small, smart restaurant at this beautiful hotel specializes in "Legacy Dining", refined household cooking that celebrates the cuisine of Costa Rica and Central America in general. Eat out on the terrace overlooking the surrounding coffee fields, where market-fresh food from local organic farmers is served in such dishes as pumpkin soup ($8) and *panko*-style pork loin with *boniato* purée and coffee sauce ($20). Advance reservation only. Daily 7–9pm.

Los Tiroleses *Chalet Tirol*, 10km north of Heredia, well signposted on the road to Los Angeles via San Rafael ⓣ2267-6222, ⓦwww.hotelchaleteltirol.com. One of Costa Rica's most acclaimed French restaurants (the chef is Cordon Bleu-trained), with an elegant dining area adorned with murals and a large and eclectically stocked wine cellar. Try the excellent bean-heavy *cassoulet*.

Café Britt

Just north of Heredia on the road to Barva, you'll see signs off the highway directing you to **Café Britt** (tours daily at 9.30am & 11am, also 3pm mid-Dec to April; $20; 1hr 30min; ⓣ2777-1600, ⓦwww.coffeetour.com), where you can get an idea of how the modern-day coffee industry operates. The *finca* grows one of the country's best-known brands and is the most important exporter of Costa Rican coffee to the world. Guides take you through the history of coffee growing in Costa Rica, demonstrating how crucial this export crop was to the development of the country, with a rather polished presentation and thorough descriptions of the processes involved in harvesting and selecting the beans. Once you've toured the plantation, roasting factory and drying patios, it's back for a coffee-cupping demo and, of course, the inevitable stop in the gift shop. For Golden Bean gourmets, there's also a "Coffee Lover's" tour to a nearby coffee mill (daily 11am; $35; 4hr including lunch).

The half-hourly **bus** from Heredia to Barva runs past the turning to Café Britt, from where it's a 400m walk. Otherwise, the *finca* can pick up visitors and return them to most San José hotels ($17 extra).

Museo de Cultura Popular

The unusual **Museo de Cultura Popular** (Mon–Fri 8am–4pm, Sun 10am–5pm; $3; ⓣ2260-1619, ⓦwww.museo.una.ac.cr), a couple of kilometres beyond the Café Britt turn-off, recreates coffee-plantation life from the late nineteenth and early twentieth century. Set in a large house with verandas, and surrounded by coffee fields, it features rooms recreated in the style of that time. The emphasis is firmly on education – access in the week is by guided tour for large groups only ($7, includes one or two cooking workshops, depending on group size; reserve in advance) – a concept that stems to the **restaurant** as well, which serves authentic food of the period, including *torta de arroz* (layered rice casserole), *pan casero* (a type of sweet bread) and *gallos picadillos* (a mixture of meat, vegetables and rice).

Finca Rosa Blanca

For an interesting alternative to large-group **coffee tours**, follow the road through Barva and northwest to Santa Bárbara de Heredia and the coffee fields at **Finca Rosa Blanca Coffee Plantation & Inn** (tours daily 8am & 11am, Nov–April also

1pm; $20; 2hr; book in advance on ⓣ2269-9392 or at ⓦwww.fincarosablanca.com). The plantation at this fantastic hotel (see p.145) is one of the country's few **organic** setups – the beans are fertilized using rich soil from the hotel's vermiculture and compost made from their restaurant refuse, while the fields are planted with various trees and plants that help the crop's growth: *pejibaye* to deter insects, bananas to help retain moisture during the dry season, palms for shade. The resident expert passionately guides visitors through the science behind this, plus there's the chance (in season) to join in the harvesting or roasting. As a renowned *barista*, his tasting tips at the closing cupping session are second to none.

INBioparque

Four kilometres southwest of Heredia in Santo Domingo, **INBioparque** (Tues–Fri 8.30am–4pm last admission 2pm, Sat & Sun 9am–4.30pm last admission 3.30pm; $23, children $13; ⓣ2507-8107, ⓦwww.inbioparque.com) is a small educational and recreational centre set up by the not-for-profit Instituto Nacional de Biodiversidad to explain, in simple terms, how biodiversity works and why it's so important. The park comprises a projection room with an audiovisual presentation on Costa Rican flora and fauna, instructive displays, and **guided trails** (30min–2hr) through four small botanical gardens filled with plants and animals from the country's main ecosystems – Valle Central forest, rainforest, tropical dry forest and wetland – as well as a small petting farm. Although mostly aimed at schoolchildren and students, the park is a good place for budding naturalists to learn to identify native species – it's home to 51 species of bird and nearly 600 native plant species. There's a café and restaurant on site. You can get here on the local **bus** from Heredia, which runs to the village of Santo Domingo (every 10min; 15min).

Parque Nacional Braulio Carrillo

PARQUE NACIONAL BRAULIO CARRILLO, 15km northeast of Heredia, covers nearly 500 square kilometres of virgin rainforest and dense cloudforest, but draws few visitors on account of its sheer size and lack of facilities – most tourists experience the majestic views of thick foliage only from the window of a bus on their way to the Caribbean coast. Those that do spend any length of time here tend to spend it tackling **Volcán Barva**, which dominates the southwest corner of the park and is accessed from the village of Sacramento.

The park is named after Costa Rica's third, and rather dictatorial, chief of state, who held office in the mid-1800s. It was established in 1978 to protect the land from the possible effects of the **Guápiles Highway**, then under construction between San José and Limón, a piece of intelligent foresight without which this whole stretch of countryside might have been turned into a solid strip of petrol stations and motels.

Note that, unfortunately, **security** is a growing problem in the park; if driving, never leave anything in your car, and always use a **guide** for longer hikes – though these are only available at Quebrada Gonzalez ($15 for 3–4hr).

Quebrada Gonzalez

Three short, circular **trails** lead off from the ranger station at **Quebrada Gonzalez** (daily 8am–3.30pm; $8; ⓣ2268-1039), on the Guápiles Highway, 2km east of the Río Sucio bridge – though as they are narrow, steep and often ungroomed, they can take longer than you might think to complete. **Las Palmas**

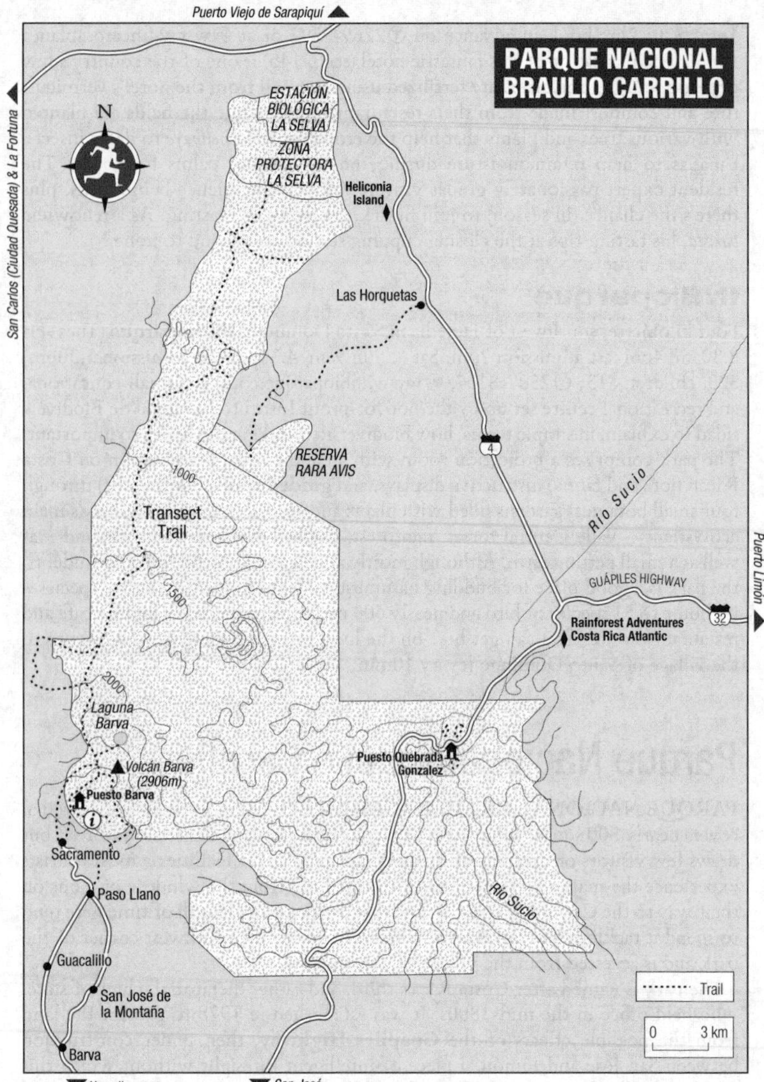

(1.6km), just behind the ranger station, is a good bet for birds; directly across the Guápiles Highway, **El Ceibo** (1km) loops down to the Río Sucio, named "Dirty River" due to its discolouration by minerals; while the high-hiking route of **Botarrama** (2.5km) is more likely to provide chance encounters with some of the park's animals.

Volcán Barva

Most people visit the more popular Barva section of the park (daily 8am–3.30pm; $8; ⓣ2261-2619) with just one aim: climbing **Volcán Barva**, a forest-clad peak

Watching wildlife in Braulio Carrillo

Due to its enormous size and varied altitude, Braulio Carrillo has one of the highest levels of biodiversity in Costa Rica, with over 530 species of **birds**, including the rare quetzal (mostly seen at higher elevations), toucans, trogons and eagles, and some 135 species of **mammals**, such as collared peccary, paca, jaguar and ocelot. The park, particularly the Barva area, is one of the few places in the country where the bushmaster (*matabuey*), Central America's largest **venomous snake**, makes its home, along with the equally poisonous fer-de-lance (*terciopelo*).

that tops out at just over 2900m. From the ranger station, **trails** (5km; 4hr round-trip) ascend through dense deciduous cover, giving fleeting panoramic views over the Valle Central and southeast to Volcán Irazú along the way. At the summit, the striking green-blue **Laguna Barva** fills the small, pristine crater, surrounded by dense forest that is often obscured in cloud. Take a compass, water and food, a sweater and rain gear, and leave early in the morning to enjoy the clearest views of the top.

The **Transect Trail**, which leads north through the park from here as far as the Estacíon Biologica La Selva (see p.246), takes around four days to complete and is strictly for highly experienced jungle hikers only; you'd need to be totally self-sufficient, and take all your food, water and camping equipment with you.

Park practicalities

Hourly **buses** from San José's Terminal de Caribe pass the **Quebrada Gonzalez** ranger station (about 45min) en route to Limón and Puerto Viejo de Sarapiqui; for the return journey, it's a case of flagging one down on the highway. For **Volcán Barva**, buses run from Heredia (Mon–Sat 6.25am, 11.45am & 3.55pm, Sun 6.30am, 11am & 4pm; 1hr 45min) to the tiny hamlet of Sacramento, from where it's a 3km walk up a steep track to the Barva ranger station; buses back to Heredia leave at 7.30am, 1pm (12.30pm on Sun) and (most conveniently) 5pm. You'll need a 4WD if **driving** to Volcán Barva, even in the dry season.

Accommodation within the park consists of a camping area (with toilets and running water) and two very basic huts at the Volcán Barva ranger station ($2 per person; reserve in advance); the huts can sleep up to four people each, although there are no mattresses on the beds. The closest lodgings to the park are at *Cabañas Las Milenas* (Ⓣ2266-0015, Ⓦwww.grupoardillas.com/milenas_index.htm; ❻, includes use of spa at weekends), around 5km south of Volcán Barva, where eleven log cabins are dotted among the trees, each with private bathroom, TV and open fireplace. The **restaurant** serves food cooked over a coffee-wood fire.

Rainforest Adventures Costa Rica Atlantic

The brainchild of American naturalist Donald Perry, the Rainforest Aerial Tram, now rebranded by some marketing whizz as the **Rainforest Adventures Costa Rica Atlantic** (daily 7am–4pm; tram $55, children $27.50, various multi-activity packages available; Ⓣ2257-5961, Ⓦwww.rainforesttram.com), lies just beyond the northeastern boundary of Parque Nacional Braulio Carrillo,

1.5km from the Guápiles Highway. Funded by private investors, and the product of many years' research, the tram was, when it opened in the mid-1990s, the first of its kind in the world (there's now another one in Costa Rica near Jacó on the Pacific coast; see p.359). Its premise is beautifully simple: twenty overhead cable cars, each holding five passengers and one guide, run slowly (and largely silently) along the 2.6km aerial track, skirting the tops of the forest and passing between trees, providing eye-level encounters along the way. The ride (45min each way) affords a rare glimpse of birds, animals and plants, including the epiphytes, orchids, insects and mosses that live in the upper reaches of the forest – wear a hat and insect repellent, and bring binoculars, camera and rain gear. For those staying in the lodge (see below), **torchlit night rides** (until 9pm) examine the canopy's nocturnal inhabitants.

To view the treetops at a faster pace, you can sign up for the new **canopy tour** ($45; no children under 12), which sends you whizzing through the forest along seven zip lines. More conventionally, you can also explore the park via a network of ground-level trails (included in the price), or on a number of full-day **guided tours**, such as birdwatching and trekking (both $82.50, including tram ride and, on the trek, breakfast and a picnic lunch). A **butterfly and frog garden** ($10) and a **serpentarium** (daily 6.30am–4pm, Mon from 9am; $10) complete the attractions.

In his book, *Life Above the Jungle Floor* (see p.460), Perry tells how he risked life and limb to get the project started. Committed to protecting the rainforest canopy and the jungle floor, he refused to allow the construction firm erecting the tram's high-wire towers to use tractors; they were unable to secure a powerful enough helicopter in Costa Rica, but Nicaragua's Sandinistas came to the rescue, loaning one of their MI-17 combat helicopters (minus the guns) to help erect the poles.

Practicalities

Hourly **buses** from San José's Terminal de Caribe to Limón and Puerto Viejo de Sarapiqui can drop you off at the turn-off for the Aerial Tram (about 1hr), from where it's a 1.5km walk; to get back to San José, you'll need to flag down buses on the highway. It's much easier to take a **tour**, either directly with the tram's San José office on Av 7, C 5/7 ($77, including return transport, guided tram ride and hiking on nature trails), or on one of the combination tours offered by several San José-based agencies (see p.123).

You can **stay** at the tram's expensive jungle lodge (Ⓣ1-866-759-8736; $300), which comprises ten luxury bungalows, all with views of the forest. Rates include two tram rides, a morning birdwatching tour, unlimited access to the trails in the company of an expert guide, and three meals a day.

Cartago and around

Founded in 1563 by Juan Vazquez de Coronado, **CARTAGO**, meaning "Carthage", was Costa Rica's capital for three hundred years before the centre of power was moved to San José in 1823. Like its ancient namesake, the city has been razed a number of times, although in this case by earthquakes instead of Romans – two, in 1823 and 1910, almost demolished the place. Most of the town's fine nineteenth-century and *fin-de-siècle* buildings were destroyed, and what has grown up in their place – the usual assortment of shops and haphazard modern buildings – is not particularly appealing. Nowadays, Cartago functions mainly as a busy

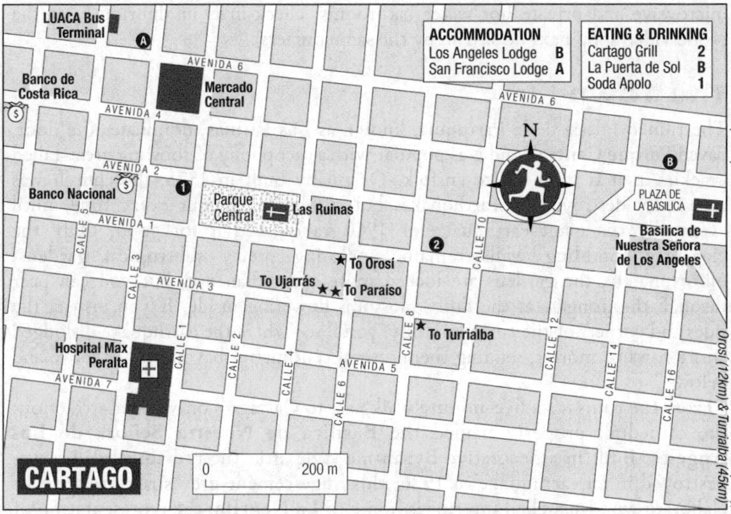

CARTAGO

ACCOMMODATION	
Los Angeles Lodge	B
San Francisco Lodge	A

EATING & DRINKING	
Cartago Grill	2
La Puerta de Sol	B
Soda Apolo	1

LUACA Bus Terminal
Banco de Costa Rica
Mercado Central
Banco Nacional
Parque Central
Las Ruinas
Plaza de la Basilica
Basilica de Nuestra Señora de Los Angeles
Hospital Max Peralta
To Orosí
To Ujarrás
To Paraiso
To Turrialba
San José
Volcán Irazú (32km)
Jardín Botánico Lankester (4km), Orosí (12km) & Turrialba (45km)
Avenida 1, Avenida 2, Avenida 3, Avenida 4, Avenida 5, Avenida 6, Avenida 7
Calle 1, Calle 2, Calle 3, Calle 4, Calle 5, Calle 6, Calle 8, Calle 10, Calle 12, Calle 14, Calle 16
0 200 m

market and shopping centre, with some industry around its periphery. The star attraction is its soaring **cathedral**, or *basílica*, dedicated to La Negrita, Costa Rica's patron saint.

Arrival and information

LUMACA **buses** leave from Av 10, C 5 in San José every ten minutes (45min), arriving in Cartago at their terminal on Calle 5. Cartago's **taxi** rank is at Las Ruinas.

Banco de Costa Rica and Banco Nacional have **ATMs** and will change **travellers' cheques**. The **post office** is ten minutes from the town centre at Av 2, C 15/17 (Mon–Fri 7.30am–6pm, Sat 7.30am–noon).

Accommodation

You're unlikely to get stranded in Cartago, but if you do need a **hotel** one of the most decent is the *Los Angeles Lodge* (ⓣ2551-0957, ⓔhotel.los.angeles@hotmail.com; ④), on the corner of Avenida 4 and Calle 16, opposite the *basílica*; the clean rooms, some large enough for a family, have private bathrooms and TV, and there's a reasonable restaurant (see p.153). Alternatively, the *San Francisco Lodge* (ⓣ2551-4804; ③), one block north of the Mercado Central on C 3, Av 6/8, has perfectly respectable rooms, all with three beds, cable TV, coffee maker, fridge,

Moving on from Cartago

LUMACA **buses** for **San José** leave every ten minutes (24hr) from their terminal at C 5, Av 6/8 (45min). In the other direction, regular buses for **Turrialba** (Mon–Fri 5.45am, 4pm & 5.45pm, Sat 6.15am, more on Sun; 1hr 20min) leave from a stop on Av 3, C 8. Local services are frequent and reliable: buses for **Paraíso** (for the Jardín Botánico Lankester; every 5min; 15min) and **Orosi** (every 30min till 8pm, then hourly till 10pm; 45min) use the stops on C 6, Av 1/3; buses for **Cachí** (for Ujarrás; 25min) leave roughly hourly from Av 3, C 4/6.

microwave and private hot-water bathrooms; check-in is insalubriously at the erotic video shop next door (run by the same owners).

The Town

The ruined Iglesia de la Parroquía, known as **Las Ruinas**, dominates the dour, paved **Parque Central**, and is as popular with a cacophony of roosting great-tailed grackles as it is with the townsfolk. Originally built in 1575, the church was repeatedly destroyed by earthquakes but stubbornly rebuilt every time, until eventually the giant earthquake of 1910 vanquished it for good. Only the elegantly tumbling walls remain, enclosing pretty subtropical gardens; unfortunately, the gardens are locked more often than not, but you can peer through the irongate at the fluffy blossoms flowering inside. If you inspect the sides and corners of the ruins carefully, you'll see where the earthquake dislodged entire rows of mortar, sending them several centimetres beyond those above and below.

From the ruins it's a five-minute walk east to Cartago's only other attraction: the cathedral, properly named the **Basílica de Nuestra Señora de Los Angeles**. Built in a decorative Byzantine style after the previous basilica was destroyed in an earthquake in 1926, this huge cement-grey structure with its elaborate wood-panelled interior is home to **La Negrita**, the representation of the Virgin of Los Angeles, patron saint of Costa Rica. On this spot on August 2, 1635, the Virgin reportedly showed herself to a poor peasant girl in the form of a dark doll made of stone. Each time the girl took the doll away to play with it, it mulishly reappeared on the spot where she had found it; this was seen as a sign, and the church was built soon after. In the left-hand antechamber of the cathedral you'll see silver *ex votos* (devotional sculptures) of every imaginable shape and size, including horses, planes, grasshoppers (representing plagues of locusts), hearts with swords driven through them, arms, fingers and hands. This is a Latin American tradition stretching from Mexico to Brazil, whereby the faithful deposit representations of whatever they need cured, or whatever they fear, to the power of the Almighty.

Eating and drinking

You'll find a few basic **restaurants** in Cartago, and a handful of **sodas** where you can fill up for under $5. Your best bet may be to pop into one of the excellent **pastry shops** and enjoy lunch on a bench in front of the *basílica*.

Cartago Grill In front of the courthouse, Av 1, C 8/10. This popular restaurant with cheerful blue and yellow decor has a crowd-pleasing menu, excellent service and pile-on-the-pound portions. Choose between chicken, hamburgers or kebabs (from $3.50), or settle for what they do best – juicy cuts of steak grilled to perfection ($8–16). Daily 11am–9pm, Sat till 10pm.

El Día de la Negrita

The celebration of the Virgin of Los Angeles (**El Día de la Negrita**) on August 2 is one of the most important days in the Costa Rican religious calendar, when hundreds of pilgrims make the journey to Cartago to visit the tiny black statue of the Virgin, tucked away in a shallow subterranean antechamber beneath the crypt in the town's *basílica*. It is a tradition in this grand, vaulting church for pilgrims to shuffle down the aisle towards the altar on their knees, rosaries fretting in their hands as they whisper a steady chorus of Hail Marys: indeed, many will have travelled like this from as far away as San José to pay their respects.

La Puerta de Sol *Los Angeles Lodge*, Av 4, C 14. The interior may be a bit gloomy, but this restaurant is still a cut above most of the others in town because of the wide range of seafood dishes it serves. Daily 10.30am–2am.

Soda Apolo Av 2, C 1. Its bar permanently propped up by locals, this lively street-corner *soda* is a good source of solid, *típico* food ($3.50 for a chicken and drink combo) and (if your Spanish is up to it) gossip. Open 24hr.

Jardín Botánico Lankester

Orchids are the chief attraction at the University of Costa Rica's **Jardín Botánico Lankester** (daily 8.30am–5.30pm, last entrance 4.30pm; $7.50; Ⓦ www.jbl.ucr.ac.cr), a research centre 4km southeast of Cartago. The large, attractive gardens (the oldest in the country) are covered with a bewildering array of tropical plant and flower species, including orchids, heliconias and bromeliads – ostentatious elaborate blooms that thrust out from the undergrowth. The most rewarding time to visit is the dry season, particularly in March and April, when the garden explodes with virulent reds, purples and yellows.

To get to the gardens, take the **Paraíso bus** which leaves every ten minutes from a stop on C 4, Av 1/3 in Cartago. The driver will drop you on the main road, from where it's a (signposted) walk of about 500m.

Parque Nacional Volcán Irazú

The blasted lunar landscape of **PARQUE NACIONAL VOLCÁN IRAZÚ** (daily 8am–3.30pm; $10; Ⓣ 2200-5025) reaches its highest point at 3432m and, on clear days, offers fantastic views all the way to the Caribbean coast. Famous for having had the gall to erupt on the day President John F. Kennedy visited Costa Rica on March 19, 1963, Irazú has been more or less calm ever since. But while its **main crater** is far less active, in terms of bubblings and rumblings, than that of Volcán Poás, its deep depression and the strange algae-green lake that fills it create an undeniably dramatic sight.

Looming 32km north of Cartago, the volcano makes for a long and entirely uphill but scenic trip, especially in the early morning before the inevitable **clouds** roll in (about 10am). While the main crater draws the crowds, it's worth noting that the shallow bowl to its right, the flat-bottomed and largely unimpressive **Diego de la Haya crater**, is the remnant of Irazú's first and largest eruption: when it blew in 1723, the eruption lasted ten months and showered San José in ash.

There's not much to do around here after viewing the main crater from the *mirador* – no official trails cut through this section of the park, though you can scramble among the grey ash dunes that have built up on **Playa Hermosa**, the buried older crater that spreads to the left of the walkway and is dotted with what little vegetation that can survive in this otherworldly environment. Stay behind the barriers at all times, though, as volcanic ash crumbles easily, and you could end up falling into the ominous-looking lake.

Park practicalities

A visit to Irazú is strictly for day-trippers, since there's nowhere to stay or camp in the park. Only one **bus** runs to the park, leaving from opposite San José's *Gran Hotel Costa Rica* on Av 2, C1/3 at 8am daily (get there early in high season to get a seat), stopping to pick up passengers in Cartago (on the corner of Las Ruinas) at

8.45am; the bus returns to San José at 12.30pm. You can also get to Irazú on any number of half-day **tours**, run by travel agencies in San José (see p.46), which whisk you back and forth in a modern minibus for around $45, not including the entrance fee.

At the crater parking area, you'll find toilets, an information board and a **reception centre** with a snack bar that serves cakes and hot drinks; coatis are regular visitors to the picnic tables here, on the scrounge for food. It can get cold (and wet) at the summit, so bring a sweater and a waterproof jacket.

Valle Orosí

After workaday Cartago, the verdant **VALLE OROSÍ**, occupying a deep bowl just 9km to the southeast, is a veritable Garden of Eden. Passing through **Paraíso**, the road drops down a ski-slope hill to the pretty villages of **Orosí** and, on the other side of Lago Cachí, **Ujarrás**, each with their own lovely church; annoyingly, although they lie less than 8km apart, no bus runs between them, so without your own transport you'll have to backtrack to Paraíso. Southeast of these lies the little-visited **Parque Nacional Tapantí-Macizo Cerro de la Muerte**, a wildlife-rich park that's one of the closest places to the capital for rainforest hiking.

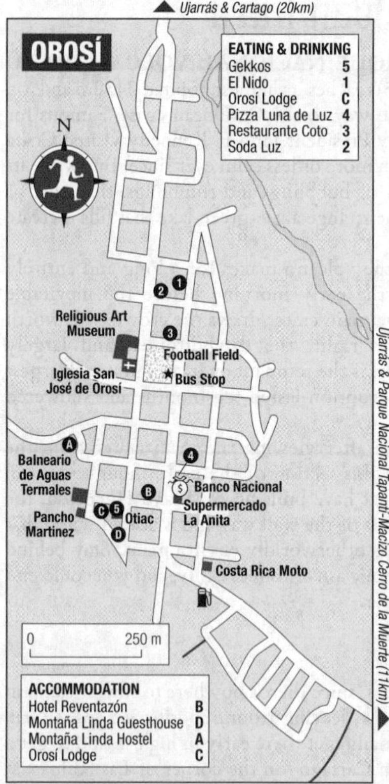

Orosí

Nestled in a little topographical bowl between thick-forested hills and coffee plantations, **OROSÍ** is one of the most picturesque villages in Costa Rica. Its bucolic charms have a way of seducing visitors, and many end up staying far longer than they intended – on a clear morning, when the lush hillsides are drenched in sunlight and with Irazú and Turrialba volcanoes hovering on the horizon, Orosí can feel like the most idyllic spot on earth.

Arrival and information

Regular **buses** leave from the stop on C 6, Av 1/3 in Cartago for the forty-five-minute journey to Orosí (every 30min till 8pm, then hourly till 10pm); the last service back to Cartago leaves at 10pm from the stops along the main street. By **car**, take the road from Cartago to Paraíso, then turn right at the Parque Central and drive straight until you begin to descend the precipitous hill to the village. **Taxis** congregate on the north side of the main square, outside *Restaurante Coto*.

For **information** about the area, stop at *Otiac* (Mon–Fri 7.30am–6.30pm, May–Oct till 4.30pm, Sat & Sun 9am–5pm; ⓣ2533-3640), 300m south of the church. It's run by the folks at *Montaña Linda* (see below) and offers a wide range of activities – from tours (including trips to Volcán Irazú; $20) and cooking classes ($15) to homestays and volunteer programmes – as well as Spanish lessons at its popular language school (see p.72). It also has a café (see p.156), and you can also buy postcards and send mail here. There's a Banco Nacional in town, 250m south of the football field, which has an **ATM** and can change travellers' cheques.

Accommodation

Orosí offers surprisingly good **accommodation**, most of which is at the southern end of town.

Chalet Teca 2km outside Orosí, on the road to Tapantí ⓣ2533-3268, ⓦwww.chaletorosi.com. See Valle Orosí map on p.157. Good-looking wood-and-stone chalet set in compact but attractive grounds on a hill south of the village. There's a well-equipped kitchen and inviting open fireplace, plus fine views from its terrace (complete with jacuzzi). ❻

Hotel Reventazón 25m south and 25m east of the Banco Nacional ⓣ2533-3838. Small, clean rooms suited to a variety of budgets; all have lovely valley vistas, private hot-water bathrooms and for those who like their creature comforts, one room even comes with funky wall art, a flat-screen TV, stereo, leather couch and desk. ❸

Hotel Tapanti Media 1km south of the church and 100m up a steep hill ⓣ2533-9090. See Valle Orosí map on p.157. Fronted by flags flapping in the breeze and offering superb views of the valley, *Tapanti Media* has clean but modest rooms, with TV, phone and private hot-water bathrooms. If you can score the top-floor far-corner room with two big bay windows, you've got it made. There's a cosy bar with comfy lounge chairs and fireplace – perfect for those chilly Orosí nights. ❺

Montaña Linda Guesthouse 25m south of Otiac ⓣ2533-3640, ⓦwww.montanalinda.com. These relaxed digs offer large, light-filled rooms with en-suite hot-water bathrooms and glorious valley views from the wraparound balcony. The communal kitchen and lounge area – complete with book exchange library, long dining table and inviting couches – is a great space to relax, study or chat with other travellers. Breakfast not included. ❸

Montaña Linda Hostel 200m south and 100m east of the football field ⓣ2533-3640, ⓦwww.montanalinda.com. Benefiting from the same chilled-out vibe as its sister accommodation, this is the best budget option in Orosí: in three pretty dorm rooms ($7.50), en-suite doubles with valley views, or camping space ($3 with own tent, $4 with hostel tent). All rooms have shared hot-water bathrooms, and there's a communal kitchen. Breakfast not included. ❷

Orosí Lodge 25m east of Aguas Termales ⓣ2533-3578, ⓦwww.orosilodge.com. Lovely little hotel whose six wood-floored rooms (top three with volcano views, bottom three with an extra bed in each) are equipped with coffee maker, minibar and fan. The split-level chalet around the back ($85) makes an excellent base, with a spacious, high-ceilinged lounge and a private balcony looking across Orosí to Irazú and Turrialba, looming on the horizon. Breakfast (extra) can be taken at the on-site café (see p.156). ❹

Sanchiri Mirador & Lodge 6.5km north of Orosí ⓣ2574-5454, ⓦwww.sanchiri.com. See Valle Orosí map on p.157. The large-windowed rooms at this family-run option make the most of their stupendous position high above the valley, though there are also new comfortable wood cabins in the grounds. The restaurant (with equally jaw-dropping views) serves tasty meals made from locally grown produce, and the hotel's friendly staff can help with local information and tours. ❺

The Town

While Orosí's laidback atmosphere is its top attraction, the village does also boast the **Iglesia San José de Orosí** (built in 1735), Costa Rica's oldest church that is still in use, which sits squat against the rounded pates of the hills behind. This simple, low-slung adobe structure, single-towered and roofed with red tiles, has an interior devoid of the hubris and frothy excess of much of Latin American religious decor. The adjacent **religious art museum** (Tues–Sat 1–5pm, Sun 9am–5pm; ¢350) exhibits fascinating *objectos de culto* from the early 1700s such as icons, religious paintings and ecclesiastical furniture, along with a faithful recreation of a monk's tiny room.

Of the two **hot springs** in the village, **Balneario de Aguas Termales** (daily 7.30am–4pm, closed Tues; $3), at the southern end of the village, is the better, attractively framed by forest-clad hills and well maintained.

Activities

There are various ways of exploring the surrounding countryside: you can ride along the valley by **bike**, available to rent from *Orosí Lodge* ($3 per hr, $10per day), who can also provide you with a map of the area featuring points of interest; or by **motorbike**, with Costa Rica Moto (Ⓣ2533-1564, Ⓦwww.costarica-moto.com), 100m east of the petrol station on the south side of the village, who rent bikes ($50 per day) and also offer tailor-made tours from $95 a day.

For a gentler excursion, you can take an early morning **horseback** ride through the valley with Francisco "Pancho" Martinez ($10/hr; Ⓣ2830-6058), who can be found just left of the Balneario de Aguas Termales.

Eating and drinking

If you're self-catering, the Supermercado La Anita (daily 7.30am–8pm), next to the Banco Nacional, is exceptionally well stocked; the town also has a couple of good fruit and vegetables stores.

Gekkos 300m south of the church. Breezy arts café in the Otiac information centre, serving half a dozen breakfast variations (from $3.75), lunch (salads, burgers and the like; from $4.75) and (local) coffee and cakes. Browse the small library while you wait or make use of the free wi-fi. Daily 6.30am–2pm.

El Nido 150m north of the football field. Pull up a saddle seat for tasty *bocas* and crispy *chicharrones* at this dark, hot but friendly bar and restaurant. Daily 11am–11pm.

Orosí Lodge 25m east of Aguas Termales. Top spot for all-day breakfasts ($7.50), home-made pastries and Orosí coffee (their own brand) while chilling to a backdrop of cool tunes on the vintage jukebox or getting competitive on the table football. Good collection of local art and World Music CDs for sale. Mon–Sat 7am–7pm.

Pizza Luna de Luz Next to the Banco Nacional. Pick up a tasty pizza loaded with fresh toppings (from $3) at this rustic joint on the main road through the village. There's around a dozen to choose from, including a decent vegetarian. Mon, Tues & Thurs 2–10pm, Fri–Sun 11.30am–10pm.

Restaurante Coto Opposite the football field. You're paying for the central location as much as anything, although the inviting terrace is as good a place as any in town for, albeit pricey, *tipíco* food. Daily 8am–10pm.

Soda Luz 100m north of the church. *Soda Luz* has been going strong for over sixty years, and the proprietors still serve up one of the best *gallo pintos* you'll find anywhere in the country. Daily 7am–4pm, Sat & Sun till 8pm.

Coffee at Cristina

One of the most interesting activities in the area is visiting **Café Cristina** (Ⓣ2574-6426, Ⓦwwww.cafecristina.com), a small-scale organic coffee farm about 9km northeast of Orosí, on the road from Paraiso to Turrialba, which has been toiled by an American family since 1977. The charismatic owners, Linda and Ernie, offer ninety-minute tours ($10; reservations essential) and take great pride in explaining every stage of the coffee-making process – from growing to milling to roasting. The tour culminates in one of the sweetest cups of coffee you'll taste in Costa Rica.

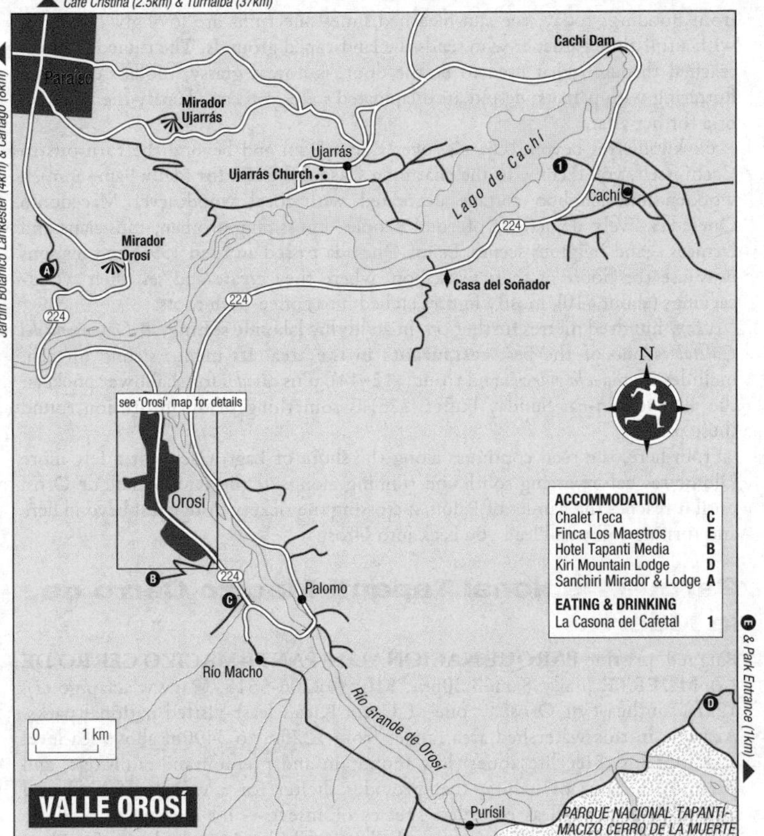

Ujarrás and around Lago Cachí

The 30km loop-road from Orosí around **Lago Cachí** makes a great half-day trip, ambling through some of the most beautiful scenery in the valley and taking in the ruins at **Ujarrás** along the way. Ujarrás and Cachí (for the Casa del Sonador) are accessible by hourly **bus** from Cartago, leaving from a stop on Av 3, C 4/6; it's far better, however, to **drive** – a tour around the lake in one of Orosí's jeep-taxis costs around $25 (see p.155) – or, if you're fit enough, **cycle**: bikes are available for rent in Orosí (see opposite).

Following the road north out of the village, you'll come to a couple of **miradors**: Orosí (daily 7am–5pm; free) and, taking the right turn further up the hill, Ujarrás (same hours; ¢50); both have *parilla* grills and fine views over Orosí and the lake.

From the second *mirador*, the road winds dramatically down to the tiny agricultural hamlet of **UJARRÁS**, home to the evocative ruins of the **Iglesia de Nuestra Señora de la Limpia Concepción** (if coming by bus, ask to be dropped at the fork for Ujarrás, from where it's a 1km walk). Built between 1681 and 1693 on the site of a shrine erected by a local fisherman who claimed to have seen the Virgin in a tree trunk, the church was abandoned in 1833 after irreparable damage from flooding; today, the sun-bleached limestone ruins are lovingly cared for, with a full-time gardener who tends the landscaped grounds. The ruined interior, reached through what used to be the door, is now a grassy, roofless enclosure fluttering with parrots; despite its dilapidated state, you can identify the fine lines of a former altar.

Six kilometres beyond Ujarrás, over Cachí Dam and beyond the turn-offs to Cachí itself, you'll come to the charming **Casa del Soñador** (daily 9am–6pm), a wooden and bamboo cottage decorated with local woodcarver Macedonio Quesada's lively depictions of rural people – gossiping women, musicians and farmers – and religious scenes. Señor Quesada passed away in 1995, and his sons now use the house as their workshop, where they create and sell their woodcarvings (about $10), mostly figures etched into coffee-bush roots.

A few hundred metres further on, in an idyllic lakeside setting, *La Casona del Cafetal* is one of the best **restaurants** in the area. Its menu, strong on fish, includes tilapia *a la plancha* and trout ($12–14), plus *casados* for shallower pockets; the all-you-can-eat Sunday buffet ($25) is something of an institution round these parts.

From here, the road continues along the shore of Lago Cachí for a few more kilometres before arcing south and running alongside the Río Grande de Orosí until it reaches the hamlet of Paloma; crossing the rickety bridge just beyond here and turning right will lead you back into Orosí.

Parque Nacional Tapantí-Macizo Cerro de la Muerte

Rugged, pristine **PARQUE NACIONAL TAPANTÍ-MACIZO CERRO DE LA MUERTE** (daily 8am–3.30pm; $10; ⓣ2206-5615, ⓦwww.aclap.go.cr), 12km southeast of Orosí, is one of Costa Rica's least-visited national parks. Altitude in this watershed area ranges from 1220m to 3490m above sea level and contains three life zones (low mountain and premontane rainforest, and paramo), a range of habitat that provides shelter for a variety of **bird and animal life**, as well as countless species of insects – it's perhaps one of the easiest places in the country to spot the beautiful Blue Morpho butterfly. Flora is equally spectacular, including bromelias, heliconia and numerous ferns and mosses; it has been estimated that each hectare contains up to 160 different species of tree. The park is divided into two sectors: **Tapantí**, accessed from Orosí (and described here), and **Macizo Cerro de la Muerte**, approached from the Interamerican Highway.

The trails

Tapantí's three densely wooded **trails** lead off from the main road that cuts through the park and are relatively short. Of the walks that skirt the Río Grande de Orosí, the easiest is the sun-dappled **Sendero La Oropendola**

Watching wildlife in Tapanti

Tapanti is chock-full of **mammals**; about 45 species live here, including the elusive tapir, as well as ocelot and margay, although you're more likely to spot paca, coati and, if you're lucky, kinkajou. **Birdlife** is abundant, particularly along the trails that winds up into the hills: look out for black guan, tinamou and chacalaca. The park's high rainfall makes it nirvana for **reptiles** and **amphibians**, too, including eye-lash viper and basilisk lizard.

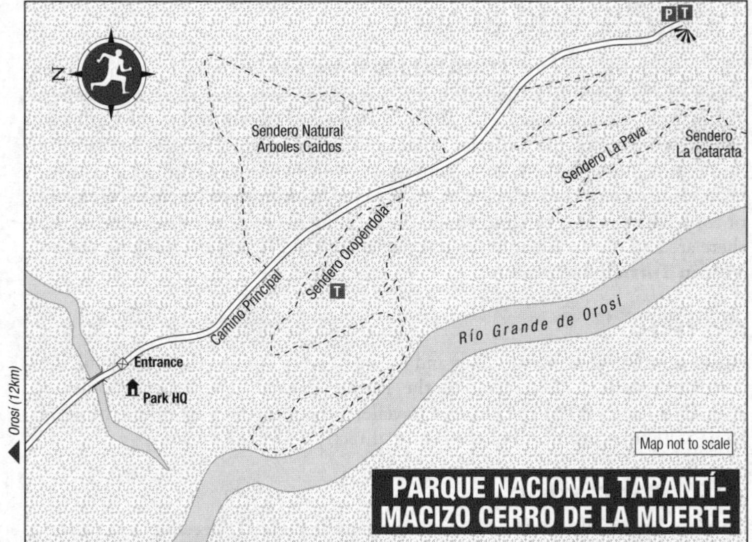

(1.2km), which, true to its name, is a good place to spot Montezuma oropendola – a flock can normally be seen in the trees near where the trail loops back. The slightly harder **Sendero La Pava-Catarata** (1.5km) descends, via a couple of little bridges, to a section of small rapids (Catarata) or a boulder-strewn spot along the river (Pava). On the opposite side of the main road, the steep and difficult **Sendero Natural Arboles Caídos** (2km) is a reliable birdwatching trail.

Park practicalities

From Orosí, take a **jeep-taxi** from the north side of the village square ($17 each way) or, with your own transport, follow the main road south to the Beneficio Orlich coffee factory, where it bends left across a small bridge; turn right (the park is signposted from here) and continue for 10km along a progressively rugged track (you'll need a 4WD in the rainy season).

Tapantí receives one of the highest average annual **rainfalls** (a whopping 7000mm) in the country. October is the wettest month, but bring rain gear whenever you go, and dress in layers – if the sun is out it can be blindingly hot, whereas at higher elevations, when overcast and rainy, it can feel quite cool. Despite its low numbers of visitors, the park has good **services**, with car-parking spaces at the trailheads and toilets and drinking water at regular intervals along the trails themselves.

The nearest **accommodation** is at *Kiri Mountain Lodge* (Ⓣ2533-2272, Ⓦwww.kirilodge.net; ④), 2.5km from the park: it's an isolated, peaceful place with basic but comfortable rooms and a restaurant and bar, and they can also arrange guided walks and trout-fishing. To **camp**, head for the *Finca Los Maestros* (Ⓣ2533-3312; $4), 1km from the park entrance; it's run by a friendly local schoolteacher who will cook on request ($3 for breakfast; $4 for lunch or dinner).

Turrialba and around

The agricultural town of **TURRIALBA**, 45km east of Cartago on the eastern slopes of the Cordillera Central, boasts sweeping views over the rugged eastern Talamancas – and not much else. With the demise of the railroad to the Caribbean and the opening of the Guápiles Highway further north, Turrialba has faded in importance, though there are a number of worthwhile day-trips around town: most visitors come through here en route to the **Monumento Nacional Guayabo** or for a **white-water rafting** trip on the thrilling *ríos* Pacuaré or Reventazón, but there are also the excellent biological gardens at **CATIE** and the smoking cone of **Volcán Turrialba** to explore.

Arrival

Buses from San José (hourly; 2hr) and Cartago (every 30min; 1hr 20min) pull into Turrialba's station, 400m west of the Parque Central. The Banco Popular on Avendia 4 has an **ATM** and changes travellers' cheques; the **post office** (Mon–Fri 8am–5.30pm) is just north of the centre, directly above the square.

Accomodation

Turrialba isn't really a tourist town, but has some perfectly decent places **to stay**; for the area's more -upmarket hotels, however, you'll have to venture further out of town.

In town

Hotel Kardey C 4, Av 2/4 ⓣ2556-0050, ⓔhotelkardey@hotmail.com. Small, respectable spot on a noisy road halfway between the bus station and the Parque Central. Rooms are clean and come with cable TV and a private hot-water bathroom, but those on the ground floor have unappealing internal windows; go for the upstairs ones, with big glass doors and superb mountain vistas. ❸

Hotel Wagelia Av 4, C 2/4 ⓣ2556-1566, ⓦwww.hotelwageliaturrialba.com. Tasteful but pricey rooms with cable TV, wi-fi and hot-water bathrooms set around a tranquil courtyard. Breakfast is included at the on-site restaurant. ❻

Interamericano Av 1, C 0/1 ⓣ2556-0142, ⓦwww.hotelinteramericano.com. Near the old train station, *Interamericano* is the town's best budget option – basic but friendly and an excellent place to meet other travellers. There are a variety of rooms on offer, hot water and wi-fi, and they can organize kayaking and other tours. Breakfast is extra. ❷–❸

Turrialba B&B C 1, Av 6/8 ⓣ2556-6651, ⓦwww.turrialbahotel.com. There's a great vibe at this rafters' crash-pad. Rooms come with queen-size beds and hot-water baths, while spacious public areas include a large kitchen, courtyard with bar and jacuzzi, and a roof terrace. Pool and darts are also on offer. Free internet. ❺

Out of town

Casa Turire 8km southeast of Turrialba on the road to La Suiza ⓣ2531-1111, ⓦwww.hotelcasaturire.com. Elegant, Swiss-owned colonial plantation mansion enfolded by Lago Angostura. The mellow, wood-floored rooms have king-sized bed, cable TV, bathtub and private balcony, while the honeymoon-worthy master suite ($350) runs over two floors and has jacuzzi, couches and breathtaking views. There's a dazzling swimming pool, fine-dining restaurant, bar and games room. The hotel has its own walking trails, and organizes birdwatching and kayaking, as well as trips to Monumento Nacional Guayabo and Volcán Turrialba. ❼

Hotel Villa Florencia 5km east of Turrialba, on the road to Siquirres ⓣ2557-3536, ⓦwww.villaflorencia.com. Set amid coffee fields near CATIE, the large, likeable rooms – wood-floored and featuring two queen-sized beds – open out onto lovely grounds, home to toucans, oropendolas and a variety of other chattering birdlife. ❼

Pacuare Jungle Lodge 35km northeast of Turrialba, on the Río Pacuaré ⓣ2225-3939, ⓦwww.junglelodgecostarica.com. Archetypal luxury hideaway (palm-thatched river-view suites, vast canopy king-sizes dressed in Egyptian-cotton sheets) with a difference – you paddle yourself

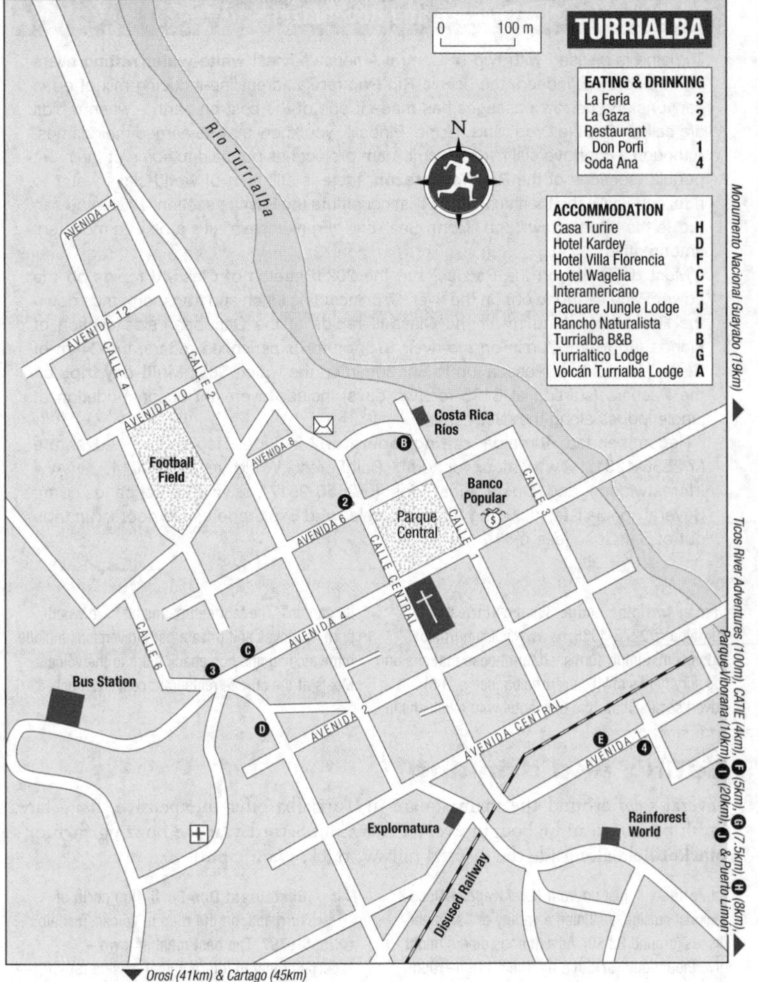

there in a raft, negotiating several kilometres of the raging Río Pacuare (see box, p.162) in order to bed down for the night in your own private piece of paradise. The WTO-certified eco-lodge part-funds a nearby jaguar research project and has started its own conservation effort by reintroducing howler monkeys into the surrounding area. Two-night packages, including rafting in and out, start at $375.

Rancho Naturalista 20km southeast of Turrialba, beyond La Suiza ⓣ2554-8100, ⓦwww.costaricagateway.com. Rustic five-bedroom lodge with four adjacent cabins that is famed among bird-watchers (more than 400 bird species have been spotted in the area). It's not cheap, but the cost includes three gourmet communal meals and guided tours and the property has its own network of rainforest trails. $290

Turrialtico Lodge 7.5km southeast of Turrialba, on the road to Siquirres ⓣ2538-1111, ⓦwww.turrialtico.com. Cosy lodge, groaning under the weight of its blossoming bougainvillea. Farmhouse-style rooms are decorated with handmade bedspreads and work by local artists; some have balconies overlooking the gorgeous surrounding countryside. They organize tours to Volcán Turrialba and Monumento Nacional Guayabo. ❺–❻

White waters: the Pacuaré and Reventazón

Turrialba is blessed with two of Central America's finest **white-water rafting** rivers on its doorstep. Indeed, the scenic **Río Pacuaré**'s adrenaline-inducing mix of open canyons and narrow passages has made it one of the best on earth – when rapids are called "Double Drop" and "Upper Pinball", you know they've earned their names. Although a controversial hydroelectric-dam project has put paid to some of the most popular sections of the **Río Reventazón**, there is still a lot of world-class water to ride, especially the technical drops that constitute the Pascua section, where you can tackle the "Corkscrew", the "North Sea" and "Frankenstein" (it's a bit of a monster), among others.

Most **day-trips** on the Pacuaré run the 29km stretch of Class-IV rapids on the Lower Pacuaré (up to 5hr on the river; $75, including lunch and transport); trips down the Reventazón tend to hit the Class-III rapids at the Caribbean-side section of Florida (up to 2hr 30min on the river; $75) or, for experienced rafters, the 24km of Class IV+ rapids at Pascua (up to 3hr 30min on the water; $85). **Multi-day trips** on the Pacuaré (starting at $195 for two days) include overnight accommodation at jungle lodges along the river.

Recommended Turrialba **rafting operators** include Tico's River Adventure (ⓣ2556-1231, ⓦwww.ticoriver.com), RainForest World (ⓣ2556-0014, ⓦwww.rforestw.com) and Costa Rica Ríos (ⓣ2556-9617, ⓦwww.costaricarios.com). Several specialists, including Rios Tropicales and Exploradores Outdoors, run trips out of San José (see p.64).

Volcán Turrialba Lodge 35km northwest of Turrialba ⓣ2273-4335, ⓦwww.volcanturrialbalodge.com. Simply furnished farmhouse that sits on the very flanks of Volcán Turrialba (see p.165) – it advertises itself as "the only hotel with a volcano in its garden". The fourteen rooms all have wood-burning stoves and private bath; diversions include birdwatching and horseback tours to the volcano. Meals at the on-site restaurant cost $12 each. ④

Eating and drinking

Several *sodas* around the main square in Turrialba offer inexpensive, *típico* fare. Fresh produce can be bought every Friday and Saturday at the buzzing **farmer's market** held alongside the disused railway tracks (7am–5pm).

La Feria Av 4, just up from *Hotel Wagelia*. Decent regional cuisine, including a variety of Caribbean dishes (around $3.50). Adventurous diners might give the tongue ($7.50) a try. Daily 11am–10pm, Tues till 2pm.

La Gaza C 0, Av 6/8. Long-standing bar and restaurant, located on the northwest corner of the Parque Central, serving cheap sandwiches and hamburgers (from $2), plus the usual range of chicken, meat and seafood dishes ($6–10). Daily 10.30am–11pm.

Restaurant Don Porfi 4km north of Turrialba, on the road to Volcán Turrialba ⓣ2556-9797. The best meal in town – expertly prepared international cuisine ($6–12) that can be paired with a bottle of fine European or Chilean wine. 11am–11pm, closed Wed.

Soda Ana Av 1, east of the *Interamericano*. An intimate, family-run *soda* where the friendly staff serve up impromptu Spanish lessons with the piping hot *casados* ($4). Daily 7am–10pm.

CATIE

Regarded as one of the world's premier tropical research stations, the **Centro Agronómico Tropical de Investigación y Enseñanza**, otherwise known by its acronym **CATIE** (ⓦwww.catie.ac.cr), is unique in Costa Rica. For the last 65 years, the agricultural research and higher education centre, 4km east of Turrialba, has worked on marrying the needs of Latin America's rural poor with those of the environment – it was here that the technique for producing *palmito* (heart-of-palm) from the *pejibaye* was developed – and at any one time it is involved in over a hundred research and development projects, from tackling climate change to producing disease-resistant tropical crops.

It's this expert knowledge that makes the tours of CATIE's landscaped **Jardín Botánico** (daily 7am–4pm, Sat & Sun from 8am, last tour at 3pm; $6, $15 with tour, reservations recommended; ⓣ2556-2700, ⓦwww.catie.ac.cr/jardinbotanico) so eye-opening. The genial guide will introduce you to some of the 472 species being preserved here, explaining the virtues of the miracle fruit (it makes sour things taste sweet) or divulging some of the 101 benefits of eating noni; the tour is very interactive, so you'll spend much of your time sniffing spices, touching tubers and munching on freshly picked tropical fruit such as mangosteen and pink ornamental bananas.

As well as hosting a number of vital germplasm projects, including one of the most important collections of coffee and cacao plants in the world ($15, $25 combined with the Jardín Botánico; 2hr), CATIE harbours a variety of **wildlife**: armadillos, coatis, sloths and caimans, and, attracted by the myriad tropical plants, 300 species of bird – the central lagoon alone is home to boat-billed heron, northern jacana and purple gallinule, and is the roosting site for a hundred or so great white herons. Keen birders can take part in the **bird-banding** research run by the Programa Monitoreo de Aves (ⓣ2558-2596, ⓦweb.catie.ac.cr/pma), part of an ongoing study into land-use transition – vital when so many Costa Rican farmers are replacing their coffee plantations with sugar cane. Volunteers can help with the catching, weighing and releasing of birds in various habitats across campus (Mon, Wed & Fri; 5–9am; $15, $25 including transport; reserve at least one day in advance). The hourly **buses** from Turrialba to Siquirres pass by CATIE; alternatively, you could take a **bike tour** of the campus with Explornatura ($55; ⓣ2556-2070, ⓦwww.explornatura.com).

Parque Viborana

About 10km east of Turrialba you'll find the **Parque Viborana** (daily 8am–4pm; phone for tour times; $10; ⓣ2538-1510), a small snake centre run by renowned herpetologist Minor Camacho, who spent years researching snake venom at the University of Costa Rica for medicinal purposes. Minor gives fascinating educational talks, focusing on the deadly fer-de-lance snake, a native (although thankfully not a very common one) of the area. Hourly **buses** from Turrialba to Siquirres run past the *serpentarium*.

Monumento Nacional Guayabo

The most accessible ancient archeological site in Costa Rica, the **MONUMENTO NACIONAL GUAYABO** (daily 8am–3.30pm; $6; ⓣ2559-1220) lies 19km northeast of Turrialba and 84km east of San José. Discovered by explorer Anastasio Alfaro at the end of the nineteenth century, the remains of the town of Guayabo, believed to have been inhabited from about 300 BC to 1400 AD, were only excavated in the late 1960s. Administered by MINAE (which also controls Costa Rica's national park system), Guayabo today suffers from an acute shortage of funds: some of the **montículos** (stone mounds) are in a poor state of repair and only a small part of the site has been excavated. With the withdrawal of the annual US aid grant, the prospects for further exploration look bleak.

The **site**, a dairy farm until 1968, is visually disappointing compared to the magnificent Maya and Aztec cities of Mexico or Guatemala – cultures contemporaneous with Guayabo – though it's well to remember that civilizations

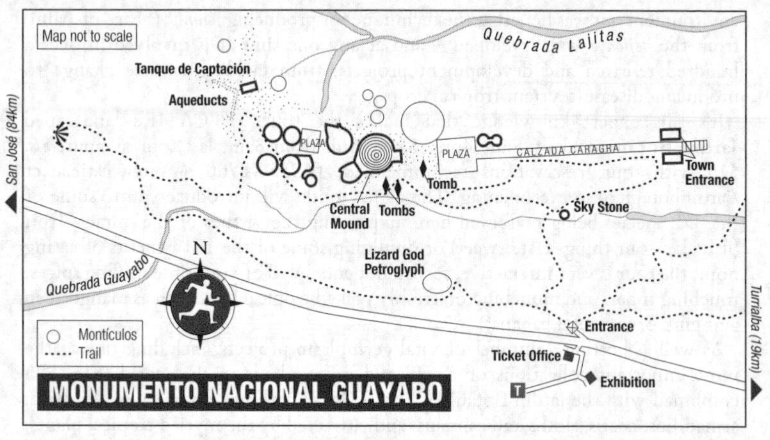

should not necessarily be judged on their ability to erect vast monuments. Facing the considerable difficulties posed by the density of the rainforest terrain, the Guayabo managed not only to live in harmony with an environment that remains hostile to human habitation, but also constructed a complex system of water management and social organization, and expressed themselves through the "written language" of petroglyphs.

The mysteries of Guayabo are amplified by today's site, which lacks anything in the way of information or interpretation; it's a good idea to hire a **guide** ($10; English-speakers not always available) to help you decipher what can otherwise look like random piles of stone. Either way, it's best to start at the gloomy **exhibition** space, which has a model showing how the town would have looked, before heading up to the *mirador* for an overview; the trail (1.6km) then weaves its way down among the mounds.

Most of the heaps of stones and basic structures now exposed were erected between 300 and 700 AD, though the (still working) **aqueducts** at the northwestern end of the site are some 2000 years old. Excavations have shown that the Guayabo were particularly skilled in water conducting – look out for the stone **tanque de captación** near here, where they stored water carried in these subterranean channels from nearby springs.

At the heart of the town is the **central mound**. Of the 43 *montículos* that make up the site, this is the tallest circular base unearthed so far, with two staircases and pottery remains at the very top. Guayabo houses were built to a hierarchial system, and it is likely that this was home to the community chief, a *cacique*, who had both social and religious power. Near the central mound, you can see some of the **tombs** (known as Tumbas de Cajón, or Drawer Tombs) that have been uncovered in various parts of the site. They were constructed in layers of rock (hence their name) brought from surrounding rivers; unfortunately, the tombs discovered so far have been plundered by looters long ago. Beyond here, at the eastern end of the site, a paved road, the **Calzada Caragra**, runs for 200m before disappearing into thick jungle; the main entrance to town, this was believed to have once stretched for 20km.

The people of Guayabo brought stones to the site from a great distance, probably from the banks of the Río Reventazón, and **petroglyphs** have been found on 53 of these – most are now in the Museo Nacional in San José (see p.105), but you can still see carvings of what appear to be lizard and jaguar gods, and an altogether more intriguingly patterned rock, the so-called **Sky Stone**, believed by some experts to represent a celestial map of the southern skies, and therefore possibly of use as an ancient calendar.

Other than this, little is known of the people who lived here, and there are no clues as to why Guayabo was ultimately abandoned, though hypotheses include an epidemic or war with neighbouring tribes.

Practicalities

Daily **buses** make the one-hour journey from Turrialba's main station (Mon–Sat 11.15am, 3.10pm & 5.20pm, Sun 9am, 3.30pm & 6.30pm), returning at 7am, 12.30pm and 4pm. The inconvenient timetable means you'll probably get too long at the site, so alternatively you can walk back to the main road, a 4km downhill hike, and intercept the bus from Santa Teresita to Turrialba, which passes by at about 1.30pm (double-check the times with the *guardaparques*); if you get stuck, you can always bed down at the monument's small campsite ($2 per person). **Driving** from Turrialba takes about thirty minutes; the last 4km is on a bad gravel road, passable with a regular car, but watch your clearance. **Taxis** charge $16 from Turrialba.

Most hotels in Turrialba run **tours** to the site, as do Explornatura (Ⓣ2556-2070, Ⓦwww.explornatura.com), who offer a guided hike for $60 (including return transport).

Parque Nacional Volcán Turrialba

The least-visited of the Valle Central's major volcanoes, **Volcán Turrialba** (3328m) erupted for the first time in 145 years on January 5, 2010, blowing a large vent in the crater's upper wall and forcing the evacuation of sixty people from local villages; dramatic cloud plumes (up to 2km high) continued to spout skyward for the first few months of the year.

The **park** (daily 8am–4pm, though no one's around to enforce this, nor collect park fees) is open again, but with **restricted access**, according to volcanic activity. Check the latest before venturing up here – and note that the Volcanological and Seismological Observatory of Costa Rica (OVSICORI) haven't ruled out the January eruption being the precursor to further, larger-scale seismic activity.

The nearest bus from Turrialba drops you 18km shy of the volcano, and driving to the summit requires a 4WD to tackle the last 10km of rough gravel road, so if you do decide to visit, it's better to come on a **tour**: Explornatura in Turrialba (Ⓣ2556-2070, Ⓦwww.explornatura.com) offers guided walks that lead through lush montane rain- and cloudforest to the top ($75, including return transport and lunch). Pack warm clothes as the temperature at the summit hovers around 15°C.

Travel details

Buses

Alajuela to: Atenas (every 30min; 1hr); Heredia (every 30min; 45min); La Fortuna (3 daily; 3hr 25min); Grecia (every 30min; 1hr); La Guácima Abajo, for the Butterfly Farm (hourly; 40min); Jacó (3 daily; 2hr 30min); Liberia (frequent; 2hr 10min); Monteverde (2 daily; 4hr); Puntarenas (frequent; 2hr 10min); Sabanilla (for Doka Estate; every 30min; 40min); San José (every 10min; 20min); San Ramón (hourly; 45min); Sarchí (every 30min; 1hr 15min); Volcán Poás (daily; 1hr 30min); Zoo-Ave (frequent; 15min).

Cartago to: Cachí (for Ujarrás; hourly; 25min) Orosí (every 30min; 45min); Paraíso (for the Jardín Botánico Lankester; every 5min; 15min);

San José (every 10min; 45min); Turrialba (1–6 daily; 1hr 20min); .

Heredia to: Alajuela (every 30min; 45min); Sacramento (for Volcán Barva; 3 daily; 1hr 45min); San José (every 5–10min; 30min); Volcán Irazú (daily; 1hr 45min).

Orosí to: Cartago (every 30min; 45min).

Parque Nacional Braulio Carrillo to: San José (hourly; 45min).

San José to: Alajuela (every 10min; 20min); Cartago (every 10min; 45min); Grecia (every 30min; 1hr); La Guácima Abajo, for the Butterfly Farm (hourly; 1hr); Heredia (every 5–10min; 30min); Parque Nacional Braulio Carrillo (hourly; 45min); San Ramón (hourly; 1hr); Sarchí (Mon–Fri 3 daily, Sat daily; 1hr 30min); Turrialba (hourly; 2hr 30min); Volcán Irazú (daily; 2hr); Volcán Poás (daily; 2hr 15min); Zarcero (every 45min; 1hr 30min).

San Ramón to: Alajuela (hourly; 45min); San José (hourly; 1hr); Zarcero (every 2hr; 1hr).

Sarchí to: Alajuela (every 30min; 1hr 15min); San José (via Alajuela).

Turrialba to: Cartago (1–6 daily; 1hr 20min); Guayabo (3 daily; 1hr).

Ujarrás to: Cartago (hourly; 25min).

Zarcero to: San José (every 45min; 1hr 30min); San Carlos (every 30min–1hr; 1hr); San Ramón (every 2hr; 1hr).

Trains

Heredia to: San José (Mon–Fri 15 daily; 20min).

San José to: Heredia (Mon–Fri 15 daily; 20min).

3

Limón Province and the Caribbean coast

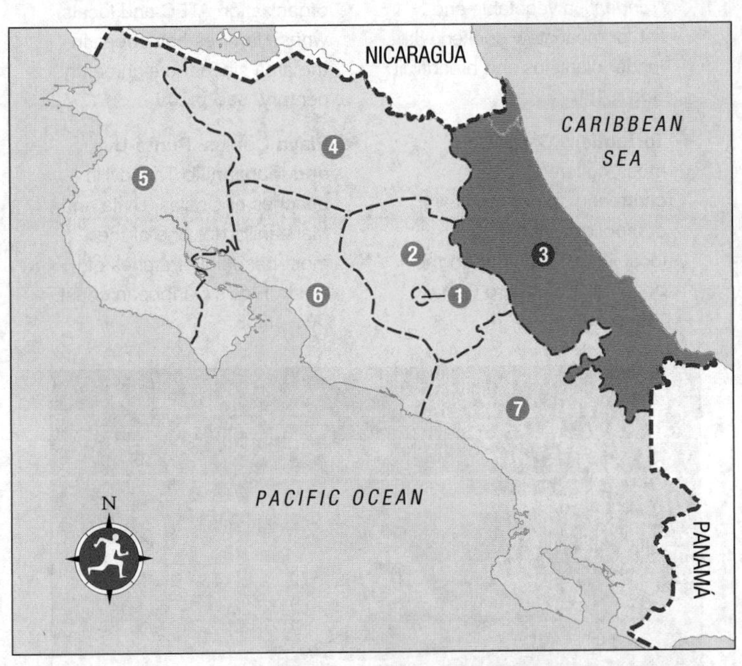

CHAPTER 3

Highlights

* **Carnival, Puerto Limón** Revellers in Afro-Caribbean costumes and spangly tops parade through the streets to a cacophony of tambourines, whistles and blasting sound systems. **See p.178**

* **Caribbean cuisine** Sample the region's traditional Caribbean cooking, from coconut-scented rice-and-beans to "*rondon*", a vegetable and fish or meat stew cooked with tender plantains and breadfruit. **See p.180**

* **Tortuguero Canal** Spot moss-covered sloths, chattering spider monkeys, crocodiles, caiman and local life as you float up the beautiful Tortuguero Canal. **See p.182**

* **Rafting the Pacuaré** The rapids come quickly and mercilessly on a white-knuckle ride down the mighty Pacuaré – and the scenery is just as breathtaking. **See p.203**

* **ATEC tours** Learn about traditional plant remedies and indigenous history on a tour to the Bribrí and Cabécar villages, led by the grassroots organization ATEC and locals whose families have been in the area since the eighteenth century. **See p.205**

* **Playa Cocles, Punta Uva and Manzanillo** The idyllic beaches of Cocles, Uvita and Manzanillo dot one of the most beautiful stretches of Costa Rica's Caribbean coast. **See p.205**

▲ Paddling up the Tortuguero Canal

3

Limón Province and the Caribbean coast

We were at the shore and travelling alongside a palmy beach. This was the Mosquito Coast ... Massive waves were rolling towards us, the white foam vivid in the twilight; they broke just below the coconut palms near the track. At this time of day, nightfall, the sea is the last thing to darken: it seems to hold the light that is slipping from the sky; and the trees are black. So in the light of this luminous sea, and the pale still-blue eastern sky, and to the splashings of the breakers, the train racketed on towards Limón.

Paul Theroux, *The Old Patagonian Express*

The Caribbean or "Miskito" coast (in Spanish, Mosquito) forms part of the huge, sparsely populated Limón Province, which sweeps south in an arc from Nicaragua to Panamá. Hemmed in to the north by dense jungles and swampy waterways, to the west by the mighty Cordillera Central and to the south by the even wider girth of the Cordillera Talamanca, Limón can feel like a lost, remote place.

Those seeking palm-fringed sands and tranquil crystalline waters that the word "Caribbean" conjures up will be disappointed. Limón has very few really good **beaches** to speak of and most are battered, shark-patrolled shores, littered with driftwood, and huge, bucking skies stretching out to sea. However, you can watch gentle giant sea **turtles** lay their eggs on the wave-raked beaches of **Tortuguero**; snorkel coral reefs at the unspoilt **Cahuita** or Punta Uva; go surfing at **Puerto Viejo de Talamanca**; or go animal- and bird-spotting in the region's many **mangrove swamps**. The interior of Limón Province is crisscrossed by the powerful Río Reventazón and Río Pacuaré, two of the best rivers in the Americas for **white-water rafting**.

Although Limón remains unknown to the majority of visitors – especially those on package tours – it holds much appeal for eco-tourists and travellers off the beaten track. The province has the highest proportion of **protected land** in the country, from the **Refugio Nacional de Vida Silvestre Barra del Colorado**, on the Nicaraguan border, to the **Refugio Nacional de Vida Silvestre Gandoca-Manzanillo** near Panamá in the extreme south. That said, however, the wildlife reserves and national parks still offer only partial resistance to the considerable ecological threats of full-scale fruit farming, logging, mining and tourism.

The Caribbean coast exudes a greater sense of **cultural diversity** than anywhere else in Costa Rica – a feeling of community and a unique and

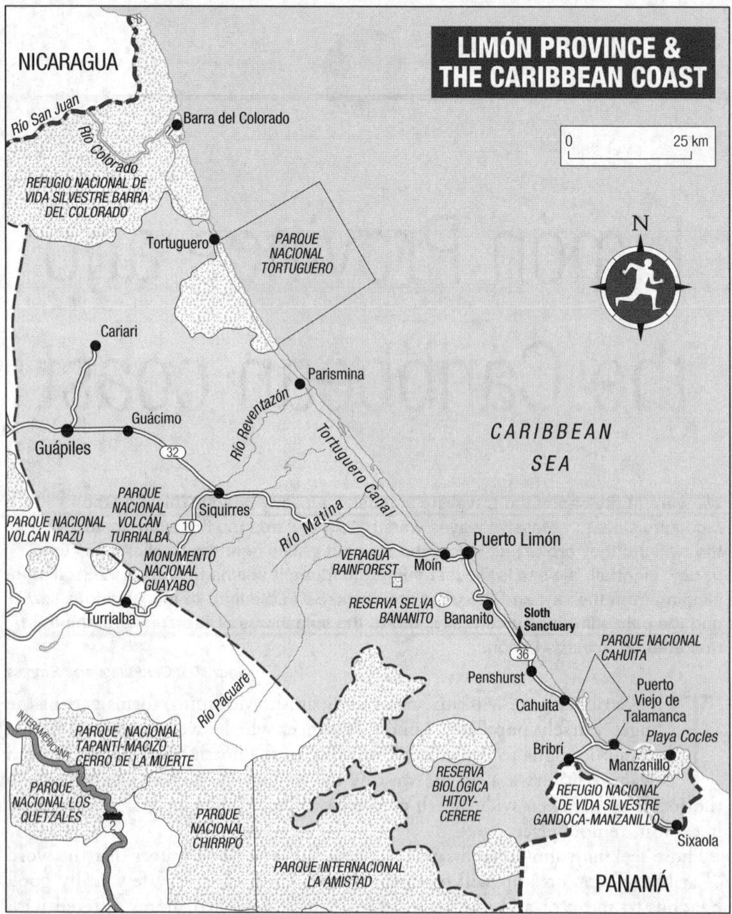

complex local history. **Puerto Limón**, the only town of any size, is one of several established "black" Central American coastal cities, like Bluefields in Nicaragua and Lívingston in Guatemala. A typical Caribbean port, it has a large, mostly Jamaican-descended **Afro-Caribbean** population. In the south, near the Panamanian border, live several communities of indigenous peoples from the **Bribrí** and **Cabécar** groups, none of whom has been well served by the national government.

The area's diverse microclimates mean there is no best **time to visit** the Caribbean coast. In Tortuguero and Barra del Colorado, you'll encounter wet weather much of the year, with somewhat drier spells in February, March, September and October. South of Limón, September and October offer the best chance of rain-free days.

Some history

Although the coast has been populated for at least ten thousand years, little is known of the ancient indigenous **Bribrí** and **Cabécar** people who inhabited the area when Columbus arrived just off the coast of present-day Puerto Limón, on his fourth and last voyage to the Americas in 1502. Well into the mid-eighteenth century, the only white people the Limón littoral saw were British **pirates**, rum-runners and seamen from the merchant vessels of the famous Spanish Main, plying the rich waters of the Caribbean, and bringing with them commerce and mayhem. Nefarious buccaneers often found refuge on Costa Rica's eastern seaboard, situated as it was between the two more lucrative provinces of Panamá and Nicaragua, from which there was a steady traffic of ships to raid. Their presence, along with the difficult terrain, helped deter full-scale settlement of Limón.

The province's development was inextricably linked to two things, themselves related: the **railway** and **bananas**. In 1871 it was decided that Costa Rica needed a more efficient export route for its coffee crop than the long, meandering river journey from Puerto Viejo de Sarapiquí to Matina (midway between Tortuguero and Puerto Limón) from where the beans were shipped to Europe. From the other main coffee port – Puntarenas on the Pacific coast – boats had to go all the way round South America to get to Europe. **Minor Keith**, an American, was contracted to build a railroad across the Cordillera Central from San José to Puerto Limón; to help pay for the laying of the track, he planted bananas along its lowland stretches. Successive waves of Highlanders, Chinese, East Indian (still locally called Hindus) and Italian immigrant

Ethnicity in Limón Province

In his book *Tekkin a Waalk*, journalist and travel writer Peter Ford uses the ingenious term "an anthropological Galápagos" to describe the ethnic and cultural oddities encountered in Limón, where the Caribbean meets Central America. There's no doubt that the province provides a touch of **multiculturalism** lacking in the rest of Costa Rica's relatively homogeneous Latin, Catholic society. In Limón, characterized by intermarriage and racial mixing, it's not unusual to find people who are of combined Miskito, Afro-Caribbean and Nicaraguan ancestry. Though the first black inhabitants of the province were the slaves of the British pirates and mahogany-cutters who had lived in scattered communities along the coast since the mid-1700s, the region's **ethnic diversity** stems largely from the influence of Minor Keith (see p.428), who brought in large numbers of foreign labourers to work on the construction of the Jungle Train. They were soon joined by turtle fishermen who had settled in Bocas del Toro, Panamá, before migrating north to escape the Panamanian war of independence from Colombia in 1903. The settlers brought their respective **religions** with them – unlike in the rest of Costa Rica, most Afro-Caribbeans in Limón Province are Protestant.

Regardless of race or religion, the coastal settlers were resourceful and independent. They not only planted their own **crops**, bringing seeds to grow breadfruit, oranges, mangoes and ackee, all of which flourished alongside native coconuts and cocoa, but also made their own salt, charcoal, musical instruments and shoes and brewed their own **spirits** – red rum, *guarapo*, cane liquor and ginger beer.

Limón's diversity has never been appreciated by the ruling and economic elite of the country. Until 1949, blacks were effectively forbidden from settling in the Valle Central or the Highlands, and while the **indigenous communities** have a degree of autonomy, their traditional territories have long since been eaten up by government-sanctioned mining and banana enterprises. Official discrimination against the province's Afro-Caribbean inhabitants ended in 1949 with a new constitution that granted them full citizenship. Black *Limonenses* now make up around 30 percent of the province's population.

labourers were brought in for the gruelling construction work, only to succumb to yellow fever. At least four thousand people died while laying the track for the Jungle Train. In the final stages, some ten thousand Jamaicans and Barbadians, thought to be immune to the disease, were contracted, many of them staying on to work on further railroad expansion or in the banana plantations. In 1890, the first **Jungle Train** huffed its way from San José via Turrialba and Siquerres to Limón, bringing an abrupt end to the Caribbean coast's era of near-total isolation. This also marked the beginning of Costa Rica's **banana boom**. Initially planted as a sideline to help fund the railroad, the fruit prospered amid this ideal climate, leading Keith to found the United Fruit Company, whose monopoly of the banana trade throughout Central America made him far wealthier than the railroad ever could.

Traditionally neglected and underfunded by the government, Limón suffered a major blow in the 1991 **earthquake**, which heaved the Caribbean coast about 1.5 metres up in the air. Already badly maintained roads, bridges and banana railroads were destroyed, including the track for the Jungle Train, one of the most scenic train rides in the world. While much has been rebuilt, an air of neglect still hangs over parts of the province, from housing and tourist infrastructure to basic sanitation.

Getting around

Options are limited in **getting around** Limón Province. From San José to Puerto Limón, you have a choice of just two roads, while from Puerto Limón south to the Panamá border at Sixaola there is but one decent route (not counting the few small local roads leading to the banana *fincas*). North of Puerto Limón there is no public land transport at all: instead, private *lanchas* ply the coastal **Tortuguero Canal**, dug in the late 1960s in order to bypass the treacherous breakers of the Caribbean. The canal connects the port of Moín, 8km north of Puerto Limón, to the Río Colorado near the Nicaraguan border.

Daily **flights** travel from San José to Barra del Colorado and Tortuguero. A reliable **bus** network operates in the rest of the province, with the most efficient and modern routes running from San José to Puerto Limón and on to Sixaola. Petrol provision is generally poor, except on the highway from San José; take a spare can with you if you plan to do much driving south of Puerto Limón or down into Panamá. **Language** can be a problem when travelling around Limón. While English is spoken widely along the coast (in Puerto Limón, Tortuguero and Puerto Viejo), don't expect everyone to know it. Your best bet is to make your first approaches in Spanish, if you can; people can then choose in which language to answer you.

San José to Puerto Limón

Two land routes head from the capital to Puerto Limón. Though the main route, the **Guápiles Highway** (Hwy-32), remains one of the best-maintained roads in the country, it's still half-jokingly referred to as the "Highway to Heaven" because of its high accident and fatality record. Nevertheless, the vast majority of buses and cars take this road, which begins in San José at the northern end of Calle 3 and climbs out of the Highlands to the northeast. This opening section of the highway is the most impressive, with Barva and Irazú volcanoes looming on either side. In general, however, the road doesn't offer quite the scenery you might expect because it's hewn from sheer walls of mountain carpeted with thick, intertwining vegetation. While one side is solid rock, the other side, in places, makes a sheer phantasmagoric drop that you can't quite see, with only the enormous, common huge-leaf plant known as "poor man's umbrella" (*sombrilla de pobre*) growing by the roadside to break the monotony.

The older, narrower and slower route, Hwy-10, often called the **Turrialba Road**, runs through Turrialba on the eastern slopes of the Cordillera Central before following the old switchbacking San José–Limón train tracks through a dense and pristine mountainous landscape, gutted by the deep cuts of the Pacuaré and Reventazón rivers. It joins the Guápiles Highway near **Siquerres**, about three-quarters of the way to Limón, beyond which the road passes through a final 80km of low flatlands to the coast. Considered dangerous and difficult to drive, the Turrialba Road now carries very little traffic, as it takes about four hours as opposed to two and a half to three hours on the Guápiles Highway.

Guápiles and around

GUÁPILES, about 60km east of San José, is the first town of any size on the Guápiles Highway and functions as a supply point for the Río Frío banana plantations and a waystation for the *bananero* workers. Today it's a commotion of shopping malls and stalls – there's even a farmer's market on Saturdays. The few **hotels** in town cater mainly to plantation workers and have cold water and thin walls. The one exception is the comparatively swish *Hotel Suerre* (across from the Technical College ⓣ2713-3000, ⓦwww.suerre.com; ❼), a country club with 55 rooms; a pool (with waterslides), jacuzzi, gym, tennis/basketball courts, and poolside bar (all of which non-guests are welcome to use for around $5). The rooms have air conditioning and satellite TV. The hotel also features a decent restaurant, two bars and a disco. You can check email at the *Café Internet Caribe* ($1 per hour; ⓣ2711-0631), in a strip mall about 100m in the town centre.

About 7km outside Guápiles, following a well-marked right turn from the highway at the *Ponderosa* restaurant, sits the *Casa Río Blanco Ecolodge* (ⓣ2710-4124, ⓦwww.casarioblanco.com; ❹), a rainforest lodge and bird-lover's paradise with comfortable *cabinas* and lush hiking trails down to the river and its waterfalls. *Cabinas* are perched on a 65-foot cliff, with one wall fully screened out to a hammocked veranda overlooking the frothy Río Blanco and its captivating rainforest environs. The owners are passionate about nature and offer birding/hiking tours.

Jardín Botánico Las Cusingas

Two kilometres east of Guápiles, a dirt road turn-off at *Soda Buenos Aires* leads to the secluded, **Jardín Botánico Las Cusingas** ($6; ⓣ2382-5805), 4km further on. Owned by Costa Ricans, Las Cusingas aims to educate visitors about tropical ecology and conservation. They offer hiking trails, horseback rides and a library. Covering 50 acres, the garden features 80 species of stunning orchids, and more than a hundred species of medicinal plants and bromeliads. Over a hundred species of birds have been recorded on the grounds. A two-hour guided tour costs $6. They also rent out a rustic yet well-appointed two-room **cabin**, which accommodates four people without difficulty, for $60.

Siquerres

Many of the package tours to Tortuguero (see p.183) make a brief stop at **SIQUERRES**, 1km northeast of the Guápiles Highway at Km-99 from San José, en route to picking up the boat at the small village of Hamburgo de Siquerres on the Río Reventazón. Most white-water raft operators also set out from here.

As the rusted hulks of freight cars and track-scarred streets show, Siquerres – which means "reddish colour" in a Miskito dialect – used to be a major railway hub for the **Jungle Train** that carted people, bananas and cacao to the Highlands. Along with Turrialba, this is where black train drivers, engineers and maintenance men would swap positions with their "white" (Spanish, *mestizo*, European or Highland) counterparts, who would then take the train into the Valle Central, where blacks were forbidden from travelling until 1949. Though the Jungle Train no longer runs, trains still haul bananas and machinery to and from Siquerres, mainly servicing the innumerable banana towns or *fincas* nearby (easily recognizable on maps from their factory-farm names of Finca 1, 2, a, b and so forth). You won't find much in the way of sights in sleepy Siquerres except for the completely **round church** on the western side of the football field. Built to mirror the shape of a Miskito hut, its authentic indigenous shape shelters a plain, wood-panelled interior.

The Standard Fruit Company of Costa Rica (which exports under the more popular name Dole) runs a tour of its **Esperanzas banana plantation** ($15; ⓣ2768-8683, ⓦwww.bananatourcostarica.com). If bananas are not your fruit of choice, you could always try the **Agri Pineapple Tour** ($17; ⓣ2282-1349, ⓦwww.agritourscr.com), which offers an inside look at Del Monte's Hacienda Ojo de Agua. Both tours are aimed at bus groups, and while drop-ins are accepted, you should call in advance outside of high season. About 1km east of the town is the rafting centre for **Exploradores Outdoors** (see p.64), which runs trips down the Río Pacuaré.

From Siquerres, it's a relatively easy 50km drive east to Puerto Limón along the well-maintained Hwy-10, though beware of truck and bus drivers speeding and overtaking on this stretch. As you drive, the countryside unfolds with macadamia nut farms set alongside small banana plots, flower nurseries and bare agricultural land dotted with humble roadside dwellings.

Puerto Limón and around

To the rest of the country, **PUERTO LIMÓN**, more often simply called Limón, is Costa Rica's *bête noire*, a steamy port raddled with slum neighbourhoods, bad sanitation and drug-related crime. The traveller may be kinder to the city than the Highland Tico, although Paul Theroux's first impressions in *The Old Patagonian Express* are no encouragement:

> **The stucco fronts had turned the colour and consistency of stale cake, and crumbs of concrete littered the pavements. In the market and on the parapets of the crumbling buildings there were mangy vultures. Other vultures circled the plaza. Was there a dingier backwater in all the world?**

Not much has changed in the thirty years or so since Theroux went through town, though the vultures have disappeared. Many buildings, damaged during the 1991 earthquake (the epicentre was just south of Limón), lie skeletal and wrecked, still in the process of falling down. Curiously, however, with its washed-out, peeling oyster-and-lime hues, Limón can be almost pretty, in a sad kind of way, with the pseudo-beauty of all Caribbean "slums of empire", as St Lucian poet Derek Walcott put it.

It's a working port but a neglected one, because most of the big-time banana boats now load at the deeper natural harbour of **Moín**, 6km up the headland toward Tortuguero. Generally, tourists come to Limón for one of three reasons: to get a **boat to Tortuguero** from Moín; to catch a bus south to the **beach towns** of Cahuita and Puerto Viejo: to join in the annual **El Día de la Raza** (Columbus

Limón patois

Limón patois combines **English phrases**, brought by Jamaican and Barbadian immigrants to the province in the last century, with a Spanish slightly different to that spoken in the Highlands. Though used less these days, the traditional greeting of "What happen?" ("Whoppin?") remains a stock phrase, equivalent to the Spanish "*¿Qué pasa?*" ("What's going on?"). In Limón, you'll also hear the more laconic "Okay" or "All right" (both hello and goodbye) taking the place of the Spanish "*Adiós*" ("hello" in Costa Rica rather than goodbye; see p.466), "*Que le vaya bien*" and "*Que Díos le acompañe*".

Yet, English might be spoken at home, and among the older Limón crowd, but Spanish is the language taught at school and used on the street, particularly among the younger generation. Older *Limonenses* sometimes refer to Spanish speakers as "Spaniamen" (which comes out sounding like "Sponyaman").

Day) carnival during the week preceding October 12; and, increasingly, to explore **Veragua Rainforest**. Less well known, but equally worth a visit, is the **Reserva Selva Bananito**, about thirty minutes to the south and one of the best birdwatching spots on the Caribbean Coast.

Arrival, information and orientation

Arriving in Limón after dark can be unnerving – get here in daylight if possible. Transportes Caribeños **buses** make the two-and-a-half-hour trip between **San José** (departing from C 0, Av 11) and **Limón** roughly hourly from 5am until 7pm, until 8pm on Sat & Sun. San José buses arrive at Limón's Gran Terminal del Caribe on C 7, Av 1/2, from where you can also catch a bus to Moín. You should buy your ticket several days in advance during *El Día de la Raza* carnival, even though extra buses run at this time. Arrivals **from the south** – Cahuita, Puerto Viejo de Talamanca and Panamá (via Sixaola) – terminate at the Transportes MEPE stop at C 3, Av 4, 100m north of Mercado Central.

There's no official **tourist office** in Limón or the entire province for that matter. Your best bet is to contact ICT in San José (see p.90) in advance of your arrival. Note that during *El Día de la Raza* carnival, everything shuts for a week, including all banks and the post office (see p.178).

While Limón isn't quite the mugger's paradise as portrayed by the Highlands media, you shouldn't linger on the pavement looking lost nor carry valuables while on the street – most of the hotels listed below have safes. When trying to **find your way around**, bear in mind that even more so than in other Costa Rican towns, nobody refers to *calles* and *avenidas* in Limón. The city does have street numbers, but virtually no signs. To confuse things further, unlike other towns in Costa Rica, *calles* and *avenidas* in Limón run sequentially, rather than in separate even- and odd-numbered sequences. Though the city as a whole spreads quite far out, central Limón covers no more than about ten blocks.

Accommodation

It's worth shelling out a bit extra for a **room** in Limón, especially if you're travelling alone – the comfort and safety of your hotel makes a big difference to your peace of mind. In midweek, the town's hotels fill up quickly with commercial travellers; try to get to Limón as early as possible if you're arriving on a Wednesday or Thursday.

Staying **downtown** puts you in the thick of things, and many hotels have communal balconies, perfect for relaxing with a cold beer and checking out the

Moving on from Limón

Shallow-bottomed private *lanchas* make the trip up the coastal canal from the docks at Moín to **Tortuguero** (3hr). It's best to arrive at the docks early (7–9am) although you may find boatmen willing to take you until 2pm. Expect to pay around $50 round-trip for a group of four to six people; if you're travelling alone or in a couple, try to get a group together at the docks. Buses for **Moín** depart from the main bus terminal at C 7, Av 1/2, but the bus has no set schedule and leaves when it's full (more or less every thirty minutes), so a taxi ($2–3) may be a better option.

Buses to San José run by Transportes Caribeños start running at 6.15am from the main bus terminal and continue hourly until 7pm (until 8pm on Sat & Sun). Prosersa buses (ⓣ2222-0610) depart from the main bus terminal to **Siquerres** and **Guápiles**, where you can make a bus connection to the capital.

Transportes MEPE buses (C 3, Av 4, ⓣ2257-8129), 100m north of the Mercado Central, serve the area **south of Limón**. Buses operate from 7am to 6pm, four times daily to Cahuita (1hr) and five times daily to Puerto Viejo (1hr 30min–2hr). The **Sixaola** bus also stops in both places. Two daily buses at 6am and 2.30pm go direct to **Manzanillo** village (2hr) in the heart of the Gandoca-Manzanillo Wildlife Refuge, via Puerto Viejo.

Taxis line up on Avenida 2 and around the corner from the main bus terminal: they do long-haul trips to Cahuita and Puerto Viejo ($30–40), and to the banana plantations of the Valle de Estrella ($20), where you can pick up another taxi to the **Reserva Biológica Hitoy-Cerere**. Prices are per car, so if you're in a group, renting a taxi can be far more convenient than taking the bus, and almost as cheap.

lively street activity below. The downside is the noise, especially at night; if you prefer to hear gentle waves lapping, try the *Park Hotel*, which stands alone on a little promontory close to the sea. There's also a group of quieter hotels outside town (about 4km up the spur road to Moín) at **Portete** and the small, somewhat misnamed **Playa Bonita**. A taxi to here costs less than $1.50, and the bus to and from Moín runs along the road every twenty minutes or so. Allow an hour to walk into town. In all but the most upmarket places, avoid drinking the **tap water**, or use a filter or iodine tablets.

Hotel prices rise by as much as fifty percent for **carnival** week, and to a lesser extent during *Semana Santa*, or Easter week. The least expensive times to stay are when rainfall is at its highest, between July and October, and December to February, which (confusingly) are considered high season in the rest of the country.

Limón has its share of dives, which tend to get booked when a big ship has docked. None of the places listed below is rock-bottom cheap. If this is what you're after, you'll find it easily enough, but always ask to see the room first and inspect the bathroom in particular.

In town

Hotel Caribe Av 2, C 1, above *Brisas del Caribe* restaurant along the pedestrian walkway by the central park ⓣ2758-0138. Bed down in these plain but spacious rooms with TV and fan, but beware that it can get noisy at night. A good place to haggle for a deal. ❷–❸

Miami Av 2, C 4/5 ⓣ&ⓕ2758-0490. This friendly, stylish spot near the central market offers large, clean rooms with ceiling fans, cable TV and private bathrooms. ❶, with a/c ❷

Park Hotel Av 3, C 1, by the *malecón* ⓣ2758-4364, ⓦwww.parkhotelcostarica.com. Popular with Ticos and travellers alike, this well-appointed hotel has 32 rooms in a range of styles: the more expensive ones come with a sea view, slightly less expensive rooms have a street view, and the cheapest, *plana turista*, have no view at all. There's a good restaurant on site and note that it's important to book in advance. ❹

Teté Av 3, C 4/5 ⓣ2758-1122. One of the best downtown hotels in this price range, friendly *Teté*

has clean, well-cared-for rooms; those on the street have balconies but can be noisy, while the darker inside rooms are quieter. ❷

Around Limón

Apartotel Cocorí Playa Bonita ⓣ2798-1670. Relax in these comfortable self-catering apartments, with fan or a/c, amid a beautiful leafy setting overlooking the ocean. Pluses include a friendly staff and a swimming pool. The lively outdoor bar-restaurant, right by the sea, has lovely views. ❸

Cabinas Maeva Portete; look for the blue-and-white sign ⓣ2758-2024. Cute, yellow hexagonal *cabinas* with small private bathrooms nestle among palm trees, a beautiful pool and Neoclassical statues. ❷

Hotel Playa Westfalia 2km south of Limón airport ⓣ2756-1661, ⓦhotelplayawestfalia.com. If you're looking for luxury within easy driving distance of Limón, this idyllic beachfront hotel is unquestionably your best choice. The eight well-appointed rooms and suites all have a/c, wi-fi and cable TV, and the hotel has a pool and a pleasant restaurant serving Caribbean cuisine. ❻

Maribú Caribe Playa Bonita ⓣ2795-4010, ⓔmaricari@racsa.co.cr. A favourite among banana-company executives, this luxurious seaside complex of round, thatched-roof huts has 1960s decor, a pool and a pleasant but pricey bar-restaurant overlooking the sea. ❻

The Town

Stroll around Puerto Limón for about fifteen minutes and you've got a decent lay of the land. **Avenida 2**, known locally as the "market street" and for all purposes the main drag, runs along both the north edge of Parque Vargas and the south side of the **Mercado Central**. At times, the market seems to contain the entire

El Día de la Raza carnival

Though carnivals in the rest of Latin America are usually associated with the days before Lent, the Limón Carnival celebrates Columbus's arrival in the New World on October 12. The festivity was first introduced to Limón by Arthur King, a local who had been away working in Panamá's Canal Zone. He was so impressed with that country's Columbus Day celebrations that he decided to bring the merriment home to Limón. Today, **El Día de la Raza** (Day of the People) basically serves as an excuse to party. Throngs of Highland Ticos descend upon Limón – buses fill to bursting, hotels brim and revellers hit the streets in search of this year's sounds and style. Rap, rave and ragga – in Spanish and English – are hot, and Bob Marley lives, or at least is convincingly resurrected, for carnival week.

Carnival can mean anything you want it to, from noontime displays of Afro-Caribbean dance to Calypso music, bull-running, children's theatre, colourful *desfiles* (parades) and massive firework displays. Most spectacular is the **Grand Desfile**, usually held on the Saturday before October 12, when revellers in Afro-Caribbean costumes – sequins, spangles and fluorescent colours – parade through the streets to a cacophony of tambourines, whistles and blasting sound systems.

Instead of taking place in Limón's streets as it has in years past (the national press reported on "sanitation" problems that threatened to bring the whole event to a halt), most of the carnival's night-time festivities now occur within the fences of the harbour authority JAPDEVA's huge docks and car park. This might sound like a soulless location, but it's a well-managed affair, and while you may not be dancing in the streets, you're at least dancing. The overall atmosphere – even late at night – remains unthreatening, with teens and grandparents alike enjoying the music. Kiosks dispense steaming Chinese, Caribbean and Tico food, and on-the-spot discos help pump up the volume. **Cultural Street**, which runs from the historic Black Star Line (the shipping company that brought many of the black immigrants here), is an alcohol-free zone, popular with family groups. Kids can play games at small fairgrounds to win candyfloss and stuffed toys. Elsewhere, bars overflow onto the street, and the impromptu partying builds up as the night goes on.

population of Limón – dowager women mind their stalls while men clutch cigarettes, chattering and gesticulating. The produce looks fresh: chayotes, plantains, cassava, yucca, beans and the odd banana (most of the crop is exported) vie for space with bulb-like cacao fruit, baseball-sized tomatoes and huge carrots. For an inexpensive, quality bite to eat, try the market's *sodas* and snack bars.

Limón, often noisy and chaotic, becomes pleasantly languid in the heat of the day, with workers drifting towards **Parque Vargas** and the *malecón* at lunch to sit under the shady palms. The park features a sea-facing **mural** (at the easternmost end of C 1 and Av 1 and 2) by artist Guadalupe Alvarea. The mural swarms with colourful, evocative images of the province's tough history. On the left of the semicircular wall, indigenous people are shown making crafts, which were later destroyed by the Catholic missionaries. Moving right, you'll note the era of Columbus, with ships being loaded with coffee and bananas by women wearing vibrant African cloth. Finally, the arrival of the Jungle Train is depicted with a wonderful Chinese dragon to symbolize the Chinese labourers who worked on it.

A small colony of **sloths** lives in the park's tall royal palms. At the end of the central promenade rises a shrine to sailors and fishermen, and also a dilapidated bandstand, the site of occasional concerts. From here, the **malecón** (a thin ledge where it's hardly possible to walk, let alone take a seaside promenade) winds its way north. Avoid it at night when muggings have been reported. At the northern end of the park is the slightly run-down **municipalidad** (town hall), with a pale facade and peeling Belle Epoque grillework. Opposite, on the shore, sits an elegant modern sculpture in the shape of a ship's prow. A small amphitheatre and stage have been cleverly built into its framework, and here you can enjoy the occasional concert or outdoor theatre performance.

The only other building of note in Limón is the landmark **Radio Casino** (corner of C 4 and Av 4), home to an excellent community-service station, broadcast by and for Limonenses, with call-in chat shows, international news and good music, including local and imported reggae. As for **swimming** in town, forget it: one look at the water from the tiny spit of sand next to the *Park Hotel* is discouragement enough. Pollution, sharks, huge banana-carrying ships and sharp, exposed coral make it practically impossible to swim anywhere nearby; the nearest possibility is at **Playa Bonita**, though even that is plagued by dangerous riptides.

Eating, drinking and entertainment

Limón has a decent variety of places to eat, with several restaurants focusing on authentic **Caribbean and Creole cuisine**. It's best to heed the warnings and not sit outside at the restaurants in the town centre, particularly around the Mercado Central, where tourists are prime targets for often aggressive beggars. Inside the market, however, it's quite safe and you'll find a host of decent *sodas* serving tasty *casados*. Gringos in general and women especially should avoid most **bars**, especially those that have a large advertising placard blocking views of the interior, which are often less than salubrious. For a drink, stick to places like *Casa Blanca* (corner of C 4 Av 4) or *Brisas del Caribe*. When you tire of the town, head to relaxing **Playa Bonita** for lunch or an afternoon beer.

In town

Brisas del Caribe C 1, Av 2, in *Hotel Caribe*. Enjoy views of Parque Vargas from this clean bar-restaurant with a soothing ambience, except when they blast the sound system. The varied menu includes Chinese fare, sandwiches, snacks and a tasty *medio casado* (half *casado*) for around $3. Mon–Fri 7am–11pm, Sat & Sun 10am–11pm.

Park Hotel Av 3, C 1, by the *malecón*. The only restaurant in town where you feel you might actually be in the Caribbean – warm breezes float in through large slatted windows that look out onto vistas of blue seas and clouds as far as the eye can see. Dine on excellent, though pricey, breakfast and standard Costa Rican fare, including *elote* (corn on the cob) and *arroz con pollo*. Daily 7am–10pm.

Soda La Estrella C 5, Av 3/4. The best lunch in town features excellent *soda* staples, delicious *refrescos*, coffee and snacks like *arreglados* (filled puff pastries), all accompanied by cordial service. Daily 10am–10pm.

Supra Pizzeria Av 3, C 4/5 ☎2758-3371. Located upstairs at the Plaza Caribe, this is a good spot to enjoy pizza (large $10) and pasta with the local set. Open till 11pm.

Playa Bonita

Quimbamba Bar & Restaurant Playa Bonita ☎2795-4805. Dine on excellent – if pricey – fresh fish cooked to order at this hopping split-level beach-bar. Live music at the weekend. Daily 8am–late.

Reina's Playa Bonita ☎2795-0879. Stylish beachside restaurant and lounge bar that's equally successful at delivering tasty Caribbean cuisine – particularly the seafood – smooth cocktails and energetic local live acts and DJs. Daily 10am–10pm.

Listings

Banks The Banco de Costa Rica, on Av 2, C 1, and Scotiabank, on Av 3, C 2, both offer money exchange and have ATMs that accept Visa and Cirrus. Load up here, as banks are a rarity along the Caribbean coast.

Hospital ☎2758-2222. Limón is home to the largest hospital on the coast, which is located on the northern edge of town, along the *malecón*; to get there, follow Av 6.

Internet At the post office; Net Café on Av 4, C 5/6; and Cyber Internet, on Av 3, C 3/4, which has a bunch of speedy machines.

Post office Av 2, C 4 (Mon–Fri 7.30am–5pm, Sat 8am–noon), though the mail service from Limón is dreadful – you're better off posting items from San José.

Creole cuisine in Limón Province

Creole cuisine is known throughout the Americas, from Louisiana to Bahía, for its imaginative use of African spices and vegetables, succulent fish and chicken dishes and fantastic sweet desserts. Sample Limón's version at any of the locally run restaurants dotted along the coast. These are often family affairs, usually presided over by respected older Afro-Caribbean women. Sitting down to dinner at a red gingham tablecloth, with a cold bottle of Imperial beer, reggae on the boombox and a plate heaped with coconut-scented rice-and-beans is one of the real pleasures of visiting this part of Costa Rica. Note that many restaurants, in keeping with age-old local tradition, feature Creole dishes at weekends only, serving simpler dishes or the usual Highland rice concoctions during the week.

Everyone outside Limón will tell you that the local speciality, **rice-and-beans** (in the lilting local accent it sounds like "rizanbin"), is "*comida muy pesada*" (very heavy food). However, this truly wonderful mixture of red or black beans and rice cooked in coconut milk is no more *pesada* – and miles tastier – than traditional Highland dishes like *arroz con camarones*, where everything is fried; it's the coconut milk that gives this dish its surprising lift. Another local speciality is **pan bon**, sweet bread glazed and laced with cheese and fruit which is often eaten for dessert, as are ginger biscuits and plantain tarts. *Pan bon* doesn't translate as "good bread", as is commonly thought; "bon" actually derives from "bun", brought by English-speaking settlers. **Rundown** (said "rondon" – to "rundown" is to cook) is a vegetable and meat or fish stew in which the plantains and breadfruit cook for many hours, very slowly, in spiced coconut milk. It may be hard to find, mainly because it takes a long time, at least an afternoon, to prepare. Though some restaurants – *Springfield* in Limón, *Miss Junie's* in Tortuguero and *Miss Edith's* in Cahuita – have it on their menus as a matter of course, it's usually best to stop by on the morning of the day you wish to dine and request it for that evening.

Favoured **spices** in Limonese Creole cooking include cumin, coriander, peppers, chillies, paprika, cloves and groundspice, while the most common vegetables are those you might find in a street market in West Africa, Brazil or Jamaica. Native to Africa, **ackee** (in Spanish *seso vegetal*) was brought to the New World by British colonists, and has to be prepared by knowledgeable cooks because its sponge-cake-like yellow fruit, enclosed in three-inch pods, is poisonous until the pods open. Served boiled, ackee resembles scrambled eggs and goes well with fish. **Yucca**, also known as manioc, is a long pinkish tuber, similar to the yam, and usually boiled or fried. Local yams can grow as big as 25kg, and are used much like potato in soups and stews. Another native African crop, the huge melon-like **breadfruit** (*fruta de pan*), is more a starch substitute than a fruit, with white flesh that has to be boiled, baked or grated. **Pejiballes** (*pejibaye* in Spanish – English-speaking people in Limón pronounce it "picky-BAY-ah") are small green or orange fruits that look a little like limes. They're boiled in hot water and skinned – and are definitely an acquired taste, being both salty and bitter. You'll find them sold on the street in San José, but they're most popular in Limón. Better known as heart-of-palm, **palmito** is served in restaurants around the world as part of a tropical salad. **Plantains** (*plátanos* in Spanish), the staple of many Highland dishes, figure particularly heavily in Creole cuisine, and are deliciously sweet when baked or fried in fritters. Right at the other end of the health scale are **herbal teas**, a speciality of the province and available in many restaurants: try wild peppermint, wild basil, soursop, lime, lemon grass or ginger.

Around Limón

While it's not worth using Limón as a base to visit Tortuguero – a day-trip there would leave you with almost no time to see either the turtles or the village – there are a couple of nearby attractions that can be easily visited in a day. About an hour or so west is the excellent **Veragua Rainforest**, in the hamlet of Brisas de Veragua in the hills above the town of Liverpool. To the south of Limón, the little-visited gem **Reserva Selva Bananito** has a slew of outdoor activities that will you keep you busy for a day – and easily longer, should you choose to stay at the reserve's lodge.

Veragua Rainforest

Opened in 2008, **Veragua Rainforest** (Tues–Sun 8am–3pm; $55; ⓣ2296-5056, ⓦwww.veraguarainforest.com) is a fascinating "research and adventure park" that provides a quick and sleek introduction to some of the region's rich biodiversity. Owned and operated entirely by Costa Ricans, Veragua holds several smartly designed animal exhibits – including one that mimics a nocturnal habitat for frogs – as well as an aerial tram, a zip line and an elevated trail through the rainforest leading to a waterfall. The highlight, though, is the research facility, where you can talk with the resident biologists and learn more about the ongoing study of the park's stunning collection of butterflies.

Empresa buses for Siquirres leave Limón's Terminal de Caribeños hourly; get off at the Liverpool town stop, about 12km from Limón – let the bus driver know you're going to Veragua. The road leading to Veragua is signposted about 50m from the bus stop. Call in advance to arrange pick-up from here, which is possible most days. If you're driving, a 4WD is necessary to negotiate the bone-rattling gravel road that covers the final 3km to the rainforest.

Reserva Selva Bananito

Twenty kilometres south of Limón, the eight-square-kilometre private **Reserva Selva Bananito** unfolds alongside the Parque Nacional La Amistad and protects an area of mountainous, virgin rainforest. The reserve is reached via an inland road from the main coastal highway that goes through the banana town of Bananito and then along a very rough track across several rivers (you'll need a 4WD). There are several activities on offer, from horseriding and tree-climbing to hiking and bird-watching (toucans, orioles, various raptors and kingfishers have all been spotted in the reserve); prices range from $20 to $45.

After making the trip here it's not easy to turn your back on the reserve's wonderfully peaceful **lodge** (ⓣ2253-8118, ⓦwww.selvabananito.com; ❽, including three meals). Eleven attractive, spacious cabins have large verandas overlooking the forest, with meals and drinks served in the main ranch. Owned and run by the environmentally conscious children of a pioneering German farmer, the lodge is built from secondhand wood discarded by loggers, has solar-powered hot water (though no electricity) and donates a percentage of its profits to the Fundación Cuencas de Limón, which helps protect the local area and develop educational programmes. If you don't have your own transport, you can call the lodge and arrange to be picked up from the bus stop at *Salon Delia* in Bananito Norte.

Parque Nacional Tortuguero

Despite its isolation – 254km from San José by road and water – **PARQUE NACIONAL TORTUGUERO** ($10; ⓣ2710-2929) is among the most visited national parks in Costa Rica. *Tortuguero* means turtle-catcher in Spanish, and turtle-catchers have long flourished in this area, one of the most important nesting sites in the world for the **green sea turtle**, one of only eight species of marine turtle. Along with the hawksbill turtle, the green sea turtle lays its eggs here between July and October.

First established as a protective zone in the 1960s, Tortuguero officially became a national park in 1975. It encompasses 190 square kilometres of protected land, including not only the beach on which the turtles nest, but also the surrounding impenetrable tropical rainforest, coastal mangrove swamps and lagoons, and canals and waterways. Except during the comparatively dry months of February, March, September and October the park is fairly wet, receiving over 3500mm of rain a year. This soggy environment hosts a wide abundance of **wildlife** – fifty kinds of **fish**, numerous **birds**, including the endangered green parrot and the vulture, and about 160 **mammals**, some under the threat of extinction. Due to the waterborne nature of most transport and the impenetrability of the ground cover, it's difficult to spot them, but howler, white-faced capuchin and spider monkeys lurk behind the undergrowth. The park is also home to the fishing bulldog bat, which fishes by sonar, and a variety of large rodents, including the window rat, whose internal organs you can see through its transparent skin. Jaguars used to thrive here, but are slowly being driven out by the encroaching banana plantations at the western end of the park; you may also spot the West Indian manatee, or sea cow, swimming underwater. It's the **turtles**, however, that draw all the visitors. The sight of the gentle beasts tumbling ashore and shimmying their way up the beach to deposit their heavy load before limping back, spent, into the dark phosphorescent waves can't fail to move.

As elsewhere in Costa Rica, logging, economic opportunism and fruit plantations have affected the parkland. Sometimes advertised by package tour brochures as a "Jungle Cruise" along "Central America's Amazon", the journey to Tortuguero is indeed Amazonian, taking you past tracts of **deforestation** and lands cleared for cattle – all outside the park's official boundaries but, together with the banana plantations, disturbingly close to its western fringes.

The most popular way to see Tortuguero is on one of literally hundreds of **tour packages**, many of which are two-night, three-day affairs that use the expensive lodges across the canal from the village. Accommodation, meals and transport (which otherwise can be a bit tricky) are taken care of, and guides point out wildlife along the river and canal. The main difference between tours comes in the standard of accommodation, and most importantly, the quality of your guide. Ask about your guide's accreditations, and don't hesitate to check his level of English. Castor Hunter Thomas ⓣ2709-8050 (his father was Tortuguero's first guide) or Bonye Scott ⓣ8844-8099 come highly recommended.

With a little planning, however, you can also get to Tortuguero **independently** and stay in *cabinas* in the village. Basing yourself in the village allows you to explore the beach at leisure – though you can't swim – and puts you within easy reach of restaurants and bars.

Getting to Tortuguero

As the **Tortuguero Canal** is impassable in most areas to all but the most shallow-bottomed of boats, *lanchas*, which go up the canal from Moín, Antigua Pavona and elsewhere, are effectively the only means of transportation. Expect a three- or four-hour trip (sometimes longer), depending upon where you embark – if you're on a package tour, it will probably be **Hamburgo de Siquerres** on the Río Reventazón; travelling independently, you'll find it logistically easier to leave from **Antigua Pavona** or **Moín**. Either way, the *lanchas* glide through mirror-calm waters past palm and deciduous trees and small, stilt-legged wooden houses, brightly painted and poised on the water's edge. The canal hums with human activity, with scores of *lanchas*, *botes* (large canoes) and *pangas* (flat-bottomed outboard-motored boats) plying the glassy waters. You may spot crocodiles and caimans basking on the canal banks, moss-covered and immobile sloths clinging to a tree or perhaps even a troupe of spider monkeys making their leaping, chattering way through the waterfront canopy.

Much less time-consuming, of course, is a **flight** from San José to the airstrip across the canal from *Tortuga Lodge*. The trip is a spectacular one, as you rise above the mountains outside the city and are afforded a bird's-eye view of the canals as you approach the park from the south.

By lancha from Moín

If you're travelling independently, you should be able to find a boat at **Moín** willing to make the four hour journey up the canal any time from 6am until as late as 2pm (depending on the tides), although the earlier you travel the better. You can arrange with your boatman your return day and time; get a phone number if possible, so you can call from Tortuguero village if you change return plans. The *lanchas* drop you at Tortuguero dock in the centre of the village, from where you can walk to the village accommodation or take another *lancha* to the more expensive tourist lodges further up the canal.

By lancha from Cariari

Alternatively, you can do as the locals do and take a 9am or 10.30am bus from San José's Terminal Gran Caribe to **Cariari**, and then switch to either the noon or 3pm bus for Rancho La Suerte (also known as Antigua Pavona), from where boats depart daily around to Totuguero (a boat is timed to leave shortly after the bus arrives from Cariari). The journey is long, but the boat ride costs only $3–10 each way, so you'll save a lot, particularly if you're travelling alone. The return boat to San José leaves daily at 6am.

By air

Sansa (Ⓣ2290-4100) and NatureAir (Ⓣ2299-6000) fly daily **from San José** (flight time 35–50min). Sansa flights depart at 6am from Juan Santamaría International Airport, while NatureAir flights depart at 6.15am from Tobías Bolaños International Airport in the Pavas district. The Tortuguero airstrip lies about 4km north of the village. There are no taxis from here to the village, though the more upscale lodges will come and pick you up; otherwise you'll have to walk.

Tour operators to Tortuguero

Several companies offer **all-inclusive packages** to Tortuguero, usually including accommodation at one of the upmarket lodges lining the canal. Budget options tend to involve some form of bus/boat transfer while the more expensive tours fly direct from San José.

Costa Rica Expeditions C Central, Av 3, San José Ⓣ2257-0766, Ⓦwww.costaricaexpeditions.com. Exceedingly well-run and attentive outfit offering upscale Tortuguero packages including flights from San José, accommodation at the comfortable *Tortuga Lodge* and three meals a day. Prices start at $358 per person for a three-day, two-night package. They also offer trips to Barra del Colorado.

Ecole Travel C 7, Av 0/1, San José Ⓣ2234-1669, Ⓦwww.ecoletravel.com. One of the longest-established companies offering Tortuguero tours, Ecole has excellent budget tours popular with students and backpackers. Tours ($189 for two nights and three days) start from the *Gran Hotel Costa Rica* in San José.

Jungle Tom Safaris Ⓣ2221-7878, Ⓦwww.jungletomsafaris.com. Long-running US-owned operator offering some of the more inexpensive tours to Tortuguero. They lead one-, two- and three-day trips from $90 from San José.

Riverboat Fracesca Tours Ⓣ2226-0986, Ⓦwww.tortuguerocanals.com. Riverboat Fracesca features two-day, one-night tours of the Tortuguero canals from $200. The price includes bus transportation from San José to Moín (where you embark on the canal tour), meals and lodging.

Information

A small, somewhat faded display on the turtles' habits, habitat and history surrounds the **information kiosk** in the village centre. This is the official place to buy tickets for turtle tours; the park rangers sell the tickets at the kiosk from 5pm to 6pm. Here you can also get contact info for local guides. Canadian naturalist and local resident Darryl Loth (Ⓣ2709-8011, Ⓦcasamarbella.tripod.com), who runs the nearby *Casa Marbella* (see p.186), has a small information centre in the village and can arrange tours, including boat trips and hikes up Cerro Tortuguero (see p.188). Another excellent source of local information is fellow Canadian and botanist Ross Ballard (Ⓣ2709-8193, Ⓔsrossballard@gmail.com) who leads ecological tours on the canals.

There are no **bank** or **money-changing** facilities in Tortuguero – bring all the cash you'll need with you – and though there's a **post office** in the middle of the village, mail may take three or four weeks just to make its way to Limón. If villagers are heading to Limón they might offer to carry letters for you and post them from there, which can be useful if you're staying here for any length of time. Tortuguero has a weekly **medical service**; otherwise emergencies and health problems should be referred to the park's administration headquarters, north of the village, near the airstrip. The purple Paraíso Tropical **souvenir shop** in the middle of the village doubles as the village's NatureAir agent, and sells tickets to San José.

Accommodation

Staying at Tortuguero on the cheap entails bedding down in one of the independent **cabinas** in the village. If you haven't booked a hotel in advance, be aware that accommodation in the village can fill up quickly during the turtle-nesting seasons (March–May & July–Oct).

Staying at Tortuguero's **lodges**, most of which are across the canal from the village, has its drawbacks. Though convenient, and in some cases quite luxurious, life as a lodger can be a rather regimented affair. Guests are shuttled in and out of the lodges with stopwatch precision and there's precious little nightlife. If you want to explore the village and the beach on your own you have to get a *lancha* across the canal (free, but inconvenient). Note, however, that outside the turtle-watching season, most lodges don't operate their boats at night. Owing to Tortuguero's perennial popularity with package tourists, the lodges seldom have space for independent travellers.

Camping on the beach is not allowed, though you can set up a tent for about $2 per day at the mown enclosure near the **ranger station** at the southern end of the village, where you enter the park. It's in a sheltered situation, away from the sea breezes, and there's drinking water and toilets. Bring a groundsheet and mosquito net, and make sure your tent is waterproof.

In the village

Cabinas Aracari South of the information kiosk and football field Ⓣ2709-8006. Run by a local family, these clean, comfortable *cabinas*, all with private bath, cold water and fan, sit amid a beautiful tree-filled garden. ❶

Cabinas Meriscar In the southern part of the village where three dirt roads converge Ⓣ2709-8202. Newer cabins come with private bathrooms, while the older, slightly gloomy but clean *cabinas* have shared spick-and-span bathrooms. It's possible to camp in the grounds for $2. ❷

Cabinas Tortuguero South of the village, towards the entry to the national park and across from the supermarket Ⓣ2709-8114, Ⓔcabinas_tortuguero@yahoo.com. Five simple en-suite rooms sit in a lovely garden. Tasty meals are offered, including Italian food, because one of the owners is from Bologna. You can also rent canoes. ❷

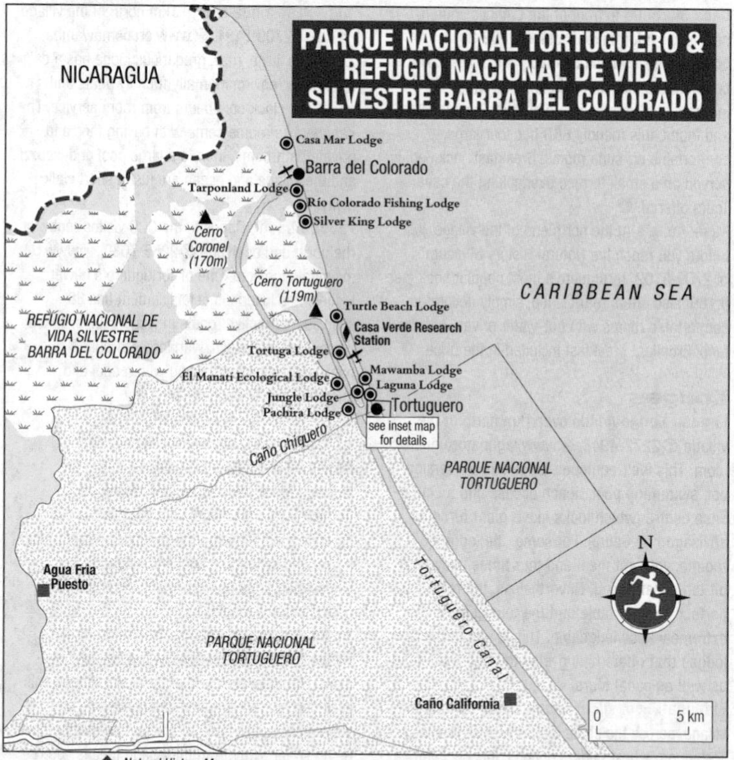

PARQUE NACIONAL TORTUGUERO &
REFUGIO NACIONAL DE VIDA
SILVESTRE BARRA DEL COLORADO
NICARAGUA
Casa Mar Lodge
Barra del Colorado
Tarponland Lodge
Río Colorado Fishing Lodge
Silver King Lodge
Cerro Coronel (170m)
Cerro Tortuguero (119m)
CARIBBEAN SEA
Turtle Beach Lodge
Casa Verde Research Station
REFUGIO NACIONAL DE VIDA SILVESTRE BARRA DEL COLORADO
Tortuga Lodge
Mawamba Lodge
Laguna Lodge
El Manatí Ecological Lodge
Jungle Lodge
Pachira Lodge
Tortuguero
see inset map for details
Caño Chiquero
PARQUE NACIONAL TORTUGUERO
Agua Fria Puesto
Tortuguero Canal
PARQUE NACIONAL TORTUGUERO
Caño California
0
5 km
N

Natural History Museum
TORTUGUERO
0
100 m
Paraíso Tropical
Private Dock
Laguna Tortuguero
CARIBBEAN SEA
Football Pitch
Public Dock
N
Parque Nacional Tortuguero & Ranger Station

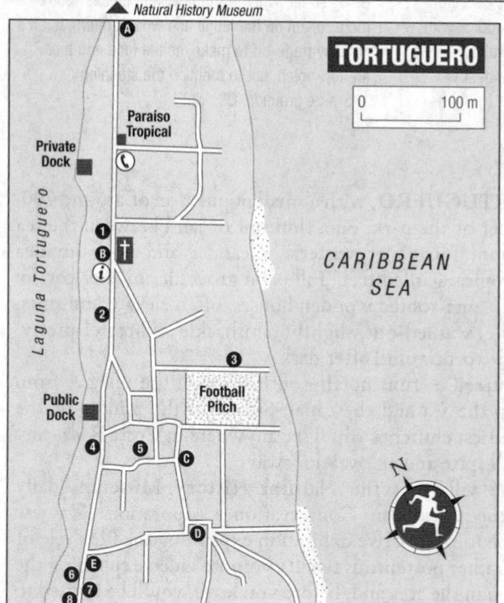

ACCOMMODATION

Cabinas Aracari	C
Cabinas Meriscar	D
Cabinas Tortuguero	E
Casa Marbella	B
Miss Junie's	A

EATING & DRINKING

Budda Café	2
Cabinas Tropical Lodge	8
Centro Social La Culebra	4
Dorling's Bakery	1
Miss Junie's	A
Miss Miriam's	3
El Muellecito	5
Sunrise	7
La Taberna	6

Casa Marbella In front of the Catholic church, next to the information kiosk ⓣ2709-8011, ⓦwww.casamarbella.tripod.com. Managed by a committed Canadian environmentalist, an inexhaustible source of info on the regional flora and fauna, this friendly B&B has four large, comfortable en-suite rooms. Breakfast, included, is served on a small terrace overlooking the canal. Tours offered. ❹

Miss Junie's At the north end of the village, just before you reach the Natural History Museum ⓣ2709-8102. Tortuguero's most popular cook (see p.189) also offers refurbished, simply decorated, comfortable rooms with hot-water private bath and fans. Excellent breakfast included in the price. ❹

Lodges

Laguna Lodge A little over 1km north of the village ⓣ2272-4943, ⓦwww.lagunatortuguero.com. This well-equipped lodge has a riverside bar, swimming pool, beach access and a conference centre (which looks like a giant turtle as envisaged by Gaudí). For some, the lodge's regime, with set meal and tour times, may be a bit too constraining. Nevertheless, the rooms are perfectly comfortable and the tour guides extremely knowledgeable. This is one of the few lodges that offers hiking trips through the jungle as well as canal tours. ❽

El Manatí Ecological Lodge 1.5km north of the village, across the canal ⓣ2383-0330. One of Tortuguero's best budget options, this peaceful family-run lodge has basic but clean rooms with hot-water private bath and fans, as well as several attractive two-bedroom *cabinas*. Breakfast is included. ❺

Mawamba Lodge 1km north of the village ⓣ2709-8181, ⓦwww.grupomawamba.com. This large, ritzy, gregarious lodge has a daily slide show, environmentally friendly boats and round-the-clock cold beers from room service. The *cabina*-style rooms come with ceiling fans and private bathrooms, there's a large pool and jacuzzi and the village and ocean are just a short walk away. ❽

Pachira Lodge Opposite the CCC visitor centre at rhe north end of village ⓣ2256-7080, ⓦwww.pachiralodge.com. One of Tortuguero's newer lodges, this luxurious establishment has 88 spacious, attractive rooms in wood cabins, linked by covered walkways, with large en-suite, hot-water bathrooms, along with a pool and imaginative tour options. ❽

Tortuga Lodge ⓣ2257-0766, ⓦwww.costaricaexpeditions.com. Owned by Costa Rica Expeditions, this is the plushest lodge in the area (but among the furthest from the village) with large, attractive en-suite rooms, exemplary service, excellent food, a riverside swimming pool and elegantly landscaped grounds from which several trails depart into the jungle. ❽

Turtle Beach Lodge About 2km north of the village ⓣ2248-0707, ⓦwww.turtlebeachlodge.com. The most removed of the major lodges, this secluded upmarket option has handsome and supremely comfortable rooms and an inviting pool. Being so far away from the village means you're more reliant on the lodge and what it offers, but it's an easy trade-off to make, as the food and tours are top-notch, not to mention the stunning 175-acre grounds. ❽

The village

The peaceful village of **TORTUGUERO**, with a small population of around 700, lies at the northeastern corner of the park, on a thin spit of land between the sea and the canal. The exuberant foliage of wisteria, oleander and bougainvillea imbues the village with a tropical garden feel. Tall palm groves loom over patchy expanses of grass dotted with zinc-roofed wooden houses, often elevated on stilts. This is classic Caribbean style: washed-out, slightly ramshackle and pastel-pretty, with very little to disturb the torpor until after dark.

A dirt path – the "main street" – runs north–south through the village, from which narrow paths lead to the sea and the canal. Smack in the middle of the village stands one of the prettiest churches you'll see anywhere in Costa Rica, tiny and pale yellow, with a small spire and an oval doorway.

At the north end of the village is the **Natural History Museum** (daily 10am–5pm; $2) run by the Caribbean Conservation Corporation (ⓦwww.cccturtle.org), with a small but informative exhibition explaining the life cycle of sea turtles. You can watch a rather portentous twenty-minute video explaining the history of turtle conservation in the area and, before you leave, you'll be invited to "adopt a turtle" for $25 for which you'll receive an adoption certificate and information so that you can track the migratory progress of your chosen beast on the internet as it makes its slow, purposeful way across the ocean.

The park

Most people come to Tortuguero to see the **desove**, or egg-laying of the turtles. Few are disappointed, as the majority of tours during **laying seasons** (March–May & July–Oct) result in sightings of the surreal procession of the reptiles from the sea to make their egg-nests in the sand. While turtles have been known to lay in the daylight (the hatchlings wait under the cover of sand until nightfall to emerge), it is far more common for them to come ashore in the relative safety of night. Nesting can take place turtle-by-turtle – you can watch a single mother come ashore and scramble up the beach just south of the village or, more strikingly, in groups (*arribadas*) when dozens emerge from the sea at the same time to form a colony, marching up the sands to their chosen spot, safely above the high-tide mark. Each turtle digs a hole in which she lays eighty or more eggs; the collective whirring noise of sand being dug away is extraordinary. Having filled the hole with sand to cover the eggs, the turtles begin their course back to the sea, leaving the eggs to hatch and return to the waves under the cover of darkness. Incubation takes some weeks; when the hatchlings emerge they instinctively follow the light of the moon on the water, scuttling to safety in the ocean.

Tortuguero is one of the best spots in Costa Rica to observe marine turtles nesting, as three of the largest kinds of endangered sea turtles regularly nest here in large numbers. Along with the **green** (*verde*) turtle, named for the colour of soup made from its flesh, you might see the **hawksbill** (*carey*), with its distinctive hooked beak, and the ridged **leatherback** (*baula*), the largest turtle in the world, which weighs around 300kg – though some are as heavy as 500kg and reach 2.4m in length. The green turtles and hawksbills nest mainly from July to October (August is the peak month), while the leatherbacks may come ashore from March to May.

Turtle tours

Turtle tours, led by certified guides, leave at 8pm and 10pm every night from the information kiosk in the village. If you're not going with an organized group from one of the lodges, you'll need to buy park entrance tickets from the kiosk, which is staffed by park rangers from 5pm to 6pm every afternoon. Be sure to get there early because the number of visitors is strictly limited. No more than 200 people are allowed on the beach at any one time and visitors must wear dark clothing, refrain from smoking, and aren't allowed to bring cameras (still or video) or flashlights. Everyone must be off the beach by midnight. There are over a hundred certified guides in Tortuguero; they charge $10 for a turtle tour (roughly half the price of a lodge tour) – if you haven't already sorted one out, they conveniently tend to hang around the ticket kiosk at 5pm in search of customers.

Hiking

The well-maintained **Jaguar Trail** (2km) starts at the ranger station at the park entrance and heads toward the coast where it turns south, paralleling the beach which remains close at hand for the length of the path. It's a mostly shaded walk, and it gives you a good chance of spotting lizards and monkeys. As for the long, wild **beach**, you can amble for up to 30km south, spotting crabs and birds along the way, and also looking for turtle tracks, which resemble the two thick parallel

Turtling

For hundreds of years the fishermen of the Caribbean coast made their living culling the seemingly plentiful turtle population, selling shell and meat for large sums to middlemen in Puerto Limón. Initially, turtles were hunted for local consumption only, but during the first two decades of the 1900s, the fashion for turtle soup in Europe, especially England, led to large-scale exports.

Turtle-hunting was a particularly brutal practice. Spears were fashioned from long pieces of wood, taken from the apoo palm or the rawa, and fastened with a simple piece of cord to a sharp, barbed metal object. Standing in their canoes, fishermen hurled the spear, like a miniature harpoon, into the water, lodging the spear in the turtle's flesh. Pulling their canoes closer, the fishermen would then reel in the cord attached to the spear, lift the beasts onto the canoes and take them ashore dead or alive. On land, the turtles might be beheaded with a machete or put in the holds of ships, where they could survive a journey of several weeks to Europe if they were given a little water.

Today, turtles are protected, their eggs and meat a delicacy. Locals around Tortuguero are officially permitted to take two turtles a week during nesting season for their own consumption – the unlucky green turtles are considered the most delicious. The recent sharp decline in the populations of hawksbill, green and leatherback turtles has been linked, at least in part, to **poaching**. This has prompted the national parks administration to adopt a firm policy discouraging the theft of turtle eggs within the park boundaries and to arm park rangers. Meanwhile, should you find a turtle on its back between July 10 and September 15, do not flip it over, as in most cases it is being tagged by researchers, who work on the northern 8km of the thirty-five-kilometre-long nesting beach.

It is not just the acquisitive hand of humans that endangers the turtles. On land, a cadre of **predators**, among them coati and raccoons, regularly ransack the nests in order to eat the unborn reptiles. Once the hatching has started – the darkness giving them a modicum of protection – the turtles really have their work cut out, running a gauntlet of vultures, barracudas, sharks and even other turtles (the giant leatherback has been known to eat other species' offspring) on their way from the beach to the sea. Only about sixty percent – an optimistic estimate – of hatchlings reach adulthood, and the survival of marine turtles worldwide is under question.

lines a truck would leave in its wake. Swimming is not a good idea, due to heavy waves, turbulent currents and sharks. Remember that you need to pay **park fees** to walk on either the beach or along the trail.

Other activities around Tortuguero

Almost as popular as the turtle tours – and with good reason – are Tortuguero's **boat tours** through the *caños*, or lagoons, to spot a jaw-dropping array of wildlife, including monkeys, caiman, crocodiles and Jesus Christ lizards, as well as birds such as nocturnal herons with bulbous eyes, dignified-looking cranes and kingfishers. Most lodges have **canoes** (some also have hydro-bikes) that you can take out on the canal – a great way to get around if you're handy with a paddle, but stick to the main canal as it's easy to get lost in the complex lagoon system northwest of the village. In the south of the village, 50m north of the ranger station and right by the water, Ruben Aragón rents traditional Miskito-style boats and canoes for about $8 an hour, or $15 with a guide-paddler.

You can also climb **Cerro Tortuguero**, an ancient volcanic deposit looming 119m above the flat coastal plain 6km north of the village. A climb up the gently sloping sides leads you to the "peak", where you can enjoy good views of flat jungle and inland waterways. Accessible only by *lancha*, this is a half-day hike, and you must go with a guide. Of the lodges, only the *Laguna Lodge* offers the guided climb as part of its package.

Eating, drinking and nightlife

Tortuguero village offers homely Caribbean food with a wide selection of fresh **fish**. Expect to pay up to twice as much for a meal as you'd pay in other parts of Costa Rica. For entertainment, the Centro Social La Culebra next to the dock has a nightly **disco**, though the clientele can be a bit rough. The **bar** at *Cabinas Tropical Lodge*, in the centre of the village on the path to the park, is a noisy and entertaining village watering hole with perfect sunset views over the river. Next door, *La Taberna*, is Tortuguero's best bet for a laid-back sundowner.

Cafés and restaurants

Budda Café ⓣ2709-8084. Relaxing spot with seats along the canal, *Budda* offers an assortment of tantalizing crepes, pizzas and specialty drinks, such as coffee with rum, ice cream and milk. Closes at 9pm

Dorling's Bakery Attached to *Cabinas Marbella*. A very basic interior belies heavenly baked goods, gut-busting breakfasts and coffee strong enough to see you through your morning. The service is friendly, too. Closes at 6pm.

Miss Junie's North end of village path, 50m before the Natural History Museum. Operating out of a dining hall, the town's most revered restaurant offers solid Caribbean food – red beans, jerk chicken, rice, chayote and breadfruit, all on the same plate – dished up by local Miss Junie. Wash it down with an ice-cold beer. The standard, though, isn't quite as high as it once was and meals can be somewhat hit or miss.

Miss Miriam's Adjacent to village football pitch (and a good spot to watch the village teams in action). This cheerful, immaculate restaurant serves Caribbean food, including chicken with rice and beans cooked in coconut milk, at very reasonable prices. Rooms also available; those upstairs have a sea view and are a bit breezier (❷).

El Muellecito In the middle of the village. One of Tortuguero's best breakfast spots, with tasty pancakes and fruit salad. For lunch and dinner the menu is heavy on Costa Rican regulars like grilled beef with rice and fried plantains. Basic rooms are available (❶). Closes at 8pm.

Sunrise Southern half of village next to *Cabinas Tortuguero*. A good spot to fill up on coffee and eat solid Caribbean fare and pizzas, too.

Refugio Nacional de Vida Silvestre Barra del Colorado

Created to preserve the area's abundant fauna, the **REFUGIO NACIONAL DE VIDA SILVESTRE BARRA DEL COLORADO** lies at the northern end of Costa Rica's Caribbean coast, 99km northeast of San José near the border with Nicaragua. This ninety-square-kilometre, sparsely populated (by humans, at least) tract of land is crossed by the Río Colorado, which debouches into the Caribbean next to the village of Barra del Colorado. The grand Río San Juan marks the park's northern boundary, which is also the border with Nicaragua. The river continues north of the border all the way to the Lago de Nicaragua and almost all traffic in this area is by water.

The small, quiet village of **Barra del Colorado**, the area's only settlement of any size, is inhabited by a mixed population of Afro-Caribbeans, Miskitos, Costa Ricans and a significant number of Nicaraguans, many of whom spilled over the border during the Civil War. The village is divided into two halves: Barra Sur and the larger Barra Norte, which stand opposite each other across the mouth of the Río Colorado. Tropical hardwoods are still under siege from illegal logging around here – you may see giant tree trunks being towed along the river and into the Caribbean, from where they are taken down to Limón. There are no public services in town (no post office, police station, internet café or hospital) except for a couple of public phones outside the souvenir shop next to the airport and near the *Los Almendros* bar.

It is extremely **hot** and painfully **humid** around Barra. Wear a hat and sunscreen and, if possible, stay under shade during the hottest part of the day. It rains throughout the year, though February, March and April are the driest months.

Activities

Very few people come to Barra on a whim. As far as tourism goes, **sports-fishing** is its *raison d'être*, and numerous lodges offer packages and transportation from San José. Large schools of tarpon and snook, two big-game fish prized for their fighting spirit, ply these waters, as does the garfish, a primeval throwback that looks something like a cross between a fish and a crocodile. The sports-fishing season runs from January to May, and September to October.

Because of the impenetrability of the cover, activities for non-fishing tourists are limited to **wildlife watching** from a boat in one of the many waterways and lagoons. The usual sloths and monkeys are in residence, and you'll certainly hear the wild hoot of howler monkeys shrieking through the still air. If you are really lucky, and keep your eyes peeled, you might catch sight of a *manatí* (manatee, or sea cow) going by underneath. These large, benevolent seal-like creatures are on the brink of becoming an endangered species. This is **shark** territory so you shouldn't swim here – even though you may see locals taking that risk.

Getting to Barra

In terms of the time it takes to get there, Barra is one of the least **inaccessible** places in the country. Most people arrive either by **lancha** from Tortuguero (1hr 45min) or Puerto Lindo (45min). For the latter you'll need to catch the 2pm bus from Cariari (2hr), which will drop you at the small dock in Puerto Lindo where a *lancha* will be waiting to pick up passengers for Barra. *Lanchas* arrive in Barra Sur, or, if you ask, will take you directly to your accommodation. The **flight** (30min) from San José to Barra (landing at Barra Sur) affords stupendous views of volcanoes, unfettered lowland tropical forest and the coast: both Sansa and NatureAir operate flights from San José.

Accommodation

Because of Barra's inaccessibility and its emphasis on fishing, hardly anyone comes here for just one night. Most lodges are devoted exclusively to **fishing packages**, although you could, theoretically, call in advance and arrange to stay as an independent, non-fishing guest. The lodges can provide details on their individual packages; generally they comprise meals, accommodation, boat, guide and tackle, and some may offer air transfer to/from San José, boat lunches, drinks and other extras. They do not include fishing licence or tips.

Casa Mar Across the river from Barra del Colorado ⓣ1-800/493-8426, ⓦwww.casamarresort.com. Luxurious, elegant cabins set in lovely gardens with hiking trails through jungle to the beach. Fishing packages only, at around $2895 for seven nights.

Río Colorado Fishing Lodge Barra Sur ⓣ2232-4063, ⓦwww.riocoloradolodge.com. Built on walkways over the river, the oldest lodge in town has lots of character. Comfortable wooden rooms are homely and come with a/c, cable TV and bathrooms. Enjoy good food and pretty Barra

The Río San Juan and the Nicaraguan border

Heading to or from Barra via the Sarapiquí area in the Zona Norte entails a trip along the Río Sarapiquí to the mighty **Río San Juan**. Flowing from Lago de Nicaragua to the Caribbean, the San Juan marks most of Costa Rica's border with Nicaragua, and the entire northern edge of the Refugio Nacional de Vida Silvestre Barra del Colorado. It's theoretically in Nicaraguan territory, but Costa Ricans have the right to travel on the river – though this eastern stretch of the San Juan has been the source of a diplomatic dispute between the two countries since late 2010 (see box, p.435). There isn't, however, an official entry point between the two countries so it's technically illegal to cross into either country along this stretch. For more details on crossing into Nicaragua see p.239.

One bizarre phenomenon local to this area is the migration of **bull sharks** from the saltwater Caribbean up the Río San Juan to the freshwater Lago de Nicaragua. They are unique in the world in making the transition, apparently without trauma, from being saltwater to freshwater sharks.

You'll notice much evidence of **logging** in the area, especially at the point where the Sarapiquí flows into the Río San Juan – the lumber industry has long had carte blanche in this area, due to the non-enforcement of existing anti-logging laws. The **Nicaraguan side** of the Río San Juan, part of the country's huge Reserva Indio Maíz, looks altogether wilder than its southern neighbour, with thick primary rainforest creeping right to the edge of the bank. Partly because of logging, and the residual destruction of its banks, the Río San Juan is silting up, and even shallow-bottomed *lanchas* get stuck in this once consistently deep river. It's a far cry from the sixteenth and seventeenth centuries, when pirate ships used to sail all the way along the Río San Juan to Lago de Nicaragua, from where they could wreak havoc on the Spanish Crown's ports and shipping.

Norte views in the dining room, where local musicians often perform in the evenings. Tours of the rainforest and Tortuguero are also offered and a tame tapir wanders the grounds. Packages from $1900 for five nights; standalone rate from $475 a night.

Silver King Lodge ⓣ2794-0139 or 1-877/335-0755, ⓦwww.silverkinglodge.net. Efficient, well-equipped fishing lodge, with spacious rooms, a bar, restaurant, swimming pool, jacuzzi and TV with US channels. Three-night fishing packages from $2255; without fishing from $135 a night. Closed July & Dec.

Tarponland Lodge Next to the airstrip in Barra Sur ⓣ2710-2141, ⓦtarponparadise.com. Large old lodge, moderately priced, with simple screened rooms with fans and private or shared baths – there are several more basic, budget *cabinas* attached. It's also one of the few places in town where you can get a reasonably priced meal and a cold drink. Fishing from $295 per day, rooms from $25. ❷

Reserva Biológica Hitoy-Cerere

Sixty kilometres, and a three-hour road-trip, south of Limón is one of Costa Rica's least visited national reserves, the **RESERVA BIOLÓGICA HITOY-CERERE** (daily 8am–4pm; $10; ⓣ2758-3996). Sandwiched between the Tanyí, Telier and Talamanca indigenous reservations, this very rugged, isolated terrain – ninety-one square kilometres of it – has no campsites or washrooms, though there is a ranger station at the entrance with a small dormitory where you can bed down for the night ($6 per person).

In the Bribrí language, *hitoy* means "woolly" (the rocks in its rivers are covered with algae, and everything else has grown a soft fuzz of moss); and *cerere* means "clear waters", of which there are many. One of the wettest reserves in all of Costa

Rica, it receives a staggering 4m of **rain** per year in some areas, with no dry season at all. Its complicated biological profile reflects the changing altitudes within the park. The top canopy trees loom impressively tall – some as high as 50m – and epiphytes, bromeliads, orchids and lianas grow everywhere beneath the very dense cover. **Wildlife** is predictably abundant, but most of the species are nocturnal and rarely seen, although you might spot three-toed sloths, and perhaps even a brocket deer. You'll probably hear howler monkeys, and may glimpse white-faced monkeys. Pacas and rare frogs abound, many of them shy and little-studied. More visible are the 115 species of **birds**, from large black vultures and hummingbirds to trogons and dazzling blue kingfishers.

Hitoy-Cerere's **Sendero Espavel**, a tough nine-kilometre hike, leads south from the ranger station through lowland and primary rainforest past clear streams, small waterfalls and beautiful vistas of the green Talamanca hills. Only **experienced tropical hikers** should attempt it, and bring a compass, rubber boots, rain gear and water. The trail begins at a very muddy hill; after about 1km, in the area of secondary forest, you'll notice the white-and-grey wild cashew trees (*espavel*) after which the trail is named. Follow the sign here; it leads off to the right and cuts through swathes of thick forest before leaving the reserve and entering the Talamanca reservation, which is officially off-limits. At the reserve's boundary, take the trail leading up a steep hill. This ends at the Río Moín, 4.5km from the start. All you can do now is turn back, taking care to negotiate the numerous fallen trees, tumbled rocks and boulders. Many of them were felled by the 1991 earthquake; older casualties are carpeted in primeval plants and mosses. The only possible respite from very dense jungle terrain are the small dried-up river beds that follow the streams and tributaries of the ríos Cerere and Hitoy.

Having a car is the most convenient way to get to **Hitoy-Cerere**. Take the right fork towards Penhurst from the coastal Limón–Cahuita Road and follow the signs to the reserve. Using public transport, you'll need to take the bus from Limón to Valle de Estrella, and get off at the end of the line at a banana town called (confusingly) both **Fortuna** and **Finca Seis** (*Finca* Six). It's 15km from here to the reserve, most of it through banana plantation. A local 4WD taxi – ask at the plantation office – can take you there, and will return to pick you up at a mutually agreed time for $15–20. The nearest **accommodation** is at the *Selva Bananito Lodge* (see p.181) or of the Sloth Sanctuary (see p.200).

Cahuita and around

Head down the paved Hwy-36, which runs from Limón to Sixaola on the Panamanian border, 43km southeast of Limón and you'll come across the tiny village of **CAHUITA**. Pay attention, as the turn-off sign is by no means blatant. Like other villages on the Talamanca coast, Cahuita has become a byword for relaxed, inexpensive Caribbean holidays, with a laidback atmosphere and great Afro-Caribbean food, not to mention top surfing beaches further south along the coast. The local "dry" season is between March and April, and from September to October, though it's pretty wet all year round. Close to the village, the largely marine **PARQUE NACIONAL CAHUITA** was created to protect one of Costa Rica's few living coral reefs; many people come here to snorkel and take glass-bottomed boat rides.

The sheltered bay was originally filled with *cawi* trees, known in Spanish as *sangrilla* ("bloody") on account of the tree's thick red sap – Cahuita's name comes from the Miskito words *cawi* and *ta*, which means "point". Most of the inhabitants descend from Afro-Caribbean settlers of the Bocas del Toro area of Panamá and from workers brought to help build the Jungle Train. Older residents remember when fishing, small-scale farming and some quadrille-dancing formed the mainstay of local life. These days, Cahuita – along with the rest of the Talamanca coast – has become very popular with backpackers and surfers, its semi-Rasta culture offering an escape from the cultural homogeneity of Highland and Pacific Costa Rica. Yet while tourism has undoubtedly brought prosperity to the village, it has also created problems in its wake – at one point Cahuita was known for its drug scene and bouts of opportunistic theft. In recent years, though, the community has made huge and largely successful efforts to clean up the village, with extra policemen drafted in to patrol the sandy streets. Still, it's worth being cautious: lock your door and windows, never leave anything on the beach and avoid walking alone in unlit places at night. Nude or topless bathing is definitely unacceptable, as is wandering through the village in just a bathing suit.

Arrival

Before the Puente Río Estrella was built in the mid-1970s, a journey from Limón to Cahuita involved a train ride, a canoe ferry across the Río Estrella and a bus over a dirt road. Access has also become dramatically easier since the opening of the Guápiles Highway in 1987. Nowadays, the easiest way to get to Cahuita from San José is by **bus** on the comfortable direct Transportes MEPE service (4 daily; 4hr) which continues on to Puerto Viejo. Taking a bus from San José to Puerto Limón (3hr) and then changing for Cahuita (4 daily) is only marginally less expensive than taking the direct bus and increases travel time by at least an hour. In Cahuita, buses arrive at the bus station on the main road into the village centre, about 100m southeast of the park.

Information

The website Ⓦcahuita.cr is the best locally generated resource for **information** on Cahuita, with comprehensive accommodation, restaurant and tour listings. The **tour companies** provide the only visitor information in the village itself. Mr Big J's (Ⓣ2755-0328, Ⓦcahuitatipsandtours.blogspot.com), towards the Parque Nacional Cahuita ranger station and beach, is particularly friendly and has a book exchange, laundry facilities ($5 for a big bag) and **bike rentals** ($7). Cahuita Tours (Ⓣ2755-0000) rents bicycles for $6 a day and has phones where you can make international calls. Turística Cahuita (Ⓣ2755-0017) sells the *Tico Times*. For **internet** access, stop by the CyberNet café, opposite *Cabinas Safari*. There's a **bank** at the strip mall attached to the bus station. The small *guardia rural* (police station) is on the last beach-bound road at the north end of the village; the **post office** next door (theoretically Mon–Fri 7.30am–5pm) keeps erratic hours, to say the least. The nearest **petrol station** is about 7km south of Cahuita on the road to Puerto Viejo.

Moving on from Cahuita

Nine daily buses head from the bus station in Cahuita to **Limón**, where you can connect for **San José**. If you're in a hurry to reach the capital, it's faster and easier to take the direct nonstop service (4 daily; 4hr) run by Transportes MEPE. For **Puerto Viejo** (40min) the local bus leaves the bus station in Cahuita eight times daily (first bus at 6am, last at 7pm), continuing on from Puerto Viejo to **Bribrí** and then **Sixaola**.

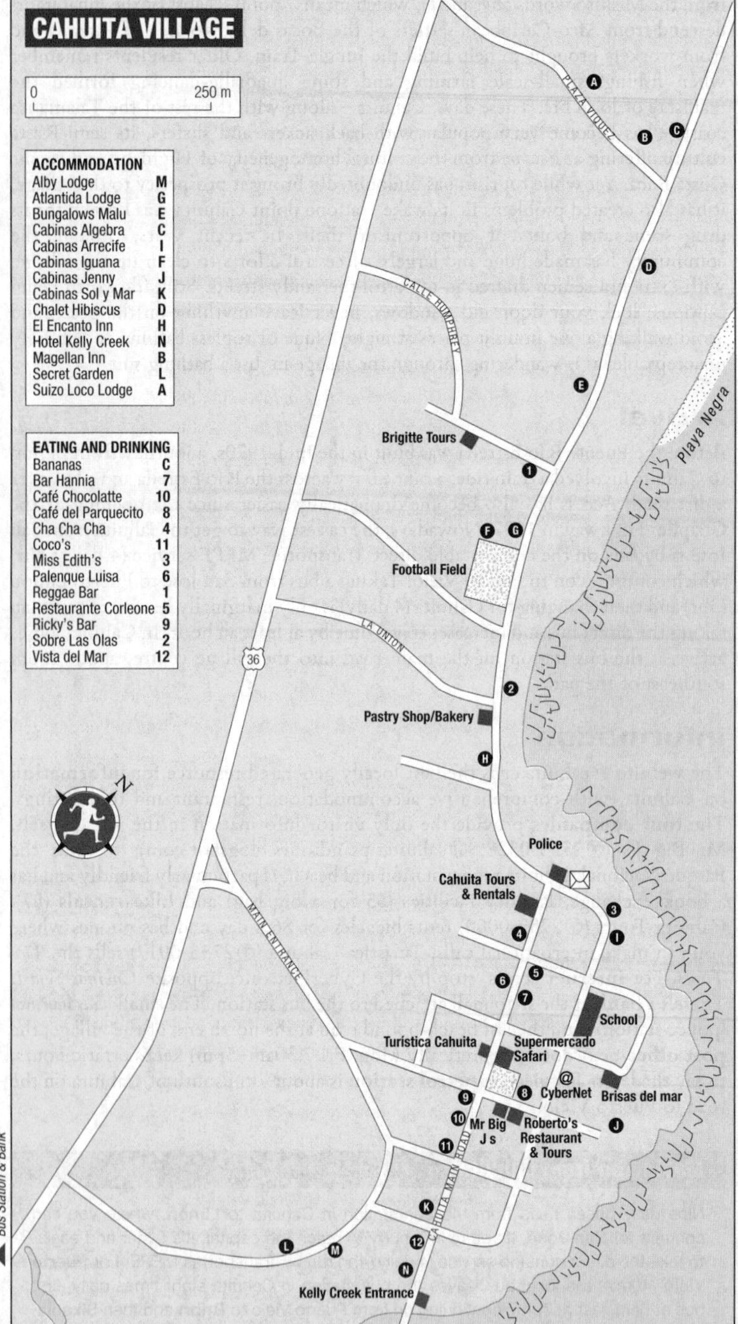

CAHUITA VILLAGE
0
250 m
ACCOMMODATION
Alby Lodge M
Atlantida Lodge G
Bungalows Malu E
Cabinas Algebra C
Cabinas Arrecife I
Cabinas Iguana F
Cabinas Jenny J
Cabinas Sol y Mar K
Chalet Hibiscus D
El Encanto Inn H
Hotel Kelly Creek N
Magellan Inn B
Secret Garden L
Suizo Loco Lodge A
EATING AND DRINKING
Bananas C
Bar Hannia 7
Café Chocolatte 10
Café del Parquecito 8
Cha Cha Cha 4
Coco's 11
Miss Edith's 3
Palenque Luisa 6
Reggae Bar 1
Restaurante Corleone 5
Ricky's Bar 9
Sobre Las Olas 2
Vista del Mar 12
PLAZA VIQUEZ
CALLE HUMPHREY
Playa Negra
Brigitte Tours
Football Field
LA UNION
36
Pastry Shop/Bakery
N
Police
Cahuita Tours & Rentals
MAIN ENTRANCE
School
Turística Cahuita
Supermercado Safari
@ CyberNet
Brisas del mar
Mr Big J s
Roberto's Restaurant & Tours
CAHUITA MAIN ROAD
Kelly Creek Entrance
Bus Station & Bank

Accommodation

Though popular with budget travellers, Cahuita is not especially cheap. If you're travelling in a group, however, you can keep costs to a minimum because most **cabinas** charge per room and have space for at least three or four people. Many rooms tend to be of the concrete-cell variety, but facilities are usually good, with fans, mosquito nets, clean sheets and bathrooms. Upstairs rooms are slightly more expensive, due to the sea breezes and occasional ocean views.

The **centre of the village** has scores of options, the best of which are listed below; staying here is convenient for restaurants, bars and the national park. There's also accommodation in all price ranges on the long (3km or so) road that runs by the sea north along **Playa Negra**. It's quieter here, and the beach is not bad, though women (even if travelling in groups) and those without their own car are better off staying in town; a number of rapes and muggings have been committed along this road, though so far only at night. You should **book ahead** on weekends during the dry season (Dec–April).

You'll find several **camping** options in the vicinity; the nicest is at the Puerto Vargas ranger station in the national park (see p.199 for details).

In the village

Alby Lodge Down the signposted path behind *Hotel Kelly Creek* at the south end of the village ⓣ2755-0031, ⓦwww.albylodge.com. Built and run by its Austrian owners, this well-equipped lodge, set in pleasant grounds, has individual thatched wooden cabins with porch, hammock and private bathroom. ❹

Cabinas Arrecife On the seafront next to *Edith's* restaurant ⓣ2755-0081, ⓦwww.cabinas arrecife.com. This relaxed, backpacker-style accommodation has cheap, simply furnished rooms (some with sea views), hammocks slung on the porch and snorkelling gear and bikes for hire. ❸

Cabinas Jenny On the beach ⓣ2755-0256, ⓦwww.cabinasjenny.com. Beautiful rooms (especially the more expensive ones upstairs) have high wooden ceilings, sturdy bunks, mosquito nets, fans and wonderful sea views. Deckchairs and hammocks are provided, there's on-site parking and stout locks on all doors. ❸

Cabinas Sol y Mar Towards Kelly Creek ⓣ2755-0237, ⓦwww.solymarcr.com. Small, basic rooms, plus larger rooms (❷)and cabins (❷), run by friendly locals who also manage the neighbouring *soda*. Clean and safe. ❶

El Encanto Inn Past the police station in the north of the village ⓣ&ⓕ2755-0113, ⓦwww.elencantocahuita.com. Bright and pleasantly furnished B&B, with a gorgeous garden, pool, spa, seven beautifully decorated doubles (❺) and a delicious breakfast included in the room rate. There's also a self-contained house that sleeps up to six. (❽)

Hotel Kelly Creek Beside the national park beach at Kelly Creek ⓣ2755-0007, ⓦwww.hotelkelly creek.com. Four vast, wood-panelled rooms right by the park entrance, with mosquito nets and a good Spanish restaurant on site. ❺

Secret Garden Near *Alby Lodge* ⓣ2755-0581. Set in a charming rock garden, this popular budget choice has cosy rooms with private bathrooms. Video movies shown on request and there's free wi-fi. ❸

Playa Negra

Atlantida Lodge Next to the football field on the road to Playa Negra, about 1km from the village ⓣ2755-0115, ⓦwww.atlantida.cr. This friendly spot is one of the village's pricier options with pretty grounds, good security, and a pool, jacuzzi and poolside bar. The cool rooms are decorated in tropical yellows and pinks, with heated water, and there's free coffee and bananas all day.❺

Bungalows Malu Beyond the football field ⓣ2755-0114. Six natural-wood octagonal-shaped *cabinas* with intricate stone and terracotta work set in a large tropical garden facing the sea, decorated with the owner's paintings. Each is spotless and comfortably furnished. ❻

Cabinas Algebra 2km or so up the Playa Negra Rd ⓣ&ⓕ2755-0057, ⓦwww.cabinasalgebra .com. Run by a friendly Austrian couple, these funky, attractive *cabinas* are some distance from town, but the owners offer free pick-up from the village, as well as haircuts and laundry service. Good long-term rates. The tasty meals at its on-site restaurant *Bananas* (see p.197) are enough to keep you from wandering far for other options. ❸

Cabinas Iguana On the first side road past the football field ⓣ2755-0005,

Ⓦ www.cabinas-iguana.com. One of the best budget spots in town, with lovely wood-panelled *cabinas* on stilts set back from the beach, a large screened veranda, laundry service, book exchange and a swimming pool with adorable waterfall and sundeck. The friendly Swiss owners also rent out two apartments and a three-bedroom house with kitchen. ❸

Chalet Hibiscus 2.5km north of village on the right Ⓣ 2755-0021, Ⓔ hibiscus@ice.co.cr. Three chalets and four cabins sit on a small point by the sea with beautiful views, good security and friendly owners. The larger chalet is open and breezy, with a veranda and hammock, rustic wooden decor, an unusual wood-and-rope spiral staircase and comfortable rooms. There's also a swimming pool, wi-fi, games room and a garden sloping down to the sea. ❹

Magellan Inn 3km up Playa Negra, on a small signposted road leading off to the left Ⓣ 2755-0035, Ⓦ www.magellaninn.com. Run by a friendly Canadian woman named Terry, this comfortable, quiet hotel has beautiful gardens dotted with pre-Columbian sculptures and a small pool. The hacienda-style rooms have rattan furniture and hot water; some also have a/c and TVs. Rates include continental breakfast, and there's also wi-fi, a bar and an excellent French Creole restaurant, though it's only open in high season and then only to guests. Secure on-site parking. ❺

Suizo Loco Lodge 200m down approach road to Playa Negra Ⓣ 2755-0349, Ⓦ www.suizolocolodge.com. Immaculate, Swiss-run, stylish hotel built with great attention to detail. The staff are particularly helpful and knowledgeable about local activities. There's a good restaurant and a great pool with whirlpool. Water is heated ecologically with solar panels. All rooms have a TV, phone, fridge and hairdryer, and there's wi-fi throughout. ❼

The village

Cahuita comprises just two puddle-dotted, gravel-and-sand streets running parallel to the sea, intersected by a few cross-streets. Though it seems like anything nailed down has been turned into some kind of small business, you'll still see a couple of private homes among the haphazard conglomeration of signs advertising *cabinas* and restaurants. Few locals drive (bicycles are popular), so most of the vehicles you see kicking up the dust belong to tourists.

Cahuita's main street runs from the national park's entrance at Kelly Creek to the northern end of the village, marked more or less by the football field. Beyond here it continues two or three kilometres north along Playa Negra. The small park at the central crossroads downtown, with its three small busts of Cahuita's founding fathers, is the focal point of the village, where locals wait for buses to San José and catch up on recent gossip. Opposite, *Coco's* disco and bar is *the* place to hang out at night, especially at weekends when its breezy veranda crams with partygoers from the city and gaggles of young backpackers soaking up the atmosphere.

You can swim at either of the village's two **beaches**, although neither is fantastic: the first 400m or so of the narrow **Playa Cahuita** (also known as the White Sand Beach and as Kelly Creek), just south of the village in the national park, is particularly dangerous because of riptides. At the northern end of the village, **Playa Negra** (or Black Sand Beach) is safe for swimming in most places but also littered with driftwood. The beach south of Punta Cahuita – sometimes called **Playa Vargas** – is better for swimming than those in the village. It's protected from raking breakers by the coral reef and also patrolled by lifeguards. It does, however, take some effort to reach it – you need to follow a trail for half a kilometre or so through thick vegetation and mangrove swamps that back the shore.

Activities

The principal daylight activity in Cahuita involves taking a boat trip out to the Parque Nacional Cahuita's coral reef to **snorkel** – any of the town's tour companies can take you (see p.193; $20) – or you can snorkel off the beach at

Pirates and ghosts

According to local history, in the 1800s the coastal waters of the Caribbean crawled with pirates. Two **shipwrecks** in the bay on the north side of Punta Cahuita are believed to be pirate wrecks, one Spanish and one French. You can sometimes see the Spanish wreck on glass-bottomed boat tours to the reef (contact one of the town's tour companies on p.193) although it has been (illegally) picked over and the only thing of interest that remains are encrusted manacles – an indication of the dastardly motives of the ship's crew.

In her excellent collection of local folk history and oral testimony, *What Happen*, sociologist Paula Palmer quotes Selles Johnson, descendant of the original turtle hunters, on the pirate activity on these shores:

...them pirate boats was on the sea and the English gunboats was somewhere out in the ocean, square rigger, I know that. I see them come to Bocas, square rigger. They depend on breeze. So the pirate boats goes in at Puerto Vargas or at Old Harbour where calm sea, and the Englishmen can't attack them because they in Costa Rican water...so those two ships that wreck at Punta Cahuita, I tell you what I believes did happen. Them was hiding in Puerto Vargas and leave from there and come around the reef, and they must have stopped because in those days the British ship did have coal. You could see the smoke steaming in the air. So the pirate see it out in the sea and they comes in here to hide.

Where you find pirates you also find pirate ghosts, it seems, doomed to guard their ill-gotten treasure for eternity. Treasure from the wrecks near Old Harbour, just south of Cahuita, is said to be buried in secret caches on land. One particular spot, supposedly guarded by a fearsome headless spirit dressed in a white suit, has attracted a fair share of treasure hunters; no one has yet succeeded in exhuming the booty, however, all of them have fainted, fallen sick or become mysteriously paralysed in the attempt.

Playa Vargas (see opposite). You can **surf** at Cahuita – Cahuita Tours and Turística Cahuita both rent out boards – though Puerto Viejo (see p.200) has better waves. Wherever you swim, either in the park itself or on Playa Negra, don't leave possessions unattended, as even your grubby T-shirt and old shorts may be stolen. All the major tour operators in Cahuita offer combined **jeep trips** to local villages and the beach ($50). Brigitte Tours in Playa Negra leads a variety of enjoyable **horseriding** tours around Cahuita, including a 6hr trip to a farm and waterfall ($75; ⓣ2755-0053), while Exploradores Outdoors in Puerto Viejo (see p.203) can pick up from Cahuita for their **white-water rafting** trips on the Río Pacuaré.

Eating, drinking and nightlife

Cahuita has plenty of places **to eat** fresh local food, with a surprisingly cosmopolitan selection. As with accommodation, prices are higher than elsewhere in Costa Rica – dinner starts at around $5. **Nightlife** in the village revolves around listening to music over a cold beer. At weekends, the village's two discos get sweaty – cranked-up sound systems play until the wee hours and revellers dance and spill out onto the street.

Restaurants and cafés

Bananas *Cabinas Algebra*, Playa Negra. Inviting, family-run restaurant serving superb Creole-Caribbean cuisine, such as roasted vegetables with rice and beans. The portions are ample and there is live music some nights.

Cahuita coral

Arcing around Punta Cahuita, the *arrecife de Cahuita*, or **Cahuita reef**, comprises six square kilometres of coral, and is one of just two snorkelling reefs on this side of Costa Rica (the other is further south at the Refugio Nacional de Vida Silvestre Gandoca-Manzanillo; see p.209). **Corals** are actually tiny animals, single-celled polyps, that secrete limestone, building their houses around themselves. Over centuries the limestone binds together to form a multilayered coral reef. The coral thrives on algae, which, like land plants, transform light into energy to survive; reefs always grow close to the surface in transparent waters where they can get plenty of sun. The white-sand beaches along this part of the coast were formed by shards of excreted coral.

Unfortunately, Cahuita's once-splendid reef is dying, soured by agricultural chemicals from the rivers that run into the sea (the fault of the banana plantations), and from the silting up of these same rivers caused by topsoil runoff from logging, and the upheaval of the 1991 earthquake. The species that survive are common **brain coral**, grey and mushy like its namesake, **moose horn coral**, which is slightly red, and sallow-grey **deer horn coral**. In water deeper than 2m, you might also spot fan coral wafting elegantly back and forth.

This delicate **ecosystem** shelters more than 120 species of fish and the occasional green turtle. Lobsters, particularly the fearsome-looking spiny lobster, used to be common but are also falling victim to the reef's environmental problems. Less frail, and thus more common, is the blue parrotfish, so called because of its "beak"; actually teeth soldered together. Unfortunately, the parrotfish is causing a few environmental problems of its own as it uses its powerful jaws to gnaw away at the coral's filigree-like structures and spines.

Café Chocolatte On the principal cross-street where it intersects the main road ☎2755-0010. Using natural ingredients this cute café makes inventive breakfasts, such as a country-style tortilla – eggs and vegetables wrapped inside a pancake. They serve freshly baked crispy cheese bread with good coffee to wash it down.

Café del Parquecito Behind the village park ☎2755-0279. This excellent breakfast spot in the village dishes up fresh juices, pancakes and French toast.

Cha Cha Cha Next door to Cahuita Tours. Fantastic, reasonably priced gourmet cuisine – exotic salads, grilled squid, seafood and Tex-Mex – prepared by a French-Canadian chef and served in a pretty setting with fresh flowers on the tables and fairy lights at night. Closed Mon.

Miss Edith's Northern end of village. Justifiably popular among tourists, *Miss Edith's* dishes up Cahuita's best Creole food. Dig into tasty rice-and-beans, *rundown*, *pan bon* and a wide range of vegetarian dishes. Top off the meal with home-made ice cream and herbal teas. The service is notoriously slow, especially at dinner, and no alcohol is served.

Palenque Luisa In the middle of the village opposite the grocery store. This popular restaurant offers an extensive menu of *casados* and fish and Creole dishes. Enjoy live calypso music on Sat nights.

Restaurante Corleone Signed down a side street at the northern end of the village. Friendly, informal pizzeria also offers other Italian staples like cannelloni and lasagna.

Sobre Las Olas At the northern end of the village, right on the beach. Atmospheric, classy hangout serving first-rate seafood – the lobster is particularly succulent – with the sound of lapping waves in the background. Also offers cheap rooms for $10–15 – handy if you can't move after stuffing yourself. Closed Tues.

Vista del Mar Near Kelly Creek. Known by locals as "El Chines", this barn-sized backpackers' favourite has a vast menu featuring Chinese food, as well as inexpensive rice-and-bean combos and fish dishes.

Bars and clubs

Bar Hannia In the village centre. Small, friendly bar serving ice-cold beer in a relaxed atmosphere.

Coco's In the centre of the village. *The* place to party in Cahuita, with a pleasant balcony over the main street, a dancefloor inside and reggae tunes. If you're a single woman you'll inevitably be chatted up by the resident dreadlocked hustlers, though they're harmless enough. Fri is Reggae Night, though it seems like every night is reggae night.

Reggae Bar Playa Negra. Laidback reggae bar directly opposite the beach with a consistently good vibe and filling Caribbean cuisine.

Ricky's Bar At the intersection of the main road into the village and the principal cross-street. The village's other disco, with a large, rather dark interior and powerful sound system, operates somewhat erratic opening times but it gets heaving with live music on Wed and Sat nights.

Parque Nacional Cahuita

One of Costa Rica's smallest national parks, 10.7-square-kilometre **PARQUE NACIONAL CAHUITA** covers a wedge-shaped piece of land that encompasses the area between Punta Cahuita and the main highway and, most importantly, the **coral reef** (*arrecife*) about 500m offshore. On land, Cahuita protects the coastal rainforest, a lowland habitat of semi-mangroves and tall canopy cover that backs the gently curving white-sand beaches of Playa Vargas to the south and Playa Cahuita to the north. Resident **birds** include ibis and kingfishers, along with white-faced capuchin monkeys, sloths and snakes, but the only animals you're likely to see are howler monkeys and, perhaps, coati, who scavenge around the northern section of the park, where bins overflow with rubbish left by day-trippers.

There are two **entrances** to the park, one at **Kelly Creek** at the southern end of Cahuita village (open during daylight hours; voluntary donation) and another at **Puerto Vargas** (8am–5pm; $7), 4km south of Cahuita along the Limón–Sixaola Road.

The park's one **trail** (7km), skirting the beach, offers a very easy, level walk, with a path so wide it feels like a road, covered with leaves and other brush, and a few fallen trees and logs. Stick to the trail, as snakes abound here. The Río Perzoso, about 2km from the northern entrance, or 5km from the Puerto Vargas trailhead, is not always fordable, unless you like wading through chest-high water when you can't actually see how deep it is. Similarly, at high tide the beach is impassable in places: ask the ranger at the Puerto Vargas entrance about the tide schedules. Walking this trail can be unpleasantly humid and buggy: best to go in the morning. It's also very likely to rain and, despite the dense cover of tall trees, you'll still get wet.

If you want to go **snorkelling** on your own, you have to enter the park at the Puerto Vargas entrance and swim the 200 to 500m out to the reef from Playa Vargas. Note the signs indicating treacherous currents, wear shoes (you will have to walk over exposed coral) and watch out for prickly black sea urchins.

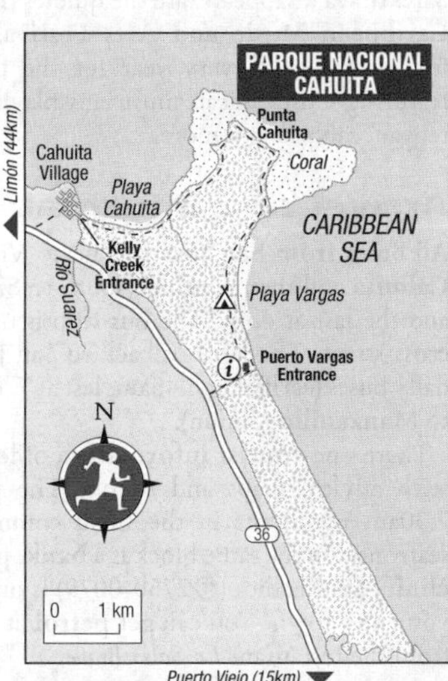

You'll find good **camping** facilities ($2 per day) at the Puerto Vargas entrance, complete with barbecue grill, pit toilets and showers, but you'll need to bring your own drinking water, insect repellent and a torch. Be careful, too, not to pitch your tent too close to the high-tide line; check with the rangers. Theft is also a problem: don't leave anything unattended and ask the rangers for advice – they may be able to look after your belongings.

The Sloth Sanctuary

About 11km north of Cahuita at the Río Estrella, the small **Sloth Sanctuary** (first tour at 7am, last one departs at 2.30pm; $15, $25 with canoe ride; ⓣ2750-0775, ⓦwww.slothrescue.org;) sits on a small island in the river's delta. The sanctuary functions as an important rehabilitation and research centre for injured and orphaned sloths, and, not surprisingly, is the best place in Costa Rica to see them up close. Several walking trails traverse the grounds and there's an observation platform for **birdwatching** (an incredible 312 species have been sighted here – bring binoculars). You may also spot white-faced, howler and spider monkeys. On the one-hour **canoe tour** through the delta you can catch a glimpse of caimans, river otters and all kinds of birds. The sanctuary's lodge (❼) has comfortable B&B accommodation in seven rooms with fans and hot-water bathrooms – it's often full, so book ahead. To reach the Sloth Sanctuary by bus from Limón, take the Cahuita service and ask to be dropped off at the entrance, just before the Puente Río Estrella.

Puerto Viejo de Talamanca and around

The twelve-kilometre coastal stretch between the languorous village of **PUERTO VIEJO DE TALAMANCA**, 18km southeast of Cahuita, and Manzanillo is among the loveliest in Costa Rica. Though not great for swimming, its beaches – **Playa Chiquita, Playa Cocles, Punta Uva** and **Manzanillo** – are some of the most picturesque on the Caribbean coast. Puerto Viejo itself is one of the most popular backpacker towns in Central America, with plenty of accommodation, plus a lively social scene, and the entire place sells out at weekends, so prepare accordingly.

It's **surfing**, however, that really pulls in the crowds; the stretch south of *Stanford's* restaurant at the southern end of Puerto Viejo offers some of the most challenging waves in the country and certainly the best on the Caribbean coast. Puerto Viejo's famous twenty-foot wave **"La Salsa Brava"** crashes ashore between December and March and from June to July; September and October, when La Salsa Brava disappears, are the quietest months of the year. Then there's the **South Caribbean Music and Arts Festival** (ⓣ2750-0062, ⓔfestival@playachiquita lodge.com) held every year for the four weekends leading up to Easter, and featuring Costa Rican musicians playing a variety of music including ska, jazz, reggae, calypso and more.

Arrival and information

All buses **from San José** to Puerto Viejo (4 daily; 4hr) stop first in **Limón** and **Cahuita** and then continue south to **Sixaola**; the first bus leaves San José at 6am and the last at 4pm. The bus stop is on the beach road at Puerto Viejo's second cross-street. The last bus back to San José leaves Puerto Viejo at 4pm, while six daily buses (earliest at 6.45am, last at 7.15pm) head south from here along the coast to **Manzanillo** (30min).

There's no **tourist information** office but the village's tour operators can help with advice, maps and so on. The **post office** (Mon–Fri 7.30am–6pm, Sat 7.30am–noon) sits in the small commercial centre two blocks back from the seafront. On the same block is a **bank**, **pharmacy** and **supermarket**. The **medical clinic**, Sunimedica (ⓣ2750-0079) is on the main road past the first cross-street as you enter town. You can get **petrol** at the east end of the village, across the road from the restaurant *La Salsa Brava*.

PUERTO VIEJO DE TALAMANCA
CARIBBEAN SEA
0 50 m
N
Reef Runner Divers
Police
To Cahuita, Limón, Sixaola, Manzanillo
ATEC Office
To San José
Alternative Missions
Playa Negra
El Buen Precio Supermercado
Terraventuras Tours
Exploradores Outdoors
Surf Rentals
Supermarket
Laundry
Medical Clinic
Baptist Church
School
Football Field
Manzanillo
H, Cahuita & Bribrí
ACCOMMODATION
Banana Azul A
Blue Conga D
Cabinas Casa Verde F
Cabinas Grant E
Cabinas Jacaranda J
Cabinas Tropical K
Coco Loco M
Hotel Guarana G
Kaya's Place C
Pura Vida L
Rocking J's B
Samasati H
Tamandua Surf Lodge I
EATING & DRINKING
Bread and Chocolate 13
El Café Rico 12
Caribbeans 5
Chili Rojo 8
Hot Rock Café 3
Koki Beach 2
Miss Sam's 14
Monita Bonita 10
Pan Pay 1
Peace and Love 7
Pizzeria Coral 11
Restaurante Tamara 9
Stanford's 4
Stashu's Con-Fusion 6

The ATEC office on the main road (daily 8am–9pm; Ⓣ&Ⓕ2750-0191, Ⓦwww.ateccr.org) arranges not-to-be-missed **tours** of the local Bribrí communities (see p.205), and has **internet** access, telephones for international calls and a fax; there's also internet access around the corner at *Jungle Café* (Ⓣ8835-9928).

Accommodation

In recent years places to stay in and around Puerto Viejo have mushroomed and you shouldn't have any problem finding accommodation, although it's still best to reserve a room in advance during high-season and surfing-season weekends (Dec–March, June & July). The majority of places in the **village** are simple *cabinas*, some without hot water, while more upmarket establishments line the **coast** south of the village. You can **camp** on the beaches, but budget travellers usually forsake their tents for the excellent *Tamandua Lodge*.

In the village

Blue Conga On the eastern edge of town Ⓣ2750-0681, Ⓦwww.bluecongacr.com. One of the better choices in the village, this brightly painted hotel has breezy, elegantly understated rooms. Breakfast is included, there's wi-fi and you can rent bikes and snorkelling gear. ❺

Cabinas Casa Verde One block south of the main drag Ⓣ2750-0047, Ⓦwww.cabinascasaverde.com. Seventeen comfortable *cabinas*, decorated with shell mobiles and washed-up coral, with sparkling clean showers, ceiling fans, mosquito nets and space to sling hammocks. Get a poolside massage or lounge in the whirlpool near the frog garden. Owner Carolina sells art to benefit local Indians and those across the border in Panamá. Bike rental and parking available. ❹

Cabinas Grant On the main road Ⓣ2750-0292. Spotless, locally run hotel with basic but serviceable rooms; those on the first floor have balconies and cost slightly more. ❷–❸

Cabinas Jacaranda Just north of the football field Ⓣ2750-0069, Ⓦwww.cabinasjacaranda.net. Basic but very clean option, with *cabinas* decorated in lively Guatemalan fabrics and set amid a lush tropical garden. ❸

Cabinas Tropical On the eastern edge of the village Ⓣ&Ⓕ2750-0283, Ⓦwww.cabinastropical.com. Small, quiet and clean hotel with ten large, comfortable rooms, and pet birds in the garden, owned by a local ecologist couple. ❸

Coco Loco Two blocks inland at the southern end of the village Ⓣ2750-0281, Ⓦwww.cocolocolodge.com. Just 150m from the beach, this lodge is one of the better options if you want to be in the village but a little apart from the attendant late-night revelry. The charming, well-kept bungalows are spread across four acres of attractive landscaped grounds and feature mosquito nets, cable TV and wi-fi. ❹

Hotel Guarana South of the main drag on the way to the football field Ⓣ2750-0244, Ⓦwww.hotelguarana.com. Run by a friendly Italian couple, this lovely small hotel has attractive rooms, tiled bathrooms, hammocks and a communal kitchen. Climb up the treehouse in the garden for great views over the village. Internet access and parking available. ❹

Pura Vida Near the football field Ⓣ2750-0002, Ⓦwww.hotel-puravida.com. This popular budget hotel has ten pleasant rooms (with both private and shared baths), ceiling fans, mosquito nets, a pleasant veranda and garden. It tends to fill quickly. Breakfast is included. ❸

Tamandua Surf Lodge Two blocks back from the main street Ⓣ2750-2087, Ⓦwww.salsabravasurfing.com. Aimed squarely at backpackers – particularly those longing to ride a wave – this budget lodge offers three private rooms ($20), a mixed dorm ($15) and camping space in the garden ($3) as well as internet access and parking. As you might expect, they also offer paddleboard and surfboard lessons, as well as equipment rental. ❶

Playa Negra and around

Banana Azul Playa Negra Ⓣ2750-2035, Ⓦwww.bananaazul.com. Colourful and creatively designed lodge set in gorgeous grounds a short walk from the beach. Each room is spacious with a unique style; those on the top floor have particularly impressive views, and there's also a secluded two-bedroom apartment (❼). The open-air lounge, restaurant and bar area look onto a pool punctuated by thatched-roof shades and vibrant flora. The on-site tour operator, Gecko

Travel Adventures (☎2756-8412, ⓦwww.geckotrail.com), can book a variety of outings, including rafting trips, zip-lining and snorkelling. ❻

Kaya's Place on the black volcanic sand beach 200m north of town ☎2750-0690, ⓦwww.kayasplace.com. Artistic and unique 26-room lodge built in Afro-Caribbean rustic style, using recycled driftwood from the beach and local materials. It's run in an ecologically sensitive manner, though there have been complaints about the service and the dust from the road. Parking available. ❸

Samasati About 4 miles north of Puerto Viejo, ☎1-880/563-9643, ⓦwww.samasati.com. If you're looking to combine a stay in Puerto Viejo with yoga classes, *Samasati* is one of the best health-focused and ecologically-minded retreats in the country. The accommodation, ranging from bungalows to a large guesthouse, is impeccably designed and furnished and blends in well with the surroundings: verandas provide spectacular views. The restaurant serves creatively prepared mostly vegetarian dishes, and there's a full-service spa. A variety of packages are offered, including daily yoga classes and spa treatments. ❻

The village

The **village** itself lies between the thick forested hills of the Talamanca Mountains and the sea, where locals bathe and kids frolic with surfboards in the waves. It's a dusty little place in daylight hours but reasonably well cared for, with bright hand-painted signs pointing the way to *cabinas*, bars and restaurants. The main drag through the centre, potholed and rough, is crisscrossed by a few dirt streets and an offshoot road that follows the shore. As in Cahuita, many Europeans have been drawn to Puerto Viejo, and have set up their own businesses; you'll find lots of places offering health foods and New Age remedies. Most locals, however, are of Afro-Caribbean descent and signs of **indigenous culture** are more evident here than in Cahuita, with the **Reserva Indígena KéköLdi**, inhabited by about two hundred Bribrí and Cabécar peoples, skirting the southern end of the town.

Puerto Viejo has become a byword for backpacker and surf-party culture, with a vibrant nightlife and an attendant drugs scene, though this is fairly low-key. Nevertheless, make sure your room is well secured at night and avoid wandering alone through the village in the small hours. The best way to negotiate Puerto Viejo's dirt-track streets is by cycling. You'll find several bicycle rental shops in town and many of the local hotels and *cabinas* also rent out bikes for about $5–7 a day.

Activities

Though a languorous day on the beach is the biggest draw for most visitors, there's no shortage of **tours** and **activities** on offer. Terraventuras, 100m south of the bus stop (☎2750-0750, ⓦwww.terraventuras.com), runs a popular zip-line canopy tour ($55), birdwatching tour ($29), a half-day trip to the Gandoca-Manzanillo reserve ($55), as well as outings further afield, to destinations such as Arenal.

The excellent Exploradores Outdoors (☎2750-2020, ⓦwww.exploradoresoutdoors.com), in the mini-mall on the main road, also runs several tours of the local area, including a **kayaking and hiking** trip to Punta Uva ($49). They also lead one of the best day-trips in the country, **rafting** on the Río Pacuaré, which includes four hours of rafting on Class III and IV sections of the river – a total of 38 rapids – and lunch ($99). Tours depart from their rafting centre in Siquerres, with pick-ups from Puerto Viejo, Cahuita or San José: they can drop you off at a different location than pick-up, which is handy if you're moving on to San José or Cahuita.

The best **dive** outfitter in town, Reef Runner Divers (☎2750-0480, ⓦwww.reefrunnerdivers.com) offers PADI certification as well as snorkelling ($35) and diving ($55) tours around Puerto Viejo; they also run a hedonistic sunset booze and **beach barbecue cruise** that includes time to swim and unlimited alcohol ($25). Surf Rentals (☎2750-1909,) on the main road at the eastern edge of the village, rents out bikes, scooters, **surf-and boogie boards** and can organize surfing lessons. **Skaters** can drop by Alternative Missions, where Bible study and skateboarding make odd bedfellows. The skate park – complete with a fun box, half pipe and bowl – is free and can provide boards and protective gear: known locally as the "Concrete Jungle", it also serves as a meeting place for the youth of Puerto Viejo.

Eating, drinking and nightlife

Puerto Viejo offers a surprisingly cosmopolitan range of **places to eat** or, for something more authentic, ATEC (see opposite) can put you in touch with village women who cook typical regional meals on request. Although relatively quiet during the day, Puerto Viejo begins thumping at **night**.

Bread and Chocolate 50m south of the post office. People already form a queue before this bakery opens – at 6.30am! Another must-eat, run by cool expats, offering hearty breakfast in the form of cinnamon-oatmeal pancakes, French toast, and creamy scrambled eggs. Lunch involves jerk chicken, tomato hummus, and roasted red peppers. Everything is homemade, even the mayo. No credit cards. Closed Mon and Tues.

El Café Rico Opposite *Cabinas Casa Verde*. Englishman Roger knows everything about the locality and can hook you up with anything you need. His legendary café serves some of the best coffee in town, made with Café Britt Arabica, as well as great fruit plates, tasty sandwiches and crepes. No dinner. He also rents out a nice room right on top of the café (❸), offering free bikes for guests. Laundry service is also available.

Caribbeans Across from the beach ☎2750-0850. Cosy local hangout serving Fair Trade coffee, chocolate and pastries: there's wi-fi too, and an enviable setting across from the beach.

Chili Rojo On the main road in the mini-mall. Newly relocated old favourite serving tasty Thai-style food, with main courses from $5–9. A good place for a sundowner, with 2 for 1 drinks at happy hour (from 5pm).

Hot Rock Café At the junction of the main street and the road leading to the police station. One of the town's more openly touristy places, this lively café-bar shows a movie (7pm nightly), usually followed by live Latin or reggae music.

Koki Beach In the centre opposite the beach ☎2750-0902. Hip open-air restaurant and lounge adorned with recycled furnishings and built around an almond tree. Serves mostly Caribbean cuisine with some international dishes. Tues–Sat 4pm–midnight.

Miss Sam's Three blocks back from the seafront. Tuck into wonderful Caribbean home cooking including rice and beans and *rondon* – at very reasonable prices.

Monita Bonita On the main road, one block east of the post office. Split-level reggae-tinged restaurant serving mostly grilled dishes, such as chicken with mango sauce, and fish tacos. The upstairs bar is a good place to start a night out.

Pan Pay On the seafront near the police station ☎2750-0081. This popular breakfast spot and bakery serves up croissants, cakes and delicious Spanish tortillas.

Peace and Love On the seafront near the police station. An attractive hippy café specializing in Italian breads.

Pizzeria Coral Just south of the main street, near the post office. Succulent, if pricey, pizzas ($4) served on a lively outdoor terrace.

Restaurante Tamara On the main road. No-frills lunch and dinner spot serving tasty Caribbean cuisine, such as house shrimp with fried plantains.

Stanford's Just east of the main street. Very popular at weekends, this restaurant-bar serves a small range of snacks and has a large outdoor disco where you can dance to the sounds of reggae and waves crashing on the shore.

Stashu's Con-Fusion On the main road leading out of town to Playa Cocoles ☎2750-0530. Formerly Loco Natural, *Stashu's* has a far-reaching menu, which includes curries, jerk chicken and tandoori dishes, all well prepared and colourful. It's a lively spot with frequent evening music performances, when the inventive cocktails are particularly popular.

The Reserva Indígena KéköLdi and ATEC

About two hundred Bribrí and Cabécar peoples live in the **Reserva Indígena KéköLdi**, which begins just south of Puerto Viejo and extends inland into the Talamanca Mountains. The reserve was established in 1976 to protect the indigenous culture and ecological resources of the area, but the communities and land remain under constant threat from logging, squatters, tourism and banana plantations. The worst problems arise from lax government checks on construction in the area which, inhabitants claim, have led to several hotels being built illegally on their land. The main obstacle between the indigenous peoples and their neighbours has been, historically, their irreconcilable views of land. The Bribrí and Cabécar see the forest as an interrelated system of cohabitants all created by and belonging to Sibö, their god of creation, while the typical *campesino* view is that of a pioneer – the forest is an obstacle to cultivation, to be tamed, conquered and effectively destroyed.

The best way to visit the reserve is on one of the **tours** ($20 for a half day, $36 for a full day with meal, or $80 for overnight tour to Yorkin reserve by motorboat) organized by the Asociación Talamanqueña de Ecoturismo y Conservación, or ATEC (Ⓣ2750-0191, Ⓦwww.ateccr.org), a grassroots organization set up by members of the local community – Afro-Caribbeans, Bribrí indigenous peoples and Spanish-descended inhabitants. If you're spending even just a couple of days in the Talamanca region, an ATEC-sponsored trip is a must; to reserve a tour, go to their Puerto Viejo office on the main road at least one day in advance. The organization's main goal is to give local people a chance to demonstrate their pride in and knowledge of their home territory, and to teach them how to make a living from tourism without selling their land or entering into more exploitative business arrangements. In this spirit, ATEC has trained about fifteen local people as **guides**, who get about ninety percent of the individual tour price. Whereas many of the hotel-organized excursions use cars, ATEC promotes **horseback and hiking** tours. They also visit places on a rotating roster, so that local hamlets don't deteriorate from foreigners traipsing through daily.

The tour does not take you, as you might expect, to villages where indigenous peoples live in "primitive" conditions. The Bribrí speak Spanish (as well as Bribrí) and wear Western clothes. But underneath this layer of assimilation lie the vital remains of their culture and traditional way of life. Although the area has seen some strife between the reserve dwellers, their neighbours and foreign hotel developments, these altercations remain largely on the level of policy. As a visitor, you won't see any overt ill-feeling between the groups. Treks usually last about four hours, traversing dense rainforest and the Talamanca Mountains. They start near the road to Puerto Viejo – where **Bribrí crafts**, including woven baskets and coconut shell carvings, are on sale – and pass cleared areas, cocoa plantings and small homesteads, and then into secondary, and finally primary, cover. In this ancient forest the guide may take you along the same trails that have been used for centuries by Bribrís on trips from their mountain homes down to the sea, pointing out the traditional medicinal plants that cure everything from malaria to skin irritations. A tour may also involve discussions about the permanent reforestation programme or a visit to the iguana breeding farm established by the local community. However, they conveniently neglect to mention one of the reasons they breed the iguanas is to eat them – especially when the females are pregnant – a major reason they are on the verge of extinction.

South to Manzanillo

The fifteen-kilometre stretch of coast south of Puerto Viejo features some of the most appealing **beaches** on the entire Caribbean coast. All the trappings of a pristine tropical paradise are here, with palm trees leaning over calm sands, purples, mauves, oranges and reds fading into the sea at sunset and a milky twilight mist

wafting in from the Talamancas. You'll find excellent accommodation along the Puerto Viejo–Manzanillo Road, but public transport is infrequent, so it's much easier with a car, especially if you want to explore the **Refugio Nacional de Vida Silvestre Gandoca-Manzanillo**, which borders the area. If you're driving, however, be aware that the coast road south of Puerto Viejo is sporadically paved and very bumpy. It was only built in 1984 – electricity came five years later – and despite the mini-invasion of hotels and *cabinas*, local life around here remains much the same as ever, with subsistence householders fishing for still-abundant lobster and supplementing their income with tourism-oriented activities.

The first two hamlets heading south from Puerto Viejo, are **Playa Cocles** (2km south) and **Playa Chiquita** (4km south) which, owing to the amount of recent development, now more or less blend into one another. Patrolled by lifeguards, Playa Cocles offers perhaps the best **surfing** in the entire region and is also home to the jungle bookstore Echo Books (ⓣ8703-8525), with excellent coffee and chocolates, and an impressive selection of reading matter. Playa Chiquita has a couple of interesting attractions nearby, plus a good selection of bars and cafés.

Punta Uva, 5km beyond Playa Chiquita, has a pristine white-sand beach set in a protected cove making it particularly good for swimming. **Manzanillo**, another 2km further on, almost at the end of the coastal road, has a large shelf of coral reef just offshore that teems with marine life and offers some of the best **snorkelling** in Costa Rica. The village itself is small and charming, with laidback locals and a couple of great places to eat and hang out.

Accommodation

There's no shortage of accommodation in the vicinity – mostly mid-range options, plus a few elegant boutique hotels and several self-catering places.

Playas Cocles and Chiquita

Cariblue Playa Cocles ⓣ&ⓕ2750-0035, ⓦwww.cariblue.com. *Cariblue* has luxurious individual *cabinas*, all with balconies and hammocks, in a well-maintained jungle setting with a top-notch Italian restaurant, a swimming pool (with pool bar) and souvenir shop. ❼

La Costa de Papito Playa Cocles ⓣ&ⓕ2750-0080, ⓦwww.lacostadepapito.com. Run by an effusive New Yorker, *La Costa de Papito* offers "bungalows for the noble savage". Its pretty gardens are home to thirteen bungalows – all with bamboo beds, pink mosquito nets and balconies – extremely friendly staff and a lovely spa. There's bike rental and internet access too. ❹

La Kukula Lodge Playa Chiquita ⓣ2750-0653, ⓦwww,lakukulalodge.com. One of the newer lodges along this stretch, *La Kukula* has smartly designed rooms and bungalows powered by a hybrid solar/electric grid. There's a pool, bar, library and wi-fi, and the staff will go out of their way to help you with local activities. ❻

Miraflores Playa Chiquita ⓣ2750-0038, ⓦwww.mirafloreslodge.com. Opposite the beach, *Miraflores* is a rustic, comfortable lodge set on an old cacao plantation. Festooned with tropical flowers, the lovely decor includes Bribrí paintings and carvings. The upstairs rooms are brighter – with mosquito nets, mirrors and high bamboo ceilings – and there's an outside breakfast area. The owner has excellent contacts with the local Bribrí community and runs imaginative tours, including trips to Panamá in a motorized dugout. ❹

Rocking J's Playa Cocles ⓣ2750-0665, ⓦwww.rockingjs.com. To say that *Rocking J's* has contributed its fair share to Puerto Viejo's reputation as a beachside backpacker's party paradise is an understatement, but it's a fun and friendly hostel nonetheless and not always as hedonistic as you may think. Accommodation includes dorm rooms ($7), cabins and a "king" suite, which has a double and single bed and a private bathroom and yard (❺). There's wi-fi, bike and surfboard rental, a communal kitchen and the staff can provide information on the village and local activities. ❷

Shawandha Lodge Playa Chiquita ⓣ2750-0018, ⓦwww.shawandhalodge.com. The long-running *Shawandha* was the one of the original lodges built along the Puerto Viejo–Manzanillo stretch and it still has a style entirely its own. Each spacious palm-roofed bungalow combines a Bali-esque look with comfortable furnishings; the tilework in each bathroom is exquisite and unique. The open-air restaurant is a real gem; see p.208. Breakfast is included. ❼

Villas del Caribe Between Playas Chiquita and Cocles ⓣ2750-0202, ⓦwww.villasdelcaribe.com. Actually within the Reserva Indígena KéköLdi, this beachside complex has standard rooms plus comfortable two-storey self-catering villas, with a terrace, hot water, fans and organic garbage disposal. The grounds are right on the beach, with great sunset views. ❼

Punta Uva

Almonds and Corals 200 metres off the main road and 100 from the beach in Punta Uva ⓣ2222-2024, ⓦwww.almondsandcorals.com. The *Almonds and Corals* luxury tent lodge lies amid a lush rainforest setting in the Gandoca-Manzanillo Refuge. Jacuzzi aside, the lodge does not aspire to be a luxury resort – more like an adventure. You sleep in a screened-in hut on stilts within the jungle. Wildlife is everywhere and deafening at night. Each of the stilt-set tents has comfortable furniture and an adjoining bathroom. The pathways are raised wood boardwalks and one must stay on them to avoid the undergrowth. Howler monkeys live in the canopy above and wake you every morning around dawn. Truly a primitive, revitalizing experience. ❾

Tree House Lodge Punta Uva ⓣ2750-0706, ⓦwww.costaricatreehouse.com. Marked by a giant iguana sculpture at the gates on the main road, this creative hotel consists of four separate houses built around six enormous trees, connected by a steel suspension bridge. There is no TV, internet or restaurant on the property though there is a/c in the bedrooms. The Beach Suite bathroom resembles a colourful UFO – with a seahorse jacuzzi – and claims to be the largest in the country. Free tours of the admirable on-site iguana conservation project. ❽

Jaguar Centro de Rescate

Founded in 2008 by Spanish expats, Playa Chiquita's **Jaguar Centro de Rescate** (guided tours Mon–Sat 9.30am & 11.30am, $12; ⓣ2750-0710, ⓦwww.jaguarrescue.com) has quickly blossomed into one of Costa Rica's most successful conservation initiatives. The aim of the small sanctuary is to eventually release the rescued animals – which include howler monkeys, margays, sloths, owls, snakes and caiman (though no jaguars) – back into the wild once they reach maturity. In the meantime, the informative guided tour allows you to interact with some of the younger animals. The centre, signposted from the road, is about a 30-minute walk from Puerto Viejo or a five-minute drive.

Chocorart

Set at the end of a 400m gravel road in Playa Chiquita, and signed off the main road, the Swiss-owned **Chocorart** (ⓣ2750-0075; call for opening times) is a chocolate lover's delight. On a two-hour tour ($20) round the cacao plantation, you'll watch various stages of the chocolate-making process, as well as have a chance to spot wildlife that live in the surrounding rainforest. The real treat, of course, is sampling the chocolate, which is predictably decadent, some even infused with fruit grown on the land.

Reserva Natural La Ceiba

A private reserve that falls within the Gandoca-Manzanillo refuge, and is accessed from Playa Chiquita, **Reserva Natural La Ceiba** (morning tour starts at 7am, last evening tour at 6pm; ⓣ8889-9184 or 8889-9258, ⓦwww.rpceiba.com) protects a dense 111-acre swatch of humid tropical forest. The reserve, run by an enthusiastic Spanish couple, is crisscrossed by several trails and occasionally hosts visiting biologists who come to study the thriving flora and fauna. At the heart is its namesake, the Ceiba, a massive tree that can live for over five hundred years and reach 50m in height.

After a spectacular survey of the surrounding forest from the elevated deck of the reserve's headquarters, the guided day hike ($45 for solo hikers, $35 for 2 or more people; 2–3hr) winds through the immediate vicinity, eventually bringing you to a massive hollowed out tree where you can gaze up at slumbering bats. It's the night tour (same prices as day tour; 3–4hr), however – when you can spot frogs, nocturnal insects, and snakes and hear the forest come alive – that should not be missed.

The road to the reserve should only be attempted in a 4WD; one with high clearance is advisable. Pick-up can be arranged if necessary.

Eating and drinking

There aren't quite as many places to eat along this stretch as there are to stay, but the choice is strong nonetheless. If you need to stock up on **food supplies**, *C & J* in Playa Chiquita (ⓣ2750-0904, ⓦwww.candjcostarica.com) is the best option. They also have a juice bar and book exchange and offer yoga classes.

Playas Cocles and Chiquita

La Biela Playa Chiquita ⓣ2750-0896. Friendly and intimate café serving pizzas, spaghetti Bolognese and fish with rice and beans. Closed Mon.

La Casa de Carol Playa Chiquita. Breezy French restaurant that makes the best quiche on the Caribbean coast. They offer freshly baked bread, sandwiches and pizzas, too, though prices aren't exactly cheap. Open Mon, Wed & Fri.

Jungle Love Playa Chiquita. Restaurant and bar known for its great menu (go for the wraps), fresh ingredients and wonderful garden setting. All recipes are the loving creations of owners Yamu and Poppy, with notable favourites such as Mango Chicken, Tokyo Tuna and home-made ravioli specials. Open at 5pm.

Luna May Café Playa Chiquita ⓣ2750-0346. Small, hip café selling mixed fruit and herb drinks, such as mango and maracuya ($2.50), as well as healthy sandwiches and pasta dishes.

Miss Holly's Playa Chiquita ⓣ2750-0131. Hearty omelettes ($6) and an assortment of sandwiches ($7) are served at this cute breakfast and lunch spot with free wi-fi and some outside eating. Wed–Mon 8am–4pm.

Shawandha Lodge Playa Chiquita (see p.207). The most elegant night out in the area, this striking open-air restaurant serves an inventive mix of delicious French and Caribbean dishes, with fresh fish and tender beef a speciality; the heart-of-palm salad is a treat, too.

Punta Uva and Manzanillo

Mamma Mia Punta Uva. An enormous selection of pizzas are doled out at this local favourite. Choose from topping-laden choices like the Atómica (tomato, mozzarella, Italian sausage, onion, peppers, pepperoni and olives) or more basic ones such as the Romana (tomato and garlic). Also serves calzones and a few select pasta dishes. Closed Wed.

Maxi's Manzanillo. Split-level restaurant and bar with great views over the beach. It's renowned for its seafood, notably lobster, and gets packed at the weekend.

Selvin's Punta Uva. You can feast on locally caught fish served with coconut-flavoured rice-and-beans at this perennially popular restaurant-bar.

Soda Mimi 25m behind behind *Maxi's*, Manzanillo. Simple *soda* with veranda seating serving heaps of Caribbean specialities, like shrimp with rice and Tico staples such as steak with rice and beans.

Refugio Nacional de Vida Silvestre Gandoca-Manzanillo

Covering over fifty square kilometres of land and a similar area of sea, the little-visited but fascinating **REFUGIO NACIONAL DE VIDA SILVESTRE GANDOCA-MANZANILLO** ($6; ⓣ506/754-2133) sits in the southeast corner of the country, with its ranger station 200 metres south of Manzanillo village. The refuge, which includes the small hamlets of Gandoca and Manzanillo, borders Río Sixaola and the frontier with Panamá. It was established to protect some of Costa Rica's last few **coral reefs**, of which **Punta Uva** is the most accessible and offers great snorkelling. There's also a protected **turtle-nesting beach** south of the village of Manzanillo, along with tracts of mangrove forests and the last *orey* **swamp** in the country. More than 358 **bird** species have been identified, many of them rare – ten years ago there were sightings of the endangered harpy eagle, believed to be extinct in the rest of the country due to deforestation. Other species found in the refuge include the *manatí*, tapir and American crocodile, who hang out along the river estuary, though you're unlikely to see them.

If you're interested in exploring the refuge, all Puerto Viejo's tour companies (see p.203) offer trips. One of the best is the excellent Aquamor Adventures (ⓣ2759-9012, ⓦwww.greencoast.com/aquamor.htm) in Manzanillo. Although principally a scuba-diving outfit, the friendly Aquamor also offers a wide range of marine activities including dolphin tours and they can put you in touch with knowledgeable local guides who lead hikes through the refuge. **Camping** is permitted within the refuge, but is really only feasible on the beach, due to the mosquitoes, snakes and other biting creatures inland.

Four kilometres from Manzanillo down a rough track, **Gandoca** provides access to the estuary of the Río Gandoca, a bird-spotter's delight with boat trips organized from the village. You can get here by walking from Manzanillo, or there's access from the Sixaola Road – if you have a 4WD – via the banana *fincas* of Daytonia, Virginia and Finca 96.

The trail to Monkey Point

Gandoca-Manzanillo has one fairly demanding but rewarding **trail** (5.5km each way), that passes primary and secondary forest as well as some pretty, secluded beaches on its way from Manzanillo to **Monkey Point** (Punta Mona). It can get extremely hot, and mosquitoes are usually out in force, so carry plenty of water, sunscreen and repellent. Beginning at the northeast end of Manzanillo village, the trail proceeds along the beach for 1km. After crossing a small creek and entering a grove of coconut trees, it becomes poorly marked and easy to lose, but should be just about visible as it climbs up a small bluff. The trail then drops to lower ground and skirts a few small shark-infested beaches before heading inland. Some of these up-and-down sections are quite steep, and if it has been raining (as it invariably has) then mud and mosquitoes can make the trip unpleasant. However, the trail does offer great opportunities for spotting

The Punta Mona Center for Sustainable Living

If you are looking for an alternative to conventional tourism and even backpacking, and want to settle in a remote spot, Punta Mona is worth a visit. **The Punta Mona Center for Sustainable Living** (Ⓦwww.puntamona.org) is an 85-acre organic farm and retreat centre located inside the Gandoca-Manzanillo Wildlife Refuge near the Panamanian border. The only way to get there is to take a boat or hike three or four hours from Manzanillo, where the coastal road ends and the rainforest begins. The café and convenience store are the last opportunity to purchase provisions until your return. Ask for Bako, the man with the boat, and if he's not around someone else will take you for about $20 per person.

If you are feeling adventurous, there is a trail that goes south along the beach, crosses a stream and on toward Punta Mona. Bear in mind this trail is usually very muddy and can be slow going. There are also paths leading off from there that go to distant indigenous villages. One wrong turn and you might find yourself dropping in on the natives, uninvited. If you take the boat, it's a thirty-minute journey until you round the bend, and lay eyes on the white sands and ears on the howler monkeys who inspired Christopher Columbus to name the place "Monkey Point".

The guerrilla gardeners who hold down the Punta Mona fort are completely dedicated to teaching environmental awareness, and they welcome everyone for visits of any length. Promoting a sustainable way of living through example, they grow their own food organically, recycle and manage all waste, use eco-technologies such as solar power, and create an amazing sense of community. You learn about the fruit and vegetables trees, gather the food, and participate in the cooking. Their architecturally impressive houses are built from fallen trees, they've constructed an incredible irrigation system, solar panels provide the electricity, and they've planted a variety of tropical fruits, nuts, spices and medicinals from around the world.

When you're not doing your share to keep the place running, you can laze on a hammock, take Spanish lessons, snorkel, kayak, hike, look for dolphins or nesting turtles (in season), play dominoes with Paddy, an old fisherman – or even surf the internet care of a satellite broadband connection. There is something very cool about signing on to chat with friends in their cubicles back home while you are tucked away in a remote stretch of Latin American rainforest.

birds and wildlife; you're almost guaranteed a sight of chestnut-mandibled and keel-billed **toucans**. The tiny flashes of colour darting about on the ground in front of you are **poison dart frogs**; watch where you're stepping, and avoid touching them. Punta Mona, at the end of the trail, is flanked by a shady beach, from where you can see across to Panamá, only about 8km to the south. From here you return to Manzanillo the same way.

Bribrí and the Panamanian border

From Puerto Viejo, the paved road (Hwy-36) continues inland to **BRIBRÍ**, about 10km southwest, arching over the Talamancan foothills to reveal the green valleys stretching ahead to Panamá. This is banana country, with little to see even in Bribrí itself, which is largely devoted to administering the affairs of indigenous reserves in the Talamanca Mountains. If you are stopping on your way into Panamá, Bribrí has a couple of basic **places to stay** including *Cabinas El Mango* (no telephone; ❶) and Cruz Roja (Ⓣ2759-0612; ❷), a few simple **restaurants** and a **bank**, the Banco Nacional, which changes money and travellers' cheques.

There are several **indigenous reserves** near Bribrí. You can't visit them without special permission both from the communities themselves and from the government, but if you're interested, anthropologist Fernando Cortés (Ⓣ2766-6800) leads small groups through the Talamanca Mountains on officially sanctioned visits to Cabécar communities. Trips (lasting around a week) begin near Cartago, from where you walk into the Talamanca region, and cost about $100 per person.

From Bribrí, a dusty gravel road winds for 34km through solid banana *fincas* to **Sixaola**. Locals cross the border here to do their shopping in Panamá, where most things are less expensive. The majority of foreigners who cross into Panamá do so simply because their tourist visa for Costa Rica has expired and they have to leave the country for 72 hours, though the pristine Panamanian island of **Bocas del Toro** just over the border offers an inviting prospect even for those who don't need an extension.

The border and on into Panamá

Sixaola–Guabito is a small crossing that doesn't see much foreign traffic, and for the most part formalities are simple, but you should still arrive as early in the morning as possible. Just walking across the rusty old bridge that looks like it's about to collapse into the river at any moment (yet somehow they are still running tractor-trailers over on lumber boards) is a life-defining experience. Bear in mind there's nowhere decent to stay before you get to Bocas del Toro – and you should leave time to look for a hotel once there. Also, bus connections in Panamá can be tricky, though many locals will be making the same connections as you.

The Sixaola–Guabito border is open daily from 8am to 5pm Panamá time (one hour ahead of Costa Rica). Tourists leaving Costa Rica need to buy a **Red Cross exit stamp** (about $2 from the pharmacy in Sixaola); citizens of some nationalities may require a **tourist card** to enter Panamá (valid for 30 days); the Panamanian Consulate in San José issues them, as does the San José office of Copa, the Panamanian airline (see p.116). Immigration requirements often change; check with the Panamanian Consulate (see p.117).

There's nowhere to **stay** in Guabito, the tiny hamlet on the Panamanian side of Río Sixaola, so your best option is to catch the bus (7am–5pm; every 30min) to the banana town of Changuinola, further into Panamá, or arrange a taxi (ask at the border post), which makes the thirty-minute trip for about $15. The bus continues on to Almirante – though you may need to change at Changuinola – from where you can get a water taxi to **Bocas del Toro**, the main settlement in a small archipelago of little-inhabited islands, with beautifully clear water, great for snorkelling and swimming. **Hotels** include the friendly *Hotel Angela* (Ⓣ507/757-9813, Ⓦwww.hotelangela.com; ❹), right on the waterfront, and the rather swanky *Swan's Cay* (Ⓣ507/757-9090, Ⓦwww.swanscayhotel.com; ❻).

Connections with the **rest of Panamá** from this northeast corner are tenuous. From Almirante, you'll need to take the ferry fifty kilometres southeast to the banana town of Chiriquí Grande, from where there are road connections to the rest of the country, and a bus service across the Cordillera Central to Chiriquí on the Interamericana, where you can get bus connections to Panamá City and back to San José.

Travel details

Buses

Cahuita to: Puerto Limón (14 daily; 1hr); Puerto Viejo de Talamanca (8 daily; 1hr 30min–2hr); San José (4 daily; 4hr); Sixaola (4 daily; 2hr).
Puerto Limón to: Cahuita (4 daily; 1hr); Manzanillo (6 daily; 1hr 45min); Moín (every hour; 1hr 30min); Puerto Viejo de Talamanca (5 daily; 1hr 30min); San José (every 30min; 2hr 30min–3hr); Sixaola (14 daily; 3hr).
Puerto Viejo de Talamanca to: Cahuita (8 daily; 1hr 30min–2hr); Manzanillo (6 daily; 30min); Puerto Limón (4 daily; 1hr 30min); San José (4 daily; 4hr 30min); Sixaola (4 daily; 2hr).
San José to: Cahuita (4 daily; 4hr); Puerto Limón (25 daily; 2hr 30min–3hr); Puerto Viejo de Talamanca (4 daily; 4hr 30min); Sixaola (4 daily; 6hr).
Sixaola to: Cahuita (4 daily; 2hr); Puerto Limón (14 daily; 3hr); Puerto Viejo de Talamanca (4 daily; 2hr); San José (4 daily; 6hr).

Boats

Cariari to: Tortuguero (10 daily; 1hr 30min).
Moín docks to: Tortuguero (private *lanchas* only; 4hr).

Flights

San José to: Tortuguero (1 daily; 30min).
Tortuguero to: San José (1 daily; 30min).

Sansa

San José to: Tortuguero (1 daily Mon, Tues & Fri; 45min).
Tortuguero to: San José (1 daily Mon, Tues & Fri; 45min).

The Zona Norte

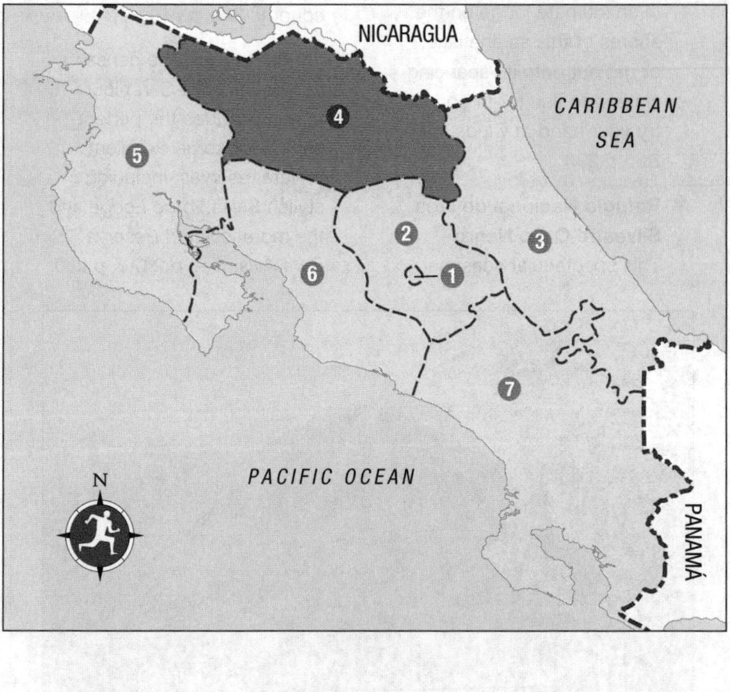

CHAPTER 4

Highlights

* **Volcán Arenal** Stunning by day, and even more memorable at night, when flows of incandescent lava illuminate its slopes. **See p.227**

* **Rancho Margot** Take a riverside yoga class or help milk the cows at this groundbreaking eco-retreat and organic farm. **See p.229**

* **Laguna de Arenal** Relax in an intimate lodge on the shores of this serene lake, or get out onto its sparkling waters, to fish for tarpon or to try your hand at windsurfing. **See p.230**

* **Refugio Nacional de Vida Silvestre Caño Negro** This spectacular seasonal floodland near the border with Nicaragua offers some of the best wildlife-watching in Central America. **See p.240**

* **Birdwatching at La Selva** Explore the vast network of trails at this renowned research station – home to nearly 500 species of birds – with some of the most informative guides in the country. **See p.246**

* **Jungle lodges** The dense rainforest of the Sarapiquí region provides the perfect setting for some excellent private reserves, including stylish *Selva Verde Lodge* and the more isolated *Reserva Rara Avis*. **See p.247 & p.250**

▲ Volcán Arenal

4

The Zona Norte

Vast by Costa Rican standards, the **Zona Norte** (Northern Zone) spans the hundred-odd kilometres from the base of the Cordillera Central to just short of the mauve-blue mountains of southern Nicaragua. Historically cut off from the rest of the country, the Zona Norte has developed a distinct character, with large segments of the population consisting of independent-minded farmers and Nicaraguan refugees. Neither group journeys to the Valle Central very often, and many here have a special allegiance to and pride in their region; indeed, the far north, which for years was mauled by fighting in the Nicaraguan civil war, feels more like Nicaragua than Costa Rica.

Topographically, the Zona Norte separates neatly into two broad, river-drained plains (*llanuras*) stretching all the way to the Río San Juan on the Nicaraguan–Costa Rican border: in the west, the **Llanura de Guatusos** is dominated by Volcán Arenal, while to the east the **Llanura de San Carlos** features the tropical jungles of the **Sarapiquí** region. Less obviously picturesque than many parts of the country, it nonetheless has a distinctive appeal, with lazy rivers snaking across steaming plains, and flop-eared cattle, originally imported from India, languishing beneath riverside trees.

Most visitors use the flourishing town of **La Fortuna** as a gateway to the active **Volcán Arenal**, which looms over the eastern end of **Laguna de Arenal**. The multitude of activities on offer here makes it the most popular destination in the Zona Norte, though the Sarapiquí region, with its tropical-forest eco-lodges and the research stations of **La Selva** and **Rara Avis**, also draws significant numbers of visitors. The regional capital, **San Carlos**, lies between the two; though devoid of actual sights, its easy-going nature – and the fact that it's a transport hub for the region – make it a decent place to stop off en route. In the north, the remote flatlands are home to the increasingly accessible wetlands of the **Refugio Nacional de Vida Silvestre Caño Negro**, home to an extraordinary number of migratory and indigenous birds. Few visitors venture any further, though a steady trickle passes through the small border town of **Los Chiles** en route to Nicaragua.

One of the prime agricultural areas in the country, the Zona Norte is carpeted with vast banana, pineapple and sugar-cane plantations (this is the home of TicoFrut, Costa Rica's major domestic fruit grower) and expansive dairy-cattle farms. The worst excesses of slash-and-burn **deforestation** are all too visible from the roadsides and riverbanks, with the matchstick corpses of once-tall hardwoods scattered over stump-scarred fields patrolled by a few cattle. Legal and illegal logging over the last two decades has cleared more than seventy percent of the region's original forest, making the creation of the

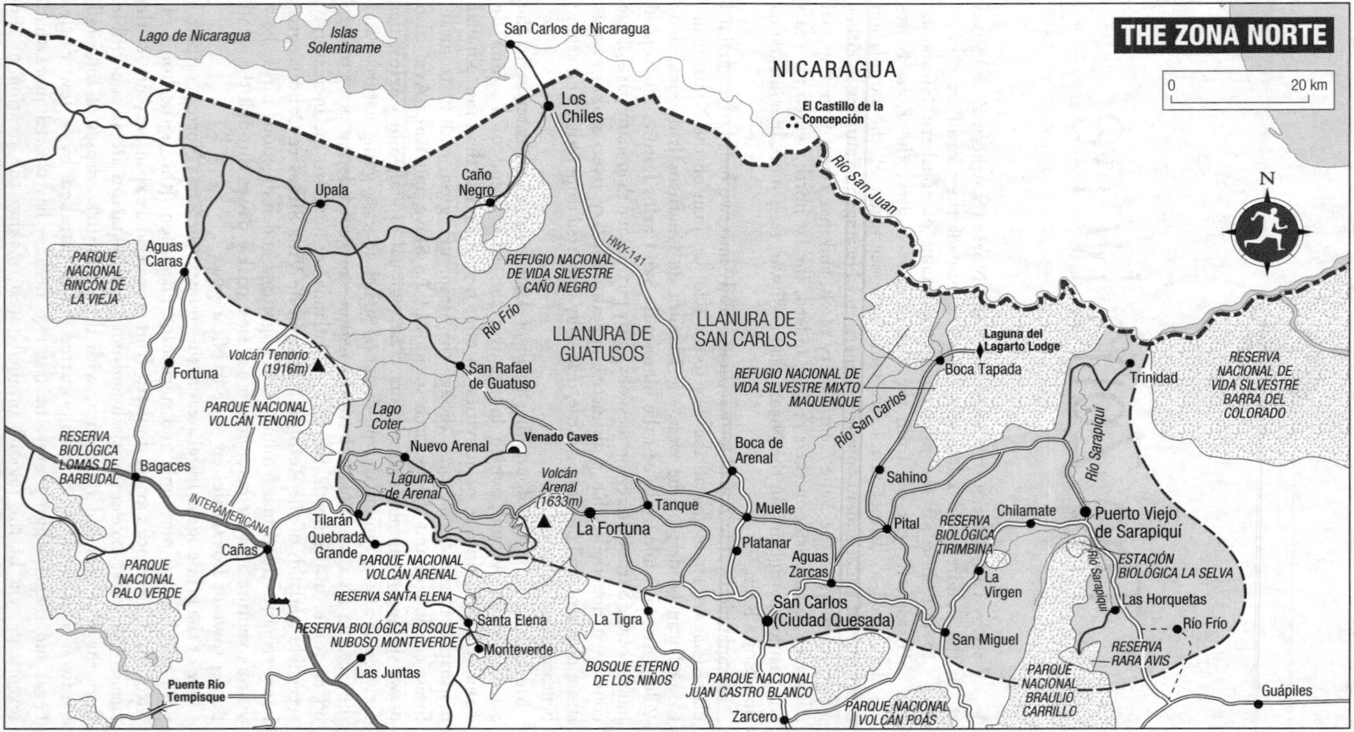

THE ZONA NORTE

0 20 km
N
NICARAGUA
Lago de Nicaragua
Islas Solentiname
San Carlos de Nicaragua
Los Chiles
El Castillo de la Concepción
Río San Juan
Caño Negro
Upala
Aguas Claras
PARQUE NACIONAL RINCÓN DE LA VIEJA
REFUGIO NACIONAL DE VIDA SILVESTRE CAÑO NEGRO
HWY-141
Río Frío
LLANURA DE GUATUSOS
LLANURA DE SAN CARLOS
Laguna del Lagarto Lodge
Boca Tapada
RESERVA NACIONAL DE VIDA SILVESTRE BARRA DEL COLORADO
Trinidad
Fortuna
Volcán Tenorio (1916m)
San Rafael de Guatuso
PARQUE NACIONAL VOLCÁN TENORIO
REFUGIO NACIONAL DE VIDA SILVESTRE MIXTO MAQUENQUE
Río San Carlos
Río Sarapiquí
Lago Coter
Venado Caves
RESERVA BIOLÓGICA LOMAS DE BARBUDAL
Nuevo Arenal
Bagaces
Boca de Arenal
Laguna de Arenal
Volcán Arenal (1633m)
Sahino
INTERAMERICANA
Tanque
Muelle
Tilarán
Quebrada Grande
La Fortuna
Pital
RESERVA BIOLÓGICA TIRIMBINA
Chilamate
Puerto Viejo de Sarapiquí
Cañas
Platanar
PARQUE NACIONAL PALO VERDE
PARQUE NACIONAL VOLCÁN ARENAL
Aguas Zarcas
ESTACIÓN BIOLÓGICA LA SELVA
La Virgen
RESERVA SANTA ELENA
1
San Carlos (Ciudad Quesada)
Río Sarapiquí
Las Horquetas
Santa Elena
La Tigra
Río Frío
RESERVA BIOLÓGICA BOSQUE NUBOSO MONTEVERDE
Monteverde
San Miguel
RESERVA RARA AVIS
BOSQUE ETERNO DE LOS NIÑOS
Las Juntas
PARQUE NACIONAL BRAULIO CARRILLO
Puente Río Tempisque
PARQUE NACIONAL JUAN CASTRO BLANCO
Guápiles
Zarcero
PARQUE NACIONAL VOLCÁN POÁS
Santa Cecilia & La Cruz
Liberia & La Cruz
Puerto Limón
Nicoya
Esparza & Puntarenas
San Ramón & San José
San José
San José

Refugio Nacional de Vida Silvestre Mixto Maquenque in June 2005, which helps link protected areas in Nicaragua with the Valle Central, all the more essential.

The Zona Norte's **climate** is hot and wet, more so in the east than in the west near Guanacaste, where there is a dry season. You'll be drenched by regular downpours, but the rain always makes for an enjoyable respite from the heat. Although many roads in the region are seriously potholed, **getting around** is easy enough, and there's a good bus network linking La Fortuna and Puerto Viejo de Sarapiquí; if you plan on travelling outside these areas, you're better off with a car.

Some history

For thousands of years before the Conquest, the original inhabitants of the Zona Norte were tribal groups – chief among them the **Corobicí** and **Maleku** – who made contact with one another via the great rivers. The **Spanish presence** was first felt in the early sixteenth century, when galleons meandered up the Río San Juan and into Lago de Nicaragua, looking for a route to the east. Pirates (mainly British) soon followed, wreaking havoc on the riverside communities. It was another two hundred years before the Spanish made a **settlement** of any size, the Quesada family coming down from San Ramón in the nineteenth century to found a village at present-day San Carlos, or Ciudad Quesada as it's also known. In the meantime, cross-border commerce carried on as it had for thousands of years via the San Juan, Frío, Sarapiquí and San Carlos rivers – the **Río Sarapiquí** in particular remained a more important highway than any road well into the eighteenth century, carrying coffee for export from Heredia out to the Caribbean ports of Matina and Limón.

La Fortuna and around

LA FORTUNA (or La Fortuna de San Carlos, as it's officially named) was once a simple agricultural town dominated by the majestic conical form of Arenal, just 6km away. True to its name, La Fortuna is now booming as a thriving base for the area's sports, activities and tours. Despite all the air-conditioned tour buses whizzing through town, however, it remains a pleasant, inviting community. There's nothing specific to see, as most of the streets are taken up by agencies selling tours, and visitors wander between them comparing prices, while gazing keenly towards the volcano and popping into *sodas* for much-needed *refrescos* to cope with the heat.

Looming at 1633m, **Volcán Arenal** seems to emerge directly from the town's fringes. On a clear day you can bask in the mesmerizing sight of lava oozing down the lip of the volcano like juice from a squashed fruit. But when it's rainy and foggy – which is more often than not – the volcano is almost totally obscured, its summit hidden behind a sombrero of cloud; indeed, locals estimate that one in two visitors never actually get a glimpse of the summit or lava. Nevertheless, its brooding presence remains palpable, and even if you can't actually see it, you'll almost certainly hear its rumblings and splutterings.

> As the town becomes increasingly popular, **theft** is on the rise; never leave anything unattended, especially in a car, and be careful about walking around alone late at night. Note, too, that there have also been a number of serious complaints (credit-card fraud and scams) from travellers about the agencies that operate out of the bus station.

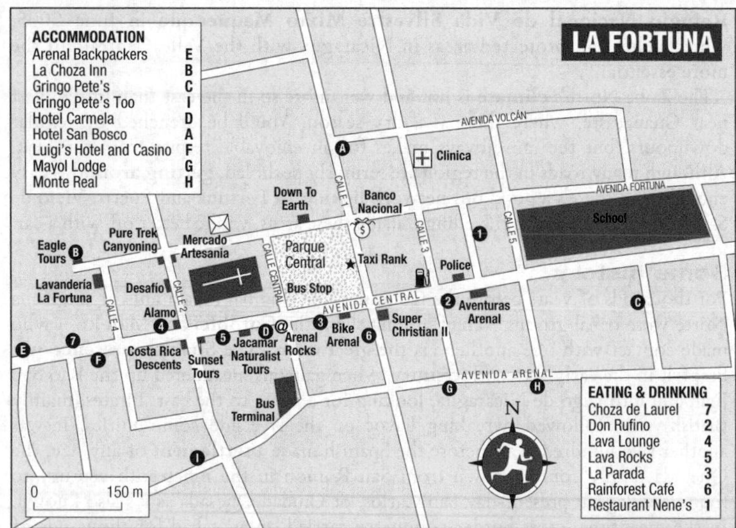

The picturesque **La Catarata de La Fortuna**, the waterfalls southwest of town, are a popular half-day diversion, while the area to the northwest offers a variety of outdoor activities, from hiking forested trails to zip-lining to bathing in steaming **hot springs** – the perfect relaxing vantage-point for observing the pyrotechnics with drink in hand.

Arrival

Three direct **buses** depart **from San José** for La Fortuna (4hr), leaving the Atlántico Norte bus terminal at 6.15am, 8.40am and 11.30am. Alternatively, take a direct bus from San José to San Carlos (hourly till 7pm; 2hr 30min), where there are frequent connections to La Fortuna (11 daily; 1hr 30min). There are also daily buses **from San Ramón** (depart 5.30am, 9am, 12.30pm & 4pm; 3hr) and **from Tilarán** (depart 7am, 12.30pm & 3pm; 3hr), with connections from **Monteverde**. Most buses terminate at the station, though some drop passengers off at the bus stop on the southern side of the Parque Central. La Fortuna's

Moving on from La Fortuna

There are two daily direct services (12.45pm & 2.45pm; 4hr) to **San José** from La Fortuna, or go to San Carlos from where you can connect with hourly buses to the capital (2hr 30min). For **Puerto Viejo de Sarapiquí**, catch a bus to **San Carlos** (10 daily; 1hr 30min), where you can pick up an onward service (12 daily; 2hr 30min). For **Monteverde**, three daily buses depart for **Tilarán** (8am, 12.15pm & 5.30pm; 3hr), at the head of Laguna de Arenal – if you catch the first one, you can connect in Tilarán with the Santa Elena service (2hr 30min) that leaves at 12.30pm; otherwise, you'll have to spend the night in Tilarán (see p.233).

Many people now opt for the "**Taxi-Boat-Taxi**" transfer to Monteverde (daily departures at 8.30am & 2.30pm; $25; 3hr); it saves time and the boat trip across the lake is spectacular. Slightly different alternatives offered by some agencies, including Desafio (see box, p.221), are a horse or bike ride on the final leg (both $85).

airport is 7km to the east ($12 taxi or shuttle service); there's one direct flight daily from San José (with NatureAir).

Accommodation

Budget travellers usually stay in or around **La Fortuna** itself, while people with their own transport and a bit of money tend to head to the lodges that line **the road to Volcán Arenal**; some of these are quite remote and local public transport is erratic, but many offer a free shuttle service into town. The nearby communities of **Chachagua**, 10km southeast of La Fortuna, and **El Castillo** (see p.229) are more relaxed alternatives to the main town but still close enough to the action.

Note that while many of the hotels listed offer tremendous **volcano vistas**, only those southwest of Volcán Arenal (ie near El Castillo and, in particular, the *Arenal Observatory Lodge*; see p.228) can currently claim views of the lava flow.

La Fortuna

All the accommodation below is marked on the La Fortuna map opposite.

Arenal Backpackers 300m west of the church ⓣ2479-7000, ⓦwww.arenalbackpackersresort.com. Great if you're a young American who wants to party, this sparkling hostel has a swanky pool with volcano views, a restaurant and double rooms with a/c, TV and private hot-water bathroom. There are also mixed dorms ($14) that are rather dark but include a/c and shared bathrooms, as well as a squadron of permanent dome tents if you'd prefer to camp ($14 per person). ❷

La Choza Inn 325m west of the Parque Central ⓣ2479-9091, ⓦwww.lachozainnhostel.com. Excellent little hotel, set on a quiet gravel side road, with light, fragrant rooms (a/c $10 more) with TV and coffee-maker. There's a fully equipped communal kitchen in the adjacent wooden cabin, which also has decent dorms (2–6 people; $7) on the first floor, sharing clean bathrooms. Eagle Tours (see box, p.223) is based here, and guests get discounted rates. ❷

Gringo Pete's 300m east of Parque Central and 100m south ⓣ2479-8521, ⓔgringopetes2003@yahoo.com. Classic, chilled-out hostel whose basic dorm beds for as low as $4 ($6 per person gets you a private double bunk with en-suite shower) are an absolute steal. There's a nice communal lounge, outdoor patio with garden and BBQ area, and the best information board in town. There are only five rooms, so if it's full, *Gringo Pete's Too* has a similar set up.

Gringo Pete's Too 225m west of the bus station ⓣ8394-7033, ⓦmrlavalava.blog.com. Run by Carlos López Ruiz, the friendly, self-styled Mr Lava Lava, the newer of Pete's two hostels has attractive wooden bunks ($5), plus simple, clean en-suite doubles. There's a communal kitchen, and, as the moniker suggests, Carlos runs tours to the volcano (he is one of the few guides to take people all the way to *Arenal Observatory Lodge*, the closest night-time volcano viewpoint; $21). ❶

Hotel Carmela Opposite the church on the main road ⓣ2479-9010, ⓦwww.hotelarenalcarmela.com. This long-established family-run hotel has inviting rooms with a/c, fridge, cable TV and shady balconies overlooking a courtyard with a good pool. There's secure parking, and breakfast is included. ❻

Hotel San Bosco 100m northeast of the Parque Central ⓣ2479-9050, ⓦwww.hotelsanboscocr.com. Quiet hotel built around a garden on the north side of town. Rooms, which come with a/c and spacious hot-water bathroom, vary in price and size. Enjoy lovely views of Arenal from the pool and hot tub as well as from the upper-level terrace. ❻

Luigi's Hotel and Casino 200m west of the church ⓣ2479-9898, ⓦwww.luigishotel.com. The setting may not be the best – it's fronted by a casino and pizza restaurant – but the cosy rooms are set around a great pool and come with a/c, phone, hot-water bath and views of the volcano. There's internet access and a laundry service. Breakfast is included. ❹

Mayol Lodge 250m east of the bus station ⓣ2479-9110, ⓦwww.mayollodge.com. Easy-to-spot old La Fortuna house (it's neon yellow and blue), with a range of good budget rooms, all with fans and private bath, and a compact pool. The room at the front of the hotel is $10 less for being nearer the road. ❸

Monte Real 100m south and 300m east of the Parque Central ⓣ2479-9357, ⓦwww.monterealhotel.com. Possibly the best deal in town, this friendly, central hotel is set in tranquil garden surrounds alongside a gurgling river. Stylish rooms – some with dead-on volcano views – are well equipped with a/c, fridge and private bath with hot water; superior ones (❻) benefit from a balcony. There's a small pool and free wi-fi. Breakfast is included. ❺

Chachagua

Finca Luna Nueva 3.5km south of Chachagua, then 2.5km down a gravel road to the right ☎2468-4006, ⓦwww.fincalunanueva lodge.com. Adjoining the Bosque Etorño de Los Niños (see p.326), this worthy eco-lodge and organic farm is a destination in itself. Good-value rooms and bungalows, made from recycled timber, provide a relaxing base for learning about its sustainable practices or indulging in a number of activities, from waterfall hikes to tours of the farm (included in the rate). A range of treatments are available at the Rainforest Spa, including the Arenal Volcanic Stone Massage (from $50 for 30min). ❻–❼

Hummingbird Cottage B&B 3.5km south of Chachagua ☎2468-0990, ⓦwww.arenalby owner.com. Cosy, quirky cottage – the spacious interior resembles a rainforest – set in landscaped tropical gardens where you can pick your own fruit; it is part of a private reserve, explorable on a number of hiking trails. The friendly owner sells her work in the adjacent Coco Loco Arts & Crafts Gallery. ❻

On the road to Arenal

All the accommodation below is marked on the Around La Fortuna map on pp.224–225.

Arenal Nayara Hotel & Gardens 7km west of La Fortuna, then 500m down a signed turn-off to the right ☎2479-1600, ⓦwww .arenalnayara.com. The attractive rooms at this tastefully furnished lodge feature super-comfy four-posters – think quality linens and feather duvets – plasma TVs and private gardens with outdoor shower; suites (from $295) come with jacuzzi-toting balconies overlooking the volcano. The hotel's restaurant, *Altamira*, is an excellent spot for dinner (see p.222). ❽

Activities around La Fortuna

You could spend weeks in La Fortuna rafting, horseriding, mountain biking and zip-lining – there are five canopy tours here alone – and still not sample all the activities on offer. The below should keep you busy for awhile, at least.

Canopy tours, aerial trams and hanging bridges

Arenal Canopy Tour *Montaña de Fuego Inn*, 9km west of La Fortuna ☎2479-9769, ⓦwww.canopy.co.cr. The original zip-lining operation in La Fortuna, with nine cables ($45), and now also offering a 40m rappel and horseriding ($55 for all three).

Arenal Hanging Bridges 20km west of La Fortuna ☎2479-0469, ⓦwww.hanging bridges.com. Fifteen bridges – up to 100m in length – on a 3km-long trail through tropical forest. You can walk the trail alone ($22) or hire a naturalist guide (recommended) to pick out the local flora and fauna ($50).

Arenal Paraíso Canopy Tour *Arenal Paraíso Resort & Spa*, 8km west of La Fortuna ☎2479-1100, ⓦwww.arenalparaiso.com. Twelve cables, the last one zipping over the Río Arenal, peaking at over 350m in length. $45

Canopy Los Cañones *Los Lagos*, 6km west of La Fortuna ☎2479-1047, ⓦwww .canopyloscanones.com. Upmarket hotel with a dozen cables running across its grounds ($45).

Ecoglide Arenal Park 3.5km west of La Fortuna ☎2479-7472, ⓦwww.arenal ecoglide.com. Fifteen cables ($45) and a Tarzan swing in a park beneath the volcano. There's also a mini cable for practie.

Sky Adventures 23km from La Fortuna, on the road to El Castillo ☎2479-9944, ⓦwww.skyadventures.travel. Aerial tram ($55), hanging bridges and a canopy tour (eight cables; $66, including the Sky Tram). One of only a few places in the country where you can go zip-lining at sunset.

White-water rafting, canoeing and canyoning

Canoa Aventura 1.5km west of La Fortuna ☎2479-8200, ⓦwww.canoa-aventura .com. Canoe specialists, with half-day trips on Laguna de Arenal ($45), a full-day

Arenal Oasis Ecolodge & Wildlife Refuge 1km west of La Fortuna, then 800m down a signed turn-off to the left ⓣ2479-9526, ⓦwww.arenaloasis.com. Rustic Hansel-and-Gretel-style *cabañas* (the beds are carved out of wood) set in its own reserve just outside of town – once grazed by cattle, it is now home to sloths, tamanduas and around 200 species of birds. Various tours available. ❺

Arenal Paraíso Resort & Spa 8km west of La Fortuna ⓣ2479-1100, ⓦwww.arenalparaiso.com. This unobtrusive hotel has *cabinas* built of varnished wood, all with hot-water bath, a/c and fridge, and huge porches that look out directly onto the volcano. The more upmarket ones further up the hill have better views. The pool has a swim-up bar, while the on-site restaurant specializes in big, juicy steaks. ❼

Catarata Eco-Lodge 400m beyond *Arenal Oasis* ⓣ2479-9522, ⓦwww.cataratalodge.com. Sitting on fertile farmland between La Fortuna and the waterfall, this eco-lodge offers a swimming pool and 21 cosy and comfortable rooms, all with fan and hot-water bath. The restaurant serves local food made with organic produce from its garden, and a hearty breakfast is included. ❺

Hotel Arenal Manoa 7km west of La Fortuna, then 800m down a signed turn-off to the right ⓣ2479-1111, ⓦwww.arenalmanoa.com. The welcome cocktail sets the tone at this beautifully done hotel, whose brightly decorated rooms boast a/c, satellite TV, fridge and private patio, complete with rocking chairs. There's a sparkling pool, and the rate includes a guided tour of the hotel's nearby dairy farm. ❼

Montaña de Fuego Inn 9km west of La Fortuna ⓣ2479-1220, ⓦwww.montanadefuego.com. Smart complex of dark-wood bungalows, plus a two-storey "family" building, all with a/c, fridge and private terrace; the higher-end rooms have rocking chairs, perfect for basking in spectacular light shows from the volcano opposite. ❼

Mountain Paradise Hotel 7km west of La Fortuna, then 500m down a signed turn-off to the

paddle in Caño Negro ($55) and a family-friendly "safari float" down the forest-fringed Río Peñas Blancas ($40–55). Prices include the services of a bilingual naturalist guide.

Costa Rica Descents On Avenida Central, opposite the southwest corner of the church, La Fortuna ⓣ2479-9419, ⓦwww.costaricadescents.com. Run by two brothers who got their white-water wings rafting in the Rockies, this is the only Class V outfitter in La Fortuna, with full-day trips on the Upper Balsa ($115). They also run the Class III–IV rapids of the Río Toro ($85), plus more gentle trips on the Class II–III Río Sarapiquí ($75) and Río Balsa ($75).

Desafío Opposite the west side of the church, La Fortuna ⓣ2479-9464, ⓦwww.desafiocostarica.com. Friendly, efficient rafting specialist running tours on the Class II–III Balsa ($65) and the Class III–IV Toro ($85); combine a ride down the Balsa with rappelling in the rainforest ($150, $90 just for the rappel).

Pure Trek Canyoning Opposite the northwest corner of the church, La Fortuna ⓣ2461-2110, ⓦwww.puretrekcostarica.com. Five rappels (four down a series of waterfalls) in a canyon near town ($90).

Horseriding

Desafío See above. In addition to their recommended rafting trips, Desafío run horseback rides to the Catarata de La Fortuna ($45); their transfer to Monteverde includes a lakeside ride on well-cared-for horses ($85;5hr).

Don Tobias *Arenal Springs Resort*, 7km west of La Fortuna, then 450m down a signed turn-off to the right ⓣ2479-1212, ⓦwww.cabalgatadontobias.com. Three-hour tours in the fields and forests around Volcán Arenal, with some creek-crossing involved. Safety-conscious, experienced guides.

Rancho Arenal Paraíso *Arenal Paraíso Resort & Spa*, 8km west of La Fortuna ⓣ2460-5333, ⓦwww.arenalparaiso.com. The hotel's ranch runs similar trips to Don Tobias, mostly on mountain trails on the slopes of Arenal.

right ⓣ2479-1414, ⓦwww.hotelmountain paradise.com. Spacious Hacienda-style *casitas* dotted in pairs among beautiful grounds that are a haven for hummingbirds. Large rooms easily accommodate two big wooden beds and come with flat-screen TV, a/c and huge bathrooms, complete with dramatic-looking "waterfall" showers. Friendly staff, and a hot-water pool with wet bar. Treatments in the on-site spa start from $50. ❼

El Silencio del Campo 5km west of La Fortuna ⓣ2479-7055, ⓦwww.hotelsilenciodelcampo.com. Though quite clustered together, these tranquil villas with volcano views are perfect for families: there are two swimming pools (one for kids only), a restaurant and a new hot-spring pool. The hotel is just 300m from Ecotermales Fortuna (see p.226), and guests get discounted entry. ❽

The Springs Resort & Spa 9km west of La Fortuna, then 4km down a side road to the right ⓣ2401-3313, ⓦspringscostarica.com. Lavish five-star whose multimillion-dollar budget didn't quite stretch to an exterior designer. The dozen different types of room all offer private terraces, sumptuous bathrooms, flat-screen TVs and wi-fi. The spa is vast, and its hot springs (18 pools) are also open to non-guests (daily 8am–11pm; $40). Numerous on-site restaurants include *Las Ventanas*, with stellar volcano views (see opposite). $395–435

Eating and drinking

While you can find the inevitable *casados*, *platos del día* and *arroz-con*-whatever, a growing number of **restaurants** in La Fortuna offer imaginative international cuisine, and there are several fine-dining options on the road west of town. At weekends, *Volcán Look*, 4km west of La Fortuna, is the liveliest *discoteca*.

La Fortuna

All the places listed below are marked on the La Fortuna map on p.218.

Choza de Laurel 400m west of the Parque Central, on the main road. Very much on the tourist-bus circuit, but atmospheric nevertheless, with hefty slabs of tender steak (around $15) and crispy, wood-roasted chicken ($8 for a quarter). Daily 6.30am–10pm.

Don Rufino 100m east of the Parque Central ⓣ2479-9997, ⓦwww.donrufino.com. The wide-ranging menu trots around Central America, but steaks are the speciality: from a ribeye for two ($20) up to a 20oz Chateaubriand carved at your table ($45). The bar (till 11.30pm) can keep willing patrons sufficiently lubricated. Daily 11am–10.30pm.

Lava Lounge 200m west of the Parque Central ⓦwww.lavaloungecostarica .com. Mouthwatering mixture of original wraps, organic salads and grilled sandwiches, such as tuna steak marinated in ginger soy sauce with wasabi aioli mustard and fruit chutney ($10). Daily 11am–11.30pm.

Lava Rocks 115m west of the Parque Central. Shady breakfast hangout (around $4; until 11am) that's a good place to grab a snack (from $3.50) or a blackberry *batido* at any time of the day. Daily 8am–10.30pm, bar until 1am.

La Parada Directly opposite the bus stop on the Parque Central. Popular *soda* that's perfect for people-watching while you fill up on *casados* ($4) or a variety of pizzas – all served up by an enthusiastic staff. Open 24hr.

Rainforest Café 75m southeast of the Parque Central. Take your time over a cup of Costa Rica's finest in this airy café that hums along to mellow tunes. Smiling waitresses serve up good lemon cake and the like. Daily 7am–8pm.

Restaurant Nene's 250m east and 50m south of the Parque Central ⓣ2479-9192. This highly regarded restaurant adorned with a mural of tropical birds is known for its ceviche ($6) but people also come from far and wide to enjoy its varied menu of sea bass, steak and pastas and a range of cocktails ($4). Daily 10am–11pm.

On the road to Arenal

All the places listed below are marked on the Around La Fortuna map on pp.224–225.

Altamira *Arenal Nayara*, 7km west of La Fortuna, then 500m down a signed turn-off to the right ⓣ2479-1600, ⓦwww.arenalnayara .com. Charming service and even better food, softly lit by Chinese lanterns. Try roasted tenderloin with jalapeno sauce ($19) followed by the fluffiest chocolate mousse you'll ever have ($4). The changing three-course set-menu is decent value at $25. Daily 5–9.30pm.

Restaurante Heliconias *Arenal Kioro Suites & Spa* ⓣ2479-1700, ⓦwww.hotelarenalkioro.com. The main restaurant at this suite-only hotel makes the most of its position at the foot of Volcán Arenal, with huge floor-to-ceiling windows (which open up) perfectly framing its smoking cone. The food (which runs along the lines of sea bass in caper sauce; $19) is top drawer, too. Daily 4–10pm.

Vagabondo 2km west of La Fortuna. This attractive, open-air restaurant serves up authentic Italian wood-fired pizzas (around $10). In the back, a large convivial bar with pool tables stays open late. Daily noon–11pm.

Las Ventanas *The Springs Resort & Spa*, 9km west of La Fortuna, then 4km down a side road to the right ⓣ2401-3313, ⓦspringscostarica.com. Hanging 300m over the Río Arenal, this fine-dining restaurant is as much about what's going on outside as what's going on your plate – seared yellow-fin tuna, organic vegetables and delicate French desserts vie for attention with some of the area's most spectacular volcano views. Daily noon–3pm & 6–10pm.

Listings

Banks The Banco Nacional on the northeastern side of the Parque Central has an ATM and changes travellers' cheques.
Bicycle rental Bike Arenal (ⓣ2479-9454, ⓦwww.bikearenal.com), on Av Central, rents mountain bikes for $20 a day.
Car rental Alamo, 200m west of the church ⓣ2479-9090; Mapache, 800m west of the church ⓣ2479-0010.
Healthcare Clinica, 125m east and 50m north of the Parque Central ⓣ2479-9501 (Mon 8am–8pm, Tues–Thurs 8am–10pm, Fri–Sun 24hr).
Internet Arenal Rocks, on Av Central, opposite the church (daily 8am–11pm; ¢450 for 30min).
Laundry Lavandería La Fortuna, 125m west and 125m north of the Parque Central (Mon–Sat 8am–9pm).
Police On Av Central, 125m east of the Parque Central ⓣ2479-9501; also a booth at the turning to Parque Nacional Volcán Arenal west of town.
Post office Opposite the north side of the church (Mon–Fri 8am–5.30pm, Sat 7.30am–noon).
Scooter rental Carlos at *Gringo Pete's Too* (see p.219) rents scooters for $8 per hr or $50 per day.

Tours

The most popular **tour** from La Fortuna is the late-afternoon hike around **Volcán Arenal**, followed by a night-time soak in the **hot springs**. The volcano hike involves a walk through rainforest, much of it uphill, and a final scramble over lava rocks – take care, as they're particularly sharp, and few guides carry a medical kit (bring a flashlight, too). The volcano in action is an amazing sight, provided you're lucky enough to be there on a clear night when there's activity – scarlet rivers of lava pour from the top, and you can hear the crunch of boulders landing as they are spewed from the volcano's mouth.

La Fortuna is also a prime setting-off point for trips to the **Venado Caves** and the remote wildlife refuge of **Caño Negro**; shorter tours to the latter will just take you on a scenic cruise down the Río Frío from Los Chiles, so make sure that you'll actually be visiting the refuge itself.

Tour operators

Aventuras Arenal 150m east of the Parque Central ⓣ2479-9133, ⓦwww.arenaladventures.com. Professional setup offering tours to the Venado Caves (7.30am & 1pm; 4hr; $55) and the Maleku Indigenous Reserve at Gautuso (8am; $99, mini of 4 people; 4hr).

Eagle Tours 325m west of the Parque Central, in front of *La Choza Inn* ⓣ2479-9091, ⓦwww.eagletours.net. Budget backpacker favourite with night-time volcano tours ($28) and a trip to the Venado Caves that's "the darkest tour in town" ($65).

Jacamar Naturalist Tours Next to *Lava Rocks* ⓣ2479-9767, ⓦwww.arenaltours.com. Runs a range of naturalist tours, including a walking tour through Parque Nacional Volcán Arenal ($49), boat ($65) and kayak ($75) trips to Caño Negro, and hiking up Cerro Chato ($80).

Sunset Tours On Avenida Central, by the southwest corner of the church ⓣ2479-9800, ⓦwww.sunsettourcr.com. Pricier than the rest but they only use professional, well-qualified guides. As well as volcano tours ($35), they run trips to Cerro Chato and the La Fortuna waterfall ($70) and hikes along the Río Celeste near Volcán Tenorio ($100).

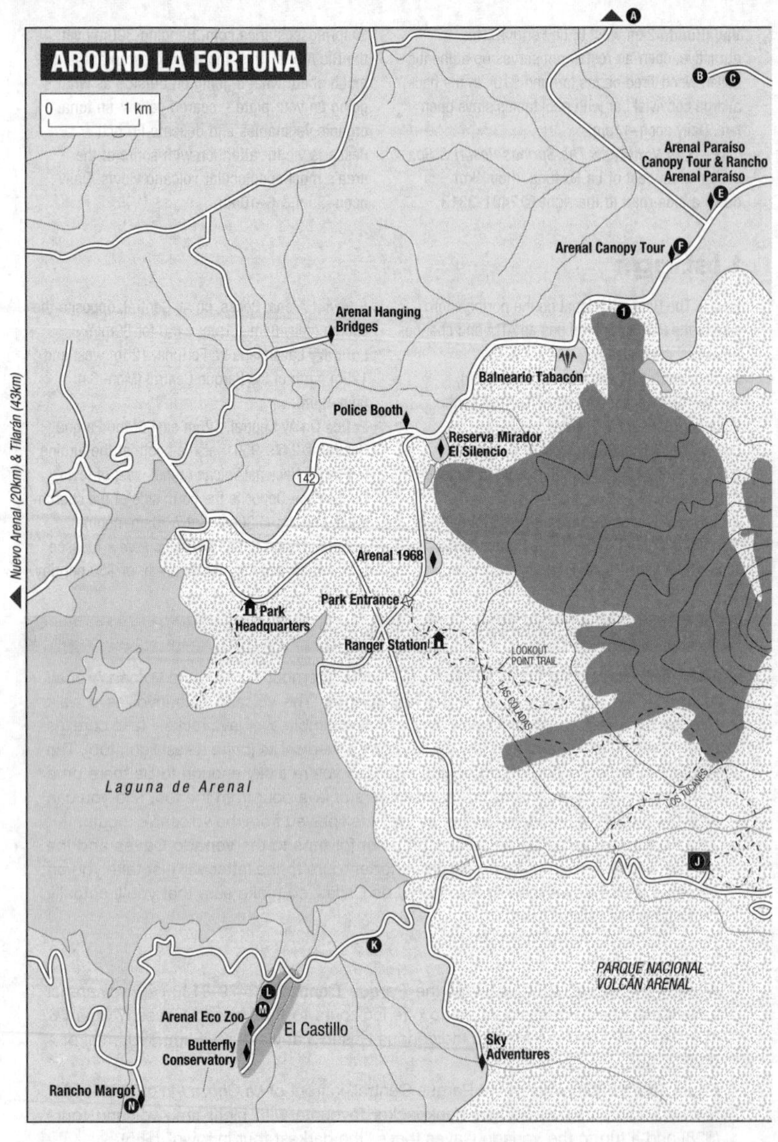

Shopping Numerous souvenir stores stock the usual tourist trinkets: the most pleasant place to browse is the Mercado Artesania, on the corner northwest of the church, with wood crafts, T-shirts, hammocks and the like (daily 8am–7.45pm). Down to Earth, opposite the north side of the Parque Central (daily 10am–7pm; ⓦ www.godowntoearth.org) is a one-stop shop for your gourmet caffeine needs, specializing in coffee chocolates and liquers.

Supermarkets Super Christian II, diagonally opposite the southeast corner of the Parque Central (Mon–Sat 7am–10pm, Sun 8am–8pm).

Taxis There's a rank on the eastern side of the Parque Central; expect to pay around $6.50 to La Catarata de La Fortuna and $18 to Parque Nacional Volcán Arenal.

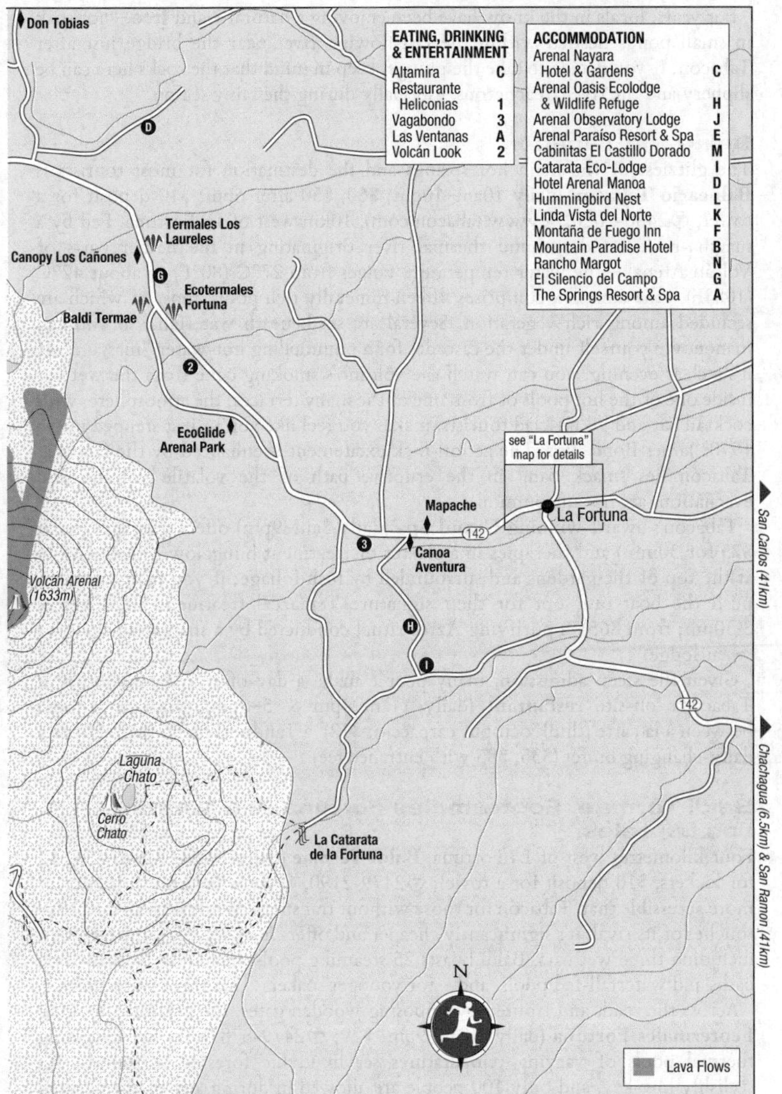

The hot springs

A number of **hot springs** line the road from La Fortuna to Arenal, all set around a variety of pools fed by thermally heated underground streams. The majority of agencies in town sell tickets and transportation to the springs, and most of the volcano evening tours end up at one spring or another, but you can easily visit them independently. A couple of the newer **hotels**, including *The Springs* (see p.222), have worked hot springs into their landscaped grounds, which are also open (for a fee) to non-guests.

For years, locals in the know have been enjoying a natural – and **free** – hot soak in small ponds nestled within the fast-flowing river near the bridge just after Tabacón. If you decide to take the plunge, keep in mind that the rocks here can be slippery and the river treacherous, especially during the rainy season.

Balneario Tabacón

The glitziest of the main hot springs and the destination for most tourists is **Balneario Tabacón** (daily 10am–10pm; $60, $50 after 6pm; $10 deposit for a towel; ⓣ2460-2020, ⓦwww.tabacon.com), 10km west of La Fortuna. Fed by a magma-boiled underground thermal river originating in the nether parts of Volcán Arenal – the water temperature ranges from 27°C (80°F) to about 42°C (108°F) – the complex comprises fifteen minerally rich pools, most of which are secluded among rich vegetation. Several are set beneath waterfalls, so you can manoeuvre yourself under the cascades for a pummelling hot-water "massage". If it's a clear evening, you can watch the volcano's smoking cone from the wet bar inside one of the hot pools or from one of the many terraces; the atmosphere, with cocktail bar and bikini-clad tourists, makes you feel like you've just stepped into a 1970s James Bond film. The action-flick excitement is enhanced by the fact that Tabacón lies smack bang in the eruptive path of the volatile volcano and evacuations are not uncommon.

Tabacon's award-winning **Grand Spa** (daily 8am–9pm) offers massages (from $75 for 30min) and therapies in a cluster of treatment bungalows, tucked away at the top of the gardens and surrounded by lush foliage; if you really want to push the boat out, opt for their signature Temazcal treatment (10.30am & 3.30pm; from $65), a purifying Aztec ritual conducted by a shaman in the spa's sweat lodge.

Given the steep admission, many people make a day of it and take lunch at Tabacón's on-site **restaurant** (daily 11am–4pm & 5–9pm); you can choose between à la carte (think octopus carpaccio; $12), a Tandoori menu ($15–20) or a daily-changing buffet ($35, $85 with entrance fee).

Baldi Termae, Ecotermales Fortuna and Termales Los Laureles

Four kilometres west of La Fortuna, **Baldi Termae** (daily 10am–10pm; $35; $5 for lockers, $10 deposit for a towel; ⓣ2479-2190, ⓦwww.baldihotsprings.cr) is more accessible than Tabacón for those without transport. While it lacks the classy touches of its rival, it's significantly cheaper and offers many of the same facilities, including three wet bars. Baldi boasts 25 steaming pools, including Roman-style baths and waterfall-fed pools, and – for younger soakers – has three waterslides.

Across the road, and fronted by imposing wooden gates, the exclusive-looking **Ecotermales Fortuna** (daily 10am–9pm; $29; ⓣ2479-8787) has five cascading thermal pools of varying temperatures set in idyllic forested surrounds. It's stylishly low-key, and only 100 people are allowed in during any of the allotted times (10am–1pm, 1–5pm & 5–9pm), so be sure to book ahead in high season. While there's no volcano view from the pools, the rainforest setting more than makes up for it. The price includes towel, locker and access to two bars and a restaurant.

One kilometre west and a further 500m down a rough road, **Termales Los Laureles** (daily 10am–10pm; $8; ⓣ2479-1431, ⓦwww.termalesloslaureles.com) is the cheapest official hot springs in the Arenal area and is popular with Ticos. Four simple pools (one with slides) are set around a very ordinary garden, but the volcano views are sensational. Bring your own food and booze and make a night of it.

La Catarata de La Fortuna

The dramatically sited **La Catarata de La Fortuna** (daily 8am–5pm; $10), 4km southwest of town, is the epitome of the picture-book cascade – a tall, thin stream plunging prettily from a narrow aperture in the rocky heights 75m above, and forming a foaming pool among rocks and rainforest vegetation below. From the ticket booth, a path leads 600m vertically down to the base of the falls, where a series of pools provide a tempting spot for a quick dip; swimming is not recommended, due to flash floods, although a lot of people do. There's a *mirador* (signposted) 200m along the trail for those who would rather look from a distance, giving great views across the steep valley and its heavily forested floor to the thin finger of the cascade. Make sure you wear waterproof shoes, and be aware that the paths can be slippery.

Most combination tours include a stop at the waterfall, but it's cheaper **to get there** by taxi ($6.50) and more fun by horseriding across the fields; Desafío (see p.221) charges $45 for four-hour trips that leave daily at 8am and 1pm. If driving or cycling (note that it's a fairly stiff uphill climb on the way there), take the road heading south from La Fortuna across the bridge, then turn west down a gravel road (it's the only turn-off in sight) and follow signs for the *cataratas*.

Parque Nacional Volcán Arenal

Volcán Arenal was afforded protected status in 1995, becoming part of the national parks system as the **PARQUE NACIONAL VOLCÁN ARENAL** (daily 8am–3.30pm; $10; ⓣ2461-8499). Though Arenal is one of the most active volcanoes in the Americas, whether you see any lava flow depends very much on the weather. If you can't see the summit, the park's visitor centre has video displays of the volcano's more spectacular activity – including its jaw-dropping night flows – and if nothing else, you'll certainly hear unearthly rumbling and sporadically feel the ground shake, especially at night.

The trails

The park contains a few good **trails**, all accessed from the main park entrance, including the **Lookout Point Trail** (1.3km), from where you can watch molten lava ebbing down the hillside, and the **Las Coladas Trail** (2.8km), which heads southeast to a lava flow from 1992. The **Los Tucanes Trail** (4km), also accessed off the road up to the *Arenal Observatory Lodge* (see p.228), takes you to the part of the forest that was flattened by the 1968 eruption. You may see some wildlife on these hikes; birds (including oropéndolas and tanagers) and agoutis are particularly common. Although the park has a simple café, it's best to take a picnic lunch and plenty of water if you intend to walk extensively.

A number of other hikes on the fringes of the park are also worth exploring. The four trails at the **Reserva Mirador El Silencio** (daily 7am–9pm; $7; ⓣ8354-4177, ⓦwww.miradorelsilencio.com), 5km north of the park entrance, lead through primary forest sheltering peccaries and spider monkeys to a lookout at the foot of the volcano. Closer to the entrance, **Arenal 1968** (daily 8am–8pm; $10; ⓣ2462-1212, ⓦwww.arenal1968.com) offers a taxing but highly worthwhile hike (3km loop) up to the original lava flow.

Practicalities

The **park entrance** is 14km west of La Fortuna; look for the well-signed driveway off to the left. **Taxis** head from La Fortuna to the west side of the

Volcán Arenal: explosions and eruptions

Volcán Arenal is the youngest and most active **stratovolcano** – the term for a steep, conical volcano created by the eruption of thick lava flows – in Costa Rica. Geologists have determined that Arenal is no more than 2900 years old; by comparison, Cerro Chato, which flanks Arenal to the south, last erupted in the late Holocene period, around 10,000 years ago. Geologists speculate that Arenal is so active because it directly taps a magma chamber located on a fault about 22km below the surface.

Arenal's growth over the ages has been characterized by massive **eruptions** every few centuries: it is thought to have erupted around 1750, 1525 and 1080 AD, and 220 and 900 BC. At the time of its most recent eruption in the late 1960s, Arenal seemed to be nothing but an unthreatening mountain, and locals had built small farms up its forested sides (take a look at Cerro Chato and you get the idea). But on **July 29, 1968**, an earthquake shook the area, blasting the top off Arenal and creating the majestic, lethal volcano seen today. Arenal killed 78 people that day, with fatalities caused by a combination of shockwaves, hot rocks and poisonous gases. The explosion created three craters, and Arenal has been active ever since, with almost daily rumblings and shakings.

While history would suggest that it's not due another major blowout for a few hundred years yet, Arenal is still very much an active volcano, so a few safety tips are worth bearing in mind: **never veer from trails** or guided tours, and do not attempt to hike anywhere near the crater, since lethal gases, ballistic boulders and molten rock, all of which occur regularly, can appear or change direction without warning. Indeed, technically everything between the volcano and the roads that run from La Fortuna to Laguna de Arenal and El Castillo lie in a **high-risk area** – a guide and a young girl were killed by a pyroclastic flow while walking "safe" trails (now closed) in the *Los Lagos* complex in August 2000 – so choose your trip with care.

volcano for $12, though you'll need to negotiate the rate if you want them to wait. Unless you're in a large group, it's cheaper – and easier – to take a tour. The **bus** from La Fortuna drops passengers off 2km from the park entrance, though the return journey can be tricky, as you'll need to connect with the bus coming from Tilarán or Nuevo Arenal.

The park can only be visited after dark on one of the **night tours** from La Fortuna. Most operators (see box, p.223) run them even when it's cloudy, in the hope that the clouds will lift or the opposite side of the volcano will be clear; none offers you a refund if you don't see anything, so you might want to wait for a clear evening before signing up. Operators in Nuevo Arenal (see p.232) run sunset boat tours where you can watch the action from Laguna de Arenal.

You can **spend the night** in the shadow of the volcano at *Arenal Observatory Lodge* (Ⓣ2479-1070, Ⓦwww.arenalobservatorylodge.com; ❻–❼; see map, pp.224–225), 5km beyond the park entrance. Just 1.8km from the crater, this is the area's best base for serious volcano-watchers. Standard rooms are rustic but comfortable, while the superior "Smithsonian" rooms (❽) have big beds and huge windows looking out at Arenal, which seems awesomely close; cheaper rooms are in *La Casona* farmhouse. Families renting the *White Hawk Villa* (sleeps 8; $480), 800m from the main lodge, can soak up the finest views of the lot. The extensive grounds include primary rainforest with trails, a small museum, pool and spa. There's a $4 charge for non-guests to enter the grounds, even if coming to eat at the overpriced **restaurant** – but you're really paying for the vista.

El Castillo

Just 23km southwest of La Fortuna but a world away in ambience, the idyllic mountain village of **EL CASTILLO** is all undulating hillsides covered with farmland and rainforest. Blessed with dead-on volcano views, this little village is also currently the best place in the Arenal area to gawk at the volcano's southwesterly lava dribbles. The turn-off for El Castillo is 15km west of La Fortuna, on the road to Nuevo Arenal; the (currently) unpaved, bumpy road which heads 8km east from here has for years kept the village off the traditional tourist trail, making it a welcome retreat from the buzzing commercial circus that is La Fortuna.

There's not much to the village itself, just one main street with a school, church, small supermarket and the **Arenal Eco Zoo** (daily 8am–7pm; $13, kids $10; Ⓣ2479-1059, Ⓦwww.arenalecozoo.com), principally a *serpentarium* housing over eighty species of snake, including a monster Burmese python that's knocking on 4m long. About 800m up the road from the school lies the enchanting **Butterfly Conservatory** (daily 8am–4.30pm; $13 with tour; Ⓣ2479-1149, Ⓦwww.butterflyconservatory.org), a regeneration project occupying a former cattle ranch, with six well-tended butterfly atriums, an insect museum, medicinal herb garden and riverside trails that weave through lush regenerating rainforest.

The main reason for coming to El Castillo, though, is to visit the extraordinary **Rancho Margot** (tours by appointment only; $20, $35 including lunch; 2hr; Ⓣ2479-7259 or 302-7318, Ⓦwww.ranchomargot.org), an organic farm, wildlife rescue centre and scenic accommodation (see below) that is well on the way to becoming the poster child for ecotourism in Costa Rica. The expansive property, set in a valley of the Río Caño Negro, is a byword for sustainability: a water-powered micro-turbine generates the ranch's electricity, the outdoor hot pool is heated using a biodigestor that converts animal waste into energy, and most of the food served in the excellent buffet-style restaurant is grown or raised on the property. A free shuttle bus runs four times daily from La Fortuna.

Accommodation

El Castillo has a growing selection of **accommodation** options (marked on the map on pp.224–225), most enjoying prime volcano views.

Cabinitas El Castillo Dorado In the centre of the village Ⓣ2479-1146, Ⓔcabinitaselcastillo@hotmail.com. A string of compact *cabinas* (opt for one of the trio of standalone cabins; $55) staggered along a ridge directly opposite Arenal, simply attired but with huge windows that make the most of the panorama. There's also a low-key restaurant on site. ❹

Hummingbird Nest In the centre of the village Ⓣ2479-1144, Ⓦwww.hummingbirdnestbb.com. Delightful American-run place with two sparkling rooms and an outdoor hot tub – all with spectacular views of the volcano. There's even a beauty therapist on hand offering pedicures. ❻

Linda Vista del Norte On the road into El Castillo Ⓣ2479-1551, Ⓦwww.hotellindavista.com. Perched on a hillside with gobsmacking lake and volcano views – you can watch the lava flow while kicking back in the pool, hot tub or restaurant, or just lord it up in one of the top-notch rooms with picture windows, attractive wood panelling and princely hot-water bathrooms. ❻

Rancho Margot 5km west of El Castillo Ⓣ2479-7259 or 8302-7318, Ⓦwww.ranchomargot.org. This terrific self-sufficient eco-retreat encourages a hands-on stay: you can milk the cows; make cheese, wine or marmalade; or help till the organic gardens. There's a riverside yoga and meditation studio, or you might opt for canyoning, kayaking, horseback-riding or one of the other activities on offer; adventurous types can even hike to Reserva Santa Elena, 8km away. Accommodation ranges from basic dormitory-style rooms in the bunkhouse with shared hot-water bathroom ($35 per person) to honeymoon-worthy hilltop bungalows with piping-hot showers, gigantic windows and wraparound terraces (❼). A free shuttle bus runs four times daily between La Fortuna and the ranch. ❺

Laguna de Arenal

The waters of **Laguna de Arenal** make what would otherwise have been a pretty area into a very beautiful one – a fact exploited by the tourist board's promotional posters showing a serene Volcán Arenal rising preternaturally out of the lake. Pretty as it is, it's actually a man-made body of water created when the far smaller original lake was dammed in 1973; the resulting Arenal Dam now generates much of the country's hydroelectricity. The lake is an excellent spot for **fishing** rainbow bass (*guapote*), an iridescent fish found only in freshwater lakes and rivers in Costa Rica, Nicaragua and Honduras, and for **windsurfing**; several schools operate out of **Tilarán**, on the southwest corner of the lake. Tourism has brought with it a sizeable colony of foreign residents, many of them Germans or Austrians attracted by the combination of a rather European-looking landscape with year-round tropical temperatures.

The road that winds its way from La Fortuna around the northern side of the lake has beautiful views of the volcano and of gentle hills, some of them given over to wind-farming – look for the giant white windmills on the hills above the north edge of the lake. About 40km from La Fortuna, lies lakeside **NUEVO ARENAL**, also known as **Arenal Town** (the original Arenal was flooded when the dam was built). Served by Tilarán-bound buses from La Fortuna, it's a quiet and pleasant place; in its centre (essentially one road that curves around to a church and football field), you'll find a post office (Mon–Fri 8am–noon & 1–5pm), a Banco de Costa Rica and a well-stocked supermarket (Mon–Fri 7am–6pm, Sat 7am–3pm).

Accommodation

There are some great **accommodation** options overlooking the lake, with the stretch between La Fortuna and Nuevo Arenal a particularly rich hunting ground for atmospheric lodgings.

Cabinas Catalinas In Nuevo Arenal, opposite the petrol station and behind *Moya's Place* ⓣ 2694-4001. This no-frills option is one of the better places to stay if you want to be in town. The rooms are light and clean, and you'll get a hot shower. ❷

La Ceiba Tree Lodge 4km from Nuevo Arenal ⓣ 2692-8050, ⓦ www.ceibatree-lodge.com. This romantic and relaxing German-run lodge just above Laguna de Arenal has six *cabinas* with private hot-water baths, fridges, carved wooden doors and tasteful artwork, as well as an excellent apartment perfect for a couple. Best of all is the big, shady communal terrace for great sunset viewing. Named after the massive 500-year-old tree in the grounds, the lodge also has a couple of walking trails. ❺

Chalet Nicholas 2km west of Nuevo Arenal ⓣ 2694-4041, ⓦ www.chaletnicholas.com. Small, beautifully kept hotel with just three rooms, all with private bathroom and hot water, looking out to the lake and distant volcano. You'll get a warm welcome from the charming hosts, not to mention their three massive Great Danes who have their own suite. Horseback-riding and birdwatching tours can be arranged, though you'll spot plenty of birds within the hotel grounds. ❻

Gingerbread 1km east of Nuevo Arenal ⓣ 2694-0039, ⓦ www.gingerbreadarenal.com. Sleep off your meal at the excellent restaurant (see p.232) in one of four themed rooms – Butterfly, Cupid, Jungle or the larger Garden of Eden (❼) – all boasting spacious, locally made beds and adorned in (literally) enchanting murals. ❻

Los Héroes Hotel 15km east of Nuevo Arenal ⓣ 2692-8012, ⓦ www.hotellosheroes.com. This small hotel perched above the lake looks transported straight from an alpine meadow. Rooms – decked out with gingerbread woodwork and some with balconies – are comfortable, and there's a hot tub, pool and quirky revolving restaurant (see p.233). ❺

Lost Iguana Resort 18km west of La Fortuna, across the dam, then 1.5km down a signed road to the right ⓣ 2461-0122, ⓦ www.lostiguanaresort.com. This peaceful, upscale jungle lodge has rooms with balconies offering volcano vistas, large, comfortable beds and a/c, satellite TV and private hot tubs, plus *Las Casitas*, two-bedroom suites set in a separate hilltop building ($425). The resort has several jungle trails and a spa, and they can also arrange any sort of local activity. ❾

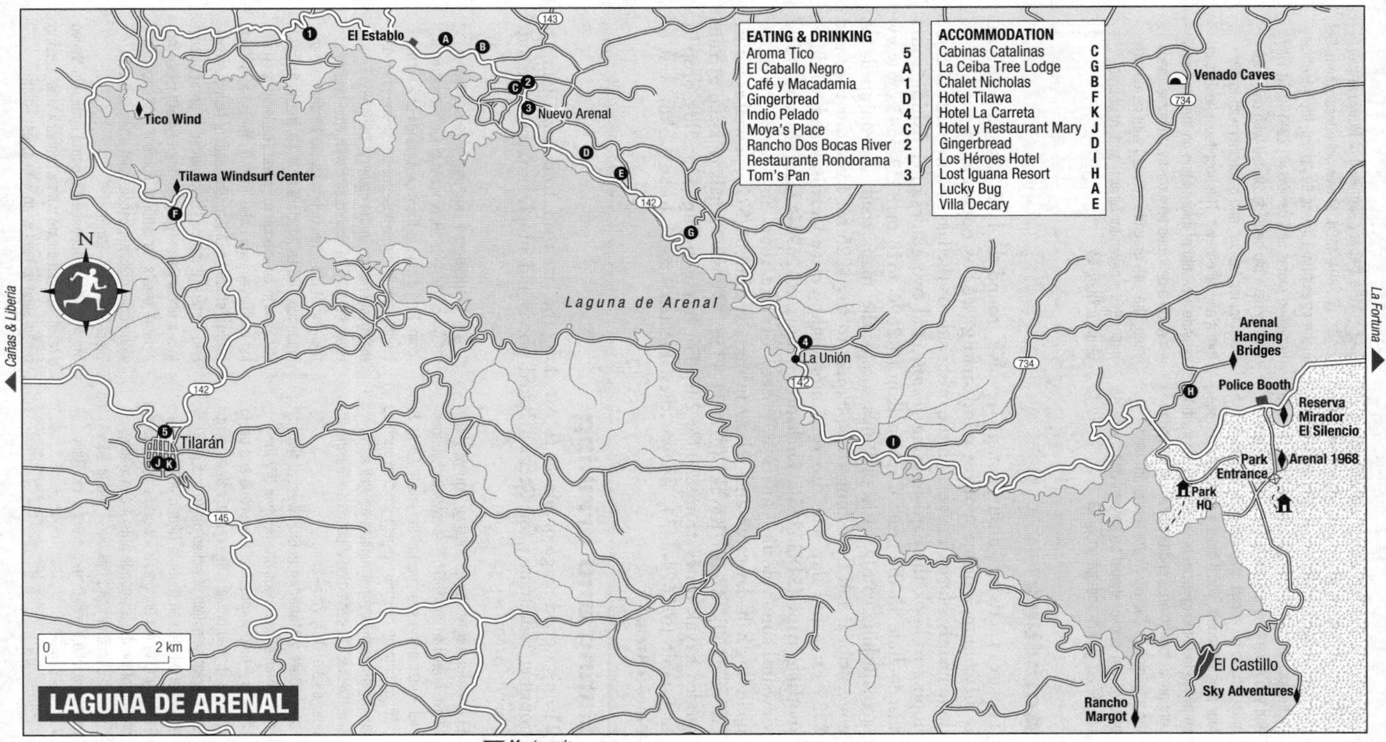
LAGUNA DE ARENAL
EATING & DRINKING
Aroma Tico 5
El Caballo Negro A
Café y Macadamia 1
Gingerbread D
Indio Pelado 4
Moya's Place C
Rancho Dos Bocas River 2
Restaurante Rondorama I
Tom's Pan 3
ACCOMMODATION
Cabinas Catalinas C
La Ceiba Tree Lodge G
Chalet Nicholas B
Hotel Tilawa F
Hotel La Carreta K
Hotel y Restaurant Mary J
Gingerbread D
Los Héroes Hotel I
Lost Iguana Resort H
Lucky Bug A
Villa Decary E
Laguna de Arenal
El Establo
Nuevo Arenal
Tico Wind
Tilawa Windsurf Center
Tilarán
La Unión
Venado Caves
Arenal Hanging Bridges
Police Booth
Reserva Mirador El Silencio
Arenal 1968
Park Entrance
Park HQ
El Castillo
Sky Adventures
Rancho Margot
La Fortuna
Cañas & Liberia
Monteverde
N
0
2 km
142
143
145
734

Lucky Bug 3km west of Nuevo Arenal ⓣ2694-4515, ⓦwww.luckybugcr.net. This bed and breakfast overlooking a pond is truly fantastical – think Alice in Wonderland goes tropical and you're on the right track. Owned by a German artist whose rainforest-inspired work graces the four themed rooms, you'll have a fine night's sleep sprawled in the king-sized beds. There's an inviting communal lounge area and breakfast is served in the adjoining *El Caballo Negro* restaurant (see below). Non-guests should be sure to visit the on-site art gallery and gift shop. ❻

Villa Decary 2km east of Nuevo Arenal ⓣ2694-4330, ⓦwww.villadecary.com. Set just metres from Laguna de Arenal, the beautifully furnished rooms and *casitas* ($129–149) at *Villa Decary* have big beds decorated with colourful Guatemalan fabrics, and balconies with lovely forest and lake views. The hospitable hosts can provide a wealth of information on the area, and serve up a delicious breakfast with home-made jams. The lush grounds, planted with rare palms, make this a haven for birds – and, of course, birdwatchers. ❻

Activities

The area's activities unsurprisingly revolve around the lake. Laguna de Arenal is the country's prime spot for **windsurfing** (see box opposite), though this is done mainly out of Tilarán, on the other side of the lake. Many visitors come hoping to hook the hard-fighting *guapote*, and two guides offer **fishing tours** that include all the gear: Captain Ron (ⓣ2694-4678 or 8339-3345, ⓦwww.arenalfishing.com), with pick-ups along the main road, is equipped for conventional and fly-fishing trips; expect to pay $225 for five-hour trips and $325 for a full day. He also runs moonlight volcano **cruises** and wildlife-spotting trips ($185–225). Enchanted Tours (ⓣ2694-4731, ⓦwww.worldviewsintl.com/volcano) offers a variety of lake tours in a pontoon boat, including half-day catch-and-release fishing expeditions ($225) as well as nature cruises ($60). Arenal Kayaks (ⓣ2694-4336, ⓦwww.arenalkayaks.com) runs guided **kayak tours** (from $30 for 2hr). For **horse-riding** ($35; 3hr), drop by El Establo (ⓣ2694-4434, ⓦwww.thestablearenal.com), located 3km west of Nuevo Arenal.

Eating and drinking

There's a good range of **places to eat** along the lake road, from pizza joints to gourmet restaurants; for German baked goods and simpler snacks, head into Nuevo Arenal.

El Caballo Negro *The Lucky Bug*, 3km west of Nuevo Arenal ⓣ2694-4757, ⓦwww.luckybugcr.net. Outstanding spot, part of the lovely *Lucky Bug* B&B, dishing up delicious vegetarian fare such as aubergine parmesan parmigiana as well as schnitzels ($16) served on a patio overlooking the hotel's lake. Daily 7am–5pm.

Café y Macadamia 6km west of Nuevo Arenal. Enormous sandwiches (try the Capresa – turkey, mozzarella, avocado and pesto on home-baked bread; $9), organic salads, soups and a great selection of cakes make this an essential pit stop en route to Tilarán or La Fortuna. Even if you're not hungry, it's worth stopping for a portion of local macadamia nuts – chocolate, coconut, cinnamon and the like – and to take in the gorgeous lake views from out the back. Daily 7.30am–5pm.

Gingerbread 1km east of Nuevo Arenal ⓣ2694-0039, ⓦwww.gingerbreadarenal.com. Fine dining in the expert hands of a French-taught Israeli chef, whose fusion cuisine is among the most creative in the country. The menu changes daily, in accordance with whatever's freshest at the time, but has a big Mediterranean influence. Dishes (starters from $9, mains from $15) are large enough to share. The lengthy wine list is stocked with Latin imports. Tues–Sat 5–9pm.

Indio Pelado La Unión, 9km east of Nuevo Arenal. Bad name – it means "Bald Indian" – great pizzas: thin-crust, Italian-style pies (from $4.50) including a meat-lover's "Argentina" number that's topped with steak, chicken, bacon, ham and pepperoni. Tues–Sun noon–10pm.

Moya's Place Opposite the petrol station in Nuevo Arenal. Cool little café with a laidback vibe, serving meals such as beef wrap with sweet potato coleslaw ($8) and basil chicken curry salad ($7). Daily 11.30am–9.30pm.

Rancho Dos Bocas River 500m west of Nuevo Arenal. A warm welcome awaits at this Tico eatery run by a local women's cooperative; they'll cook a whole fish for you, and also make a fine *chimichanga* ($5). Daily 9am–9pm.

Restaurante Rondorama *Los Héroes Hotel*, 15km east of Nuevo Arenal ⓣ2692-8012, ⓦwww.hotellosheroes.com. It's just as much fun getting to the revolving restaurant at this alpine-esque hotel as it is eating there – it's reached on a miniature railway ($10; reservations required), which whisks visitors 3km through tunnels, over bridges and up a hill, where you can feast on both the food (mains $5–18) and the panoramic valley views. Daily 11am–3pm.

Tom's Pan On the main road in Nuevo Arenal. Stock up on everything from rye and pumpernickel to apple strudel and gingerbread, or tuck into German sausages while enjoying lake views from the outdoor terrace. Daily 7.30am–5pm.

Tilarán and around

Unhurried **TILARÁN** lies 40km northwest of Monteverde and roughly 60km west of La Fortuna. The town's wide streets channel the vigorous breezes that breathe life into an otherwise lazy tropical hamlet – these same winds create the best **windsurfing and kitesurfing** conditions in the country at nearby Laguna de Arenal, 5km away. On the last weekend in April, Tilarán celebrates its ranching roots with a well-attended rodeo festival.

Practicalities

Buses from La Fortuna (daily 8am, 12.15pm & 5.30pm; 3hr), Santa Elena (daily 4.30am & 12.30pm; 2hr 30min) and San José (5 daily; 4hr) pull in 100m north of the Parque Central. In addition to the services to Santa Elena (for Monteverde; daily 7am & 4pm), there are connections west to Cañas and the Interamericana (6 daily; 30min), from where you can head north to Liberia and the Guanacaste beaches, or east to La Fortuna (daily 7am, 12.30pm & 3pm; 3hr) and south San José (7 daily; 4hr).

On the lakeshore east of town, *Hotel Tilawa* (ⓣ2695-5050, ⓦwww.hotel-tilawa.com; ❺) has large **rooms** and *cabinas*, a great swimming pool and a hot tub, and arranges windsurf rentals and lessons (see box below); after a day on the waves,

Windsurfing and kitesurfing

Thanks to its unusually consistent conditions, Laguna de Arenal is the best place in Costa Rica for **windsurfing and kitesurfing** – the strong winds that buffet the surface of the lake from December to April can reach speeds of up to 25mph, drawing experienced riders from around the world. The wind peaks between mid-December and February, so aim for the late-season months if you're looking to learn.

Operators

Ticowind About halfway between Nuevo Arenal and Tilarán ⓣ2692-2002 or 8383-2694, ⓦwww.ticowind.com. Well-respected outfit with over twenty years' experience. They rent quality equipment (from $50/$58 for windsurfing/kitesurfing for a half-day), while windsurfing classes cater for first-timers ($120) and those looking to improve their technique ($200). Their comprehensive beginner's kitesurfing course includes nine hours on the water ($540).

Tilawa Windsurf Center *Hotel Tilawa*, 5km east of Tilarán ⓣ2695-5050, ⓦwww.windsurfcostarica.com. Hotel-affiliated centre offering older windsurfing kit (from $45 for the half-day, $35 for hotel guests), plus a range of lessons, from gybe tuition ($30; 1hr) to jumps and loops (both $10; 20min).

guests can enjoy home-brewed beer at the hotel bar. In town, the best option is the welcoming *Hotel La Carreta* (ⓣ2695-6593, ⓦwww.lacarretacr.com; ❺), 150m south of the Banco de Costa Rica, whose smart rooms are brightened by elegant, hand-painted murals. The parkside *Hotel y Restaurant Mary* (ⓣ2695-5479; ❷) has clean, bright rooms (ask to see a few before making a decision) with cable TV and private hot-water bathroom, friendly staff and free coffee. At *Aroma Tico* (ⓣ2695-3065, ⓦwww.aromatico.net), 300m north of the church at the intersection of the road to Cañas and Nuevo Arenal, you can get local **information** from English-speaking staff, surf the **internet**, shop for souvenirs and eat at the pricey **restaurant**.

North of La Fortuna

The area north of La Fortuna, on the western fringes of the Llanura de Gautusos, is a world away from the activity-driven hubbub of town. The long road that runs from La Fortuna via Tanque sees little traffic, and peters out beyond the village of **San Rafael de Gautuso** into seemingly endless bumpy tracks that head northeast to Caño Negro or northwest to the border with Nicaragua. This is, however, one of the few places outside the Caribbean where you can interact with the country's indigenous peoples: San Rafael is the modern-day home of the **Maleku**, and visitors are welcome to call in at the **Reserva Indígena Maleku**, just south of the village. On the way here – though more often visited on a tour – the **Venado Caves** provide a rare opportunity to head underground, their labyrinthine system of bat-filled caverns proving an interesting alternative to the ubiquitous canopy tours.

Venado Caves

About 30km northwest of La Fortuna, on a paved road near the tiny mountain town of **Venado** ("Deer"), are the **Venado Caves** (Nov–April dawn to dusk; $15; ⓣ2478-8008). This small network of subterranean caverns is quite accessible, provided you aren't afraid of bats and don't mind getting wet, as you'll need to walk through waist-high water to get to some of them. Inside is a spooky and unique tangle of stalactites and smoothed-out rock formations; look out for the Papagayo Rock, shaped (with a little imagination) like a parrot. Using the services of a **guide** is a very good idea – the caves are linked by a labyrinth of narrow passages (check that you can fit before you begin the crawl) – and you should bring a flashlight and rubber boots; you may be able to rent them from your hotel if you're staying locally.

Several companies in La Fortuna offer **tours**, including guide and entrance fee (see box, p.223). Otherwise, two daily **buses** head from San Carlos to Venado (departing 7.30am & 2.30pm, returning 1.30pm & 6.40pm), more than 2km from the entrance to the caves; you can also catch these from the El Tanque intersection 5km east of La Fortuna. More frequent buses from La Fortuna to Guatuso will drop you off at a private farm, from where it's a walk of several kilometres along a gravel road and marked trail to the caves.

San Rafael de Guatuso and the Reserva Indígena Maleku

Ten kilometres north of Venado, the village of **SAN RAFAEL DE GUATUSO** (known locally as Guatuso) lies at the heart of Costa Rica's few remaining **Maleku communities**, who live in *palenques* (straw huts) on the **Reserva**

Indígena Maleku, established by the government in the 1960s. Historically part of the Corobicí tribal group, the present-day Maleku (also known as Guatuso) are a group of interrelated clans that have inhabited northwestern Costa Rica and southern Nicaragua for thousands of years. Now numbering about 600, their history and the story of their steady decline is a familiar one for tribal peoples in the area. Victims of disease, intertribal kidnapping and slavery to Spanish settlers in Nicaragua, they were dealt further blows in the 1700s and 1800s by the efforts of the Nicaraguan and Costa Rican Catholic churches to convert them to Christianity.

Though the Maleku speak their own language – broadcast by Radio Sistema Cultural Maleku and taught in schools – you won't see native dress or any outward signs of tribal identity around Guatuso. The best place to get a sense of traditional indigenous culture is at the reserve itself, set in bucolic countryside 7km south of the village. On the excellent guided tours at the **Centro Ecológico Maleku Araraf** (daily 8am–4pm; $35, ask for Luis Denis; 4hr; Ⓣ8839-0540, Ⓔcentro ecologicomalekuararaf@yahoo.es) you'll learn about medicinal plants, get insight into local religious beliefs and burial practices (for example, they bury their dead directly beneath their homes), hike a rainforest trail and eat traditional food. There's also an on-site museum with a modest selection of artefacts and handicrafts. Similar activities are available at the **Centro Ecocultura Maleku TAFA** (daily 7am–8pm; $30; Ⓣ2464-0443 or 8838-1320, Ⓔeco_cultura_maleku_tafa@yahoo.ca), run by the family of former Maleku leader Wilson Morera Elizondo ("TAFA"). The centre gives demonstrations of religious ceremonies and organizes language classes; some of the handmade crafts you can buy here include masks and drums constructed out of iguana skin.

If you decide to spend the night hereabouts, try *Cabinas El Milagro* (Ⓣ2464-0037; ❷), a friendly spot with tidy, basic rooms offering cold-water bathrooms. A number of daily **buses** travel to Guatuso from La Fortuna (1hr–1hr 30min) and San Carlos (2hr–2hr 30min).

San Carlos and around

Perched on the northern slopes of the Cordillera Central, 650m above sea level, **SAN CARLOS** (also known as **Ciudad Quesada**, or simply Quesada) has a decidedly rural atmosphere – fresh produce overflows from market stalls onto the streets, and *campesinos* with weathered faces hang out in the main square in front of the church. You're likely to pass through here on the way from or to La Fortuna; there's little to actually do – locals only come into town to have a drink on Friday night or to sell their wares at the Saturday market – though therein lies its charm. Strolling about town, you get a real feel for what drives Costa Rica's economy: much of the nation's milk, beef, citrus fruit and rice come from the large-scale agricultural holdings in these parts. Positioned at the heart of cattle country, San Carlos is also something of a **saddlery** centre; it's well worth dropping by one of the expert saddlers, if only to watch them skilfully working the supple leather.

Arrival and information

Daily **buses** for San Carlos depart from **San José**'s La Coca-Cola terminal hourly until 5.30pm (2hr 30min), stopping in the centre of town before heading to the bus station, 1km north of Parque Central. There are also services from **La Fortuna** (10 daily; 1hr 30min), **Los Chiles** (12 daily; 2hr 30min) and **Puerto Viejo de Sarapiquí** (12 daily; 2hr 30min).

Moving on from San Carlos

San Carlos is the gateway to the Zona Norte, and buses depart frequently for a range of destinations, including **La Fortuna** (11 daily; 1hr 30min), **Los Chiles** (12 daily; 2hr 30min) and **Puerto Viejo de Sarapiquí** (12 daily; 2hr 30min). There's also an hourly service until 6pm to **San José** (2hr 30min). To get to the bus station from the town centre, take one of the frequent local buses labelled "Terminal".

The Zone Norte's **tourist information centre** (Mon–Fri 8am–4pm; ⓣ2461-1112), lies at the far southern end of Calle Central, though the sparsity of information on offer hardly warrants the hike out here. In town itself, you can change cash and **travellers' cheques** at the Banco de Costa Rica on the south-western corner of the Parque Central. For **medical emergencies**, the Hospital de San Carlos (ⓣ2460-1176), 750m south of the town centre, is the best in the Zona Norte. As befits its setting, San Carlos hosts various horseriding shows throughout the year – the biggest is the **San Carlos International Expo**, a ten-day event at the end of April featuring horse parades, rodeos and cattle auctions.

Accommodation

You'll find plenty of budget options in San Carlos, but if you're looking for more luxurious **accommodation**, try one of the likeable lodges outside town.

In town

Hotel Conquistador Calle Central, 700m south of Parque Central ⓣ2460-0546, ⓕ2460-6311. Looking much grander than it actually is, the *Conquistador's* imposing facade gives way to functional rooms – some offering valley views – with tiled floors, TV, fan (a/c rooms are $9 more) and hot-water bath. Those with a car will appreciate the secure parking. ❸

Hotel Don Goyo C 2, Av 4 ⓣ2460-1780, ⓔhoteldongoyo@hotmail.com. One of the most pleasing options in town, these clean, quiet, brightly painted rooms, all with private hot-water bath and fan, are in a modern building near the centre. There's also parking and a reputable restaurant downstairs. ❸

Hotel del Valle Av 3, C2/4 ⓣ2460-0718 or 8305-1485, ⓔhoteldelvalle2010@gmail.com. Situated on a quiet central street, this little hotel has stuffy rooms with TV, bathroom and fan. The mattresses are a bit too submissive for some tastes, but comfy nonetheless. ❷

Around town

La Garza Opposite the sports field in Platanar, 15km northeast of San Carlos ⓣ2475-5222, ⓦwww.hotellagarza.com. Named for the herons (*garzas*) that nest in the grounds, this hotel is part of a working dairy farm. Rustic, comfortable polished-floor bungalows have fans or a/c and are decorated in Guatemalan fabrics. Hammock-laden verandas look out onto the river, home to a variety of frogs. There's also a restaurant (reached across a hanging bridge) and pool. ❺

Hotel Lodge La Quinta 15km north of San Carlos, just after the sugar mill on the southern outskirts of Platanar ⓣ2475-5260, ⓕ2475-5921. The best budget option in the area (and accessible by bus from San Carlos), this friendly family-run accommodation has seven attractive doubles (a/c $3 more), some overlooking the river, and two fully equipped self-catering apartments (for 6 or 11; both $36). Iguanas frequent the huge pool (with a slide). There's also an on-site restaurant for guests. ❶

Termales de Bosque 7km northeast of San Carlos ⓣ2460-4740, ⓦwww.termalesdelbosque.com. This self-contained resort with a plethora of modest *cabinas* boasts hot-spring pools set in lush jungle surrounds; the newer deluxe bungalows ($152) are plusher, and can sleep up to six. There's an on-site restaurant and a spa offering various thermal-themed treatments. See also opposite. ❻

Tilajari Resort Hotel 800m west of Muelle, 22km north of San Carlos ⓣ2469-1212, ⓦwww.tilajari.com. This quiet, beautifully situated resort hotel sits on an out-of-the-way cattle ranch by the croc-populated Río San Carlos (which many of the rooms overlook). Double rooms have bathroom, a/c, terrace and satellite TV, and there's a restaurant, pool and tennis and basketball courts. Iguanas roam the landscaped grounds, and horseriding and rainforest walks can be arranged. ❻

The Town

San Carlos fans out around the attractive **Parque Central**, dominated by a startling modern church with a gigantic Jesus figure looming above worshippers. On the north side of the park, the cooperative **Mercado de Artesanía de San Carlos** (Mon–Sat 8.30am–6pm) sells leatherwork and other crafts and is a less frenetic place to browse for souvenirs than some of the more touristy stores in nearby Sarchí (see p.135).

You can watch local leatherworkers making intricate Costa Rican saddles in any of the **saddlers' stores** (*talabarterías*) that are dotted around town – one of the best is Talabartería La Moderna (daily 6.30am–6.30pm), two blocks north of the Parque Central, at Av 3, C 0/1, which also sells a good range of cowboy paraphernalia. The artisans in San Carlos are known for the quality of their work, and while you may not have room in your luggage for a full-sized saddle (handcrafted ones are available from $200, a bargain if you're into that sort of thing), they can normally fashion you something smaller while you wait.

Eating and drinking

There are several cheap and cheerful **sodas** around town, but as San Carlos is known for its fine beef it's worth trying out one of the various steakhouses dotted around town. On weekend evenings, the town offers a genuine Tico experience far removed from the tourist-oriented **nightlife** in other parts of the country.

Coca Loca Steakhouse C 2, Av 0/2. Popular spot overlooking the Parque Central, with generous slabs of local steak and fries going for around $9. Daily 11am–10.30pm.

Los Geranios C 4, Av 0. Start your bar crawl at this hopping first-floor bar 100m south of the Parque Central, with breezy upstairs seating overlooking the street. Daily 4pm–12.30am.

Restaurante Plaza In the food market, on the northern side of the Parque Central. The best of the market's budget *sodas*, with a long wooden counter where they serve up meals and snacks, including *gallos*, soups and excellent *batidos*. Daily 6am–6pm.

La Terraza C 0, Av 5/7. Airy first-floor restaurant with a balcony overlooking Calle Central. Meat, of course, tops the list – Argentinian steak served with chimichurri sauce will set you back $9.50 – but the bar's varied *boca* menu (ceviche, *papas a la francesa*, etc) takes some beating. Daily 11am–11pm.

Around San Carlos

The sleepy villages of **Muelle**, **Platanar** and **Aguas Zarcas**, set in the beautiful country around San Carlos, feature the area's best accommodation (see opposite) and have a couple of minor sights between them.

Seven kilometres along the road to Aquas Zarcas, the self-styled ecological park of **Termales del Bosque** (daily 9am–9.30pm; $12, children $6; ⓣ2460-4740, ⓦwww.termalesdelbosque.com) is centred around seven riverside hot springs and has a spa offering a variety of treatments, from hydrotherapy to volcanic clay masks. About 2km further north, the family-run **La Marina Wildlife Rescue Center** (daily 8am–4pm; $8, children $5; ⓣ2474-2202, ⓦwww.zoocostarica.com) houses some five hundred animals (over eighty species) that have been saved from illegal owners or areas where their habitat has been destroyed. Though acting on a very tight budget – the centre relies completely on donations from its visitors – it has established a successful breeding programme, including tapirs, spider monkeys and the endangered great green macaw, releasing a number of these into the wild.

Muelle itself, 22km north of San Carlos, is a useful stopoff on the road between La Fortuna, Puerto Viejo de Sarapiquí and Los Chiles (there's a petrol station here). It's worth stretching your legs at the *Restaurante Las Iguanas* (daily 7am–8pm) by the bridge across the Río San Carlos, the trees around which are a favoured basking spot for a large group of **iguanas**.

The far north

The **far north** of the Zona Norte is an isolated region, culturally as well as geographically, closer in spirit to Nicaragua than to the rest of the country and mostly devoted to sugar cane, oranges and cattle. Years of conflict during the Nicaraguan civil war made the region more familiar with CIA men and arms-runners than with tourists, but it's all quiet now.

Most visitors are here to see the **Refugio Nacional de Vida Silvestre Caño Negro**, a vast wetland that makes up one of the most remote wildlife refuges in the country. Located at a key point on the migratory route between North and South America, it acts as the resting place for hundreds of migrant bird species and is considered by the Ramsar Convention on Wetlands to be the third most important wetland reserve in the world.

Caño Negro is accessed from **Los Chiles**, near the Nicaraguan border, and the only village of any size in the far north. The drive up here, along an unnervingly straight stretch of road from San Carlos, takes you through a flat landscape of rust-red soil and open pasture, broken only by roadside shacks, with the Llanura de Guatusos stretching hot and interminably to the west. During the Nicaraguan civil war, Los Chiles was a Contra supply line. Nowadays, there's a climate of international cooperation, helped by the fact that many of the residents are of Nicaraguan extraction, and **crossing the border** is straightforward, as long as your documents are in order. Incidentally, the **Río San Juan** is technically Nicaraguan territory – the border is on the Costa Rican bank – though Costa Rica is allowed free use of the river.

Los Chiles

The only reason tourists make it to **LOS CHILES**, a border settlement just 3km from the Nicaraguan frontier, is to break their journey on the way to **Caño Negro**, 25km downstream on the Río Frío (see p.240), or to cross the Nicaraguan border – although the majority of travellers still cross at Peñas Blancas, further west on the Interamericana. There's little to do in town other than soak up its end-of-the-world atmosphere – the highway peters out just beyond Los Chiles in the direction of the Río San Juan, leaving nowhere to go but the river – though you can while away some time wandering down to the docks, where the tumble-down houses evoke a forlorn, France-in-the-tropics feel.

Arrival

Two **buses** do the daily run from **San José** (C 12, Av 7/9) to Los Chiles (5.30am & 3.30pm; 5hr), returning at 5am and 3pm. Hourly buses depart from **San Carlos** (2hr 30min), heading back on the hour from 6am to 5pm. For **Caño Negro**, you'll need to take one of the three daily buses signed "Upala" (5am, noon & 4.30pm; 1hr 15min). Buses stop in Los Chiles at the small station just west of where the main road turns left down to the port.

Driving from San Carlos, Hwy-141 heads north along a reasonable road through the tiny settlements of Florencia and Muelle, and then along the 66km stretch of virtually empty highway, potholed in places, from Boca de Arenal to Los Chiles. There are few service stations north of Muelle: make sure you have plenty of petrol.

Information

The best source of **information** in town is *Heliconia Tours & Restaurant*, 100m east of the docks (daily 7am–8pm; ☎2471-2096 or 8307-8585,

Into Nicaragua

The **border at Los Chiles** has a turbulent history: during the Nicaraguan civil war, US-sponsored Contras were supplied through here, and it was not unusual to see camouflaged planes sitting on the airstrip on the edge of town, disgorging guns. In the past, the border was closed to foreigners, and for a period also to Nicaraguans and Costa Ricans, though it's now possible for anyone to **enter Nicaragua** from here.

Crossing the border

The proposed road crossing at Tabillas, 7km north of Los Chiles, is continually plagued by delays, and for the time being the only way to reach Nicaragua is **by boat on the Río Frío**: daily services leave the docks in Los Chiles at noon and 1pm. From the border control point, it's a fourteen-kilometre trip up the Río Frío to the small town of **San Carlos de Nicaragua** ($12; 45min) on the southeast lip of huge Lago de Nicaragua. The Los Chiles *migración* officials are relatively friendly, and you may be able to confirm boat times with the groups of Nicas or Ticos who hang around the office. Make sure that the **Nicaraguan border patrol**, 3km upriver from Los Chiles, stamps your passport, as you will need proof of entry when leaving Nicaragua. Few nationalities require a **visa** for Nicaragua, but if needed, this must be done at the Nicaraguan consulate in San José (see p.117). Note that if you needed a visa to enter Costa Rica, make sure you've got a double-entry stamp or you won't be allowed back into Costa Rica.

You'll need some **local currency** upon arrival in San Carlos de Nicaragua; change a few colones for *córdobas* at the bank in Los Chiles. From San Carlos de Nicaragua, it's possible to cross the lake to **Granada** and on to **Managua**, but check with the consulate in San José because this is an infrequent boat service and without forward planning you could end up stuck in San Carlos for longer than you'd hoped.

Day-trips

In the current atmosphere of relative political stability in Nicaragua, you can go on **organized day-trips** from Los Chiles to Nicaraguan **San Carlos**, **Lago de Nicaragua** and even the **Islas Solentiname**. Visitors may even be able to see the fortress **San Juan** (also called the Castillo de la Concepción or Fortaleza) on Lago de Nicaragua, one of the oldest Spanish structures (1675) in the Americas, built as a defence against the English and pirates (often one and the same) plying the Río San Juan, though note that these trips can be very expensive (from $250). For more details, contact *Rancho Tulipán* in Los Chiles (see p.240).

Ⓔcocas34@hotmail.com), where you can check the bus schedules and the times of the *colectivo* boat to Nicaragua, and get details of travelling on to Granada; they also organize early-morning trips up the Río Frío, spotting birds, reptiles (iguanas and turtles) and monkeys en route ($30; 3hr), and can arrange transportation to San Carlos de Nicaragua should you want to leave earlier than the public boat ($12).

Though Los Chiles is quite isolated, it has most of the facilities you'll need: you can **change dollars** and travellers' cheques, and pick up Nicaraguan *córdobas* at the Banco Nacional on the north side of the football field (Mon–Fri 8am–3.30pm), which also has an ATM. The **post office** (Mon–Fri 8am–noon & 1–5.30pm) is opposite the bus station. For **supplies**, head to Supermercado Carranzo, on the western side of the football field (daily 7am–8pm).

Accommodation

There are a couple of options if you need to **stay the night** in Los Chiles before crossing the border or heading on to Caño Negro. The best budget lodging in town is the simple, clean and comfortable *Cabinas Jabirú* (Ⓣ2471-1496, Ⓔjcarlos0829@hotmail.com; ❷), signed to the right half a block north of the bus station; it offers air-conditioned rooms with fridges and private hot-water bathrooms. Another good option is the *Rancho Tulipán* (Ⓣ2471-1414, Ⓔsergioca7@hotmail.com; ❸), opposite the *migración*, whose air-conditioned, en-suite rooms are large and come with hot water. They also have an on-site restaurant (daily 6am–10pm) and internet café, and can arrange tours to Caño Negro ($70) and Nicaragua ($250).

Eating and drinking

A number of decent, inexpensive **sodas** dot the town: try *Soda Pamela* (daily 6am–7pm), by the bus station, which serves up excellent *batidos*, cool shakes that are a godsend in the heat. On the south side of the football field, *Restaurante El Parque* (daily 7.30am–10pm) has a relaxed vibe and you can fill up on *tipíco* food for around $5, while *Heliconia Tours and Restaurant* (daily 7am–10pm), 100m south of the docks, cooks up a fine rainbow bass, plucked straight from the murky waters meandering just metres from the restaurant entrance.

Refugio Nacional de Vida Silvestre Caño Negro

The largely pristine **REFUGIO NACIONAL DE VIDA SILVESTRE CAÑO NEGRO** (daily 8am–4pm; $10), 25km southwest of Los Chiles, is one of *the* places in the Americas to view enormous concentrations of both migratory and indigenous **birds**, along with mammalian and reptilian **river wildlife**. Until recently, its isolation kept it well off the beaten tourist track, though access has improved and nowadays numerous tours are offered from San José, La Fortuna and – best of all – the adjacent village of **Caño Negro**.

The refuge is created by the seasonal flooding of the Río Frío, so depending on the time of year you may find yourself whizzing around a huge 800-hectare lagoon in a motorboat or walking along mud-caked riverbeds. There's a 3m difference in the water level between the rainy season (May–Nov), when Caño Negro is at its fullest, and the dry season (Dec–April); while the mammalian population of the area stays more or less constant, the birds vary widely. The **best time to visit** is between January and March, when the most migratory species are in residence and you'll see scores of caiman basking on the riverbanks.

Arrival

Daily **buses** leave Los Chiles for the village of Caño Negro (signed "Upala") at 5am, noon and 4.30pm, stopping outside *Soda La Palmera*, opposite the Parque Central, and the Coopecane Cooperativa; they return at 4.50am, 11am and 4pm (1hr 15min each way). If **driving**, it's nineteen bone-shuddering kilometres from the turn-off south of Los Chiles.

Alternatively, you could take a **tour** from San José, La Fortuna (see box, p.223), Los Chiles (from where most tour boats leave) or some of the more upmarket Zona Norte hotels, but bear in mind that the first 25km of the trip down the Río Frío (taking an hour or more by *lancha*) does not take you through the wildlife refuge, which begins at the mouth of the large flooded area and is marked by a sign poking out of a small islet. Make sure your boatman takes you into Caño Negro – some operators will skimp on the time, petrol and refuge entrance fee and take you nowhere near the real thing – or better still, that your tour company drives all the way to Caño Negro village and starts the boat tour from there.

Watching wildlife in Caño Negro

The wildlife that calls Caño Negro home includes a staggering variety of **birds** such as **storks**, **cormorants**, **kingfishers** and **egrets**. You should be able to tick off a number of the **heron** species that inhabit the riverbanks (including green, boat-billed and rufescent tiger herons), along with **northern jacana** and **purple gallinule**. The lagoon itself is a good place to spot the elegant, long-limbed **white ibis**; its shimmering dark-green cousin, the **glossy ibis**; and perhaps the most striking of all the reserve's avifauna, the **roseatte spoonbill**, a pastel-pink bird that is usually seen filtering the water with its distinctive flattened beak. The most common species are the sinuous-necked **anhingas** (snakebirds), who impale their prey with the knife-point of their beaks before swallowing, though Caño Negro is also home to Costa Rica's only colony of **Nicaraguan grackle**.

Reptiles are abundant, particularly the large **caiman** that lounge along the river and on the fringes of the lagoon, though you'll also spot plenty of pot-bellied **iguanas**. Look out, too, for the strikingly green **emerald basilik lizard**; **swimming snakes**, heads held aloft like periscopes, bodies whipping out behind; and the various **turtles** (yellow, river and sliding) that can be seen resting on logs at the water's edge.

Large **mammals** that live in Caño Negro include pumas, jaguars and tapirs, but these private creatures are rarely spotted. **Howler monkeys** are at least heard if not seen – it helps to have binoculars to distinguish their black hairy shapes from the surrounding leaves in the riverside trees – though it takes a good guide to pick out a **sloth**, camouflaged by the green algae often covering their brown hair. The rows of small grey triangles you might see on tree trunks are **bats**, literally hanging out during the day.

Perhaps the reserve's most unusual inhabitant (in the wet season, at least) is the **tropical garfish**, a kind of in-between creature straddling fish and reptile. This so-called living fossil is a fish with lungs, gills and a nose, and looks oddest while it sleeps, drifting along in the water.

Information

Unless you're an expert in identifying wildlife, the most rewarding way to enjoy Caño Negro is to use the services of a local **guide** who knows the area and can point out animals and other features of river life. The **Real Tour Association** (daily 8am–4pm; ⓣ2471-1621; ⓔreal.tour@hotmail.com), on the southwest corner of the *parque*, near the refuge entrance, represents all official tour operators in the community and charges a set rate of $40 (1hr), $60 (2hr; the minimum time needed to get into the main lagoon) or $70 (3hr) per boat for a wildlife-spotting cruise in the refuge. They can also arrange guided canoeing ($30; 4hr), horseriding ($25; 2hr) and hiking ($10; 2hr). If the office is closed, your hotel or just about anyone in Caño Negro can hook you up with a local guide. The $10 **entrance fee** is sometimes included, but if not you'll need to pay it at the MINAE office (daily 8am–4pm; ⓣ2471-1309), 250m east and 300m north of the Real Tour Association.

The reserve is also hugely popular with anglers, who trawl the murky waters during the **fishing** season (Aug–May) for snook, tarpon and rainbow bass; you'll need to come prepared, as until Incopesca finish building their Caño Negro office, permits ($21) are only available from their branch in Florencia, 100km southeast of the village, just north of San Carlos.

Accommodation

There are a handful of options in the village of Caño Negro, including a couple of **homestays**, and all can help arrange tours in the wildlife refuge. You can **camp** by the river at the *Albergue Caño Negro*, 150m west of the school ($5, including bathroom access).

Caño Negro Natural Lodge 200m east and 100m north of the Parque Central ⓣ2471-1000, ⓦwww.canonegrolodge.com. Surprisingly plush, given the modesty of the village, *Caño Negro Natural Lodge*'s elegant en-suite terraced rooms are set in manicured gardens and come with a/c and hot water. Facilities include a good restaurant (see below) and a swanky swimming pool with wet bar. ❼

Casa Avalos Jiménez 50m south of the refuge entrance ⓣ2471-1301. Simple spare room for rent, with a butterfly garden in the backyard (see below); breakfast is $5 extra, and for another $6 they'll rustle up lunch or dinner as well. ❶

Casa Sequera 100m east of the Parque Central ⓣ2471-1369. Shack up with the friendly proprietors of the *Kingfisher Lodge*, who rent out a basic en-suite room (3 beds) attached to their house. ❷

Hotel de Campo Caño Negro Near the entrance to the village, about 100m from the Los Chiles/Upala junction ⓣ2471-1012 or 8877-1212, ⓦwww.hoteldecampo.com. Occupying fruit-tree-filled grounds on the edge of a large lagoon, the bungalow rooms at *Hotel de Campo Caño Negro* have big beds, a/c and private bathrooms. There's a good pool, and the kitchen serves up mostly organic produce – the proprietor might even cook you fresh fish reeled in from the Río Frío. ❻

Kingfisher Lodge 100m east and 400m north of the Parque Central; reception at *Casa Sequera* (see above) ⓣ2471-1116 or 8870-0458, ⓦwww.kingfisherlodgecr.com. Five tasteful cabins that sleep up to five surrounded by groomed gardens; the private bathrooms include hot-water showers and you can pay $10 more for a/c. ❹

Caño Negro village

The tiny village of Caño Negro is a loose collection of ramshackle houses and *sodas* set around a sweltering, dusty grid. Few people here speak English, but the locals are a patient and welcoming bunch. Aside from tours in the refuge, the town has a couple of other attractions to keep visitors lingering for a few hours. **Criadero de Tortugas** (ⓣ2876-1181), 600m west of the football field, is a turtle conservation project run by local volunteers, where turtle eggs are collected and hatchlings looked after for a year and a half before being released into the wild. Fifty metres south of the refuge entrance, **Mariposa La Reinita** ($3), is a lovingly tended butterfly garden behind the home of the Avalos Jiménez family.

Eating

The best **place to eat** is at the airy *Restaurant Jabiru*, within the *Caño Negro Natural Lodge* (daily 11am–2pm & 7–10pm); the good-value menu runs the gamut from hamburger and chips ($5) to *lomita a la plancha* ($10). Some 100m south, the open-air *Restaurant El Pueblo* (daily 7am–7pm) boasts a pretty garden setting and serves *casados* for around $5. Opposite the Real Tours Association, *Soda La Palmera* (daily 7am–8pm) is a dingy-looking joint dishing up perfectly good Tico fare.

Laguna del Lagarto Lodge

Set in the heart of the Refugio Nacional Vida Silvestre de Mixto Maquenque, **Laguna del Lagarto Lodge** (ⓣ2289-8163, ⓦwww.lagarto-lodge-costa-rica.com; ❺, breakfast not included) is one of the most remote lodges in the country – and only 16km from the Nicaraguan border. Set within 1250 acres of virgin tropical rainforest, the ecolodge is home to an incredible variety of trees, plants and animals, and offers some of the best birdwatching in the country – it's one of the very few places in Costa Rica where you might still see the highly endangered **great green macaw** (see box, p.251), as well as a large resident colony of more common oropéndolas. **Rooms** are rustic but comfortable, with private bathrooms and peaceful views from their balconies. There are 10km of well-marked **rainforest trails** to explore, as well as canoeing (included in the rate) and boat trips ($26; 4hr) on the San Carlos and San Juan rivers.

To reach the lodge **by car** from San José or San Carlos, head east through Aguas Zarcas to Pital and then – on good gravel roads – to Boca Tapada; the lodge is 7.5km to the east of Boca Tapada, also on a reasonable road, although a 4WD is recommended. **Buses** leave daily from San José (Av 9, C 12) at 5.30am and 12.30pm, and every half-hour from San Carlos to Pital (1hr 15min), from where you can connect with buses north to Boca Tapada (9.30am & 4.30pm; 2hr). The lodge will pick you up from here and can also arrange transfers from San José, La Fortuna or Puerto Viejo de Sarapiquí.

The Sarapiquí region

Costa Rica's **Sarapiquí region** stretches around the top of Parque Nacional Braulio Carrillo and west to the village of San Miguel, from where Volcán Arenal and the western lowlands are easily accessible by road. Tropical and carpeted with fruit plantations, the area bears more resemblance to the hot and dense Caribbean lowlands than the plains of the north and, despite large-scale deforestation, still shelters some of the best-preserved **premontane rainforest** in the country.

The largest settlement in the area, sleepy **Puerto Viejo de Sarapiquí**, attracts few visitors and is primarily a river transport hub and a place for the plantation workers to stock up on supplies, though it can make a good base for exploring the superb **Estación Biológica La Selva**. The region's chief tourist attractions, however, are the rainforest lodges of **Rara Avis** and **Selva Verde**, which offer access to some of the last primary rainforest in Costa Rica.

Unsurprisingly, the region receives a lot of **rain** – as much as 4500mm annually, and there is no real dry season (although less rain is recorded Jan–May), so rain gear is essential. The rain also helps create a variety of white-water thrills for kayakers and rafters who flock to the area around **La Virgen** for runs on the **Río Sarapiquí**.

Until the road via Vara Blanca is repaired following the Cinchona Earthquake (see box, p.141), the only route **from San José or the Valle Central** is via the **Guápiles Highway** through Parque Nacional Braulio Carrillo, heading left at the Las Horquetas/Puerto Viejo de Sarapiquí turn-off at the base of the mountain pass.

Puerto Viejo de Sarapiquí and around

Just short of 100km northeast of San José, **PUERTO VIEJO DE SARAPIQUÍ** (not to be confused with Puerto Viejo de Talamanca on the Caribbean) is an important hub for banana plantation workers and those who live in the isolated

Fruits of their labour

Despite harbouring some of the largest remaining tracts of primary rainforest in the country, the Sarapiquí region is also home to a frightening number of **banana** and **pineapple farms**, while south of Puerto Viejo de Sarapiquí, the land around the small town of Las Horquetas is the sight of the biggest **palmito** (heart-of-palm) plantations in the world. As in the rest of Costa Rica, it's a difficult balance between preserving the rainforest (land rendered useless by monobiotic methods employed in the cultivation of pineapples, for example, can take up to fifty years to recover), and appeasing the needs of the local workers – *palmitos*, along with bananas and pineapples, form the core of the regional economy.

For a closer look into the everyday lives of these workers (ironically, many of them Nicaraguan migrants), you can take a tour of the organic pineapple plantation at **Finca Corsicana** (tours daily at 8am, 10am & 2pm; $24; 2hr; reserve in advance on ⓣ2761-1700, ⓦwww.fincacorsicana.com), 8km northeast of La Virgen, or the Dole banana plantation at **Finca Zurqui** (phone for tour times; $15; 1hr 30min; ⓣ2768-8683, ⓦwww.bananatourcostarica.com), 5km southeast of Puerto Viejo de Sarapiquí.

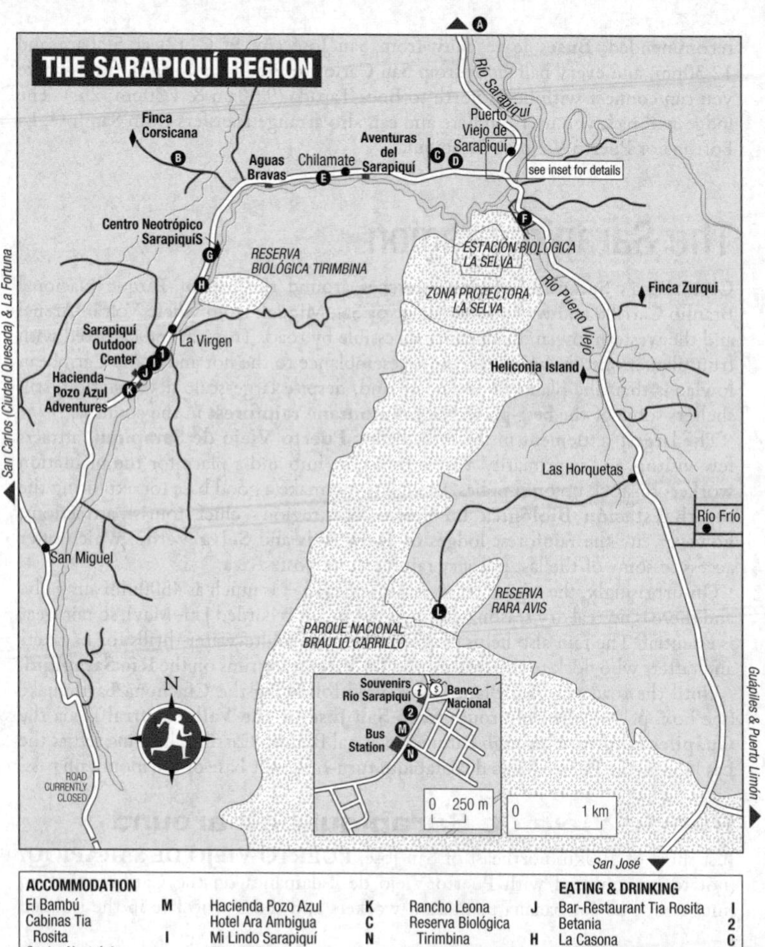

ACCOMMODATION						EATING & DRINKING	
El Bambú	M	Hacienda Pozo Azul	K	Rancho Leona	J	Bar-Restaurant Tia Rosita	I
Cabinas Tia Rosita	I	Hotel Ara Ambigua	C	Reserva Biológica Tirimbina	H	Betania	2
Centro Neotrópico SarapiquíS	G	Mi Lindo Sarapiquí	N	Reserva Rara Avis	L	La Casona	C
Estación Biológica La Selva	F	Posada Andrea Cristina	D	Selva Verde Lodge	E	Hacienda Pozo Azul	K
		La Quinta de Sarapiquí Country Inn	B	Trinidad Lodge	A	Marisqueria San Si	1
						Mi Lindo Sarapiquí	N
						La Terrazza	E

settlements between here and the coast. Life in Puerto Viejo is inextricably linked with the Río Sarapiquí, and most cargo, both human and inanimate, is still carried by river to the Río San Juan and the Nicaraguan border to the north, and to the canals of Tortuguero and Barra del Colorado in the east.

A humid jungle outpost, Puerto Viejo serves as a jumping-off point for visiting the nearby **rainforest reserves**, and the research station at **La Selva**; everything in town itself focuses on the main street, lined with coconut trees, and the small docks at its eastern end. Puerto Viejo plods along during the week, though things can get a bit lively on Friday evenings when the plantation workers are paid.

Arrival

Numerous **buses** leave San José's Gran Terminal del Caribe for Puerto Viejo de Sarapiquí (those marked "Río Frío" also serve Puerto Viejo), running **via the**

Moving on from Puerto Viejo de Sarapiquí

Puerto Viejo is a transport hub for the entire Zona Norte and eastern side of the country. **Buses** run to **San José** via the Guápiles Highway (12 daily; 2hr), and you can also cut across the country west to **San Carlos** (12 daily; 2hr 30min) and on to **La Fortuna** (3–4hr 15min, depending on connection) and Volcán Arenal. **Local buses** for La Virgen (and attractions in between) run on the hour, and can be hailed from any roadside bus stop.

It's possible to continue **by boat** north along the Río Sarapiquí to the Nicaraguan border and then east along the Río San Juan to Barra Colorado and Parque Nacional Tortuguero, though it'll be a pricey trip – you'll have to rent a private *lancha*, which can take anywhere between four and five hours (you're going upstream) and will cost around $700 for up to ten people. Ask at Souvenirs Río Sarapiquí (see below).

Guápiles Highway and Las Horquetas (9 daily; 2hr). There are also a dozen daily services from La Fortuna via San Carlos (2hr 30min from the latter). The **taxi** rank is next to the football field.

Information

The best source of general **information** is Souvenirs Río Sarapiquí (daily 8am–5.15pm; ⓣ2766-6727), diagonally across from the Banco Nacional on the main road. It's run by the knowledgeable Luís Alberto Sánchez, who can make reservations for the area's lodges and arrange tours to the Tortuguero/Barra del Colorado area as well as **riverboat rides** on the Río Sarapiquí ($30; 2hr) to see caimans, crocodiles, sloths and monkeys lounging around in the heat – note, though, that the river is heavily populated by Costa Rican standards and its wildlife has suffered following the Cinchona Earthquake (see box, p.141).

The **post office** (Mon–Fri 8am–noon & 1–5pm) is on the corner where the main street joins the road to the dock; the Banco Nacional opposite has an **ATM**.

Accommodation

Puerto Viejo de Sarapiquí's **accommodation** is quite varied considering the town's size, though Friday and Sunday nights can get booked up with plantation workers. To experience the region's dense rainforest, however, you may prefer to stay at one of the nearby **jungle lodges**, such as *Selva Verde Lodge* (see p.250) and *Reserva Rara Avis* (see p.247).

El Bambú On the main street opposite the football field ⓣ2766-6005, ⓦwww.elbambu.com. The plushest accommodation in the centre of town, this hotel has nicely decorated rooms (all with fans, TV and hot water), a bar and restaurant set around the massive stand of bamboo that gives the place its name, as well as a good-sized pool and a gym. A range of tours can be arranged, including boat trips along the Río Sarapiquí. ❻

Hotel Ara Ambigua 1.5km west of Puerto Viejo, 400m down a signed gravel road to the right ⓣ2766-7101, ⓦwww.hotelaraambigua.com. Lovely rustic cottages, nicely furnished and impeccably clean. Beautifully decorated with pastel shades and pictures of birds, the rooms come with private bath, hot water and a/c. There's a swimming pool, sauna and a frog garden. It's worth a visit alone for the tasty food dished up in the hotel's rustic restaurant (see p.246). ❺

Mi Lindo Sarapiquí On the main street by the football field ⓣ2766-6281. The best budget accommodation in town features well-scrubbed rooms with fan and private bath beside a good restaurant. Ask for one of the quieter rooms at the back. ❶

Posada Andrea Cristina 1km west of Puerto Viejo ⓣ2766-6265, ⓦwww.andreacristina.com. This family-owned operation has simple rooms with fan and private bath, some in A-frame cabins with high wooden ceilings, plus a new tree house – all with top-notch breakfasts and coffee. One of the owners, Alex Martínez, is a qualified nature guide and can offer good advice on what to do in the local area. ❹

Trinidad Lodge 35km up the Río Sarapiquí in the community of Trinidad ⓣ2397-2349. It's a spectacular boat ride up the crocodile-infested river to this rustic lodge located by the Nicaraguan border. The extremely basic rooms have private bathrooms and you can eat dinner with the owners for an extra $12. The daily *colectivo* boat for Trinidad ($15) leaves the docks in Puerto Viejo at 2pm for the 2hr journey and returns at 5am. ❸

Eating and drinking

Mi Lindo Sarapiquí (daily 9am–10pm) on Puerto Viejo's main street is the best place **to eat** in town, with an extensive menu of freshly prepared *típico* food. Alternatively, try *Betania* (daily 6am–10pm), a decent *soda* 50m north of the bus station, which dishes up good fish *casados* for $4. For a snack, a few **fruit stalls** on the main street sell seasonal treats like *mamones chinos*, the spiky lychees that look like sea anemones. If you have transport or don't mind the walk, it's worth venturing 2km west of town to *La Casona*, attached to *Hotel Ara Ambigua*, where you can sample Costa Rican standards and some mighty fine pizza in a laidback, rustic barn (call in advance on ⓣ2766-6401).

Estación Biológica La Selva

The fully equipped research station of **ESTACIÓN BIOLÓGICA LA SELVA** (ⓣ2766-6565; in San José ⓣ2524-0607, ⓦwww.ots.ac.cr or www.threepaths.co.cr), 4km southwest of Puerto Viejo de Sarapiquí, is one of the best **birdwatching** destinations in the Sarapiquí, if not the country. You can spot over half of Costa Rica's bird species here (489 in total), including the red-capped manakin – La Selva is a regular port of call for documentary makers looking to capture their energetic mating displays. An equally staggering number of tree species (some 350) have been identified, as well as 113 species of mammals, including anteaters, sloths (both two- and three-toed) and monkeys.

Leading biologists from around the world have studied here, and its facilities are extensive: a large swath of premontane rainforest shouldering the northern part of Parque Nacional Braulio Carrillo forms the natural laboratory, while the research facilities include lecture halls and accommodation for scientists and students.

Trails and tours

The terrain at La Selva extends from **primary forest** (sixty percent of the reserve's total area) through abandoned plantations to pastureland and brush, and is crossed by an extensive network of about 25 **trails** totalling just over 60km. The trails vary in length from short to more than 5km long, and some are accessible to pushchairs and travellers with disabilities. Tourists tend to stick to the main routes within the part of La Selva designated as the **ecological reserve**, next to the Río Puerto Viejo; these radiate from the river research station and lead through dense primary growth, the close, tightly knotted type of tropical forest that the Sarapiquí area is famous for. Most trails are in very good condition and clearly marked, but only visitors staying at the complex are allowed to walk them unsupervised; day-trippers have to take one of two daily **guided walks** (8am & 1.30pm; $30 half day; $38 full day; 3hr), though when the guides are as good as they are at La Selva, that's hardly a drawback.

Twitchers may prefer to take a private **birdwatching tour** (daily at 5.45am; $40; 2hr), recommended for both the quality of the guiding and the birding – you've a good chance of seeing slaty-tailed trogon and rufous motmot. For beginner birders, the full-day **birdwatching workshop** ($48) is a detailed introduction to habitats and behaviour that includes a guided walk on which you'll learn how to look for birds and then identify them. You can also join a **night tour** (daily at 7pm; $40; 2hr) in search of porcupines and kinkajou, or, for a glimpse of what life is like for the 350 or so researchers that study in the reserve each year, sign up for the **Scientist for a Day** workshop ($48), where you'll be taught how to use scientific methodology to help record the station's flora and fauna.

Note that all guided walks, tours and workshops should be **booked in advance**.

Practicalities

Local **buses** from Puerto Viejo de Sarapiquí (every 30min) run past the turn-off to La Selva on their way to Las Horquetas and Guápiles; it's a fifteen-minute walk from the road. Buses **from San José** to Puerto Viejo can also drop you off at the entrance. A **taxi** from Puerto Viejo costs about $7.

It's impossible to overstate La Selva's popularity – if you want **to stay** you need to reserve months in advance (particularly Nov–April) online or by email (Ⓔ edu @ots.ac.cr). The cabin **accommodation** (❻) includes private bathroom, three buffet-style meals a day served in the communal dining hall, and one half-day guided walk (additional guided walks cost $15).

Heliconia Island

Set on a five-acre island on the Río Puerto Viejo, 8km south of Puerto Viejo de Sarapiquí, the immaculately landscaped gardens of **HELICONIA ISLAND** (daily 8am–5pm; $10, $15 with tour; Ⓣ 2764-5220, Ⓦ www.heliconiaisland.com) boast over 400 varieties of heliconia, and as the island's microclimate makes it blissfully cooler than Puerto Viejo, it has become a refuge for sloths, howler monkeys, river otters and more than 300 species of **birds**, including various hummingbirds (the exclusive pollinator of the heliconia). Plant-lovers will get a kick out of the fragrant ylang ylang tree, torch gingers and Phenomenal sperm – a flowering Guyana native.

Local **buses** for Las Horquetas and Guápiles run approximately every half-hour from Puerto Viejo; ask the driver to let you off at the turn-off on the main highway, then follow the signs down a dirt track before crossing a narrow metal bridge to the island. A **taxi** from Puerto Viejo costs $14. You can **stay on the island** in one of four attractive fan or air-conditioned *cabinas* featuring bamboo furniture and spacious balconies (❺, including guided tour of the gardens).

Reserva Rara Avis

Remote **RESERVA RARA AVIS**, 17km south of Puerto Viejo and about 80km northeast of San José, offers one of the most thrilling and authentic ecotourism experiences in Costa Rica. Bordering the northeastern tip of pristine Parque Nacional Braulio Carrillo, the reserve features both primary rainforest and some secondary cover dating from about 35 years ago and boasts an incredibly diverse rainforest **flora**. The area is home to a number of unique **palm species**, including the stained-glass palm tree, a rare specimen much in demand for its ornamental beauty, and the walking palm, whose tentacle-like roots can propel it over a metre of ground in its lifetime as it "walks" in search of sunlight. **Orchids** are also numerous, as are non-flowering bromeliads, heliconias, huge ancient hardwood trees smothered by lianas, primitive ferns and other plants typically associated with dense rainforest cover.

Established in 1983 by American Amos Bien (a former administrator of the Estación Biológica La Selva), forest ranger Robert Villalobos and biologist Carlos Gómez, Rara Avis combines the functions of a tourist lodge and a private rainforest reserve, and is dedicated to both the conservation and farming of the area. A pioneer in the country's ecotourism movement, its ultimate objective is to show that the rainforest can be profitable, giving local smallholders a viable alternative to clearing the land for cattle. Rara Avis supports a number of endemic plants that have considerable economic potential, including *geonoma epetiolata*, or the stained-glass palm, which was until recently believed to be extinct. Another significant part of the reserve's mandate is to provide alternative sources of employment in nearby Las Horquetas, where most people work for the big fruit companies or as day-labourers on local farms.

Rara Avis also functions as a **research station**, accommodating student groups and volunteers whose aims include development of rainforest products – orchids, palms and so forth – as crops, as well as the silk of the golden orb spider.

Arrival

Rara Avis is extremely isolated – it's what makes the place so special – and getting here is something of an endurance test. Local **buses from Puerto Viejo** run to the school in **Las Horquetas** (20min), 100m from the reserve's office; Puerto Viejo-bound buses **from San José** (1hr 30min) can drop you at the turn-off to the village, a five-minute walk away. **Taxis** from Puerto Viejo cost around $16. The lodge can also arrange a **transfer from San José** ($75). If **driving**, you can leave your car at the office.

The reserve itself is still 15km away. At the office, guests are fitted out with rubber boots and loaded onto a **truck-pulled cart** (departs 9am; if coming direct from San José, you'll need to catch the 6.30am bus via the Guápiles Highway to make this connection), which laboriously ascends the first arduous 12km (2hr); alternatively, horses are available to hire for this section of the journey (until 2pm; $35; 3–4hr). Remarkably, the road gets even worse after this, and it's necessary to complete the final 3km in a **tractor-pulled cart** (1hr), which slithers and slides down pitted hills – though visitors have the option of hiking this final leg on a rainforest trail (1hr 30min), a fine way to build up a lunchtime appetite (and a necessity if you've come this far on horseback).

Leaving Rara Avis, the tractor departs at 2pm, in time to connect with the last bus for San José that passes Las Horquetas around 6pm.

Accommodation and eating

There are three **places to stay** at ★ *Rara Avis* (two-night minimum stay; reserve in advance on Ⓣ2764-1111, Ⓦwww.rara-avis.com; ❽), with rates at each including all meals, transport by tractor to and from Las Horquetas, and two guided walks a day. The main accommodation complex is the comfortable **Waterfall Lodge**. Set 200m from a picture-perfect cascade, it has no electricity, but the rooms do have hot water, private baths, kerosene lamps and spacious wrap-around balconies with hammocks and fantastic views of pristine rainforest and the hot lowland plains stretching towards the Caribbean. Less than 50m from the dining area, it's an idyllic place to stay: the only sounds heard at five or six in the morning are the echoing shrieks of birds and howler monkeys, and the light, especially first thing, is sheer and unfiltered, giving everything a wonderfully shimmering effect.

A ten-minute rainforest hike away, the **River Edge Cabin** ($10 more) is even more isolated and peaceful, with just the gurglings of the Río Atelopus for company. It enjoys solar-powered lighting, but if you stay here, you'll need to be unfazed by walking through the forest at night with only a torch or a lamp. Five minutes from the *Waterfall Lodge* is the reserve's cheapest accommodation, **Las Casitas** ($55 per person), consisting of six rooms each sleeping four people in bunk beds. Facilities are comfortable enough, with shared bathroom, although you'll also have to hike from the dining area through dense forest at night.

All **meals** are served in the *Waterfall Lodge*'s communal dining area, home to a small naturalist library and board games (perfect for those rainy afternoons). The meals are delicious: breakfasts consist of heaped platters of eggs, *gallo pinto*, bread, fresh fruit and coffee, while lunches and dinners are filling, delicately flavoured dishes.

Activities

Rara Avis has a 30km network of excellent **trails**, which are well marked and offer walks of thirty minutes to several hours. The informative **guided walks** are run by knowledgeable guides, most of whom have lived at or around the reserve for some time, although guests are welcome to go it alone: you'll be given a map at the lodge reception, but you should always let the staff know which trail you are following and about how long you intend to be. Rain gear is essential, as is insect repellent.

The lodge offers a couple of tours in addition to the walks included in the rate. With its incredible array of birdlife, the **birdwatching tour** (daily 6am; $15; 1hr 30min) is highly worthwhile, heading out early each morning in search of some of the 386 species that have been spotted in the reserve (see box below). At the other end of the day, the **night walk** (daily 7.30pm; $15) reveals a different side of the rainforest, and offers the chance to spot a variety of insects, amphibians and nocturnal mammals, such as the arboreal four-eyed opossum.

A short walk below the *Waterfall Lodge*, a 50m-high waterfall plummets into a deep pool – **swimming** in the ice-cold pool, shrouded in a fine mist, is a wonderful experience, but keep an eye on the weather and check with the staff regarding approaching floodwaters, an occasional but deadly hazard up here. Within 50m of the main hotel, guests are free to wander around the small **butterfly garden**, home to the exquisite Blue Morpho butterfly. Also nearby is the wooden **"Spider House"**, where golden orb spiders are studied and their shimmering golden silk – supposedly stronger than steel – is harvested for research purposes.

Watching wildlife at Rara Avis

A mind-boggling number of **bird species** have been identified at Rara Avis, and it's likely that more are yet to be discovered. As well as the fearsome black, turkey and king vultures and the majestic osprey, you might see nine species of parrot, over twenty types of antbird, thirty different species of hummingbird, both chestnut-mandibled and keel-billed toucans, and the unlikely named great potoo. The endangered great green macaw also nests here, and trogons, bare-necked umbrellabirds and the distinctive-looking three-wattled bellbird can also be spotted.

Among the more common **mammals** are opossums, monkeys, armadillos, anteaters, sloths and bats (eleven species in total). The reserve harbours five of the country's six cat species, though the closest you'll probably come to an ocelot or jaguar is discovering their tracks on a muddy trail. You may also encounter the Watson's climbing rat that frequents the *Waterfall Lodge* and has a voracious appetite for hand soap.

Amphibians and reptiles are abundant, ranging from the tree-climbing salamander to the white-lipped mud turtle, and including eight species of tree frog alone. Along with other vipers, the fer-de-lance and bushmaster **snakes**, two of the most venomous in the world, may lie in wait, so take extra care on the trails by looking everywhere you step and put your hand. Boa constrictors also hang out here; if you do see one, be careful as the generally torpid boa can get aggressive when bothered.

Selva Verde Lodge

One of the most luxurious rainforest lodges in Costa Rica and a paradise for birdwatchers, **SELVA VERDE LODGE** (Ⓣ2766-6800, in the US Ⓣ1-800/451-7111, Ⓦwww.selvaverde.com; ❼) sits aside two square kilometres of preserved primary rainforest alongside the Río Sarapiquí. The lodge comprises an impressive complex of accommodation blocks, dining hall, lecture rooms and a lovely riverside restaurant-bar where monkeys chatter above and the Sarapiquí bubbles below. It's set in tropical gardens rather than dense overgrowth, though the vegetation around the lodge is still home to toucans, sloths and howler monkeys, while iguanas and basilisk lizards are frequent poolside visitors. Wilder, primary rainforest stretches off into the distance the other side of the river, accessed on a guided tour, and provides habitat for one of the region's most endangered species, the **great green macaw** (see box opposite).

Arrival

Selva Verde is signed off the road near the village of Chilamate, 8km west of Puerto Viejo de Sarapiquí and 9km east of La Virgen; taxis from the former cost around $9. Buses running westwards from Puerto Viejo will drop you at the entrance. The lodge has its own private transport and can pick up or drop off at San José's airport ($75).

Accommodation and eating

Accommodation at ⛤ *Selva Verde* is split between two complexes. The comfortable **River Lodge** rooms, from which the Sarapiquí's gentle gurglings can be heard, are connected to each other by a walkway and have dark-wood floorboards contrasting with bright walls. You can lounge on hammocks and there's electric light after dark, so night owls have the option of reading (everybody at *Selva Verde* seems to go to bed early – the bar empties out by 9pm). Sometimes the lodge is full of tour or study groups (it's often possible to join one of their evening talks), in which case the more private and air-conditioned **Bungalows** ($30 more), a short walk from the main lodge on the other side of the road, can prove an attractive alternative.

Rates include breakfasts but not lunch or dinner, which are either served buffet-style in a room overlooking the Sarapiquí ($15 for each) or taken in *La Terrazza* downstairs, arguably the best **restaurant** in the area, whose Italian-influenced menu includes home-made spinach and ricotta ravioli ($10) and lemon tilapia with capers ($12), as well as half-a-dozen varieties of pizza baked to perfection in the wood-fired oven (from $7).

Activities

Selva Verde's expanse offers an excellent variety of walks along well-marked trails through primary and secondary forest, riverside, swamps and pastureland. The **guided walks** through the denser section of premontane forest across the Río Sarapiquí ($15; 2hr) are a must – the informative guides are top-notch and can make uncannily authentic bird calls to get the attention of trogons and toucans as well as pointing out poison-dart frogs, primitive ferns and complex lianas. You can take a **self-guided walk** in the section of secondary rainforest across the road from the lodge – ask for a map at reception – which is explored in greater detail on one of the free **birdwatching tours** (6am & 4pm; 1hr). Other tours include white-water rafting, horseback rides and boat trips on the Río Sarapiquí.

The lodge is also heavily involved in the local community and is home to the nonprofit **Sarapiquí Conservation Learning Center** (Ⓣ2766-6482,

The great green macaw: back from the brink?

The Sarapiquí region harbours the country's last flocks of **great green macaw** (*lapa verde*), the largest parrot in Central America. Globally endangered, it is estimated that less than 200 birds remain in Costa Rica, with fewer than 30 breeding pairs, but the fact that they survive here at all – in what constitutes just ten percent of their original home range – is only due to some sterling conservation work. Continued deforestation across the Zona Norte has caused a dramatic decrease in the population of the great green macaws, whose unfortunate fate is to rely on the **almendro tree** (a popular tropical hardwood) for their existence, nesting in its boughs and feeding on the large nuts it produces.

The *almendro* is now, belatedly, protected, but the first major step in the fight to save this beautiful bird was the creation of the **San Juan–La Selva Biological Corridor** (Ⓦwww.greatgreenmacaw.org), which ecologically links the Reserva Biológica Indio-Maíz in Nicaragua with the Cordillera Central – great green macaws require a wide area for breeding and foraging, and the corridor acts as a vital migratory pathway. Its conservational focus is the **Refugio Nacional de Vida Silvestre Mixto Maquenque**, a multi-use wildlife refuge encompassing more than 500 square kilometres of wetlands, lagoons and lowland Atlantic forest that was established in 2005, after ten years of hard lobbying.

Mixto Maquenque plays a vital role in sustaining Costa Rica's great green macaw population, though the bird's future depends as much on the continuity of the corridor, which can only really be achieved through the creation of private eco-reserves that provide a financial incentive for conserving their habitat. The first of these initiatives, the **Costa Rican Bird Route** – which includes Reserva Biológica Tirimbina (see p.253), *Selva Verde Lodge* (see opposite) and Estación Biológica La Selva (see p.246) – was set up to improve bird tourism in the region, thus delivering greater economic opportunities to local communities. The development of the Bird Route (see p.69 for more) has resulted in another fifteen square kilometres of forest being newly protected as official private reserves.

Ⓦwww.learningcentercostarica.org), which can arrange visits to local communities ($24) and schools ($18), as well as tree-planting activities and dance classes.

La Virgen and around

Lying on a bend in the Río Sarapiquí, the rafting hub of **LA VIRGEN** sprawls for 5km along the busy road between San Miguel and Puerto Viejo de Sarapiquí, the latter 17km to the east. The town is second only to Turrialba as Costa Rica's prime **rafting and kayaking centre**, and between July and December, outdoor types with well-toned arms come here by the bus-load to brave the variety of nearby runs. Less vigorous pursuits are available at the **Reserva Biológica Tirimbina**, 2km to the east, where hiking trails lead into dense rainforest, and the adjoining **Centro Neotrópico SarapiquíS**.

Arrival and information

Buses from San José travel via the Guápiles Highway and Las Horquetas (12 daily; 2hr) and terminate in Puerto Viejo (see p.243), from where you can hop on one of the hourly local buses for the half-hour journey to La Virgen or take a taxi ($14). The town centre has a Banco Nacional with 24-hour **ATM**, a pair of internet cafés and two modestly stocked supermarkets.

White-water thrills: the Puerto Viejo and the Sarapiquí

The wild Río Pacuaré near Turrialba may lure adrenaline junkies to Costa Rica, but the churning waters around La Virgen have plenty of thrilling white-water action on offer. The relaxing **Class I–II** run that puts in on the **Río Puerto Viejo** is essentially a scenic float along a jungle-lined river, suitable for wildlife-watchers and small children (from 3). Moving up a grade, the **Class III** runs, which start on the **Río Sarapiquí** around La Virgen, require good physical fitness but can be ridden by anyone over 8. If you want to tackle the ferocious and technically more demanding **Class IV** runs on the Upper Sarapiquí, you must be over 16 and have plenty of experience wielding a paddle.

Tour operators

A number of companies in and around La Virgen offer guided white-water rafting and kayaking tours, each charging around $50 for two- to three-hour trips, most of which include lunch and transportation.

Aguas Bravas Roble, 12km east of La Virgen ⓣ2766-6524 or 2992-2072, ⓦwww.aguas-bravas.co.cr. Perhaps the largest rafting company in the country, with runs on Class I–II, III (both $45) and IV ($60) rapids. Pick-ups from San José and La Fortuna ($30–35 extra).

Aventuras del Sarapiquí 12km east of La Virgen ⓣ2766-5101, ⓦwww.sarapiqui.com. Rafting ($50), canoeing ($80) and tubing trips, as well as private full- and four-day kayaking courses ($150/600). They also run mountain-biking and hiking trips and have a zip-line canopy tour that shoots strapped-in victims across two rivers ($50).

Hacienda Pozo Azul Adventures 2km west of La Virgen ⓣ2761-1360, ⓦwww.haciendapozoazul.com. Rafting Class I and II–III rapids ($50; 2hr) is just part of the package at this one-stop-shop for outdoor adventure sports; other activities include rappelling ($28; 1hr 30min), horseriding ($35; 2hr) and a nine-cable canopy tour ($45).

Sarapiquí Outdoor Center 1.5km west of La Virgen ⓣ2761-1123. Established rafting and kayaking company offering 2hr trips on the Puerto Viejo and Sarapiquí (both $55). Riverside camping ($5) and dark dorms ($10 per person) also available on site.

Accommodation

In addition to the **accommodation** listed below, there is also local lodging at Tirimbina (see opposite), the Centro Neotrópico SarapiquiS (see opposite) and *Selva Verde Lodge* (p.250).

Cabinas Tia Rosita 1km west of La Virgen ⓣ2761-1032. Although lacking in atmosphere, these four clean and basic cabins are good value, each with TV and a hot-water bathroom. ❶

Hacienda Pozo Azul 2km west of La Virgen ⓣ2761-1360, ⓦwww.haciendapozoazul.com. Large tourist centre offering a couple of accommodation options: *Hacienda Pozo Azul Tent Suites* (❻), 25 luxury tents set in the forest just metres from the bubbling Río Sarapiquí; and the solar-powered *Magsasay Jungle Lodge*, 2.5km further on the fringes of Parque Nacional Braulio Carillo, whose ten delightful rooms with bunk beds are only available to groups of 10 or more ($55 per person). Both options include shared bathrooms, and, at *Magsasay*, three meals a day.

La Quinta de Sarapiquí Country Inn 5km east of La Virgen, then 1.5km up a side road on the left ⓣ2761-1052, ⓦwww.laquintasarapiqui.com. On the banks of the Río Sardinal, this comfortable lodge has 32 spacious *casitas*, all with ceiling fans and hot-water bathrooms with power showers; they're set amid heliconia plants, so there's plenty of hummingbird activity to watch from the rocking chair or hammock on your veranda. Activities include swimming in the pool, tubing down the river and exploring the lodge's butterfly house and frog pond. ❼

Rancho Leona 1km west of La Virgen ⓣ2761-1019, ⓦwww.rancholeona.com. This tired-looking riverside lodge has some of the cheapest lodgings in the area: $12 dorm beds, well liked by backpackers, and very rustic rooms with shared bathroom. There's a communal kitchen, laundry facilities and internet access. ❷

Eating and drinking

Treat yourself to the best seafood in the Zona Norte at *Marisqueria San Si* (daily 11am–10pm), less than 1km west of La Virgen, where heaving portions of fried fish ($10) and river prawns ($50) are dished up to famished rafters in a swanky timber rotunda. A hundred metres west, the most popular *soda* around these parts, *Bar-Restaurant Tia Rosita* (Mon–Fri 7am–9pm, Sat 8am–9pm, Sun 8am–4pm) serves above average Tico specialties for $5. The adventure centre at *Hacienda Pozo Azul*, 2km west of La Virgen, has a decent restaurant where you can munch on delicious *enyucados* ($3) while taking in the view over the Río Sarapiquí from its outdoor deck.

Reserva Biológica Tirimbina

The thrilling **RESERVA BIOLÓGICA TIRIMBINA** (daily 7am–5pm; $15; ⓣ2761-1579, ⓦwww.tirimbina.org), 2km east of La Virgen, is a small private reserve with 9km of trails weaving through primal rainforest and across a couple of suspension bridges, one of which is 272m long and straddles the gurgling Río Sarapiquí. While the trails here are well marked and maintained, this is no sanitized rainforest experience: hidden cameras have captured jaguars, margay, ocelots and Baird's tapir going about their business.

A variety of **guided walks** are offered, including night hikes ($19; 2hr;), frog tours ($19; 2hr), bird-spotting strolls ($24; 2hr 30min) and even a chocolate tour explaining the cacao fruit's journey from tree to chocolate bar ($20; 2hr 30min). Perhaps the most interesting, though, is the **bat programme** ($19; 2hr), one of only two activities in the country dedicated to this misunderstood mammal (the other is in Monteverde; see p.326); part of an ongoing research project, the programme uses bats caught in drift nets that evening to explain their physiology and feeding habits.

You can **stay** at the reserve in one of twelve comfortable flagstone-floored rooms, equipped with air conditioning, hot-water bathrooms and wi-fi (❹–❺); price includes entry to the reserve, valid for three consecutive days.

Centro Neotrópico SarapiquíS

Part-funded by the Belgian government and set up as both a hotel and nonprofit educational centre, the various parts of the **CENTRO NEOTRÓPICO SARAPIQUÍS** (daily 8am–6pm; $9, $15 with a guide; ⓣ2761-1004, ⓦwww.sarapiquis.org) seem to be pulling in different directions, giving the place a rather disjointed feel. Essentially an archeological park built on the site of a six-hundred-year-old pre-Columbian tomb, it also features a museum that explores the relationship between indigenous cultures and the rainforest, plus botanical gardens. Most of the **hotel**'s 36 rooms are housed in large *palenques*; all have a private terrace and bath with solar-heated hot water (❻, not including breakfast), but you still have to pay to enter the educational centre.

Travel details

Buses

Los Chiles to: San Carlos (12 daily; 2hr 30min); San José (2 daily; 5hr).
La Fortuna to: San Carlos (10 daily; 1hr 30min); San José (2 daily; 4hr); San Ramón (4 daily; 3hr); Tilarán (3 daily; 3hr).
Puerto Viejo de Sarapiquí to: San Carlos (12 daily; 2hr 30min); San José (10 daily; 2hr).
San Carlos to: Los Chiles (12 daily; 2hr 30min); La Fortuna (11 daily; 1hr 30min); Puerto Viejo de Sarapiquí (12 daily; 2hr 30min); San José (hourly; 2hr 30min).
San José to: Los Chiles (2 daily; 5hr); La Fortuna (3 daily; 4hr); Puerto Viejo de Sarapiquí (8 daily; 2hr); San Carlos (hourly; 2hr 30min); Tilarán (5 daily; 4hr).
Tilarán to: La Fortuna (3 daily; 3hr); San José (5 daily; 4hr); Santa Elena (for Monteverde; 2 daily; 2hr 30min).

Flights

La Fortuna to: San José (daily; 25min).
San José to: La Fortuna (daily; 25min).

5

Guanacaste

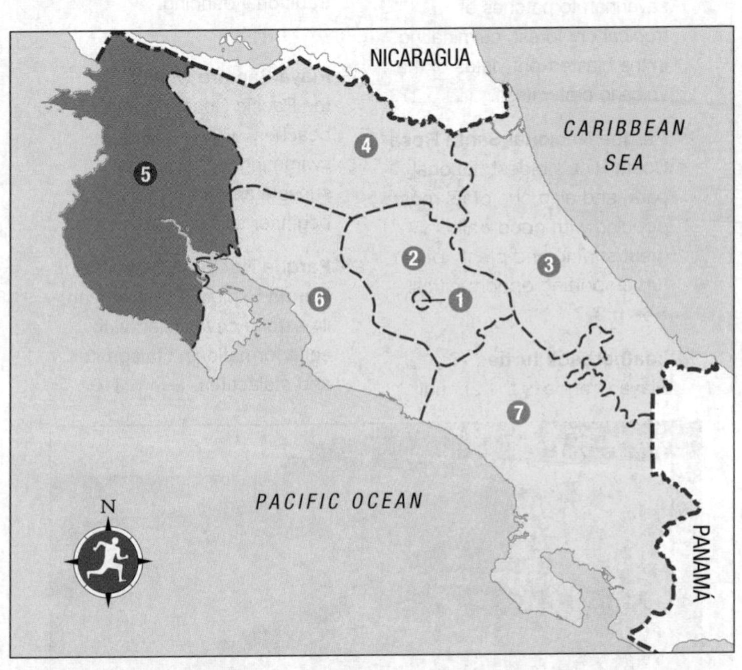

CHAPTER 5

Highlights

* **Cowboys** Skilful and self-reliant, Guanacaste's cowboys – or *sabaneros* – encapsulate the history of Costa Rica's vibrant rural communities. **See p.259**
* **Parque Nacional Rincón de la Vieja** The beautiful landscapes of Volcán Rincón de la Vieja encompass terrains varying from rock-strewn savannah to patches of tropical dry forest, culminating in the blasted-out vistas of the volcano crater itself. **See p.273**
* **Parque Nacional Santa Rosa** Costa Rica's oldest national park, and also one of its most popular, with good trails, great surfing and plenty of turtle-spotting opportunities. **See p.277**
* **Leatherback turtles** Playa Grande is the annual destination for hundreds of leatherback turtles, the largest of the four species of marine turtle that lay their eggs along Costa Rica's shores. **See p.290**
* **Fiestas** Lively community fiestas celebrate Guanacaste's livestock heritage with bullfights, rodeos, processions and traditional dancing. **See p.299**
* **Playa Sámara** One of the Pacific Coast's finest beaches, with excellent swimming, spectacular sunsets and good waves for beginner surfers. **See p.302**
* **Parque Nacional Barra Honda** Explore subterranean, limestone caves filled with eerie formations, stalagmites and stalactites. **See p.310**

▲ Nesting leatherback turtle

5

Guanacaste

For the majority of the Tico population, the **Guanacaste Province**, hemmed in by mountains to the east and the Pacific to the west, and bordered on the north by Nicaragua, is distinctly apart. Guanacastecos still sometimes refer to Valle Central inhabitants as "Cartagos", an archaic term dating back to the eighteenth century when Cartago was Costa Rica's capital. Though little tangible remains of the dance, music and folklore for which the region is distinct, there is undeniably something special about the place. Granted, much of the **landscape** has come about through the slaughter of tropical dry forest, but it's still some of the prettiest you'll see in the country, especially in the wet season, when wide-open spaces, stretching from the ocean across savannah grasses to the brooding humps of volcanoes, are awash in earth tones, blues, yellows and mauves.

The dry heat, relatively accessible terrain and panoramic views make Guanacaste the best place in the country for **walking** and **horseriding**, especially around the mud pots and stewing sulphur waters of the spectacular **Parque Nacional Rincón de la Vieja** and through the tropical dry forest cover of **Parque Nacional Santa Rosa**. Beyond Cañas, protected areas administered by the **Area de Conservación Tempisque** (ACT) encompass **Parque Nacional Palo Verde**, an important site for migratory birds, **Reserva Biológica Lomas Barbudal**, and the deep underground caves of **Parque Nacional Barra Honda** on the Nicoya Peninsula, just across the Río Tempisque.

For many travellers, however, Guanacaste means only one thing: **beaches**. Most are found where the **Nicoya Peninsula** joins the mainland. Roughly two-thirds of the mountainous peninsula is in Guanacaste, while the lower third belongs to the Puntarenas Province, covered in Chapter 6. Beaches range from simple hideaways such as quiet Nosara to large resorts aimed at the North American winter market. Several beaches are also nesting grounds for marine turtles – giant leatherbacks haul themselves up onto Playa Grande, near Tamarindo, while Parque Nacional Santa Rosa is the destination for olive ridley turtles. The only **towns** of any significance for travellers are the provincial capital of **Liberia**, and **Nicoya**, the main town on the peninsula. If you are overnighting on the way to **Nicaragua**, La Cruz makes a useful base.

Highlands Ticos tend to describe Guanacaste as a virtual desert, liberally applying the words *caliente* (hot) and *seco* (dry). Certainly it is dry, in comparison to the rest of the country: parts of it receive only 500mm of rain a year, ten times less than the Caribbean coast. To some extent irrigation has helped, but in summer (Dec–April), Guanacaste still experiences some drought. This is when you'll see an eerie landscape of bare, silver-limbed trees glinting in the sun, as many shed their leaves in order to conserve water. The province is significantly greener, and

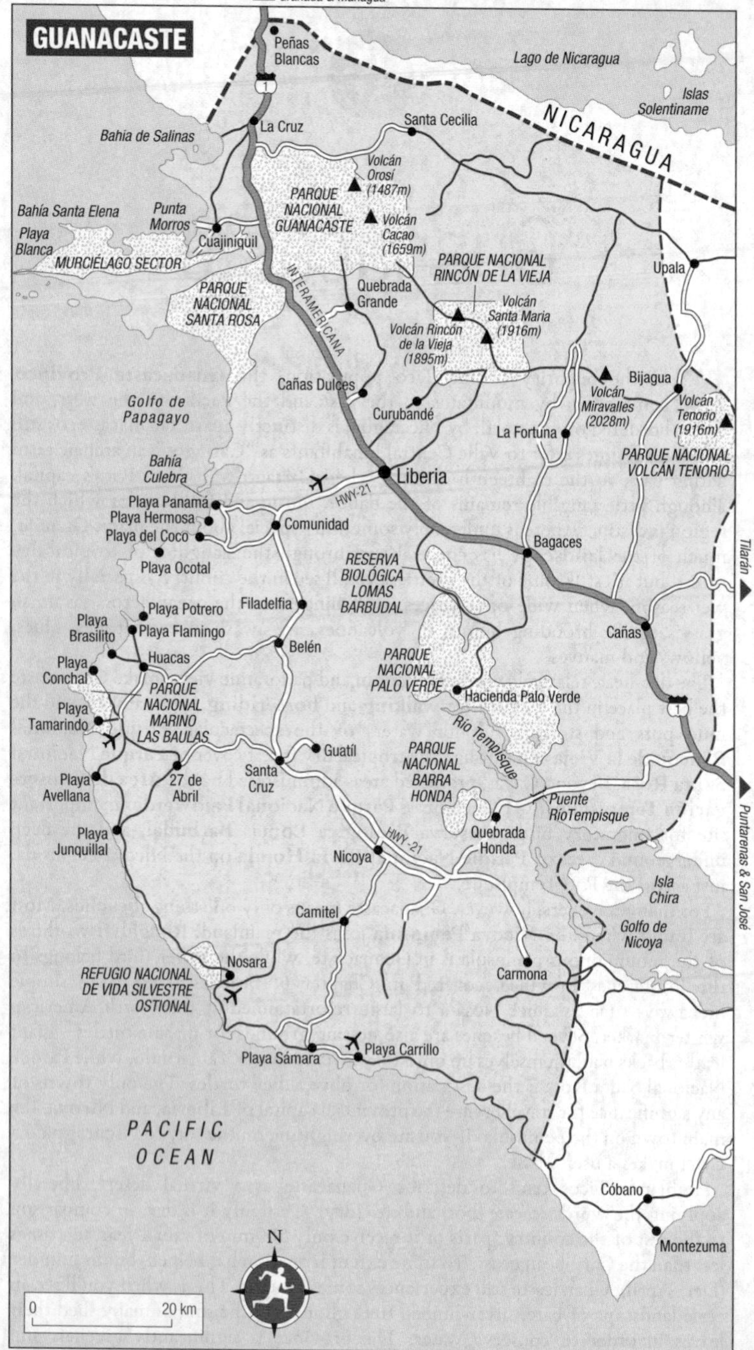
GUANACASTE
Granada & Managua
Peñas Blancas
Lago de Nicaragua
Islas Solentiname
NICARAGUA
La Cruz
Santa Cecilia
Bahia de Salinas
Volcán Orosí (1487m)
PARQUE NACIONAL GUANACASTE
Volcán Cacao (1659m)
Bahía Santa Elena
Punta Morros
Cuajiniquil
Playa Blanca
MURCIÉLAGO SECTOR
PARQUE NACIONAL SANTA ROSA
INTERAMERICANA
Quebrada Grande
PARQUE NACIONAL RINCÓN DE LA VIEJA
Volcán Santa Maria (1916m)
Volcán Rincón de la Vieja (1895m)
Upala
Bijagua
Volcán Miravalles (2028m)
Volcán Tenorio (1916m)
PARQUE NACIONAL VOLCÁN TENORIO
La Fortuna
Cañas Dulces
Curubandé
Golfo de Papagayo
Bahía Culebra
Liberia
HWY-21
Playa Panamá
Playa Hermosa
Playa del Coco
Comunidad
Playa Ocotal
RESERVA BIOLÓGICA LOMAS BARBUDAL
Bagaces
Tilarán
Filadelfia
Playa Potrero
Playa Brasilito
Playa Flamingo
Cañas
Belén
Huacas
Playa Conchal
PARQUE NACIONAL PALO VERDE
Hacienda Palo Verde
PARQUE NACIONAL MARINO LAS BAULAS
Playa Tamarindo
Río Tempisque
Guatíl
PARQUE NACIONAL BARRA HONDA
Santa Cruz
Playa Avellana
27 de Abril
Puente RíoTempisque
Puntarenas & San José
Quebrada Honda
Playa Junquillal
HWY-21
Nicoya
Isla Chira
Camitel
Golfo de Nicoya
Nosara
Carmona
REFUGIO NACIONAL DE VIDA SILVESTRE OSTIONAL
Playa Sámara
Playa Carrillo
PACIFIC OCEAN
Cóbano
Montezuma
N
0
20 km

Cowboy culture in Guanacaste

Much of Guanacaste has long been turned into pasture for cattle ranching, and a huge part of the region's appeal is its **sabanero** (cowboy) culture. As in the US, the *sabanero* has acquired a mythical aura – industrious, free-spirited, monosyllabic, and a skilful handler of animals and the environment – and his rough, tough body, clad in jeans with leather accoutrements symbolizes "authenticity" (women get assigned a somewhat less exciting role in this rural mythology: the *cocinera*, or cook). In reality, however, the life of the *sabaneros* is hard; they often work in their own smallholdings or as *peones* (farmworkers) on large haciendas owned by relatively well-off ranchers.

To witness the often extraordinary skills of the *sabaneros*, head for the smaller towns – particularly on the Nicoya Peninsula – where during the months of January and February weekend **fiestas** are held in the local *redondel de toros* (bullring). More a rodeo than a bullfight, unlike in Spain, no gory kills are made: the spectacle comes from amazing feats of bull riding and roping. You'll see cowboys riding their horses alongside the Interamericana highway, too, often towing two or three horses behind them as big transport trucks steamroll past on their way to Nicaragua. This dependence on cattle culture has its downside. Much of Guanacaste is degraded pastureland, abandoned either because of its exhaustion by grazing or as a result of continually poor domestic and foreign markets for Costa Rican meat. Although impressive efforts to regenerate former tropical dry forest are under way – at Parque Nacional Santa Rosa and Parque Nacional Guanacaste, for example – it is unlikely that this rare life-zone will recover its original profile.

prettier, in the wet season (May–Nov), which is generally agreed to be the **best time** to come, with the added benefit of fewer travellers and lighter rainfall than the rest of the country receives during these months.

These days, Guanacaste is changing fast. An enormous number of hotels, some all-inclusive resorts, are being built on the Pacific coast, and with the opening of the Liberia airport to international traffic, **winter charter tourism** has truly arrived. Inland, mass tourism is less evident, and, despite the presence of *McDonald's* in its dignified streets, Liberia itself remains one of the most charming towns in the country. There seems to be no getting away from "progress", however, and the province may become many tourists' first, and perhaps only, glimpse of the country.

Access to most of Guanacaste from San José is easy via the Autopista General Cañas to the Puntarenas turn-off, then the Interamericana (Hwy-1), which runs right through to the Nicaraguan border at Peñas Blancas. This being Central America, common **road hazards** include falling mangoes, dead monkeys, iguanas, cyclists and schoolchildren. Follow the road rules, particularly on the Interamericana, which is heavily patrolled by traffic cops. Modern, comfortable **buses** ply the highway, with good services to Cañas, Liberia and the border. The national parks of Rincón de la Vieja and Santa Rosa are trickier to reach, however, and bus travellers may have to walk, hitch or take a taxi for part of the journey. All the beaches are accessible by bus and car, though the roads are not in fantastic shape, and journeys from San José can take several hours.

The **ACT regional office** (Mon–Fri 8am–4pm; ⓣ2671-1455), on the Interamericana opposite the turn-off to Parque Nacional Palo Verde, is not geared up for tourists, though staff can advise on current road conditions. For general **information**, it's best to head to Palo Verde itself or contact the ACT head office in Nicoya (ⓣ2686-4967).

The flowering trees of Guanacaste

Guanacaste's many flowering trees dot the landscape with pastel puffs of colour. Trees blossom in a strange way in the dry lands of Guanacaste, flowering literally overnight and then, just as suddenly, shedding their petals to the ground, covering it in a carpet of confetti colours. The **corteza amarilla** bursts into a wild Van Gogh-like blaze in March, April and May, and is all the more dramatic being set against a landscape of burnt siennas, muted mauves and sallow yellows. The **guanacaste** tree itself, also called the "elephant ear", is a majestic wide-canopied specimen and an emblem of the nation. Its cream-coloured flowers appear in May, and its curious seed pods feed the cattle and horses.

In November the deciduous **guachipelín** tree blooms, with its delicate fern-like leaves; in January it's time for the pastel-pink floss of the **poui**, followed in March by the equally pretty **tabebuia rosea**. By the end of the dry season the red flowers of the **malinche** explode into colour.

Some history

Due to significant excavations in the area and some contemporaneous Spanish accounts, Guanacaste's **pre-Columbian** history is better documented than in the rest of Costa Rica. Archeologists have long been interested in the **Chorotegas**, considered to have been the most highly developed of all Costa Rica's scattered and isolated pre-Columbian peoples, but whose culture predictably went into swift decline after the Conquest. In archeological terms it belongs to the **Greater Nicoya Sub-area**, a pre-Columbian designation that includes some of western Nicaragua, and which continues to yield buried clues to the extent of communication between the Maya and Aztec cultures to the north and smaller groups inhabiting Mesoamerica from the fifth to the fifteenth centuries.

Following the Conquest, the region became part of the administrative entity known as the **Capitanía General de Guatemala**. Guanacaste was annexed by Nicaragua in 1787, but in 1812 the Spanish rulers about-turned and donated the province to Costa Rica, so that its territory became large enough for it to be officially represented in the Captaincy. When the modern-day Central American nations declared independence from Spain, and the Captaincy was dissolved in 1821, Guanacaste found itself in the sensitive position of being claimed by both Costa Rica and Nicaragua. In an 1824 vote the province's inhabitants made their allegiances clear: the Guanacastecos in the north, traditionally cattle ranchers with familial ties to Nicaragua, voted to join that country, while the inhabitants of the Nicoya Peninsula wished to maintain links with Costa Rica. The peninsular vote won out, by a slim margin.

As the nineteenth century progressed, **cattle ranching** began to dominate the landscape, providing the mainstay of the economy until well into the twentieth century. Despite the continuing presence of the cattle culture and the *sabanero* (see box, pp.262–263) in Guanacaste, however, beef prices have been dropping in Costa Rica for some years now, after the boom years of the 1960s and 1970s when deforestation was rife. In contrast, as in the rest of the country, the **tourist industry** is becoming increasingly important to the local economy.

Cañas and around

Sleepy, arid **CAÑAS**, 168km northwest of San José, is the heart of agricultural commerce for the surrounding area. In town, activity is decidedly at a minimum; what there is of it mostly takes place within a few blocks of the unremarkable grassy and concrete **central square**. It's a pleasant town of single- and two-storey traditional buildings with only one real sight to speak of, the incongruous modernist **church**, on the east side of the square. The barn-like structure is replete with colourful, Gaudí-esque mosaics which reach a bright blue crescendo in the steeple, capped by an understated cross. Its interior is significantly more subdued, marked by a ceiling covered with stained wood blocks and a minimalist altar backed by a wall patterned with limestone rectangles.

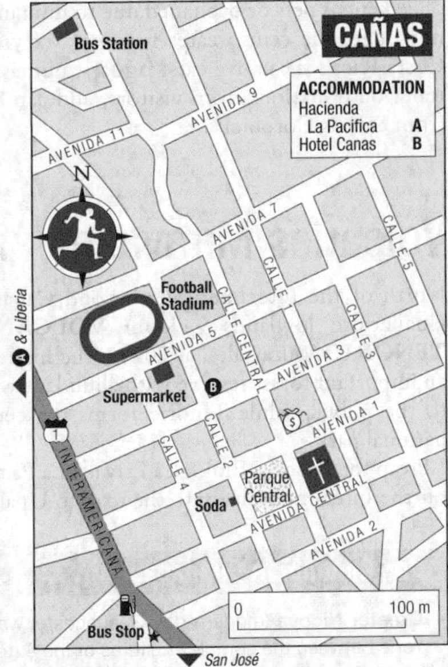

The town has no tourist office; the staff at *Hotel Cañas* (see below) are a good source of area information. The most central **bank** is the Banco Nacional branch on Calle Central at Avenida 1, and there's a **petrol station** on the Interamericana at Avenida 2, on the western edge of town. There are a couple of good **sodas** on the square; the best one is on the west side facing the church, where you can fill up on hearty portions of *comida típica*. The most refined meal in the area can be had at the **restaurant** of *Hacienda La Pacifica,* where most of the ingredients are grown or raised on the ranch's land.

Accommodation

It's only really worth staying overnight in Cañas if you arrive late or are planning to use it as a base for a trip into Palo Verde. Though the **accommodation** choices are limited, there are a couple of decent places to consider.

Hacienda La Pacifica 5km NE of town on the Interamericana ⓣ2669-6050, ⓦwww.pacificacr.com. Set in the grounds of a large cattle ranch, this hotel has country-style *cabinas* furnished with wi-fi, sleek bathrooms and comfortable, ornate beds. ❻

Hotel Cañas C 2 at Av 3 ⓣ2669-0039. A couple of blocks from the main square, this central option has 36 bland, but clean rooms; some have TV and a/c. The restaurant is not exactly memorable but serves straightforward good-value food. ❷

Rafting the Río Corobicí

Five kilometres west of Cañas on the Interamericana, the long-established **Safaris Corobicí** (trips depart daily from 7am–3.30pm; ⓣ2669-6191, ⓦwww.safaricorobici.com;), specializes in gentle floating trips on the Río Corobicí (2hr to half a day; $45–60 depending on duration, snacks included). Knowledgeable guides row while you observe the local mammals and reptiles, including howler and spider monkeys, surprisingly large crocodiles, iguanas and caimans. The trip also provides a prime opportunity for birdwatching, as several species, including mot-mots, cuckoos, falcons, ospreys herons and the endangered Jabirú stork, can all be spotted along the river's length.

Las Pumas Rescue Shelter

For about forty years, **Las Pumas Rescue Shelter** (daily 8am–4pm; $8; ⓣ2669-6044, ⓔlaspumas@racsa.co.cr) has provided a refuge for native wildlife once kept as pets or orphaned due to human activity. Although its enclosures are not huge, the centre cares for over sixty species of animal, including five of Costa Rica's six native cats: jaguars, pumas, margays, jaguarundi and ocelots. It relies on donations from visitors, and can be found about 500m up a side road from Safaris Corobicí.

Volcánes Miravalles and Tenorio

North of the Interamericana beyond Cañas – and clearly visible from the hot Guanacaste lowlands – loom **VOLCÁN MIRAVALLES** and **VOLCÁN TENORIO**. Miravalles, at 2028m the highest volcano in Guanacaste, is home to an important forest reserve with abundant wildlife and birds, though it's not open to the public, while Tenorio forms the centrepiece of an increasingly popular national park.

From the Reserva Biológica Privada La Pacífica, 7km north of Cañas, turn north off the Interamericana onto the road to Upala, a paved and reasonably maintained

Pre-Columbian Guanacaste

Greater Nicoya (modern-day Guanacaste) was an archeological and cultural buffer zone between the complex cultures of the Aztecs and the Maya to the north, and the simpler agrarian cultures to the south, who had more in common with the prehistoric peoples of the Amazon basin. Greater Nicoya was occupied from an indeterminate date by the **Nicoyans**, about whom little is known, but most of the historical and archeological facts discovered about the region relate to the peoples known as the **Chorotegas**, who arrived in Nicoya in 800 AD, though some sources date their arrival as later, fleeing social and political upheavals far to the north.

The central Mexican empire of Teotihuacán, near the Mexico City of today, had fallen into disorganization by about 650 AD, and was abandoned about one hundred years later, at the same time that the Classic Maya civilizations of modern-day Yucatán and northern Guatemala also collapsed. New **fragmented groups** were created, some of whom forged migratory, militaristic bands. In the eighth century, harassed by their territorial enemies the Olmecs, groups of Maya and Aztecs migrated south. Among them were the people who would become known as Chorotegas. The word Chorotega derives from either their place of origin, Cholula, or from two words in the Chorotegan language: *cholol* (to run or escape) and *teca* (people) – "the people who escaped".

Evidence of immediate and long-term cultural upheaval in the area after 800 AD includes a significant increase in the number of Nicoyan **burial sites** found dating from around this time. The use of objects associated with elites – like ceremonial skulls, jades and elaborate metates – suddenly declined almost to the point of disappearing completely, and populations seem to have migrated from the interior toward the coasts. While this evidence could suggest a natural disaster (a volcanic eruption, perhaps) it also bears the hallmarks of what could be termed an invasion.

The Chorotegas' first contact with the **Spanish** was calamitous. The 1522 Spanish expedition from Panamá up the Pacific coast to Nicaragua brought smallpox, the plague and influenza to the indigenous people of Greater Nicoya. Imprisonment and slavery followed, with coastal peoples raided, branded and sold into slavery in Panamá and Peru. The demise of the Chorotegas from the sixteenth century was rapid and unreversed.

Excavations in Guanacaste and the Nicoya Peninsula reveal something of the Chorotegas' **belief systems** and social arrangements. Near Bahía Culebra, fifty-eight-kilometre stretch that runs between the two volcanoes, and from which you can contemplate the spectacular colour changes and cloud shadows on their flanks. Located roughly equidistant between the two volcanoes is the small hamlet of **Bijagua**, an impressively enterprising community that is home to a number of ecotourism projects, including an ecology centre, organic farms and a collective of female artisans.

Parque Nacional Volcán Tenorio

An active volcano, although so far without spectacular eruptive displays, **TENORIO** (8am–5pm; $10) was designated a national park in 1995. Though most people come to the park to glimpse the surreal waters of the **Río Celeste**, wildlife also thrives within the park's borders, and you may be lucky enough to spot tapirs, agoutis and howler monkeys.

A **trail** departs from the ranger station at the entrance to the park and enters the forest where it eventually splits into a few well-marked loops. Don't wander from the trails, for the area is geothermically active; there are *fumaroles* (little columns of hot vapour escaping from the ground) and mud pots – one false move and you

anthropologists unearthed pottery shards, utensils and the remains of hearths, along with a burial ground holding twenty females, children and infants. Chorotega villages were made up of longhouse-type structures – common to many indigenous cultures of the Americas – inhabited by entire extended families, and centred on a large square, site of religious ceremonies and meetings.

Like the Maya and Aztecs, the Chorotegas had a belief system built around **blood-letting** and the **sacrifice** of animals and humans. Although it is not known if beating hearts were ripped from chests, virgins were definitely thrown into volcano craters to appease their gods, about whom little is known. Chorotegas also believed in **yulios**, the spirit alter ego that escaped from their mouths at the moment of death to roam the world forever. Although pagan, Chorotega priests shared a number of duties and functions with the Catholic priests who worked to destroy their culture. Celibate, they may also have heard confessions and meted out punishments for sins.

Few Chorotega **rituals** are documented. One known practice was the formation of a kind of human maypole, consisting of *voladores*, or men suspended "flying" (actually roped) from a post, twirling themselves round and round while descending to the ground. Originating with the Aztecs, the ritual was dedicated to the Morning Star, considered to be a deity; the four *voladores* represented the cardinal points. While no longer displayed in Costa Rica, it is still performed in the Mexican state of Veracruz and in certain villages in Guatemala.

The Chorotega **economy** was based on maize (corn). They also cultivated tobacco, fruit, beans and cotton, using cacao beans as currency, and the marketplace was run by women. All land was held communally, as was everything that was cultivated and harvested, which was then distributed throughout the settlement. This plurality did not extend to social prestige, however. Three strata characterized Chorotega society: at the upper echelon were chieftains (*caciques*), warriors and priests; in the middle were the commoners, and at the bottom were the slaves and prisoners of war. The Chorotegas were the only indigenous peoples in Costa Rica to have a written **language**, comprising hieroglyphs similar to those used by the Maya. They were also skilled artisans, producing ornamental jewellery and jade, and colouring cotton fabrics with animal and vegetable dye. It was the Chorotegas who made the bulk of the distinctive **ceramics** so celebrated in the country today, many of which can be seen in San José's Museo Nacional (for more on Chorotega pottery, see box, p.300).

could step into skin-stripping superheated volcanic soil. The main trail climbs steadily and opens up to a spectacular view of Volcán Miravalles, before eventually leading to a striking waterfall of the Río Celeste where you can take a dip. The highlights of the park, though, are a stunningly blue lagoon, the **Laguna Azul**, and similarly coloured *teñidores* (bright blue sections of the river) that flow alongside the trail – all created by a rare mix of sulphur, copper sulphate and calcium carbonate.

Accommodation and eating

No **camping** is allowed in the park, and most of the choices for **accommodation** in the area are centred around the village of Bijagua, about 18km from the park entrance. Alternatively, you can stay near Volcán Miravalles on the side facing Volcán Rincón de la Vieja (see p.274). There are a couple of small unremarkable *sodas* in Bijagua, but the only place **to eat** in the park is the friendly *Restaurante Los Pilones* in a whitewashed building opposite the ranger station, with outside seating overlooking the park. It serves reasonably priced, well-made *comida típica*, such as chicken with rice and beans ($6).

Albergue Ecoturística Heliconia 3km north of Bijagua on the road to Upala ⓣ2466-8483, ⓦwww.heliconiaslodge.com. At 750m elevation in a private forest reserve right between the volcanoes, this beautifully sited lodge holds several hiking trails, waterfalls and natural hot springs. The accommodation consists of six cabins with private bath, and four smartly designed spacious cottages (❻): there's also a restaurant and stunning views from around the grounds. The lodge can arrange walking tours of Parque Nacional Volcán Tenorio as well as trips to the Refugio Nacional de Vida Silvéstre Caño Negro (see p.240), travelling via the spectacular road to Upala, from where you can glimpse Lago Nicaragua and the Islas Solentiname shimmering in its blue waters. Breakfast is included. ❺

La Carolina Lodge 7km northeast from Bijagua, in the hamlet of San Miguel ⓣ8380-1656, ⓦwww.lacarolinalodge.com. The rustic *La Carolina Lodge* is set on a working farm well off the beaten path amid tranquil surroundings. There are private or shared rooms (one sleeping up to seven people). By the lodge is a (swimmable) river where toucans, green parrots and hummingbirds nest, and where you might also catch a glimpse of sloths and anteaters. Included in the very reasonable price are delicious home-style meals, a guided walk and a horseback-ride. Trips to Parque Nacional Tenorio can be arranged ($65 per person includes three meals and a guide), and the owners offer transport from Liberia ($75 per carload); alternatively, there are five buses daily from Cañas to Bijagua, from where a taxi to the lodge costs about $12. ❻

Casitas Tenorio About 3km east of Bijagua ⓣ8312-1248, ⓦwww.casitastenorio.com. Two charming and comfortable *casitas* set on a farm with views of Volcán Miravalles. There is an outdoor kitchen, and camping is possible on site ($6). The friendly owners can arrange guided hikes and tours of the areas as well as homestays. ❺

Parque Nacional Palo Verde

About 30km west of Cañas on the northern bank of the Río Tempisque lies the **PARQUE NACIONAL PALO VERDE** (daily 8am–5pm; $10), created in 1982 to preserve the habitat of the **migratory birds** that nest in the estuary of the Tempisque and a large patch of relatively undisturbed lowland dry forest. With a distinctive topography featuring ridged limestone hills – unique to this part of the country, and attesting to the fact that certain parts of Guanacaste were once under water – the park shelters about fifteen separate ecological habitats. From December to May, Palo Verde can dry out into baked mud flats, while in the wet season, extensive flooding gives rise to saltwater and freshwater lakes and swamps. Following the wet season, the great floodplain drains slowly, creating marshes, mangroves and other habitats favoured by migratory birds. Little visited by tourists, the park is mainly of interest to serious **birders**, but what you see depends

Beware the killer bees

In recent years swarms of **Africanized bees** – sometimes sensationally termed "killer bees" – have taken to colonizing Palo Verde. Africanized bees are aggressive, and may pursue – in packs – anyone who unwittingly disturbs one of their large, quite obvious, nests. They are known to attack dark colours, so if attacked remove all dark clothing and cover dark hair. The conventional technique is to cover your head and run in a zigzag pattern so that you can dodge the cloud of pursuing bees. Although, luckily, this occurs very rarely, you should take special care if you are sensitive to stings, and ask the rangers about the presence of nests on or around trails. Bees are also found in the Reserva Biológica Lomas Barbudal (see p.266).

on the time of year – by far the **best months** are at the height of the dry season (Jan–March), when most of the 250 or so migratory species are in residence. In the wet season, flooding makes parts of the park inaccessible.

The park is home to one of the largest concentrations of **waterfowl** in Central America, both indigenous and migratory, with more than three hundred species of birds, among them the endangered Jabirú stork and black-crowned night heron. Further from the riverbank, in the tree cover along the bottom and ridges of the limestone hills, you may spot toucans, and perhaps even one of the increasingly rare scarlet macaws. At evening during the dry season, many birds and other species – monkeys, coatis and even deer – congregate around the few remaining waterholes; bring binoculars and a torch. Note, though, that you shouldn't swim in the Río Tempisque (or anywhere else), as it's home to particularly huge crocodiles – some, according to the park rangers, are as much as 5m long.

The trails

From the administration building (see p.266), two **trails** lead up to the top of hills, from where you can see the expansive mouth of the Río Tempisque to the west and the broad plains of Guanacaste to the east. A number of other **loop trails**, none more than 4km long, run through the park. The shortest of the trails, at just 300m, is **Las Calizas**; others include **El Manigordo** ("ocelot"; 1.5km), **El Mapache** ("raccoon"; 2km) and **El Venado** ("deer"; 2km), all of which give you a good idea of the landscape and a chance of viewing the animals after which they're named. You've also got a good chance of seeing collared peccaries, abundant in this area, or a coati, which you may see or hear foraging in the undergrowth. White-tailed deer also live here, but they're very shy and likely to dart off at the sound of your approach.

For longer treks, try the **Bosque Primario** trail (about 7km), through, as the name suggests, primary forest cover. You can also walk the 6km (dry season only) to the edge of the Río Tempisque from where you'll see the aptly named **Isla de los Pájaros** (Bird Island). Square in the mouth of the river, the island is chock-full of our feathered friends all year, with black-crowned night herons swirling above in thick dark clouds. Many hotels and tour agencies in the province offer boat trips around the island, but landings are not permitted, so you have to content yourself with bird-spotting and taking photographs from the boat.

Check with rangers regarding **conditions** before walking on any of the trails: access is constantly subject to change, due to flooding and sometimes bee colonies. The Río Tempisque walk in particular can be muddy and unpleasantly insect-ridden in all but the driest months. You should bring plenty of water, as the heat and humidity are considerable.

Practicalities

Getting to Palo Verde takes a while, though it is possible with a regular non-4WD vehicle. From the well-signed turn-off from the Interamericana at Bagaces (opposite the ACT regional office, where you can check out current road conditions), it's a thirty-kilometre drive to the entrance hut, and a further 9km to the administration building. There are signs all along the road to the park, but at long intervals, and the road forks unnervingly from time to time without indicating which way to go. If in doubt, follow the tyre tracks made by the rangers. This road is theoretically passable year-round without a 4WD.

The Organization for Tropical Studies (OTS) has a field station at Palo Verde, originally set up for comparative ecosystem study and research into the dry forest habitat. If you contact their San José office (Ⓣ2524-0607, Ⓦwww.ots.ac.cr) in advance you may be able to stay in their rustic field station, next door to the administration building providing it's not full of scientific researchers. **Accommodation** (❻) is in clean dormitories, and meals are included in the rate. There's also a basic but perfectly comfortable *albergue* at the ranger station, about 10km from the entrance. The six rooms here each contain six bunk beds ($15 per person), including mosquito nets and fans, and meals are available (breakfast $3; lunch and dinner $6). You can also **camp** ($2 per day; Ⓣ2671-1290 or 2671-1062) at the small site next to the administration building, where there are lavatories, but it's best to call ahead to check that there's space. If there's not, there are several accommodation options along the Interamericana in and around Bagaces.

Reserva Biológica Lomas Barbudal

The **RESERVA BIOLÓGICA LOMAS BARBUDAL** (daily 8am–4pm; $10) is an impressive, though small-scale, initiative about 20km west of Bagaces, just north of Parque Nacional Palo Verde. Home to some of the last vestiges of true **tropical dry forest** in the region, Lomas Barbudal means "bearded hills" and that's just what they look like, with relatively bare pates surrounded by sideburns of bushy deciduous trees. Stretches of savannah-like open grassland are punctuated by the thorny-looking **shoemaker's tree** and crisscrossed by rivers and the strips of deciduous woods that hug their banks. The reserve also features isolated examples of the majestic **mahogany** and **rosewood** trees, whose deep-blood-red timber is coveted as material for furniture.

Lomas Barbudal is also rich in **wildlife**. If you don't spot a howler monkey, you'll at least likely hear one. And, this is practically the only place in Guanacaste where you have a reasonable chance of seeing the **scarlet macaw**. Like Parque Nacional Santa Rosa to the north, Lomas Barbudal hosts an abundance of **insects** – some 200 to 300 **bee species** alone, around 25 percent of the species of bees in the entire world. Those allergic to stings or otherwise intolerant of insects might want to give Lomas Barbudal a miss; they're everywhere, including the aggressive Africanized bees (see p.265).

Practicalities

Although you could take a **taxi** (about $30 return) to Lomas Barbudal from Bagaces, it's best reached with your own transport. Take the road north from Bagaces, and after about 7km follow the road off to the left; note that it's in pretty bad condition. The administration office lies 6km further, prettily set on the banks of the Río Cabuyo. You can **camp** ($4 per night), but bring your own water and food; there are no lavatories. There are also two swimmable rivers, a small network of trails designed and cleared by local volunteers, and a visitor centre.

Tropical dry forest

With its mainly deciduous cover, Guanacaste's **tropical dry forest**, created by the combination of a Pacific lowland topography and arid conditions, looks startlingly different depending upon the time of year. In the height of the dry season, almost no rain falls on lowland Guanacaste, the trees are bare, having shed their leaves in an effort to conserve water, and the landscape takes on a melancholy, burnt-sienna hue. In April or May, when the rains come, the whole of Guanacaste perks up and begins to look comparatively green, although the dry forest never takes on the lush look of the rainforest.

The story of the demise of the tropical dry forests in Mesoamerica is one of nearly wholesale destruction. In all, only about two percent of the region's pre-Columbian dry forest survives, and what was once a carpet stretching the length of the Pacific side of the isthmus from southern Mexico to Panamá now exists only in besieged pockets. Today, dry forests cover just 518 square kilometres of Costa Rica, almost all in Guanacaste, concentrated around the Río Tempisque and, more significantly, north in the Parque Nacional Santa Rosa. Due to deforestation and climatic change, tropical dry forests are considered a rare life-zone. Their relative dryness means they are easily overrun by field fires, which ranchers light in order to burn off old pasture. Hardy grasses spring up in their wake, such as the imported African jaragua, which gives much of Guanacaste its African savannah-like appearance.

Along with the leafy trees, tropical dry forest features **palms** and even a few **evergreens**. At the very top of a good thick patch of dry forest you see the umbrella form of **canopy trees**, although these are much shorter than in the tropical rainforest. Dry forest is a far less complex ecosystem than the humid rainforest, which has about three or four layers of vegetation. Like temperate-zone deciduous forests, the tropical dry forest has only two strata. The ground shrub layer is fleshed out by thorn bushes and tree ferns, primitive plants that have been with us since the time of the dinosaurs. Unlike rainforest, dry forest has very few epiphytes (plants growing on the trees), except for bromeliads (the ones that look something like upside-down pineapple leaves). The most biologically diverse examples of tropical dry forest are in the lower elevations of Parque Nacional Santa Rosa, where the canopy trees are a good height, with many different species of deciduous trees. There are also some pockets of mangroves and even a few evergreens in the wetter parts of the park.

Tropical dry forests can support a large variety of **mammal life**, as in the Parque Nacional Santa Rosa–Parque Nacional Guanacaste corridor. Deer and smaller mammals, such as the coati and paca, are most common, along with large cats, from the jaguar to the ocelot, provided they have enough room to hunt. You may see the endangered **scarlet macaw**, which likes to feed on the seeds of the sandbox tree, in a few remaining pockets of Pacific dry forest, including Lomas Barbudal and, further south, around Río Tarcoles and Parque Nacional Carara (see p.353), itself a transition zone between the dry forests of the north and the wetter tropical cover of the southern Pacific coast. In addition, the staggering number and diversity of **insects** are of great interest to biologists and entomologists: there are more than two hundred types of bee in Lomas Barbudal, for example, and a large number of butterflies and moths in Parque Nacional Santa Rosa.

Liberia and around

True to its name, the spirited provincial capital of **LIBERIA** (from *libertad*, meaning liberty) is distinctively friendly and progressive, its wide, clean streets the legacy of the pioneering farmers and cattle ranchers who founded it. Known colloquially as the "Ciudad Blanca" (white city) due to its whitewashed houses, Liberia is the only town in Costa Rica that seems truly colonial in style and

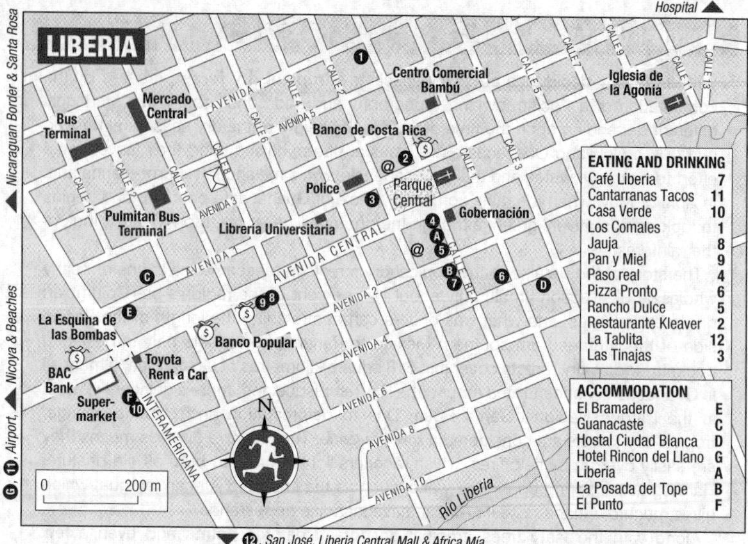

character. Many of the white houses still have their **puerta del sol** – corner doors that were used, ingeniously, to let the sun in during the morning and out in the late afternoon, thus heating and then cooling the interior throughout the day – an architectural feature left over from the colonial era and particular to this region.

At present, most travellers use Liberia simply as a jumping-off point for the national parks of **Rincón de la Vieja** and **Santa Rosa**, an overnight stop to or from the **beaches** of Guanacaste, or a break on the way to Nicaragua. However, Liberia is an appealing town, with everything you might need for a relaxing day or two – well-priced accommodation (although limited in choice) and a couple of nice places to eat and drink. The nearby international airport delivers busloads of visitors to the western beaches, but Liberia happily remains unchanged: it's still the epitome of dignified (if somewhat static) provincialism, with a strong identity and atmosphere all its own.

Liberia also boasts several lively local **festivals**, including the **Fiestas Cívicas de Liberia** in early March. The festival has its origins as an annual livestock fair and is now celebrated over ten days with parades, bands, fireworks and bulls wreaking havoc on daring but alcohol-addled young locals. Most of the action takes place in the fairgrounds in the northwest corner of town. On July 25, **El Día de la Independencia** celebrates Guanacaste's independence from Nicaragua with parades, horseshows, cattle auctions, rodeos, fiestas and roving marimba bands. If you want to attend, make bus and hotel reservations as far in advance as possible.

Arrival and information

Twelve kilometres west of the town, Liberia's international **airport** is connected to San José by regular Sansa and NatureAir flights; you can take a taxi from here into town ($10) unless you fancy a fifteen-minute walk from the terminal to the main road, where any eastbound bus will take you to town. Liberia's clean and efficient **bus terminal** is on the western edge of town near the exit for the Interamericana – it's a ten-minute walk at most from here to the centre of town – and serves all destinations except San José. At the bus station is an elaborate list of departure times;

Moving on from Liberia

Liberia is a main regional **transport hub**, providing easy access to Guanacaste's parks and beaches, the Nicaraguan border and **San José** (11 direct Pulmitan de Liberia buses daily; 4hr 30min). If you're heading for **the border**, take one of the hourly buses to La Cruz or Peñas Blancas, the border's official name (1hr). Through-buses from San José to Managua stop at the main bus terminal in Liberia, although it can be tricky to get a seat; the bus station also sells tickets to Managua if there is a vacant seat, otherwise it's a question of jumping on the bus, paying the driver and hoping you can grab a seat. *Hotel Guanacaste* can also sell bus tickets to Managua ($15 one-way).

For **Parque Nacional Santa Rosa** (40 min), take a La Cruz or Peñas Blancas bus. You should take the earliest bus possible to give yourself time for walking; ask the driver to let you off at Santa Rosa – it takes about an hour to walk from here to the park's administration centre. You can also reach the park by *colectivo* taxi ($15 per car), shared between four or five people. Catch one at the northwestern corner of Parque Central. *Colectivo* taxis are also good value if you're heading to **Parque Nacional Rincón de la Vieja** or the lodges near Las Pailas ranger station (roughly $25 for four people). Pretty much the best way to get to Rincón de la Vieja is to travel with one of the Liberia hotels – *La Posada del Tope*, *Hotel Liberia* and *Hotel Guanacaste* can all arrange transport to the park. All services are open to non-guests, though hotel guests get first option.

The more northerly of Guanacaste's **beaches** are served by direct buses. For Playa Hermosa and Playa Panamá, five buses leave daily (1hr); for Playa del Coco, six leave per day (1hr). Heading south, six daily buses serve **Tamarindo** (2hr); you can also easily get to **Santa Cruz** (hourly 5.30am–7.30pm; 1hr), from where you can hook up with buses to beaches further south. Buses for **Nicoya** (2hr) leave on the hour from 5am to 7pm, and those to **Puntarenas** (3hr) leave at 5am, 8.30am, 10am, 11am and 3pm. Not for those in a rush – these buses stop everywhere and are notorious for improvising on their routes.

these are pure fiction, so you must check with the ticket office. San José buses arrive at and depart from the **Pulmitan terminal**, a block southeast of the bus station. If you're coming by car, the exit off the Interamericana is at an intersection with traffic lights and three petrol stations – known as La Esquina de las Bombas (Gas Station Corner). Turning left (if coming from the south) takes you to the beaches, while a right takes you along the town's **Avenida Central**, lined with floppy mango trees. **Addresses** in Liberia are most often given in relation to the **church**, the **Parque Central**, or the large, white **Gobernación**, the regional government building across from the church on the corner of Calle Real and Avenida Central.

There's no tourist office in town, but *La Posada del Tope* (see p.270) can usually help with **information**.

Accommodation

Pleasant Liberia is a convenient **place to spend the night** along this northern stretch of the Interamericana. In the popular dry season, it's best to book a room in advance.

El Bramadero La Esquina de las Bombas ⓣ2666-0371, ⓦwww.hotelelbramadero.com. The setting, beside the fuel pumps on the Interamericana, isn't the loveliest, but it's convenient for the beaches and popular with Ticos. The rooms are fairly nondescript, but surprisingly quiet (try to get one at the back), and there's a decent open-air restaurant and a pool. A good bet if everything else is full. ❺

Guanacaste Av 1, 300m south of the bus station ⓣ2666-0085, ⓦwww.higuanacaste.com. Popular, HI-affiliated hostel, with a traveller-friendly cafeteria-restaurant. The rooms are simple, clean and dark; the doubles aren't great value compared to the town's other options, but there are a few dorm places available ($7). The hostel fills up quickly, so book ahead. With an HI card you get a 15 percent discount, and you might wangle a further 10 percent with a student ID. The management organizes a daily transfer ($20) to Rincón de la Vieja and sells bus tickets to Nicaragua. ❷–❸

Hostal Ciudad Blanca Av 4, 200m south and 150m east of the Gobernación ⓣ2666-3962. Spotless hotel in a stately rancher's mansion with a small breakfast terrace/bar, and twelve modern, a/c rooms with TV, private bath and ceiling fans. Popular with American travellers bedding down before heading out to the beach. Breakfast included. ❺

Hotel Rincón del Llanó 3 miles west of the airport ⓣ2667-0981. Spotless, newly opened hotel that's a good option if you want to stay near the airport. The rooms are unimaginatively designed and have a chain hotel feel, but they're comfortable and come with a good range of amenities, including large TVs, a/c and wi-fi. There's a decent restaurant, pool and adjacent bar, and the hotel runs an airport shuttle. ❹

Liberia C 0, 75m south of Parque Central ⓣ2666-0161. Well-established, friendly youth-hostel-type hotel with a jolly papaya-orange exterior. The bare and basic rooms with shared cold-water bathroom are set around a sunny courtyard. The newer rooms in an annexe to the rear are better and have their own bath, though they cost an extra $4. The hotel staff can organize transport to Rincón de la Vieja. The hotel is popular, so a reservation and deposit are required in the high season: Visa accepted. ❷

La Posada del Tope C 0, 150m south of the Gobernación ⓣ&ⓕ2666-3876. Popular, cheap budget hotel in a beautiful historic house. The six basic rooms with fan and shared showers in the old part of the hotel are a bit stuffy, but clean; the more modern rooms across the street in the annexe Casa Real cost only slightly more (❷), come with cable TV, and are set around a charming courtyard. The shared bathrooms aren't great, but there's plenty of character here, as well as a friendly staff, parking and a rooftop telescope for stargazing. The manager runs transport to Rincón de la Vieja for $10 per person round-trip, as well as trips to Palo Verde. ❶

El Punto ⓣ2665-2986, ⓦwww.elpuntohotel.com. Vibrantly coloured B&B in a converted school run by an enthusiastic local artist. Set in leafy landscaped grounds, it has six colour-themed rooms, each with an unfussy layout, high ceilings, a/c, wi-fi, mini-fridge and a loft that can accommodate additional guests. A well-prepared breakfast is included and Liberia's finest restaurant, *Casa Verde*, is just a few metres away. Easily the best deal in town. ❸

The Town

Liberia's wide, clean streets are used more by cyclists and horseriders than motorists. Despite the lack of standout sights, it's a pleasant place to walk around in the shade provided by the mango trees, though in March and April watch out for the ripe fruit plopping down full-force at your feet. The town is arranged around a large **Parque Central**, officially called Parque Mario Cañas Ruiz, named after a twentieth-century poet and musician whose songs paid tribute to *sabanero* culture. The Parque is dedicated to *el mes del anexión*, the month of the annexation (July), celebrating the fact that Guanacaste is not in Nicaragua. Liberia's Parque Central is one of the loveliest central plazas in the whole country, ringed by benches and tall palms that shade gossiping locals. On the eastern edge of the Parque is the town **church**, a contemporary structure whose startlingly modernist – some would say downright ugly – form looks a little out of place in this very traditional town.

Far more appealing is the colonial, mottled yellow **Iglesia de la Agonía** that sits about 600m away on Avenida Central at the eastern end of town. On the verge of perpetual collapse – it has had a hard time from successive earthquakes – it's almost never open, but try shoving the heavy wooden door and hope the place doesn't collapse around you if it gives way.

The most historic street in town is the **Calle Real** (marked as Calle Central on some maps). In the nineteenth century this street was the entrance to Liberia, and practically the whole road has been restored to its original colonial simplicity.

Tours from Liberia

Several of Liberia's hotels, including *La Posada del Tope*, run **tours** to attractions in the surrounding area, including Rincón de la Vieja ($15–20), Palo Verde ($25–35) and the Guanacaste beaches. One of the best independent operators in town, Offi Tours (T 8899-8149, E offitempisque@yahoo.com), run by the affable José Chamorro, leads similar excursions as well as day-trips to Parque Nacional Volcán Tenorio ($120) and Granada, Nicaragua ($140). Prices are per car, so it makes sense to go with a group.

Stately white adobe homes feature large windows with ornate wooden frames and wide overhanging eaves under which locals pass the evenings in cane armchairs.

Eating, drinking and entertainment

Liberia has several **restaurants** that serve local dishes such as **natilla** (soured cream) eaten with eggs or *gallo pinto* and tortillas. For a real feast, try **desayuno guanacasteco**, a hearty local breakfast of tortillas, sour cream, eggs, rice and beans, and sometimes meat. This is *sabanero* or, more properly, **criollo** food, to be worked off with hard labour. For rock-bottom cheap **lunches**, try the stalls at the bus terminal or head to one of the fried chicken places, the bar *Las Tinajas*, or *soda Rancho Dulce*. You can pick up Guanacastecan **corn snacks** from stalls all over town.

The town's main **disco**, *Kurú*, about 200 metres west of the Interamericana down the road to the beaches, gets lively with salsa and merengue, especially on weekends and holidays. *Tsunami*, across the road and down a side street, is also popular and fills with young dancing locals on the weekends. The main Saturday evening activity, however, involves watching the locals parading around the Parque Central in their finery, having an ice cream, and maybe going to the movies at the **Cine Liberia**, located in the shopping mall 1km south of the main Interamericana intersection.

Restaurants, bars and sodas

Café Liberia C Real Av 2/4 T 8992-4865. Wonderful café and arts centre set in a historic house that screens films and hosts occasional live performances. The best place in town to relax with a cup of coffee and hear locals discuss the region's latest political and arts developments.

Cantarranas Tacos 5km down the road towards the beaches, 50m back from the road on the right. Mexican restaurant on the road from Liberia to the beaches – a bit of a local secret. Delicious tacos served inside or alfresco. Great atmosphere and staff.

Casa Verde Next door to El Punto T 2665-8901. Hip, stylish restaurant and lounge with startlingly good food and exemplary service. The menu features a wide range of well-executed dishes, from surf 'n' turf to Thai specialities, with main courses costing $15–20. There's also an extensive selection of sushi on offer, some using an inventive mix of ingredients. Open for lunch and dinner.

Los Comales C Real, Av 5/7, 200m north of the northeast corner of Parque Central. A typical Costa Rican *soda*, very popular with locals for its generous portions of tasty rustic food, with *gallos* and *pintos* costing a mere $2, and *casados* $3; there are also several rice dishes on offer.

Jauja Av Central, C 8/10. One of the better restaurants in town, though very touristy. Large and tasty pasta dishes and pizzas cost around $7, and there are also typical steaks and fish dishes. It's all served in a pleasant, outdoor garden setting, although the big-screen TV can be off-putting.

Pan y Miel Av Central, C 8/10. Order straightforward Tico specialities in this frequently packed *soda*, where locals visit in droves for the large portions at great prices ($5–7 for lunch).

Paso Real Av 0 on the south side of the plaza. Popular second-floor restaurant looking out over the Parque Central and church. Its extensive menu includes moderately priced *comida típica* dishes, as well as fish entrées and straightforward international fare like burgers. Open till 10pm.

La cocina Guanacasteca: corn cooking

Corn is still integral to the regional cuisine of Guanacaste, thanks to the Chorotegas, who cultivated maize (corn) to use in many inventive ways. One pre-Columbian corn concoction involved roasting and grinding the maize, and then combining the meal-like paste with water and chocolate to make the drink *chicha*. Although you can't find this version of *chicha* any more you can still get **grain-based drinks** in Guanacaste, such as *horchata* (made with rice or corn and spiced with cinnamon), or *pinolillo* (made with roasted corn), both milky and sweet, with an unmistakeably grainy texture.

Corn also shows up in traditional Guanacastecan snacks such as **tanelas** (like a cheese scone, but made with cornflour) and **rosquillas**, small rings of cornflour that taste like a combination between tortillas and doughnuts. You can buy these at roadside stalls and small shops in Liberia. Served throughout the country, **chorreados** crop up most often on menus in Guanacaste: they're a kind of pancake made (again) with cornflour and served with *natilla*, the local version of sour cream.

Pizza Pronto C 1, Av 4. Rustic-chic local favourite where dark-wood tables are covered with Guanacaste topographical maps. Select from over twenty kinds of pizza, all baked in an adobe clay oven.

Restaurante Kleaver Av 1, C 0. Basic *soda* with counter seating and small tables churning out staples like grilled chicken with rice and beans and fried plantains. Though it lacks atmosphere, it's one of the few places in town where you can get a late-night meal. Open 24hr.

Rancho Dulce C Real, Av 0/2, 50m south of the Gobernación. A reliable choice at any time of day, this small and lovable *soda* serves *casados* ($3), sandwiches, *empanadas* and *refrescos*. You can sit at the tiny outdoor stools (if you have a small bottom) or tables.

La Tablita On the Interamericana, 1km south of Liberia ⓣ2666-7122. This is cattle country, and the steaks (around ($10–15) at *La Tablita Steak House* couldn't be juicier.

Las Tinajas West side of Parque Central. Liberia's best bar, with regular live music, also serves basic *casados* and excellent hamburgers ($3). The outdoor tables on the veranda of this old house are a pleasant spot to watch the goings-on in the *parque* while enjoying a *refresco* or beer, the latter available on tap and served in chilled glasses.

Listings

Banks There are plenty of banks, many on Av Central, leading into town, several with ATMs. The Banco de Costa Rica, across from Parque Central, will change travellers' cheques.

Bookshop Librería Universitaria on Av 1, 100m east of Parque Central sells the *Miami Herald* and *New York Times* newspapers.

Car rental Liberia is a useful place to rent a car, with many operators, mostly along the road to the beaches; in town, Toyota Rent a Car (ⓣ2668-1212, ⓦwww.toyotarent.com), Av Central at the Interamericana, is a good choice. Most hotels can also arrange car rental, with *La Posada del Tope* consistently offering the best deals. It's definitely worth considering a four-wheel-drive, as the potholed roads can easily cause a flat tyre in a smaller car.

Hospital Just off C 13 east of the football stadium, ⓣ2666-0011.

Internet Cybermania (daily 8am–10pm), in a small business centre on the north side of Parque Central, is efficient, friendly, air-conditioned and cheap, as is the handy Planet Internet (daily 8am–10pm) on C Real just off Parque Central: both cost about $2 per hour.

Post office Av 3, C 8 (Mon–Fri 7.30am–6pm, Sat 7.30am–noon). The efficient post office is a bit hard to find: it's between Av 3 and Av 5 in the low-slung white house across from an empty square field bordered by mango trees.

Africa Mía

Ten kilometres southeast of Liberia on the Interamericana outside the town of El Salto is one of Guanacaste's most curious and highly touted attractions, **Africa Mía** (8am–6pm, last entry at 5pm; $18 for hike and ride around the perimeter of some sections; $65 for 2hr ride inside the park in a 4WD; Ⓦ www.africamia.net). Eight years in the making, the newly opened preserve has taken the region's resemblance to the African savannah one step further by populating several hundred acres with animals endemic to the continent, such as giraffes, zebras, giant elands, ostriches and warthogs; for good measure you can spot native wildlife too, including monkeys and various bird species. All of the animals roam free (there are no predators), and your best chance of seeing a good number of them is on one of the safari vehicle tours. The somewhat curious decision to import exotic animals into a country already teeming with wildlife aside, the preserve is exceedingly well run and there's no denying the thrill of seeing animals galloping about you that you might have only previously glimpsed in the confines of a zoo. There are two cafés, a restaurant and several shops on site and accommodation is planned for 2011.

Parque Nacional Rincón de la Vieja

The beautifully dry landscape of **PARQUE NACIONAL RINCÓN DE LA VIEJA** (daily 8am–4pm; $10), about 30km northeast of Liberia, encompasses terrains varying from rock-strewn savannah to patches of tropical dry forest, culminating in the blasted-out vistas of the volcano crater itself. The land here is actually alive and breathing: Rincón de la Vieja's last major eruptions took place in 1995 and 1998, and were serious enough to evacuate local residents. The danger has always been to the northern side of the volcano, facing Nicaragua (the opposite side from the two entrance points), and the most pressing **safety** issue for tourists is to be aware that rivers of lava and hot mud still boil beneath the thin epidermis of ground. While danger areas are clearly marked with signs and fences, you still have to watch your step: walkers have been seriously burned from crashing through this crust and stepping into mud and water at above-boiling temperatures.

With the right amount of caution, however, this is an enchanting place: brewing **mud pots** (*pilas de barro*) bubble, and puffs of steam rise out of lush foliage,

signalling sulphurous subterranean springs. This is great terrain for **camping**, **riding** and **hiking**, with a comfortable, fairly dry heat, though it can get damp and cloudy at the higher elevations around the crater. **Birders**, too, enjoy Rincón de la Vieja, as there are more than two hundred species in residence.

Getting to the park

The local dry season (Dec–March especially) is the **ideal time** to visit Rincón de la Vieja, when the hiking trails and visibility as you ascend the volcano are at their best. The park has been split into two **sectors**: Sector Las Pailas ("cauldrons") and Sector Santa María, each with its own **entrance** and ranger station. The two are linked by an eight-kilometre walking trail. From Liberia most people travel through the hamlet of Curubandé, about 16km northeast, to the **Las Pailas** sector. The other ranger station, **Santa María**, lies about 25km northeast of Liberia. The **casona** that houses the ranger station here is a former retreat of US president Lyndon Baines Johnson.

Both routes to the park are along stony roads, not at all suitable for walking. People do, but it's tough, uninteresting terrain, and it's really more advisable to save your energy for the trails within the park itself. Options for getting here from Liberia are covered in the box on p.271 – transfers run by hotels such as *La Posada del Tope* are convenient and good value. **Hitching** is also an option if you can find a truck driver making a delivery, possibly at the petrol station at La Esquina de las Bombas on the Interamericana at Liberia. Alternatively, you could **rent a car** (you'll more or less need a 4WD) and stay in one of the upmarket tourist lodges such as the *Hacienda Guachipelín* or *Rincón de la Vieja Lodge* (see opposite).

To get to the **Las Pailas sector**, where most of the lodges are, take the Interamericana north of Liberia for 6km, then turn right to the hamlet of Curubandé. Here you'll see signs for the *Guachipelín* and *Rincón de la Vieja* lodges. A couple of kilometres before *Guachipelín* there's a barrier and toll booth, where you'll be charged $1.75 to use the road. If you don't have your own transport, both lodges will pick you up from Liberia for an extra charge ($10–25 return); they also offer **packages** from San José, with transport included. The **Santa María sector** and the *Rinconcito Lodge* are reached by driving through Liberia's Barrio La Victoria in the northeast of the town; ask for the *estadio* – the football stadium – from where it's a signed twenty-four-kilometre drive to the park.

Accommodation

The Rincón de la Vieja area boasts some very good **lodges**, most of which offer their own tours, either on horseback or by foot. There's a basic **campsite** near the Las Pailas ranger station, and another slightly better equipped one at the Santa María ranger station (both $2 per person), where there are lavatories and water, though you should take your own cooking utensils, food and water. If you have a sleeping bag, and ask in advance, you can also stay inside the musty bunk rooms in the Santa María ranger station (phone the ACG office at Santa Rosa for permission on ⓣ2666-5051).

Borinquen Mountain Resort ⓣ2690-1900, ⓦwww.borinquenresort.com. Upmarket, expensive lodge with its own spa centre, mudpools and sauna, set in a stunning landscape at the skirts of Volcán Rincón de la Vieja. Accommodation is in luxurious villas and bungalows. There's a classy restaurant, full disabled access and facilities for kids. They also run horseback trips and ATV (all-terrain vehicle) excursions to the volcano. ❾

Buena Vista Lodge 31km northeast of Liberia ⓣ2665-7759, ⓦwww.buenavistalodgecr.com. A working cattle ranch – you can even ride with the cowhands if your horsemanship is up to it – with stupendous views over Guanacaste and some great trails through pockets of rainforest on the flanks of the volcano and up to the crater. Double rooms are housed in individual bungalows, many set around a small lake in which you can swim. A restaurant serves up wholesome meals, and there are reasonably priced horseback and hiking tours available – the place even has its very own canopy tour. If you're driving here, a 4WD is recommended; alternatively, you can arrange to be picked up from Cañas Dulces (accessible from Liberia by bus). ❻

Hacienda Guachipelín 5km beyond Curubandé on the edge of the park ⓣ2666-8075, ⓦwww.guachipelin.com. A working ranch, the *Guachipelín* looks every inch the old cattle hacienda, with comfortable doubles in the main house. There's a fantastic swimming pool, and breakfast is included in the price. Attractions include a nearby waterfall, mud pots and some well-marked trails; guides are available for a variety of tours, including riding and hiking to the volcano. Pick-ups from Liberia can be arranged for a fee. ❽

Rincón de la Vieja Lodge 5km northwest of *Guachipelín* and 3.5km from the Las Pailas park entrance; follow the signs ⓣ2661-8198. Popular lodge with simple, rustic accommodation, including doubles with private bath and hot water (❹), and bungalows decorated in attractive *sabanero* style (❺). There's a pool and reading area and the restaurant serves tasty, filling meals. Horse riding, mountain biking, a canopy tour and swimming at nearby waterfalls can all be arranged. ❻

Rinconcito Lodge In San Jorge ⓣ2200-0074, ⓦwww.rinconcitolodge.com. The cheapest option close to the park, this farm is owned by a friendly family and has plain but good-value *cabinas* with cold-water shared or private bathroom. The owners are a good source of advice on local transport, guides and directions, and can also arrange horse riding, guided tours and pick-ups from Liberia (about $35 return per car). Meals available (breakfast $5, lunch and dinner $8). ❸

Visiting the park

Costa Rica's most memorable national park is utterly dominated by the massive and majestic Volcán Rincón de la Vieja. The most direct approach to the crater and summit of the volcano is via the Las Pailas entrance, along a marked trail. From here, you can also take a circular walk that highlights some of the volcanic features, or walk to the Santa María station, 8km away. **Warning**: the trail to the summit is often closed due to low visibility or high winds, so it's definitely worth ringing ahead on ⓣ2661-8139 to check conditions.

This is quite simply the best hiking in the country. A variety of elevations and habitats reveals hot springs, sulphur pools, bubbling mud pots, fields of *guaria morada* (purple orchids) – the national flower – plus a great smoking volcano at the top to reward you for your efforts. **Animals** in the area include all the big cats (but don't expect to see them), the shy tapir, red deer, collared peccary, two-toed sloth, and howler, white-faced and spider monkeys. There's a good chance you will see a brilliant flash of fluttering blue – this is the **Blue Morpho** butterfly, famous for its electric colours. **Birders** may spot the weird-looking three-wattled bellbird, the Montezuma oropendola, the trogon and the spectacled owl, among others.

Rincón de la Vieja is becoming more and more popular, and the trails may soon become over-walked. If you stay at one of the lodges and take their summit tours, either by horseback or on foot, you may pass through areas not covered in this section. Also, bear in mind that Rincón de la Vieja is an active volcano, and the trails described may be altered due to periodic **lava flows**. Before setting out, you should always check current conditions at one of the ranger stations, or call the Area de Conservación de Guanacaste (ACG) headquarters at the Parque Nacional Santa Rosa (ⓣ2666-5051, Spanish only). It's also advisable to carry all your **drinking water** – streams might look inviting, but often carry high concentrations of minerals (like sulphur) that can lead to extreme stomach upset if drunk.

The trails

From the Las Pailas ranger station, you have several walking options, with trails leading west to the *cataratas escondidas* (hidden waterfalls) and east to the Santa María station, along an eight-kilometre path. The most popular and least demanding trail heads east on a very satisfying six-kilometre circuit past many of the highly unusual natural features with which the park abounds, including a mini-volcano and "Pilas de Barro" **mud pots**; listen out for strange bubbling sounds, like a large pot of water boiling over. Mud pots, which should be treated with respect, are formed when mud, thermally heated by subterranean rivers of magma, seeks vents in the ground, sometimes actually forcing itself out through the surface in great thick gloops. It's a surreal sight: grey-brown muck blurping out of the ground like slowly thickening gravy. Another feature is the geothermal **hornillas** (literally, "stoves"), mystical-looking holes in the ground exhaling elegant puffs of steam. You almost expect to stumble upon the witches of *Macbeth*, brewing spite over them. Make sure not to go nearer than a metre or so, or you'll be steamed in no time. The combined effect of all these boiling holes is to make the landscape a bit like brittle Swiss cheese – tread gingerly and look carefully where you're going to avoid the ground crumbling underneath you. Many hikers have been scalded by blithely strolling too close to the holes. The trail also takes you through forest with abundant fauna and flora and be prepared to ford a couple of streams.

The hike to the summit

The highlight of the park is definitely the hike to the summit, a trail that heads north from Las Pailas. It's hard to get lost, but the top is 7.7km away, so you should start early to get up and down without hurrying too much. The walk takes you through forest similar to lower montane rainforest, densely packed, and lushly covered with epiphytes and mosses. Cool mist and rain often plague this section of the trail: if you are anywhere near the top and lose visibility, which can happen very suddenly, you're advised to stay away from the crater, whose brittle and ill-defined edges become more difficult to see, and consequently more dangerous, in cloudy weather.

At the **summit**, Rincón de la Vieja presents a barren lunar landscape, a smoking hole surrounded by black ash, with a pretty freshwater **lake**, Lago los Jilgueros, to the south. Quetzals are said to live in the forest that surrounds the lake, though you're unlikely to see them. When clear, the **views** up here are ample reward for the uphill sweating, with Lago de Nicaragua shimmering silver-blue to the north, the hump of the Cordillera Central to the southeast and the Pacific Ocean and spiny profile of the Nicoya Peninsula to the west. You can get hammered by wind at the top; bring a sweater and windbreaker.

Bosque Encantado trail

From Santa María, it's a more difficult and longer walk to the crater, but there are a number of other worthwhile trails, including the three-kilometre **Bosque Encantado** (Enchanted Forest) trail. It leads to a small forest and some hot springs next to a creek, which hikers love to leap into after a wallow in the springs, imitating a sauna effect. The temperature is usually just about right for soaking, but you should never jump into any thermal water without first checking current temperatures at the ranger station.

Border checks in Guanacaste

Driving along the Interamericana north of Liberia, don't be surprised to see a blue-suited *policia de tránsito* (traffic cop) or a light-brown-suited *guardia rural* (border police officer) leap out, kamikaze-like, into the highway directly in front of you – you'll need to stop and show your driver's licence and passport (which you must have on you at all times). These are routine checks, mainly to deter undocumented Nicaraguans from entering Costa Rica. The nearer the border you get, the more frequent the checks become. Make sure you drive carefully: knocking over a policeman is not a good move.

Parque Nacional Santa Rosa

Established in 1971 to protect a stretch of increasingly rare dry tropical forest, **PARQUE NACIONAL SANTA ROSA** (daily 8am–4pm; $10), 35km north of Liberia, is Costa Rica's oldest national park. Today it's one of the most popular in the country, thanks to its good trails, great surfing (though poor swimming) and prolific turtle-spotting opportunities. It's also, given a few official restrictions, a great destination for **campers**, with a couple of sites on the beach.

Santa Rosa has an amazingly diverse topography for its size of 387 square kilometres, ranging from mangrove swamp to deciduous forest and savannah. Home to 115 species of mammals (half of them bats), 250 species of **birds** and 100 of **amphibians** and **reptiles** (not to mention 3800 species of **moths**), Santa Rosa is a rich biological repository, attracting researchers from all over the world. Jaguars and pumas prowl the park, though you're unlikely to see them; what you may spot – at least in the dry season – are coati, coyotes and peccaries, often snuffling around watering holes.

The appearance of the park changes drastically between the **dry season**, when the many streams and small lakes dry up, trees lose their leaves, and thirsty animals can be seen at known waterholes, and the **wet months**, which are greener, but afford fewer animal-viewing opportunities. From July to November however, you may be able to witness hundreds of **olive ridley turtles** (*lloras*) dragging themselves out of the surf and nesting on Playa Nancite by moonlight; September and October are the months on which you are most likely to see them. Turtles arrive singly or occasionally in *arribadas*, a phenomenon unique to this species where thousands of females arrive en masse to lay their eggs. In an attempt to avoid the disturbances caused by big tour groups which have been a problem at places like Tortuguero, a maximum of twenty visitors are allowed access to the nesting area each day; reserve your place on ⓣ2666-5051 or ask at the administration centre when you arrive. Though too rough for swimming, the picturesque **beaches** of Naranjo and Nancite, about 12km down a bad road from the administration centre, are popular with serious **surfers**. They're also great places to hang out for a while, or do a little camping and walking on the nearby trails.

Visiting the park

Many of Santa Rosa's **trails** are intended for scientific researchers rather than tourists, and so are not well signed. If you do set off to walk, it's a good idea to hire a guide (about $10 per person); ask at the administration centre or, preferably, phone beforehand (ⓣ2666-5051) to arrange it. If you walk only one trail in the entire park, make it the very short (1km) and undemanding *sendero natural*, which provides an introduction to the unique features of the tropical dry forest. Curving around from the road just before the *casona*, it's signed as the **Sendero "Indio Desnudo"**, after the peeling-bark trees of the same name (also tongue-in-cheekily called "sunburned-tourist trees"). Along the trail you'll see acacia and **guapinol** trees, whose colloquial name is "stinking toe" on account of its smelly seed pods. Look out for monster iguanas hiding innocuously in tree branches, and for the ubiquitous bats.

From the administration centre a rough (but signposted) track leads past La Casona camping area, with several trails branching off along the way. Some of these may be restricted at any one time for research purposes; check first at the administration centre, however, as you can usually walk where you want as long as you let someone know. After about 5km you come to a fork, bearing left to Playa Naranjo, and right to Playa Nancite, both of them about 3km further on.

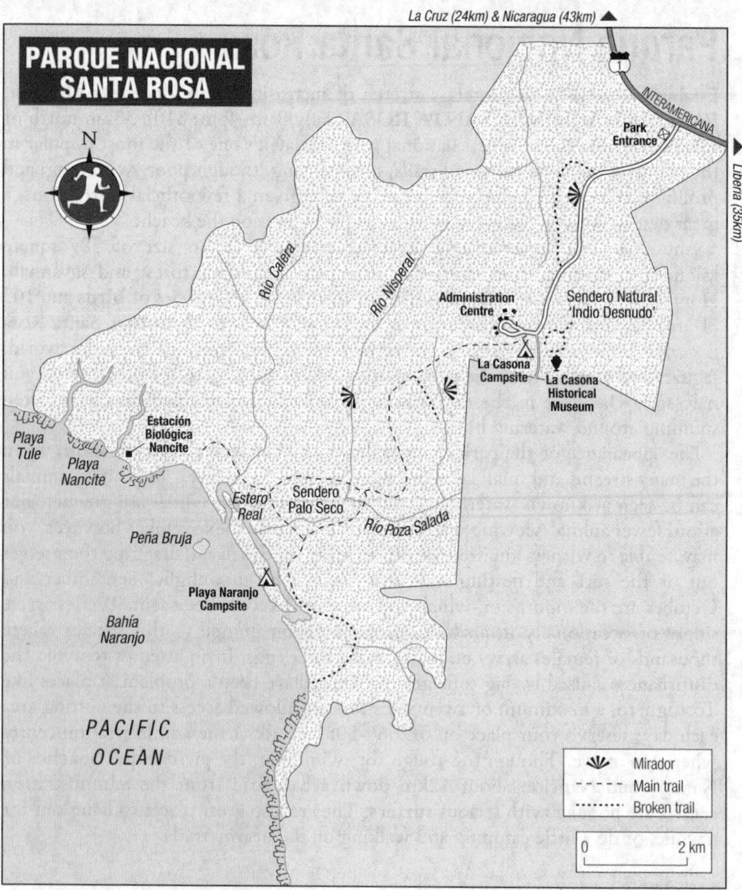

Playa Nancite is a lovely grey sand beach and when the tide has just gone out, it's as lustrous as a wet seal's skin. It is also the nesting home of the **olive ridley turtles**, a species which nests only here and at Ostional near Nosara on the Nicoya Peninsula (see p.309). With none of the large tour groups you find at other Costa Rican turtle beaches, it's a great place to watch the **arribadas**, during which up to eight thousand turtles – weighing on average around 40kg each – come ashore on any given evening, virtually covering the beach: for more on the *arribadas*, see box, p.310. According to estimates, more than eleven million eggs can be deposited by the turtles during a single *arribada*.

Due to riptides, Playa Nancite is no good for swimming but, as is usually the case, it's good for **surfers**, with huge rolling, tubular waves. For the best surf, though, you should head for **Playa Naranjo** (also known as Witch's Rock). Theoretically you can hike between the two (2hr) on a narrow trail across the rocky headland, which opens out on top into hot, dry scrub cover, but you have to watch the tide, since the trail crosses the deep Estero Real, the drainage point for two rivers. Ask for the *marea* (tidal times) from the administration centre before setting out.

La Casona

About 400m from the administration building is the formidable wooden and red-tiled homestead **La Casona** (Big House), one of Costa Rica's most famous historical sites. For many years it was the centre of a working hacienda until the land was expropriated for the national park in 1972. In 2001, it was burned down by poachers who were retaliating against arrests by park rangers. However, phoenix-like, it stands again after being lovingly (and painstakingly) reconstructed in less than a year – this time, with the addition of smoke alarms.

Information panels recount the various instances of derring-do which have occurred at La Casona, with resumés of the battles of March 20, 1856 (the confrontation between William Walker's filibusters and the Costa Rican forces; see p.280), of 1919 (against the Nicaraguans), and of 1955, against another Nicaraguan, the dictator Anastasio Somoza García, who ruled the country from 1936 until his assassination in 1956. His hulk of a tank can still be seen, rusting and abandoned, along a signed road just beyond the entrance hut.

La Casona, set around a flowering courtyard, is full of rustic character. It's now entirely given over to **exhibitions**, and you are free to clamber up and down the steps and wander around the dark rooms, which have a significant population of resident bats. Many of the exhibits were destroyed in the fire, but there's some information on the life of the notorious William Walker and the great battle of 1856, remnants of dead animals and archeological remains. At one side of La Casona, a stair path leads up to a viewpoint with a magnificent perspective of the twin volcanoes of Rincón de la Vieja National Park.

Murciélago sector

Few tourists go to Santa Rosa's **Murciélago sector**, an area of reserve to the northwest of – and entirely separate from – the main sector of the national park. It's a kind of reforestation laboratory in which former cattle pasture is slowly being regenerated, though there's also a campsite and a beach that's safe for swimming. To get there, drive along the Interamericana from the main Santa Rosa entrance about 10km north then take the left turn 8km to the hamlet of **Cuajiniquil**. A poor road continues here another 9km to the ranger station (open daily 7am–7pm, joint entry with Santa Rosa or $10). Be sure to take the dirt road, not the paved one. You'll almost certainly need a 4WD, at least in the wet season, when there are two creeks to ford. At the ranger station you can camp ($2) and arrange meals with prior notification (at the Santa Rosa administration centre). Dirt roads lead from the Murciélago ranger station to a series of fine swimming beaches (this part is known as the **Area Recreativa Junquillal**), accessible by walking or by 4WD. The westernmost of these, **Playa Blanca**, a small white stretch of sand, is the prettiest and one of the most isolated and least visited in the country. There's a ranger station here, with a camping area, limited water and simple toilet facilities. **Border checks** (see box, p.276) are particularly vigilant in this area. As usual, have your passport and all other documents in order.

Just 30km from the border, Murciélago is home to the remains of the training grounds used by the CIA-backed **Contras** during the Nicaraguan civil war. They're overgrown and scrubby today, with no sign that anything was ever there. It was also the location of the famous "secret" airstrip built, on Oliver North's orders, in direct violation of Costa Rica's declared neutrality in the conflict. Originally given the go-ahead by President Alberto Monge, the airstrip was eventually destroyed under President Oscar Arias's subsequent administration – a unilateral action that led to the US reducing its financial and political support for Costa Rica.

Practicalities

Santa Rosa's **entrance hut** is 35km north of Liberia, signed from the Interamericana. After paying the park fee, pick up a map and proceed some 6km or so, taking the right fork to the **administration centre** (ⓣ2666-5051), which also runs Guanacaste and Rincón de la Vieja national parks. As well as checking road conditions and getting your camping/turtle-watching permits, you can visit La Casona and make reservations (at least 3hr in advance) for a simple lunch in the

The great pretender: William Walker

Born in Tennessee in 1824, **William Walker** was something of a child prodigy. By the age of 14 he had a degree from the University of Nashville, notching up further degrees in law and medicine just five years later before setting off to study at various illustrious European universities. However, upon his return to the US, Walker failed in his chosen professions of doctor and lawyer and, somewhat at a loose end, landed up in California in 1849 at the height of the Gold Rush. Here he became involved with the **pro-slavery** organization Knights of the Golden Circle, who financed an expedition, in which Walker took part, to invade Baja California and Mexico to secure more land for the United States. Undeterred by the expedition's failure, Walker soon put his mind to another plan. Intending to make himself overlord of a Central American nation of five slave-owning states, and then to sell the territory to the US, Walker invaded Nicaragua in June 1855 with mercenary troops. The next logical step was to secure territory for the planned eleven-kilometre canal between Lago de Nicaragua and the Pacific. Gaining much of his financial backing from Nicaraguan get-rich-quick militarists and North American capitalists who promptly saw the benefits of a waterway along the Río San Juan from the Pacific to the Atlantic, in 1856 William Walker, and several hundred mercenary troops, invaded Costa Rica from the north.

Meanwhile, Costa Rican president **Juan Rafael Mora** had been watching Walker's progress with increasing alarm and, in February 1856, declared war on the usurper. Lacking military hardware, Costa Rica was ill-prepared for battle, and Mora's rapidly gathered army of nine thousand men was a largely peasant-and-bourgeois band, armed with machetes, farm tools and the occasional rusty rifle. Marching them out of San José through the Valle Central, over the Cordillera de Tilarán and on to the hot plains of Guanacaste, Mora got wind that Walker and his band of three hundred buccaneers were entrenched at the **Santa Rosa Casona**, the largest and best-fortified edifice in the area. Although by now Mora's force was reduced to only 2500 (we can only guess that, in the two weeks that it took them to march from San José, heat exhaustion had left many scattered by the wayside), on March 20, 1856 they routed the filibusters, fighting with their *campesino* tools. Mora then followed Walker and his men on their retreat, engaging them in battle again in Nicaraguan territory, at **Rivas**, some 15km north of the border, where Walker's troops eventually barricaded themselves in another wooden *casona*. It was here – and not, as is commonly thought, at Santa Rosa – that **Juan Santamaría**, a nineteen-year-old drummer boy, volunteered to set fire to the building in which Walker and his men were barricaded, flushing them out, and dying in the process. Walker, however, survived the fire, and carried on filibustering, until in 1857 a US warship was dispatched to put an end to his antics which were increasingly embarrassing for the US government, who had covertly backed him. Undeterred after a three-year spell in a Nicaraguan jail, he continued his adventuring until he was shot dead by the Honduran authorities in September 1860.

Later, Mora, no devotee of democracy himself, rigged the 1859 Costa Rican presidential election so that he could serve a second term – despite his military victories against Walker, there was strong popular opposition to his domestic policies – but he was deposed later that year. He attempted a coup d'état, but was subsequently shot in 1860, the same year that his former adversary met his Waterloo in Honduras.

comedor. The food – *casados* with fish, chicken or meat and salad – is good, and this is a great place to get talking to rangers or other tourists. From here a rough road leads to the beaches; to drive to these, even in the height of the dry season, you need a sturdy 4WD. The administration discourages any driving at all beyond the main park road; nevertheless, people – surfers, mainly – insist on doing so, and survive. Most park their vehicle at the administration centre and walk. One thing is for sure: don't try to drive anywhere in the park (including the Murciélago sector to the north, and the road to Cuajiniquil, detailed on p.279) in the rainy season without asking rangers about the state of the roads. You could get bogged down in mud or stopped by a swollen creek. Before setting off, you can always phone the Area de Conservación de Guanacaste (ACG) headquarters (Ⓣ2666-5051, Spanish only) to check the current state of the roads in the park.

If you're walking down to the beach, a ranger or fellow tourist will probably give you a ride, but on no account set out without **water** – you'll need a couple of litres per person, at least, even on a short jaunt. Particularly convenient are the easy-to-carry bottles of water with plastic handles sold at the petrol stations on the road outside Liberia; stock up before you come. You can also buy drinks, including small bottles of water, at the administration centre.

Camping facilities at Santa Rosa are some of the best in the country. There are two sites, each costing $2 per person, payable as you arrive at the administration centre and valid for the length of your stay. The shady **La Casona** campground has bathrooms and grill pits, while **Playa Naranjo**, on the beach (and only open outside the turtle-nesting season), has picnic tables and grill pits, and a ranger's hut with outhouses and showers, plus, apparently, a boa constrictor in the roof. Wherever you camp, watch your fires (the area is a tinderbox in the dry season), take plastic bags for your food, do not leave anything edible in your tent (it will be stolen by scavenging coati) and, of course, carry plenty of water.

Parque Nacional Guanacaste

Located 36km north of Liberia on the Interamericana, much of **PARQUE NACIONAL GUANACASTE** was not long ago nothing more than cattle pasture. Influential biologist D.H. Janzen, editor of the seminal *Costa Rican Natural History*, who had been involved in field study for many years in nearby Santa Rosa, was instrumental in creating the park virtually from scratch in 1991. Raising over $11 million, mainly from foreign sources, he envisioned creating a kind of biological corridor in which animals, mainly mammals, would have a large enough tract of undisturbed habitat in which to hunt and reproduce.

The **Santa Rosa–Guanacaste** (and, to an extent, Rincón de la Vieja) **corridor** is the result of his work, representing one of the most important efforts to conserve and regenerate tropical **dry forest** in the Americas. Containing tropical wet and dry forests and a smattering of cloudforest, Parque Nacional Guanacaste also protects the **springwell of the Río Tempisque**, as well as the ríos Ahogados and Colorado. More than three hundred species of **birds,** including the orange-fronted parakeet and the white-throated magpie jay, have been recorded, while mammals lurking behind the undergrowth include jaguar, puma, tapir, coati, armadillo, two-toed sloth and deer. It's also thought that there are about five thousand species of moths and **butterflies**, including the giant owl butterfly.

The park is devoted to research rather than tourism, and the administration staff at Santa Rosa (see opposite) discourage casual visitors. There are three main research stations, and it is sometimes possible to stay at them if you show enough

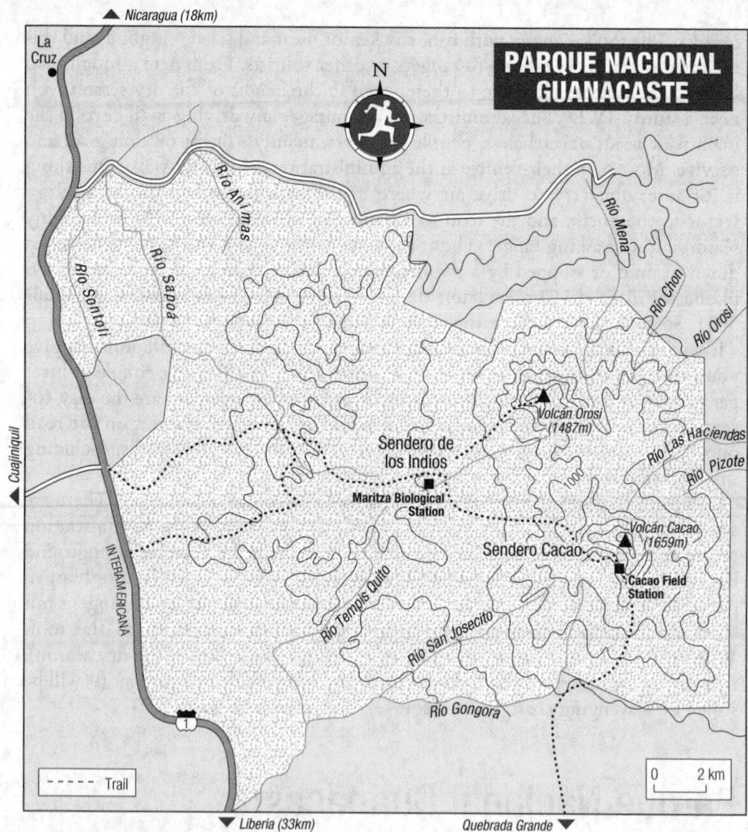

interest and contact the Santa Rosa administration centre well in advance. Apart from the primary rainforest that exists at the upper elevations, the park's highlight is an astonishing collection of **pre-Columbian petroglyphs** at El Pedregal. A trail leads to the site from the Maritza field station.

Practicalities

Facilities at Guanacaste are still minimal. **Access** is very difficult, unless (as usual) you've got a Range Rover or some other tank of a vehicle. The road to Cacao field station, on the slopes of the volcano of the same name, leaves the Interamericana 10km south of the Santa Rosa turn-off. It leads to a hamlet called Potrerillos; once there, head for Quebrada Grande (on some maps called García Flamenco) and continue for about 8km. It's passable most of the way, but the boulders from hell appear 3km from the entrance; at this point you have to ditch non-4WD vehicles and walk. There's very basic **lodge** accommodation of four rooms with a capacity of 32 people max ($20 per person) at Cacao and Maritza field stations. Call the Santa Rosa administration (☎2666-5051) to check if it's open. They'll try to discourage you, so make your interest clear. To reach Maritza station from the Interamericana, take a right turn opposite the left turn-off to Cuajiniquil (see p.279), and continue along the poor road for about 15km. In addition to the path to the petroglyphs, there's also a trail that connects Maritza with Cacao station.

La Cruz, Bahía Salinas and the border

Set on a plateau north of Parque Nacional Guanacaste, overlooking Bahía Salinas and the Pacific Ocean to the west, the tiny, sleepy town of **LA CRUZ** is the last settlement of any size before the border, just 20km away, and makes a reasonable stopover if you're heading up to Nicaragua. The views at sunset are incredible, and there are a couple of good **places to stay** in town, although if you're spending any length of time in the area you'd do better at one of the nearby tourist lodges such as *Finca Cañas Castilla* (Ⓣ8381-4030, Ⓦwww.canas-castilla.com; ❹), a Swiss-run ranch on 150 acres of land alongside the River Sapoa. The farm has several groves of fruit trees, including orange and bananas, while free-range chickens produce fresh eggs daily for guests and the local market. Mainly hilly terrain with thick forests as well as expansive grassland for grazing, the ranch can be explored on horseback – in addition to the livestock you might catch a glimpse of sloths and anteaters. To get to the farm from La Cruz, head north on the Interamericana and turn right after 5km onto an unpaved road which leads to the village of Sonzapote; continue for another 2km from here and you'll see signs to the *finca*.

In La Cruz itself, the quirky *Amalia's Inn* (Ⓣ2679-9181; ❹), about 100m south of the town's Parque Central, has spacious rooms, a pool and a spectacular view over the bay. It's well worth paying extra for a room with a view. Casual, friendly *Cabinas Santa Rita*, across from the courthouse (Ⓣ2679-9062), offers clean, simple rooms with shared or private bath (❸), along with more upmarket, air-conditioned doubles in an annexe at the back (❹); there's also secure parking. **Eating** options aren't so rosy – *La Orquidea* and *Thelma*, on the main road, are the town's best *sodas* though neither is particularly memorable. For more interesting fare, head to one of the hotels out of town or to the *Hotel Bella Vista* near the square, which has a bar, restaurant and fine views. You can check your email at BT, just east of the town square.

Bahía Salinas

To the west of La Cruz a road leads for about 12km to the windswept kitesurfing mecca of **BAHÍA SALINAS**. Prevailing conditions produce gusts throughout the year, but they tend to intensify from November to July which is when the bay sees the most visitors. While the reliable (and often quite forceful) winds attract professional kitesurfers from around the world, it's also a good place for beginners to try their hand at the sport. For **kitesurfing lessons**, the best choice in the bay is the Kitesurfing 2000 School based at the *Blue Dream Hotel* (Ⓣ8826-5221, Ⓦwww.bluedreamhotel.com; ❸), on the left of the approach road to Bahía Salinas. The longest-running school of its kind in the country, it rents all the gear you'll need to get up on the water and provides lessons ranging from hourly ($30; minimum of two people) to a four-day package for $229. *Blue Dream* also has some of the most comfortable **accommodation** on the bay, with nine pleasant rooms and four newer, larger rooms in wooden bungalows with balconies. Its lively on-site **restaurant** serves mostly Mediterranean fare and wood-oven pizzas.

Though most of the pretty bay's **beaches** are predictably windy throughout the year, if you're looking to rest on the sand without having it blown in your face, the most sheltered spot is at **Playa Jobo**, on the bay's southern arm.

Note that much of the road to Bahía Salinas is prone to being mud-laden at certain times of the year; check about the road's condition in La Cruz before setting out.

The Nicaraguan border: Peñas Blancas

Peñas Blancas (7am–8pm daily), the main crossing point into Nicaragua, is emphatically a border post and not a town, with just one or two basic *sodas* and no hotels. Aim to get here as **early** as possible, as procedures are ponderous and you'll be lucky to get through the whole deal in less than ninety minutes. If you come on a Ticabus, things are smoother – all passengers are processed together and have some priority. Both Costa Rican and Nicaraguan border officials are quite strict, and there are many checks to see that your paperwork is in order. Buses on both sides of the border are far more frequent in the morning. If you're arriving from Nicaragua, the last San José-bound bus leaves at 3.30pm (5.30pm Fri–Sun), and the last Liberia bus at 5pm. After that, the only alternative is to take a costly taxi.

Exit stamps are given on the Costa Rican side, where there is a restaurant and a helpful, well-organized Costa Rican **tourist office** (daily 6am–noon & 1–8pm). Money-changers are always on hand and can change colones, *córdobas* and dollars. After getting your Costa Rican exit stamp it's a short walk north to the barrier from where you can get one of the regular shuttle buses ($2), 4km north to the Nicaraguan shantytown of Sapoa, where you go through Nicaraguan *migración*.

An **alternative** way to cross into Nicaragua from Liberia is to take a Peñas Blancas service, then pick up a local bus to **Rivas**, the first Nicaraguan town of any size, 37km beyond the border. This might not be convenient if you are going all the way to Managua, but the formalities are far less cumbersome than on the Tica and SIRCA services. As there's so much regular local traffic and fewer (potentially visa-holding) foreigners on these buses, they are generally processed much more quickly.

The Guanacaste beaches

The **beaches of Guanacaste** are scattered along the rocky coastline that runs from Bahía Culebra in the north near Liberia to Sámara on the west of the Nicoya Peninsula. Few of those in the north could truthfully be called beautiful, and most are quite small, located in coves or sheltered bays that makes them good for swimming, and relatively safe – though they lack the impressive expanse of Playas Flamingo and Tamarindo a bit further down the coast. The waters in the **Bahía Culebra** (marked on some maps as Playa Panamá) are some of the clearest and most sheltered in the country, with good snorkelling.

The landscape of the Nicoya Peninsula is changing rapidly and many of the northern beaches, such as Tamarindo and Playa Panamá, are being aggressively developed for mass tourism. The nearby airport in Liberia exists mainly to service the package and charter market along this coast. Sprawling across nearly the entire Bahía Culebra is the **Papagayo Project**, the country's largest tourist development consisting of hotels, condos, a mall and a golf course.

The signs of mass tourism lessen as you head further south towards **Parque Nacional Marino Las Baulas**, where droves of **leatherback turtles** come ashore to lay their eggs between October and February. The beaches here have drawn foreign expatriates in pursuit of paradise, and these cosmopolitan enclaves are in sharp contrast to the rest of the region, with resorty **Tamarindo** being the top spot for surfing. The beaches of the southern part of the Nicoya Peninsula are covered in the Central Pacific and Southern Nicoya chapter.

It can take a long time to get to the Guanacaste coast from San José (4–5hr minimum, unless you fly) and in some places you feel very remote indeed. **Getting around** can take time, too, as the beaches tend to be separated by rocky headlands or otherwise impassable formations, with barren hilly outcroppings coming right down to the sea, carving out little coves and bays, but necessitating considerable backtracking inland to get from one to the other. Although bus connections with the capital are good, travelling from beach to beach on the peninsula by **bus** is tricky, and you'll have to ask locals to figure out the peninsular services, whose schedules are not formally published, but which locals will know. By far the most popular option is to **rent a car**, which allows you to beach-hop with relative ease. Roads are not bad, if somewhat potholed – you'll do best with a **4WD**, though this can prove expensive. Another possibility for couples or small groups is to **hitch**, as there's a fair amount of tourist traffic around here.

Bahía Culebra

Sheltered from the full force of the Pacific, the clear blue waters around **Bahía Culebra** boast some of the best beaches in the country for swimming and snorkelling. The calm waters quietly lap at the grey volcanic sands of **Playa Panamá**, the northernmost beach of the bay. Unusually for this dry, hot zone of Guanacaste, **Playa Hermosa**, on the southern edge of the bay, is blessed with soothing shade, calm waters and gorgeous sunset views of the Pacific and offshore islets (be aware that there are two beaches named Playa Hermosa in Costa Rica – the other is farther south in Puntarenas). If you want to go **diving** off Playa Hermosa, contact the family-run Diving Safaris (Ⓣ2672-1259, Ⓦwww.costaricadiving.net), next door to *Hotel Playa Hermosa Bosque del Mar*, for trips or lessons; they also lead snorkelling tours and rent equipment.

Arrival

Both Panamá and Hermosa beaches are easily accessible by **car** from Liberia. Take the turn-off to the right just after the hamlet of Comunidad – signposted to Playas Hermosa, Panamá and Coco – and continue for several kilometres over the good paved road. There's another turn-off to Hermosa and Panamá on the right. Five daily **buses** head from Liberia to Playa Hermosa and Playa Panamá. From San José, there's also a direct daily bus to the two beaches (5hr) at the ungodly hour of 3.25am, returning at 5am.

Accommodation

Bahía Culebra is dotted with upmarket **hotels**, many of them Italian run.

La Finisterra Up a steep dirt road off the southern access road to Playa Hermosa Ⓣ2672-0227, Ⓦwww.lafinisterra.com. A charming, small hotel with a superb setting on the cliff at the southern end of the beach. Enjoy stunning sunset views, a swimming pool and warm hospitality. The excellent restaurant offers tasty international dishes (see p.286) and breakfast is included in the price. ❼

Hilton Papagayo Resort At the end of the Playa Panamá beach road Ⓣ2672-0000, Ⓦwww.hilton.com. Plush all-inclusive complex that has just about everything you might need plus quite a bit more, this unabashedly over-the-top hotel has an infinity pool, spa, fitness centre and several restaurants and bars. The rooms and bungalows are elegantly furnished with a minimalist design and have a wide range of amenities. ❾

Hotel Giardini di Papagayo On a plateau overlooking Playa Hermosa Ⓣ2672-0067. Well-located hotel offering immaculate rooms decorated in the Californian-Spanish colonial style favoured by upmarket hoteliers hereabouts. Rates include all meals, but you pay extra for sea views. Free snorkelling and kayaking trips are included. ❼

Hotel Playa Hermosa Bosque del Mar On Playa Hermosa Ⓣ2672-0046, Ⓦwww.hotelplayahermosa.com. Situated in a great spot right on the beach, with lush gardens featuring hundred-year-old trees near a large swimming pool with jacuzzi. This hotel is owned and managed by Ticos offering old-fashioned hospitality, with a beachfront restaurant that's also open to non-residents. Rooms have hot water, a/c, and cable TV. ❽

Iguana Inn On the northern access road to Playa Hermosa Ⓣ2672-0065,

Ⓦwww.playahermosahotel.com. A stone's throw from the beach, this pleasant budget option has simple, colourful rooms with fan and small hot-water bathrooms. There's also a swimming pool and a well-equipped shared kitchen. ❷

Occidental Grand Papagayo Off the northern access road to Playa Hermosa ⓣ2672-0191. An all-inclusive gated property with two lovely pools, a handful of posh restaurants and bars and a fitness centre. The rooms, some of which have ocean views, are decorated with muted colours and dark-wood furniture and have a/c, cable TV and safes; all have balconies. ❾

El Velero Off the northern access road to Playa Hermosa ⓣ2672-1017, Ⓦwww.costaricahotel.net. Friendly hotel with split-level rooms with balconies. Enjoy sea views from the lovely gardens that are filled with birds and lizards; a short path leads from the hotel down to the beach. There's also a good restaurant and a small pool.

Eating

Bistro Restaurant *La Finisterra* (see p.285). Creatively prepared dishes like ceviche and beef tenderloin and an impressive wine list in an elegant setting. It's less expensive than you might expect, and the views of the Pacific are spectacular.

Ginger On the main road, 2km inland from Playa Hermosa ⓣ2672-0041. Chrome, glass and sharp angles cantilevered in the hills, *Ginger* is popular with the trendy expat community. The menu consists of a diverse range of Asian-fusion/Mediterranean-inspired small plates designed for sharing. Tapas galore is on offer, but don't look for *comida típica* here. Open Tues–Sun.

Pescado Loco Opposite *El Velero* (see above). For the best cheap eats, head to this low-key restaurant where freshly caught fish costs $8–10, and roast chicken is $7.

Playa del Coco

Some 35km west of Liberia, with good road connections, booming **Playa del Coco** was the first Pacific beach to hit it big with weekending Costa Ricans from the Valle Central. The beach itself is nothing special, but it's kept clean by rubbish-collecting brigades organized by local residents, and the town's accessibility and budget accommodation make it a useful base to explore the better beaches nearby. It also has many good restaurants, all within walking distance, and is a good place from which to take a snorkelling or diving tour.

Arrival and acccommodation

A direct **bus** (5hr) leaves San José for Coco three times daily at 8am, 2pm and 4pm, returning at 4am, 8am and 2pm. You can also get to Coco on nine daily local services from Liberia (1hr).

Coco has plenty of fairly basic **cabinas**, catering to weekending nationals and tourists. In the high season you should **reserve** at weekends, but you can probably get away with turning up on spec midweek, when rooms may also be a little cheaper. In the low season bargains abound. There's **camping** ($4) at *Chopin* (ⓣ2391-5998), on the road heading right 100m before the beach.

B&B Villa del Sol 1km north of the village; turn right off the main road 150m before the beach ⓣ8301-8848, Ⓦwww.villadelsol.com. Small, welcoming hotel in a quiet location with rooms set around a large plain grassy space – all have private bath with hot water and ocean views. Pleasantly decorated by the friendly French-Canadian owners, the hotel also has a large pool and tasty meals. ❺

Casa Vista Azul On a hill about 4km from the beach ⓣ2670-0678, Ⓦwww.hotelvistaazul.com. Small boutique hotel with seven compact rooms that have a/c, ceiling fans, safe-deposit boxes, private baths and a magnificent ocean view. Breakfast included. ❻

Hotel Coco Palms On the beach, next to the football pitch ⓣ2670-0367, Ⓦwww.hotelcoco palms.com. Like a motel in style, but nice and clean with a gringo vibe. It's Coco's only sushi spot, with wi-fi, a bookswap and the *Lazy Frog* sports bar on site. ❻

Pato Loco Inn On the road coming into town, about 300m before the village ⓣ2670-0145. The "Crazy Duck" offers nice airy rooms with private bath and fan (❹) or a/c (❺) – along with cordial, personal treatment. There are a couple of long-stay apartments with kitchen, as well as internet access for guests.

La Puerta del Sol Off the road leading to the right 100m before you reach the beach ⓣ2670-0195, ⓦwww.lapuertadelsolcostarica.com. Friendly Italian-run retreat set in quiet gardens; rooms have a/c, phone and cable TV and a small terrace and lounge area. The thoughtfully arranged complex has a pool, gym and the *Sol y Luna* restaurant (see p.288) serving top-notch Italian food. Breakfast is included in the price. ❻

Rancho Armadillo On a hill about 5km from the beach ⓣ2670-0108, ⓦwww.ranchoarmadillo.com. Run by an easy-going American former chef, this stunning hilltop estate with centuries-old sculptures spread throughout the grounds is quite unlike anything else in the area. The rooms are exceedingly comfortable, well appointed and decorated with striking wood furnishings, the communal areas invite extended lingering, the pool is beautiful and the views of the Pacific are unmatched. That said, what truly makes the place memorable is the care and attention of the staff, who make you feel right at home. ❽

The Town

El Coco town spreads out right in front of the beach, with a tiny **parquecito** as the focal point. The minimal services include a miniscule **post office** (Mon–Fri 7.30am–5pm) and public **telephones** on either side of the park. The Banco Nacional, on the main road as you enter town, will change dollars and travellers' cheques and has an **ATM**. **Taxis** gather by the little park on the beach. There's **internet** access at *Leslie's*, and a good supermarket, Luperón, next to the Banco Nacional.

Playa del Coco is a popular **snorkelling** and **diving** centre: the staff at Rich Coast Diving (ⓣ2670-0176, ⓦwww.richcoastdiving.com), on the main road about 300m from the beach, speak English, organize snorkelling and scuba trips ($50–80 for a two-tank dive) and rent out mountain bikes. Across the street in the precinct of the *Coco Beach* hotel, another good option, Deep Blue Diving (ⓣ2670-1004, ⓦwww.deepblue-diving.com) runs similar trips.

Eating, drinking and nightlife

Coco has two very distinct types of places to **eat and drink**: those catering to Ticos and those that attempt a cosmopolitan vibe to hook the gringos. There's a lively **nightlife** – over two dozen bars and nightclubs rock through the night. Much of it emanates from the *Lizard Lounge* and *Zouk Santana* on the main street, two bars with plenty of cocktails, shooters and moody bass beats. A little further up the street is *Banana Surf*, an upstairs bar with a balcony. *Coconuz* is a sports bar with free wi-fi and a lovely little pond where turtles swim. At weekends, the *Cocomar Discoteca* by the beach gets hopping Tico-style. A quietish but atmospheric bar is *La Vida Loca*, reached across a narrow footbridge 100m south of the park – look for the flashing cross.

Andre's Beach Bar Opposite *Zouk Santana*. A low-key spot favoured by expats. It's not on the beach, but still worth a stop for filling, Chicago-style hot dogs and decent pizzas. Daily 8am–late.

Bar Coco Opposite the *parquecito*. A popular place in a prime position, *Bar Coco* offers good seafood lunches and dinners or just a beer in the evening.

Lizard Lounge On the main road, 100m before the beach, on the right. Relaxing bar and restaurant serving Tico fare and Western burgers and steaks – all at reasonable prices. It's a pleasant spot to grab a snack, chill out listening to music or catch the latest sporting events and news on the big screen. Daily 4pm–2am.

Las Olas On the main road, about 100km before the beach, on the right. Newish restaurant serving some of the best food in town, including salads and chicken and pasta dishes. The speciality is fish and seafood – don't miss the stuffed red snapper ($15). Open daily for lunch and dinner.

Papagayo On the main drag, 100m before the beach. If it's fresh and available, you'll find it on the menu at Coco's best seafood restaurant, run by the family of the big shot of the local fishing fleet. The "catch of the day" will set you back $7, while a delectable mixed seafood platter comes in at $15. The fish is prepared in a wide variety of styles, but the quality is consistently excellent. Daily noon–10pm.

Sol y Luna In the *Puerta del Sol* hotel (see p.287). An attractive and intimate setting where you can sample expertly prepared Italian food, including home-made pasta seasoned with herbs. The owners make a big effort to import authentic ingredients, and there's also a decent wine selection. Mains dishes are $8–10. Wed–Mon 5–10pm.

Tequila Bar On the main road, near the *parquecito*. Although the building looks a little ramshackle, the Mexican food here is high quality. Filling plates start at $5 and the Mexican owner extends a warm welcome to diners. Daily noon–11pm.

La Vida Loca On the beach south of the main road just past the wooden pedestrian bridge. Popular with expats, this American-owned beachfront bar with a buxom mermaid out front is a good spot for an afternoon drink and can get pretty lively when most other places close for the night. Open for lunch until late.

Zouk Santana On the main road, near the *parquecito. The* place to eat, drink and dance in Coco. With a fresh vibe and somewhat upmarket style, *Zouk* is a good stop for aperitifs, and a smoke at the cigar bar. Doors open 7am every morning, when they serve lavish breakfasts of brioches, muffins and cappuccino or espresso. There's even a gift shop. Daily 5pm–2am.

Playa Ocotal

Past the rocky headland south of Coco, the upmarket enclave of **PLAYA OCOTAL** is reached by taking the signed turn-off to the left 200m before reaching the beach at Coco. Ocotal and its surroundings have lovely views over the ocean and across to the Papagayo Gulf from the top of the headland, and the small beach is better for swimming than Coco, but the real attractions are the marlin and other "big game" fish that glide through these waters: many of Ocotal's **hotels** are often tied in with sports-fishing packages.

Most of the big hotel resorts have their own **restaurants**, but a popular local choice is *Father Rooster Bar and Grill* on the beach (Ⓣ2670-1246), where you can try tasty dishes such as fish tacos and shrimp kebabs, at reasonable prices served by fun staff. To get there, pass Ocotal's gate, then take the first right and continue to the end: open till 10pm.

Accommodation

Bahia Pez Vela Follow the sign to *Ocotal Beach Resort* off the main road, and after 1km you'll see another sign for *Bahía Pez Vela* Ⓣ2670-0129, Ⓦwww.bahiapezvela.com. Upmarket resort with forty two-storey villas, in beautiful grounds with two pools, a wading pool, and a gorgeous lawn area above a nice private beach ideal for swimming. The bar and restaurant *Picante* is open-air, casual and by the pool, but pricey by local standards. ❾

Ocotal Beach Resort Signposted on the turn-off from the road to Playa del Coco Ⓣ2670-0321, Ⓦwww.ocotalresort.com. Set on top of a hill, this top-end hotel has stunning views over the Pacific and elegantly furnished rooms with TV, hammocks, a/c and fridges. In addition to sports-fishing packages, it also offers tennis, swimming and scuba-diving packages. ❼

Villa Casa Blanca Signposted off the road to *Ocotal Beach Resort* Ⓣ2670-0448, Ⓦwww.hotelvillacasablanca.com. A small, quiet and very accommodating B&B that offers boat tours, deep-sea fishing, scuba diving to the Islas Murciélagos near Santa Rosa, and horseriding trips. The Spanish-style villas feature colourful and bright canopy beds. There's a charming bridged pool, a tennis court in the grounds and rates include breakfast. No restaurant, however. ❼

Playas Flamingo, Brasilito, Potrero and Conchal

Despite its name, there are no flamingoes at the upmarket and expensive gringo enclave of **PLAYA FLAMINGO**, a place that feels more Cancún than Costa Rica – some of the big beach houses lining the white sands are owned by the odd movie star. It does, however, have the best beach on this section of the coast, with white sand, gentle breakers and picturesque rocky islets offshore. There's also great

Adventure travel

With its two coastlines, smoking volcanoes, mountainous backbone, dripping-wet jungles, churning rivers and wildlife-rich offshore islands, Costa Rica naturally lends itself to outdoor adventures. This tiny country certainly knows how to make the most of what it's got, and while nature provides the setting, adventure-tour outfitters provide the means – kitting you out, strapping you in and sending you on the ride of your life, be it bungee jumping, white-water rafting, surfing or

Monteverde is the home of zip-lining in Costa Rica ▲

Leap from a bridge over the Río Colorado ▼

Rafting on the Pacauré near Turrialba ▼

Flights of fancy

The most ubiquitous of Costa Rica's outdoor thrills is the **zip-line** or **canopy tour** – an adrenaline-fuelled flight above the jungle canopy. Zip-lining started in the cloudforests around **Monteverde** (see p.323) – and with half a dozen operators, this is still the place to experience Costa Rica's longest, fastest and highest rides – but nowadays, it seems that every one-*pulpería* town has a zip-wire operator; **La Fortuna** alone has five different canopy tours (see p.220). No matter where in the country you zip, they all essentially subscribe to the same formula: using gloved hands to apply pressure to the cables, you can control the speed you zip, creating a ride that can be as hair-raising or as leisurely as you want.

If zip-lining brings out your inner Tarzan/Jane, you might want to move things up a notch in the terror stakes and try **bungee jumping**, from a bridge over the **Río Colorado** (see p.134), or leaping from a lofty platform with full-frontal views of the **Pacific Ocean** (see p.359).

Riding the rapids

White-water rafting and **kayaking** are among the few outdoor adventure activities that actually improve during the rainy season. Costa Rica's rivers flow between jungle-flanked banks and sheer mountain gorges, offering rides as beautiful as they are exhilarating. There are runs to suit all skill levels, with floats your grandmother could happily sip a cup of tea on without spilling a drop, and others that will make you squeal for mercy as you battle wall upon wall of sheer white foam. The star of Costa Rica's rivers is the Valle Central's **Río Pacuaré** (see p.162), though the **Río Sarapiquí** (see p.252), near La Virgen, is growing in popularity.

reserve, created in 1995 to protect the nesting grounds of the critically endangered **leatherback turtles**, which come ashore here to nest from November to February. Leatherbacks have probably laid their eggs at **Playa Grande** for millions of years, and it's now one of the few remaining such nesting sites in the world. The beach itself offers a beautiful sweep of light-coloured sand, and outside laying season you can surf and splash around in the waves, though swimming is rough, plagued by crashing waves and riptides. Despite its proximity to an officially protected area, developers have been given carte blanche to build at Playa Grande: the *Rancho Las Colinas Golf and Country Club*, which includes an eighteen-hole golf course and over two hundred separate villas, is symptomatic of the lack of planning, the short-termism and the plain daftness (the golf course is located in an area with a long, hot dry season and a history of water shortages) that characterizes so much recent tourist development in Costa Rica. What effect the development will have on the ancient nesting ground of the turtles remains to be seen.

Getting to the park

There are two official entrances to Playa Grande, though **tickets** to enter the reserve can only be bought at the southern entrance, where the road enters the park near the *Villa Baula* (see below). Playa Grande has in the past been a magnet for tour groups from upmarket Guanacaste hotels as well as day-trippers from Tamarindo and Coco. Nowadays, however, visitor numbers are regulated and you are no longer allowed to walk on the beach during nesting season (get the rangers to tell you stories of what people used to do to harass the turtles and you'll see why).

There are no bus services to the park. To **drive to Las Baulas**, take the road from Huacas to Matapalo, and turn left at the football field (a 4WD is recommended for this stretch during the wet season). Most people, however, visit the park by **boat** from Tamarindo, entering at the southern end rather than from the Matapalo road.

Accommodation

Although most visitors to Las Baulas stay in Tamarindo, a few kilometres to the south, you'll find several excellent **hotels** at Playa Grande.

Bula Bula At the southern end of the Playa Grande ⓣ2653-0975, ⓦwww.hotelbulabula.com. In a splendid setting between Playa Grande and the river that runs behind the beach, this brightly coloured hotel offers ten rooms, plus some bungalows (sleeping 4–6), all with wi-fi, a/c and cable TV. Excursions include kayaking, sport-fishing, horseriding and mountain biking. The restaurant serves fantastic food, particularly the large continental and Costa Rican breakfasts (included in the room rate). ❼

Las Tortugas Hotel Centre of Playa Grande ⓣ2653-0423, ⓦwww.lastortugashotel.com. The area's longest established hotel, with pool, restaurant and luxurious a/c rooms and suites. The conscientious owners have kept the light the hotel reflects onto the beach to a minimum (turtle hatchlings are confused by light coming from land), and designed the building so that it will block light from any future developments to the north. They also rent surfboards, can advise on turtle tours and horseriding and have hillside apartments available for extended stays. ❹

Villa Baula South end of Playa Grande ⓣ2653-0493, ⓦwww.hotelvillabaula.com. Nestled among the trees on the beach, *Villa Baula* has comfortable seaside rooms with ceiling fans, plus some attractive private bungalows, all with private bath and hot water (some also have a fridge). There are two lovely pools in the grounds and a good restaurant serving Indonesian and international dishes. ❺

Turtle nesting

Turtle nesting takes place only in season and at **night**, with moonlit nights at high tide being the preferred moment. Note that you are not guaranteed to see a nesting turtle on any given night, and it's definitely worth calling in at El Mundo de la Tortuga (see p.292) before your visit, both to see the informative exhibition

Surf's up

Surfers are spoilt for choice in Costa Rica. There are reef breaks and point breaks, beach breaks and rivermouths, and with two coastlines to choose from, waves are usually pummelling in fast and furious on at least one front. Costa Rica is the ideal place for beginners to find their feet: there are a plethora of surf schools with English-speaking instructors and the warm ocean means wetsuits are never necessary. As for the **best places to catch a wave**? Well, serious surfers would never divulge such secrets, but **Playa Naranjo** (or Witch's Rock; see p.295) has one of the finest breaks in the country, and there is usually plenty of action at **Playa Hermosa** (see p.360) and **Playa Dominical** (see p.390), with some of the best consistency on the Pacific coast.

Alternative adventures

▸▸ Windsurf on Laguna Arenal Consistent winds and a number of local outfitters make this vast lake the best place in the country to try your hand at windsurfing. See p.233

▸▸ Abseil into a ravine Strap in for a heart-stopping series of rappels (some down waterfalls) in a gushing canyon near La Fortuna. See p.220

▸▸ Go caving Grab a torch and get down and dirty among the bats and bugs in the cavernous chambers of Parque Nacional Barra Honda. See p.310

▸▸ Climb a volcano Skirt the lava flows of the western hemisphere's most active volcano on a hiking tour of Parque Nacional Volcán Arenal. See p.227

▸▸ Saddle up with a cowboy Grab your horse and ride with the *sabaneros* across the flat, open landscapes of Guanacaste. See p.259

▲ Mal País is a popular surf spot

▼ Explore the bat-filled caves of Barra Honda

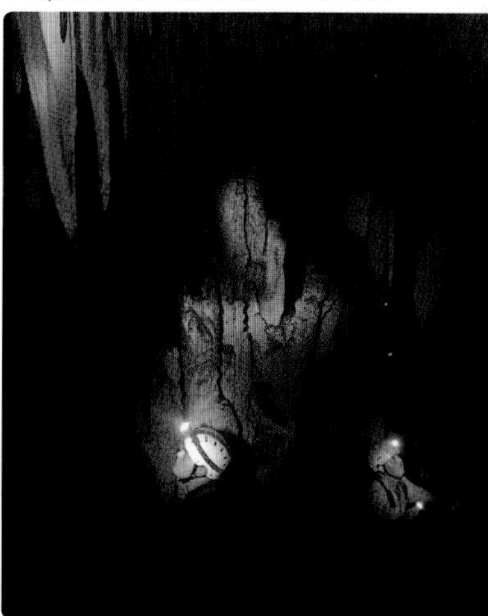

▼ Abseiling near La Fortuna

Swimming with sharks ▲

Tropical fish off the Isla del Coco ▼

Hiking on Cerro Chirripó, the country's highest peak ▼

Snorkelling and diving

Snorkelling and diving are gaining in popularity in Costa Rica, with tour operators taking advantage of the country's abundant coral reefs, marine wildlife, tropical fish and mysterious shipwrecks. On the **Caribbean coast**, Parque Nacional Cahuita (see p.199) and the Refugio Nacional de Vida Silvestre Gandoca-Manzanillo (see p.209) are within striking distance of impressive coral reefs; on the **Pacific coast**, Parque Nacional Marino Ballena (see p.394) protects a large tract of coral reef and is coming into its own as a diving destination. Some 535km off the mainland, the incredible **Isla del Coco** (see p.337) is one of the world's most exclusive **scuba-diving** destinations, offering diving on an entirely different scale altogether: a subterranean world of hammerhead and white-tipped reef sharks, green turtles, grouper and manta rays.

Take a hike

Costa Rica's extensive network of national parks means **hikers** have no shortage of places to muddy their boots. The classic ain't-no-mountain-high-enough trek is to **Cerro Chirripó** (see p.386), a steep 16km ascent through the ever-changing scenery of the Talamanca cordillera, which, if you time it right, culminates in a breathtaking sunrise at the top. In Guanacaste, the tropical dry forest of **Parque Nacional Santa Rosa** (see p.217) is a favourite haunt for hikers and campers alike, while for off-the-beaten-track rainforest adventures, try a multi-day trek in the outer reaches of the **Bosque Eterno do Los Niños** (see p.326) or in **Parque Nacional Corcovado** on the Osa Peninsula (see p.408), where rainforest paths traverse shark-infested rivers, wildlife-rich jungle and picture-perfect beaches.

sports-fishing: almost all the resort-style hotels in the area cater to siasts or sun-worshippers on packages. It's approached via the road unappealing **PLAYA BRASILITO**, a scruffy beach with darkish sa about 5km before Playa Flamingo's marina.

To escape the rather static and standoffish atmosphere of Flaming north to **PLAYA POTRERO**, a small cove that opens onto a dec shaped beach whose calm waters are good for swimming.

The most southerly of the four beaches, **PLAYA CONCHAL** ("Sh set in a steep broad bay a couple of kilometres south of Playa Brasilit by a rocky headland, it has appealing pink-coloured sand, with mo shells and quiet waters that are good for swimming and snorkelling.

Arrival

To reach the beaches by **car**, take the Liberia–Nicoya road to Belén right off the main road and follow a side road to the hamlet of Hu beyond Belén, from where the beaches are signposted. From San José, T direct **buses** to Flamingo (3 daily; 5hr). There are also two buses daily Cruz (see p.298) to Brasilito, Flamingo and Potrero beaches arriving e morning or mid-afternoon. To get to Conchal from Flamingo, yo backtrack inland, turning right at the village of Matapalo. It's quicke along the sand from Brasilito, but you'll need a 4WD or a tug-of-war t

Accommodation

The majority of the decent **accommodation** options are in Playa Flam prices tend to be less than you might expect. Alternatively, you can **ca** relaxed *Mayra's* (Ⓣ2654-4213; $5) right on the seashore in Playa Potrero

Bahia Esmeralda Playa Flamingo Ⓣ2654-4480, Ⓦwww.hotelbahiaesmeralda.com. Friendly and tranquil Italian-run option with rooms located in a complex of cabins, plus a large pool and a small restaurant. ❹

Cabinas Cristina Playa Potrero Ⓣ2654-4006, Ⓦwww.cabinascristina.com. Bright, comfortable rooms and apartments with a/c, cable TV and wi-fi. There's a pool, and the helpful owners rent boats and can arrange tours. ❺

Flamingo Beach Resort Playa Flamingo Ⓣ2654-4444, Ⓦwww.resortflamingobeach.com. Large, fairly characterless hotel though it boasts a pretty setting across from the beach, a good pool, a restaurant and bar, a casino, spa and spacious rooms. The hotel can arrange charter flights and will pick you up from the airstrip. ❽

Flamingo Marina Resort Playa Flamingo Ⓣ2654-4141, Ⓦwww.flamingomarina.com. A popular resort that has modern rooms as well as enormous suites with jacuzzis. There are several pools, a tennis court, restaurant, lively bar and tour service. ❼

Hotel Brasilito Playa Brasilito Ⓣ2654-4 Ⓦwww.brasilito.com. The best budget o area and right on the beach. The 17 spac are sparsely furnished but with large bed hot-water bathrooms. The hotel rents kay $10 per day, and its reasonably priced *Pe* restaurant serves typical regional fare as v more eclectic choices such as Thai curries

Hotel Paradisus Conchal Playa Conchal Ⓣ2654-4123, Ⓦwww.solmelia.com. Set b from the beach between Playas Brasilito a Conchal is this plush Spanish-owned touris complex, whose arrival dramatically chang character of the area from a sleepy low-key community to an exclusive resort boasting hundreds of suites and a golf course. ❾

Mariner Inn Playa Flamingo Ⓣ2654-4081. the cheaper options in Playa Flamingo with 1 clean a/c rooms. It's a pleasant spot to hang especially at the appealing bar, named *Sprea* where fishermen's tall tales are swapped ove beers and tasty burgers. ❹

Parque Nacional Marino Las Baulas

On the Río Matapalo estuary between Conchal and Tamarindo, **PARQ NACIONAL MARINO LAS BAULAS** (daily 9am–4pm, open for guided ni tours in season; $10, including tour; Ⓣ2653-0470) is less a national park tha

The leatherback turtle

Leatherback turtles (in Spanish, *baulas*) are giant creatures. Often described as a relic from the age of the dinosaurs, they're also one of the oldest animals on earth, having existed largely unchanged for 120 million years. The leatherback's most arresting characteristic is its sheer size, reaching a length of about 2.4m and a weight of 500kg. Its front flippers are similarly huge – as much as 2.7m long – and it's these which propel the leatherback on its long-distance migrations (they're known to breed off the West Indies, Florida, the northeastern coast of South America, Senegal, Madagascar, Sri Lanka and Malaysia). Leatherbacks are also unique among turtles in having a skeleton that is not firmly attached to a shell, but which consists of a **carapace** made up of hundreds of irregular bony plates, covered with a leathery skin. It's also the only turtle that can regulate its own body temperature, maintaining a constant 18°C even in the freezing ocean depths, and withstanding immense pressures of over 1500 pounds per square inch as it dives to depths of up to 1200m.

Since the 1973 Convention on the International Trade of Endangered Species, it is illegal to harvest green, hawksbill, leatherback and loggerhead turtles. Unlike olive ridleys or hawksbills, leatherbacks are not hunted by humans for food – their flesh has an unpleasantly oily taste – though poachers still steal eggs for their alleged aphrodisiac powers. Even so, leatherbacks still face many human-created hazards. They can choke on discarded plastic bags left floating in the ocean (which they mistake for jellyfish, on which they feed), and often get caught in longline fishing nets or wounded by boat propellers – all added to a loss of nesting habitats caused by beachfront development and the fact that, even in normal conditions, only one in every 2500 leatherback hatchlings makes it to maturity.

The number of nesting females at Las Baulas alone dropped from 1646 in 1988 to 215 in 1997, although numbers have since increased to over 800. At Las Baulas, authorities have established a hatchling "farm" to allow hatchlings to be born and make their trip to the ocean under less perilous conditions than would normally prevail, though this will not affect adult mortality, which is believed to be the root cause of the drop in leatherback numbers. While the population is healthier than it was fifteen years ago, it continues to be plagued by longline fishing, large-scale rubbish dumping, ocean contamination and other factors contributing to fertility problems.

If you're interested in **volunteering**, Earthwatch (Ⓦwww.earthwatch.org) have run conservation holidays on Playas Grande and Langosta for a number of years, documenting numbers of nesting turtles and their activity patterns.

and to ask if tides and weather are favourable for nesting – alternatively you could ask the rangers at the entrance hut.

Those who see a nesting are often moved both by the sight of the turtles' imposing bulk, and also by their vulnerability, as they lever themselves up on to the beach. Each female can nest up to twelve times per season, laying a hundred or so eggs at a time, before finally returning to the sea – after which she won't touch land again for another year. Eggs take about sixty days to hatch, and the female turtle **hatchlings** that make the journey from their eggs to the ocean down this beach will (if they survive) return here ten to fifteen years later to nest themselves.

While it's worth seeing a nesting, it's difficult not to feel like an intruder. Groups of up to fifteen people are led to each turtle by guides (some of them "rehabilitated" former poachers), who communicate via walkie-talkie – and if it's a busy night there might be several tour groups after the same turtle. When the guide locates a turtle ready to lay her eggs you trudge in a group along the beach and then stand around watching the leatherback go through her procreative duty, while from time to time the turtle will cast a world-weary glance in the direction of her fans. It's hard not to think it would be better for the turtle if everyone just stayed away and bought the video, although the viewing is well managed and fairly considerate, and the revenue does help to protect the turtles' habitat.

El Mundo de la Tortuga

Around 200m from the park entrance, the impressive and educational **El Mundo de la Tortuga** exhibition (daily 2–6pm, or until much later when turtles are nesting; $5; ⓣ2653-0471) includes an audio-guided tour in English and some stunning photographs of the turtles. You'll gain an insight into the leatherbacks' habitats and reproductive cycles, along with the threats they face, and current conservation efforts. There's also a souvenir shop and a small café where groups on turtle tours are often asked to wait while a nesting turtle is located. It's open late at night – often past midnight – depending on demand and nesting times.

Playa Tamarindo

Perennially popular **Tamarindo** stretches for a couple of kilometres over a series of rocky headlands, and attracts surfers and holiday spring-breakers. Sprawling and occasionally snobby, **TAMARINDO** village boasts a decent selection of restaurants, a lively beach culture (think beautiful young things parading up and down the sand) and a healthy nightlife, at least during high season. Many come here to learn to surf – indeed, the gentle breakers are an ideal training ground – or simply to laze on the beach, which is undeniably gorgeous. Tamarindo is the least Costa Rican of places, with locals completely outnumbered by tourists and expats. Even by its own trendy terms, the village is booming, with small complexes of shops springing up in the concrete mini-mall-style favoured hereabouts, while internet cafés, flashy restaurants and estate agents colonize the centre of the village, as foreigners rush in to snap up their plots in paradise.

Arrival, information and transport

You can **fly** into Tamarindo on NatureAir and Sansa, both of which have offices in town; **buses** arrive by the village loop at the end of the main road. This loop effectively constitutes Tamarindo's small centre and is lined by restaurants, New -Age jewellery stalls and surf shops. There are many **banks** in town, several with ATMs, and you'll be hard-pressed to find anywhere that doesn't accept dollars as currency. There are **public telephones** at the loop and several **internet cafés** (around $2 per hour), including Tamarindo.Net at the junction north of the loop. The Supermercado Tamarindo and Supermercado Pelicano

Moving on from Tamarindo

All buses leave from the bus stop at the village loop, with three daily heading **to San José**, departing at 3am, 5.30am and 7am (6hr), and six daily to **Liberia** (1hr 30min). To head further south down the peninsula, take one of the six daily buses **to Santa Cruz** (1hr), where you can link up with buses to Sámara or Nosara. As always, bus timetables are likely to change.

Interbus is also a useful option that runs daily to destinations all over the country ($36 to San José; $30 to Monteverde; $50 to Manuel Antonio) and will pick you up from your hotel in the morning. It can be reserved through various agents in town.

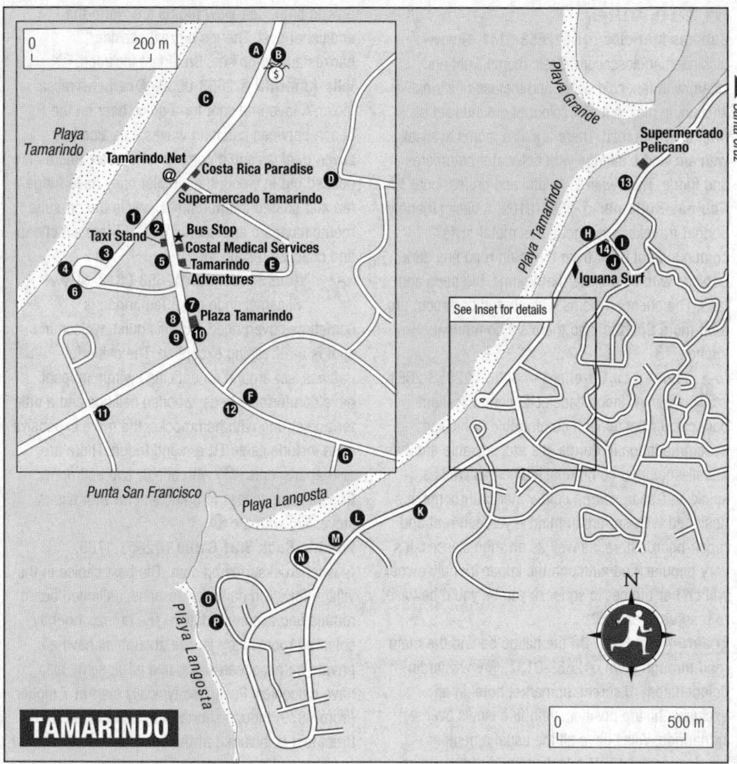

ACCOMMODATION

B&B Casa Sueca	N	Hostel La Botella de Leche	G
B&B Sueño del Mar	O	El Jardín del Eden	D
B&B Villa Alegre	P	El Milagro	I
Cabinas El Mono Loco	K	Pasatiempo	F
Cabinas Marielos	B	Tamarindo Diría	C
Cabinas Rodamar	J	Villa Amarilla	A
Capitán Suizo	M	Villas Macondo	E
Casa Cook	L	Witch's Rock Surf Camp	H

EATING AND DRINKING

Babylon	5	Lazy Wave	10
Buon Appetito	1	Nougi's	4
Capitán Suizo	M	The Oasis	F
Falafel Mundo	9	Pachanga	12
Frutas Tropicales	14	Sunset Lounge	6
El Jardín del Eden	D	Voodoo Lounge	7
Kahiki	11	Walter's	3
La Laguna del Cocodrilo	13	Wok and Roll	8
		Zullymar	2

sell basic foodstuffs, and you can wash clothes at Lavandería Mariposa by Iguana Surf. For **medical attention**, contact Coastal Medical Services (Ⓣ2653-0611 or 2653-1974).

For getting around the area, and out to Playa Langosta, the beach just south of the village, you could **rent a scooter** or **mountain bike** from Costa Rica Paradise (see box, p.296) among other places. Several places **rent cars**, including Economy and Alamo, both on the main road at the northern entrance to the village. **Taxis** congregate on the loop across from the bus stop.

Accommodation

Many of Tamarindo's **hotels** are very good, if expensive. Playa Langosta's upmarket **B&Bs** and hotels offer a retreat from the sometimes hectic Tamarindo beachside scene, and are a fifteen- to twenty-minute walk from the heart of the action.

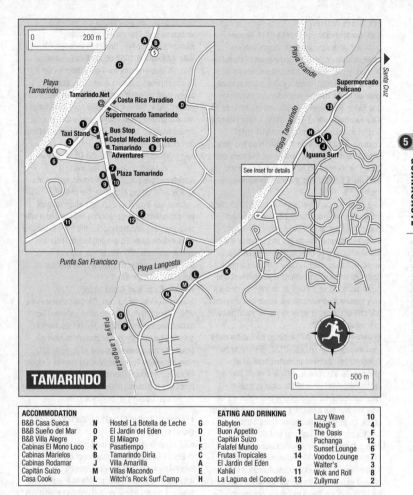

In the village

Cabinas Marielos ⓣ&ⓕ2653-0141, ⓦwww.cabinasmarieloscr.com. Basic rooms, light and clean, with fan, cold water and the use of a small kitchen, in pleasant and colourful grounds set back from the main road. There are also rooms available with a/c, and a handful with hot-water bathrooms and fridge. The owner is helpful and professional. ❸

Cabinas Rodamar ⓣ2653-0109. A basic, friendly budget traveller's hangout, this motel-style compound set back from the main road has dark *cabinas* with cold-water bathrooms, big beds and fans. The cheaper rooms with shared bathroom are a bit more Spartan, and there's a communal kitchen. ❷

Hostel La Botella de Leche ⓣ2653-2061, ⓦwww.labotelladeleche.com. Excellent backpacker hostel with comfortable bunk-bed accommodation in dorms. It's a/c, sociable and has a well-equipped communal kitchen as well as spick-and-span shared cold-water bathrooms. It's designed with surfers in mind – you can rent and repair boards here, as well as arrange classes. It's very popular, and although the super-friendly owner will do her utmost to squeeze you in, you'd be wise to reserve ahead. ❸

El Jardín del Eden On the hilltop behind the main road through town ⓣ2653-0137, ⓦwww.jardindeleden.com. Discreet, upmarket hotel in an exclusive hilltop position, with fine views over Tamarindo. Villas have all the usual amenities – a/c, fans, satellite TV, telephone and fridge – plus nice touches like tiled bathrooms and wicker chairs on the large private balconies. There's also a landscaped pool, jacuzzi, bar and an excellent French restaurant. Breakfast included. ❼

El Milagro ⓣ2256-3665, ⓦwww.elmilagro.com. A long-time Tamarindo favourite, featuring nicely decorated *cabinas* with private hot-water bathroom, cable TV and a/c. Some rooms are generously proportioned, with French windows opening onto flowered terraces. The poolside restaurant serves great food. Breakfast included. ❻

Pasatiempo ⓣ2653-0096. Popular hotel with a relaxed and friendly atmosphere. The spotless rooms have a/c, wi-fi, hot water and CD players. The larger rooms sleep 5 and are a good deal for groups. The atmosphere is homely, with hammocks strung outside the rooms and around the pool. There's also a lively restaurant and bar (that can get loud in high season). ❻

Tamarindo Diría ⓣ2653-0031, ⓦwww.tamarindodiria.com. One of Tamarindo's oldest hotels, set in shady palm groves on the beach. Arranged around two swimming pools looking out to the ocean, the large rooms all have a/c, cable TV, telephone and private bath. Sea-view rooms are worth the additional cost. There's a great seaside bar/restaurant on site. Breakfast included. ❽

Villa Amarilla ⓣ2653-0038, ⓔcarpen@racsa.co.cr. A favourite spot for a quick beer on the beach between catching waves, this also has seven *cabinas* and a communal kitchen. Rooms are decked out in wood; the simpler ones have fridge, fan and shared bathroom (❹), while the en-suite rooms have a/c and cable TV (❺). There's a cheap and cheerful restaurant.

Villas Macondo ⓣ2653-0812, ⓦwww.villasmacondo.com. Tamarindo is sometimes overpriced, but this quiet, welcoming spot is a refreshing exception. The colourful *cabinas*, set around an enticing swimming pool, have comfortable beds, wooden ceilings and a little terrace strung with hammocks; the more expensive ones include cable TV, a/c and fridge. There are also apartments (❼) with one or two bedrooms. Guests have access to a kitchenette with gas stove. ❸; with a/c ❹

Witch's Rock Surf Camp ⓣ2653-1705, ⓦwitchsrocksurfcamp.com. The best choice in the village for all-in daily surf lessons, unlimited board rentals and accommodation. The breezy, brightly coloured rooms vary in size, though all have a/c, private baths, ocean views and wi-fi; some also have balconies. Packages typically start at 7 nights (from $879) though shorter stays can be arranged. Breakfast is included at the open-air restaurant, *Eat at Joe's* and there's an on-site surf shop.

Playa Langosta and around

B&B Casa Sueca On the road to Playa Langosta ⓣ2653-0021, ⓦwww.tamarindocs.com. Beautifully appointed, cosy apartments, all artistically decorated, with private bath, hot water, fans and breezy balconies. You can rent surfboards and get advice on local surf hot-spots. Good weekly discounts. ❺

B&B Sueño del Mar Playa Langosta ⓣ2653-0284, ⓦwww.sueno-del-mar.com. Swing in a hammock on the ocean-facing veranda of this beautiful Spanish hacienda-style house, with tiled roofs and adobe walls. The charming and luxurious rooms and *casitas* all come with pretty tiled showers. Rates include a tasty and filling breakfast. Rooms ❽, *casitas* ❾

B&B Villa Alegre Playa Langosta ⓣ2653-0270, ⓦwww.villaalegrecostarica.com. Relaxing, Californian-owned B&B in a quiet location on the beach in Playa Langosta. The five rooms, with large, comfortable beds, are bright and tastefully decorated. The generous breakfast is served on the veranda by

Surf schools

The Tamarindo area has always been a surfing paradise, and its credibility was upped several notches when Bruce Brown's seminal surfing docudrama *Endless Summer II* was partly filmed here. Most surfers ride the waves at Tamarindo, Playa Grande and adjacent Playa Langosta, an excellent surf beach a couple of kilometres south. The friendly and professional **Iguana Surf** (Ⓣ2653-0148, Ⓦwww.iguanasurf.net), 500m southwest along the road to Playa Langosta, will almost certainly have you standing on a board by the end of your first class; cost is around $45 including board rental. Another popular school is **Tamarindo Adventures** in an unmistakeable round building with a huge sign reading "hightide" (Ⓣ2653-0108, Ⓦwww.tamarindo aventuras.com), who also rent out ATVs, dirt bikes and kayaks, while **Witch's Rock Surf Camp** (see opposite), named after one of the best breaks in the area, also offers lessons and board rentals. All schools rent surfboards; typical prices are $25 for a day's rental of a long board, or $100 for a week. You can also rent boogie boards, windsurfing equipment and masks and snorkels.

the pool. Also available are a pair of villas (accommodating 2–5 people) with kitchen facilities. ❽

Cabinas El Mono Loco About 300m up the road to Playa Langosta Ⓣ2653-0238, Ⓦwww.hotelmonoloco.com. Run by a relaxed Tico family, this clean little hotel is set around a tranquil garden with a small plunge pool. There are dorm beds ($15 per person) as well as large simple rooms with a/c and hot water – try and get room 1, which receives considerably more sunlight than the others. Some rooms sleep up to seven, so it's good value for groups. The owners also rent bikes and prepare meals. ❺

Capitán Suizo On the road to Playa Langosta Ⓣ2653-0075, Ⓦwww.hotelcapitansuizo.com. Popular, upmarket Swiss-run hotel set in spacious, landscaped grounds on the beach. The *cabina*-style rooms all have a balcony or terrace, fridge, ceiling fans or a/c, bathtub, hot water and an outside shower. The palm-shaded pool is bigger than most, and the atmosphere friendly and relaxed. There's also a cocktail bar, restaurant (see p.296), beautiful beach views and a buffet breakfast. ❾

Casa Cook On the road to Playa Langosta Ⓣ2653-0125, Ⓦwww.casacook.net. Small, beautiful hotel with beachfront *cabinas*, a *casita* and a studio apartment, each pleasantly furnished and with a full range of amenities, including a/c, wi-fi and cable TV. There's a pool, and the affable staff are an excellent source of information on the area. *Cabinas* and *casita* ❾, apartment ❽

The Town

Though fishing still plays a small part in the local economy, Tamarindo's transformation from village to beach resort has been rapid, with the usual associated worries about drugs and the loss of community. **Swimming** isn't great around Tamarindo, because of choppy waters and occasional riptides. Most people are content to paddle in the rocky coves and tide pools south of the town. Tamarindo is, however, an ideal **surf** spot because of the reliable, but relatively gentle, waves and the beach attracts a combination of enthusiastic surfers and well-to-do Costa Ricans, who own holiday houses in the vicinity.

If you tire of soaking up the sun on the beach, eating fresh fish and hanging out with fellow foreigners, you can take daily **yoga and pilates** classes at the Ser movement studio (Ⓣ8346-8005), above Cine-Mas (Ⓣ8703-4853), a cosy **cinema** in Plaza Tamarindo that shows films at the end of their runs and serves the requisite popcorn and hot dogs in a space not much larger than your average living room. In the evening, the main activity is watching the typically opulent **sunsets**, as the sun disappears into the Pacific just beyond the rocky headland that marks the southern end of the beach, but attention soon shifts to the bar with the cheapest drinks specials.

North of the Tamarindo river estuary begins the long sweep of Playa Grande (see p.290), where the **leatherback turtles** lay their eggs. Turtles also come ashore at

Tours around Playa Tamarindo

Many operators in town run a popular two-hour **boat excursion** ($40 per person) that takes you around the river estuary where you might spot monkeys, birds and crocodiles. In leatherback nesting season (Nov to mid-Feb), you can head out on a **turtle tour** ($30 per person; about 2hr); trips leave in the evening, the exact hour depending on the tide. During the rest of the year, turtles also nest further south at Refugio Nacional de Vida Silvestre Ostional (see p.309), usually only on a couple of days each month, depending on the moon. A trip there and back costs around $40. Numerous Tamarindo operators run these and other trips; one of the most professional and helpful is **Costa Rica Paradise** (Ⓣ2653-0031, Ⓦwww.crparadise.com), also known as the Costa Rica Tourist Information Centre, just north of the turn-off to Playa Langosta. Another well-run operator is **Destination Adventures** (Ⓣ2653-3842, Ⓦwww.destinationadventures.net), who lead snorkelling trips around Tamarindo ($55; 3hr), horseback riding along the beach ($45; 2hr 30min) and day-trips further afield, including a popular trip to Parque Nacional Rincón de la Vieja which includes climbing, rappelling and zip lines ($125; 12hr).

Tamarindo, but in much smaller numbers. Officially, Tamarindo is within the boundaries of Parque Nacional Las Baulas, in so far as the ocean covered by the protected area extends out in an arc, encompassing Tamarindo beach. The Servicio de Parques Nacionales (National Parks Service) has bought up the beach south of Tamarindo to Playa Langosta, too, preventing further hotel development and allowing turtles to continue coming ashore along this entire stretch.

Eating, drinking and nightlife

Tamarindo has a number of excellent, cosmopolitan restaurants, many serving delicious fresh seafood and also world and fusion cuisine. **Nightlife** centres on the restaurants and bars – a couple of them with pleasant beachfront locations – in the heart of the village. *Las Palmas*, 200m north of the loop, is a trendy spot to unwind and watch the sun set after a day in the surf. The spacious *Babylon* is the place to be on Thursday and Friday evenings ($3 including first drink); later in the night, the action continues at *La Bodega*, just to the south. On Saturdays, the scene shifts further south along the beach to *Big Bazaar*, which has more of a dance music vibe.

Buon Appetito Across from *Zullymar*. Italian-owned café serving sandwiches on fresh ciabatta bread as well as filling breakfasts and fruit shakes. Open for breakfast, lunch and dinner.

Capitán Suizo *Capitán Suizo* hotel. Popular, inviting open-air restaurant fronted by the hotel's gorgeous pool and with views of the ocean. Though the menu changes regularly, it features creative and reasonably priced healthy dishes prepared with sustainable ingredients. The fish and seafood in particular is worth sampling, as it typically includes fresh, home-made sauces. Open for lunch and dinner.

Falafel Mundo On the road about 50m east of the loop. Shawarma and falafel sandwiches ($6) are the specialities at this cute roadside restaurant run by an Israeli. Open daily for lunch and dinner.

Frutas Tropicales On the main road, at the north end of town. One of the few genuinely cheap places in Tamarindo. The name says it all: all kinds of tropical fruit are on offer, including delicious fruit *refrescos*. They also serve good *casados* ($4) and hamburgers ($4) – and even rent out a couple of *cabinas* (❹). Daily 8am–10pm.

El Jardín del Eden In the *El Jardín del Eden* hotel (see p.294). Romantic, upmarket (but reasonably priced) restaurant in tropical gardens serves high-quality French and Italian cuisine made with top-notch ingredients. The lobster, seafood brochettes and *pargo* (snapper) are all recommended. Count on spending around $30 per person. Daily noon–10pm.

Kahiki South of the loop on the road to Playa Langosta Ⓣ2653-3816. Sip exotic tropical fruit Kahikiritas while enjoying a Polynesian-themed dining experience beneath an open-air traditional thatched roof rancho. The New-York-trained chef's menu features creative dishes from Kona Mountain black bean hummus to Thai shrimp spring rolls with mango sauce. Closed Tues.

La Laguna del Cocodrilo At the northern end of Tamarindo ⓣ2653-0255. Classy Mediterranean restaurant in a palm-fringed garden (with resident crocodile) right on the beach. Starters include an exquisite tuna carpaccio ($6); for main course, try the seafood, steak and other exotic offerings such as fried camembert in honey sauce or chicken stewed in a spicy beer sauce, all for $8–11. Stock up on picnic fare at the on-site French bakery. Daily 6am–10pm.

Lazy Wave Opposite the entrance to Tamarindo resort, 100m up the Playa Langosta turn-off from the beach road ⓣ2653-0737. This outdoor restaurant may look casual, but it dishes up some of the best cooking in the region, if not the country. The very fairly priced menu (changes daily) is distinguished by the delicacy and inventiveness of its ingredients and flavours and includes sushi, seared tuna steaks and beef Wellington in giant portions. The bakery-patisserie is worth a visit, too. Sat–Thurs 6–10pm.

Nougi's ⓣ2653-0059. On the Tamarindo loop. Long-running favourite where you can dine on smoked pork chops with fruit salsa ($14), sandwiches and local fish dishes. Closed Wed.

The Oasis In the *Pasatiempo* hotel. Perennially good and reasonably priced restaurant serves crowd-pleasers like Caesar salad ($4), a wonderfully succulent blackened fish with greens and chicken breast with mango stuffing ($8). If nothing else, try the superlative fruit cocktails and a few nibbles. Live music twice a week in high season. Open for lunch and dinner.

Pachanga Near the *Pasatiempo* hotel. Turn left up towards Playa Langosta; as the road bends right, go straight ahead. Intimate, candlelit restaurant, tastefully decorated and with a French-influenced gourmet menu. The fish tartar ($6) is exquisite, as is the snapper fillet ($11), but it's also worth considering the enticing daily specials. Cash only. Closed Sun.

Sunset Lounge On the Tamarindo loop. Casual café that serves excellent breakfasts, with good breads, pastries and coffees, which you can either eat at the breezy seaside tables or take away. Also, try the fine snacks such as fish tacos and fresh fillets of fish. Open Fri–Sun.

Voodoo Lounge Just east of the loop ⓣ2653-0100. Upmarket restaurant serving an assortment of tasty international dishes such as chicken curry with pineapple ($11) and mahi mahi in white sauce with shrimp ($14). Open for dinner until 2am.

Walter's On the beachfront about 25m north of the loop. One of the few places in the village where you're likely to encounter more locals than foreigners, this relaxed and reasonably priced open-air spot serves *comida típica*, shrimp specialties and filling breakfasts, like rice, beans, eggs and coffee for $7. Open for breakfast, lunch and dinner.

Wok and Roll Right in the centre of town, next to Essence Day Spa and across from the Tamarindo Plaza ⓣ2653-0156. As its name suggests, it serves stir-fries (you choose ingredients) and sushi (with fresh fish caught daily). Service isn't exactly hurried but the food is enticing. Closed Sun.

Zullymar On the Tamarindo loop ⓣ2653-0140. Unbeatable beachfront location – everybody seems to come here for a drink while watching the sun go down – and good food, with main dishes for $7–10. Service is slow, so plan on sitting and watching the crabs scuttling across the sand while waiting. All will be forgiven, however, once your tasty *corvina* or *dorado* arrives. Inexpensive pizzas are served during the day only. Open for lunch and dinner.

South to Playa Avellanas

It's not possible to continue straight down the coast from Tamarindo: to pick up the road south you have to return a couple of kilometres inland to the hamlet of Villareal. Don't head south in the rainy season without a 4WD, and not at all unless you like crossing creeks – there are plenty on this stretch, and they can swell worryingly fast in the rain.

In the dry months you should be all right with any vehicle as far as the surfing hotspot of **PLAYA AVELLANAS**, 11km south of Tamarindo, but it may not do the car any good, and further south the roads become discouragingly rough. There are a few surfers' hangouts where you can **stay** at Avellanas, with spartan but good-value accommodation, though if you're not a surfer, you'll feel a bit out of it, and may prefer the more upmarket option of *Cabinas Las Olas* (ⓣ2652-9315, ⓦwww.cabinaslasolas.co.cr; ❻) set back from the beach with pleasant light bungalows and swinging hammocks among mangroves. It also has wi-fi and a surf shop where you can rent equipment as well as kayaks and mountain bikes. At the nearby *Lola's on the Beach* (Ⓣ2652-9097) you'll see Lola herself, a 400kg porky pig splashing around in the surf, but most come to enjoy the succulent fresh fish, relax with a few cocktails and to take in the action out on the waves.

Playa Junquillal

Ten kilometres beyond Avellana, lovely **PLAYA JUNQUILLAL** has a long, relatively straight beach. It's ideal for **surfing**, pounded by breakers crashing in at the end of their thousand-kilometre journeys, but far too rough for swimming. If you're looking for seclusion and quiet, however, it's a great place to hang out for a few days – there's precious little to do, and nothing at all in the way of nightlife.

One **bus** daily arrives in Junquillal from San José (via Santa Cruz). This service currently gets you to Junquillal after dark: as with all the places along the west coast of Nicoya, make sure you book a room in advance. The bus returns to San José at 5am.

Accommodation

Junquillal has several very good **hotels**, many perched up above the beach on a small cliff, with stupendous views. There's also a **campsite**, *Los Malinches* (Ⓣ2658-8429; $5 per person), south of *Hotel Iguanazul*.

El Castillo Divertido On a hillside about a third of a mile from the beach Ⓣ2658-8428, Ⓔcastillodivertido@hotmail.com. Enchanting, small white turreted "castle" run by entertaining hosts. The rooms have fans, some have an ocean view and there's a bar, restaurant and rooftop terrace. ❹

Guacamaya Lodge 2km south of Junquillal Ⓣ2658-8431, Ⓦwww.guacamayalodge.com. Swiss-run hotel in a serene setting with comfortable, semicircular rooms, lovely views, friendly management and a pool. There's also an on-site bar and restaurant serving Swiss specialities and a few Tico staples. ❺

Hotel Iguanazul 3km north of Playa Junquillal Ⓣ2658-8123, Ⓦhoteliguanazul.com. Friendly hotel in a great setting overlooking the sea: it has bright rooms decorated with indigenous art, plus a pool, bar and restaurant with a lovely view of the beach. It offers fishing, diving and horseback tours, as well as excursions to Las Baulas. Call ahead to reserve and ask about road conditions, especially in the rainy season. ❼

Santa Cruz and Nicoya

After spending time on some of the Pacific's upscale beaches, venturing inland to the heart of traditional Guanacaste can be a little jarring. About 35min east of Playa Junquillal, **Santa Cruz** is a bastion of the region's distinctive folk heritage and provides good access to several of the Pacific beaches as well as to **Nicoya**, 25km to the south at the northern edge of its namesake peninsula. Costa Rica's oldest city and home to its oldest church, Nicoya's role today is as the peninsula's major travel and agricultural centre, though it also retains a strong indigenous presence.

Santa Cruz and around

Generally regarded by travellers as little more than somewhere to pass through on the way from Liberia or San José to the beach, the sprawling town of **SANTA CRUZ**, some 30km inland from Tamarindo and 57km south of Liberia, is actually "National Folklore City". Much of the music and dance considered quintessentially Guanacastecan originates here, like the various complex, stylized local dances,

Dance and music in Guanacaste

In their book *A Year of Costa Rican Natural History*, Amelia Smith Calvert and Philip Powell Calvert describe their month on Guanacaste's **fiesta** circuit in 1910, starting in January in Filadelfía, a small town between Liberia and Santa Cruz, and ending in Santa Cruz. They were fascinated by the formal nature of the functions they attended, observing: "The dances were all round **dances**, mostly of familiar figures, waltzes and polkas, but one, called '*el punto*' was peculiar in that the partners do not hold one another but walk side by side, turn around each other and so on."

At Santa Cruz, "All the ladies sat in a row on one side of the room when not dancing, the men elsewhere. When a lady arrived somewhat late then the rest of the guests of the company, if seated, arose in recognition of her presence. The **music** was furnished by three fiddles and an accordion. The uninvited part of the community stood outside the house looking into the room through the open doors, which as usual were not separated from the street by any vestibule or passage." The Calverts were also delighted to come across **La giganta**, the figure of a woman about 4m high; actually a man on stilts "with a face rather crudely moulded and painted". What exactly *La giganta* represented isn't known, but she promenaded around the streets of Santa Cruz in her finery, long white lace trailing, while her scurrying minders frantically worked to keep her from keeling over. *La giganta*, along with other oversized personalities, still features in nearly every large village fiesta, usually held on the local saint's day.

including the "Punto Guanacasteco" ("*el punto*"), which rivals Scottish country dancing for its complexity and has been adopted as the national dance. That said, however, they're not exactly dancing in the streets of Santa Cruz; life is actually rather slow, much of it lived out in contemplative fashion on the wide veranda of the town's old houses.

Unless you arrive during the **Fiesta Santa Cruz** (mid-Jan), when the town comes alive with bullfights and fireworks and the streets overflow with revellers, Santa Cruz offers little reason to linger longer than it takes to catch the bus out. There are few facilities too, apart from the **Banco Nacional** on the way into town. In the unlikely event that you need a **hotel**, choose from the *Paraje del Diría*, 4km north of town (ⓣ2680-1826; ❹), which has two pools and 50 air-conditioned rooms with TV; or *Hotel La Estancia*, one block west of the central plaza (ⓣ2680-0476; ❸), whose rooms have TV, wi-fi, private bath (though no hot water) and fans, but can be stuffy. For **food**, join the locals at the popular *Coopetortillas*, a barn-sized tortilla-making cooperative just off the central plaza with its own restaurant that serves chicken, Guanacastecan *empanadas* and sweet cheese bread, as well, of course, as tortillas.

Santa Cruz is a regional **transport** hub, with good connections inland and to the coast. Tralapa (ⓣ2221-7202) and Alfaro (ⓣ2222-2666) run daily buses to San José (5hr) which depart more or less hourly from the bus terminal on the west side of the central plaza. There are also numerous local bus services to Liberia. A number of buses leave for **Tamarindo** including a direct service at 8.30pm (about 1hr) returning from Tamarindo at 6.45am. For **Junquillal** a bus leaves at 6.30pm and returns to Santa Cruz at 5am. You can also get to **Playas Flamingo** and **Brasilito**, via Tamarindo, with services leaving daily at 6.30am and 3pm (1hr 30min) and returning to Santa Cruz at 9am and 5pm.

Guaitíl

The one town in Guanacaste where you can still see crafts being made in the traditional way is **GUAITÍL**, 12km east of Santa Cruz, well known throughout Costa

Chorotega pottery

The chief characteristics of **Chorotega pottery** are the striking black and red on white **colouring**, called *pataky*, and a preponderance of panels, decorated with intricate anthropomorphic snake, jaguar and alligator motifs. Archeologists believe that pieces coloured and designed in this way were associated with the elite, possibly as mortuary furniture for *caciques* (chiefs) or other high-ranking individuals. In the Period VI (an archeological term for the years between 1000 BC and 500 AD) the *murillo appliqué* style emerged, an entirely new, glossy, black or red pottery with no parallel anywhere else in the region, but curiously similar to pottery found on Marajó Island at the mouth of the Amazon in modern-day Brazil, thousands of kilometres away.

After the Conquest, predictably, pottery-making declined sharply. The traditional anthropomorphic images were judged to be pagan by the Catholic Church and subsequently suppressed. Today you can see some of the best specimens in San José's Museo Nacional (see p.105) or watch them being faithfully reproduced in Guaitíl.

Today, potters in Guaitíl use local resources and traditional methods little-changed since the days of the Chorotegas. To make the clay, local rock is ground on ancient *metates*, which the Chorotegas used for grinding corn. The pigment used on many of the pieces, *curiol*, comes from a porous stone that has to be collected from a natural source, a four-hour walk away, and the ceramic piece is shaped using a special stone, also local, called *zukia*. *Zukias* were used by Chorotega potters to mould the lips and bases of plates and pots; treasured examples have been found in Chorotega graves.

Rica for its **ceramics**. On the site of a major Chorotega potters' community, the present-day artisans' cooperative (*cooperativo artesanía*) was founded more than twenty years ago by three local women whose goal was to use regional traditions and their own abilities as potters and decorators for commercial gain. Today the artisans are still mainly women, keeping customs alive at the distinctive, large, dome-shaped kilns, while the men work in agricultural smallholdings.

Every house in Guaitíl seems to be in on the trade, with pottery on sale in front of people's homes, on little roadside stalls and in the Artesanía Cooperative on the edge of the football field. Some of the houses are open for you to wander inside and watch the women at work. Wherever you buy, don't haggle and don't expect it to be dirt cheap, either. A large vase can easily cost $20 or $25. Bear in mind, too, that this is decorative rather than functional pottery, and may not be that durable.

Guaitíl is on the old road to Nicoya; to get there from Santa Cruz, head east on the smaller road instead of south on the new road; turn off to the left where you see the sign for Guaitíl.

Nicoya

Bus travellers journeying between San José and the beach towns of Sámara and Nosara (see p.302 & p.305) need to make connections at the country town of **NICOYA**, inland and northeast of the beaches. Set in a dip surrounded by low mountains, Nicoya is the peninsula's main settlement. The town is permeated by an air of infinite stasis but is undeniably pretty, with a lovely **Parque Central**, cascading bougainvillea, colourful plants and the white adobe church, the **Parroquis San Blas**. Founded in 1644, the church has survived multiple earthquakes and has recently undergone extensive renovation. Nicoya has a considerable Chinese presence, with many of the town's restaurants, hotels and stores owned by descendants of Chinese immigrants.

Practicalities

Eight **buses** a day arrive in Nicoya from San José, a journey of around six hours. Buses also arrive from a number of regional destinations, including Liberia (10 daily), Santa Cruz (16 daily), Sámara (4–8 daily) and Nosara (5 daily). Most buses arrive at Nicoya's spotless **bus station** on the southern edge of town, a short walk from the centre; the Liberia service pulls in across from the *Hotel Las Tinajas*.

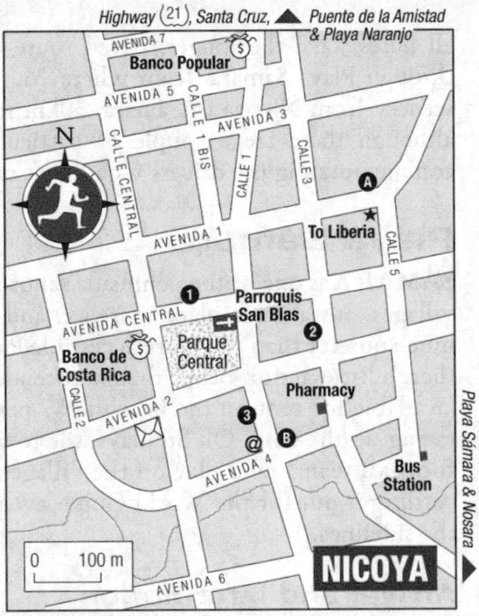

Most services are clustered around the Parque Central, including the **post office** and **banks**, several with ATMs, as well as **taxis**, which line up by the parque (or call Coopetico on ⓣ2658-6226). There's an **internet** café 100m south of Parque Central, opposite the friendly *Hotel Jenny* (ⓣ2685-5050; ❸), the cheapest **place to stay** in town, with 28 old, basic rooms with TV and phone (only four have a/c). The *Hotel Las Tinajas* (ⓣ2285-5081; ❹), 100m northeast of Parque Central, is cleaner and somewhat more modern, with dark rooms inside the main building and lighter *cabinas* around the back.

Good **restaurants** include the *Cafetería Daniela*, 100m east of the parque, for breakfast and pastries; the *sodas* by the parque (*El Nuevo Horizonte* is the best) for large *casados*; and, for quick serve Chinese food, the *Restaurant El Teyet*, across from *Hotel Jenny*.

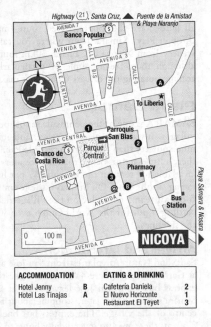

ACCOMMODATION		EATING & DRINKING	
Hotel Jenny	B	Cafetería Daniela	2
Hotel Las Tinajas	A	El Nuevo Horizonte	1
		Restaurant El Teyet	3

Nicoya Peninsula beaches

For a peaceful beachside break, a good bet is to head down to **Sámara** or **Nosara** on the Nicoya Peninsula. A road runs the 35km between Nicoya and the coast at Nosara, via Caimital, though it's only negotiable with a 4WD. Most drivers, and

The Friendship Bridge

Opened in 2003, the 780-metre **Puente Tempisque** connects the mainland with the Nicoya Peninsula, spanning from near Puerto Moreno (17km east of the Nicoya–Carmona road) on the peninsula to a point 25km west of the Interamericana on the mainland. The bridge replaced a time-consuming ferry connection and saves at least two hours on the journey between San José and Sámara. The $26 million bridge was financed by Taiwan in exchange for commercial fishing rights in Costa Rican waters, which were quickly rescinded due to abuse. It's partly held up by suspension cables connected to towers that, at 80m, make it the tallest structure in Costa Rica.

all buses, take the longer, paved route (marked as Route 150 on some maps) through Playa Sámara, from where you can loop north back up the coast. The scenery from Nicoya to Sámara, 30km south, is rolling, rather than precipitous, although there are a couple of particularly nasty corners, marked by crosses commemorating the drivers who didn't make it.

Playa Sámara

SÁMARA is one of the peninsula's most peaceful and least developed beachside villages. It's a great place to relax, and its distance from the capital makes it much quieter than the more accessible Pacific beaches. Even at the busiest times, there's little action other than weekenders tottering by on stout *criollo* **horses** (available for rent on the beach at $7 per hour) and the occasional dune buggy racing up the sand. On Sundays, the town turns out in force to watch the local **football** teams who play on the village field as if they're Brazil and Argentina battling it out for the World Cup – even weekending Ticos shun the beach for the sidelines.

Arrival and information

Sansa and NatureAir **planes** from San José arrive at the airstrip 6km east of town at Carrillo, from where 4WD taxis make the trip to Sámara for about $6. The express **bus** from San José leaves daily at 12.30pm and 6.15pm, and arrives at Sámara some 5 hours later, stopping about 50m in front of the beach right at the centre of the village. The express bus **back to San José** leaves at 4.30am and 8.30am; there are also several daily buses **to Nicoya** (2hr).

You can buy **tickets** for some bus services from the Transporte Alfaro office (daily 7am–5pm) in the centre of the village, which also sells potato chips, suntan lotion and bottles of cold water and is home to the village's **public telephone**. Sámara's **post office** – a small shack really – 50m before the entrance to the beach,

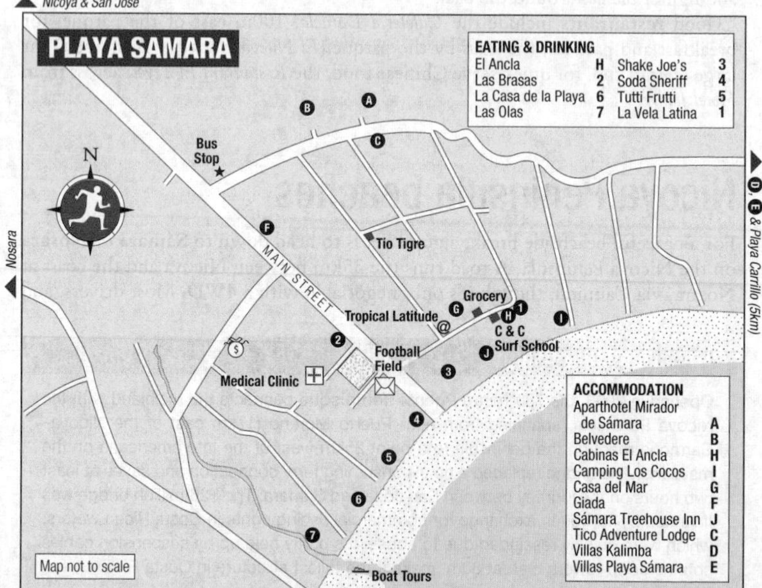

offers minimal services. There's a **Banco Nacional** (with an ATM) located down the first road to the right off the main street as you enter the village. *Tropical Latitude*, near the *Hotel Casa del Mar*, offers **internet access**; for **laundry**, head for Lava Ya. There's a **medical clinic** (Mon–Fri 8am–4pm; ⓣ2656-0166) a few blocks north of the main street near the beach: for emergencies contact the Red Cross on ⓣ2685-5458.

Accommodation

Staying in Sámara is getting pricier, with few cheap *cabinas*. During high-season weekends you'll need an advance **reservation** no matter what price range. The best spot in the village to pitch a tent is *Camping Los Cocos* (ⓣ2656-0496; $6), on the beach, which is clean and well run, with cooking grills.

Aparthotel Mirador de Sámara First left as you come into Sámara and 100m up the hill from the *Marbella* ⓣ2656-0044, ⓦwww.miradordesamara.com. Huge apartments (5–7 people) with large bathrooms, bedrooms, living rooms, kitchen and terrace, all with panoramic views of the town and beach. The bar is in an impressive tower with spectacular sunset views, and there's a small pool with wooden sundecks. Good low-season and extended-stay discounts. Better value for four or more people, rather than couples. ❻

Belvedere 100m down the road to Carrillo ⓣ2656-0213, ⓦwww.belvederesamara.net. This wonderfully pleasant hotel has ten rooms and two apartments with either a/c or fan (the latter $10 less), and all are brightly furnished in light wood, with mosquito nets and solar-heated water. There's also a jacuzzi and swimming pool, and a good German breakfast is included. ❹

Cabinas El Ancla On the beachfront road 200m south of the centre ⓣ2656-0254. Simply furnished rooms, with cold-water bathroom and fan, right on the beach. The upstairs rooms are a bit hotter but still better than the dark and oppressive downstairs rooms. There's a friendly *dueña* and good beach-front seafood restaurant. ❸

Casa del Mar 50m north of the entrance to beach on the left ⓣ2656-0264, ⓦwww.casadelmarsamara.net. Large, good-value rooms (although a bit sparsely furnished) close to the beach. The downstairs rooms are clean and white, but rather dark; ask for an upstairs room with shared bath and palm-fringed sea view. The price includes breakfast. With a/c and private bath ❻; with fan and shared bath ❹

Giada About 100m before you come to the beach, on the left ⓣ2656-0132, ⓦwww.hotelgiada.net. Small hotel set around a compact pool, with spotless banana-yellow rooms, good beds, overhead fans, private baths and tiled showers – the upstairs rooms are better for views and breeze. There's also a friendly Italian restaurant. ❻

Sámara Treehouse Inn On the beach ⓣ2656-0733, ⓦwww.samaratreehouse.com. Four beachfront units built on tree-trunk stilts, with hammocks beneath. They have modern ceramic-tiled bathrooms, and there's a shady open patio with BBQ as well as wi-fi throughout. Includes breakfast. ❻

Tico Adventure Lodge On the third road back from the beach ⓣ2656-0628, ⓦwww.ticoadventurelodge.com. A fantastic deal, this smartly designed American-run hotel has nine cheerful rooms with a/c and balconies, a house set alongside the pool and an upstairs apartment for larger groups. There's wi-fi throughout and the friendly owner is a great source of local information. They can also arrange surfing lessons with C & C Surf Shop (see p.304). ❹

Villas Kalimba On the road to Carillo ⓣ2656-0929, ⓦwww.villaskalimba.com. The six Southwestern-style villas are set around a pool and jacuzzi and have handcrafted wooden windows and furniture and a/c. ❽

Villas Playa Sámara On the road to Carrillo ⓣ2656-0372, ⓦwww.villasplayasamara.com. Upmarket resort, wildly popular amongst wealthy Costa Rican families, with both all-inclusive and accommodation-only tariffs. The well-built villas come with large, spacious kitchens and sitting rooms, plus outside terrace and hammock but the whole effect (golf carts for your luggage; see-your-neighbour proximity) is a bit suburban, and the management could be more efficient – although the beachside setting at the quiet south end of the beach is lovely. ❽

Activities

Sámara boasts some of the calmest waters, making it ideal for **swimming**. The long, gorgeous stretch of sand is protected by a reef about a kilometre out, which takes the brunt of the Pacific's power out of the waves. The effect also makes the beach one of the best spots on the Pacific coast to learn to **surf**; the waves are strong enough without being too unforgiving on beginners. At the south end of the beach, C & C Surf Shop (Ⓣ2656-0628, Ⓦwww.ticoadventurelodge.com/lesson.html) offers expert instruction ($40 for 1hr lesson) plus surf-and boogie board rentals.

Alexis Boat Tours (Ⓣ8358-0793), on the beach at the north end of town, runs a variety of fishing and **watersports excursions**, as well as wildlife-spotting trips to the Refugio Ostional (see p.309). Tío Tigre (Ⓣ2656-0098) can instruct you in the art of **sea-kayaking** and also runs **dolphin-watching cruises**. Pura Vida Dive (Ⓣ2656-0273) arranges **dives** and PADI courses.

Eating, drinking and nightlife

Sámara has a couple of very nice places to **eat**, where you can also enjoy a cold beer by the lapping waves. **Nightlife** is quiet, except at weekends, when the dark *Tutti Frutti* disco on the beach gets going. It's open until 3am, and costs $1 to enter. A little further north is the much more pleasant *Las Olas*, a casual open beach bar with pool tables and a cheery vibe. By far the most peaceful and stylish spot for a drink is *La Vela Latina*, south of the centre on the beach where you can sip a daiquiri while relaxing on a rocking chair.

El Ancla On the beach. Waterside restaurant with an extensive menu of fish dishes that attracts plenty of holidaying Ticos who know good seafood when they smell it. Closed Thurs.

Las Brasas Town centre Ⓣ2656-0546. Split-level restaurant serving Spanish dishes such as paella or an entire suckling pig (with advance notice). The fillet steaks ($10) are tasty, as is the guacamole, but the pasta dishes are nothing special. Daily noon–10pm.

La Casa de la Playa On the beach. Relaxing arty café and restaurant offering healthy juices and salads. Seafood dishes include a tasty coconut curry ($7) or grilled prawns. Open for breakfast, lunch and dinner.

Shake Joe's On the beach. Low-key restaurant that attracts a lot of students from the language school up the beach. A good spot for a burger and a shake, and they also do a couple of refreshing salads. Opens at 11am; closed Mon.

Soda Sheriff On the beach. Pleasant, no-frills *soda* serving *comida típica* including noteworthy *casados* in the $6–9 range. Daily 8am–10pm.

Playa Carrillo and around

Aficionados of Pacific sunsets will want to head 6km east of Sámara to **PLAYA CARRILLO**, a ninety-minute walk along flat sands. Known for its spectacular evening light and colours, beautiful palm-fringed Carrillo is also safe for swimming, though the fact that more and more people are setting up hotels and restaurants means the beach no longer has the sleepy, end-of-the-line feel it once had. Try the *Mirador* restaurant, just behind Playa Carrillo up on a hill, where you can enjoy a drink and a **meal** (though the food is rather plain) to the sound of crashing waves, while watching pastel mauves, pinks and oranges blend into each other as the sun goes down. Just behind the *Mirador*, *El Colibrí* (Ⓣ2656-0656, Ⓦwww.cabinaselcolibri.com; ❹) has good budget **accommodation**, run by super-friendly Argentines: the rooms have tiled floors, hot showers and above-average beds, there's a BBQ restaurant on site and breakfast is included.

East of Carillo

The stretch east of Carrillo is for off-road driving nuts only, and should not be attempted without a 4WD (make sure the clearance is high). You need a good **map**, because roads go haywire in this part of the peninsula, veering off in all directions, unsigned and heading to nowhere, some ending in deep creeks (unpassable at high tide even in Range Rovers and Land Rovers). The further south you go, the tougher it gets, as dirt roads switch inland and then through the hamlets of Camaronal, Quebrada Seca and Bejuco, all just a few kilometres apart but separated by frequent creeks and rivers. It's best not to drive down here alone, as there's a very good chance you'll get stuck (rising to a virtual certainty in the rainy season, whatever vehicle you have) and settlements are few and far between. There are **filling stations** in Sámara and Cóbano: bring a spare can with you just in case, because the distance between the two, in total, is about 70km. Also, be sure to carry lots of drinking water and food, and, if possible, camping gear. You can **camp** on the deserted beaches, and there are a few budget and upmarket places **to stay** in the settlement of Playa San Miguel, about 30km southeast of Carrillo. The most luxurious option in the area is the isolated *Hotel Punta Islita* (Ⓣ2656-2020, Ⓦwww.hotelpuntaislita.com; ❾), 8km beyond Playa Carrillo, with hillside rooms boasting majestic views. The atmosphere is exclusive and facilities include a driving range, tennis courts, pools, restaurants and a canopy tour, while snorkelling, mountain-biking and fishing trips can also be arranged.

Nosara and around

The pretty drive from Sámara 25km northwest to the village of **NOSARA** runs along shady, secluded dirt and gravel roads punctuated by a few creeks. It's passable with a regular car (low clearance) in the dry season (though you'll still have to ford two creeks except at the very driest times of year), but you'll need a 4WD or high clearance in the wet. The road follows a slightly inland route; you can't see the coast except where you meet the beach at **Garza**, about ten minutes before Nosara. This little hamlet is a good place to stop for a *refresco* at the *pulpería*, and perhaps take a dip in the sea.

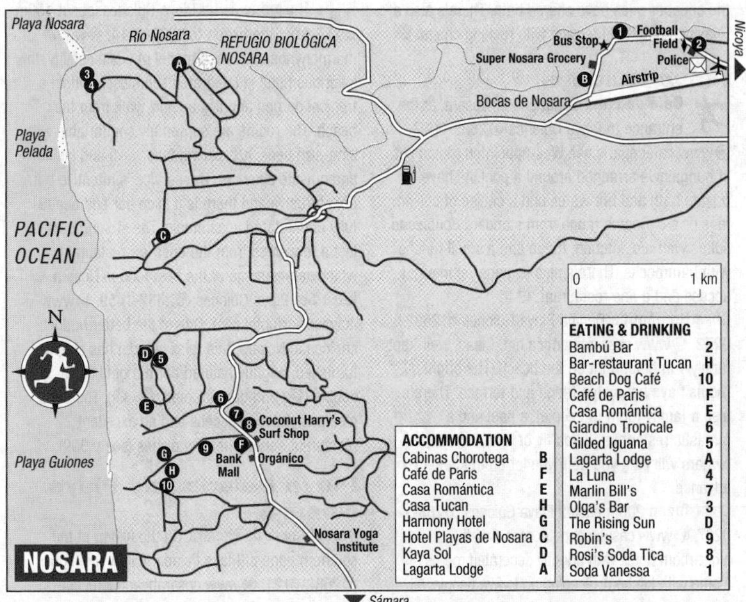

In contrast to Sámara, the vast majority of people who come to Nosara are North Americans and Europeans in search of quiet and natural surroundings. Indeed, the two main tourist attractions hereabouts are nature reserves: the bird-rich **Reserva Biológica Nosara** and the **Refugio Nacional De Vida Silvestre Ostional**, famed for its *arribadas* of olive ridley turtles.

Arrival and information

Though most people drive to Nosara, there's also a daily **bus** from San José as well as two daily buses from Nicoya and Playa Sámara: all pull in at the stop adjacent to the Super Nosara Grocery. NatureAir and Sansa **fly** daily to Nosara from San José, landing at the small airstrip. The Tuanis tour agency and souvenir shop, near the football field, has **internet** access, books for sale and **rents bikes**; they also have a useful notice board with local events. The small **post office** and local **Red Cross** station (Ⓣ2682-0175) are next to the airstrip. There's a **bank** in the mini plaza to the left as you enter Playa Guiones.

Accommodation

Nosara has some excellent beachside **accommodation** if you've money to spend, and the owners and managers tend to be more environmentally conscious than at many other places on the peninsula. Indeed, a local civic association keeps a hawkish eye on development in the area, with the aim of retaining Nosara's natural charms and preventing it from becoming another Tamarindo or Montezuma. The cheaper accommodation options are in or near the village, but you'll need to rent a bike or count on doing a lot of walking to get to the ocean.

In the village

Cabinas Chorotega In the village, by the supermarket Ⓣ2682-0129. Pleasant *cabinas* with large rooms. Upstairs *cabinas* are best, though you'll have to climb an extremely steep staircase; the cheaper ones have shared bath. There's also a relaxing communal terrace with rocking chairs. ❸

Playa Guiones

Café de Paris South end of Nosara, at the entrance to Playa Guiones Ⓣ2682-0087, Ⓦwww.cafedeparis.net. Well-appointed rooms set in bungalows arranged around a pool. All have private bath and hot water, and a choice of ceiling fans or a/c. Rooms range from standard doubles to suites with a/c, kitchen, fridge and a small rancho with hammocks. There's also (expensive) internet access and a fine restaurant. ❺

Casa Romántica Behind Playa Guiones Ⓣ2682-0272, Ⓦwww.casa-romantica.net. Clean, well-kept family-run hotel right on the beach. The bright rooms have hot water, fridge and terrace. There's also a family room (5 people), a pool and a fantastic restaurant. If you fly or take the bus, the owners will pick you up if you let them know in advance. ❻

Casa Tucan 200m east of Playa Guiones Ⓣ2682-0287, Ⓦwww.casatucanhotel.com. Small, eight-room hotel, with brightly decorated rooms (some with kitchen), sleeping up to five people; all have private bath, hot water, fridge, and fan or a/c. There's a good restaurant and bar, a juice bar and a pool. In peak period you have to book a package deal including surf lessons, yoga classes and full meals; these are also available throughout the year. ❻

Harmony Hotel Playa Guiones, about 150m from the beach Ⓣ2682-4114, Ⓦwww.harmonynosara.com. A model of sustainability, this luxurious hotel is integrated seamlessly within a tropical garden and lies a short walk from the beach. The rooms are supremely comfortable with king-size beds, a/c, ceiling fans, wi-fi and inside and outside showers. The service is attentive but not obtrusive and there is a juice bar and beautifully understated yoga studio. The striking pool is just a few steps from the open-air restaurant, which serves some of the best food in Nosara. ❾

Kaya Sol Playa Guiones Ⓣ2682-1459, Ⓦwww.kayasolsurfhotel.com. One of the better budget choices in Nosara, this relaxing spot has simply furnished, brightly painted dorm rooms ($18), double (❶) and group rooms (❹–❺). There's a nice pool, kitchen access and an excellent restaurant serving healthy dishes (see p.309).

Playa Pelada and Playa Nosara

Hotel Playas de Nosara On the hilltop at the southern edge of Playa Pelada; follow the signs Ⓣ2682-0121, Ⓦwww.nosarabeachhotel.com.

Dramatically situated hotel on a headland overlooking the beach and pine-clad coastline. Its stunning design includes a 360-degree observation lounge that makes the structure look like a mosque from afar. The large, clean, cool rooms with fans are priced according to the quality of the view (not all rooms overlook the beach). There's a pool but few other services. ❻

Lagarta Lodge Signposted from the village near the mouth of the Río Nosara ⓣ2682-0035, ⓦwww.lagarta.com. Set on the edge of the Reserva Biológica Nosara (see p.309) southwest of the village, this lodge has excellent birdwatching and stunning coastal views. The rooms above the pool overlooking the ocean boast one of the best panoramas in the country. Rooms have private bath, hot water and fridges. A healthy buffet breakfast (not included) as well as other meals is also available. ❻

The village: Bocas de Nosara

Nosara is more of a widely scattered community than a village as such; it spreads along three beaches and the hinterland behind them. The centre, if you can call it that, is known as **Bocas de Nosara** and is set about 4km inland, backed by a low ridge of hills. The atmosphere in Bocas de Nosara itself is shady and slow, with the

The *recorrido de toros*

If you're in Nosara on a weekend in January or February, or on a public holiday such as the first of May, be sure not to miss the **recorrido de toros** (rodeo). *Recorridos*, held in many of the Nicoya Peninsula villages, are a rallying point for local communities, who travel long distances in bumpy communal trucks to join in the fun.

Typically, the village **bullring** (*redondel*) is no more than a rickety wooden circular stadium, held together with bundles of palm thatch. Here local radio announcers introduce the competitors and list the weight and ferocity of the bulls, while travelling bands, many of them from Santa Cruz, perform oddly Bavarian-sounding oom-pah-pah music at crucial moments in the proceedings. For the most fun and the best-seasoned rodeo jokes, sit with the band – usually comprising two saxophones, a clarinettist, a drummer and the biggest tuba known to man – but avoid the seat right in front of the tuba.

The *recorrido* usually begins in the afternoon, with "Best Bull" competitions, and gets rowdier as evening falls – after dark, a single string of cloudy white light bulbs illuminates the ring – and more beer is consumed. The *sabanero* tricks on display are truly impressive: the mounted **cowboy** who gallops past the bull, twirls his rope, throws it behind his back and snags the bull as casually as you would loop a garden hose, has to be seen to be believed. The grand finale is the **bronco bull-riding**, during which a sinewy cowboy sticks like a burr to the huge spine of a Brahma bull who leaps and bucks with increasing fury. During the intervals, local men and boys engage in a strange ritual of wrestling in the arena, taking each other by the forearm and twirling each other round like windmills, faster and faster, until one loses his hold and flies straight out to land sprawling on the ground. These displays of macho bravado are followed by mock fights and tumbles, after which everyone slaps each other cordially on the back.

The *recorrido* is followed by a **dance**: in Nosara the impromptu dancefloor takes up the largest flat space available – the airstrip. The white-line area where the planes are supposed to stop is turned into a giant outdoor bar, ringed by tables and chairs, while the mobile disco rolls out its flashing lightballs and blasts out salsa, reggae and countrified two-steps. Wear good shoes, as the asphalt is super-hard: you can almost see your soles smoking after a quick twirl with a hotshot cowboy.

The atmosphere at these events is friendly and beer-sodden: in villages where there's a big foreign community you'll be sure to find someone to talk to if your Spanish isn't up to conversing with the *sabaneros*. **Food** is sold from stalls, where you can sample the usual *empanadas* or local Guanacastecan dishes such as *sopa de albóndigas* (meatball soup with egg).

sweet smell of cow dung in the air and excitable voices drifting out from the local Evangelical church. People are friendly, and Nosara is still low-key, though it does get busy in the high season when foreigners flock here in search of seclusion. The area around the village can be very confusing, with little dirt and gravel roads radiating in all directions. To counter the lost-tourist effect locals have erected copious signs – though there are so many at certain intersections that they simply add to the confusion. Resign yourself to driving around looking lost at least some of the time.

The beaches

The three beaches in the area – **Nosara, Guiones and Pelada** – are fine for **swimming**, although you can be buffeted by the crashing waves, and there are some rocky outcrops. Playa Guiones is the most impressive of the beaches: nearly 5km in length, populated by pelicans, and with probably the best swimming, though there's precious little shade. It's also popular for **surfing**, though not so suitable for beginners as Sámara (see p.302). One of the favourite local pastimes is watching the mass of surfers at sunrise and sunset – that is, if you're not among those out on the waves. The whole area is a great place to go beachcombing for shells and driftwood, and the vegetation, even in the dry season, is greener than further north. Some attempts have been made to limit development, and a good deal of the land around the Río Nosara has been designated a wildlife refuge.

Eating and drinking

The Nosara area has a profusion of very good **restaurants**, and prices are not as high as you might expect, given the area's relative isolation. There are a number of places in the village, most of them on and around the road leading to the beach or on the road into town, though many of the better restaurants are huddled together near Playa Guiones, where the majority of tourists eat. There are a couple of small **grocery stores** in the village, while in Playa Guiones there's *Orgánico*, a natural food market.

In the village

Bambú Bar Next to the Abastecedor general store. A bit dark, and with pounding music, though it's still a decent place to have a beer and watch the kids kick balls around the football field.

Soda Vanessa In Nosara village. A typical *soda* with filling *casados* for under $3, as well as other snack-style fare. Open for breakfast, lunch and dinner.

Playa Guiones

Bar-restaurant Tucan Next to the *Casa Tucan* hotel. The menu features seafood in adventurous fruit-based sauces, chicken, pasta and steaks (all $9–15), served in a pleasant rancho strung with inviting hammocks and coloured lights. A new juice bar offers "create-your-own" drinks. Open for lunch and dinner.

Beach Dog Café Behind Playa Guiones. An expat favourite, this open-air café is the closest spot to the beach for a meal. American-style breakfasts, such as waffles and *huevos rancheros*, are served along with fruit smoothies and a nice selection of coffee. Free wi-fi. Breakfast and lunch only.

Café de Paris At the southern entrance to Playa Guiones ⓣ2682-0087. The brioche and pain au chocolat confirm this bakery as a bona fide overseas *département* of France, while the pleasant poolside restaurant serves sandwiches and pizzas for lunch ($4–9). Open for lunch and dinner.

Casa Romántica In the hotel of the same name. Some of the most ambitious food in town, featuring a changing menu of fish, steak and pasta dishes ($9–12). There's a decent wine list, too – possibly the only good one in Nosara. Dining is in a small outdoor area, lit with candles at night. Open for lunch and dinner.

Giardino Tropicale South end of Nosara, on the road towards Sámara ⓣ2682-0258. Superior-quality real Italian pizza cooked in a wood oven and served in a pretty plant-strewn dining area ($6–9). Other well-crafted Italian dishes are also on offer, and there's takeaway.

Gilded Iguana Behind Playa Guiones ⓣ2682-0259. Upmarket gringo bar with Mexican food that attracts the local expats. Reasonably priced lunch specials, including fillet of *dorado* ($5) and fish and chips ($3). Closed Mon, Tues & Sun.

Marlin Bill's Playa Guiones. Fairly pricey but well-prepared grilled seafood (the *corvina*, sea bass, is particularly tasty) served in a setting just above the growing village near Playa Guiones. Closed Sat & Sun.

The Rising Sun *Kaya Sol*. Inventive and cheerful restaurant serving some of the best health food in Nosara. Standouts include a beet burger that exudes flavour and a dragon bowl that includes tofu, steamed vegetables, rice and a tantalizing chipotle cashew sauce. Closed Sun.

Robin's Playa Guiones. Cute café where you can munch on feel-good wraps and gorge on decadent crepes stuffed with chocolate and other savouries. The main draw for many, though, is the selection of sorbet and ice cream and the home-made cones it's served in. Closed for dinner.

Rosi's Soda Tica On a small hill above the road leading into Playa Guiones. Small, friendly, family-run restaurant (one of the few in the area run by locals) serving excellent *comida típica*, including *casados* ($4–6) for lunch and *gallo pinto* ($3–5) for breakfast. Mon–Sat 8am–3pm.

Playa Pelada and Playa Nosara

Lagarta Lodge In the hotel of the same name. Although the changing menu is perfectly fine, it's the setting rather than the food that makes this place special, as you dine to the sound of the Pacific crashing gently below. The sociable seating arrangement has all guests sitting around a big mahogany table – a good way to meet people. Closed Tues.

La Luna Just below the Playa Nosara hotels. ☎2682-0122. A loveable spot above Playa Pelada, with tranquil terrace tables overlooking the sea. The constantly changing menu features lip-smacking international dishes and seafood, with main dishes around $6–9. Highlights include salads, home-made bread as well as Thai soups and curries. The cheerful owners dream up some sinful desserts, including vanilla toffee pudding and chocolate fudge cake. Daily 11am–10pm.

Olga's Bar On Playa Pelada. Cold beer, good *casados* and fish, and ocean views, but watch the bill – they don't itemize your food and drinks. One of the best spots to watch the setting sun. Daily 10am–10pm.

Reserva Biológica Nosara

Accessed through the *Lagarta Lodge* (see p.307), the **RESERVA BIOLÓGICA NOSARA** (daily 8am–4pm; $6) protects nearly 100 acres of mangroves and dense forests that are home to a bewildering number of bird species, such as blue-footed boobies, ospreys and peregrine falcons. There is quite a bit of terrestrial wildlife too, including crocodiles and caiman. An **elevated walkway** (2hr round-trip) passes through a beautiful section of mangrove swamp where the calls of birds and frogs seem jarring against the often ghostly silence. Consider hiring a guide at the *Lagarta Lodge* (an additional $5) for the chance to learn more about the fascinating reserve and enable you to spot far more animals than you're likely to see on your own.

Refugio Nacional de Vida Silvestre Ostional

Eight kilometres northwest of Nosara, **Ostional** and its chocolate-coloured-sand beach make up the **REFUGIO NACIONAL DE VIDA SILVESTRE OSTIONAL**, one of the most important nesting grounds in the country for **olive ridley turtles** who come ashore to lay their eggs en masse. If you're in town during the first few days of the *arribadas* (see box, p.310), you'll see local villagers with horses, carefully stuffing their big, thick bags full of eggs and slinging them over their shoulders. This is quite legal: villagers of Ostional and Nosara are allowed to harvest eggs, for sale or consumption, during the first three days of the season only. Don't be surprised to see them barefoot, rocking back and forth on their heels as if they were crushing grapes in a winery; this is the surest way to pick up the telltale signs of eggs beneath the sand. You can't swim comfortably at Ostional though, since the water's very rough and is plagued by sharks, for whom turtle nesting points are like all-you-can-eat buffets.

Arribadas

One of only two species of marine turtles who nest in mass numbers (Kemp's ridleys being the other), **olive ridley turtles** emerge from the sea in their tens of thousands onto the beaches of Ostional to lay their eggs, mainly in the rainy season from August to December. These **arribadas** (the Spanish word for arrivals) can last over twelve hours, with a steady stream of females crawling slowly out of the water to a free patch of sand beyond the high tide line where they will begin to lay their eggs.

Each individual will lay around one hundred eggs over the course of a few days; collectively **several million eggs** may be deposited on the shores of Ostional during a single *arribada*. It is the sheer number of eggs that is the evolutionary reason behind the unusual behaviour of the olive ridleys: the more eggs there are, the better chance the offspring have of survival. With so many eggs and hatchlings for predators to prey on, the likelihood of a hatchling making it out to sea increases dramatically. Despite the mass layings, however, the odds are still stacked overwhelmingly against the young turtles – only one out of three hundred hatchlings from the protected beaches of Ostional will reach adulthood.

It takes about fifteen minutes to drive the gravel-and-stone road from Nosara to the refuge; alternatively you can bike it or take a taxi (about $8–10). There are a couple of places to stay and eat in the village.

Parque Nacional Barra Honda and around

The **PARQUE NACIONAL BARRA HONDA** (Dec–April daily 8am–4pm; $10), about 40km east of Nicoya and 13km west of the Río Tempisque, is popular with spelunkers for its forty-odd subterranean **caves**. A visit to Barra Honda is not for claustrophobes, people afraid of heights (some of the caves are more than 200m deep) or anyone with an aversion to creepy-crawlies.

The landscape around here is dominated by the **limestone plateau** of the Cerro Barra Honda, which rises out of the flat lowlands of the eastern Nicoya Peninsula. About seventy million years ago this whole area – along with Palo Verde, across the Río Tempisque – was under water. Over the millennia, the porous limestone was gradually hollowed out, by rainfall and weathering, to create caves and weird karstic formations.

The caves form a catacomb-like interconnecting network beneath the limestone ridge, but you can't necessarily pass from one to the other. Kitted out with a rope harness and a helmet with a lamp on it, you descend with a guide, who will normally take you down into just one. The **main caves**, all within 2km of each other and of the ranger station, are the Terciopelo, the Trampa, Santa Ana, Pozo Hediondo and Nicoa, where the remains of pre-Columbian peoples were recently found, along with burial ornaments and utensils thought to be over two thousand years old. Most people come wanting to view the huge needle-like **stalagmites** and **stalactites** at Terciopelo, or to see subterranean wildlife such as bats, blind salamanders, insects and even birds.

Down in the depths, you're faced with a sight reminiscent of old etchings of Moby Dick's stomach, with sleek, moist walls, jutting rib-like ridges and strangely smooth protuberances. Some caves are big enough – almost cathedral-like, in fact, with their vaulted ceilings – to allow breathing room for those who don't like enclosed spaces, but it's still an eerie experience, like descending into a ruined subterranean Notre Dame inhabited by crawling things you can barely see. There's even an "organ" of fluted stalagmites in the Terciopelo cave; if knocked, each gives off a slightly different musical note.

Above ground, three short **trails**, not well marked, lead around the caves. It's easy to get lost, and you should walk them with your guide or with a ranger if there is one free, and take water with you. Some time ago, two German hikers attempted to walk the trails independently, got lost and, because they were not carrying water, died of dehydration and heat exhaustion.

The endangered **scarlet macaw** sometimes nests here, and there are a variety of ground mammals about, including anteaters and deer. As usual, you'll be lucky to see any, though you'll certainly hear howler monkeys.

Practicalities

You need to be pretty serious about caves to go spelunking in Barra Honda. Quite apart from all the planning, what with the entrance fee, the payment to the guide and the price of renting equipment ($25), costs can add up. It's obligatory to go with a **guide**, who will also provide **equipment**; to do otherwise would be foolhardy, not to mention illegal. You pay your entry fee at the **ranger station**, which will give you information and perhaps supply a guide, but to save a trip, it's worth checking conditions and availability of guides first, either at the ACT regional headquarters (see p.259) on the Interamericana or in Nicoya. Anyone who wants to follow the **trails** at Barra Honda has to tell the rangers where they are intending to walk and how long they intend to be gone for.

If you speak Spanish, another good way to hook up with guides is to call Sr Olman Cubillo, president of the local community development association, at the Complejo Ecoturístico Las Delicias (Ⓣ2685-5580) in **Santa Ana**, the nearest hamlet to the caves. Recommended by both the SPN and the ACT, he can also provide **local information** about food, lodging, camping and horseback tours.

Driving to Barra Honda is possible even with a regular car. From the Nicoya–Tempisque road, the turn-off, 13km before the bridge, is well signed. It's then 4km along a good gravel road to the hamlet of Nacaome (also called Barra Honda), from where the park is, again, signed. Continue about 6km further, passing the hamlet of Santa Ana until you reach the ranger station, where most people arrange to meet their guide.

There's a **campsite** inside the park, with picnic tables and drinking water ($2 per person), but most people who come to Barra Honda, stay in Nicoya (see p.300), or across the Río Tempisque on the mainland.

Cave architecture

Created by the interaction of water, calcium bicarbonate and limestone, the distinctive cave formations of stalagmites and stalactites are often mistaken for each other. **Stalagmites** grow upwards from the floor of a cave, formed by drips of water saturated with calcium bicarbonate. **Stalactites**, made of a similar deposit of crystalline calcium bicarbonate, grow downwards, like icicles. Both are formed by water and calcium bicarbonate filtering through limestone and partially dissolving it. In limestone caves, stalagmites and stalactites are usually white (from the limestone) or brown; in caves where copper deposits are present colours might be more psychedelic, with iridescent greens and blues. They often become united, over time, in a single column.

Travel details

Buses

Cañas to: Liberia (9 daily; 50min); San José (11 daily; 3hr 30min).
Liberia to: Bagaces (11 daily; 40min); Cañas (11 daily; 50min); Cuajiniquil (1 daily; 1hr 30min); La Cruz (14 daily; 1hr); Nicoya (10 daily; 2hr); Parque Nacional Santa Rosa (5 daily; 1hr); Peñas Blancas (6 daily; 2hr); Playa del Coco (12 daily; 1hr); Playa Hermosa (8 daily; 1hr 20min); Playa Panamá (8 daily; 1hr 20min); Puntarenas (5 daily; 3hr); San José (11 daily; 4hr 30min); Santa Cruz (14 daily; 1hr); Tamarindo (6 daily; 1hr 30min–2hr).
Nicoya to: Liberia (10 daily; 2hr); Nosara (1 daily; 2hr); Playa Sámara (7–10 daily; 1hr 30min); San José (8 daily; 6hr); Santa Cruz (16 daily; 40min).
Nosara to: Nicoya (1 daily; 2hr); Playa Sámara (2 daily; 40min); San José (1 daily; 6hr).
Peñas Blancas to: Liberia (6 daily; 2hr); San José (3 daily; 6hr).
Playa Brasilito to: San José (3 daily; 6hr); Santa Cruz (2 daily; 1hr 30min).
Playa del Coco to: Liberia (9 daily; 1hr); San José (3 daily; 5hr).
Playa Conchal to: San José (3 daily; 6hr); Santa Cruz (2 daily; 1hr 30min).
Playa Flamingo to: San José (3 daily; 6hr); Santa Cruz (13 daily; 1hr 40min).
Playa Hermosa to: Liberia (8 daily; 1hr 20min); San José (1 daily; 6hr).
Playa Junquillal to: San José (1 daily; 5hr); Santa Cruz (4 daily; 1hr 30min).
Playa Panamá to: Liberia (8 daily; 1hr 20min); San José (1 daily; 6hr).
Playa Potrero to: San José (3 daily; 6hr); Santa Cruz (2 daily; 2hr).
Playa Sámara to: Nicoya (10–14 daily; 1hr 30min); Nosara (2 daily; 40min); San José (2 daily; 5hr).
San José to: Cañas (11 daily; 3hr 30min); Nicoya (8 daily; 6hr); Nosara (1 daily; 6hr); Parque Nacional Santa Rosa (4 daily; 6hr); Peñas Blancas (3 daily; 6hr); Playa Brasilito (3 daily; 6hr); Playa del Coco (3 daily; 5hr); Playa Flamingo (3 daily; 6hr); Playa Hermosa (1 daily; 5hr); Playa Junquillal (1 daily; 5hr); Liberia (11 daily; 4hr); Playa Panamá (1 daily; 6hr); Playa Potrero (3 daily; 6hr); Playa Sámara (3 daily; 5hr); Santa Cruz (5 daily; 5hr); Tamarindo (2 daily; 6hr).
Santa Cruz to: Liberia (14 daily; 1hr); Nicoya (16 daily; 40min); Playa Brasilito (2 daily; 1hr 30min); Playa Flamingo (2 daily; 1hr 30min); Playa Junquillal (4 daily; 1hr 30min); Playa Potrero (2 daily; 2hr); San José (5 daily; 5hr); Tamarindo (6 direct daily; 1hr).
Tamarindo to: Liberia (6 daily; 1hr 30min–2hr); San José (2 daily; 6hr); Santa Cruz (6 direct daily; 1hr).

Flights (Sansa)

San José to: Liberia (1 daily; 1hr 15min); Nosara (1 daily; 1hr 10min); Playa Sámara (Mon–Sat 1 daily; 1hr); Tamarindo (3 daily; 50min).

Flights (NatureAir)

San José to: Liberia (4 daily; 1hr 45min); Nosara (3 daily; 1hr 10min); Playa Sámara (4 daily; 1hr).

6

The Central Pacific and southern Nicoya

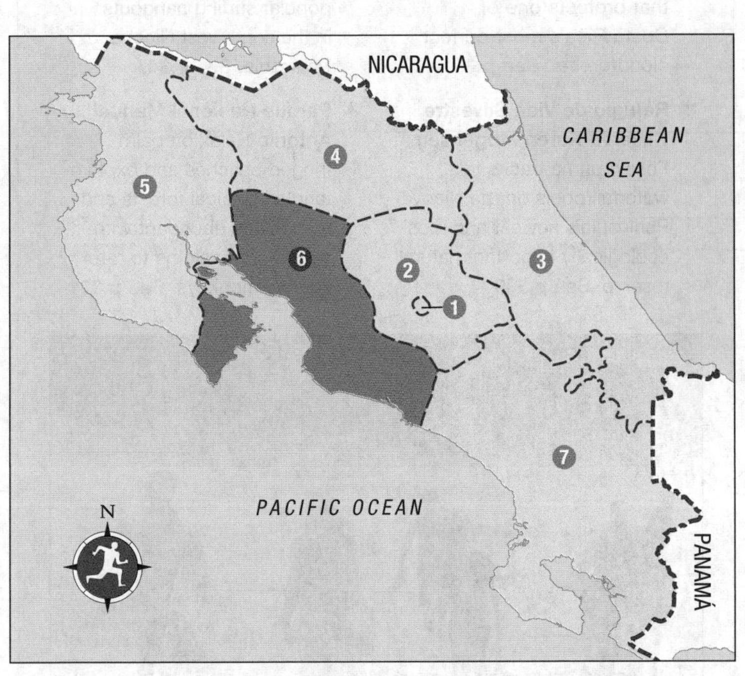

CHAPTER 6

Highlights

* **Monteverde night walk** The jungle comes alive after dark – take an eerie hike through Monteverde's dense rainforest on the lookout for bats, frogs and tarantulas. **See p.330**

* **Reserva Santa Elena** Search for the elusive quetzal in this lush reserve that protects one of Costa Rica's most perfect cloudforests. **See p.331**

* **Refugio de Vida Silvestre Reserva Karen Mogensen** Follow puma tracks to waterfall pools on the Nicoya Peninsula's newest and most ecologically important nature reserve. **See p.339**

* **Reserva Natural Absoluta Cabo Blanco** Costa Rica's oldest piece of protected land features unique Pacific lowland tropical forest and is home to howler monkeys, white-tailed deer and flocks of pelicans. **See p.346**

* **Mal País and Santa Teresa** Ride the waves at these popular surfing hangouts in the southwest Nicoya Peninsula. **See p.347**

* **Parque Nacional Manuel Antonio** Relax on palm-fringed beaches and explore tangled tropical forests and mangroves abundant with wildlife, from sloths to rare squirrel monkeys. **See p.371**

▲ Surfers at Mal País

6

The Central Pacific and southern Nicoya

Costa Rica's **Central Pacific** region boasts several of the country's most popular tourist spots, including the number-one attraction, the **Reserva Biológica Bosque Nuboso Monteverde** (the Monteverde Cloudforest Biological Reserve), draped over the ridge of the Cordillera de Tilarán. Along with nearby **Reserva Santa Elena**, Monteverde protects some of the last remaining pristine **cloudforest** in the Americas. **Southern Nicoya**, effectively cut off by bad roads and a provincial boundary from the north of the peninsula (covered in Chapter 5), is part of **Puntarenas** province, whose eponymous capital, a steamy tropical port across the Gulf of Nicoya on the mainland, is the only town of any size in the entire area.

The area is home to some of Costa Rica's best-known **beaches**, several of which are easily accessed from San José on the new Caldera Highway. Each offers a distinct experience, from the coves of chilled-out **Montezuma**, a former fishing village, to the forest-flanked coastline of **Mal País** and **Santa Teresa**, to the huge waves of **Jacó** and **Playa Hermosa**, two of the most popular places to surf in the country. Further south, **Parque Nacional Manuel Antonio** has several extraordinary beaches, with white sands and azure waters.

With the exception of the cool **climate** of Monteverde, the region is tropical and drier than in the south of the country – temperatures can be uncomfortably high, with a dry-season average of about 30°C (86°F), and even in the much quieter wet season (Quepos and Manuel Antonio, in particular, receive torrential afternoon rains) temperatures don't cool down by much.

Three **routes** connect San José with the Central Pacific coast, taking between 45 minutes and two hours. The **Interamericana** climbs over the Cordillera Central before dropping precipitously into the Pacific lowlands and levelling out at the town of Esparza, a few kilometres before the turn-off for Puntarenas. A more direct route for travellers aiming for Playa Jacó and Parque Nacional Manuel Antonio is the **Caldera Highway**, a fast toll road that runs due west of the capital; opened in March 2010, it shadows **Hwy-3** as far as Orotina, where it continues on to Puerto Caldera, while the older road heads south to Jacó. Overall, Hwy-3 is the more pleasant experience, with great views and good roadside stalls selling fudge, nuts and *galletas* (cookies); furthermore, it's in very good condition for most of the way between Orotina and Jacó, offering some of the least stressful driving in the country. By contrast, **the journey to Monteverde** can be quite an

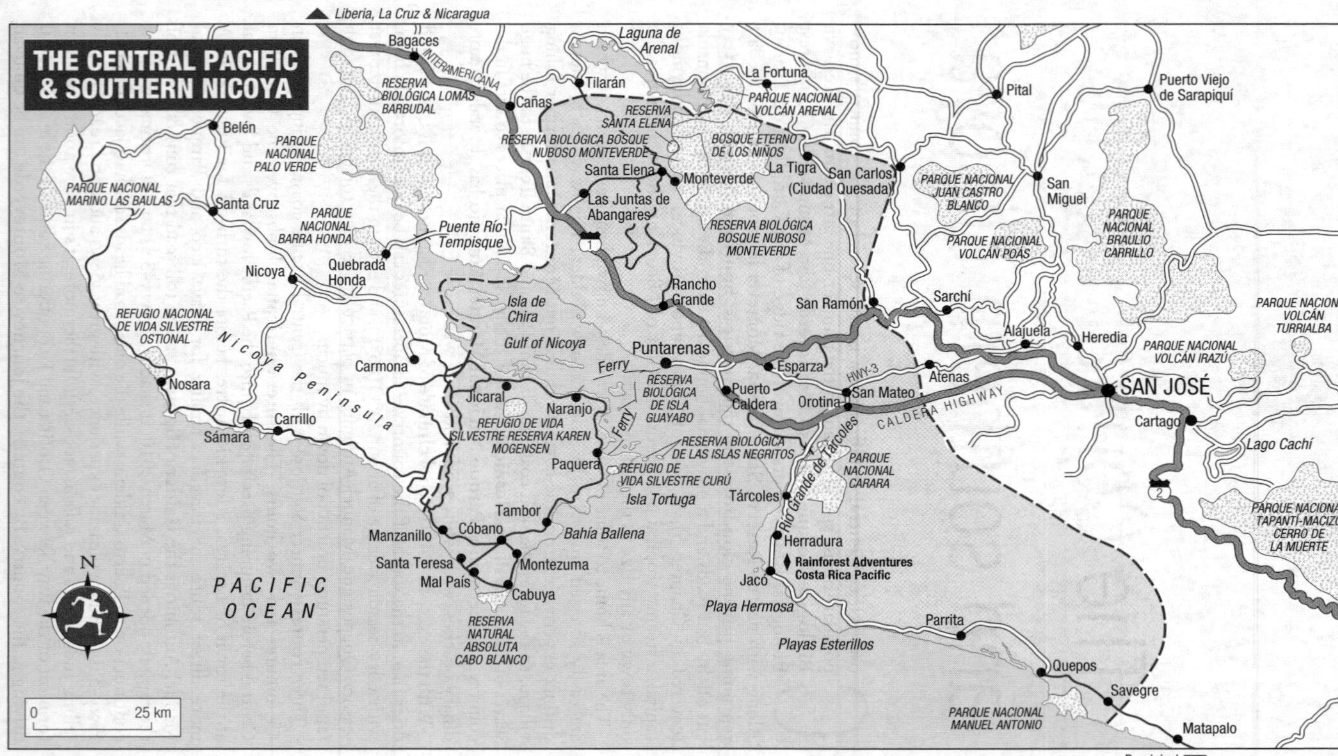
THE CENTRAL PACIFIC & SOUTHERN NICOYA
Liberia, La Cruz & Nicaragua
Golfito & Osa Peninsula
Dominical
Bagaces
INTERAMERICANA
RESERVA BIOLÓGICA LOMAS BARBUDAL
Cañas
Tilarán
Laguna de Arenal
La Fortuna
PARQUE NACIONAL VOLCÁN ARENAL
Pital
Puerto Viejo de Sarapiquí
RESERVA SANTA ELENA
RESERVA BIOLÓGICA BOSQUE NUBOSO MONTEVERDE
BOSQUE ETERNO DE LOS NIÑOS
Santa Elena
Monteverde
La Tigra
San Carlos (Ciudad Quesada)
PARQUE NACIONAL JUAN CASTRO BLANCO
San Miguel
PARQUE NACIONAL BRAULIO CARRILLO
Belén
PARQUE NACIONAL PALO VERDE
PARQUE NACIONAL MARINO LAS BAULAS
Santa Cruz
Las Juntas de Abangares
PARQUE NACIONAL BARRA HONDA
Puente Río Tempisque
RESERVA BIOLÓGICA BOSQUE NUBOSO MONTEVERDE
PARQUE NACIONAL VOLCÁN POÁS
1
Nicoya
Quebrada Honda
Rancho Grande
San Ramón
Sarchí
PARQUE NACIONAL VOLCÁN TURRIALBA
Isla de Chira
REFUGIO NACIONAL DE VIDA SILVESTRE OSTIONAL
Nicoya Peninsula
Gulf of Nicoya
Alajuela
Heredia
PARQUE NACIONAL VOLCÁN IRAZÚ
Puntarenas
Carmona
Ferry
RESERVA BIOLÓGICA DE ISLA GUAYABO
Esparza
HWY-3
Atenas
SAN JOSÉ
Nosara
Jicaral
Naranjo
Puerto Caldera
San Mateo
Orotina
CALDERA HIGHWAY
Cartago
REFUGIO DE VIDA SILVESTRE RESERVA KAREN MOGENSEN
Carrillo
Sámara
Ferry
RESERVA BIOLÓGICA DE LAS ISLAS NEGRITOS
Río Grande de Tárcoles
Lago Cachí
PARQUE NACIONAL CARARA
Paquera
REFUGIO DE VIDA SILVESTRE CURÚ
2
Isla Tortuga
Tárcoles
PARQUE NACIONAL TAPANTÍ-MACIZO CERRO DE LA MUERTE
Tambor
Manzanillo
Cóbano
Bahía Ballena
Herradura
Santa Teresa
Montezuma
Rainforest Adventures Costa Rica Pacific
Mal País
Jacó
N
PACIFIC OCEAN
Cabuya
Playa Hermosa
RESERVA NATURAL ABSOLUTA CABO BLANCO
Parrita
Playas Esterillos
Quepos
Savegre
0
25 km
PARQUE NACIONAL MANUEL ANTONIO
Matapalo

expedition – although it's only 180km from San José, the final 35km is along a poor and unpaved road. The majority of visitors cross over to the **southern Nicoya Peninsula** from Puntarenas on the **ferries** to Naranjo (for Nicoya) or Paquera (for Tambor and Montezuma), though the bridge across the mouth of the Río Tempisque is an alternative route for drivers.

Monteverde and around

Though generally associated only with its eponymous cloudforest reserve, **MONTEVERDE** actually covers a larger area, straddling the hump of the Cordillera de Tilarán between Volcán Arenal and Laguna de Arenal to the northeast and the low hills of Guanacaste to the west. Along with the reserve, you'll find the spread-out Quaker community of Monteverde village; the neighbouring town of **Santa Elena** – with the majority of the area's amenities and budget accommodation – and, further afield, its own cloudforest reserve; as well as several small hamlets, including **Cerro Plano**. Throughout the region, the enchantment of the cloudforests is magnified by a combination of tranquil beauty, invigorating weather and the odd mix of Swiss-style farms and tropical botanical gardens.

Seeking autonomy and seclusion, the **Quaker** families living here arrived from Alabama in the United States in the 1950s. The climate and terrain proved ideal for **dairy farming**, which fast became the mainstay of the economy – the region is famed throughout the country for its dairy products, and you'll see a variety of

The Quakers of Monteverde

Quakerism (*cuáquerismo*), also called the Society of Friends (ⓦwww.quaker.org), is an altruistic, optimistic belief system founded by an Englishman, **George Fox** (1624–91), who instilled in his followers the importance of seeing God in everybody. From the beginning, Quakers placed themselves in opposition to many of the coercive instruments employed by the state and society – a philosophy that subjected them to severe discrimination when they first arrived in the New World in 1656 – and they continue to embody a blend of the conservative with an absolute resistance to state control.

In the early 1950s, a group of Quakers from Alabama fled the US, having been harassed to the point of imprisonment for refusing the draft (**pacifism** is a cornerstone of Quaker beliefs). Attracted by the fact that Costa Rica had abolished its army a few years earlier in 1948, they settled in Monteverde. At the time, the remote village was home to only a few Costa Rican farming families; there was no road, only an ox-cart track, and the journey to San José took several days. The Quakers bought and settled some twelve square kilometres of mountainside, dividing the land and building their houses and a school.

Quakerism doesn't impose any obvious standards of dress or appearance upon its followers – you're not going to see the jolly old man from the oatmeal box sauntering by – nor does it manifest itself in any way that is immediately obvious to visitors, except for the area's relative lack of bars. The Quakers manage their **meeting houses** individually, with no officiating minister and purely local agendas. Gatherings focus on meditation, but anyone who is moved to say a few words or read simply speaks up – all verbal offerings in context are considered valid. The meeting houses welcome outsiders, who are never subject to being converted. In Monteverde, visitors can attend meetings at the **Friends Meeting House**, held on Wednesdays at 9.30am and Sundays at 10.30am.

its cheeses in most *supermercados*. Abroad, however, Monteverde is known for its pioneering private nature reserves. Of these, the **Reserva Biológica Bosque Nuboso Monteverde** is the most popular, although the **Reserva Santa Elena** offers equally pristine cloudforest cover and, because it receives fewer visitors, may prove the more fruitful of the two for spotting wildlife. The huge **Bosque Eterno de los Niños** (Children's Eternal Rainforest), established with funds raised by school kids from all over the world, surrounds Monteverde; day and night walks are offered in the Bajo del Tigre section, the easiest part of the reserve to explore. To avoid the inevitable crowds, consider visiting at the beginning or end of the **wet season** (May–Nov), when you should still get decent weather.

Note that the **roads** to Monteverde, built purely to serve small rural communities, are generally in poor condition. While tour operators bemoan their state, the **Monteverde Conservation League** (MCL) and the wider community have resisted suggestions to pave them, arguing that easier access would increase visitor numbers to unsustainable levels and threaten the integrity of local communities. Whatever the future holds, it's unlikely that Monteverde will be

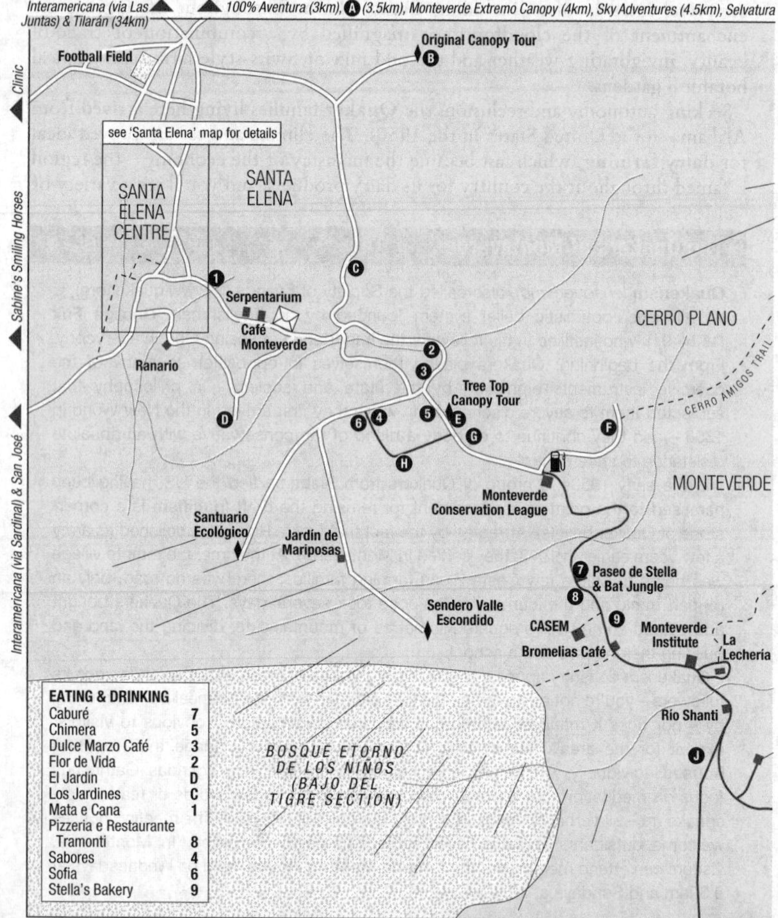

ruined: the community is too outspoken and organized to let itself be overrun by its own success.

Arrival

Most people coming **by bus from San José** (C12, Av 7/9) arrive on one of the two direct services (6.30am & 2.30pm; 4hr 30min); demand is high, so book your tickets a few days in advance in high season. Buses also run here from **La Fortuna** via Tilarán (leaving the latter at 4.30am & 12.30pm; 2hr 30min) and **Puntarenas** (7.50am, 1.50pm & 2.15pm; 3hr). The **bus stop** is next to the church in Santa Elena, at the top of the town centre "triangle". Numerous **taxis** line the street next to the bus station.

Another immensely popular way of getting here from La Fortuna is on the **Taxi–Boat–Taxi** transfer (see box, p.218), a superb (and time-saving) way to travel between two of the country's major attractions; alternative versions replace the final leg with either a bike or horse ride.

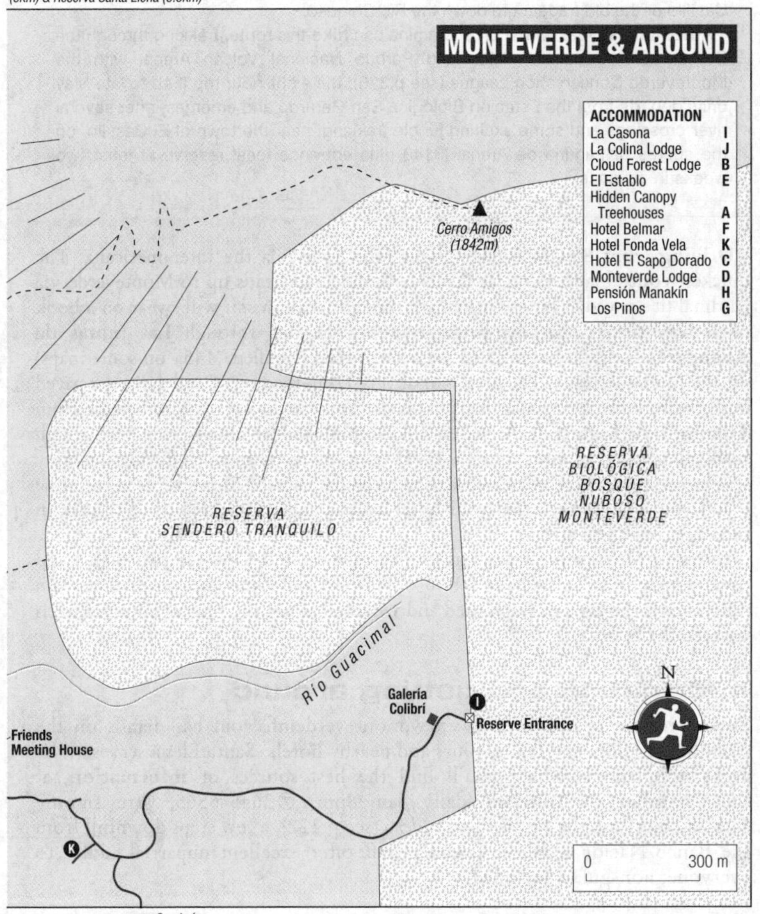

Moving on from Monteverde

Buses for **San José** leave daily at 6.30am and 2.30pm (4hr 30min). Buses also run from Santa Elena to **Tilarán** (daily 7am & 4pm; 2hr 30min) for connections to La Fortuna, and **Puntarenas** (daily 4.30am, 6am & 3pm; 3hr). The first Puntarenas service stops in **Las Juntas** (2hr) from where you can get to **Liberia** and points north in Guanacaste; otherwise, take the San José-bound bus and get off just after the bus turns onto the Interamericana, at the intersection for Chomes, from where you can hail northbound buses to Liberia and elsewhere. Check at the ticket office at the Santa Elena bus stop for **timetables** to all buses and to buy tickets for the more popular routes in advance (daily 5.30–7am, 7.30–11am & 1.30–5pm, till 3pm on Sun).

The **"Taxi-Boat-Taxi" transfer to La Fortuna**, near Volcán Arenal (daily departures at 8am & 2pm; $25; 3hr), involves a ninety-minute minibus journey to the shores of Laguna de Arenal, then a spectacular ride across the water with the volcano looming above, and finally another vehicle to La Fortuna. Desafío Expeditions and Sabine's Smiling Horses (see box, p.325) can arrange a Horse-Boat-Taxi alternative ($85; 5hr), riding along the shore of Laguna de Arenal or, in the dry season (Dec–July), via El Castillo or the old trade route down the Río Chiquito.

Adventurous types with a bit of stamina can **hike** this route, trekking through the Bosque Eterno de los Niños and Parque Nacional Volcán Arenal with the Monteverde Conservation League (see p.326); the eight-hour trip (Feb to late May only) departs from the Estación Biológica San Gerardo and emerges, after several river crossings and some exciting jungle trekking, near the town of El Castillo, on the shores of Laguna de Arenal ($140 plus entrance fees; reserve at least two weeks in advance).

Driving from San José takes about four hours via the Interamericana. The quickest **route** branches off at Rancho Grande and heads up to Monteverde via Sardinal (it's paved as far as Guacimal), though local *taxistas* will swear on a book of lottery tickets that the better route is the one through **Las Juntas de Abangares**, a tiny town reached via a small road (labelled "145" on some maps) off the Interamericana. The first 7km of this 37km road, via Candelaria, are paved but beware some spectacular hairpin bends. You can also reach Monteverde from **Tilarán**, near Laguna de Arenal, a 40km uphill judder along often very rough roads. Regardless of your route, a **4WD** is highly recommended during the rainy season – some agencies even refuse to rent regular cars for Monteverde at this time – and you should check that your hotel has parking, as it's impossible to park in the street once you arrive.

Tours to Monteverde from San José average around $350 for two nights and usually include accommodation, return transport and sometimes meals. The main difference is the type of hotel used and whether or not the reserve entrance fee is covered in the price.

Information and getting around

For a preview of the area, Ⓦwww.monteverdeinfo.com has details on the cloudforest's flora and fauna, tours and nearby hotels. Santa Elena serves as the area's hub, and is where you'll find the best sources of **information**, at the **Chamber of Tourism** (daily 8am–8pm; Ⓣ2645-6565, Ⓔturismomv@racsa.co.cr) and the *Pensión Santa Elena* (see p.322), a few steps downhill from the Banco Nacional, whose friendly staff offer excellent impartial advice to everyone, non-guests included.

The village of Cerro Plano lies 1km to the east of Santa Elena, with the reserves a long walk, uphill, in either direction – **shuttle buses** run from Sant Elena's Info Center Camino Verde to the Monteverde reserve (daily 6.15am, 7.30am, 1.20am & 3pm, returning 6.45am, 11.30am, 2pm & 4pm; 30min; $1 each way) and the Santa Elena reserve (daily 6.30am, 8.30am, 10.30am, 12.30pm & 3pm, returning 11am, 1pm & 4pm; 30min; $2 each way). **Jeep-taxis** charge around $10 one-way from the town to the former and $8 to the latter.

Accommodation

Santa Elena offers the area's cheapest accommodation – it's mostly basic, but you'll get heated water to go with a warm welcome, and the owners usually offer an array of services, from home cooking and laundry to horse hire. In contrast, hotels in and around the **Monteverde** community aspire to European mountain-resort facilities – large rooms, orthopedic mattresses and even saunas and hot tubs are the norm –and tend to be expensive, appealing to those who like their wilderness deluxe. These hotels often have a restaurant and meals may be included. Aside from illustrated nature talks, nightlife within the hotels is low-key to nonexistent – some have a small bar, and that's about it.

Santa Elena and around

The accommodation listed below is marked on the Santa Elena map on p.324, unless otherwise stated.

Arco Iris Up a side street just east of the town centre ⓣ2645-5067, ⓦwww.arcoirislodge.com. Relax in spacious, well-appointed cabins amid quiet landscaped gardens near the town centre. You can also stay in cheaper rooms with double or bunk beds (❹). The delicious breakfast ($7) of hearty German bread, granola, fresh fruit, eggs and toast is also available to non-guests (daily 7–9am). ❻

Cabinas Eddy 100m southwest of the supermarket ⓣ2645-6618, ⓦwww.cabinas-eddy.com. The well-scrubbed rooms here (some with private bath) can accommodate up to seven people and are a cut above most of the other budget options in town. Combine this with friendly owners, free tea, coffee and internet, and mountain views from the wraparound balcony, and you're onto a winner. Breakfast is $5 extra. ❷

Cabinas Vista Al Golfo 300m southwest of the church ⓣ2645-6682, ⓦwww.cabinasvistaalgolfo.com. One of the best budget options in Monteverde boasts bright, clean dorms ($8) and rooms, some with bath, plus fully equipped apartments with private balconies (❹). Enjoy fantastic views of the Gulf of Nicoya and hang out with fellow travellers in the sociable shared kitchen. There's free internet, and the cheery owners can organize tours. ❷

Casa Tranquilo 100m downhill from the supermarket ⓣ2645-6782, ⓦwww.casatranquilohostel.com. This cheerful terracotta-coloured hangout buzzing with seasoned travellers has seven clean, bright rooms (some with private bathroom) and comfortable mattresses to boot. Free internet and on-site laundry service are a plus. ❷

Claro de Luna 300m southwest of the church, opposite *Cabinas Vista Al Golfo* ⓣ2645-5269, ⓦwww.clarodelunahotel.com. Nine pretty rooms with blissfully comfortable beds (deluxe rooms have four-posters; ❼) and luxurious bathrooms occupying an exquisite wooden house with a dramatically sloped roof. ❻

Cloud Forest Lodge 500m northeast of Santa Elena ⓣ2645-5058, ⓦwww.cloudforestlodge.com. See Monteverde and around map on p.318. Set in seventy acres of primary and secondary forest high above Santa Elena, this secluded, surprisingly low-priced hotel is one of the classiest in the area. The well-appointed wood-panelled cabins have cable TV, large private bathroom and terraces with dizzying views, and the hotel has its own 5km system of trails. ❼

Hidden Canopy Treehouses 4km north of Santa Elena, on the road to the reserve ⓣ2645-5447, ⓦwww.hiddencanopy.com. See Monteverde and around map on p.318. Fantastic treehouses, the sort you dreamed of as a kid, perched up in the canopy, with oversized beds and huge windows that make the most of the superb views down to the Gulf of Nicoya. Bathrooms have exotic waterfall showers, and two (split-level) treehouses even have jacuzzis on their balconies. There are also rooms in the main house if you haven't got a head for heights. Rooms ❽, treehouses from $245.

Hotel El Sueño 25m east of the supermarket ⓣ2645-6695, ⓦwww.hotelelsuenocr.com. Stay in cosy, rustic wooden rooms right in the heart of Santa Elena. The main building houses the cheaper ones with shared bath, while modern, split-level en-suite rooms occupy the annexe (❺). Start your day with a tasty breakfast cooked up by the friendly owners. ❹

Pensión Santa Elena 25m downhill from the Banco Nacional ⓣ2645-5051, ⓦwww.pensionsantaelena.com. Perennially popular central hostel – the helpful owners are a wealth of local information – offering four- and six-bed dorms ($7) with shared hot-water bathrooms, some decent doubles with private bath out back and new, attractive *cabinas* (❸). Amenities include a kitchen, cheap internet and large communal area where you can yap the night away with fellow backpackers. ❷

Sleepers 200m southwest of Santa Elena ⓣ2645-7133, ⓦwww.sleeperssleepcheaperhostels.com. Simple accommodation in a variety of clean (mixed) dorms ($7.50) and rooms (sleeping up to 4) that ticks all the boxes for backpackers: cheap lodgings, communal atmosphere, shared kitchen and free tea, coffee, pancakes and internet. ❶

Tree House Hotel On the main street ⓣ2645-5004, ⓦwww.monteverdeinfo.com/tree-house-hotel. Built around a fifty-year-old strangler fig, this central hotel offers superb value for money. The rooms (try to get one with a balcony) are fresh and light and can sleep up to seven people; most come with private bathroom. They've done their best with sound insulation, but bear in mind that the hotel is next door to rowdy *Bar Amigos*. It's a good source of local knowledge – the owners run monteverdeinfo.com – and the *Treehouse Café* downstairs is the funkiest in town (see p.327). ❹

Cerro Plano

All the accommodation listed below is marked on the Monteverde and around map on p.318.

El Establo 1.3km east of Santa Elena ⓣ2645-5110, ⓦwww.elestablo.com. Large-scale luxury lodgings with copious facilities (heated swimming pools, tennis and basketball courts and a canopy tour; see box opposite) should you still have energy to burn after a hike in the reserve – and a spa for those that don't. Carpeted rooms are a decent size given the layout and come with two queen beds and large bathrooms. ❽

Hotel Belmar 2km east of Santa Elena ⓣ2645-5201, ⓦwww.hotelbelmar.net. The oldest of the area's many Swiss-style hotels, the perennially popular *Belmar* sits on a hillside above Cerro Plano, with sweeping views of the gulf. Pricier rooms are somewhat larger and equipped with a fan, rarely a necessity in blustery Monteverde. ❼

Hotel El Sapo Dorado 500m east of Santa Elena ⓣ2645-5010, ⓦwww.sapodorado.com. Take in stupendous views of the Gulf of Nicoya from these spacious, rustic wooden chalets perched on a hill. The Mountain Suites are set higher than the others and come with open fireplaces, while the Sunset Suites lower down benefit from a spacious terrace. The restaurant serves tasty fare using mostly organic ingredients and can cater to special diets (see p.328). ❼

Monteverde Lodge 400m southeast of Santa Elena ⓣ2645-5214, ⓦwww.costaricaexpeditions.com. The Monteverde outpost of this well-regarded tour operator has tasteful rooms with super-comfy beds and corner windows overlooking thick forest, plus three cheaper garden lodgings ($111). After a walk in the reserve, settle down in the cosy bar (with open fire) for afternoon tea and cake. Staff are exceedingly helpful, and the on-site restaurant is superb (see p.327). ❽

Pensión Manakín 1.3km east of Santa Elena ⓣ2645-5080, ⓦwww.manakinlodge.com. This family pension with the forest as its backyard offers some of the friendliest budget accommodation in the area, including family rooms that almost disappear into the trees ($50). Guests also have access to laundry service and internet. The owner can whip up traditional or vegetarian food on demand. ❸

Los Pinos 1.5km east of Santa Elena ⓣ2645-5252, ⓦwww.lospinos.net. A terrific family hideaway, these great-value self-catering cabins set amid forested gardens are far enough from each other to guarantee privacy. The six-bed, three-bathroom cabins are a good deal at $125 and come with large kitchens and lounge area. Guests can pick their own dinner from the hydroponic greenhouse. ❺

Monteverde

All the accommodation listed below is marked on the Monteverde and around map on p.318.

La Casona Reserva Biológica Bosque Nuboso Monteverde ⓣ2645-5122, ⓦwww.cct.or.cr. Accommodation is in basic dorms (some with private bathrooms), but there's an infectious environmental buzz about this lodge located just inside the reserve. It's often packed with researchers and students (tourists are second priority), so advance reservations are essential.

Canopy tours and hanging bridges

The ever-popular **canopy tours** that now seem an obligatory part of any activities centre in Costa Rica were pioneered in Monteverde, using techniques developed by cavers and canyon rappellers to let visitors experience the rainforest from a bird's-eye view. For a different – but no less exhilarating – forest adventure, take a hike along one of the **hanging bridges**, which thread through the treetops for several kilometres; bring binoculars, for here's your chance to spot birds and howler monkeys at their own level.

100% Aventura 3.5km north of Santa Elena ⓣ2645-6959, ⓦwww.monteverdeadventure.com. A dozen cables interspersed with a Tarzan swing and rappelling ($40), plus 2.5km of hanging bridges ($25).

Monteverde Extremo Canopy 4.5km north of Santa Elena ⓣ2645-6058, ⓦwww.monteverdeextremo.com. The newest company on the block, with adrenaline-fuelled tours of fifteen cables through secondary forest ($40); the Superman ($5 extra), requires adopting the eponymous arms-out, legs-up pose down a kilometre-long wire hanging 180m above the trees.

Original Canopy Tour Office next to the Banco Nacional in Santa Elena, reserve located near the *Cloud Forest Lodge* ⓣ2645-5243, ⓦwww.canopytour.com. They're not fibbing: the first canopy tour in Monteverde (and therefore the world) may be smaller than its competitors, but it's more in harmony with its surroundings – stepladders run up the trees themselves (and even through one old fig tree), and the platforms barely get beyond poking out from their boughs. Tours ($45) include a rappel and a Tarzan swing, and there's also the option of a night ride (daily 5.30–8pm).

Selvatura Office opposite the church in Santa Elena, reserve located 6.5km north of Santa Elena ⓣ2645-5929, ⓦwww.selvatura.com. Similar set-up to Sky Adventures, with sixteen-cable canopy tours ($45) and a network of hanging bridges ($40 with a guide), plus a number of wildlife exhibits, the most interesting of which is the Jewels of the Rainforest, one of the largest collections of insects in the world ($12). Transport runs from Santa Elena at 8am, 10.30am 12.30pm & 2pm to coincide with the canopy tour times.

Sky Adventures Office next to the Santa Elena bus station, reserve located 5km north of Santa Elena ⓣ2645-5238, ⓦwww.skyadventures.travel. After a tram ride up above the trees, zip along ten high-tension cables, including one that's a whopping kilometre in length ($60); you can also take an interesting hike with a well-informed naturalist guide along their impressive series of hanging bridges and paths ($30).

Tree Top Canopy Tour El Establo, 1.3km east of Santa Elena ⓣ2645-5110, ⓦwww.elestablo.com. The sixteen cables on this luxury-hotel canopy tour ($40) enjoy great views of the Gulf of Nicoya; there are also rope bridges and a Tarzan swing to try out.

Rates include entrance to the reserve and three meals a day. ❹

La Colina Lodge About 2km before the entrance to the Monteverde reserve ⓣ2645-5009, ⓦwww.lacolinalodge.com. This handy, rustic spot near the reserve has cute, country-cottage-style rooms with homely wooden furnishings. Rooms have private or shared bath, and some have a balcony. Dorms with shared bathroom cost $10, or you can camp in the grounds for $5 per person. ❹

Hotel Fonda Vela About 1.5km before the entrance to the Monteverde reserve ⓣ2645-5125, ⓦwww.fondavela.com. Near the reserve amid quiet grounds, this old-fashioned family-run hotel is expertly managed by an attentive staff. Newer suites ($130) aim for deluxe, with huge bathrooms and beautiful furniture, while the older, rustic rooms have attractive wood-panelled walls and huge windows – the better to enjoy the astonishing views, particularly at sunset. Breakfast is an additional $10. ❼

Santa Elena

As well as being the transport and commercial centre for the region, **SANTA ELENA** is also home to a number of good nature museums. In town, the **Jardín de Orquídeas** (daily 8am–5pm; $10; 30min tour; ⓣ2645-5308, ⓦwww.monteverdeorchidgarden.com) features more than 425 species of orchids, all of them local to the region, including the world's smallest, which can be observed with a magnifying glass. On the road to the reserve sits the **Serpentarium** (daily 9am–8pm; $9, $11 with a guide), home to numerous slithering snakes, including deadly pit vipers and coral snakes, along with various other reptiles; the serpents tend to be more active in the afternoon. Also just outside Santa Elena, accessed off the main road down to the Interamericana, the **Ranario** frog pond (daily 9am–8.30pm; $12; ⓣ2645-6320, ⓦwww.ranario.com) is home to an array of colourful amphibians, including poison-dart frogs and the incredible translucent glass frog. As with the snakepit, your ticket is valid for multiple entries, and in this case it's well worth making a visit during the day and one at night, when different species emerge from beneath their lily pads.

If you haven't yet been (un)lucky enough to get intimate with Costa Rican insects in the privacy of your hotel room, you may want to check out the **Mundo de los Insectos** (daily 9am–7pm; $10, ⓣ2645-6859), just beyond the turning to the *ranario*; it's home to a collection of 25 species of live creepy-crawlies from Costa Rica, united by an alarmingly short life span.

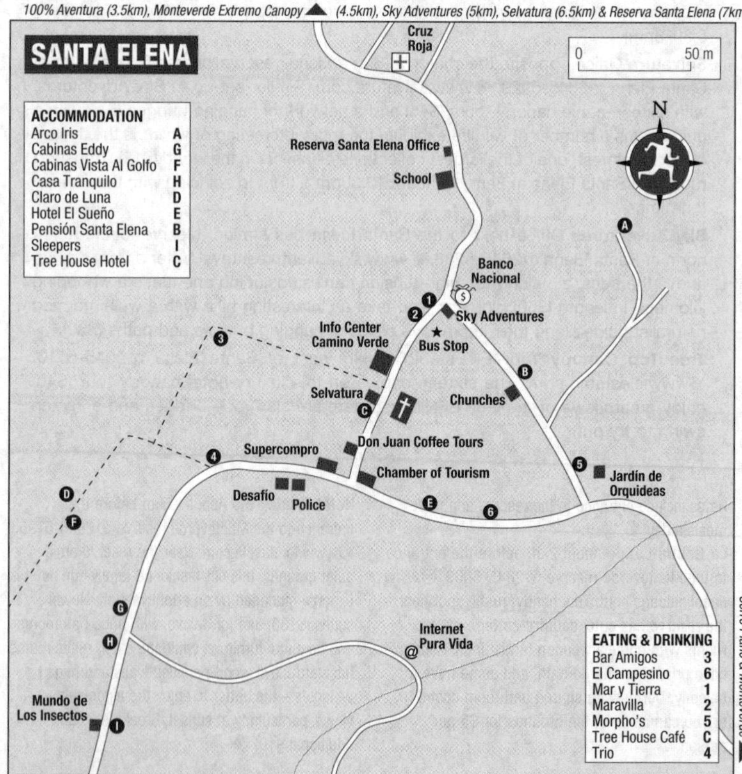

Horseriding around Santa Elena

The efficient and friendly Desafío (Ⓣ2645-5874 or 8379-9827, Ⓦwww.monteverdetours.com), opposite the *supermercado* in Santa Elena, specializes in scenic **horse-riding tours**. Their standard tour takes in forest and farmland ($32; sunset tour at 3pm; 2hr 30min), while other trips head along the Continental Divide ($47; 4hr) or to the San Luís Waterfall ($62 including entrance fee; 5hr 30min). Sabine's Smiling Horses (Ⓣ2645-6894 or 8385-2424, Ⓦwww.smilinghorses.com) also offers journeys on healthy, well-cared-for steeds; owner Sabine knows the stunning countryside around Santa Elena well, and arranges trips that stop at various panoramic views of the Pacific and the Nicoya Peninsula ($45; sunset tour at 3.30pm; 3hr) as well as monthly Full Moon rides ($50; 3hr).

Cerro Plano

Up the road from Santa Elena in the cute village of **CERRO PLANO**, a signposted side road leads to the **Jardín de Mariposas** (daily 9am–4pm; $12; Ⓣ2645-5512, Ⓦwww.monteverdebutterflygarden.com), the oldest butterfly farm in the country, with four individual butterfly gardens and a leafcutter ant colony; the butterflies are at their most active on sunny mornings. The entry fee includes a guided tour, which begins in the on-site natural history museum.

Several private reserves in Cerro Plano offer walks along well-maintained trails in search of sloths, monkeys and birds. Signposted down a right-hand turn in the centre of the village, the **Santuario Ecológico** (daily 7am–5pm; $10, $25 with guided tour; Ⓣ2645-5869, Ⓦwww.santuarioecologico.com) encompasses a swathe of transition forest and can be a good place to spot a diverse range of species; night walks (daily 5.30pm; $20 includes transport from your hotel; 2hr) head out each evening to spot porcupines, kinkajous and bats. Trails on the nearby **Sendero Valle Escondido** (daily 7am–4pm; $20 with guided tour; Ⓣ2645-6601, Ⓔinfovalleescondido@yahoo.com), eleven hectares of former farming land, run past a cascading waterfall and afford panoramas of the Pacific; their night walk (daily 5.30pm; $20 includes transport from your hotel; 2hr) allows free access to the reserve during the day. In the **Reserva Sendero Tranquilo** you can take guided walks (daily 7.30am & 1.30pm; $35; 3hr; with transport from your hotel; Ⓣ2645-5010, Ⓦwww.sapodorado.com) around an 85-hectare reserve bordering the Reserva Biológica Bosque Nuboso Monteverde, as well as a night walk that leaves later than most (daily 6pm; 2hr).

Monteverde

Just off the main road east of Santa Elena sprawls the settlement of **MONTEVERDE**, a timeless place where modest houses perch above splendid forested views, and farmers trudge along the muddy roads in sturdy rubber boots. Established in 1954 by the original Quaker settlers (see p.317), **La Lechería** forms the heart of the community and, along with ecotourism, is its economic mainstay. The cheese factory produces a range of European-style cheeses, of which Monte is the best known, along with yoghurts and cream. You can buy fresh cheese at La Lechería's shop (daily 6.30am–5pm) or take an informative tour, which is as much about the area's history as it is about the cheese-making process (Mon–Sat 9am & 2pm; $10; reservations on Ⓣ2645-7090, Ⓦwww.crstudytours.com).

A few hundred metres northwest along the same road, the arts and crafts collective **CASEM** (Mon–Sat 8am–5pm, Sun 10am–4pm) holds exhibits of local artists and craft for sale. Founded thirty years ago by eight women, CASEM has long

Coffee in the cloudforest

Monteverde is probably the best place outside the Valle Central (see box, p.216) to learn about Costa Rica's golden beans. Two companies here offer **tours** of their coffee fields and processing plants, enabling you to follow the journey from bush to bag. The co-operative **Café Monteverde** (ⓣ2645-5901, ⓦwww.monteverde-coffee.com) was the country's first sustainable coffee producer and offers a hands-on tour of an organic plantation in San Luis ($30; 3hr), where you can visit their water-powered coffee mill, as well as a shorter trip to an agro-ecological, organic farm just north of Santa Elena ($22; 1hr 30min); you can sample their beans without leaving town, at the *Casa del Café Monteverde* (daily 8am–5pm), near the post office on the road to Cerro Plano. **Don Juan Coffee Tour** (ⓣ2645-7100, ⓦwww.donjuancoffeetour.com), with an office on the Santa Elena triangle, runs similar trips to a small farm 2km north of the village ($25; 1hr 30min).

played an important role in this small community and supports over a hundred local artisans. Just up the road towards Santa Elena is the distinctive Paseo de Stella, a hilltop colonial-style complex housing the **Bat Jungle** (daily 9am–7.30pm, feeding times 9am, noon & 3pm; $10; ⓣ2645-6566, ⓦwww.batjungle.com). The first of its kind in the world, this worthy little attraction aims to dispel stereotypes of bats as bloodthirsty, disease-ridden creatures of the night. The exhibit and 45-minute guided tour takes visitors through a simulated tropical rainforest to view cute little Monteverde bats (eight of the region's sixty species) going about their business – roosting, munching on bananas and flying about in their bat cave.

Bosque Eterno de los Niños

Central America's largest private reserve, the vast **Bosque Eterno de los Niños** (Children's Eternal Rainforest), known colloquially as the "BEN", stretches over 210 square kilometres and accounts for half of the Zona Protectora de Monteverde. Initiated in 1987 by Swedish school children, the reserve is run by the **Monteverde Conservation League** – their information office is opposite the pertrol station in Cerro Plano (ⓣ2645-5003, ⓦwww.acmcr.org) – and encompasses cloudforest, rainforest and montane evergreen forest, harbouring over fifty percent of Costa Rica's known vertebrate species. The most accessible section is at **Bajo del Tigre** (daily 8am–4pm; $8), between CASEM and La Lechería, which has 3.5km of easy-going trails and offers birdwatching tours (5.30am) and guided day (8am & 2pm) and night (5.30pm) walks, the latter a memorable trek through transition forest, with a good chance of spotting tarantulas, frogs and roosting birds; all walks last two hours and cost $30.

You can stay at the reserve's two **field stations**, though you'll be vying for space with scientists and researchers: *Estación Biológica San Gerardo*, 7.5km north of Santa Elena, has access to 5km of trails and is a good spot for birdwatching, while *Estación Biológica Pocosol* is on the far eastern fringes of the BEN, with 10km of trails leading to a natural lagoon and bubbling mud pots; accommodation at both is in bunks ($48 per night, including three meals a day). *San Gerardo* is a 3.5km hike from the Reserva Santa Elena, but to get to *Pocosol* – which is actually easier to reach from La Tigra, on the road between San Ramón and La Fortuna – you'll need to embark on a two-day trek from the Monteverde reserve ($285, plus entrance fees), overnighting at a refuge along the way. This is real bushwhacking stuff, on unmarked trails (pumas have been spotted around the refuge), and each trip is escorted by two fully equipped rangers trained in first aid; you'll need to carry all your food in, plus a sleeping bag.

Eating and drinking

Santa Elena and neighbouring Cerro Plano are home to a number of cheap *soda*-style **eateries** as well as a number of classier options; several of these are hotel restaurants that are open to non-guests. You can pick up fresh fruit and vegetables, home-baked bread, cheese and pickles from the **Farmers' Market** (Sat 6am–noon) at the Colegío Santa Elena.

Drinking is kept to a minimum in the Quaker community of Monteverde – and even in gringo-packed Santa Elena, bars aren't all that prevalent. Still, you can usually find folks slinging back beers at *Bar Amigos* (daily noon–midnight; Ⓦwww.baramigos.com), down a side street opposite the church in Santa Elena, with live music every Friday. Later in the evening, the action often moves to *Mata e Cana*, a rum bar 25m north of the Banco Popular on the road to the *Serpentariun* (open till 1am), where the dancefloor fills to a mix of salsa, merengue and international pop. In February and March, the amphitheatre *Bromelia's Café*, up a driveway opposite CASEM, is the setting for the **Monteverde Music Fest**, which showcases top Costa Rican artists.

Santa Elena

All the listings below are marked on the Santa Elena map on p.324.

El Campesino On the southern side of the Santa Elena triangle. Legions of stuffed toys hang from the ceiling of this quirky little Tico-run eatery. The pricey menu features steaks and seafood for $12–17; take the owner's recommendations for specials of the day and you won't be disappointed. Daily 10am–11pm.

Mar y Tierra Above Panadería Jiménez, opposite the Banco Nacional. Good range of tempting meat and fish dishes, including shrimp ceviche ($7) and sesame-breaded mahi-mahi ($11), served with organic vegetables from their garden. Daily 11am–10pm.

Maravilla Opposite the bus stop. This bustling, no-frills *soda* is typically packed and for good reason: the food is simply delicious and the portions generous. For dinner, you can't go wrong with the grilled fish with mashed potatoes and veggies ($7), washed down by a strawberry milkshake. Daily 7am–9pm.

Morpho's Next to the Jardín de Orquídeas. This stylish split-level restaurant decorated with unusual hanging butterflies and an extravagant wraparound mural serves excellent dishes like passion fruit chicken ($10) and Monteverde blue-cheese tenderloin ($16), as well as cheaper soups and subs ($5–12). Daily 11.30am–9.30pm.

Tree House Café Next to the *Treehouse Hotel* Ⓦwww.treehouse.cr. The eclectic menu includes huge platters, but you're better off opting for something simpler – pancakes and granola for breakfast (til 11am) or a creamy *guanabana batido* ($3) – as you're really here for the eponymous tree: a huge fig growing right through the centre of the restaurant. Daily 7am–10pm.

Trio 50m west of the supermarket Ⓣ2645-7254. Cool new restaurant from the Karen Nielsen stable (the brains behind Cerro Plano's *Chimera* and *Sofia*) with an unusual menu – ribs with sugarcane syrup and beer ($5), sea bass with spiced watermelon sauce – served on an attractive terrace: dinner only. Daily 6–9pm.

Cerro Plano

All the listings below are marked on the Monteverde and around map on p.318.

Chimera On the main road through Cerro Plano Ⓣ2645-6081. Excellent (and expensive) Latin-infused tapas, with a small menu of tasty morsels including roasted aubergine and smoked *provolone* ($3.50) shrimp, butter-soft fried calamari with coconut-chilli dip ($6.50) and yucca fries ($3.25). Daily 11.30am–9.30pm.

Dulce Marzo Café In the centre of Cerro Plano. This cheerful café is your one-stop shop for gourmet coffee, massive mozzarella and tomato sandwiches (on home-baked bread), creamy soups ($3–6) and home-made cookies. Mon–Sat 11am–7pm, Sun 10am–2pm.

Flor de Vida Cerro Plano. Enjoy forest views at this relaxed café and restaurant that serves bagels, vegetable stir-fries ($8) and other international fare. Non-smoking. Daily 7am–10pm.

El Jardin *Monteverde Lodge* 400m southeast of Santa Elena Ⓣ2645-5214. Beautifully presented dishes such as succulent beef tenderloin with red-wine sauce ($16.50) and chicken coconut curry ($11) hit the spot every time. Considering the quality of the food, the prices are keen and the (imaginative) salads are tremendous value (from $5.50). The first-rate service manages to combine efficiency with friendliness. Daily noon–2.30pm & 6–8.30pm.

Los Jardines *Hotel El Sapo Dorado*, 500m east of Santa Elena. Take in jaw-dropping views over the Gulf of Nicoya at this classy restaurant with a romantic atmosphere (mains $12–20). It's worth coming here for the happy-hour cocktails and superb vistas alone. Daily 6.30am–9.30pm.

Sabores Opposite the bullring in Cerro Plano. Sample the region's natural dairy produce at this popular ice-cream parlour. Pick from a variety of flavours, including tropical fruit, macadamia and coffee. Mon & Wed–Sun noon–8pm.

Sofia Opposite *Sabores* ⓣ2645-7017. The creative "Nuevo Latin" cuisine at this stylish restaurant with a candlelit interior won't disappoint. Sweet-and-sour fig-roasted pork loin ($15) is a real hit, and the cocktail list is top notch. Daily 11.30am–9.30pm.

Monteverde

The listings below are marked on the Monteverde and around map on p.318.

Caburé In the Paseo de Stella complex on the road to the Monteverde reserve ⓦcabure.net. Relish the coastal sunset views from the lofty balcony over a glass of Malbec at this great little Argentine restaurant and *chocolatería*. The menu covers Milanesas ($12.50) and Indian curries, and you can treat yourself to sumptuous home-made truffles and chocolates for afters. Daily 8am–8.30pm.

Pizzeria e Restaurante Tramonti Opposite the Paseo de Stella complex on the road to the reserve ⓣ2645-6120. Don't leave Monteverde without dining at this divine Italian restaurant. Many of the ingredients are sourced from Italy and you can taste the Mediterranean in everything from the Caprese salad ($6) to the wood-fired pizzas ($9–16). Mon–Sat 11am–10pm.

Stella's Bakery Opposite CASEM. Pleasant little coffee shop that does delicious soups, strudel and brownies; its walls are adorned with said Stella's artwork. Daily 6am–10pm.

Listings

Banks The Banco Nacional (with an ATM) sits at the northern apex of the triangle in Santa Elena.

Bookshops Chunches book and coffee shop, south of the bank, sells espresso, snacks and second-hand paperbacks.

Internet access Internet Pura Vida, in an old school bus just outside Santa Elena on the road to Monteverde (daily 10am–8pm; $1/30min).

Laundry Internet Pura Vida (see above) charges $1 per lb.

Medical care The clinic on the road that runs past the football field north of Santa Elena is open 24hr (ⓣ2645-7778).

Post office Just east of *Casa del Café Monteverde*, on the road from Santa Elena to Cerro Plano (Mon–Fri 8am–noon & 1–4.30pm).

Supermarkets Supercompro, on the southwest corner of the triangle in Santa Elena (daily 7am–9pm).

Yoga Río Shanti, near La Lechería (ⓣ2645-6121, ⓦwww.rioshanti.com) holds various classes (Mon–Sat), from meditation (1hr; free) to rigorous Astanga (1hr 30min; $10) in a mellow sixty-year-old building in Monteverde village; massages cost $70 for 1hr.

Reserva Biológica Bosque Nuboso Monteverde

Attracting visitors in their droves, the **RESERVA BIOLÓGICA BOSQUE NUBOSO MONTEVERDE** (Monteverde Cloudforest Biological Reserve; daily 7am–4pm; $17; ⓣ2645-5122, ⓦwww.cct.or.cr) is one of the last sizeable pockets of primary cloudforest in Mesoamerica. At an altitude of 1440m and straddling the Continental Divide, the reserve was established in 1972 by George Powell (an American biologist) and Wilford Guindon (a local Quaker) to protect the country's rapidly dwindling pristine cloudforest. Today, it encompasses ten square kilometres of protected land and is administered by the nonprofit Centro Científico Tropical (Tropical Science Centre), based in San José.

The reserve's sheer diversity of **terrain** – from semi-dwarf stunted forest on the wind-exposed areas to thick, bearded cloudforest vegetation elsewhere – supports six different **life zones**, or eco-communities, hosting an estimated 3000 species of

plants, more than 100 types of mammals, some 490 species of butterflies and over 400 species of birds, including the resplendent quetzal and the three-wattled bellbird. The cloudforest cover – dense, low-lit and heavy – can make it difficult to spot wildlife, though the amazing diversity of tropical plants and insects more than makes up for this, with guided walks leading past thick mosses, epiphytes, bromeliads, primitive ferns, leaf-cutter ants and poison-dart frogs.

The trails

Nine **trails** wind through 13km of the reserve and most are contained in a roughly triangular pocket known as **El Triángulo**. They're clearly marked and easily walkable (at least in the dry season), and many of them are along wooden or concrete pathways that help prevent slipping and sliding on seas of mud.

If you're keen to plunge straight into the cloudforest, make for the **Sendero Bosque Nuboso** (1.8km). The forest canopy along this trail is literally dripping with moisture, each tree thickly encrusted with moss and epiphytes. You'll probably hear howler monkeys and the unmistakable "boink" of the three-wattled bellbird, but it's difficult to spot either in this dense cover – your best bet for bird-watching is at the beginning of the trail. The spongy terrain efficiently preserves animal tracks, and in the morning especially you may see tracks from agouti or coati. One creature that you will see on this trail is the clearwing butterfly, whose transparent wings are as fragile as the thinnest parchment.

At the end of the trail, a small *mirador*, **La Ventana**, has vistas of the thickly forested hills on the other side of the Continental Divide. It's reached via a staircase of cement-laid steps that lead to a lookout point suspended over an amazingly green expanse of hills – a surreal place, with only the sound of wind as company.

The **Sendero Camino** (2km), higher in elevation than the others, is stony, deeply rutted in spots and often muddy, but as this trail (which also leads to La

The cloudforest

The most obvious property of the cloudforest is its dense, dripping **wetness**. Cloudforests are formed by a constant, near-one-hundred-percent humidity created by mists, produced here when northeasterly trade winds from the Caribbean drift across the high ridge of the Continental Divide to cool and become dense clouds settling over this high-altitude forest.

The cloudforest environment can be rather eerie, due to the sheer layering of vegetation, and the preponderance of **epiphytes** – plants that grow on other living plants for physical rather than nutritional support. Everything seems to be stacked on top of each other, and when walking the Monteverde and Santa Elena trails you'll notice that green mosses wholly carpet many trees, while others seem to be choked by multiple layers of strangler vines, small plants, ferns and drooping lianas.

The **leaves** of cloudforest plants are often dotted with scores of tiny holes, as though they were gnawed by insects that soon gave up – which is, in effect, exactly the case. Many cloudforest plants produce toxins to deter insects from eating an entire leaf or plant. The plants are able to produce these poisons because they harbour excess energy that would otherwise be used to protect themselves against adverse weather conditions, such as a prolonged dry season or heavy winds and rain. The insects, in turn, guard themselves by eating only a little of a leaf, and by sampling a wide variety, so that they are not overwhelmed by one powerful toxin.

For an in-depth look into cloudforests, check out *An Introduction to Cloudforest Trees*, by William Haber, Willow Zuchowski and Erick Bello, available at the reserve visitor centre and in bookshops in San José.

Ventana) is wider than the others, it gets more sunlight, attracting greater numbers of birds and butterflies. Often quite steep, the **Sendero Pantanoso** (1.4km) passes through sun-dappled swamp forests and leads past magnolias and the rare *podocarpus* – the reserve's only conifer. It links with **Sendero El Río** (1.1km) to bring you, in a long arch, back to the park's entrance. The **Sendero Wilford Guindon** features a 100m suspension bridge that takes you high up into the trees for great birds'-eye views of the cloudforest canopy.

The tours

The reserve runs excellent two- to three-hour **guided tours** ($17) at 7.30am, noon and 1.30pm, with knowledgeable guides who have a knack for spotting wildlife you'd never see on your own – ask in your hotel or contact the reserve office (Ⓣ2645-5122, Ⓔreservaciones2@cct.or.cr) a day in advance to secure a place. They also run early-morning **birdwatching tours** ($64; 6hr) and a fascinating if eerie **night walk** ($17; 2hr), departing every evening at 6.15pm; transport to the reserve visitor centre ($3) leaves from Santa Elena at 5.40pm. Many of the reserve's animals are nocturnal, and your chances of seeing one, albeit only as two brilliant eyes shining out of the night, are vastly increased after dark – you may spot tarantulas, toucans with their beaks tucked between their feathers, and some guides will even catch bats. Although the guides carry a powerful flashlight, it's useful to bring your own, as well as rain gear.

Reserve practicalities

Several **buses** make the 6km run from Santa Elena to the reserve (daily 6.15am, 7.30am, 1.20am & 3pm, returning 6.45am, 11.30am, 2pm & 4pm; $1 each way; 30min); alternatively, a **taxi** costs about $8.

The reserve imposes **a quota** on the number of people allowed in the cloudforest at any given time (220), so it's a good idea to arrive early. In addition to the **official**

Watching wildlife in Monteverde and Santa Elena

What you might see...

Ever since **National Geographic** declared that Monteverde might just be the best place in all of Central America to see the **resplendent quetzal**, spotting one has become almost a rite of passage, and many zealous, binocular-toting birders come here with this express purpose in mind. This slim bird, with a sweet face and tiny beak, is extraordinarily colourful, with shimmering green feathers on the back and head, and a rich, carmine stomach. The male quetzal is the more spectacular, with a long, picturesque tail and fuzzy crown. About a hundred pairs of quetzals mate at Monteverde, in monogamous pairs, between March and June. During this period, they descend to slightly lower altitudes than their usual stratospheric heights, coming down to about 1000m to nest in dead or dying trees, hollowing out a niche in which to lay their blue eggs. Your best chance of seeing one is on a guided tour, or arrive on your own just after dawn, the most fruitful time to spot birds.

Another bird to look out for, particularly in Santa Elena (and from March to August), is the bizarre-looking **three-wattled bellbird**, whose three black "wattles", or skin pockets, hang down from its beak; even if you don't see one, you'll almost certainly hear its distinctive metallic call, which has been likened to a pinball machine. The far rarer **bare-necked umbrella bird** can only be seen in Santa Elena, and not very often at that, but those lucky enough to witness its spectacular mating routine will never forget it.

Several types of endangered **cats**, including puma, jaguar, ocelot, jaguarundi and margay, live in the reserve, which provides ample space for hunting. You're unlikely to come face to face with a jaguar, but if you're lucky, you may hear the growl of a big cat coming out of the dense forest – usually unnerving enough to cure you of your desire to actually see one.

And what you definitely won't...

Another famous resident (now thought to be extinct) of the Monteverde area is the vibrant red-orange *sapo dorado*, or **golden toad**. First discovered here in 1964, the golden toad hasn't been spotted in many years and is thought to have either been killed off by global warming – the mean minimum temperature in Monteverde has risen from 15°C in 1988 to 17°C in 2010 – or to have succumbed to the chytrid fungus that has decimated amphibian populations worldwide over the last few decades.

tours, which depart from the well-stocked **visitors' centre** at the entrance, a number of experienced local guides can lead you through the reserve; try the services of AGUINAMON (Ⓣ2645-6282), the Association of Naturalist Guides of Monteverde. Serious birders, wildlife spotters and those who would prefer to walk the trails in peace should **avoid the peak hours** of 8–11am, when tour groups pour in.

Temperatures are cool at this altitude (15°C or 16°C is not uncommon, though in the sun it often feels more like 22°C to 25°C), and the average **rainfall** is 3000mm per year, so dress in layers and carry an umbrella and light rain gear. You should also bring **binoculars** and **insect repellent**; you might get away without **rubber boots** in the dry season, but you'll most definitely need them in the wet – the reserve office rents out both boots and binoculars.

Reserva Santa Elena

Less touristed than Monteverde, the **RESERVA SANTA ELENA** (daily 7am–4pm; $14; Ⓣ2645-5390, Ⓦwww.reservasantaelena.org), 7km northeast of Santa Elena, offers an equally memorable cloudforest experience. Poised at an elevation of 1650m, the three-square-kilometre reserve is higher than Monteverde and boasts

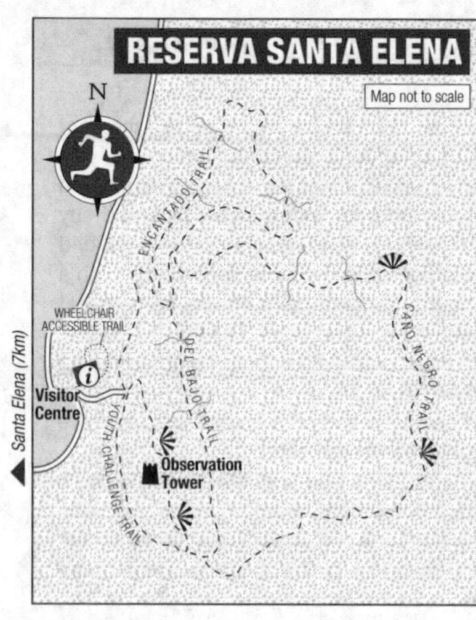

steeper, more challenging trails and a slightly better chance of seeing quetzals (and three-wattled bellbirds) in season. Established in 1992, the self-funded reserve is supported by entrance fees and donations and depends largely on volunteers, particularly foreign university students. It's run by the local high school board, whose students help maintain the trails year-round.

Several **buses** run from Santa Elena to the reserve (daily 6.30am, 8.30am, 10.30am, 12.30pm & 3pm, returning 11am, 1pm & 4pm; $2 each way; 30min); alternatively, a **taxi** costs about $10. The **visitor centre** at the reserve entrance has a small interpretative display documenting the life of the cloud-forest ecosystem and the history of the reserve itself, and hands out a helpful leaflet on cloudforests, epiphytes and some of the mammals you might see here. It also rents out rubber **boots** and has a **cafeteria** that provides coffee, cold drinks and sandwiches.

The trails

Santa Elena's 12km network of **trails** are confined to an area just east of the entrance – cut wood and mesh cover some trails, while others are rough tracks. The easiest is the hour-long **Youth Challenge Trail** (1.4km) with an observation tower halfway along, from where it's possible to see Volcán Arenal on clear days; for the best chance of viewing the volcano, arrive early before cloud, mist and fog roll in to obliterate vistas. The longest, the **Caño Negro Trail** (4.5km), named after the river that flows from here north to the border with Nicaragua, takes about four hours to complete and crosses two streams en route. There's also a **wheelchair-accessible trail** that loops from the visitors' centre, passing a couple of lookouts and a small orchid garden.

You'll see plenty of hummingbirds – strung along the entrance path is a line of feeders that draw many of the multicoloured birds – but for a better chance of viewing all the wildlife that lives here, sign up for one of the highly recommended **guided walks** (daily 7.30am & 11.30am; $15; 3hr).

Volunteering in the reserves

Both the Santa Elena and Monteverde reserves depend significantly on **volunteer labour**. Volunteers are assigned tasks according to their experience – activities include trail maintenance, teaching English and helping with conservation projects. At **Monteverde**, volunteers are expected to work Monday to Friday from 7am to 4pm and Saturday from 7am to 11.30am, for a minimum of two weeks. The reserve charges $20 per day, which includes accommodation with a local family, three meals a day and laundry; you can download an application form at Ⓦwww.cct.or.cr. For more information on volunteering at **Santa Elena**, email the reserve on Ⓔreservaciones@reservasantaelena.org.

Puntarenas and around

Heat-stunned **PUNTARENAS**, a thin, island-like finger of sand pointing out into the Gulf of Nicoya 115km west of San José, has the look of raffish abandonment that haunts so many tropical port cities. What isn't rusting has long ago been bleached to a generic pastel. Old wooden buildings painted in faded tutti-frutti colours line the town's cracked, potholed streets and mop-headed mango trees provide the only shade from the relentless sun. It's hard to believe now, but in the seventeenth century this was a prosperous port – the export point for much of Costa Rica's coffee to England – and a popular resort for holidaying Ticos.

Today, most vacationing Costa Ricans have abandoned its dodgy beaches and somewhat tawdry charms in favour of the ocean playgrounds of Manuel Antonio and Guanacaste, and foreign tourists, who never spent much time here anyway, come only to catch a ferry across to southern Nicoya. In recent years, the town's tourist trade has been somewhat revived by daily visits from the giant **cruise ships** that call at the site of the old docks. More importantly, this working port remains a jumping-off point for boats to pristine **Isla Tortuga** (see p.338) and for trips to two of Costa Rica's least-explored islands: **Isla de Chira**, a sleepy community a short boat ride away that is slowly opening up to tourism; and **Isla del Coco**, one of the world's most exclusive diving destinations that lies 535km southwest of the mainland.

Arrival and information

Hourly **buses** from San José (2hr) terminate at the bus station, on the corner of Calle 2 and Paseo de los Turistas, just southeast of the Casa de la Cultura, as do

Moving on from Puntarenas

While the bridge across the Río Tempisque north of Puntarenas has made access to the **Nicoya Peninsula** easier, **ferries** are still popular, particularly if you're heading to Montezuma and other destinations around the peninsula's southern tip. The ferry dock sits at the northwestern end of Puntarenas, a fifteen-minute walk from the city centre; buses (labelled "FERRY") run up and down Avenida Central from the centre.

Navieras Tambor (Ⓣ2661-2084, Ⓦwww.navieratambor.com) travels **to Paquera** (7 daily, roughly every 2hr from 5am to 9pm; $1.50, cars $12; 1hr 15min), from where buses run on to **Montezuma** (2hr), via Cóbano; note that the 5pm ferry is the last one that connects with this service. You'll need to change buses in Cóbano for Mal País and Santa Teresa (daily 10.30am & 2.30pm). Ferries make the return journey every two hours from 9am to 7pm. CONATRAMAR (Ⓣ2661-1069) travels **to Playa Naranjo** (daily 6.30am, 10am, 2.30pm and 7.30pm; $1.75, cars $12; 1hr), from where buses travel on to **Nicoya** (4 daily; 2hr); return ferries leave at 8am, 12.30pm, 5.30pm and 9pm. It can be a slow process buying a **car ticket**, so in high season arrive at least an hour before departure and park in the queue before purchasing your ticket.

In addition to the ferry, there are two daily **lanchas to Paquera**; these speedier passenger-only boats leave from the dock near the *mercado* in the town centre at 11am and 4pm ($1.50), returning at 7.30am, 12.30pm and 2pm. A *lancha* also leaves from here for **Isla de Chira** (daily 1.30pm; $7.50; 2hr), returning at 6am.

Buses for **San José** (hourly; 2hr) and **Liberia** (8 daily; 3hr) depart from the bus station just off Paseo de los Turistas on Calle 2. For **Manuel Antonio**, take the Quepos service (6 daily; 3hr), which also leaves from here, and runs via Jacó. Buses for Santa Elena (for **Monteverde**; daily 7.50am, 1.50pm & 2.15pm; 3hr 30min) depart from the bus stop just over the road, on the Paseo de los Turistas itself.

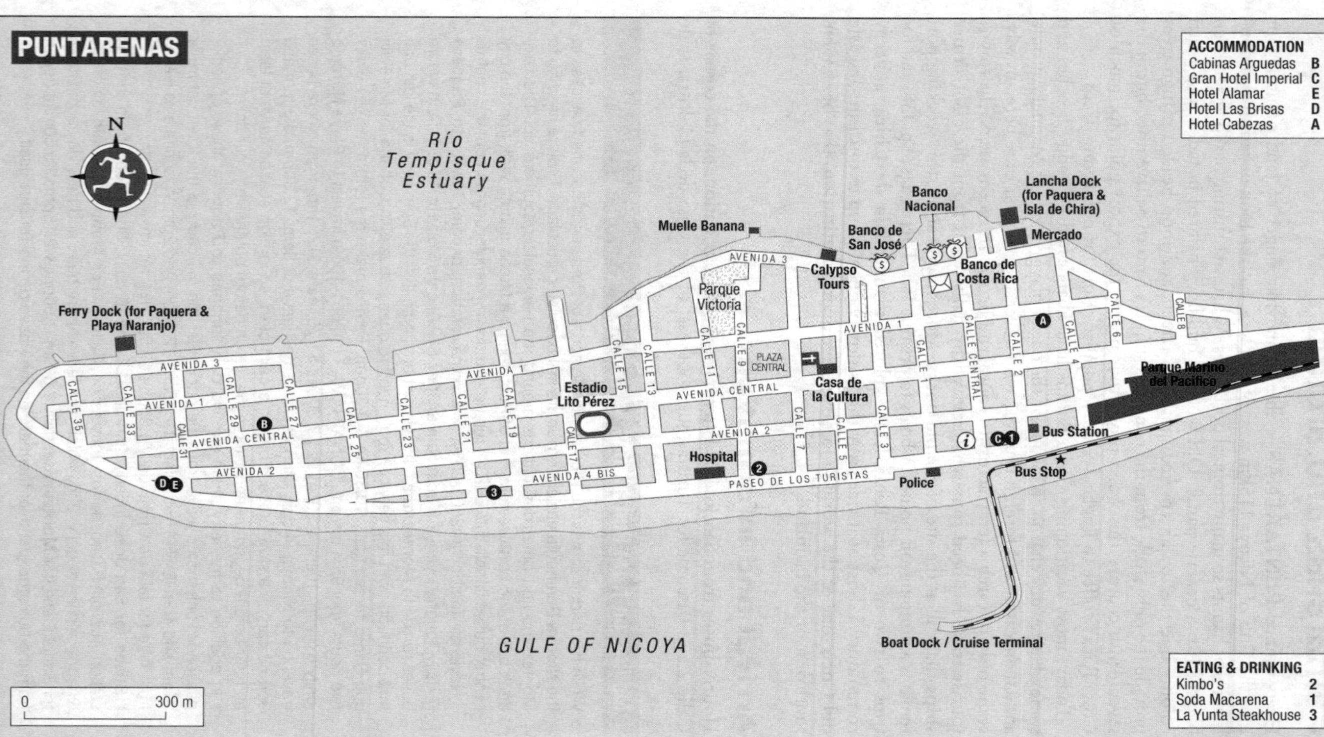
PUNTARENAS
ACCOMMODATION
Cabinas Arguedas B
Gran Hotel Imperial C
Hotel Alamar E
Hotel Las Brisas D
Hotel Cabezas A
EATING & DRINKING
Kimbo's 2
Soda Macarena 1
La Yunta Steakhouse 3
N
Río Tempisque Estuary
GULF OF NICOYA
San José (116km)
Lancha Dock (for Paquera & Isla de Chira)
Mercado
Banco Nacional
Banco de San José
Banco de Costa Rica
Calypso Tours
Muelle Banana
Parque Victoria
Plaza Central
Casa de la Cultura
Estadio Lito Pérez
Hospital
Police
Bus Station
Bus Stop
Parque Marino del Pacífico
Boat Dock / Cruise Terminal
Ferry Dock (for Paquera & Playa Naranjo)
Paseo de los Turistas
Avenida 3
Avenida 1
Avenida Central
Avenida 2
Avenida 4 Bis
Calle 8
Calle 6
Calle 4
Calle 2
Calle Central
Calle 1
Calle 3
Calle 5
Calle 7
Calle 9
Calle 11
Calle 13
Calle 15
Calle 17
Calle 19
Calle 21
Calle 23
Calle 25
Calle 27
Calle 29
Calle 31
Calle 33
Calle 35
0
300 m

those from Liberia (9 daily; 3hr) and Manuel Antonio (6 daily; 3hr), via Quepos (2hr 30min) and Jacó (1hr). Services from Santa Elena (daily 4.30am, 6am & 3pm; 3hr 30min) pull in at the bus stop on the opposite side of the *paseo*.

There's a **tourism information office** (Mon–Fri 8am–5.30pm, Sat 8am–12.30pm; ⓣ2661-2980) on the second floor of the Plaza del Pacífico, the large white building opposite the Capitanía de Puerto, where you can pick up maps and brochures. In the town centre, just a few blocks northwest of the bus station, you'll find the **post office** (Mon–Fri 8am–5pm, Sat 8am–noon), **banks** – the Banco de Costa Rica, Banco de San José and Banco Nacional, virtually next to each other on Avenida 3, have **ATMs** and currency exchange – the municipal market and a slew of cheap hotels.

Accommodation

If you're catching an early ferry to Paquera, you may find the **cheap hotels** around the north-shore docks quite handy, though be warned that at night this area can be seedy, and at some of the more dismal hotels the clientele may not be there for sleeping. Even considering Costa Rica's tropical climate, Puntarenas stands out as an exceptionally hot town – wherever you stay, make sure your room has a **fan** that works, otherwise you'll be as baked as a ceramic pot by morning.

Cabinas Arguedas Av Central, C 27/29 ⓣ2661-3508. It's only a short stroll to the ferry terminal from these simple yet well-equipped en-suite rooms with a/c and fridge. Parking also available. ❹

Gran Hotel Imperial Paseo de los Turistas, C 0/2 ⓣ2661-0579. Housed in an old clapboard house, this ramshackle-looking hotel has dark but spacious rooms with private bath; some of the shared-bath rooms have a dilapidated wooden balcony. It's extremely handy for the bus station, but pricey for what's on offer. ❺

Hotel Alamar Paseo de los Turistas, C 31/33 ⓣ2661-4343, ⓦwww.alamarcr.com. One of the nicest options on the seafront strip, the spacious, sparkling rooms in this family-friendly hotel have a/c, cable TV and private hot-water bathrooms. There are two pools, a hot tub, secure parking and a restaurant. ❻

Hotel Las Brisas Corner of Paseo de los Turistas & C 33 ⓣ2661-4040, ⓦwww.lasbrisashotelcr.com. Relax at this cheerful, clean waterfront hotel on the peninsula's southwestern tip. Rooms come with cable TV, phone and a/c and some have balconies overlooking the Gulf of Nicoya. Splash about in the swimming pool and enjoy Greek fare at the breezy café. ❻

Hotel Cabezas Av 1, C 2/4 ⓣ2661-1045. A couple of blocks from the dock, this airy budget option is painted in pink and yellow tones and has a number of clean, basic rooms with fans. All have shared bathrooms. ❶

The Town

Though Puntarenas appears to be slowly expiring in the equatorial sun, it seems to do so with affecting elegance – and its decaying streets exude a certain melancholy charm. The southerly promenade is optimistically called **Paseo de los Turistas**, though these days the only *turistas* to be seen are off the cruise ships or here on high-season weekends, when the entire town decamps to the gritty strip of **beach** fronting the *paseo*.

From the eastern end of the *paseo*, the long, skinny finger of the old dock crooks out into the gulf. This is where bananas and coffee were loaded, before all the big shipping traffic shifted 18km down the coast to the deeper harbour of Puerto Caldera; it's now used by the cruise ships that pull in daily during the dry season. The docks on the northern, **estuary** side, however, are a quite different matter, with a jungle of ketches and sturdy mini-trawlers testifying to a thriving fishing industry. Despite the aura of hot lassitude, plenty of business is conducted in the few blocks surrounding the docks, especially in the hectic **mercado**, a cacophony of noise and pungent smells. Though safe enough during the day, it's best to avoid the docks at night.

A few metres south of nearby Parque Victoria in the centre of town, the orange colonial-style **Casa de la Cultura** (Mon–Fri 8am–4pm; free; ⓣ2661-1394) exhibits evocative *fin-de-siècle* photographs documenting Puntarenas' lost prosperity. Sepia images of tough fishermen hang alongside photos of white-clad ladies whose husbands made their wealth from coffee exports. More interesting – and the pride of Puntarenas – is the Casa's **Museo Histórico Marino** (Tues–Sun 9.45am–noon & 1–5.15pm; free; ⓦwww.museosdecostarica.com), with a rundown of the region's archeology, biology and history, focusing on the town's relationship with the sea that virtually surrounds it. Two blocks east of the bus station, **Parque Marino del Pacífico** (Tues–Sun 9am–5pm, $7, children $4; ⓣ2661-5272, ⓦwww.parquemarino.org) is a small aquarium and rescue centre dedicated to Costa Rica's marine life.

Eating, drinking and nightlife

Perhaps because of its history as a bona fide resort, eating out in Puntarenas is more expensive than most other places in Costa Rica; even fish – probably caught no more than a couple of hundred of metres away – can be pricey. Pick up a cheap meal and a *refresco* in the **mercado**, but avoid drinking anything made with the local water. Or, linger over a quiet drink or a seafood lunch at the beachside *sodas* and kiosks near the **old dock**.

For **nightlife**, the Casa de la Cultura hosts concerts on summer weekends (Dec–April). Some of the larger hotels have discos that draw crowds on Saturday nights and holiday weekends, and you can always enjoy drinks at the open-air **bars** along the Paseo de los Turistas.

Kimbo's Paseo de los Turistas, C 7/9. This lively restaurant and bar serves fried fish, grilled prawns and the like (around $10). Tico tourists pop in for drinks at night, when the music, from salsa and merengue to Costa Rican karaoke classics, cranks up. Daily 7am–2.30am.

Soda Macarena Opposite the bus station. This small *soda* with ocean views serves up cheap, delicious fare, from fruit plates to toasted sandwiches; try their "Churchills" ($5), similar to a crushed-ice *granizado* but made with ice cream. Daily 10am–midnight.

La Yunta Steakhouse Paseo de los Turistas, C 19/21. Carnivores can enjoy superb ocean vistas while tucking into succulent slices of meat (around $15), and there's plenty on offer for fish fanatics, from seafood risotto to octopus ceviche ($10). Open 24hr.

Isla de Chira

Shaped like a dinosaur skull and surrounded by crocodile-infested mangrove swamps, untouristed **ISLA DE CHIRA** is like stepping back in time to Costa Rica three decades ago. At 42 square kilometres, it is the largest island in the Gulf of Nicoya, home to three thousand Ticos who eke out a simple existence through small-scale fishing and subsistence farming. Inhabited since pre-Columbian times, more than a third of the island is mangroves, the remainder essentially farmland and tropical dry forest. Running water and the first car didn't arrive until the early 1990s, and you can still count on one hand the number of vehicles that pass daily along the island's rough main road.

On the surface it seems there would be little to entice visitors, but one of Costa Rica's most inspiring rural ecotourism projects is underway here. In 2000, with over-fishing impacting on the island's traditional economy, a group of local women resolved to generate an alternative income based on promoting the responsible use of Isla de Chira's natural resources. Their decision to establish the island's first proper tourism initiative (consisting of a small hotel, restaurant and nature tours) was met with scepticism by the community – many feared tourism would

Parque Nacional Isla del Coco

Rising dramatically out of the Pacific Ocean 535km southwest of the Costa Rican mainland, **PARQUE NACIONAL ISLA DEL COCO** (☎2258-8570 or 2250-7295) is revered among divers, biologists and treasure-hunters. Gigantic waterfalls plunge off jungle-strewn cliffs straight into an underwater world that has made this national park a veritable "Costa Rican Galapagos". It's the only island in this part of the Pacific that receives enough rain to support the growth of rainforest and is home to 150 endemic species that are found nowhere else in the world, including the Cocos flycatcher and the Cocos gecko. In addition, more than 250 species of fish – including one of the world's largest concentrations of hammerhead and white-tipped reef **sharks** – patrol the surrounding waters. The rugged, mist-shrouded volcanic island itself appeared as "Dinosaur Island" in Steven Spielberg's blockbuster **Jurassic Park**: in the opening frames of the film, a helicopter swoops over azure seas to a remote, emerald-green isle – that's Coco.

Nearly 25 square kilometres in size, Isla del Coco is one of the world's largest uninhabited islands, yet few would be able to locate it on a map. Perhaps that's why pirates found it such a perfect hideout during the seventeenth and eighteenth centuries. Legend has it the golden spoils from fruitful church-looting expeditions to Lima were buried here; known as the "Lima Booty", the stories sparked a frenzy of treasure-seeking missions. More than 500 tried their luck (and failed) before Isla del Coco was declared a national park in 1978, ending all gold-digging expeditions. Though evidence suggests that the island was known by pre-Columbian seagoing peoples from Ecuador and Colombia, in the modern age it was "discovered" by the navigator and sea captain Joan Cabezas in 1526. Attempts were made to establish a colony here in the early twentieth century, and nowadays wild descendants of the would-be settlers' pigs and coffee plants have upset the island's ecosystem.

Today, however, conservation is the order of the day on this **UNESCO World Heritage Site**, although illegal fishing, shark-finning in particular, within the 15km restriction zone is rife, and park rangers and marine organizations lack the resources to bring it under control. Despite this, Isla del Coco remains an increasingly coveted destination for experienced **scuba divers**. More than a thousand a year brave the gut-wrenching **32-hour boat journey** from Puntarenas to spend a week or so moored in the island's sheltered harbour on live-aboard boats. The subterranean treasures range from underwater caves and technicolour coral reefs to schools of manta rays and, off the northeastern side of the island, the occasional whale shark. The real danger here, however, is not sharks but **strong currents**, and divers often wear gloves to grip onto rocks to stop themselves from drifting away. Water temperatures are a balmy 22–26°C and the best time of year for seeing sharks is the rainy season (May–Nov). Two sheltered bays provide access to the island itself, and during the day visitors can venture onshore to hike the steaming tropical forests.

Two diving **companies** make the trip year-round from Puntarenas: packages with Agressor (☎2289-2261 or US 1-800/438-2628, ⓦwww.aggressor.com) start at $3600 for eight days, while Undersea Hunter (☎2228-6613 or 1-800/203-2120, ⓦwww.underseahunter.com) runs similar expeditions, with ten-day trips from $4750.

For more information on the island, contact the **Fundación Amigos de La Isla del Coco** (☎2256-7476, ⓦwww.cocosisland.org), which was founded in 1994 to help preserve the unique terrestrial and marine biodiversity of Coco.

bring prostitution, and some of the husbands felt threatened by their wives' entrepreneurship, accusing them of visiting San José to find new boyfriends rather than attend business meetings. But with international funding, the **Asociación de Damas de la Isla de Chira** soldiered on, buying a small plot of forested land and the materials to build a lodge, restaurant and small fibreglass boat. *La Amistad Lodge*

(Ⓣ2248-9470, Ⓦwww.actuarcostarica.com; ⑤) is the fruits of their labour, sleeping up to 30 people and consisting of partially open basic bungalows (bring a mosquito net) and a dorm with private cold-water bathrooms. Hiking trails lead from the lodge to lookout points, and bikes can be borrowed to explore the island. Boat tours are offered to mangrove swamps and to Isla Paloma, a tiny aquatic bird sanctuary that is an important nesting site for pelicans, frigates, great egret and cormorant. About 2km east of the lodge an association of female artisans have a shop where they make and sell locally produced jewellery and crafts.

Practicalities

The easiest way to get to Isla de Chira is **from Puntarenas**: a *lancha* leaves daily from the dock near the *mercado* at 1.30pm ($7.50; 2hr), and is met by a public bus, which can stop on request at *La Amistad Lodge*, 10km east; the *lancha* returns at 6am. You can also catch a ferry from Costa de Pájoros, 33km northwest of Puntarenas (daily 5.45am, 7.30am & 2.30pm; $7.50; 45min), reached by taking any bus heading towards Cañas and transferring in Chomes; the ferry returns at 7am, 12.30pm and 3.30pm.

Tours can be arranged through ACTUAR (Ⓣ2248-9470, Ⓦwww.actuarcostarica.com), whose overnight package ($122) includes accommodation at *La Amistad Lodge* with three delicious home-cooked meals, bike trips, a birdwatching tour and a boat ride through the mangroves, plus the ferry from Costa de Pájaros; they also offer a day-trip departing from San Pablo, southwest of the Río Tempisque Bridge ($62). ACTUAR can arrange direct transfers from Isla de Chira to the Refugio de Vida Silvestre Reserva Karen Mogensen (see opposite) on the southern Nicoya Peninsula.

The southern Nicoya Peninsula

Most visitors' first sight of the **southern Nicoya Peninsula** is from the soothing, slow-paced ferry from Puntarenas: you'll see its low brown hills rising up in the distance, ringed by a rugged coastline and pockets of intense jungly green. Much of the region, though, has been cleared for farming or cattle grazing, or, in the case of the surf towns on its far southwestern tip, given over to tourism.

The area's main town is **Cóbano**, a dull transport hub with a petrol station, a post office and a Banco Nacional with an ATM, a rare convenience in these parts. Most tourists pass straight through on their way to the thriving coastal towns of **Mal País**, **Santa Teresa** or **Montezuma**, one of Costa Rica's most popular beach hangouts. The partly paved road to Montezuma, lined by acres of cattle pasture, offers a startling – and disconcerting – vision of the future of the deforested tropics. Once covered with dense primary Pacific lowland forest, today only stumps dot the fields. Still, heroic efforts are being made by local conservationists to create a biological corridor throughout the peninsula, with the wildlife refuges of **Reserva Karen Mogensen** and **Curú** proving that nature can – and is – making a comeback. For details of ferries to and from the southern Nicoya Peninsula, see box on p.333.

Isla Tortuga

One of the most popular day-trip destinations in Costa Rica, **ISLA TORTUGA** is actually two large uninhabited islands (over three square kilometres in total), just off the coast of the Nicoya Peninsula near Paquera. Characterized by its poster-perfect white sands, palm-lined beaches and lush, tropical deciduous vegetation, it's certainly a picturesque place, offering quiet – during the week, at least – sheltered swimming and snorkelling. At the weekend, however, boatloads of passengers come ashore roughly at the same time, somewhat marring the islands' image as an isolated pristine tropical paradise.

Cruises to Isla Tortuga usually leave from Puntarenas and take around two hours each way. There's plenty of opportunity for spotting **marine animals**, including large whale sharks, depending upon the season. You also pass by Negritos and Guayabo island sanctuaries, where swarms of **sea birds** nest, including brown pelicans and magnificent frigatebirds. On the island, there's time for lunch (usually included in the tour price) and **snorkelling**, followed by sunbathing or a little walking.

One of the biggest **operators** is the fairly luxurious Puntarenas-based Calypso Tours (Ⓣ2256-2727, Ⓦwww.calypsotours.com; $119 includes return transport from San José, Jacó or Quepos), who also run exclusive cruises to their private nature reserve Punta Coral, set in tropical dry forest on the Nicoya Peninsula. Bay Island Cruises (Ⓣ2258-3536, Ⓦwww.bayislandcruises.com) also offer day-trips from San José. A slower-paced and cheaper option is to take a tour from the Refugio de Vida Silvestre Curú, near Tambor (see p.341) or from Montezuma (see p.342); trips are also available from Mal País and Santa Teresa (see p.347).

Refugio de Vida Silvestre Reserva Karen Mogensen

The wildlife-rich **REFUGIO DE VIDA SILVESTRE RESERVA KAREN MOGENSEN**, 20km southwest of Playa Naranjo, offers the most rewarding ecotourism experience on the southern Nicoya Peninsula. This nine-square-kilometre patch of primary and secondary dry-humid tropical forest functions as both a private reserve and tourist lodge and has become the most crucial link in an expanding biological corridor that runs between the Reserva Natural Absoluta Cabo Blanco, 85km south at the end of the peninsula, and Parque Nacional Barra Honda, 50km north in Guanacaste. Named after the late Karen Mogensen, the Danish conservationist who was instrumental in creating Cabo Blanco (see p.346), the reserve was established in 1996 by the local not-for-profit ASEPALECO (Ⓣ2650-0607, Ⓦwww.asepaleco.com) – a name that references the peninsula's three main towns, Paquerea, Lepanto and Cóbano.

Fence removal, tree planting and natural regeneration has returned this former patch of farmland into a fully functioning jungle ecosystem. Endangered **plant species** such as rónrón, mahogany, teak and ebony grow in the reserve, while white-faced and howler **monkeys** abound, and deer roam the forest, preyed on by elusive pumas. More than 240 species of **birds** have been spotted, including great curassows, motmots, long-tailed manakins, spectacled owls and three-wattled bellbirds.

Five kilometres of well-maintained **hiking trails** run through the reserve, leading to lookouts with jaw-dropping views of the Gulf of Nicoya as well as to one of the most breathtaking waterfalls in the country – the 18m **Catarata Velo de Novia** (Bridal Veil Falls), which cascades down a rounded cliffside before dropping to a deep, turquoise swimming hole.

Practicalities

The reserve is best accessed from the village of **San Ramón de Río Blanco**, 16km southwest of Jicaral by rough road; **buses** for Jicaral meet the ferry at Playa Naranjo, or you can get here from San José, on one of the two daily buses that leave from C 12, Av 7/9 (6am & 3.30pm; 4hr), or from Nicoya (5am, 9am, 1pm & 5pm; 1hr 30min). Once in Jicaral, you'll need to take a taxi to the reserve entrance (around $25) or arrange 4WD transport with ASEPALECO. Leaving, there are buses from Jicaral to Playa Naranjo (6.30am, 10.30am, 2.30pm & 6.30pm; 1hr 30min), Nicoya (same times as above) and San José (4.45am & 2.30pm; 4hr).

Visitors who want **to stay** in the reserve can spend the night at the remote but comfortable *Cerro Escondido Lodge* (ⓣ2650-0607 or 2248-9470 for English, ⓦwww.asepaleco.com or www.actuarcostarica.com; ❻), featuring four solar-powered cabins with private cold-water bathrooms and wide balconies; the adjacent open-air restaurant serves delicious buffet-style meals, and at night local musicians provide entertainment. Rates include three meals and the services of a local guide, and all money from tourism is reinvested in purchasing more land and planting trees.

Getting to the lodge is half the adventure, as it is only accessible by either a 3km uphill hike from the village of San Ramón de Río Blanco or a one-hour horse ride from the town of Montaña Grande, 6km northeast; due to the effort involved, visitors are encouraged to stay at least two nights. ASEPALECO can store excess luggage in their office in the town of Jicaral. The **temperature** drops a few degrees on the mountain at night, so be sure to pack something warm and waterproof. Rubber boots are essential, as you'll be crossing five rivers on the hike up to the lodge; the reserve office can supply them for average sizes.

Tambor

Since 1992, when the Spanish hotel group Barceló unveiled its four-hundred-room *Hotel de Playa Tambor*, the small village of **TAMBOR** has become synonymous with large-scale tourist-resort development (see box below). Despite the presence of the mega-hotel – set off by itself, with its own road, grounds and guards – the whole area remains rather remote, and the village, surrounded on two sides by thickly forested hills, exudes a friendly, laidback vibe missing in some of the peninsula's more touristed resorts. Its sandy beach stretches along a narrow horseshoe strip at the western end of the sheltered **Bahía Ballena** where, true to its name, you can sometimes spot *ballenas* (whales).

Practicalities

Flights from San José to Tambor (7 daily; 25min) land at the small airstrip about 4.5km out of town. The **bus** that runs between Montezuma and Paquera (6 daily, from 6am until 6pm; 50min) stops in the village.

A block back from the beach, chilled-out *Cabinas Cristina* (ⓣ2683-0028, ⓔcabinascristina@ice.co.cr; ❸) is the best budget **accommodation** in town, with

Hotel de Playa Tambor: Paradise Lost?

The building of the **Hotel de Playa Tambor** is a textbook example of the type of development environmental agencies are increasingly struggling to prevent from tarnishing Costa Rica's well-earned eco credentials. The hotel has been plagued by controversy since before it even opened, and throughout its construction the backers at times seemed wilfully bent on acting out every environmental and social gaffe possible. Barceló was convicted of both **illegally draining and filling mangrove swamps**, an ecologically valuable resource similar to those protected by the nearby Refugio de Vida Silvestre Curú. They were also accused of **violating Costa Rican law** dictating that the first 50m of any beach is public property, with no development or habitation allowed. Despite an order ruling that the project be stopped, the government, in the end, appeared unwilling to close them down. Grupo Barceló now owns several other hotels throughout Costa Rica.

nine basic but clean rooms, most with private bathroom and one with kitchen (❻). The Tico owners dish up lovingly prepared meals at the popular on-site restaurant and can arrange tours. Nearby, the friendly new owners of *Hotel Costa Coral* (ⓣ2683-0105, ⓦwww.hotelcostacoral.com; ❼) are currently upgrading the ten rooms at their boutique hotel, which have air conditioning and cable TV with DVD player; most have a private terrace overlooking the pretty pool area and tropical gardens. The best place to stay in town, though, is the good-looking *Hotel Tambor Tropical* (ⓣ2683-0011, ⓦwww.tambortropical.com; ❽), set in palm gardens facing languid Playa Tambor, with an inviting pool, hot tub and beautiful wooden *cabinas* with large kitchens; no children under 16 are accepted. It's also the base for Seascape Kayak Tours, which runs recommended trips to nearby Curú (see below).

You can dine on fresh fish directly hauled in from the incoming boats at the *Bahía Ballena Yacht Club* **restaurant**, just south of town (daily 11am–10pm), where conger eel ($8) is usually among the day's catch.

Refugio de Vida Silvestre Curú

The small, semi-privately owned **REFUGIO DE VIDA SILVESTRE CURÚ** (daily 7am–3pm; $10; ⓣ2641-0100), 16km northeast of Tambor, protects a wide variety of flora, including deciduous forest and many endangered mangrove species. Pretty white-sand beaches, dotted with rocky coves and backed by exuberantly chaotic palm fronds, unfold along the reserve's coasts where, at low tide, rocky pools yield crabs and assorted shellfish.

A network of **trails** fans out through the reserve (you can pick up a map from the office): the long Sendero Quesara and Sendero Posa Colorado trails lead down to picturesque beaches, while the shorter Sendero Finca de los Monos passes through mangroves and is a good place to spot some of the reserve's great variety of **wildlife**, including northern tamanduas, iguanas and agoutis. You're also likely to see or hear monkeys – white-faced capuchin, howler and squirrel, who were re-introduced a few years ago after being driven to extinction on the Nicoya Peninsula. Of the many bird species in evidence, the most exciting to spot are the **scarlet macaws**, which can sometimes be seen foraging for almonds along the coast. Extinct locally since the late 1960s, they were reintroduced to Curú in 1999 and have successfully bred in the years since.

Practicalities

Buses from Tambor to Paquera (every 2hr from 7am to 7pm) pass by the reserve entrance, from where it's a 2km walk to the administration office. You can **stay** in the reserve at some very basic cold-water *cabinas* ($10), which are located on the beach; they're popular with students and researchers, so you'll need to book in advance. Meals ($7 each) are available at the on-site *comedor*.

Turismo Curú (ⓣ2641-0004, ⓦwww.curutourism.com), by the administration office, organizes **guided walks** ($15; 1hr 30min) and **horseback rides** ($10 per hour) around the reserve, as well as **night walks** ($20; 1hr 30min) for overnight visitors, which can help pick out some of the wildlife that you might otherwise miss. It also offers trips to nearby **Isla Tortuga**, by boat (daily 9am; $45 including BBQ lunch, snorkel rental and entrance to the refuge; 3hr 30min) or kayak ($45; 2hr), as well as the chance to see some of the island's underwater life on a scuba dive (from $90).

Seascape Kayak Tours (ⓣ8314-8605, ⓦwww.seascapekayaktours.com), based at the *Hotel Tambor Tropical* (see above) runs excellent small-group **kayak trips** in the waters off Curú, with an emphasis on wildlife-watching and learning about the local environment; you're likely to see dolphins, turtles and spotted eagle rays en route. The half-day ($74) or full-day ($135, including gourmet lunch and snorkelling) tours run from November to April and include entrance to the reserve. It also runs multi-day trips, camping overnight on white-sand beaches.

Montezuma

The popular beach resort of **MONTEZUMA** lies about 40km southwest of Paquera, near the southern tip of the Nicoya Peninsula. Some three decades ago, a handful of foreigners seeking solitude fell in love with Montezuma and decided to stay. In those days, it was just a sleepy fishing village, largely cut off from the rest of the country, but today Montezuma draws tourists galore, and virtually every establishment in town offers gringo-friendly food and accommodation and sells tours. Nevertheless, it still feels like a village because large-scale development has been kept to a minimum – and it's still a bit of an effort to get here.

Montezuma and the area south to the Reserva Absoluta Cabo Blanco features some of Costa Rica's loveliest coastline: leaning palms and jutting rocks dot the white-sand beaches. Here you can enjoy uninterrupted views of the Pacific, especially arresting when the occasional lightning storm illuminates the horizon and silky waters. Inland, thickly forested hills, including rare Pacific lowland tropical forest, dominate the landscape.

Arrival and information

Buses from Paquera (7 daily; 2hr) and San José (at 6am & 2pm; 5hr) pull in behind *El Sano Banano Hotel*. The **taxi-boat** from Playa Herradura, 7km north of Jacó

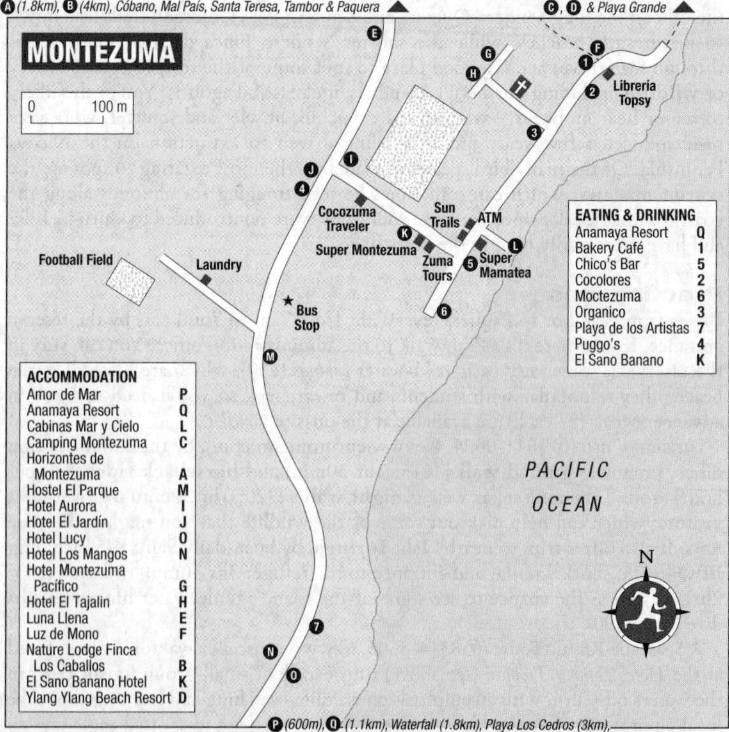

Moving on from Montezuma

Buses for Paquera (for the **ferry**; 6 daily; 2hr) and **San José** (daily 6am & 2.30pm; 5hr) leave from behind the *El Sano Banano Hotel*; for **Mal País and Santa Teresa**, you'll need to take the 10am or 2pm Paquera bus and change in Cóbano (30min), to connect with the onward services there (daily 10.30am & 2.30pm; 30min). The Paquera bus also passes the airstrip near Tambor, for **flights to San José** (7 daily; 25min). The **taxi-boat** to Jacó (departs 9.30am; $40; 1hr) is also useful for connections south to **Manuel Antonio**.

(departs 10.45am; $40; 1hr), is by far the quickest way of getting here from the Central Pacific.

On the main drag, the helpful multilingual folks at Zuma Tours (Ⓣ2642-0024, Ⓦwww.zumatours.net) offer **information** and the largest range of **tours** in town, such as day-trips to Isla Tortuga (daily 9.30am; 6hr; $50, including lunch and snorkelling tour) and horseriding along the beach to El Chorro Waterfall (daily 9am & 2pm; 4hr; $50). Cocozuma Traveler (Ⓣ2642-0911, Ⓦwww.cocozumacr.com), the other side of *El Sano Banano Hotel*, offers similar trips to Isla Tortuga, as well as to the Reserva Natural Absoluta Cabo Blanco (daily 7.30am; $40, including lunch; 6hr).

Accommodation

Accommodation prices are moderate in Montezuma as the village caters to a younger crowd who can't afford the rates of, say, Manuel Antonio. While convenient, staying in the **village** can be noisy due to traffic and the shenanigans at *Chico's Bar*. Elsewhere, you'll find it peaceful, with choices out on the **beach**, on the road that heads southwest to the Reserva Natural Absoluta Cabo Blanco, and on the sides of the steep hill about 1km above the village.

Camping is prohibited on the beach; instead, you can stay on the edge of town at the beachside *Camping Montezuma* (Ⓣ2642-0703) where $4 gets you a pitch, shared toilet and shower.

In the village

Cabinas Mar y Cielo By the beach, down a lane behind Super Mamatea Ⓣ2642-0261. The clean rooms in this rambling wooden house come with fridge, private bath – and if you're upstairs – a balcony with ocean views and sea breezes. The hammock-filled garden is a great place to relax, though *Chico's Bar* can be noisy. ❹

Hostel El Parque Just southeast of the centre, near the bus stop Ⓣ2642-0164, Ⓦwww.montezumahostel.com. Cleaner than some of the other budget places at this end of town, *El Parque* backs onto the beach, where you can laze in hammocks under the trees. Rooms are dark but cool; the four-bed dorms ($9) near the front are lighter. There's a communal kitchen and laundry, and a bar, conveniently, next door. ❷

Hotel Aurora On the northern edge of the park Ⓣ2642-0051, Ⓦwww.playamontezuma.net/aurora.htm. Take your pick among the varied en-suite rooms at this pleasant, environmentally conscious *pensión*: all come with a/c, fridge and private terrace or balcony. Guests also have use of a well-equipped kitchen and there's a great communal lounge. ❹

Hotel El Jardín At the entrance to town Ⓣ2642-0074, Ⓦwww.hoteleljardin.com. Relax in attractive, spacious cabins with wooden ceilings, tiled bathrooms and terraces with leather rocking chairs; upstairs rooms have views over the town and sea. You can also melt in the hot tub or cool off in the enticing pool surrounded by tropical plants. The two separate two-bedroom villas ($115) have their own kitchens and hammock-strewn terraces. ❻

Hotel Montezuma Pacífico Just north of the church Ⓣ2642-0204, Ⓔmontezumapacific-hotel@hotmail.com. The rooms at this hotch-potch hotel are rather characterless but clean and quiet, and come with a/c, fridge, good-sized beds and hot water. Try to get one of the front rooms with decent views or a room with a balcony. ❹

Hotel El Tajalin Just west of *Hotel Montezuma Pacífico* ⓣ 2642-0061, ⓦ www.tajalin.com. In a quiet location just northwest of the centre, this hotel – named after the purple-clawed crabs that frequent the hillside behind the village – has attractively simple wood-floored rooms with a/c; the airier ones on the top floor ($10 more) have sea views. They also have a communal lounge with television, books and coffee. ❹

Luna Llena 200m north of the village, on the road to Paquera ⓣ 2642-0390, ⓦ www.lunallenahotel.com. This surfer-friendly hostel sits peacefully on a forested hillside, with a regular troupe of monkeys as visitors. Attractive rooms (one is en suite) have fans and sleep up to five; most are a combination of double beds and bunks (extra guests $10 each). There are two shared kitchens, a BBQ and a sociable TV lounge. ❸

Luz de Mono At the eastern end of the village, 50m from the beach ⓣ 2642-0090, ⓦ www.luzdemono.com. Set between the jungle and the beach, with en-suite rooms (queen beds, satellite TV) or *casitas* (jacuzzis, terraces). There are two pools (one for kids), a restaurant and a bar (serving wine from their Playa Grande vineyard). ❺

El Sano Banano Hotel In the centre of town above the restaurant of the same name ⓣ 2642-0638, ⓦ www.ylangylangresort.com. This is a good central option if you manage to score a room without a brick-wall view. Mexican bedspreads brighten up the small and clean rooms, all with private hot-water bath, a/c and a TV. The price includes breakfast at the on-site restaurant and guests can use the pool at *Ylang Ylang Beach Resort* (see below). ❻

Around the village

Amor de Mar 600m southwest of the village on the beach, just across the bridge ⓣ 2642-0262, ⓦ www.amordemar.com. Richly rustic seafront hotel with its own tide pool sitting in pretty landscaped gardens on a rocky promontory. Hammocks hang between giant palm trees, and a nice selection of rooms come with and without bathroom; those upstairs and facing the sea are best, most of which have a veranda and ocean views. The two *casas* ($200) can sleep up to six people and are a great deal for families. ❹

Anamaya Resort 500m up the hill, accessed on the road next to *Amor de Mar* ⓣ 2642-1289, ⓦ www.anamayaresort.com. Yoga-centric wellness hotel set high up on the cliffs behind Montezuma, and offering stylish, individually designed *cabinas*, most with superb ocean views, and a gorgeous saltwater infinity pool where it feels like you're swimming out into the Pacific. The mostly organic, mostly local restaurant is also open to non-guests (see opposite). Week-long retreats (everything from cleansing and raw-food to aerial yoga and tantric sex) start at $995. ❽

Horizontes de Montezuma 1.8km before Montezuma, on the road from Paquera ⓣ 2642-0534, ⓦ www.horizontes-montezuma.com. Perched in the hills above Montezuma, this small, distinctive, tropical-Victorian-style hotel has spacious, airy rooms with hot-water private bath and balcony looking over the jungle. There's a nicely lit pool and the owners offer intensive private Spanish lessons. Breakfast (home-made German wheatbread and jams) is $4 extra. ❺

Hotel Lucy 500m south of the village ⓣ 2642-0273. This Montezuma stalwart, still operating even though the government once attempted to have it torn down because it violates the *zona maritime* prohibiting building on the first 50m of beach (the same can't be said for their restaurant, which has had to move to Santa Teresa; see p.352), offers clean, cute rooms with cold-water showers on a small stretch of grey-sand beach; a couple of rooms have private bath. ❷

Hotel Los Mangos 500m south of the village ⓣ 2642-0384, ⓦ www.hotellosmangos.com. Split-level hotel set amid mango trees, with brightly decorated doubles and quads, plus expensive-looking but slightly dark bungalows (❻), which come with fan and large, hot-water showers; some have their own verandas and rocking chairs. There's also a pool and hot tub, and regular yoga classes ($12, hr 30min) are held in an airy wooden pavilion. ❸

Nature Lodge Finca Los Caballos 4km before Montezuma, on the road from Paquera ⓣ 2642-0124, ⓦ www.naturelodge.net. Set in tropical gardens with a small pool, this casual lodge has twelve good-value rooms with hot-water private bath and a restaurant serving gourmet international cuisine – the more romantic rooms come with huge beds, views of the Pacific and either a balcony or an outdoor shower (❼). The owners offer highly recommended horse tours (from $40 for a two-hour trip to Playa Grande). ❺

Ylang Ylang Beach Resort A 10min walk along the beach from the village (your bags will be taken care of) ⓣ 2642-0638, ⓦ www.ylangylangresort.com. One of Costa Rica's most characterful hotels, this truly romantic retreat offers secluded circular *cabinas* ($265) all with beachfront verandas and outside showers. The newer split-level apartments, perfect for families, boast beach views, and there are also luxury tents ($160) in the dry season. There's a lovely freeform swimming pool with a waterfall, beautifully landscaped gardens and an on-site spa (massages from $50 for 30min). Rates include breakfast and candlelit dinner at the seafront restaurant. ❽

The village and around

It's Montezuma's atmosphere, rather than its activities, that draws visitors, and other than hanging out and sipping smoothies, there's not much to do in the village itself. Despite the palm-fringed, white-sand beaches, swimming isn't very good immediately north of Montezuma – there are lots of rocky outcroppings, some hidden at high tide, and the waves are rough and currents strong. Your best bet is to head further north along a lovely **trail** (1.5km) that dips in and out of several coves before ending at **Playa Grande**. Here, you'll find reasonable swimming, decent surfing and a small waterfall at the beach's eastern edge. Experienced surfers head in the other direction, to **Playa Los Cedros**, a left-hand reef break 3km south of Montezuma, and, a kilometre further on, the right-hand point break at the mouth of the **Río Lajas**, a very rocky spot best surfed at high tide.

A number of **waterfalls** lace Montezuma and its environs; the closest lies about a kilometre south down the road towards Cabo Blanco and then another 800m on a path (signposted to the *catarata*) through dense vegetation. Bring your swimsuit if you want to bathe, but always take care, especially in the wet season when flash floods may strike. Under no circumstances should you try to climb the waterfalls; many people have been injured – sometimes fatally – in the attempt. Sun Trails (Ⓣ2642-0808, Ⓦwww.montezumatraveladventures.com) offers a **canopy tour** (daily 9am, 1pm & 3pm; $40) that also stops at the waterfalls for a quick dip.

Eating, drinking and nightlife

Just a few years ago, all you could eat in Montezuma was fresh **fish**, served practically straight off the hook. Nowadays, varied menus offer not just *comida típica* but a slew of tourist favourites like vegetarian pizza, granola, mango shakes and paella. Self-caterers can stock up at Super Montezuma on the main street (daily 7am–10pm) or sample the organic produce at the Saturday morning market in the park opposite (10am–noon).

Nightlife centres on *Chico's Bar*, where an interesting mix of local kids – who arrive packed in the back of pick-ups – and tourists guzzle from a wide choice of alcohol. It closes at 2am, after which people tend to adjourn to the beach for some alfresco drinking. More retiring types can take in the very popular movie shows (in English) at the *Hotel El Sano Banano*'s restaurant nightly at 7 or 7.30pm ($4).

Anamaya Resort 500m up the hill, on a road next to *Amor de Mar* Ⓣ2642-1289, Ⓦwww.anamayaresort.com. Three-course ultra-healthy set menu ($35), changing daily but including such dishes as grilled mahi-mahi with macadamia-nut butter and miso-seared yellow-fin tuna with coconut quinoa. Non-guests can arrive at 3pm to walk the waterfall trail and take a dip in the infinity pool. Tues–Sat 7pm (reserve by 1pm).

Bakery Café Opposite *Luz de Mono*. Stop by for the tasty home-made sandwiches, cakes and pastries served on a soothing, shady terrace – perfect for lunch after a morning spent on the nearby beach. Daily 6am–10pm.

Cocolores This intimate restaurant in a garden by the beach serves tasty coconut fish curry ($11), Lebanese salad ($7) and a good range of vegetarian dishes – all accompanied by fresh baked bread. Tues–Sun 5–10pm.

Moctezuma Gaze straight out to sea at this split-level, waterfront restaurant in the centre of the village where the Spanish chef conjures up a mean seafood paella ($12). Sop it all up with hunks of fresh bread. Daily 7.30am–10pm.

Organico Organic down to its vanilla cardamom ice cream, the emphasis here is on delicious, wholesome cuisine. The vitamin-infused menu includes brown rice, fajitas and vegetarian lasagne – washed down with a shot of Aloe Vera. Mon–Sat 11am–9pm.

Playa de los Artistas 500m south of the village Ⓣ2642-0920. Beachside dining doesn't get any better – an unhurried candlelit dinner of fresh fish and lobster, vegetable dishes and delectable sushi (Fri) at hewn wood tables or on cushions on the sand. Main courses hover around $15 – the tuna and snapper are particularly recommended. Mon–Sat 10.30am–9.30pm.

Puggo's Just beyond the main turning down into the village. This mellow, mat-floored place at the top of the village serves up a small choice of alternative breakfasts, good starters, including crispy risotto balls ($6) and a range of stir-fried noodle dishes ($8). Mon & Wed–Sun 8am–9.30pm.

El Sano Banano Come here for excellent American breakfasts and filling lunch and dinner specials, including the fillet of fish, vegetarian pizzas and cannelloni with spinach, most of which feature organic produce (mains $8–13). At the very least, sample an incredible smoothie made with fresh fruit and yoghurt ($5). Films are screened every evening, so come early to get a seat.

Listings

Banks and money Montezuma has an ATM, but the nearest bank is in Cóbano, 7km away. Dollars are accepted everywhere.

Bookshops Librería Topsy on the beachfront road sells newspapers and books (Mon–Fri 8am–1pm & 3–5pm; Sat 8am–noon).

Laundry There's a simple *lavendaría* up the road opposite the bus stop (daily 7am–5pm; $1.50/kg)

Medical care The nearest clinic is in Cóbano (Ⓣ2642-0208).

Scooter rental *Hostel El Parque* (see p.343) rents scooters for $35/day.

Cabuya

Laidback **CABUYA**, 7km south of Montezuma, is a pleasant village that draws a growing community of permanent foreign residents who enjoy the slow pace of life, relative isolation and unspoiled scenery. It's everything its neighbour isn't, so if you're looking to escape the crowds and loll on secluded beaches, this is the place to come; it's also just a twenty-minute walk from the nearby Reserva Natural Absoluta Cabo Blanco. When the tide is low, it's possible to walk on a stony trail out to the village **cemetery** located on the otherwise uninhabited **Isla Cabuya**; it's a great spot for snorkelling but bear in mind that the path is covered by the ocean during high tide. To get there, walk west of the main intersection and follow the first road south of town.

Practicalities

The **bus** from Montezuma to Cabo Blanco (see opposite) runs past Cabuya; the road is rough, so you'll need a 4WD if driving yourself. Another rough, and hilly, road links Cabuya with Mal País; it's only driveable in a 4WD, and a water crossing often makes the road impassable in the rainy season.

Welcoming *El Ancla de Oro* (Ⓣ2642-0369, Ⓦwww.caboblancopark.com/ancla; ❷) has rustic **cabins**, with mosquito nets and fans, placed among fruit trees; there are also some self-catering "jungalows". Nearby, the *Hotel Cabo Blanco* (Ⓣ&Ⓕ2642-0332; ❹) is set right on a gentle beach with good swimming; the rooms come with fan or air conditioning and TV, and there's a swimming pool if you just can't face the short walk to the beach. Just before you enter the village, *Hotel Celaje* (Ⓣ2642-0372, Ⓦwww.celaje.com; closed Sept to mid-Nov; ❻) is a Belgian-owned beachside beauty with six palm-roofed bungalows that come with two beds with mosquito nets and small bathrooms. There's an inviting swimming pool, a bar and restaurant. You can stock up on groceries at two mini-markets or eat cheap typical food at Cabyuya's two *sodas*; about 200m north of town, munch on decent pizza, washed down with a thick fruit smoothie, at *Café el Coyote*.

Reserva Natural Absoluta Cabo Blanco

RESERVA NATURAL ABSOLUTA CABO BLANCO (Wed–Sun 8am–4pm; $8; Ⓣ2642-0093, Ⓦwww.caboblancopark.com), 9km south of Montezuma, is Costa Rica's oldest protected piece of land, established in 1963 by Karen Mogensen, a Danish immigrant to Costa Rica, and her Swedish husband Olof Wessberg. Until 1989, no visitors were allowed into the twelve square kilometres of reserve, which covers nearly the entire southwestern tip of the Nicoya

Watching wildlife in Cabo Blanco

The **best time for animal spotting** is around 8am, or on Wednesday mornings, after the reserve has been closed for two days. The heat chases a lot of the wildlife into the more heavily forested sections of the reserve, which are off-limits to visitors, but you're still likely to see **howler monkeys**, **white-faced capuchin monkeys** and **white-tailed deer**; **agoutis** and **coati** are also common. Harder to spot mammals include the **margay**, **northern tamandua** and **collared peccary** – Cabo Blanco has what is thought to be the last herd of these boar-like creatures on the Nicoya Peninsula.

Birdlife is astonishingly plentiful, in the forest itself (where you might catch a glimpse of a **long-tailed manakin** or a **sulphur-winged parakeet**) but particularly down by the shore – you'll often see scores of **pelicans** and clouds of **magnificent frigatebirds**, while Costa Rica's largest community of **brown boobies** nests on Isla Cabo Blanco, the guano-encrusted island that lies 2km offshore.

Peninsula. Though hard to believe today, most of the reserve was pasture and farmland until the early 1960s. Since its inauguration, Cabo Blanco has been allowed to regenerate naturally; a small area of original forest that had escaped destruction served as a "genetic bank" for the re-establishment of the complex tropical forest that now fills the reserve.

Pay your entrance fee at the **ranger hut**, and they'll supply you with a trail map (there are only two), which also outlines the history of the reserve and the species living here; walking the trails here can be very hot work, so head out early. The **Sendero Sueco** (5km; 2hr) leads from the entrance through tropical deciduous forest to **Playa Cabo Blanco**, a lovely, lonely spot (in low season, anyway). Swimming, however, isn't great around here; due to the high tide (*marea alta*), you'll need to walk back along the trail rather than the coast. Ask the ranger at the entrance when and where you'll likely get cut off if you want to venture along the beach.

Practicalities

An old, road-hardened **bus** runs along the rough road from Montezuma to the reserve (30min), leaving the village's *parque* daily at 8am, 10am, 2pm, 4pm and 6pm, returning from Cabo Blanco at 1pm, 3pm and 5.30pm, although it may not always run in the rainy season. **Jeep-taxis** make the trip for $10 per person. You'll need a 4WD to get there yourself, except in the very driest time of year, and even then you'll need to keep an eye out for the two creeks, which are deep at high tide. Note that it's also very **hot**: 30°C is not uncommon, so, if possible, hike the trails early, and bring a hat, suncream and plenty of water.

Mal País and Santa Teresa

Just over a decade ago, the long grey-sand surf beaches fronting the virtually seamless towns of **MAL PAÍS** ("Bad Land") and **SANTA TERESA**, 12km southwest of Cóbano and also accessible via a steep and very bumpy road from Cabuya, began luring an increasing number of travellers. First came the surfers, then the hippies, and not long after, curious yuppies, celebrities and families started trickling in. A building boom over the past decade, particularly in Santa Teresa, has transformed this formerly sleepy stretch of Pacific coast into a trendy beach resort, and foreigners now outnumber Tico residents. The developers, banks and car rental chains show no signs of leaving town, and the fear on these dusty, rutted streets is that the neighbouring towns are well on their way to becoming "the next Jacó". But as long as the roads here remain

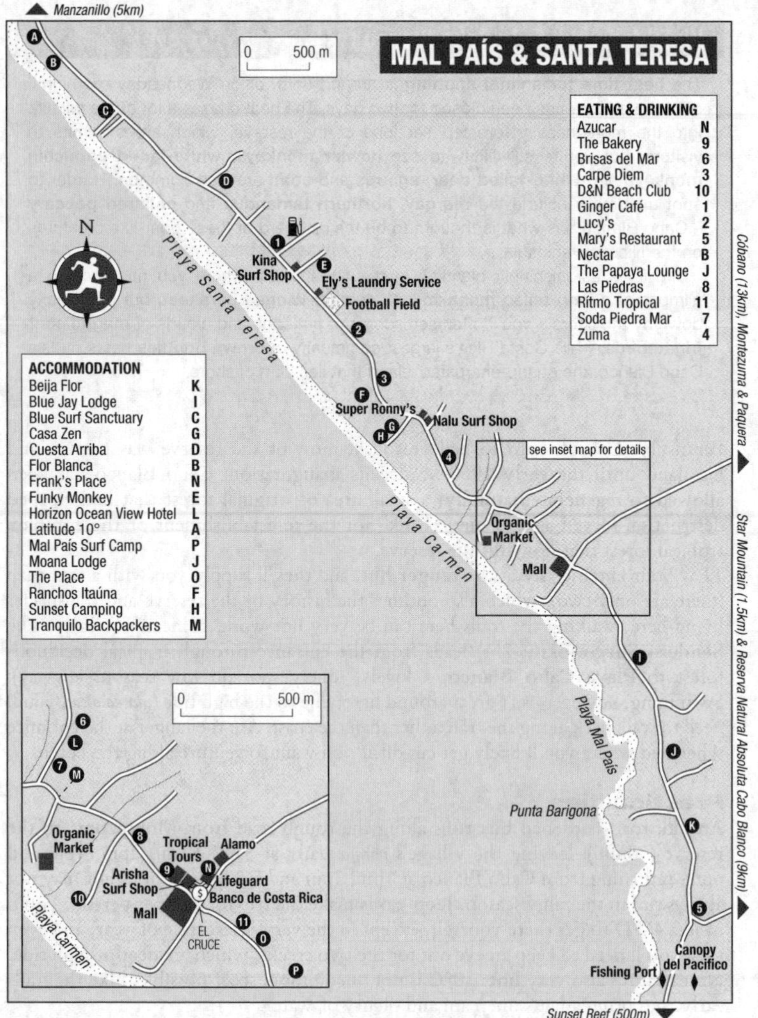

appalling, the area seems certain to retain its laidback charm; and in the rainy season at least, you can still walk along jungle-flanked surf beaches for hours and see few other people.

Arrival and orientation

There are two direct **buses from San José** to Mal País and Santa Teresa (6am & 2pm; 5hr). Buses from **the ferry** (and **Montezuma**) serve Cóbano, 12km northwest, where you can connect with one of the daily services to Mal País (10.30am & 2.30pm; 30min). If **driving from Montezuma** (in a 4WD), you could also take the road via Cabuya. A taxi from Cóbano to Mal País or Santa Teresa will set you back around $20.

The straggly oceanfront communities spread along 8km of rough road and three separate **beaches** – Mal País, Carmen and Santa Teresa. The intersection

Moving on from Mal País and Santa Teresa

Three daily **buses** make the short but jarring journey up the hill to **Cóbano** (7am, 11.30am & 3.30pm; 30min), from where you can catch another bus to the ferry at **Paquera** (7 daily, connecting services every 2hr from 8.30am to 4.30pm; 1hr 30min) or back down the other side of the peninsula to **Montezuma** (7 daily; 30min). The direct service to **San José** leaves at 6am and 2pm.

At low tide, the beach north of Santa Teresa becomes an unofficial highway linking Manzanillo with the dirt road that heads north along the coast towards **Sámara** (see p.302). In the rainy season, the drive isn't recommended; the creeks – at least a dozen of them – that cut the dirt road between Manzanillo and Sámara are likely to be so high you won't make it in anything less than a large truck.

by the hotel *Frank's Place*, known as **"El Cruce"**, is the traditional boundary: turning south takes you along the **Mal País** section of the beach strip, which is quieter and more peaceful than Santa Teresa; straight over the intersection lies **Playa Carmen**; while turning north leads quickly into **Santa Teresa**. Beyond Santa Teresa lies **Manzanillo**, a rocky beach with a couple of point breaks on the western side of the peninsula; while there were few facilities here at the time of writing, the Manzanillo coastal strip looks set to experience the next development boom.

Accommodation

The recent construction boom has brought with it a smorgasbord of boutique **hotels** and even the budget options here are surprisingly modern. The majority of the accommodation is set along the shores of Playa Carmen and Playa Santa Teresa, and most places are equipped with kitchens to suit the long-term surfer clientele; as it can be hot day and night, it's well worth splashing out on air conditioning. **Camping** is officially prohibited on the beach, but several campgrounds operate anyway, including *Sunset Camping* ($4), 1.5km north of the intersection, by *Casa Zen*; you can also pitch your tent at *Tranquilo Backpackers* ($7) and the *Mal País Surf Camp* ($10), both listed below. Most places, like the towns themselves, shut down during September and October.

Santa Teresa

The following places are listed in the order you encounter them heading north from the intersection.

Frank's Place ⓣ2640-0096, ⓦwww.franksplacecr.com. A local landmark and one of the area's most established hotels, the central location makes this a popular place to bed down, especially with holidaying Ticos. All rooms come with private bath, a/c, kitchen and fridge: the more upmarket ones are considerably roomier. You can hang out on hammocks around the pool, framed on one side by a decent restaurant (see p.352). ❻

Tranquilo Backpackers ⓣ2640-0546, ⓦwww.tranquilobackpackers.com. "Tranquilo" is probably not the best name for this popular hostel that attracts a boisterous gringo crowd. Set in a stylish two-storey ranch flanked by plenty of hammocks, the loft-style dorms ($13) can pack in six people and some have private hot-water bathrooms; doubles are also either shared bathroom or en suite. A communal kitchen, DVD movie room, pool table and ping pong complete the picture. ❸

Horizon Ocean View Hotel ⓣ2640-0524, ⓦwww.horizon-yogahotel.com. Staggered up the hillside overlooking jungle and Playa Carmen, these romantic bungalows are small but have expansive views that make up for it. Rooms come with a/c, firm mattresses, hot-water bathrooms and balconies adorned with hammocks and bamboo wind chimes; there are also two villas, one with a private pool (❽). You can munch vegetarian food, bliss out in the intimate triangular swimming pool, or stretch yourself in an outdoor yoga class (see p.351). ❼

Casa Zen ⓣ2640-8523, ⓦwww.zencostarica.com. The pick of the area's hostels, this stylish wooden house features

Asian-inspired trimmings and plenty of space. Just 50m from the beach, accommodation options include dorm rooms ($15), doubles and *cabinas* (❻). Upstairs is an apartment sleeping up to 14 people ($50–156 depending on numbers). There are morning yoga classes, movie nights and a restaurant serving mouthwatering Thai cuisine. ❷

Ranchos Itaúna ☎2640-0095, Ⓦwww.ranchos-itauna.com. This beachfront property lies smack bang between the surf breaks of Playa Carmen and Playa Santa Teresa. With just four comfortable octagonal rooms (two have kitchens and all have one double bed, a bunk bed, a/c, fridge and private hot-water bath), this place oozes tranquillity. The owners can arrange massage and surf lessons, and Brazilian fare is served in the restaurant (closed Sun). The lively bar hosts regular DJ sets and live music. ❼

Funky Monkey ☎2640-0272, Ⓦwww.funky-monkey-lodge.com. This hillside lodge with a swish pool and sushi restaurant is part boutique hotel, part upmarket backpackers hangout. Whether staying in a bamboo bungalow with outdoor shower (❻), a self-contained apartment with ocean views (❼) or bunking down in a dorm ($12) with shared cold-water bathroom, you can enjoy the lodge's excellent facilities and mingle with other travellers in the bar-side communal area. ❻

Cuesta Arriba ☎2640-0607, Ⓦwww.santateresacostarica.com. Mixed dorm beds ($12) are arranged six to a room in this sparkling hostel, ideally located for the Playa Santa Teresa breakers. Rooms are cleaned daily and come with lockers, fan and a bathroom with hot shower. There's plenty of space in the upstairs TV lounge or downstairs communal kitchen.

Blue Surf Sanctuary ☎2640-1001, Ⓦwww.bluesurfsanctuary.com. Upmarket surf camp, sponsored by Billabong and appealing to boardriders with bigger budgets – the swanky bungalows (just four) have luxurious bathrooms and treetop views from their balconies. All-inclusive surf lessons and board rental available. Seven-night surf packages start at $1195. ❼

Flor Blanca ☎2640-0232, Ⓦwww.florblanca.com. Positioned on a small beach between *playas* Santa Teresa and Hermosa, this beachside haven is fit for honeymooning Hollywood celebrities, and their wallets – the Honeymoon Suite costs $850. Its Balinese-style villas set in groomed grounds come with large open-air lounge areas and outdoor "jungle" bathrooms with sunken baths. There's also a pool, spa, yoga studio, bar and snazzy restaurant (see p.352). ❾

Latitude 10° ☎2640-0396, Ⓦwww.latitude10resort.com. Ultra-exclusive boutique hotel that manages to retain a relaxed and welcoming ambience. The five suites are beautifully furnished and completely open, allowing them to benefit from the sea breezes; the Master Suite ($440), with four-poster bed (and foot-high mattress) and spacious outdoor bathroom, must be among the finest in the country. There's a lovely little chemical-free pool, and bodyboards available for surfing on the beach out front. ❾

Mal País

The following places are listed in the order you encounter then heading south from the intersection.

The Place ☎2640-0001, Ⓦwww.theplacemalpais.com. Crisply furnished rooms and chic beach hut-style bungalows ($120) set around a chill-out lounge and garden pool. Movies are played on a big screen hanging over the pool on Tues & Fri at 7pm. ❻

Mal País Surf Camp ☎2640-0061, Ⓦwww.malpaissurfcamp.com. There's a good community vibe at this surfer centre near the top of Mal País, thanks to its mix of guests – accommodation ranges from $15 dorms through to large *casas* ($115), dotted around a nice pool – and chilled-out restaurant area. Stacks of magazines and on-loop surfing films should get you in the mood. Daily lessons also available ($45; 1hr). ❸

Blue Jay Lodge ☎2640-0089, Ⓦwww.bluejaylodgecostarica.com. The intimate, widely spaced bungalows at this easy-going place sleep two to three people. Head up the hillside for the best bungalows, with ocean views and plenty of nearby wildlife; for a relaxing break, cool off in their swimming pool. ❻

Moana Lodge ☎2640-0230, Ⓦwww.moanalodge.com. Run by a chatty Irishman and his Tica wife, this boutique hotel is one of the area's most romantic and stylish. Set on a forested slope, the lovely rooms have been tastefully decorated with African-inspired trimmings and come with a/c, hot-water bathrooms and large beds draped with silk throws. Try to score one of the higher ones with a balcony for nice ocean breezes, or – if your budget allows – the superb Honeymoon Suite, right at the top of the hill, with panoramic views from the jacuzzi and a private deck. You can while away the day in suspended beds by the pool before taking sunset drinks in the recommended restaurant (see p.352). ❼

Beija Flor ⓣ2640-1007, ⓦwww.beijaflorresort.com. Line of thatched-roof rooms minimally furnished in a design hotel kind of way, with partial outdoor showers. There are also garden-view doubles ($118) and a master suite that can accommodate five. The on-site restaurant fronts an attractive kidney-shaped pool and a popular yoga deck (Mon, Wed & Fri 9am; $15; 2hr). ❻

Activities

Despite the long stretches of sand, all the beaches here are prone to riptides and therefore not ideal for **swimming**, though there are often good tidal pools for splashing about in. They are, however, excellent for **surfing** (see box below).

Land activities include **horseriding** along the beach or in the surrounding jungle; try Star Mountain (ⓣ2640-0101, ⓦwww.starmountaineco.com), who will take you for a two-hour trot through the waves at Playa Carmen (daily 8.30am & 3pm; $50). A **canopy tour** ($40) offered by Canopy del Pacifico (ⓣ2640-0071, ⓦwww.canopydelpacifico.com) is further proof of Mal País' ascendancy on the tourist circuit, affording blurry Pacific views as you whizz through treetops adjoining the Reserva Natural Absoluta Cabo Blanco. The daily **yoga and pilates** classes held on the panoramic deck at *Horizon Ocean View Hotel* (Mon–Sat 9am, Sun 5pm, $10; ⓣ2640-0524, ⓦwww.horizon-yogahotel.com), 500m north of the intersection, are open to the public. Tropical Tours (ⓣ2640-0811, ⓦwww.tropicaltours-malpais.com), opposite Budget, arrange a variety of

Surf's up

Surfing put Mal País and Santa Teresa on the map, and the two communities still very much revolve around the rollers just offshore. **Playa Carmen** is an excellent beach for beginner and intermediate surfers, with a long right and a shorter left breaking over sand. More experienced types head north to the steeper waves at **Playa Santa Teresa**, where there are beach breaks and point breaks; on high swells, particularly between March and July, **Suck Rock**, at its northern end, peels into long, right-handed tubes. Only pro surfers and masochists ride **Sunset Reef** (also known as Playa de los Suecos), an extremely dangerous shallow reef-break with a fast take-off at the far southern end of Mal País; rocky outcrops along the rest of **Playa Mal País** render it uninviting for both swimmers and surfers, though **Punta Barrigona**, a slow, long left-hander halfway between Sunset Reef and the intersection, works well on a high-tide swell.

Equipment and tuition

The **shops** listed below all rent boards, organize surfing lessons and sometimes even run multi-day regional tours; surfer-centric **hotels** such as *Blue Surf Sanctuary* (see opposite) and the *Mal País Surf Camp* (see opposite) also offer lessons. You can get local **tide tables** online at ⓦmalpaissurfcam.com.

Arisha Surf Shop Just north of the intersection ⓣ2640-0228. A good range of surf gear, plus daily bodyboard ($5) and surfboard ($10) rental. Lessons are available on demand ($45; 1hr 30min), and they also do ding repair. Daily 9am–7pm.

Kina Surf Shop 2.2km north of the intersection ⓣ2640-0627, ⓦkinasurfcostarica.com. Wide range of boards for rent; beginner, intermediate and advanced lessons ($40; 1hr 30min); plus clothing, accessories and general surfing advice. Mon–Sat 9am–5pm, Sun 10am–4pm.

Nalu Surf Shop Next to Super Ronny's, 1km north of the intersection ⓣ2640-0391 or 8358-4436, ⓦwww.nalusurfschool.com. Rent boards for $10 per day, run professional surf classes ($40; 2hr) and lead one- ($35), three- ($105) and five-day ($175) courses. Daily 9am–6pm.

tours, including day-trips to Isla Tortuga (see p.338; $70 including BBQ lunch and snorkelling), as well as five-hour guided tours of the Reserva Natural Absoluta Cabo Blanco (see p.346; $75).

Eating and drinking

Mal País and Santa Teresa's large expat population translates into a wide range of **restaurants**, though the municipal government's decision to shut down the beachfront establishments has diluted the scene a bit, which fluctuates at the best of times (restaurants come and go with alarming frequency). **Nightlife** isn't the area's strong point, and most of the drinking and dancing action happens at the *D&N Beach Club* (ⓦwww.dayandnightbeachclub.com), just north of the intersection (open except Tues until 3am – or 5am if the police aren't on the case).

Santa Teresa

The following places are listed in the order you encounter them heading north from the intersection.

Azucar *Frank's Place.* Light lunches, such as pizza bagels ($9), and a more diverse selection in the evenings, when the culinary background of the London-trained Cuban chef is reflected in the daily specials. Daily 8am–3pm & 6–9.30pm, closed Tues eve.

The Bakery Settle down with something savoury (fresh bread, of course, but also soups, quiches or salads) or lip-lickingly sweet, including crépes and Belgian waffles. Daily 7am–10pm.

Las Piedras Delicious wood-fired chicken (plus grilled steak), prepared by a beaming Argentinian chef who knows he's onto a winner. Daily 8.30am–2pm & 6–10pm, closed Sun morning.

Soda Piedra Mar This dirt-cheap *soda* may have lost its legendary views after its forced relocation away from the beach, but it still serves great *comida típica*, including huge $5 *casados*. Daily 8am–9pm.

Zuma A buzzing local eatery that serves up Israeli favourites like falafel ($7), *shakshuka* and creamy bowls of hummus ($6) to dunk your pitta in. 9am–4pm & 6–10pm, closed Sat.

Brisas del Mar ⓣ2640-0941. It's a long way to the top of a very steep hill, but fish restaurants don't come much better than this – fresh, creative and with generous portions. Sample the spread of seafood tapas or tuck into tuna in port or delicious shrimp with bourbon-spiked Cajun cream (mains $13–17). 4–10pm, closed Mon.

Carpe Diem Seize the daily specials at this welcoming Argentinian place, cooking such gaucho staples as meat *empanadas* ($3.50) and steak *a la parilla* in Malbec sauce ($11). Daily 6–10pm.

Lucy's Relocated from Montezuma, but still serving tasty seafood (shrimp, tuna, swordfish) in a low-key setting. Mains around $12. Open evenings only, from 5pm.

Ginger Café Great spot for a bite of breakfast on the way to Playa Santa Teresa or for a lunch break just back from the beach, either roadside out front or on the funky backyard terrace. Daily 7.30am–2pm.

Nectar *Flor Blanca* ⓣ2640-0232, ⓦwww.florblanca.com. Artistic, Asian-influenced cuisine, heavily focused on seafood: dishes range from ginger, coconut and coriander ceviche ($12) to sugarcane skewered jumbo prawns ($20). The strong sushi menu is matched by some high-quality sakes. Daily noon–3pm & 6–9.30pm.

Mal País

The following places are listed in the order you encounter them heading south from the intersection.

Rítmo Tropical ⓦwww.hotelritmotropical.net. Soak up your antipasti ($11) with five types of focaccia; the real draw is the tasty thin-crust pizzas that dominate the menu (around $9). Daily 5.30–10.30pm.

The Papaya Lounge *Moana Lodge* ⓣ2640-0230, ⓦwww.moanalodge.com. The home-made Latin food changes daily but usually includes some mouthwatering fish dishes (think sea bass in coconut broth or peanut-encrusted mahi-mahi in ginger) as well as meaty mains like tamarind BBQ ribs. The great views – as far as Punta Islita – can also be enjoyed over sunset drinks and *bocas* (from 5pm). Mains around $15. 6–10pm, closed Tues.

Mary's Restaurant Locals pack the tables and booths at this buzzing restaurant to tuck into a wide variety of Mexican and Asian dishes, plus seafood (cangrejo filet with cherry tomatoes; $12) and pizzas such as roasted squash and goats' cheese ($11). 5–10pm; closed Wed.

Listings

Banks and money Both the Banco Nacional (Mon–Sat 1–7pm), next door to Budget, and the Banco de Costa Rica (Mon–Fri 9am–4pm) can change travellers' cheques and have an ATM.
Bike rental Most hotels and hostels rent bikes, as does Arisha Surf Shop, just north of the intersection ⓣ2640-0228 ($10 per day).
Car rental Budget, housed in the white strip mall at the main intersection (ⓣ2640-0500, ⓦwww.budget.co.cr); Alamo, east of *Frank's Place* (ⓣ2640-0526, ⓦwww.alamocostarica.com).
Internet access Tropical Tours, opposite Budget (50¢ for 10min).
Laundry Ely's Laundry Service, 2.4km north of the intersection (Mon–Sat 8am–6pm).
Markets An organic fruit and vegetable market is held beachside every Saturday near the intersection (3–5pm).
Medical care Paradise Medical Services, in the mall at the intersection ⓣ2640-1010. Open 24hr.
Supermarkets Self-caterers will find several well-stocked supermarkets, including Super Ronny's (daily 7am–10pm).

South of Puntarenas

On the mainland south of Puntarenas, the coast road (sometimes signposted as the **Costanera Sur**) leads down to Quepos and continues, in various states of paving, south to Dominical (covered in Chapter 7). At first, the landscape is sparse and hilly, with the coast coming into view only intermittently, but things improve considerably once you're past the huge trucks heading to the container port and refineries at hideous **Puerto Caldera**, the terminus of the new toll road linking San José and the Pacific. About 30km southeast of Puerto Caldera, just across the wide crocodile-ridden mouth of the Río Tárcoles, **Parque Nacional Carara** encompasses a range of habitats and is known for its rich birdlife. Beyond Carara, and a different beast altogether, is the resort of **Jacó**, which thanks to its relative proximity to San José is more popular than it might otherwise be. Better beaches (and an expanding surf scene) lie further south, particularly at **Playa Hermosa** and **Playas Esterillos**. From here, it's an uneventful 45km to Quepos and Parque Nacional Manuel Antonio, the last stretch along the coast from the hamlet of Parrita comprising a long corridor of African oil-palm plantations, a moody landscape of stout, brooding tree sentinels.

Parque Nacional Carara

Ecologically vital **PARQUE NACIONAL CARARA** (daily 7am–4pm, May–Nov from 8am; $10; ⓣ2637-1080), 90km west of San José, occupies a transition area between the hot tropical lowlands of the north and the humid, more verdant climate of the southern Pacific coast. Consequently, the park teems with **wildlife**, from monkeys to margays and motmots to manakins.

Carara's well-maintained **trails** are split between the heavily canopied area near the park's ranger station and the more open terrain around Laguna Meándrica, an oxbow lake that is home to crocodiles: it's accessed from a trailhead 2km north along the highway, towards the Río Tárcoles Bridge (see p.354). At the ranger station, the loop trails of **Sendero Las Aráceas** (1.2km; 1hr) and **Sendero Quebrada Bonita** (1.5km; 1hr 30min) take in primary and transitionary forest and are reliable places to spot agouti and other small rodents; you can also often see great tinamou on the paths here, and sometimes even catch the spectacular leks of orange-collared manikins. Both routes are reached via the **Sendero Encuentro de Ecosistemas**, a 1.2km loop near the ranger station that is accessible to wheelchair users. Birdwatching is perhaps even better along the rivers and in the clearings on the **Sendero Laguna**

Watching wildlife in Carara

Much of Carara's bounty of wildlife is of the unnerving sort: huge **crocodiles** lounge in the bankside mud of the Río Tárcoles ("Carara" means "crocodile" in the language of the pre-Columbian inhabitants, the Huetar), while **snakes** (19 out of Costa Rica's 22 poisonous species) slither about. Mammals include **monkeys** (mantled howler and white-faced capuchin), **armadillos, agoutis** (commonly seen), aggressive **collared peccaries** and most of the large cats, including **jaguars** and **ocelots**. Birding is excellent, and this is one of the best places in the country to see the brightly coloured **scarlet macaw** in its natural habitat – at dawn and dusk, they migrate between the lowland tropical forest areas and the swampy mangroves, soaring over in a burst of red and blue against the darkened sky. Other birds that frequent the treetops include trogons (five species), toucans (both chestnut-mandibled and keel-billed) and **guans**, while riverside birds include **anhingas** (or snake birds), the coot-like **purple gallinule** and **storks**.

Meándrica (4.3km; 2–4hr), where the wide range of avifauna includes boat-billed herons. Whichever trail you take, it's worth hiring a **guide** ($20 per person for 2hr) from the ranger station, as they can also take you into areas that tourists aren't allowed on their own.

Park practicalities

To get to Carara **from San José**, take either the Caldera Highway or Hwy-3, following the latter over the long bridge that crosses the Río Tárcoles; the park entrance is 3km after the bridge. Several agencies offer **tours** here from San José; try Costa Rica Expeditions (ⓣ2257-0766, ⓦwww.costaricaexpeditions.com), whose all-inclusive full-day trips with naturalist guides, transport, lunch and entry fee cost $199 per person (min four people).

The **ranger station** has toilets and picnic tables, and staff here hand out basic maps and answer questions about the reserve's wildlife. There have been several **thefts** in the area, so leave your vehicle in sight of the guards at the ranger station (even if walking the Laguna Meándrica trail). Note that it's extremely **hot** in Carara, so hit the trails early (the wildlife will be much less evident by 10am); if you want to stay overnight to get an early start, there are a number of **accommodation** options in nearby Tárcoles and the surrounding area (see opposite).

Tárcoles and around

The village of **Tárcoles**, 2km south of Parque Nacional Carara and a further 1km west along a rough road, sprawls along a dusty street and parallels a beach that is too polluted for even the briefest of toe-dippings.

The main attraction here – apart from visiting the nearby national park – is the **Río Tárcoles**, or more correctly the huge **crocodiles** that bask on its muddy banks. You can spot them at the estuary just northwest of town and from the **Río Tárcoles Bridge** – it's one of the best free attractions in Costa Rica, although there have been robberies on the bridge and a police booth is now positioned on the southern side for added security – or take to the water and view them from the comfort of a boat. Two local companies run **crocodile tours** on the river, complete with crocodile-feeding antics straight out of the Steve Irwin school of shameless wildlife harassment; Jungle Crocodile Safari (4 daily; $35; 2hr; ⓣ2236-6473, ⓦwww.junglecrocodilesafari.com) is the less brazen of the two.

Less of a moral dilemma are the **birdwatching tours** run by Costa Rica Birding Journeys (4 daily; $50; 3hr; ⓣ8889-8815, ⓦwww.costaricabirdingjourneys.org), which explore the mangroves at the mouth of the river in search of herons, egrets and the endemic mangrove hummingbird; the price includes transfer from local hotels.

Accommodation

Accommodation around Tárcoles has improved in recent years, and there are a number of decent options. Most lodges can meet you off the bus from San José; some also offer transport from the capital, or from nearby Jacó or Quepos.

Cerro Lodge 3km down a side road, signed off the road 3km north of the Río Tárcoles Bridge ⓣ2427-9910 or 8871-3523, ⓦwww.cerrolodge.net. The newest lodge in the area, offering eight good-value *cabinas* on a quiet working farm (trails run through the property): it's set in lush surrounds, with a pool to cool off in after a walk in Carara. Start the day watching scarlet macaws feeding in the trees opposite the on-site restaurant. ❺

Los Cocodrillos Just north of the Río Tárcoles Bridge. ⓣ2200-5623. These three basic *cabinas* are old, musty and depressingly bare, but are the only real choice round these parts for budget travellers; they come with a/c, TV and private cold-water bathrooms. It's next door to a popular restaurant of the same name. ❸

Hotel Carara In Tárcoles ⓣ2637-0178, ⓦwww.hotelcarara.com. On the beach, this much-improved hotel has clean, modest rooms with cable TV and hot-water bathrooms set around a small pool; $15 more buys you a spacious room with a/c. It's on the flight path between Carara and the coastal mangroves, so sightings of macaws are almost guaranteed early morning and late afternoon. ❹

Villa Lapas 500m east of the turn-off to Tárcoles, signed from the road just past the Río Tárcoles Bridge ⓣ2203-3553, ⓦwww.villalapas.com. Set in landscaped gardens near the river, this well-equipped hotel has large a/c rooms, a pool and – rather oddly – a replica of an old Costa Rican "town", complete with church, *cantina*, large restaurant and even larger souvenir shop. There's also a Sky Walk ($28), canopy tour ($48) and small network of trails in their nearby private reserve. ❼

Catarata Manatial de Agua Vida and the Pura Vida Gardens and Waterfalls

About 5km east of the turn-off to Tárcoles village and set amid a pristine rainforest valley is the **Catarata Manatial de Agua Viva** (daily 8.30am–4pm; $20; ⓣ2645-1017); at 200m high, this cascading waterfall, also known as Bijagual Waterfall, is supposedly the highest in the country, and it's a difficult 2km climb downhill to reach its base. While there's no designated place for swimming, there's nothing stopping you from cooling off in the river.

If you'd like the vista without the climb, head 1km up the road just before the village of Bijagual to **Pura Vida Garden & Waterfalls** (daily 8am–5pm; $20; ⓣ2645-1001, ⓦwww.puravidagarden.com). Only avid hikers can get close to the waterfalls from this private botanical garden, although a lookout point does provide dead-on views of the falls as well as the surrounding valley and Pacific coast; there are also four smaller waterfalls on the grounds. The jungle has been tamed into submission here, but as Parque Nacional Carara is next door, visitors are very likely to see scarlet macaw and poison-dart frogs while strolling the manicured nature trails.

Jacó and around

Just over two hours from San José, **Jacó** sits in a hot coastal plain behind the broad **Playa Jacó**, the closest beach to the capital. An established seaside attraction, the resort draws a mix of surfers, package tourists, holidaying Ticos and retired North American baby-boomers, along with a less savoury selection of drug dealers and

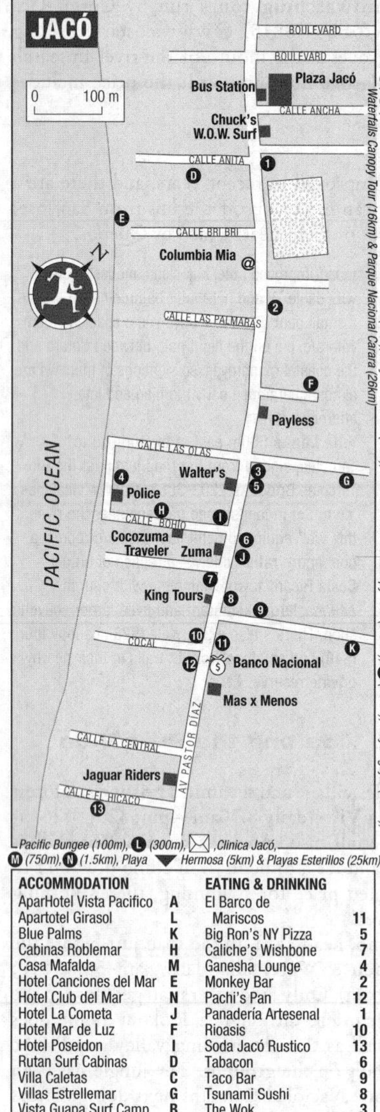

prostitutes. Jacó has seen some of the most excessive development along the Pacific, but the partying crowd don't seem to mind too much. And as a base from which to explore the surf beaches along this stretch of coast, its multitude of amenities takes some beating.

Arrival and information

Buses from the Coca-Cola bus terminal in San José (7 daily; 2hr 30min), Puntarenas (6 daily; 1hr 30min) and Quepos (6 daily; 1hr 30min) stop at Plaza Jacó at the north end of Avenida Pastor Diaz, the 3km road that constitutes the town's main drag. A **taxi-boat** from Montezuma runs to Playa Herradura, 7km north of Jacó (9.30am; $40; 1hr); the price includes transfer in to town.

Locals advise against **walking on the beach at night**: hold-ups have been reported. Otherwise, strolling about town, even at night, should be safe, especially as bike-riding police patrol the streets. Part of their mandate is to crack down on the use of recreational drugs, and snap searches are not uncommon.

Accommodation

Jacó's cheapest **cabinas** generally cater to weekending Josefinos or surfers; much of the mid-range accommodation is **self-catering**, useful if you're in town for more than a couple of days, and there are also a number of upmarket places. In general, be prepared to pay more than either the town or, in some cases, the accommodation, merits. Staying on the main road can mean **traffic noise**, particularly on busy weekends.

North of Jacó

AparHotel Vista Pacifico Perched on a hill at the far north end of town, signed off the Boulevard ⓣ2643-3261, ⓦwww.vistapacifico.com. An intimate hideaway, this tranquil hotel has it all: sweeping coastal views, mountaintop breezes and an attractive garden setting. Clustered around a sparkling blue pool, the studios and suites are bright and spotless and come with hot-water bathrooms, a/c and cable TV. ❺

Villa Caletas 15km north of Jacó, signed off the Costanera Sur ⓣ2637-0505,

Moving on from Jacó

Buses to San José (8 daily; 2hr 30min) depart from the north end of Jacó, outside the Plaza Jacó shopping centre; the buses from Puntarenas (6 daily; 1hr 30min) continue on to **Quepos**. If you're travelling at a weekend in high season, buy your ticket at least three days in advance.

Many companies in town offer the one-hour water **taxi-boat** ride from Jacó to **Montezuma** (departs 10.45am; $40), a fast-paced trip that offers the possibility of spotting dolphins, turtles and other marine life; the boat leaves from Playa Herradura; it's a beach landing, so wear shorts and water shoes.

Ⓦ www.hotelvillacaletas.com. Perched on a clifftop above the Pacific, this is one of Costa Rica's most extravagant boutique hotels. Beautifully decorated villas sit amid landscaped grounds that resemble a film set, with a small Greek theatre and Doric columns surrounding the pool; there are stunning views all round, especially at sunset. The restaurant serves gourmet cuisine with prices to match. A shuttle takes guests down the precipitous 1km trail to the private beach. ❾

Vista Guapa Surf Camp At the far north end of town, signed 500m off the Boulevard Ⓣ 2643-2830 or 8364-3155, Ⓦ www.vistaguapa.com. As the name implies, this surf hangout located high on the hill overlooking Jacó enjoys handsome views, so you can check out the breaks over breakfast. It's run by a former national champion – the staff are always on hand for surfing advice – while the smart bungalows themselves have a/c and hot-water bathrooms. Week-long packages including lessons, board hire and food start at $1000; weekend deals also available.

Central Jacó

Blue Palms 350m east of *Pops Heladeria*, on a street just south of Calle Bohío Ⓣ 2643-0099, Ⓦ www.bphotel.com. This bright two-storey hotel with pool and wrap-around balcony is good value for money. The crisp and comfortable rooms are equipped with telephones, a/c, cable TV, safe deposit and hot-water bathrooms. One room, sleeping up to six, has a kitchen ($70). ❹

Cabinas Roblemar Near the beach, on Calle Bohío Ⓣ 2643-3173. This fairly quiet establishment has smallish *cabinas* with large, comfortable beds, sharing (one between two) a simple kitchen and cold-water bathroom. ❸

Hotel Canciones del Mar On the beach, at the end of Calle Bri Bri Ⓣ 2643-3273, Ⓦ www.cancionesdelmar.com. The colourful apartments in this appealing, bamboo-framed beachfront hotel come with large beds, patio and modern kitchen. Other pluses include an ample pool and worthwhile discounts for weekly and monthly stays. ❼

Hotel La Cometa On Av Pastor Diaz, south of Calle Bohío Ⓣ 2643-3615, Ⓔ cometadejaco@yahoo.com. Right in the centre of town, these ten basic *cabinas* with charming French-Canadian owners are clean and good value. Some rooms have TV and a/c, while the three cheaper fan rooms share a bathroom. There's also a communal kitchen and parking. ❸

Hotel Mar de Luz In the town centre, on the landward side of Av Pastor Diaz Ⓣ 2643-3000, Ⓦ www.mardeluz.com. This well-kept, family-friendly hotel sits amid soothing, landscaped grounds. Colourful modern apartments (sleeping up to five) surround two large pools and a garden. Large rooms are crammed with furniture and come with TV, a/c, microwave and kitchenette, plus there's a lounge and small library. The Dutch owners speak English, Spanish, Italian, German and French. ❻

Hotel Poseidon Calle Bohío Ⓣ 2643-1642, Ⓦ www.hotel-poseidon.com. The recently refurbished rooms at this two-storey, white stucco hotel are elegantly decorated and come with smart bathrooms and all modern conveniences, including cable TV and DVD player. There's a tiny pool if you can't face the 30m walk to the beach. ❼

Rutan Surf Cabinas Calle Anita, near the beach at the northern end of town Ⓣ 2643-3328, Ⓦ www.rutansurfcabinas.com. A relaxed surfing vibe pervades this unpretentious little spot with dorms ($12), simple rooms with battle-weary mattresses and cold-water bathrooms. The BBQ area increases the social element. ❶

Villas Estrellemar On the eastern side of Calle Las Olas Ⓣ 2643-3102, Ⓦ www.estrellamar.com. Set in landscaped gardens around a 25m pool, this unpretentious holiday complex is a terrific family option. Rooms come with private hot-water bathrooms, a/c, cable TV and safe boxes; villas (one to three bedrooms) also have a kitchen and private terrace (from $84). There's a bar and restaurant, table tennis, bike rental and palm-roofed chill-out area. ❻

South Jacó

Apartotel Girasol Calle Los Almendros, at the southern end of town ⓣ2643-1591, ⓦwww.girasol.com. Relax right on the beach in these spacious tiled apartments (sleeping up to four) with fan, a/c, a full kitchen and a cane-furnished lounge area. There's a lovely swimming pool and garden, plus secure parking. ❼

Casa Mafalda Calle Hidalgo, off C Pastor Diaz ⓣ2643-1687, ⓦwww.casamafaldacr.com. Cute rooms and friendly service define this arty little beachfront hotel with just five rooms (some a/c, some fan, all with hot-water private bathrooms) and a funky thatched-roof breakfast bar overlooking the beach. ❺

Hotel Club del Mar 1.5km south of Jacó, off the Costanera Sur ⓣ2643-3194, ⓦwww.clubdelmarcostarica.com. Set on a quiet stretch of beach, these English-owned, luxury rooms and apartments (from $224) have a family-friendly atmosphere and a huge range of amenities, including pool, restaurant, spa, small library and games room. ❽

The Town

Jacó's appeal is, of course, its long, spacious **beach** – when covered in mist and backed by a spectacular Pacific sunset, the wide sands look quite attractive. It's popular with novice surfers (though the water isn't the cleanest and you do have to watch out for riptides), while more advanced riders head for the beaches nearby, including **Playa Herradura**, 7km north, a calm spot frequented by Ticos but now dominated by the lavish monstrosity of *Los Sueños Marriot Ocean and Golf Resort*, and **Playa Hermosa** (see p.360) and **Playas Esterillos** (see p.361), wild, untamed stretches to the south of town.

Eating and drinking

Jacó offers a surprisingly wide assortment of **restaurants**, many specializing in fresh seafood. **Nightlife** is predictably hedonistic, with young holidaymakers jostling for bar space with prostitutes and their clientele; discos are definitely of the meat-market variety. The most respectable spot is *Tabacon* (daily 8am–midnight, Fri & Sat till 2am), in the centre of town, which has a winning combination of cold beer and quality live music, while the spacious, air-conditioned *Monkey Bar* (daily from 9pm; ⓦwww.monkeybarcr.com), across the bridge in the northern part of town, draws a happy young tourist crowd who socialize to pop and light dance music. For a large night out, hit *Ganesha Lounge* (ⓦwww.ganeshaloungejaco.com), at the beach end of Calle Bohío, which has something on every evening but really gets going at the weekend, with guest DJs spinning a mix of hip-hop and electronica on Saturdays (10pm–2.30am).

El Barco de Mariscos Av Pastor Diaz, in the town centre. This informal venue specializes in well-prepared fresh shellfish and fish dishes (around $11). They also run a popular café and ice-creamery next door. 11am–11pm, closed Wed.

Big Ron's NY Pizza Av Pastor Diaz, just south of Calle Las Olas. Simple but satiating pizza joint, serving all the classics, either as a (huge) whole pizza or by the slice ($4, with a drink). Takeaway (ⓣ2643-2643) is also available.

Caliche's Wishbone Av Pastor Diaz, in the town centre. Running the gamut from sushi to Mexican, stuffed pitta sandwiches to *casados* and pizzas to potato salads, this recommended restaurant has just about all your cravings covered (mains $11). Daily noon–10pm.

Pachi's Pan Opposite Banco Nacional. Come here for your fill of cakes, pastries, fresh bread, *empanadas* and sandwiches, which you can tuck into on the upstairs terrace. Daily 6am–10pm.

Panadería Artesenal Av Pastor Diaz, just north of Calle Anita. Chic little bakery near Chuck's serving croissants, crusty baguettes and home-made loaves. Daily 6am–1pm & 3–8pm.

Rioasis Cnr Av Pastor Diaz & Calle Cocal. Wood-fired pizzas and Mexican favourites are dished up with fervour at this cavernous eatery: there's a relaxed outdoor area and an indoor bar that throbs with loud music. Daily 11.30am–10pm.

Soda Jacó Rustico Calle Hicaco. Join the queue of hungry locals and load your plate with Tico standards at this cheap, buffet-style *soda*. Ask for takeaway and eat your feast on the beach just 50m away. Mon–Sat 7am–7pm, Thurs till 5pm.

Activities

Although **surfing** is the be-all-and-end-all for many visitors, there are plenty of other activities on offer, from **kayaking** to zip-lining, as well as tours to nearby **Parque Nacional Carara** or **Isla Tortuga** (see p.338).

Surfing and kayaking

You can rent boards at a number of competing places in Jacó: the staff at **Walter's Surf Shop** (☎2643-1056, Ⓦwww.waltersurfshop.com), opposite Budget on Avenida Pastor Diaz, can match you with the right board and offer rentals for $10 a day and two-hour lessons for $40. Drop into **Chuck's W.O.W Surf** (☎2643-3844, Ⓦwww.wowsurf.net), on Plaza Palma, at the northern end of town, for tide tables and an excellent free "surf treasure map": board hire here is pricier at $15–20 a day, and a two-hour lesson will set you back $45.

For a less extreme water workout, **Kayak Jacó** (☎2643-1233, Ⓦwww.kayakjaco.com) runs daily excursions (8.15am & 2.30pm; $70; 2hr) from its base in nearby Playa Agujas, which can include snorkelling and fishing if you like; it can also organize tailor-made multi-day itineraries.

Canopy tours and bungee jumping

The canopy craze is alive and well here, with **Waterfalls Canopy Tour** ($60; ☎2643-3322) offering a zip-line rush that includes a rappel, suspension bridges and Tarzan swing (you can whizz through the air under the cover of darkness on their night canopy tour), and **Vista Los Sueños Canopy Tour** ($55; ☎2637-6020, Ⓦwww.canopyvistalossuenos.com), whose thirteen cables (including the longest in the area) are accessed by tractor-pulled cart.

The daredevils at **Pacific Bungee** (☎2643-6682, Ⓦwww.pacificbungee.com) can send you plunging off a 40m crane towering above the Pacific, with the option of a "water touchdown", plus a Big Swing and a Rocket Launcher (all $45; multi-activity packages available).

Tours

King Tours (☎2643-2441, Ⓦwww.kingtours.com) runs numerous excursions, including rafting on the Class II–III Río Savegre (daily 7am; $120), half-day tours of Parque Nacional Carara (daily 7am & 2.30pm; $79) and full-day whale-watching trips to Parque Nacional Marino Ballena (Wed, Sat & Sun; $139) for the chance to spot humpbacks (mid-July to mid-Nov & mid-Nov to March). **Cocozuma Traveler**, on Calle Bohío (☎2643-5196, Ⓦwww.cocozumacr.com) has a similar list of tours.

Taco Bar Between Calle Bohío and Calle Cocal, at the start of the road out towards the Costanera Sur Ⓦtacobar.info. Top lunch spot, and very novel: order your taco – fish (mahi-mahi, wahoo, snapper, tuna) is the speciality – get it grilled or fried, and then smother it in BBQ, spicy or coconut sauce before scoffing it in one of the barside swings. Also huge burritos ($8.50) and hummus combos ($5); a good all-you-can-eat salad bar is included with most dishes. Daily 7.30am–10pm, Mon from noon.

Tsunami Sushi Upstairs in the Il Galeone Mall. Stick your chopsticks into raw fish, tempura rolls and chicken teriyaki (around $13) from the air-conditioned confines of a curved leather chair. It's not cheap, but the produce is top-notch – and half-price on Monday nights. Daily 11am–10pm.

The Wok Cnr Av Pastor Diaz & eastern side of Calle Las Olas. Popular pit stop for a quick stir-fry, doing a brisk trade in roasted pork, chicken and tofu with noodles ($6–7.50). The choice of five sauces includes coconut and ginger and peanut butter. Mon–Sat 11.30am–10pm.

Listings

Banks and money Several on Av Pastor Diaz, the main drag, including a Banco Nacional that accepts foreign-issued credit cards and changes travellers' cheques.

Bike and scooter rental Many places rent out bikes (about $10 per day); try Jaguar Riders on Av Pastor Diaz (☎2643-0180) for scooters ($35 per day).
Car rental Agencies include Zuma (☎2643-1528) and Payless (☎2643-5409), both on Av Pastor Diaz.
Internet access Columbia Mia, just south of C Bri Bri (daily 9am–9pm; $1 per hour).
Laundry Lava Max, next to *Big Ron's NY Pizza*.
Medical care Clinica Jacó, opposite the post office (☎2643-1767).
Post office At the southern end of town (Mon–Fri 8am–4.30pm, Sat 8am–noon).
Supermarkets Mas x Menos is smack in the centre of Jacó (daily 8am–10pm).

Rainforest Adventures Costa Rica Pacific

Sister operation of the groundbreaking aerial tram just outside Parque Nacional Braulio Carillo (see p.149), the catchily titled **Rainforest Adventures Costa Rica Pacific** (daily 6.30am–4pm, Mon from 9am; tram $55, children $27.50, various multi-activity packages available; ☎2257-5961, Ⓦwww.rainforestadventure.com), 3km northeast of Jacó, lets you view the rainforest canopy from the surrounds of a slow-moving gondola; the price includes access to nature trails and a *serpentarium*. You can combine the ride with a ten-cable canopy tour – the "**Tranopy Tour**" – to pick up the pace a little ($70), or hit the trails with a naturalist guide on an early-morning birdwatching tour before taking a closer look at the canopy dwellers from the comfort of the tram ($82.50).

Playa Hermosa

Grey-sand **Playa Hermosa**, 5km south of Jacó, has long been a playground for hot-shot surfers. Pummelled by formidable waves, the 10km-long strip rivals Dominical for having the most consistent **beach breaks** on Costa Rica's Pacific coast. Given its proximity to Jacó, it was inevitable the development craze would reach here, too, and condos are now going up along the beachfront at a rapid pace. The area is being sold as a more upmarket version of Jacó – a coastal getaway without the noise, pollution, drugs and prostitution plaguing its neighbour…at least for now.

Hermosa is definitely not a beach for a casual dip (the riptides here are formidable), nor for novice surfers. Steep sand bars cause waves to break hard, fast and close to the shore, most impressively during the rainy season between May and August – with the best breakers in front of *Terraza del Pacifico* and the *Backyard Hotel*. On Saturday afternoons, you can watch how it should be done, when local surfers and gung-ho visitors tackle the waves as part of the **Backyard Surf Series** (4pm; free to enter).

Further south of the hotel strip, the **Refugio Nacional de Vida Silvestre Playa Hermosa y Punta Mala** protects a nesting site for olive ridley turtles, which come ashore to lay their eggs between August and December; it's off-limits to the public, but you can visit the turtle hatchery at the ranger station, a gridded block of beach being used to monitor the species' reproduction rates in this part of the Pacific.

You can **get to Playa Hermosa** from Jacó by catching a Quepos-bound bus and asking to be let off at the relevant stop; taxis cost $8.

Accommodation

Condos and luxury **hotels** rising up along the beachfront are starting to bulldoze or overshadow Hermosa's more humble dwellings, although for the moment there are still plenty of budget options for thrifty surfers.

Backyard Hotel 500m south of the football field ⓣ2643-7011, ⓦwww.backyardhotel.com. The top choice for surfers with money, the sprightly rooms in this beachfront hotel have a/c, cable TV and hot-water bathrooms. You can do laps in the swimming pool, just outside your balcony, party at the popular bar and restaurant next door (see below) and enjoy one of Hermosa's best surf breaks on your doorstep. ❼

Cabinas Playa Hermosa 400m north of the football field ⓣ2643-2640, ⓦwww.fbsurfboards.com. When there's a surfboard factory on site, you know the place is the real deal. A crash-pad for pro surfers, each of the well-appointed *cabinas* sleep up to four people and have walk-in wardrobes and private bathrooms with hot water. Hang out in the communal kitchen and small TV lounge. ❹

Cabinas Rancho Grande Just south of the football field ⓣ2643-7023, ⓦwww.cabinasranchogrande.com. The cheapest option on the strip, this sprucely renovated hostel buzzes with friendly surfers who congregate in the outdoor communal kitchen to cook in after a hard day battling Hermosa's tubes. The private en-suite doubles have good facilities for the price – a/c, cable TV, etc – and a bunk in a shared room will set you back just $15. ❸

Las Olas Hotel 300m south of the football field ⓣ2643-7021, ⓦwww.lasolashotel.com. Hang surfside with a sociable crowd at these rustic two-storey teak wood ranchos (sleeping up to seven; $100) or in the two-room main house. There's a modest swimming pool and beachfront restaurant with jaw-dropping views that dishes up hearty portions all day long. The laidback owner also arranges "stormchaser surf tours" around Costa Rica. ❺

Terraza del Pacifico 500m north of the football field ⓣ2440-6862, ⓦwww.terrazadelpacifico.com. One of the most established and upmarket hotels on the beach, the 62 light-filled rooms here come with cable TV, wi-fi and a/c, and most have private balconies. The spacious grounds have two pools, a bar and restaurant virtually on the sand. ❼

Eating and drinking

The **restaurants** along Playa Hermosa rise to the challenge of feeding lines of hungry surfers. Just off the Costanera Sur, and marked by a striking mural, the *Jungle Surf Café* (7am–9pm) is the stomach-filling spot of choice and does a roaring trade in banana pancakes and seared tuna (mains around $7). At lunchtime, a young surfer crowd congregates beneath the palm-fringed roof of *Las Olas Hotel's* beachfront restaurant (daily 7am–9pm, closed Mon morning) to scoff enormous portions of burgers and fries while watching their fellow surfers get barrelled just metres away. Late afternoon, the action moves to the *Backyard Bar* (daily 8am–11pm), next to the *Backyard Hotel*, a great spot to watch the sun melt into the horizon over sunset happy-hour drinks (4.30–7.30pm); at weekends, live music livens up the joint, while ladies night (Wed till 1am) draws a large and boisterous crowd.

Playas Esterillos

South of Playa Hermosa, some 25km from Jacó, palm-fringed **Playas Esterillos** fulfils the archetypal image of a tropical paradise beach: a long wedge of chocolate-brown sands, backed by jungle and stretching into the spray-shrouded distance. Rocks and river split the coastline here into three sections, each accessed by a different side road off the Costanera Sur; the most attractive beaches are **Esterillos Centro** and **Esterillos Este**, 3km apart by road, the latter home to one of the coolest hotels on the Central Pacific. The waves that pummel Esterillos' shores break further out than at Jacó and Playa Hermosa, and will appeal to more advanced **surfers** than those that ride the rollers further north.

Quepos-bound **buses** from Jacó can drop you off on the highway, from where it's just under a kilometre to the beach.

Accommodation

Esterillos' **accommodation** is dotted along the coast, most of it a few metres' walk from the sand. As with the beaches themselves, the best options are in Esterillos Centro and Esterillos Este.

Alma de Pacifico Esterillos Este ⓣ1-866-495-7625, ⓦwww.legendarylodging.com/costarica. This fantastic beachfront boutique hotel stared life as *Xandari by the Pacific*. The coastal sister of the equally excellent *Xandari Resort & Spa* near Alajuela, it has put Esterillos well and truly on the map (see p.130) and the same touches that made their Valle Central property such a revelation when it opened – unique architecture, artworks by the owner – are evident here, along with personal plunge-pools in the swankier Beachfront Maxima suites ($415). Now owned by *RockResorts*, it has a top-notch spa and the on-site restaurant is also superb. ❾

Hotel Monterey del Mar Esterillos Este ⓣ2778-8787, ⓦwww.montereydelmar.com. This relaxing spot, just metres from the beach and with hammocks strung around its grounds, has a variety of rooms and garden- or ocean-view bungalows, let down slightly by their dated furnishings. The beachfront pool has a wet bar, and there's a romantic ambience to the softly lit open restaurant. ❼

Hotel Pelican Esterillos Este ⓣ2778-8105, ⓦwww.pelicanbeachfronthotel.com. Small beachfront hotel with fourteen tiled-floor rooms featuring a/c and fan and en-suite hot-water bathrooms. Guests have free use of bodyboards, and the hotel also rents out surfboards and runs lessons; after tackling the waves, hit the on-site restaurant for sandwiches or ceviche. Rates include a welcome cocktail. ❻

Parque Nacional Manuel Antonio and around

Small but perfectly formed, **Parque Nacional Manuel Antonio** ranks among the top tourist destinations in the country – visitors descend in droves to experience its stunning, picture-postcard setting, with spectacular white-grey sand beaches fringed by thickly forested hills. The striking *tómbolo* formation of **Punta Catedral**, jutting out into the Pacific, accounts for much of the region's allure, and as you watch a lavish sunset flower and die over the ocean, it does seem as though Manuel Antonio may be one of the more charmed places on earth.

That said, the huge tourist boom has undeniably taken its toll on the area, and the small corridor of land between the old banana-exporting town of **Quepos** and the little community of **Manuel Antonio** is one of the most crowded pieces of real estate in the country, featuring an unbroken line of hotels and lodges that run right down to the park's perimeter.

Quepos and around

Arriving in **QUEPOS** from San José, Puntarenas or Jacó, it's immediately apparent that you've crossed into the lush, wetter southern Pacific region. The vegetation grows thicker and greener than further north, and more often than not it has just started or finished raining. Backed up against a thick hill, with a muddy – and polluted – beach in front (obscured by the seaside road out to the old dock), Quepos can look pretty ramshackle, though the **Marina Pez Vela**, a sparkling new dock built on reclaimed land southwest of town, promises to add a far glossier sheen. What Quepos does enjoy is close proximity to **Parque Nacional Manuel Antonio** and its beaches, as well as the very different, and much more low-key, **Reserva Los Campesinos**; Quepos' range of (affordable) hotels, bars and restaurants and frequent bus services to the park make it the most useful base in the area.

Once a banana-exporting town, Quepos (the name is derived from the indigenous language of the Quepoa people, who occupied this area for at least a thousand years before the arrival of the Spanish in 1563) was severely hit by the Panamá disease, a devastating banana virus, which prompted United Fruit to pull out in the 1950s. With the establishment of the nearby African oil-palm plantations, though, the area has gone through something of a resurgence in recent

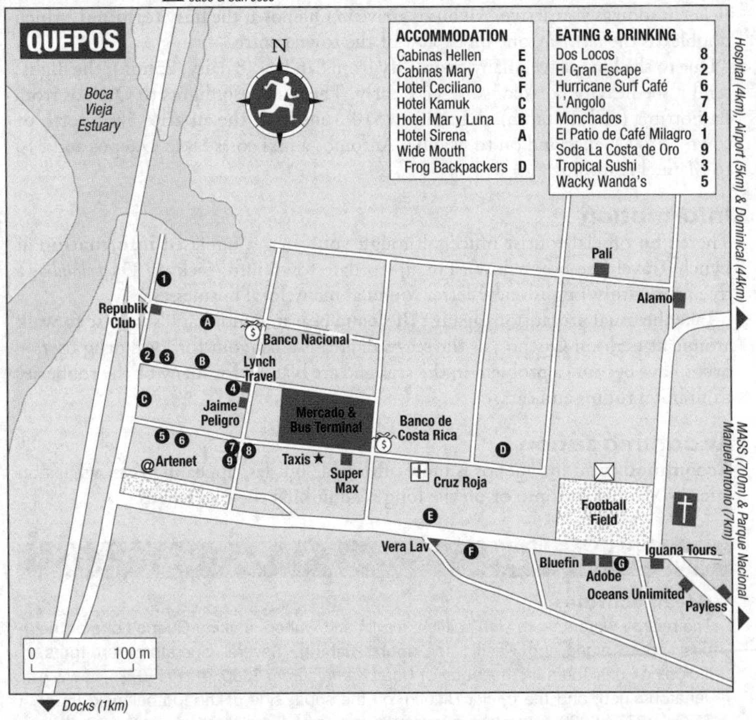

decades, and thanks to the bounty of big fish occupying its waters offshore, has also developed into one of the country's prime **sports-fishing** destinations.

Arrival

Buses from San José's La Coca-Cola bus station run to Quepos (9–12 daily; 3hr 30min–4hr 30min); the six (5 on Sat & Sun) slower regular buses continue to Manuel Antonio, dropping off at hotels on request. There are also services from Puntarenas (6 daily; 3hr) via Jacó (1hr 30min), and from Dominical (depart 7am, 11.30am & 1.30pm; 1hr 30min). On weekends, holidays and any time during the dry season, buy your bus ticket at least three days in advance, and your return

Moving on from Quepos

Buses make the short journey to **Manuel Antonio** every half-hour from 7am to 7pm (20min), departing from the main terminal. Buses also head north from here to **San José** (9–10 daily) and **Puntarenas** (6 daily), via **Jacó**, as well as south to **Dominical** and **Uvita** (depart 5.30am, 11.30am & 1.30pm). **Taxis** line up at the rank at the south end of the *mercado*; the journey to Manuel Antonio costs $14.

If you're **driving**, you can get to San Isidro, Golfito, the Osa Peninsula and other points in the Zona Sur via Dominical, 44km south of Quepos – although the road is usually in terrible condition and you'll need a sturdy 4WD, it beats going all the way back to San José and taking the Interamericana south.

You can **fly** direct from Quepos to San José (8 daily; 25min) and La Fortuna (daily 40min); for tickets and schedules, visit Lynch Tours (see p.364).

ticket as soon as you arrive. All buses arrive in Quepos at the busy **terminal**, which doubles as the *mercado*, one block east of the town centre.

Due to the long drive, many people **fly** from San José (8 daily; 25min); the flights tend to be heavily booked, so reserve early. There are also flights to Quepos from La Fortuna (daily; 40min). A minibus ($10) runs from the airstrip, 5km north of town, into Quepos and on to Manuel Antonio; a taxi costs $8 to Quepos and $16 to Manuel Antonio.

Information

There's no official tourist office, although you can get unbiased **information** at Lynch Travel (see box below). For up-to-date town info, pick up *Quepolandia*, a free bi-monthly English newsletter found at many local businesses.

Take the usual precautions against **theft** and bear in mind that it's unwise to walk around at night in Quepos, as the sea-wall area is a hangout for local drug users – drugs have become a problem in the area and are blamed for many of the robberies from hotel rooms and cars.

Accommodation

Accommodation in Quepos is more affordable but less appealing than what's on offer in Manuel Antonio or on the long road linking the two towns.

Tours and activities

Ocean activities

The nearby waters teem with sailfish, marlin and wahoo, making Quepos one of the best spots along the Pacific for **sports-fishing**. Several operators run tours, including Luna Tours, in the lobby of *Hotel Kamuk* (from $380; ⓣ2777-0725, ⓦwww.lunatours.net), and the pricier Bluefin, on the south side of the football field (from $575; ⓣ2777-0000, ⓦwww.bluefinsportfishing.com). If you'd rather see the fish than catch them, Oceans Unlimited (ⓣ2777-3171, ⓦwww.oceansunlimitedcr.com) runs half-day **scuba-diving** excursions ($139) and multi-day PADI courses (from $350), while MASS (ⓣ2777-4842, ⓦwww.masurfschool.com) offers three-hour **surfing** lessons ($65) on Playa Espadilla in Manuel Antonio.

Inland activities

Inland options include **white-water rafting** tours with operator Amigos del Río (ⓣ2777-0082, ⓦwww.amigosdelrio.net), who run tours to the Class II–III Río Savegre and Class III–IV Río Naranjo ($95 for the full day). There's no shortage of **canopy tours**: Dreamforest Canopy ($60; ⓣ2777-4567, ⓦwww.dreamforestcanopy.com) is the company of choice for adrenaline junkies, while the ride with Titi Canopy Tour ($55, $65 for their night canopy tour; ⓣ2777-3130, ⓦwww.titicanopytours.com) is slower and more suitable for families.

Tours

The biggest operator in town is the friendly and reputable **Lynch Travel** (ⓣ2777-1170, ⓦwww.lynchtravel.com). You can book white-water rafting and canopy tours through them, and their many local tours include horse rides to a waterfall ($65) and perennially popular daytime or sunset cruises, some specifically to see dolphins (both $75). They also run trips to Dominical, Corcovado and Bahía Drake, and can organize transfers to Panamá.

Iguana Tours (ⓣ2777-2052, ⓦwww.iguanatours.com) can also arrange horseriding and white-water rafting, as well as hiking in Parque Nacional Manuel Antonio ($48, includes entrance fee) and boat and kayak trips around Isla Damas, a wildlife-rich mangrove estuary just north of Quepos (both $65).

Cabinas Hellen A block south and east of the bus station ⓣ2777-0504. These secure *cabinas* at the back of a family home are equipped with private bath, fridge and fans. They offer decent single rates ($20), and there's also a small patio and parking. ❸

Cabinas Mary On the south side of the football field ⓣ2777-0128. An odd setup – the (cold-water) en-suite rooms surround what is effectively a busy car workshop – but the cheery owners keep everything spotlessly clean and you won't find cheaper digs in Quepos. ❶

Hotel Ceciliano Near the football field on the south side of the street ⓣ&ⓕ2777-0192. Dark but clean and breezy *cabinas* with fan and shared bath; the comfortable en-suite *cabinas* have a/c and TV ($30). ❶

Hotel Kamuk On the western avenue ⓣ2777-0811, ⓦwww.kamuk.co.cr. This airy *Best Western* offers rooms around a nice pool, with a/c and cable TV and – in the pricier ones (❻) – balconies with sea views. The café and restaurant centre on seafood – they'll cook up the fish you catch. ❺

Hotel Mar y Luna Just northwest of the bus station ⓣ2777-0394. Central and friendly, with an attractive plant-filled communal balcony, this hotel has dim rooms with private bath and fans – and hot-water and a/c ones for $16 more. ❷

Hotel Sirena On first road to the left as you enter Quepos ⓣ2777-0572, ⓦwww.lasirenahotel.com. Pretty little hotel, whose charming blue-and-white rooms – those upstairs receive more light – come with private bath, hot water and a/c. The small pool is flanked by a bar and restaurant; the bountiful breakfast served here is all either home-made or locally sourced. ❺

Wide Mouth Frog Backpackers 150m east of the bus station ⓣ2777-2798, ⓦwww.widemouthfrog.org. The best place to stay if on a budget. The efficient Kiwi–British owners at this sociable hostel offer a swimming pool, TV lounge, breakfast, internet and tight security. The dorms ($11) are a bit institutional, but the new rooms (some en suite) have been nicely done. Rules pasted everywhere can get a bit tedious, but they don't detract from the relaxed vibe. ❸

Eating and drinking

The **restaurants** in Quepos fall into two categories: gringo-owned and -geared eateries and cheaper ones owned by locals and frequented by Ticos. **Fish** is predictably good – order grilled *pargo* (dorado) and you can't go wrong.

Midweek, **nightlife** is more or less limited to excited fishermen debating the merits of different tackle; at the weekends, *Wacky Wanda's* gets lively with a cheerful mix of tourists and locals who hang out until fairly late at night.

Dos Locos Just southwest of the bus station. Enjoy the usual range of fajitas, burritos and tacos, plus Mexican pizza (mains $8–13), while taking in street views from the open dining area. Wash it all down with a margarita or two. Daily 7am–11pm.

El Gran Escape On the sea wall. Decent, if fairly pricey, salads, burgers and seafood (no marlin, despite the statue) and a good selection of drinks at the bar draws an overwhelmingly American fishing crowd. The pleasant, plant-filled seating area opens to the street – and weekend nights can get rowdy. 8am–10pm, closed Tues.

Hurricane Surf Café 100m west of the bus station. Funky little place doing a relaxed take on smoothies, ice creams, shakes and *batidos*. Browse their range of Rusty clothing while you wait for your freshly made sandwiches ($4). Mon–Sat 8am–9pm.

L'Angolo 25m west of the bus station. Make up your own panini (from $3) using the range of Italian meats and cheeses on offer at this gourmet deli, or try one of the salads or fresh pasta dishes from an extensive list. Daily 8am–8pm.

Monchados 50m west of the bus station. Good-value Mexican-Caribbean fare with plenty of flair (mains around $9), including burritos, chimichangas and orange honey chicken, plus just-pulled-out-of-the-Pacific seafood; the crab dip is a popular choice. Happy-hour cocktails (4.30–6.30pm) help get things started.

El Patio de Café Milagro Facing the sea wall ⓦwww.elpatiobistrolatino.com. The coffee here is among the best in the country; try the delicious Queppuccino ($3) or buy a bag of roasted beans to take home from the shop two doors down. They also serve *refrescos* (in flavours like vanilla nut chill or iced raspberry mocha) and cakes, as well as selling English-language newspapers and magazines. The breakfasts are creative and hearty, and by night it turns into a quality restaurant serving Latin-influenced cuisine, from pulled-pork corn cakes and coconut rum shrimp. There's also a branch on the road to Manuel Antonio (see p.370). Mon–Sat 6.30am–10pm.

Soda La Costa de Oro Next to Banco Popular. The best and cheapest *soda* in town – nosh on chicken *casados* ($4) amid a busy lunchtime crowd of locals and tourists. Daily 6am–7pm.

Tropical Sushi Brightly coloured sushi shack serving fresh tuna hauled out of the Pacific that morning – as well as maki rolls and sashimi – in an all-you-can-eat sushi extravaganza ($20), eaten either in the cramped interior or on the patio out back. Daily 4.30–11pm.

Listings

Banks and money Banco Nacional, just northwest of the bus station, changes money and travellers' cheques and has an ATM; also Banco de Costa Rica, opposite the bus station. Most businesses in town accept and change dollars.

Bookshop Jaime Peligro, next to Lynch Travel, sells new and secondhand books and CDs (Mon–Fri 9.30am–6pm, Sat 11am–5pm; Ⓦwww.queposbooks.com).

Car rental Abode (Ⓣ2777-4242), opposite the football field; Alamo (Ⓣ2777-3344), near the Palí supermarket; Payless (Ⓣ2777-0115), on the road towards Manuel Antonio.

Internet access Many places, including Artenet, opposite the park (Mon–Sat 9am–7pm).

Laundry Vera Lav, 100m west of the football field (Mon–Sat 8am–5pm).

Markets The *mercado* sells fish and fresh fruit and veg (Mon–Sat 6.30am–5pm); there's also a weekend (Fri 6–9pm, Sat 6am–2pm) *feria* offering fruit, veg and home-made bread.

Medical care Hospital Dr Max Teran (Ⓣ2777-0922) near the airport, or the Red Cross (Cruz Roja; Ⓣ2777-0116) between the bus station and the football field.

Post office The post office (Mon–Fri 8am–noon & 1–4.30pm, Sat 8am–noon) is near the football field, at the eastern end of town.

Supermarkets Supermax is the most convenient, opposite the south side of the bus station (daily 8am–8pm, Sun till 1pm).

Reserva Los Campesinos

If you want to experience an authentic Costa Rican peasant lifestyle, **Reserva Los Campesinos** (Ⓣ2248-9470, Ⓦwww.actuarcostarica.com), set in a small mountain community 25km east of Quepos along a rough road, offers a memorable day-long eco-adventure ($30). The reserve is managed by the Quebrada Aroyo community, an association of local vanilla producers who are creating a biological corridor to Parque Nacional Manuel Antonio, and activities involve guided hikes to waterfall pools and a ride on an old-school aerial tram; additional tours include trips to local organic farms, horseriding and white-water rafting on the Río Savegre. You can extend your trip by staying overnight in a rustic cabin with hot-water bathrooms and balconies ($73, including three meals).

Manuel Antonio

Southeast of Quepos, a 7km stretch of road winds over the surrounding hills, pitching up at the entrance to the village of **MANUEL ANTONIO** and Parque Nacional Manuel Antonio. Manuel Antonio was one of the first places in the country to feel the effects of the 1990s tourist explosion – drawn by its lavish beauty, hoteliers and businesses rushed to the area, and these days the entire road from Quepos is lined with some sort of hotel or restaurant.

At the road's end, just north of the park entrance, lies **Playa Espadilla** (also sometimes called Playa Primera or Playa Numero Uno), one of the most popular beaches in Costa Rica, and boasting wide, smooth, light-grey sands and stunning sunsets; MASS (Ⓣ2777-4842, Ⓦwww.masurfschool.com) has an outlet here, offering three-hour surf lessons ($65). The beach is plagued by **riptides** (travelling up to 10kph), however, though lots of people do also swim here – or rather, paddle and wade – and live to tell the tale. Lifeguards now patrol in high season, so it's considerably safer.

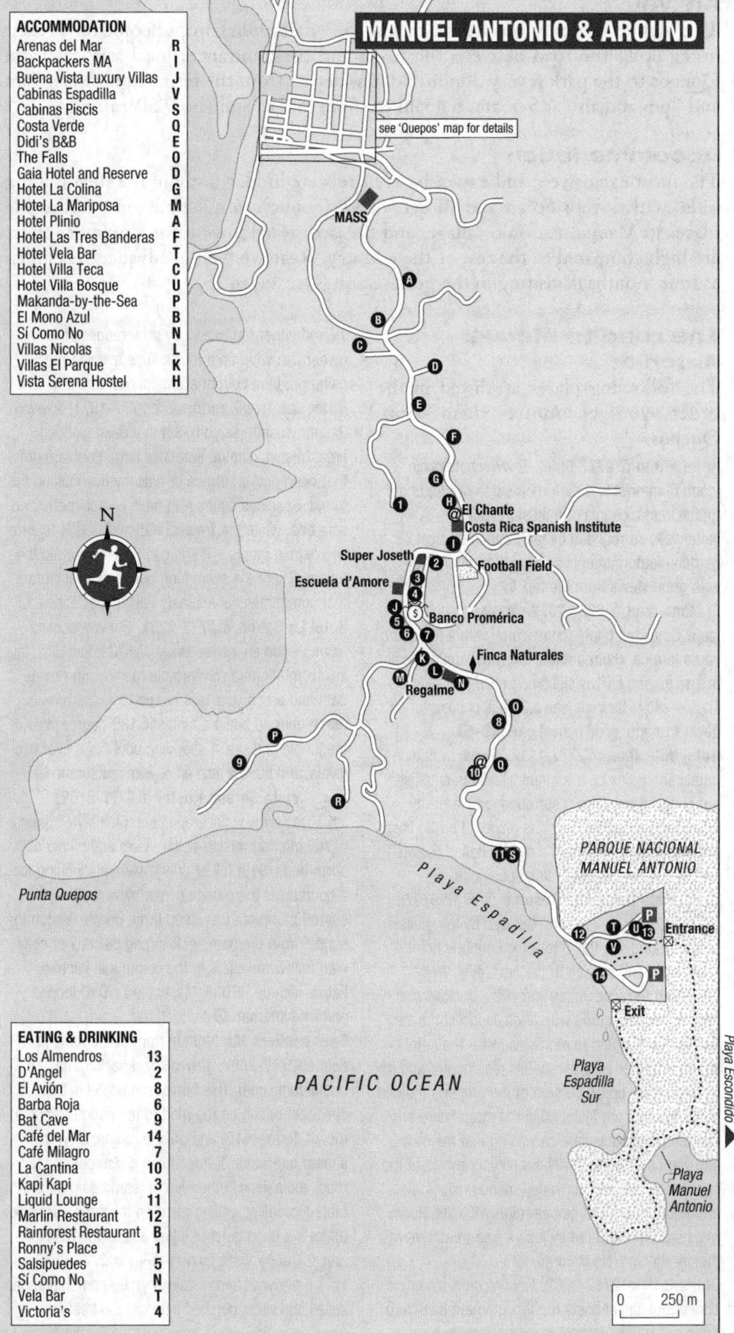

Jacó (69km)
Hospital (3.5km), Airport (4.5km) & Dominical (39km)
MANUEL ANTONIO & AROUND
ACCOMMODATION
Arenas del Mar R
Backpackers MA I
Buena Vista Luxury Villas J
Cabinas Espadilla V
Cabinas Piscis S
Costa Verde Q
Didi's B&B E
The Falls O
Gaia Hotel and Reserve D
Hotel La Colina G
Hotel La Mariposa M
Hotel Plinio A
Hotel Las Tres Banderas F
Hotel Vela Bar T
Hotel Villa Teca C
Hotel Villa Bosque U
Makanda-by-the-Sea P
El Mono Azul B
Sí Como No N
Villas Nicolas L
Villas El Parque K
Vista Serena Hostel H
see 'Quepos' map for details
MASS
El Chante
Costa Rica Spanish Institute
Super Joseth
Football Field
Escuela d'Amore
Banco Promérica
Finca Naturales
Regalme
Punta Quepos
Playa Espadilla
PARQUE NACIONAL MANUEL ANTONIO
Entrance
Exit
Playa Espadilla Sur
Playa Escondido
Playa Manuel Antonio
PACIFIC OCEAN
EATING & DRINKING
Los Almendros 13
D'Angel 2
El Avión 8
Barba Roja 6
Bat Cave 9
Café del Mar 14
Café Milagro 7
La Cantina 10
Kapi Kapi 3
Liquid Lounge 11
Marlin Restaurant 12
Rainforest Restaurant B
Ronny's Place 1
Salsipuedes 5
Sí Como No N
Vela Bar T
Victoria's 4
0 250 m
N

Arrival

The Manuel Antonio **bus** from San José (5–6 daily; 5hr) drops people off at their hotel along the road between the town and park entrance; local services from Quepos to the park (every 30min; 20min) depart from the terminal between 7am and 7pm and also at 5.45am, 6.45am & 10pm (Sat & Sun also 9.30am).

Accommodation

The most exclusive – and expensive – **hotels** are hidden away in the surrounding hills, with lovely ocean and sunset views. Though you'll find some affordable places in Manual Antonio village, and the occasional low-season discount, prices are high compared to the rest of the country. **Reserve** well in advance – as much as four months if visiting in the peak season (Dec 1–Jan 15).

The road to Manuel Antonio

The following places are listed in the order you encounter them from Quepos.

Hotel Plinio ⓣ2777-0055, ⓦwww.hotelplinio.com. Comfortable if dark rooms (fan or a/c) under thatch, and a couple of multistorey jungle suites (❻) surrounded by landscaped tropical gardens featuring a pool and a 4km nature trail with great views from the top. ❺

El Mono Azul ⓣ2777-2572, ⓦwww.monoazul.com. Small but bright rooms come with a fan or a/c and a terrace, centred round lovely swimming pools; across the road, villas sleep up to five ($85–125). The on-site restaurant (see p.370) is popular for its down-to-earth, good honest grub. ❻–❺

Hotel Villa Teca ⓣ2777-1117, ⓦwww.villatecahotel.com. Relax on a tranquil hillside in smallish but cheerful bungalows surrounded by a pretty flowering garden that attracts plenty of birds. There are a couple of pools and a decent Italian restaurant in a spacious, open-sided palenque. ❼

Gaia Hotel and Reserve ⓣ2777-9797, ⓦwww.gaiahr.com. Beloved by the glossy-brochure brigade, this ultra-chic boutique hotel takes style and service to the next level. Well-appointed terraced suites and villas, decked with natural flooring, come with huge, cloud-soft beds, flat-screen TVs and rainforest views – the hotel is set on a former wildlife rehabilitation centre and its reserve takes up 85 percent of the property (guided morning tours are included in the rate). There are two tempting pools, one cascading into the other, and you could quite easily eat all your meals at the fine restaurant, with its varied menu (including afternoon tapas) and globetrotting wine list. Room rates start at $260 but include a free treatment at the on-site spa. No children. ❾

Didi's B&B ⓣ2777-0069, ⓦwww.didiscr.com. Thoughtful Italian hosts run this intimate B&B with three colourfully decorated rooms including cable TV and either fan or a/c. By prior request, the owner can whip up a four-course evening meal using produce bought at the market that day. ❻

Hotel Las Tres Banderas ⓣ2777-1871, ⓦwww.hoteltresbanderas.com. Set in a quiet wooded area, this welcoming hotel has large double rooms that open onto a terrace or balcony overlooking the forest. Spacious suites (❼) have a kitchenette and sofa bed, while the Tropical Hideaways (❾) feature two deluxe rooms – if you can find them amid the foliage. There's a swimming pool and a restaurant that sometimes serves tasty Polish specialities. ❻

Hotel La Colina ⓣ2777-0231, ⓦwww.lacolina.com. Set on an incline locals call "Cardiac Hill", this lovely hotel offers comfortable rooms with private bath and a/c; if your legs are up to it, apartments (❻) higher up boast a fantastic 180-degree view of the jungle and sea. A sparkling pool flows over two levels, and there's also an on-site restaurant. ❺

Vista Serena Hostel ⓣ2777-5162, ⓦwww.vistaserena.com. Clean, welcoming hostel offering million-dollar views and plenty of dorm beds ($10) full of gringo students looking for a good time; the private ocean-view rooms with shared bathroom can sleep three people. Watch the sunset from the hammock-strung balcony or cook with fellow travellers in the communal kitchen. Extras include BBQ nights, cable TV/DVD lounge and free internet. ❹

Backpackers MA Right in front of the football field ⓣ2777-2507, ⓦwww.backpackersmanuelantonio.com. This family-run hostel is the cheapest option on the road to the park, offering a mix of dorms ($10) and private rooms, all with shared hot-water bathrooms. It's also one of the most sociable, whether you're teaming up on the table football or grilling meat on the patio out back (there's a good butcher's just across the road). ❸

Buena Vista Luxury Villas ⓣ2777-0580, ⓦwww.buenavistaluxuryvillas.com. High-spec suites and villas, perched amongst the treetops, enjoy sweeping views down over the Pacific. Villas, in particular, are beautifully furnished and kitted out with just about anything you could ever need – the open kitchens are chock-full of designer goods; bedrooms in the stunning Premium Villas ($650) have their own private terraces in addition to the jacuzzi-toting main balcony, plus outdoor rainwater showers. If you can drag yourself away, there are three pools (one for families) and an exclusive beach complete with (free) bodyboards and kayaks. ❾

Hotel La Mariposa ⓣ2777-0355, ⓦwww.lamariposa.com. Manuel Antonio's original luxury hotel offers villas set in lovely gardens around a pair of swimming pools. Take in Punta Catedral views from many of the luxurious rooms or treat yourself to the unsurpassed views from the penthouse suite, complete with floor-to-ceiling glass walls and private hot tub ($450). Enjoy excellent meals at the prestigious (and overpriced) Mediterranean restaurant or settle for a sunset cocktail. ❾

Arenas del Mar ⓣ2777-2777, ⓦwww.arenasdelmar.com. Set over large grounds on the headland at the northern end of Playa Espadilla (golf carts whizz you about), this upmarket but friendly place has spacious rooms with huge bathrooms, flat-screen TVs and comfy sofa-beds, starting at $320; some have great views down over Punta Catedral. It's strong on sustainability – the hotel incorporates everything from solar-powered hot water to recycled roof tiles – and the owners spent twenty years replanting the area (it was formerly a plantain farm) before it opened in 2008, so there's plenty of wildlife on site, from howler monkeys to black iguanas. ❾

Makanda-by-the-Sea ⓣ2777-0442, ⓦwww.makanda.com. Surrounded by quiet gardens with ocean views, these elegant luxury studios and villas ($400) feature beautiful hardwood ceilings and long wraparound sofas. The many amenities include fully equipped kitchenettes and CD players and iPod docks in the lounge. No children under 16. ❾

Villas El Parque ⓣ2777-0096, ⓦwww.hotelvillaselparque.com. Self-catering suites and duplex villas, most with kitchen, balcony and screened dining area. Some also have a/c, and many boast views of the Pacific and Punta Catedral. The large suite (sleeping up to 4) is particularly good value at $130. ❻

Villas Nicolas ⓣ2777-0481, ⓦwww.villasnicolas.com. Set high above the surrounding greenery, these classy villas come with hot-water private bath and ceiling fans; some have kitchens, and there's also a small pool. Rooms with views go for $30 more. No children under 6. ❼

Sí Como No ⓣ2777-0777, ⓦwww.sicomono.com. Enjoy beautiful views of the Pacific and Punta Catedral from this award-winning complex set high on a hill. Lovely, brightly furnished rooms vary from well-appointed doubles to fully equipped villas ($305); extensive facilities include a hot tub, two pools, swim-up bar, spa and a small cinema with nightly screenings. The two restaurants (see p.370) serve excellent food. The hotel also runs a small forest reserve, Fincas Naturales, with a butterfly garden and wildlife refuge/zoo (daily 8am–4pm; tours from $15; ⓣ2777-0850, ⓦwww.wildliferefugecr.com). ❾

The Falls ⓣ2777-1332, ⓦwww.fallsresortcr.com. Individually designed suites offering comfortable four-poster beds, large bathrooms and a pleasant patio with views of the tropical gardens – plenty of animals, including toucans and sloths, can be spotted in the waterfall-laced grounds. There's also a small infinity pool that seems to "hang" out over the foliage. ❼

Costa Verde ⓣ2777-0584, ⓦwww.costaverde.com. Spacious rooms and studio apartments, all constructed out of beautiful hardwood, with ocean-view balconies and lovely details like decorative tiles, plus arguably the most distinctive suite in the country: a salvaged Boeing 727, furnished with teak, which appears to be launching right out of the hillside ($500). Choose from three swimming pools with stupendous vistas, and cap off the day with a fine meal in the restaurant. ❼

Manuel Antonio village

Cabinas Espadilla ⓣ2777-2113, ⓦwww.espadilla.com. Set in attractive gardens with a pool, these pleasant, airy *cabinas* have large beds, hot-water private bath, a kitchen and fan or a/c, though are better value for groups of three to four people. Guests have use of the tennis court at the nearby sister hotel, and there's easy access to Playa Espadilla. ❻

Cabinas Piscis ⓣ2777-0046. One of the few budget places left in Manuel Antonio, these dark but clean rooms have cement floors and cold-water shared or private bath. You can access the beach via a lovely garden and the small restaurant (high season only) serves sandwiches and juices. Popular, so book ahead. ❹

Hotel Vela Bar ⓣ2777-0413, ⓦwww.velabar.com. This small hotel near the beach and surrounded by tropical gardens, has basic, pleasant rooms with private bath and fan or a/c. Apartments come with lounge, kitchenette and terrace. ❹

Hotel Villa Bosque ⓣ2777-0463, ⓦwww.hotelvillabosque.com. Light, bright rooms in a whitewashed, terracotta-tile-topped villa with wicker chairs, private hot-water bathrooms and a/c. There's also a pleasant outdoor reading and TV area, a decent restaurant and bar, and a small oval swimming pool. ❼

Eating and drinking

Eating in Manuel Antonio is notoriously expensive, and the area's few reasonably priced **restaurants** are understandably popular. For **nightlife**, there's live music and/or dancing at *Barba Roja*, *Salsipuedes* and *La Cantina* (all listed below); *Liquid Lounge* (8pm till late, closed Mon), further down the hill from *La Cantina*, is particularly popular on Thursdays (open bar for $10) and Fridays (live DJs). If you fancy boogeying inside a natural grotto, try the quirky *Bat Cave* (daily 7pm–midnight), an underground **bar** – complete with bats flittering around the ceiling – in the depths of *La Mansion* hotel, just beyond *Makanda-by-the-Sea* on the side road to Punta Quepos.

The road to Manuel Antonio

The following places are listed in the order you encounter them from Quepos.

Rainforest Restaurant *El Mono Azul.* Generous plates of chicken and fish along with tasty hamburgers, nachos and pizza (mains around $9). Proceeds at the shop next door (daily 7am–10pm) go to a local project run by children to preserve the squirrel monkeys' habitat (ⓦwww.kidssavingtherainforest.org). Daily 6am–10pm.

Ronny's Place Simple food – grilled chicken, steaks and pricey seafood specials – but sensational sunsets, the real reason you've come to this rustic place perched on the edge of the coast. Order a jug of headachingly strong sangria and plop yourself down at the tables lined up along the ridge. Daily noon–10pm.

D'Angel Fill up with the cheapest and best *casados* on the hill – five types, including liver (from $4.50) – at this charming and unpretentious *soda*, home to just a few tree-trunk tables. Daily 9am–9pm.

Kapi Kapi ⓣ2777-5049, ⓦwww.restaurantekapikapi.com. The select menu at this fine-dining restaurant specializes in seafood, such as fire-roasted red snapper ($17.50) and macadamia-encrusted mahi-mahi ($20). Sinful desserts include a one-is-not-enough chocolate soufflé ($5.50). 4–10pm, closed Mon.

Victoria's Delicious gourmet pizzas using home-made pesto and house mozzarella among other fine ingredients, though at these prices (the menu features what is surely Central America's first $32 pizza) you're better off sharing – 16-inch pizzas start at $18. Pastas, including fruits de mer, are a similar price. Daily 4–10pm, Fri 7 Sat till 11pm.

Salsipuedes Lively restaurant serving tapas-style dishes – so little portions of fajitas, grilled mahi-mahi, white-bean stew and the like (around $7) – which you can upgrade to mains ($8–17). Soak up the great balcony vistas with a (*guaro* sour) cocktail in hand. 7am–10pm, closed Tues.

Barba Roja This friendly, popular restaurant dishes up quality American cuisine, including grilled fish, tenderloin steaks, chunky burgers and lip-smacking BBQ ribs. Come and nurse a quiet drink while watching the sunset (happy hour 4.30–6.30pm), or crank things up a gear on Saturday nights, when live music is on the menu (from 8pm). Tues–Sun 3–10.30pm, Sat till 11pm.

Café Milagro Pop by for one of the best breakfasts around, or drop in any time to enjoy delicious home-made pastries washed down with excellent locally roasted coffee or a perfect cappuccino. The main branch in nearby Quepos (see p.365) doubles as a great little evening bistro. Mon–Sat 7am–6pm.

Si Como No Succulent fish brochettes and other grilled treats (around $12) at the *Rico Tico Grill* (daily 6.30am–9.30pm), which has a good children's menu and features nightly live music, or more upmarket dining at the poolside *Claro Que Si* (daily 5–10pm), a Caribbean-influenced seafood restaurant dishing coconut shrimps ($23) and the like; both overlook forest that is home to squirrel monkeys and coati. Diners at *Claro Que Si* can also catch a complimentary film afterwards in the hotel's private cinema.

El Avión Dine or drink inside an US aircraft used in the 1980s for arms-trafficking at this appropriately named restaurant. In truth, dining is more enjoyable in the open-air section, with sensational views, but the whole place exudes character. The menu includes average burgers, pastas and fajitas. Daily noon–midnight.

La Cantina Split-level, open-air bar serving up a meaty concoction of BBQ steak, chicken ribs and seafood, plus kebabs (mains from $12), and running a lengthy (and pricey) wine list. There's normally some sort of live music (7–11pm). Internet access is available in an adjoining railway carriage (see opposite). Daily 4–11pm.

Manuel Antonio village

Los Almendros *Los Almendros.* Juicy grilled steaks ($13) and tasty Argentinian *empanadas* are the stars at this pleasant, open-sided hotel restaurant. Daily 7am–9pm.

Café del Mar On the beach. This popular thatched *chiringuito* kiosk serves up salads (from $6) and cold beers to thirsty beach-goers; relaxing music adds to the vibe. Daily until 8.30pm.

Marlin Restaurant 300m from the park entrance. One of the cheaper places to eat in Manuel Antonio, this cheerful terrace restaurant serves up fresh seafood, Tex-Mex sandwiches and salads (mains $6–11) to crowds of hungry tourists. Daily 7am–9pm.

Vela Bar 50m from the park entrance. Dine on grilled fish, paella and an assortment of vegetarian dishes (around $13–22) in this dark, thatched restaurant, the swankiest in the village, or push the boat out and go for the seafood platter ($32). Daily 7am–9.30pm.

Listings

Banks and money Banco Promérica, 400m south of the football field, opposite *Barba Roja*, has an ATM.

Bookshop Regalame (daily 7am–10pm), *Sí Como No's artesanía* shop, next to the hotel, sells glossy coffee-table books and also stocks the work of local painters and craftsmen.

Internet access In *La Cantina*'s restored carriage (daily from 4pm), brought all the way from Chile; otherwise, El Chante (Mon–Sat 9am–9pm).

Language schools Several including reputable Escuela d'Amore (Ⓣ2777-1143, Ⓦwww.escueladamore.com) and the Costa Rica Spanish Institute (Ⓣ2234-1001, Ⓦwww.cosi.co.cr); from $350 for one week of classes.

Medical care The nearest hospital is in Quepos (see p.366).

Supermarket Super Joseth: 150m south of the football field (daily 7.30am–9.30pm, Sun from 8am); and at Playa Espadilla (daily 8am–9pm).

Tours Iguana Tours (Ⓣ2777-2052, Ⓦwww.iguanatours.com) offer hiking in the national park ($48, includes entrance fee), as well as boat and kayak trips around Isla Damas, a mangrove-fringed island north of Quepos (both $65).

Parque Nacional Manuel Antonio

PARQUE NACIONAL MANUEL ANTONIO (Tues–Sun 7am–4pm; $10; Ⓣ2777-5185, Ⓦwww.manuelantonio.com), some 150km southwest of San José

Manuel Antonio beaches

The **beaches** around Parque Nacional Manuel Antonio can be confusing, since they're called by a variety of different names. It's important to know which beach you're on, however, because some are unsafe for swimming; check with the rangers about conditions. From north to south, the beaches are as follows:

Playa Espadilla (also called Playa Primera or Playa Numero Uno). This long, popular curve of sand fronting Manuel Antonio village runs down to the park exit, just outside the park itself (see p.366).

Playa Espadilla Sur (also called Playa Dos or Playa Segunda). Espadilla Sur is the last beach you come to inside the park – the main trail towards the exit runs along the back of the beach. It's on the north side of Punta Catedral, and while usually fairly calm, it's also the most dangerous in rough conditions – beware the currents.

Playa Manuel Antonio (also called Playa Tres or Playa Blanca). Immediately south of Punta Catedral, and in a deeper and more protected bay than the others, Manuel Antonio is by far the best swimming beach, though you can still get clobbered by the deceptively gentle-looking waves as they hit the shore. Unfortunately, it's quite narrow and can get crowded (the best time to come is before 10am).

Playa Puerto Escondido (also called Playa Cuatro). Reached along the Sendero Puerto Escondido, this is a pretty, white horseshoe-shaped beach. Don't set out without first checking with the rangers about the *marea* (tide), because at high tide you can't get across the beach, nor can you cross it from the dense forest behind. At best, it'll be a waste of time; at worst, you'll get cut off on the other side for a few hours. Rangers advise against swimming here, as the currents can be dangerous.

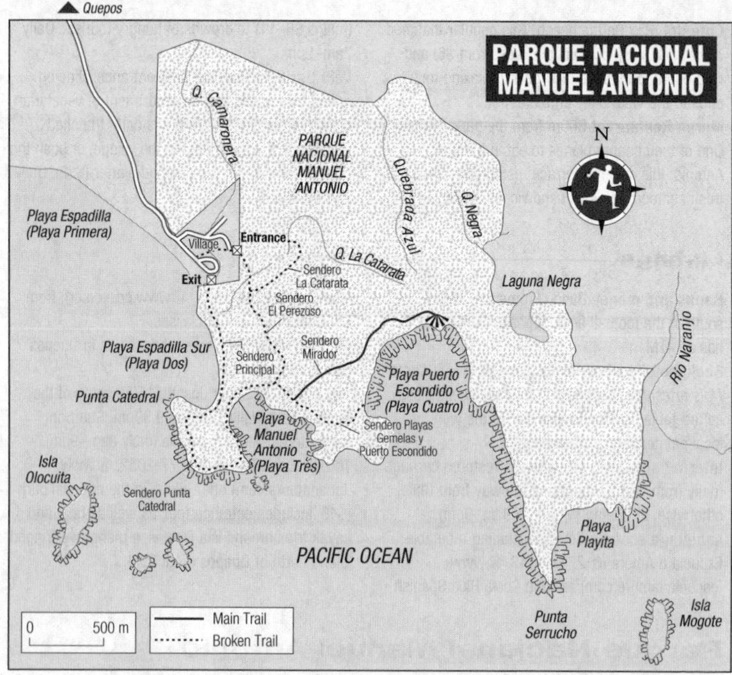

as the crow flies, may be Costa Rica's smallest national park but it's also its most popular. Considering the number of hotels and restaurants sidling up to the park's borders, one can easily imagine the fate that might have overtaken its limestone-white sands had it not been designated a national park in 1972. Even so, the park suffers from a high number of visitors (over 300,000 in 2010), and came within days of being closed down by the Ministry of Health in January 2009, after its then-inadequate facilities (much improved since) caused the pollution of local rivers and coastline. The park does close on Mondays, however, to give the animals a rest and the rangers and trail maintenance staff a chance to work.

Covering an area of only 6.8 square kilometres, Manuel Antonio preserves not only the lovely **beaches** and the unique *tómbolo* formation of Punta Catedral (Cathedral Point), but also **mangroves** and humid tropical **forest**. Visitors can only visit the part of the park that faces the sea – the eastern mountain section, off-limits to the public, is regularly patrolled by rangers to deter poaching, which is rife in the area, and incursions into the park from surrounding farmers and *campesinos*.

The trails

Manuel Antonio has a tiny system of short **trails**, all easy, except in rainy conditions, when they can get slippery. From the park entrance, the main trail, **Sendero El Perezoso**, runs for 1.3km down to Playa Manuel Antonio, providing, as the name suggests, a fair chance of spotting sloths in the guarumo trees along the way, as well as squirrel and howler monkeys. About 400m in, the short **Sendero La Catarata** (900m) leads to the pretty little waterfall after which it's named.

At the end of the trail, most people continue straight down to Playa Manuel Antonio, but for more rainforest hiking you can either head inland on the

Watching wildlife in Manuel Antonio

Manuel Antonio is one of the few remaining natural habitats of the **squirrel monkey**, the smallest of Costa Rica's primates, with close-set bright eyes and a delicate, white-haired face – their cuteness is their own nemesis, and they were once a prime target for poachers. You might spot them springing through the canopy above the park trails or outside the park in the Manuel Antonio area in general – local schoolchildren have set up a project to build overhead wooden "bridges" for the monkeys to cross the increasingly busy road from Manuel Antonio to Quepos (ask at *El Mono Azul* for details; see p.368).

You also have a good chance of seeing other smaller **mammals**, such as coati, agouti, two- and three-toed sloth and white-faced capuchin monkeys. The abundant **birdlife** includes the shimmering green kingfisher, the brown pelican, which can often be seen fishing off the rocks, and the laughing falcon.

Big **iguanas** hang out near the beaches, often standing stock-still for ten minutes at a time, providing good photo opportunities, though beware the **snakes** that drape themselves over the trails and look like vines – be careful what you grab onto.

Due to the park's high visitor numbers, some of the wildlife is unnervingly familiar with humans, and white-faced capuchin monkeys in particular have no qualms raiding backpacks in the hope of finding a bite to eat. You can **help the animals** by not feeding them (for which you can be fined), being quiet as you walk the trails and by not leaving any litter.

Sendero Mirador (1.3km), which ends at a viewpoint overlooking Playa Puerto Escondido, or take the beachside **Sendero Playas Gemelas y Puerto Escondido** (1.6km), which heads through relatively dense humid tropical forest cover, crossing a small creek before eventually reaching the rocky beach itself; a turn-off halfway along leads to Playas Gemelas. You can clamber across Playa Puerto Escondido at low tide – but check tide times with the rangers before leaving to avoid getting cut off.

Playa Manuel Antonio is the park's best swimming beach and, predictably, its most crowded – both with people and with white-faced capuchin monkeys, who seem to be running a competition with the local raccoon population as to who can steal the most backpack snacks. At the southern end of the beach, low tide reveals a pile of stones believed to have been used as **turtle traps** by the area's indigenous peoples – green turtles have probably nested in Manuel Antonio for thousands of years. Beyond here, it's worth embarking on the **Sendero Punta Catedral** (1.4km), an energetic loop offering wonderful views of the Pacific, dotted with jagged-edged little islands; like all *tómbolos*, Punta Catedral was once an island that, over millennia, has been joined to the mainland through accumulated sand deposits.

The trail out of Manuel Antonio, the **Sendero Principal** (2.2km), runs along the back of the long **Playa Espadilla Sur**. It's usually calm and less crowded than Playa Manuel Antonio, but isn't often supervised, so be careful of currents.

Park practicalities

Buses from Quepos (every 30min from 7am to 7pm; 20min) and San José (5–6 daily; 5hr) drop passengers off 200m before the park entrance. If you're staying at a hotel on the road to the park and want to travel by **taxi**, it's cheaper to flag one down on the road rather than calling from the hotel. If you're driving, note that you'll be charged ($4–6) to leave your car at one of the supervised car parks on the road loop at the end of Manuel Antonio village, or anywhere on the main street.

You can take informative **tours** with guides at the park entrance ($20 per person; 2hr). You may be approached by "guides" offering their services in the village, so check their ICT (Costa Rican Institute of Tourism) photo ID first. Whether you walk the trails guided or not, make sure you take plenty of water – the **climate** is hot, humid and wet, all year round, with temperatures easily climbing to 30°C and above – and hit the trails early, as much to avoid the influx of visitors that flood in mid-morning as the searing heat.

Note that there have been problems with **theft** in Manuel Antonio, usually as a result of people leaving valuables (like cameras) on the beach; take care also if walking the trails alone, as there have been a number of robberies, most significantly when armed robbers stole $20,000 from rangers (the day's takings) as they left the park one evening in January 2009.

Travel details

Buses

Cóbano to: Santa Teresa/Mal País (2 daily; 30min).
Jacó to: Puntarenas (6 daily; 1hr 30min); Quepos (6 daily; 1hr 30min); San José (8 daily; 2hr 30min).
Montezuma to: Paquera (6 daily; 2hr); Reserva Natural Absoluta Cabo Blanco (5 daily; 30min); San José (2 daily; 5hr); Santa Teresa/Mal País (via Cóbano; 2 daily; 1hr).
Paquera to: Cóbano, for Santa Teresa/Mal País (6 daily; 1hr 30min); Montezuma (6 daily; 2hr); Nicoya (4 daily; 2hr); Tambor (6 daily; 50min).
Puntarenas to: Jacó (6 daily; 1hr 30min); Liberia (8 daily; 3hr); Quepos (6 daily; 3hr); San José (hourly; 2hr); Santa Elena, for Monteverde (3 daily; 3hr 30min).
Quepos to: Dominical (3 daily; 1hr 30min); Jacó (6 daily; 1hr 30min); Manuel Antonio (frequent; 20min); Puntarenas (6 daily; 3hr); San José (9–10 daily; 3hr 30min–4hr 30min); Uvita (3 daily; 1hr 30min).
San José to: Jacó (7 daily; 2hr 30min); Manuel Antonio (5–6 daily; 4hr 30min); Montezuma (2 daily; 5hr); Puntarenas (hourly; 2hr); Quepos (9–12 daily; 3hr 30min–4hr 30min); Santa Elena, for Monteverde (2 daily; 4hr 30min); Santa Teresa/Mal País (2 daily; 5hr).
Santa Elena to: Puntarenas (3 daily; 3hr 30min); San José (2 daily; 4hr 30min); Tilarán (2 daily; 2hr 30min).
Santa Teresa/Mal País to: Cóbano (3 daily; 30min), for Montezuma & Paquera; San José (2 daily; 5hr).

Ferries

Naranjo to: Puntarenas (4 daily; 1hr).
Paquera to: Puntarenas (10 daily; 1hr 15min).
Puntarenas to: Isla de Chira (daily; 45min); Naranjo (4 daily; 1hr); Paquera (9 daily; 1hr 15min).

Flights

Quepos to: La Fortuna (daily; 40min); San José (8 daily; 25min)
San José to: Quepos (8 daily; 25 min); Tambor (7 daily; 25min).
Tambor to: San José (7 daily; 25min).

7 The Zona Sur

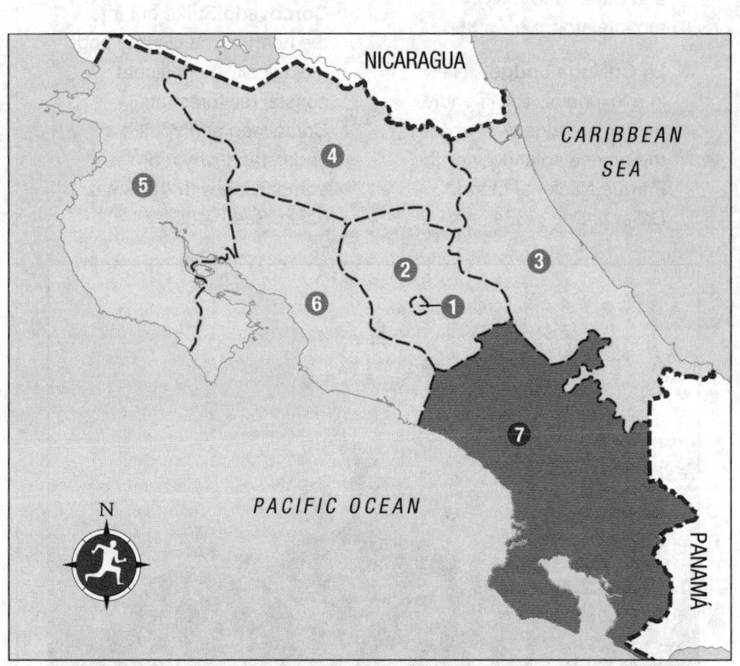

CHAPTER 7

Highlights

* **San Gerardo de Dota** Try your hand at fly-fishing or set off in search of quetzals from this remote mountain village in a jaw-dropping setting. **See p.381**

* **Climb Cerro Chirripó** The hike up Costa Rica's highest peak is a long but varied ascent through cloudforest and paramo to rocky mountaintop. **See p.386**

* **La Cusinga Lodge** Relax in a luxurious, eco-friendly rainforest lodge overlooking the marine splendour of the Parque Nacional Marino Ballena. **See p.394**

* **Bahía Drake** Explore the stunning natural scenery and marine life of remote Bahía Drake. **See p.401**

* **Isla del Caño** Snorkel among coral beds and spot dolphins, manta rays and whales at Costa Rica's premier dive spot. **See p.404**

* **Parque Nacional Corcovado** Strike out into the heart of the visually and biologically magnificent coastal rainforest at Corcovado and you'll understand why it draws comparison with the Amazon basin. **See p.408**

▲ On top of Cerro Chirripó

7

The Zona Sur

Costa Rica's **Zona Sur** (southern zone) is the country's least-known region, both for Ticos and for visitors, though tourism has increased significantly in recent years. The geographically diverse Zona Sur encompasses the high mountain peaks of the Cordillera de Talamanca at its northern edge, the agricultural heartland of the Valle de El General, the river-cut lowlands of the Valle de Diquis around Palmar and the coffee-growing Valle de Coto Brus, near the border with Panamá. The region is particularly popular with hikers, many of whom come to climb Cerro Chirripó in the Talamancas – one of the highest peaks in Central America – set in the chilly, rugged terrain of the **Parque Nacional Chirripó**. Experienced walkers also venture into the giant neighbouring **Parque Internacional La Amistad**, a UNESCO Biosphere Reserve and World Heritage Site that protects an enormous tract of land along Costa Rica's southern border.

Halfway down the region's Pacific coast, the **Playa Dominical** area was originally a surfing destination, but its tropical beauty now draws an ever-increasing number of visitors (not to mention property developers), especially since road improvements have made it accessible without a 4WD. Further south down the coast, the **Península de Osa** is the site of the **Parque Nacional Corcovado**, one of the country's prime rainforest hiking destinations, whose soaring canopy trees constitute the last chunk of tropical wet forest on the entire Pacific side of the Central American isthmus. The Península de Osa is also home to the remote and picturesque **Bahía Drake**, from where tours depart to the nearby **Reserva Biológica Isla del Caño**, still home to a few lithic spheres fashioned by the local Diquis. On the opposite side of the Golfo Dulce from the Península de Osa, near the border with Panamá, is **Golfito**, the only town of any size in the region, and one that suffered from an unsavoury reputation for years after the pull-out of the United Brands fruit company's banana operations in 1985. It has been attracting more visitors of late since being made a tax-free zone for manufactured goods from Panamá, though for foreign visitors it's more useful as a base from which to move on to the Península de Osa and Corcovado.

Despite the region's profusion of basic, inexpensive **accommodation**, you may find yourself spending more money than you bargained for simply because of the time, distance and planning involved in getting to many of the region's more beautiful spots – this is particularly true if you stay in one of the very comfortable private **rainforest lodges** in the Osa, Golfito and Bahía Drake areas. Many people prefer to take a package rather than travel independently, and travellers who stay at the rainforest lodges often choose to fly in. Bear in mind, too, that many of the region's communities are not used to seeing strangers – certainly women travelling alone will attract some curiosity.

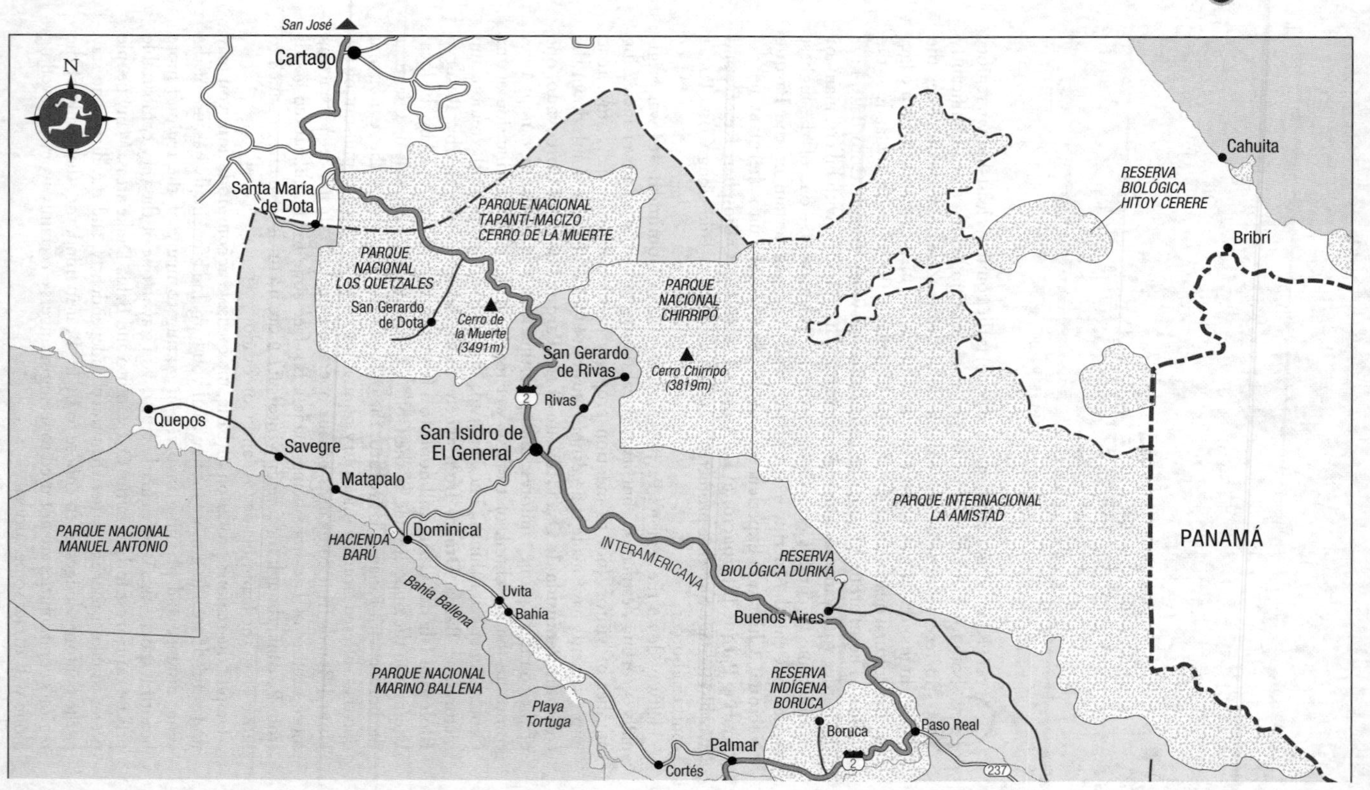
N
San José
Cartago
Santa María de Dota
PARQUE NACIONAL TAPANTÍ-MACIZO CERRO DE LA MUERTE
PARQUE NACIONAL LOS QUETZALES
San Gerardo de Dota
Cerro de la Muerte (3491m)
PARQUE NACIONAL CHIRRIPÓ
Cerro Chirripó (3819m)
San Gerardo de Rivas
Rivas
2
San Isidro de El General
Quepos
Savegre
Matapalo
Dominical
HACIENDA BARÚ
PARQUE NACIONAL MANUEL ANTONIO
Bahía Ballena
Uvita
Bahía
PARQUE NACIONAL MARINO BALLENA
Playa Tortuga
Cortés
Palmar
INTERAMERICANA
Buenos Aires
RESERVA BIOLÓGICA DURIKÁ
RESERVA INDÍGENA BORUCA
Boruca
Paso Real
237
PARQUE INTERNACIONAL LA AMISTAD
PANAMÁ
RESERVA BIOLÓGICA HITOY CERERE
Cahuita
Bribrí

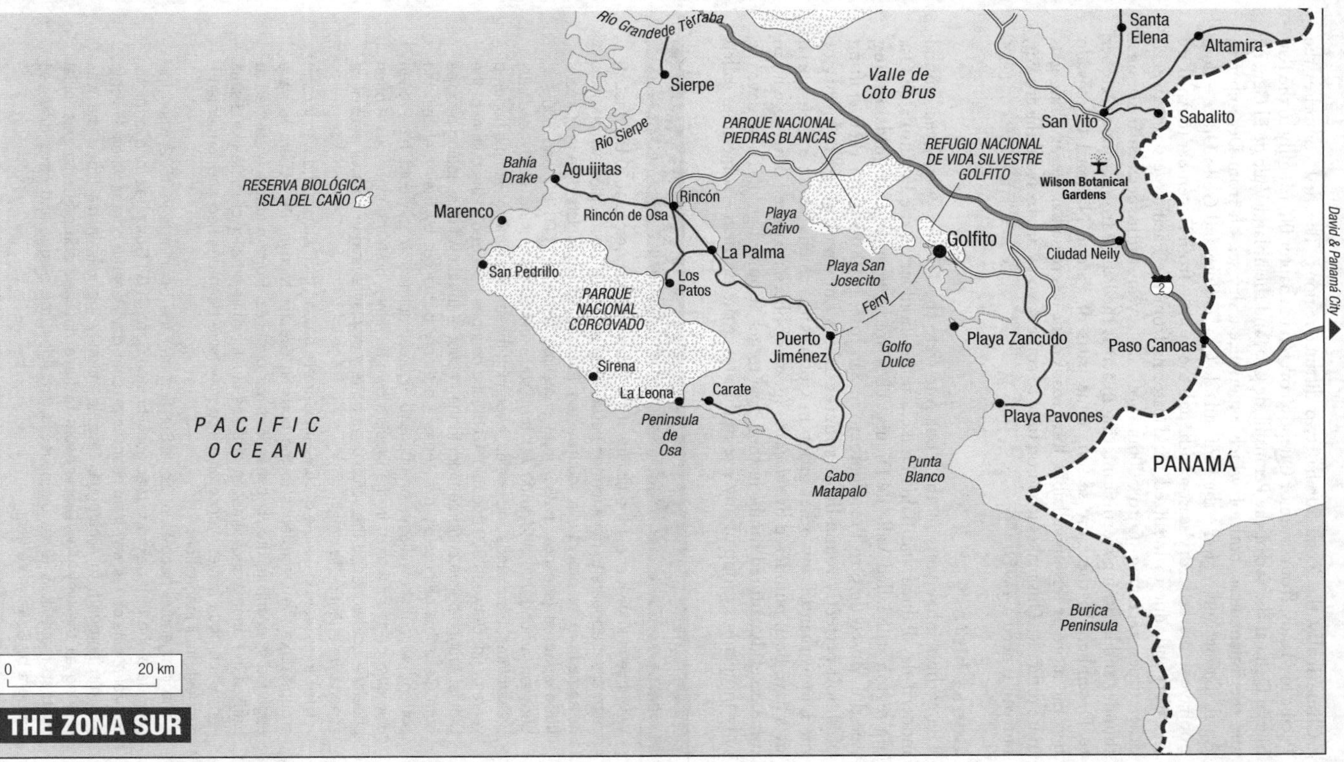
THE ZONA SUR
0
20 km
David & Panamá City
Río Grande de Térraba
Sierpe
Santa Elena
Altamira
Sabalito
San Vito
Valle de Coto Brus
Wilson Botanical Gardens
PARQUE NACIONAL PIEDRAS BLANCAS
REFUGIO NACIONAL DE VIDA SILVESTRE GOLFITO
Río Sierpe
Bahía Drake
Aguijitas
Rincón
Rincón de Osa
RESERVA BIOLÓGICA ISLA DEL CAÑO
Marenco
Playa Cativo
Golfito
Ciudad Neily
2
La Palma
San Pedrillo
Los Patos
Playa San Josecito
PARQUE NACIONAL CORCOVADO
Ferry
Puerto Jiménez
Playa Zancudo
Paso Canoas
Golfo Dulce
Sirena
La Leona
Carate
Playa Pavones
Peninsula de Osa
PACIFIC OCEAN
Punta Blanco
Cabo Matapalo
PANAMÁ
Burica Peninsula

Climatically the Zona Sur has two distinct regions. The first comprises the Pacific lowlands, from south of Quepos (covered in chapter 00) roughly to the Río Sierpe Delta at the top of the Península de Osa, and the upland Valle de El General and the Talamancas, both of which experience a dry season from December to April. The second region – the Península de Osa, Golfito and Golfo Dulce – does not have so marked a dry season (although the months from December to April are less wet) and, due to localized wind patterns from the Pacific, gets very wet at other times, receiving up to 5000mm of rain a year, with spectacular seasonal thunder and lightning storms cantering in across the Pacific from around October to December. In the rainy season, some parts of Parque Nacional Corcovado become more or less unwalkable, local roads can't be crossed and everything gets more difficult. This makes it a good time to come if you want to avoid the crowds, but you'll need a 4WD.

Some history

The earliest inhabitants of the Zona Sur were the **Diquis**, who lived around modern-day Palmar and Bahía Drake, on the shoulder of the Península de Osa – a region still called Valle de Diquis. They are best known for **goldsmithing** (see the Museo de Oro Precolombino in San José, p.100) and for their crafting of almost perfectly round **lithic spheres**. Less is known of the early history of the Diquis than of any other group in Costa Rica, chiefly because their burial sites have been plundered by *huaqueros* (grave-robbers/treasure hunters), who in some cases dynamited tombs in their zeal to get at buried gold. These days the only indigenous group of any size in the area is the Borucas – sometimes called

The Diquis

Very little is known about the history of the **Diquis region** before 1000 BC, though culturally it appears to have formed part of the Greater Chiriquí region, which takes its name from the province in southwestern Panamá. Archeologists date the famous **lithic spheres** (see box, p.395) from sometime between 1000 BC and 500 AD; between around 700 and 1600 AD the Diquis began fashioning **gold** pendants, breastplates, headbands and chains, becoming master goldsmiths within a hundred years or so. Between 500 and 800 AD drastic changes occurred in the culture of the Diquis. Archeologists attribute them to the impact of the arrival of seagoing peoples from Colombia or possibly the Andes – a theory borne out by their metates and pottery, which show llama or guanaco figures, animals that would have been unknown on the isthmus. In the Diquis's own artisanry, both the ingenious – often cheeky – goldwork and the voluptuous pottery display a unique humour as well as superlative attention to detail.

The Diquis were in a state of constant **warfare** among themselves and with foreign groups. Like the Chorotegas to the north in Greater Nicoya, they seem to have engaged in sacrifice, ritually beheading war captives. Huge metates unearthed at Barilles in Panamá show images of these rituals, while smaller crucible-like dishes – in which coca leaves, yucca or maize may have been crushed and fermented – suggest ritual inebriation.

The indigenous peoples of Zona Sur first met the Spaniards in 1522 when the *cacique* of the Térraba group graciously hosted Captain **Gil González** for a fortnight. González was on his way from near the present-day Panamá border, where his ship had run aground, to Nicaragua. Despite infirmity (he was in his fifties), he was walking all the way. The Diquis seem to have declined abruptly after this initial contact, most likely felled by influenza, smallpox, the plague and other diseases brought by Spanish settlers.

The road to Cerro de la Muerte and beyond

The **Interamericana** south of San José heaves with international transport trucks and other large vehicles. Yellow-topped kilometre markings line the highway, and villages and hamlets are often referred to by these numbers (Briseño, for example, is usually called "kilómetro treinta y siete"). The ease of travel from the capital, via Cartago, to San Isidro depends on the current condition of the highway. Rock- and mudslides are frequent and there have been isolated reports of drivers being flagged down and robbed by bandits, although this normally happens to intercontinental truckers rather than tourists. Still, it's not a good idea to drive at night – not just because of the chance of robbery, but more crucially because of reduced visibility, particularly on the ride up **Cerro de la Muerte** and the descent that ensues. Fog, mist and rain are a constant threat at all times, and the road lacks shoulder or meridian markings. The biggest problem you'll likely face, though, are the long tailbacks caused by lack of overtaking opportunities. Ticos frequently risk life and limb passing large trucks on blind corners, but don't be tempted to follow suit – Costa Rica has one of the world's highest road-accident rates.

the Bruncas – a subgroup of the Diquis. (See box, p.396, for details of their Fiesta de los Diablitos.)

The modern history of the Zona Sur has been defined by its isolation. Before the building of the **Interamericana** in the 1950s, transport across the Cerro de la Muerte was by mule only. **Charcoal-burning** was until very recently the main economic activity up in these heights, using the majestic local oaks, but *campesinos* in the area are now being discouraged from charcoal-burning, due to its deforesting effects. For a glimpse of how the charcoal-burners lived before the building of the Interamericana, read the short story "The Carbonero" by Costa Rican writer Carlos Salazar Herera, translated into English and anthologized in *Costa Rica: A Traveller's Literary Companion* (see p.461).

San José to San Isidro

The market town of **San Isidro de El General**, 136km southwest of San José, sits amid a lush agricultural landscape, and makes for a welcome respite after negotiating the rigours of the Interamericana, also known as Hwy-2. The Interamericana winds its way about 2000m up from the bowl of Cartago's enclosing valley to the chilly heights of the 3491-metre **Cerro de la Muerte** ("Mountain of Death") pass. En route, it passes turn-offs for the beguiling mountain village of **San Gerardo de Dota** and Costa Rica's newest national park, **Parque Nacional Los Quetzales**, one of the few places in the world where you stand an excellent chance of spotting quetzals in the wild and a must-stop for birders.

San Gerardo de Dota and around

About 80km south of San José, a turn-off leads to the lovely hamlet of **SAN GERARDO DE DOTA** – you'll need a 4WD to get here, since the road down from the Interamericana is treacherously steep in parts. The village enjoys a spectacular setting along the Río Savegre, with lush valley walls looming on either side of it. Though it has long been known by ornithologists for the staggeringly high number of species found in the area, particularly the striking resplendent quetzal, it has always had a bit of a forgotten feel to it, and makes an ideal base for visiting the nearby Parque Nacional Los Quetzales.

There's not much to the village itself, beyond a preponderance of apple and peach trees. Other than making trips to the Parque Nacional Los Quetzales, the most popular pastime around here is **fishing** – lure fishing from December to March and fly-fishing mostly in May and June; *Hotel de Montaña Savegre* rents out equipment and is a good choice for fishing outings on the river.

There are no **buses** to San Gerardo de Dota, though San José buses bound for San Isidro de El General will stop for you at the turn-off on the Interamericana, 8km from the village. Make arrangements in advance for your hotel to pick you up from there.

Accommodation and eating

For such a small village, there are some absolutely wonderful **places to stay**, both in San Gerardo de Dota and the surrounding area. Bear in mind that although it's set in a valley, the village lies at over 2000m; it can get chilly at night. The best **place to eat** around San Gerado de Dota is *Comida Típica Miriam* (Ⓣ2740-1049), about 300m or so uphill from *Dantica* (see below) on the road to the village, an inviting family-run *soda* serving hearty Costa Rican staples.

Albergue Mirador de Quetzales On a side road at km70 Ⓣ8381-8456. About 10km before the San Gerardo de Dota turn-off, this lodge, also known as *Finca Eddie Serrano*, sits at a nose-bleed altitude of 8500 feet. This 100-plus acre cloudforest reserve is run by a local family who have many of the quetzals' favourite trees on their land. The *albergue* itself is cosy and reasonably priced, with an eight-room lodge (shared bathrooms) and several wooden *cabinas* with private baths overlooking a misty valley. Bedside electric heaters warm you through near-freezing night-time temperatures. You can enjoy delicious home-cooked meals for about $10 extra. El Robledal, the *finca*'s 4km trail, winds past 1500-year-old cypresses and 14-million-year-old marine fossils, offering vistas from which to admire the eponymous resplendent quetzal, the bird the Aztecs worshipped. Guided hikes depart at 6am daily. Day visitors can pay about $7 to walk the trail. You can also take a horse-ride past an old plane wreck down to a waterfall. ❺

Cabinas El Quetzal In the centre of the village Ⓣ2740-1036, Ⓦwww.cabinaselquetzal.com. A good bargain, these clean and nicely furnished cabins on the main road are a great option if you're on a budget. ❺ includes three meals a day.

Dantica Cloud Forest Lodge About halfway down the road to San Gerardo de Dota, 4km from the village Ⓣ2740-1067, Ⓦwww.dantica.com. Striking modern lodge and art gallery with seven villas and a suite, all of which have south-facing terraces, comfy furnishings, jacuzzi, satellite TV and, most crucially, floor-to-ceiling windows, with jaw-dropping views. Breakfast is included and there's a restaurant in the gallery where you can dine on creative beef and pork dishes, as well as locally caught trout. ❼

Hotel de Montaña Savegre In the village Ⓣ2740-1028, Ⓦwww.savegre.co.cr. Long-running eco-lodge well known among birdwatchers for the number of quetzals that nest on or near its land. The rooms are straightforward and comfortable, with homely furnishings. The very friendly *dueños* have trail maps, can arrange guides (which cost extra) and offer bird-spotting tips, trout-fishing trips in the Río Savegre and horseriding on their 400-hectare private reserve. ❼ with breakfast, ❽ with all meals included

Trogon Lodge In the village Ⓣ2740-8181, Ⓦwww.grupomawamba.com. The *Trogon Lodge* has comfortable heated cabins (though they can still get chilly at night) and beautifully landscaped grounds, with several trout ponds, marked trails through the woods and a zip-line tour. There are also normally many quetzals to be seen around here. ❻

Parque Nacional Los Quetzales

Opened in 2005, **Parque Nacional Los Quetzales** (daily 7.30am–3.30pm; $10) covers an area of over 12,000 densely forested acres. Set higher in elevation – between 2000 and 3000m – than many of the other national parks, Los Quetzales is covered mostly in cloudforest, an ideal habitat for numerous animal species, including coyotes, jaguars, Baird's tapirs and, of course, the eponymous quetzals. The quetzals feed on the reserve's abundant aguacatillo trees, and the best time to spot them is during their nesting season, from March to June.

Currently the park has no facilities for tourists, so is best visited on a tour with one of the lodges in San Gerardo de Dota (see opposite). A couple of poorly maintained **trails** depart from the park entrance, which is signposted about 1km beyond the km75 marker, before the turn-off to San Gerardo de Dota.

San Isidro de El General

The spectacular descent into **SAN ISIDRO DE EL GENERAL**, just 702m above sea level, brings you halfway back into tropical climes after the chilly ride over Cerro de la Muerte. In Costa Rica, San Isidro is regarded as an increasingly attractive place to live, with its clean, country-town atmosphere. While the Talamancas are a non-volcanic range – and the Valle de El General therefore lacks the incredibly fertile soils of the Valle Central – there is still considerable local agricultural activity, and pineapples grow particularly well. The town hosts an **agricultural fair** in the first week in February on the Parque Central, when farmers don their finery, put their produce up for competition and sell fresh food in the streets. May is the **month of San Isidro** – patron saint of farmers and animals – and is celebrated by fiestas, ox-cart parades, dog shows and the erection of gaudy Ferris wheels. The town's one museum, the **Museo Regional del Sur** (Tues–Sat 8am–4.30pm in theory), is 75m northwest of the modern church on the Parque Central's eastern side: it's devoted to the *campesino* history of the area and features occasional displays of local artwork.

Arrival and information

San Isidro's main **bus terminal** is adjacent to the town's central market at Av 6, C 0/2, but most buses from here head to local destinations. To and from San José, TRACOPA buses stop at the terminal on the Interamericana and Calle 2, while MUSA buses pick up passengers across the road. The Banco Nacional on the main square changes **travellers' cheques** and has an **ATM**, as does the Banco de Costa Rica on Av 4, C 0. There are two **internet cafés** on the main square (BTC Internet and Brunca Café Internet) and you'll find the post office on C 1, Av 6/8.

Information about the Parque Nacional Chirripó and Parque Internacional La Amistad is available from the regional office of the national parks service (Mon–Fri 8am–4pm; ⓣ2771-3155, ⓔaclap@ns.minae.go.cr) at C 2, Av 4/6, south of the

Moving on from San Isidro

If you're travelling **south** from San Isidro to Palmar (2 daily; 4hr), Golfito (2 daily; 5hr) or Paso Canoas (2 daily; 6hr), it's better to get a bus that originates in San Isidro rather than one that's coming through from San José, as they're often full and you could find yourself standing all the way to Panamá. If you want to try for one of the through-services, visit TRACOPA's ticket office (Mon–Sat 7am–4pm) at Calle 3 and the Interamericana; you can buy tickets if there are seats available, and schedules are posted telling you what time the buses pass through town. Buses for **Quepos** (4 daily; 3hr 30min) and **Dominical** (5 daily; 1hr 20min) leave from the TRACOPA terminal, at Calle 2 and the Interamericana. Buses for **San Gerardo de Rivas** leave at 5am and 2pm (1hr 40min) from the main (El Mercado) bus terminal at Av 6, C 0/2. For all local services, buy your ticket on the bus.

Parque Central. It's worth stopping off here to ask about current conditions and, if possible, to make reservations for Chirripó (see below). On C 4, Av 1/3 are the offices of **CIPROTUR** (Ⓣ2772-5911, Ⓦwww.ecotourism.co.cr), a nonprofit organization, with a useful website, that promotes ecotourism mainly in the Zona Sur: its helpful staff can book hotel rooms and answer queries.

Accommodation

Of the budget choices in town, the best **accommodation** is at the large *Hotel Chirripó*, C 1, Av 2/4 (Ⓣ2771-0529; ❶), which has simple rooms with private bath and hot shower, a decent restaurant and free parking. Alternatively, the *Hotel del Sur Country Club and Casino* (Ⓣ2771-3033; ❺) is set in quiet, pleasant grounds about 6km southwest of San Isidro on the Interamericana and has en-suite rooms, wi-fi, tennis courts, a swimming pool and a good restaurant.

Eating and drinking

The region's fresh and varied local produce is put to good use, and San Isidro has several worthwhile places to **eat**. The best place for breakfast is the pavement café at the *Hotel Chirripó*, which serves *gallo pinto* and toast and eggs with excellent local coffee daily from 6.30am. Almost next door is the *Taquería Mexico Linda* (Ⓣ2771-8222), a brightly decorated and cheerful little café that dishes up delicious Mexican food. For superb seafood, try *Marisquería Marea Baja* (Ⓣ2771-0681) on C 2, Av 4/6 or put together your own meal at the bustling Mercado Central, adjacent to the bus station.

Parque Nacional Chirripó

Some 20km northeast of San Isidro, **PARQUE NACIONAL CHIRRIPÓ** is named after the Cerro Chirripó, which lies at its centre – at 3819m the highest peak in Central America south of Guatemala. Ever since the conquest of the peak in 1904 by a missionary priest, Father Agustín Blessing (local indigenous peoples may of course have climbed it before), visitors have been flocking to Chirripó to do the same, finding accommodation in the nearby villages of **San Gerardo de Rivas** and **Rivas** (see p.387).

The park's terrain varies widely, according to altitude, from cloudforest to rocky mountaintops. Between the two lies the interesting alpine **paramo** – high moorland, punctuated by rocks, shrubs and hardy clump grasses more usually associated with Andean heights. The colours here are muted yellows and browns, with the occasional deep purple. Below the paramo lie areas of **oak forest**, now much depleted through continued charcoal-burning. Chirripó is also the only place in Costa Rica where you can observe vestiges of the **glaciers** that scraped across here about thirty thousand years ago: narrow, U-shaped valleys, moraines (heaps of rock and soil left behind by retreating glaciers) and glacial lakes, as well as the distinctive **crestones**, or heavily weathered fingers of rock, more reminiscent of Montana than Costa Rica. The land is generally waterlogged, with a few bogs – take care where you step, as sometimes it's so chilly you won't want to get your feet wet.

Many **mammals** live in the park, and you may see spider monkeys as you climb from the lower mountain to the montane rainforest. Your best bet for **bird-spotting** is in the lower elevations: along the oak and cloudforest sections of the trail you may spot hawks, trogons, woodpeckers and even quetzals, though in the cold and inhospitable terrain higher up, you'll only see robins and hawks.

The **weather** in Chirripó is extremely variable and unpredictable. It can be hot, humid and rainy between May and December, but is clearer and drier between January and April (the peak season for climbing the mountain). Even then, clouds may roll in at the top and obscure the view, and rainstorms move in very fast. The only months you can be sure of a dry spell are March and April. **Temperatures** may drop to below 0°C at night and rise to 20°C during the day, though at the summit, it's so cold that it's hard to believe you're just 9° north of the equator. Be advised that it's not possible to climb Chirripó in October or the last two weeks in May, when the trail is closed for maintenance.

Visiting the park

Visiting the Parque Nacional Chirripó requires advance planning. First you have to reserve a place, since no more than forty hikers are allowed in the park at any one time, and demand far outstrips capacity in the popular travel seasons (around March and April, especially Easter, and Christmas) – although there are sometimes cancellations. When making reservations you should state your preferred dates, bearing in mind that it's not possible to book for the high season (which starts in January) before November 1. Most hikers find two or three nights sufficient. You may have to pay in advance (by money transfer) and in full – $15 for two days, $10 for every day after that, plus $10 per night for accommodation if you are staying in the park itself (see p.387).

To **reserve a place**, call the MINAE parks office in San Gerardo (Mon–Fri 6.30am–4.30pm; ⓣ2742-5083). Once you have your reservation you're required to check in at the ranger station – even if you're heading for the camping trail that starts from Herradura. If you turn up without a reservation, there's a small chance you may be able to secure one of the ten daily **walk-in tickets** available from the MINAE office in San Gerardo, next to the bus stop.

While Chirripó is hot at midday, it frequently drops to freezing at the higher altitudes at night. You should bring **warm clothing** (temperatures can fall to –7°C at night) and a proper **sleeping bag** (though these can be rented on site), a blanket, water, food and a propane gas stove. A short list of clothing and other essentials might include a good pair of boots, socks, long trousers, T-shirt, shirt, sweater, woolly hat and jacket, lots of insect repellent, sunglasses, first aid (for cuts and scratches), gloves (for rocks and the cold), binoculars and a torch – the accommodation huts only have electricity between 6 and 8pm.

Detailed contour **maps** of the park are available from the Instituto Geográfico in San José, who sell four maps covering the entire climb. Otherwise, the staff at the entrance can supply you with an adequate map of the park, showing some altitude markings. You can also hire a horse to carry your gear up to the accommodation huts. The services of a **guide** can be useful and interesting in helping to identify local species and interpreting the landscapes you pass through – again, ask at the ranger station at the entrance for recommendations.

Cerro Chirripó

Almost everyone who climbs Chirripó goes up to the accommodation huts first, rests there overnight, and then takes another day or two to explore the summit, surrounding peaks and paramo – it's not really feasible to climb Chirripó in one day. During high season, you'll have company on the path up the mountain, and the trail is well marked with signs stating the altitude and the distance to the summit. Watch out for **altitude sickness**, though; if you have made a quick ascent from the lowland beach areas, you could find yourself becoming short of breath, experiencing pins and needles, nausea and exhaustion. If this happens, stop and rest; if symptoms persist, descend immediately. The main thing to keep in mind is **not to go off the trail** or exploring on your own without telling anyone, especially in the higher areas of the park. Off the trail, definite landmarks are few, and it's easy to get confused.

The **hike** begins at 1219m and ends at 3819m, the summit. It's almost entirely uphill and so exhausting that you may have trouble appreciating the scenery. On the first day most hikers make the extremely strenuous fourteen-kilometre trek to the accommodation huts – reckon on a minimum of seven hours if you're very fit (and the weather is good), up to twelve hours or more if you're not. In San Gerardo de Rivas you can hire a porter to carry your gear for you (around $60 per 20kg). On the second day you can make the huts your base while you hike to the summit and back, which is easily done in a day, perhaps taking in some of the nearby lagoons.

The walk begins in a cow pasture, before passing through thick, dark cloud-forest, a good place to spot **quetzals** (March–May are the best months). After a relatively flat stretch of several kilometres, where you're likely to be plagued by various biting insects, you'll arrive at a **rest station** halfway to the accommodation huts. Some people stay here, splitting the hike into a less-taxing two days, but conditions are extremely rustic, with three sides open to the wind. The **Cuesta de los Arrepentidos** ("Hill of the Repentants", meaning you're sorry at this point that you came) is the real push, all uphill for at least 3km. At **Monte Sin Fé** ("Faithless Mountain"), about 10km into the trail, is another patch of tropical montane forest, more open than the cloudforest. Keep your eye out for the *refugio natural*, a big cave where you can sleep in an emergency, from where it's just 3km to the **accommodation huts**. At the huts, the land looks like a greener version of

Scotland: bare moss cover, grasslands and a waterlogged area where the lagoons congregate. There are no trees, and little wildlife in evidence.

The **rangers** based up here are friendly, and in the high season (Jan–April) you can ask to accompany them on walks near the summit to avoid getting lost. Do not *expect* this, however, as it is not their job to lead guided walks. It's just ninety minutes' walk from the accommodation huts along a well-marked trail to **the summit** – there's a bit of scrambling involved, but no real climbing. You'll need to set off by dawn, as clear weather at the peak is really only guaranteed until 9 or 10am. There's also a little book in a metal box where you can sign your "I did it" message; bring a pen. From the top, if it's clear, you can see right across to the Pacific. However, you're above the cloud line up here, and the surrounding mountains are often obscured by drifting milky clouds.

Accommodation

The only **accommodation** in the park itself is the block at Los Crestones, which has fifteen rooms (each sleeping four people), cold showers, a cooking area and a big sink where you can wash clothes: accommodation costs $10 per person and can be booked through the San Gerardo MINAE office (see p.385 for details). Alternatively, you can **camp** in the park, although this takes a bit more planning. You'll need to make a special reservation at the MINAE office and hire a local guide (obligatory; $25 per day for up to ten people; $50 for groups of 10–16) in the nearby hamlet of Herradura: ask at the *pulpería* or the ranger station at the park entrance for recommendations, or check Ⓦwww.sangerardocostarica.com/activities/hire-a-guide, which has a list of guides currently leading hikes to the summit. If you're camping, you'll enter the park from Herradura: the trail to the summit of Chirripó via the campsite is longer and more arduous than the more common trek via the accommodation block at Los Crestones – you'll need a minimum of three days. Note if you're camping that no fires are allowed in the park, since forest fires frequently devastate the area.

However, most people stay in the tiny town of **San Gerardo de Rivas**, 3km west of the park and 17km northeast of San Isidro. It is home to a park ranger station and has several very reasonably priced, friendly places to stay – try to get somewhere with hot water, though, as it can get very cold at night. There are also a couple of attractive family-run hotels a few kilometres further back down the road towards San Isidro in the village of **Rivas**.

In San Gerardo

Cabinas El Descanso 200m beyond the ranger station, San Gerardo de Rivas Ⓣ2742-5061, Ⓦwww.sangerardocostarica.com/accommodations/el-descanso. Private house close to the ranger station with basic rooms, some with shared bathroom others with private bathroom. It also has an excellent restaurant serving Costa Rican comfort food, horses for hire and free transport to the park entrance, 3km away. ❸

Hotel y Restaurante Roca Dura San Gerardo de Rivas Ⓣ2742-5071, Ⓔhotelrocadura@hotmail.com. Seven smallish but clean rooms – one is built into the large slab of rock after which the hotel is named– four of which have private bath and hot water (❷). The café and restaurant are a hive of activity. It's possible to camp onsite ($5) and the hotel offers free transport to the park entrance. ❶

Hotel y Restaurante Urán 50m from the Chirripó trailhead, San Gerardo de Rivas Ⓣ2742-5003, Ⓦwww.hoteluran.com. Thirteen neat, small rooms come with shared bathrooms (❶) and eight slightly bigger ones have private bathrooms; all rooms have hot water. They offer free pick-up from the ranger station and the on-site restaurant serves up big platefuls of good, solid Tico food – the perfect preparation for a long day's hike. ❸

In and around Rivas

Albergue de Montaña Talari 7km off the Interamericana on the road to Rivas Ⓣ2771-0341, Ⓦwww.talari.co.cr. Eight brightly coloured rooms, all of which offer private bathroom with solar-heated shower, mosquito nets, fridge and a small terrace, set in twenty acres of tranquil riverside forest, with walking trails and a pool. An excellent restaurant prepares dishes according to local market availability, with a three-course evening meal costing $15. They also offer guided packages to Chirripó ($390 for three nights). ❺

Monte Azul Across the bridge to the right of the bus stop in Rivas ⓣ2752-5222, ⓦwww.monteazulcr.com. Posh, high-end boutique hotel that exudes a level of artistic style and refined comfort few places in the country can match. Choose from one of four spacious riverside *casitas*, each with bold colours and lines, a private garden and terrace and kitchen artwork. There's wi-fi throughout, free international calls, a gorgeous restaurant serving organic meals, a spa and a network of trails in its own nature reserve. Not an inexpensive option, but a fantastic deal nonetheless. ❽

Rancho La Botija del Sur Rivas ⓣ2770-2146, ⓦwww.rancholabotija.com. Eight *cabinas* with pretty bamboo ceilings, plus a freshwater swimming pool and a viewing tower overlooking the farm's coffee and banana plantations. Several large petroglyphs carved with pre-Columbian indigenous patterns have been discovered on the property, including the mysterious "Rock of the Indian", and can be seen on a daily tour (7–9am; $5 per person). ❻

Eating and drinking

Most of the hotels listed above have **restaurants** serving food well suited to loading up on before starting a hike to the summit. Alternatively, the long-established *Restaurante El Bosque*, (ⓣ2742-5020), diagonally opposite the ranger station in San Gerardo, serves tasty *bocas* and *casados*, and has table football and gorgeous views over the river below. There's a **pulpería**, Abastecedor Las Nubes (6.30am–8pm), across from the bus stop where you can stock up on supplies.

Dominical and around

The popular surfing town of **DOMINICAL**, 44km southeast of Quepos and 25km southwest of San Isidro, may represent the face of things to come along this stretch of the Pacific coast. Previously a secluded fishing village, it has, since the paving of the coastal road and the laying down of electricity and phone lines,

The Reserva Biológica Dúrika

Completely off the beaten track, the isolated **RESERVA BIOLÓGICA DÚRIKA** (ⓣ2730-0657, ⓦwww.durika.org) is a compelling mix of a agricultural-based community and private reserve where you can go on hikes and explore a working farm. Nestled within 21,000 acres of largely untouched and unexplored wilderness, it consists of only thirty or so permanent members (though it also is home to over twice as many semi-permanent residents and visitors). The community's farm has enabled them to be entirely self-sufficient, and they offer **tours** where you can learn firsthand about their organic approach to farming. Members also lead guided **hikes** to nearby Bribrí and Cabécar villages and into the wildlife-rich reserve, where a variety of habitats are home to several endangered species, including Baird's tapir. Guides also lead multi-day treks up one of Costa Rica's highest peaks, Cerro Dúrika (3280m), part of the Cordillera Talamanca that cuts through the reserve.

The nearest town of any size to the reserve is **Buenos Aires**, about 50km south of Chirripó, and signposted a few kilometres north off the Interamericana on a paved road. In town the foundation's office, just south of the Banco Nacional, can make reservations and provide information on the various tours and extended stay possibilities (call well in advance if you're considering the latter). The reserve is 17km northeast from Buenos Aires on a gravel road: a 4WD car is recommended for the journey, though it is possible to hire a taxi in town.

begun to expand dramatically. A glut of new hotels, shops and restaurants have opened in town, while the coastal areas to the south, still largely made up of unspoilt stretches of beach and rainforest, are rapidly being bought up by hungry property developers and hotel chains. It is, however, a good place to chill out by the beach and visit the nearby **Hacienda Barú** rainforest reserve, while the newly paved road to Quepos, which was finally completed in 2009, makes for easy access to the laidback village of **Matapalo**, 15km north.

Arrival and information

Buses from Quepos arrive daily at around 6.30am and 3pm, and continue onto San Isidro (2hr). There are 5 daily buses from San Isidro, which go on to Uvita. Nowadays you get to Dominical in any **car**, although it makes sense to rent a 4WD if you want to explore the surrounding area. **From San José** it is more convenient and faster to come via San Isidro; **from Guanacaste** and the Central Pacific, it's best to take the paved road south from Quepos.

The village's small **tourist office** (no phone; irregular hours) is in the central plaza on the turn-off from the highway just past the bridge. It has a good deal of information on the area and the beaches further south and offers internet access. There's a **bank** in the small plaza on the highway to the west of the turn-off into the village, with Dominical's biggest **supermarket** two doors down.

Accommodation

There's a broad range of good **accommodation** in the Dominical area. In the town itself, most lodgings are basic and cater to the surfing community, but you'll also find a number of more upmarket places, usually owned by foreigners. The most expensive hotels include some wonderful hideaways, good for honeymooners, romantics and escapists. There are also a string of increasingly lavish hotels and B&Bs along the coast road towards Uvita.

In Dominical

Cabinas San Clemente Down the main street and on the beach to the right ⓣ2787-0026. Attractive en-suite rooms (❸) plus basic but very clean dormitories with shared bathrooms ($16) for the surfer crowd who relax on the hammocks strung up on the balcony facing the sea. Surf-and boogie board rental available.

Cabinas Sun Dancer On the main street 50m west of the school ⓣ2787-0189. Twelve budget *cabinas* aimed squarely at the surfing community with basic, clean rooms, a small pool, the ubiquitous hammocks and a garden. They offer very cheap long-term rates. ❷

Domilocos 150m past the fork on the left ⓣ2787-0244, ⓦwww.domilocos.net. Something of a mixed bag, this attractive hotel on the beach has enviable features such as nicely furnished rooms with a/c and an excellent restaurant (see p.391). That said, the rooms are not always as tidy as you might expect; ask to see other rooms if you're not satisfied with what you're shown. ❺

Diuwak Hotel & Beach Resort Just off the main street 50m from the beach in front of the ICE electrical sub-station. ⓣ2787-0087, ⓦwww.diuwak.com. A glimpse into Dominical's future, *Diuwak* is an upmarket mini-resort offering 18 well-equipped *cabinas*, all with private bath (some with a/c) and wi-fi, extensive gardens, a supermarket, an internet café, a tour service and private parking. ❻

Río Lindo On the right as you enter Dominical ⓣ2787-0028, ⓦwww.riolindoresortcostarica.com. Eight comfortable rooms with private bathroom, a/c, some with satellite tv. There's also a lovely round pool, bar and whirlpool on the grounds and they offer horseriding, fishing and ATV tours. Price Includes breakfast. On Sunday there's a rotisserie BBQ with live music. ❻

Tortilla Flats Next to *Cabinas San Clemente* on the beach ⓣ2787-0033, ⓦtortillaflatsdominical.com. Popular surfers' hotel with eighteen brightly decorated en-suite rooms and a beachfront restaurant and bar where crowds gather in the evening to watch the sunset. They can arrange a variety of tours as well as spa treatments. ❸

Villas Río Mar Down a track to the right as you enter the village ⓣ2787-0052, ⓦwww.villasriomar.com. Comfortable, upmarket rooms in individual chalets with wi-fi and satellite tv; some have a/c. The rooms front extensive terraced gardens with a swimming pool, bar, spa, tennis court and jacuzzi. ❻

South of Dominical

Costa Paraiso 2km south of Dominical ⓣ2787-0025, ⓦwww.costa-paraiso.com. Set in beautifully landscaped grounds spreading down to a rocky coastline, this eye-catching hotel has just five exceedingly comfortable rooms, all with either a queen- or king-size bed, a/c, mini-fridge, microwave and wi-fi; some also have a stove. Breakfast (not included) is served in the open-air restaurant, with both a pool and the ocean a few steps away. ❼

Pacific Edge 3km south of Dominical in Escalaras; follow the signed left-hand fork ⓣ2787-8010, ⓦwww.pacificedge.info. Secluded, simple and comfortable, on a ridge 600m above the sea, with beautiful views of Cerro Chirripó and the beach. The four roomy chalets each have a private shower and hammocks. Delicious meals, including bangers and mash (one of the owners is English), can be ordered in advance. ❺

Roca Verde 1.5km south of Dominical ⓣ2787-0036, ⓦwww.rocaverde.net. Small, ritzy hotel in a wonderful position right on the beach. All rooms have en-suite bath, a/c and balcony, and there's also a swimming pool, table tennis and a restaurant serving Tex-Mex and American food. ❻

Villa Ambiente About 2.5km south of Dominical ⓣ2787-8453, ⓦwww.villaambiente.net. Striking whitewashed B&B nestling in the hills south of town and run by a Swiss family. The eight rooms are nicely appointed with a/c, TVs and terraces or balconies with prime views of the ocean below. The alluring large oval pool is almost worth a stay alone and the owners will do their best to make you feel right at home. ❼

The Town

Dominical consists of a dusty or muddy, unpaved, unnamed main street (where you'll find most of the town's bars and restaurants) and a beachfront road heading south from the Río Barú lined with hotels and surf schools. And that's about it – no park, no main square, no museums. In fact, there's no official town centre, unless you count the plaza that greets you as you turn off the highway. Dominical is expanding all the time, however, as more and more foreigners (principally but not exclusively Americans), lured by the promise of cheap accommodation and ever-improving facilities (not to mention the great surfing) decide to set up home and businesses here. The number of massage parlours and New Age remedy shops seems to grow by the month. **Bamboo Yogaplay**, (ⓣ2787-0229, ⓦwww.bambooyogaplay.com) on the right side of the main road toward the beach, offers some of the finest yoga classes in the area in an open-air studio ($12 per class). Beyond that, and aside from the surfing, sunbathing and other beach-based activities, there's not actually a great deal to do in the town itself. Events are staged throughout the year, usually catering to the sensibilities of the surfing crowd – Halloween and dance parties, film screenings and so on.

Activities

Surfing is the main draw in Dominical, and thousands of visitors flock here every year to ride the big waves that crash onto the town's dark-sand beach. Dominical is home to half a dozen surf schools offering lessons for around $50 per person for a two-hour session: the Green Iguana Surf Camp just back from the seafront (ⓣ2787-0157, ⓦwww.greeniguanasurfcamp.com) is a good bet. As is usual with surfing beaches, the **swimming** varies from not great to downright dangerous, and is plagued by riptides and crashing surf. About twenty minutes' walk south along the beach brings you to a small cove, where the water is calmer and you can paddle and snorkel.

There's also a good range of tours available from town, including the recommended **kayak** and **snorkelling trips** (from $60 per person) to the Parque Nacional Marino Ballena (see p.394) and Isla del Caño (see p.404) run by Costa

Rica Southern Expeditions, on the main road into the village (Ⓣ2787-0100, Ⓦwww.southernexpeditionscr.com). Away from the water, the best way to pass a half-day is on **Don Lulo's Nauyaca Falls Tour** ($45 per person including meals; Ⓣ&Ⓕ2787-0541, Ⓦwww.cataratasnauyaca.com;). The tour begins with a one-hour horse ride to Don Lulo's home and small private zoo for breakfast, before continuing on horseback through lush rainforest with knowledgeable guides to the two cascades that make up the Nauyaca Falls – the principal one drops 46m into a sparkling pool where you can swim. A *típico* lunch cooked over an open flame on the return trip completes the day. You'll need to reserve a place on the tour as far in advance as possible.

Eating and drinking

There's a handful of decent **places to eat** in and around the village as well as plenty of lively bars, the best being the beachfront *Tortilla Flats*, an expat hangout with great views of the sunset over the Pacific.

Café Delicias At the turn-off into the village Ⓣ2787-0097. Small café serving coffee and breakfast as well as inexpensive fruit smoothies, healthy sandwiches and baked goods throughout the day.

Coconut Spice At the end of the turn-off into the village Ⓣ2787-0033, Ⓦwww.coconutspice.com. Refined riverside restaurant serving up bona fide Southeast Asian flavour. The hot-and-sour Tom Yan Goong soup is recommended if you can take the chilli heat. There are also jumbo prawns, satays, curries and other Thai-influenced dishes. The atmosphere is much nicer and temperature much cooler out on the terrace.

ConFusione Inside *Domilocos* (see p.389). *ConFusione* would fit in just as well in Milan or Rome. A class act, and the only restaurant in town with linen napkins. Try the carpaccio di salmone ($9) or the seafood risotto ($9) and you'll see why the *Tico Times* said it's the best restaurant in the south of Costa Rica. Kitchen open till 11.30pm.

Kebab Divina Across from the tourist office in the central plaza Ⓣ8932-2207. Small kebab shack with a few outdoor tables. Though the setup is simple enough and the choices are limited, the friendly owners have clearly decided to focus on what they know best. A juicy chicken kebab with a Persian iced tea comes to about $8 and is the best quick meal in the village.

La Parcela 5km south of Dominical; take a signed right fork down to the beach, which then winds up onto the rocky point above; part of a gated luxury community Ⓣ2787-0016, Ⓦwww.laparcela.net. Fancy Italian restaurant with excellent food and great sea views. The only place where you can finish meals like ceviche and other seafood specialties with a delicious tropical flambé dessert prepared at your table.

San Clemente Bar and Grill On your left as you enter the village, just past the football pitch Ⓣ2787-0055. Large, breezy Tex-Mex restaurant that's popular with the surf crowd; there's a pool table and half-price cocktails on Tuesdays.

Soda Nanyoa On the main street opposite *Posada del Sol* Ⓣ2787-0164. This pleasant, airy diner serves a hybrid menu catering to the town's cosmopolitan population: *gallo pinto* and *casados* for the local Ticos; nachos and Philly cheese steak sandwiches for the American contingent.

Hacienda Barú

About a kilometre north of Dominical, the private rainforest reserve at **Hacienda Barú** (Ⓣ2787-0003, Ⓦwww.haciendabaru.com) comprises over three square kilometres of rainforest, mangroves and protected beach. There's enough here to occupy the best part of a day, with climbing trips where you winch yourself up extremely tall trees, hiking trails and an exhilarating canopy tour ($35), which involves swooping from platform to platform through primary rainforest on long steel cables, accompanied by guides who impart a wealth of forest folklore; a 16hr overnight hiking tour ($90) is also available. A great spot for birders and orchid lovers – 250 varieties grow around the reserve – there's also a butterfly enclosure and observation tower set high in the forest canopy. Take time to chat with the hacienda's owner, Jack Ewing, a committed environmentalist with lots of local knowledge. You can even stay on site in one of the comfortable self-catering chalets or in one of the lodge's rooms (❺).

Matapalo

Some 15km north of Dominical, **MATAPALO** is a sleepy village stretching for less than a kilometre along a sweeping grey-sand surf beach. Backed by mountains, the straggly seaside community is a blissfully underdeveloped blip on the Pacific coast and provides a rare glimpse of the Costa Rica of yesteryear. Here, sunbathing iguanas share the dusty street with children on bicycles, while a growing community of foreigners lives alongside a small Tico population.

Buses chugging between Quepos (1hr 30min–2hr) and Dominical (30min) can drop you off at the turn-off to the village, marked by *Pulpería la Espiral*, from where it's a 2km walk to the ocean and hotel strip. The **beach**, which enjoys monster waves and strong currents, has a dedicated team of local lifeguards patrolling on request. **Horse rides** along the beach and in the surrounding jungle ($30 for two hours) can be arranged through the *Jungle House* (see below), whose helpful American owner is the area's unofficial source of tourist **information** and can also arrange sports-fishing, **canopy tours**, **snorkelling** and **white-water rafting** excursions.

Accommodation

For its size, Matapalo has a wide range of **accommodation**, owned mostly by foreigners who have been waiting for years for the regional government to finally pave the road south from Quepos.

Albergue Suiza Near the entrance to the village ☎2787-5220. One of the better budget options, and particularly popular with Germans: six of its nine clean and straightforward *cabinas* have a/c; those that don't are a bit cheaper ($25). ❸

Cabinas el Coquito del Pacifico On the beach ☎2787-5031, Ⓦwww.elcoquitohotel.com. Six bungalows with private bath and fan (three have a/c), a bar-restaurant, a swimming pool and direct access to a wide and mostly deserted white-sand beach, good for bathing (but ask about currents). ❺

Dos Palmas A few hundred metres down the road from *Alberque Suiza* ☎2787-5037, Ⓦwww.dos-palmas.net. An intimate beachside bed and breakfast with two of the loveliest, brightest rooms in town. ❻

Dreamy Contentment ☎2787-5223, Ⓦwww.dreamycontentment.com. The last accommodation along the strip is also the most expensive. This beachside whitewashed colonial property set in landscaped tropical grounds has two self-contained bungalows with kitchenettes and a/c as well as a spacious main house ($150 a night) that can sleep four people and has a kitchen, lounge area, bathtub and laundry. ❻

Jungle House On the beach ☎2787-5005, Ⓔjunglehouse@gmail.com. More bachelor pad than nature lodge, *Jungle House* has a number of dark wooden-panelled rooms with leopard-print curtains and a/c. There's also a two-storey open-air cane house for those who aren't fazed by furry visitors. ❺

Eating

Given the lack of distractions, **eating** is a seriously popular pastime in Matapalo.

Restaurant Bay Bambú Up the road from *Tico Gringo* ☎2787-5013. American-run restaurant that boasts an artery-clogging international menu ranging from pork crackling to chicken and pasta in vodka sauce. Opens for breakfast at 8am.

Tico Gringo On the beach ☎2787-5023. Those craving a hamburger or perhaps some fried calamari and buffalo wings should drop by this friendly, surfside spot, where Eddie (the gringo) and his Tica wife Betty will set you up with an ice-cold beer under a thatch roof.

South of Dominical

The stretch of coast that runs south from Dominical to the lovely shallow bay at **Playa Tortuga** is one of the most pristine in Costa Rica. As a consequence, it's continually under siege from real-estate agents, who buy and sell plots of land as fast as they can persuade local fishermen and farmers to part with them. For the moment, though, this area encompasses a string of gloriously empty beaches as well as **Parque Nacional Marino Ballena** – fifty-six square kilometres of water around Uvita and Bahía created to safeguard the ecological integrity of the local marine life.

Bahía Ballena

Access to the lovely **BAHÍA BALLENA**, south of Dominical, is relatively easy, though the tiny hamlets of **Bahía** and **Uvita** are less visited that their northern neighbour, and not nearly as geared up for tourism. Visitors here will be amply rewarded with wide beaches washed by lazy breakers, palms swaying on the shore, and a hot, serene and very quiet atmosphere. This will no doubt change, as more people discover Bahía Ballena, but for the time being it's unspoilt.

There's not a lot to do here, but if you like hanging out on the beach, **surfing**, walking along rock ledges and spotting **dolphins** frolicking in the water, you'll be happy. You can also take **boat tours** around the bay and to the Isla del Caño or, if you have your own equipment, you can **snorkel** to your heart's content directly off the beaches.

From San Isidro, **buses** leave from the Transportes Blanco bus station, C 1, Av 4/6, twice daily at 9am and 4pm, heading for Uvita and Bahía via Dominical (1hr 30min).

Uvita

Of the two villages on Bahía Ballena, **Uvita**, which winds inland at the crossroads just north of the Río Uvita, is more developed. The Uvita **Information Center** (Mon–Sat 9am–noon and 1–6pm; Ⓣ8843-7142), across from the Banco de Costa Rica on the highway at the northern edge of the village, should be your first stop. Its extremely helpful staff can book a wide assortment of tours, both on the water and further inland: its boat trips include snorkelling and sports-fishing, though make sure that the boat has a good outboard motor and lifejackets on board, as you'll be out on the open Pacific.

There are a couple of decent **accommodation** options in the village, including the budget *Tucan Hotel* (Ⓣ2743-8140, Ⓦwww.tucanhotel.com), with backpacker-style dormitories for $10 as well as spartan private rooms (❷): wi-fi is available throughout and they can arrange surfing lessons ($30; 2hr). Taking a left at the second road north from the bus stop will bring you to *Cascada Verde* (Ⓣ2743-8191, Ⓦwww.cascadaverde.org; ❸), a great place for the nature-loving budget traveller. Five minutes' walk away from beautiful waterfalls and swimming holes, and only a few more minutes from Uvita's coconut-laden beaches, it has rustic private rooms (❸) and a dormitory loft ($12). It also offers vegetarian food, organic gardens, a kitchen, an ocean-view yoga deck, body and mind workshops, tours, Spanish classes and work exchange.

In the centre of the village, the modern Rincón de Uvita development houses **shops**, a gym, an indoor football field, a small Saturday morning **farmer's market** and a couple of **restaurants**. The better of the two is the moderately priced *Que Pura Vida* (Ⓣ2743-8387), with open-air seating: it serves home-made *comida típica* such as chicken with rice and beans as well as a few seafood dishes. Alternatively, the excellent *Gecko* restaurant at *La Cusinga Lodge* (see p.394) serves up the best meals in the area: dishes such as dorado with mango sauce are moderately priced and mostly made from locally grown or caught ingredients. Reservations are required for non-guests. The best place to stock up on **groceries** is La Carona, next to the Banco de Costa Rica at the northern edge of the village.

Bahía

Just over a kilometre or so further south from Uvita and accessed via two dirt roads branching off from the highway, tiny **Bahía** has a better location, on the lovely beach next to the Parque Nacional Marino Ballena, but a more limited tourist infrastructure. There are a few **hotels** to choose from, including the pleasant *Cabinas Bahía Uvita* (ⓣ2743-8016; ❺), to the right of the T-junction where the two dirt roads intersect: it has comfortable rooms with air conditioning, small huts (❶) and places to camp ($4). Alternatively, the more worn *Cabinas Punta Uvita* (ⓣ2743-8015; ❶), about 50m toward the beach from the T-junction, has basic, clean rooms and also permits camping in its grounds ($4). However, if you're keen on exploring the area in depth, and have the funds to finance it, your best bet is to book a stay at *La Cusinga Lodge* (ⓣ2770-2549, ⓦwww.lacusingalodge.com; ❼), just past the Puente Uvita. One of the country's best eco-lodges and one of the few owned and run by Ticos, it occupies a gorgeous rainforest setting overlooking the Parque Nacional Marino Ballena and is an excellent example of how the environment can be preserved for both the benefit of tourists and the local community. Its seven *cabinas* are all made of wood from the lodge's sustainable teak plantation; all the electricity is provided by solar and hydro power; and there's an education centre where local children can come and learn about the area. It has an excellent restaurant (see p.393), as well as trails leading down from the lodge through rainforest (inhabited by howler and white-faced monkeys) to a beautiful stretch of quiet beach.

Parque Nacional Marino Ballena

Created in 1990, the **PARQUE NACIONAL MARINO BALLENA** ($10; ⓣ2743-8236; ⓦwww.marinoballena.org) protects an area of ocean and coastline south of Uvita that contains one of the biggest chunks of **coral reef** left on the Pacific coast. It's also the habitat of **humpback whales**, who come here from the Arctic and Antarctica to breed – although they are spotted very infrequently (Dec–April is best) – and **dolphins**. The main threats to the ecological survival of these waters is the disturbance caused by shrimp trawling, sedimentation as a result of deforestation (rivers bring silt and pollutants into the sea and kill the coral) and dragnet fishing, which often entraps whales and dolphins.

On land, the sandy and rocky beaches fronting the ocean are also protected, as is **Punta Uvita** – a former island connected to the mainland by a narrow land bridge. At low tide, you can walk from the point along the 1km **Tómbolo of Punta Uvita trail**, which stretches out into the sea and resembles a whale's tail. At certain times of the year (usually May–Oct), olive ridley and hawksbill **turtles** may come ashore to nest, but in nowhere near the same numbers as at other turtle nesting grounds in the country. If you want to see the turtles, talk first to the rangers (see below) and, whatever you do, remember the ground rules of turtle-watching: come at night with a torch, watch where you walk (partly for snakes), keep well back from the beach and don't shine the light right on the turtles. Note that the coastline is patrolled by volunteers working for the Parque Nacional Marino Ballena, who walk the beaches at night warning off poachers. Other than spotting nesting turtles or dolphins and whales frolicking from the shore, the best way to take in the park's abundant marine life is either **snorkelling** (tours and prices vary), or in a **kayak** ($75; 5hr), both of which can be arranged at the Uvita information centre (see p.393).

The park has four **beach entrances**, from north to south at playas Uvita, Colonia, Ballena and Pinuela, with **ranger stations** at each entrance. All the ranger stations provide **information** about the park, nearby picnic areas, as well as basic shower and toilet facilities, except at Uvita. It is possible to **camp** within the park, but only at spots well away from the high tide line; ask a ranger first.

Playa Tortuga

Heading south on the coastal road, Highway 34 (also known as the Costanera Sur), you'll come to **PLAYA TORTUGA**, about halfway between Dominical and Palmar. The beach here is one of the cleanest in Costa Rica, and it's an idyllic, sleepy place that sees few foreigner visitors. You'll find a couple of very good **hotels** close to the beach: *Posada Playa Tortuga* (Ⓣ2384-5489; ❻) has comfortable rooms, a large swimming pool with Jacuzzi and an amazing view, while *Villas Gaia* (Ⓣ2244-0316, Ⓦwww.villasgaia.com; ❺) offers twelve brightly coloured *cabinas* – some with air coditioning – a pool and an attractive restaurant. It also runs a range of tours including snorkelling at Isla del Caño and boat trips around the local mangrove swamps.

Palmar and around

Some 30km south of Playa Tortuga, where Highway 34 joins the Interamericana, and about 100km north of the Panamá border, the small, prefab town of **PALMAR** serves as the hub for the area's banana plantations. This is a good place to see **lithic spheres** (see box below), which are scattered on the lands of several nearby plantations and on the way to Sierpe, 15km south on the Río Sierpe. Ask politely for the "*esferas de piedra*"; if the banana workers are not too busy they may be able to show you where to look. Palmar also makes a useful jumping-off point for visiting the nearby **Reserva Indígena Boruca**, where you can buy local crafts from the indigenous population.

Palmar is divided in two by the Río Grande de Térraba: **Palmar Sur** contains the airport, which is scheduled to be the third Costa Rican airport to take international flights, while most of the services, including hotels and buses, are in **Palmar Norte**. Osa Tours (Ⓣ2786-7825, Ⓔcatuosa@racsa.co.cr) in the Centro Comercial del Norte in Palmar Norte, has **tourist information**, can help with reservations and transport and also sells stamps; you can make international telephone calls and

Lithic spheres

Aside from goldworking, the Diquis are known for their precise fashioning of large stone **spheres**, most of them exactly spherical to within a centimetre or two – an astounding feat for a culture without technology. Thousands have been found in southwestern Costa Rica and a few in northern Panamá. Some are located in sites of obvious significance, like burial mounds, while others are found in the middle of nowhere; they range in size from that of a tennis ball up to about two metres in diameter.

The spheres' original function and meaning remain obscure, although they sometimes seem to have been arranged in positions mirroring those of the constellations. In many cases the Diquis transported them a considerable distance, rafting them across rivers or the open sea (the only explanation for their presence on Isla del Caño), indicating that their placement was deliberate and significant. (Ironically, some of the posher Valle Central residences now have stone spheres – purchased at a great price – sitting in their front gardens as lawn sculpture.)

You can see lithic spheres in and around **Palmar** (there are a few sizeable ones in the park across from the airport) and also on **Isla del Caño**, which is mostly easily accessed on a tour run by one of the lodges in Bahía Drake (see p.401).

receive Western Union money transfers here too. The town's **accommodation** options are fairly limited: *Casa Amarilla*, 300m east of the TRACOPA bus stop (Ⓣ2786-7251; ❶), has clean rooms with private bath and fan; the upstairs ones have balconies and better ventilation. A more comfortable choice is the *Brunka Lodge* (Ⓣ2786-7489, Ⓦwww.brunkalodge.com; ❹) a block and a half south of the Interamericana, just beyond the Banco Nacional: the 25 cabins are pleasantly furnished and have cable TV and wi-fi and there are two pools and a restaurant.

From **San José**, TRACOPA **buses** run to Palmar Norte seven times daily and take five and a half hours, with the last one returning to the capital at 6.30pm. Transportes Térraba buses for **Sierpe** leave Palmar Norte from in front of the Banco Coopealianza (6 daily; 30min), with the first bus leaving at 4.30am. Buses heading north to **Uvita** (45min) and **Dominical** (1hr 30min) leave from the bus stop at the intersection with coastal Highway 34.

Boruca and the Reserva Indígena Boruca

About 13km east of Palmar on the Interamericana, and then 18km up a car- and body-rattling road, is the village of **BORUCA**, within the **Reserva Indígena Boruca.** The village is known for its local **crafts**, with the women making small tablecloths and purses on home-made looms, while the men fashion balsa-wood masks, some of which are expressly intended for the *diablitos* (little devils) ceremony (see box below) and procession that takes place on New Year's Eve. You can buy either from the artisans themselves or from the local cooperative, the Boruca Artesanías Group – it'll help if you have at least a working knowledge of Spanish. Local people have little other outlet for their crafts (you won't find them in the San José shops), so a visit can be a good way of contributing to the local economy. Note that you'll need a 4WD to get here.

South to Panamá

At Palmar, travellers heading south face a choice: most people intent on the quickest route to Panamá stick to the Interamericana, which heads south for the

The Borucas and the Fiesta de los Diablitos

Many indigenous peoples throughout the isthmus, and all the way north to Mexico, enact the **Fiesta de los Diablitos**, a resonant spectacle that is both disturbing and humorous. In Costa Rica the Borucas use it to celebrate New Year and to re-enact the Spanish invasion, with Columbus, Cortez and his men reborn every year. The fiesta takes place over three days and is a village affair: foreigners and tourists are not encouraged to come as spectators.

On the first day a village man is appointed to play the bull; others disguise themselves as little devils (*diablitos*), with burlap sacks and masks carved from balsa wood. The *diablitos* taunt the bull, teasing him with sticks, while the bull responds in kind. At midnight on December 30 the *diablitos* congregate on the top of a hill, joined by musicians playing simple flutes and horns fashioned from conch shells. During the whole night and over the next three days, the group proceeds from house to house, visiting everyone in the village and enjoying a drink or two of home brew (*chicha*). On the third day, the "bull" is ritually killed. The symbolism is indirect, but the bull, of course, represents the Spaniard(s), and the *diablitos* the indigenous people. The bull is always vanquished and the *diablitos* always win – which of course is not quite how it turned out, in the end.

final 100km to Panamá. This section of the trip down to the **Paso Canoas** border crossing is through an empty featureless, frontier region, with the refuelling point of **Ciudad Neily** the only point of minor interest.

The alternative route is to head east along the Interamericana, which switchbacks its way to the small, sleepy town of **Paso Real**, 20km away, following the wide and fast-running **Río Grande de Térraba** as it cuts a giant path through the almost unbearably hot lowland landscape, its banks coloured red with tropical soils. Rainstorms seem to steamroller in with the express purpose of washing everything away, and you can almost see the river rise with each fresh torrent. This stretch is prone to landslides in the rainy season, when you can find yourself stranded by a sea of mud.

At Paso Real, you can pick up the paved **Hwy-237**, which takes you south through some spectacularly scenic country. Steep and winding, with beautiful views, it is little used by tourists except those few heading to the pretty mountain town of **San Vito**, the jumping-off point for the **Wilson Botanical Gardens**, **Parque Internacional La Amistad** and the **Río Serena** border crossing. Even though the roads around here have improved, it's much easier with a 4WD to deal with occasional washouts and landslides, especially from May to November.

San Vito and the Wilson Botanical Gardens

Settled largely by post-World War II immigrants from Italy, **SAN VITO** is a clean, prosperous agricultural town with a lovely setting in the Talamancas. At nearly 1000m above sea level it has a wonderfully refreshing climate, as well as great views over the Valle de Coto Brus below. The town is growing as Costa Ricans discover its qualities, and will soon be an important regional hub, though for now there's nothing to do around here but visit the nearby **Wilson Botanical Gardens** (daily 7.30am–4.30pm; $10), 6km to the south. The gardens are among the best in the country, and on the itineraries of many specialist birdwatching and natural history tours. The huge tract of land is home to orchids, interesting tropical trees and exotic flowers such as heliconias. There's good **birding** too, on the paths and in the surrounding lands, home to more than 300 species in total. They make an excellent day-trip if you happen to be in the area, but unless you have a keen interest in birds and regional and exotic flora it's probably not worth making a special trip from San José. You can **stay** at the gardens in bunkhouses (❷) or *cabinas* with private bath (❻). Students and researchers with ID get reduced rates. Contact the Organization for Tropical Studies, or OTS (Ⓣ2524-0607, Ⓦwww.ots.ac.cr) for details; you must reserve in advance.

Parque Internacional La Amistad

Created in 1982 as a biosphere reserve, the **PARQUE INTERNACIONAL LA AMISTAD** (daily 8am–3.45pm; $10) is a joint venture by the governments of Panamá and Costa Rica to protect the Talamancan mountain areas on both sides of their shared border. Amistad also encompasses several **indigenous reserves**, the most geographically isolated in the country, where Bribrí and Cabécar peoples are able to live with minimal interference from the Valle Central. It is the largest park in the country, covering 2070 square kilometres of Costa Rican territory.

In 1983 Amistad was designated a World Heritage Site, thanks to its immense scientific resources. The Central American isthmus is often described as being a crossroads or filter for the meeting of the North and South American eco-communities; the Amistad area is itself a "biological bridge" within the isthmus, where an extraordinary number of habitats, life zones, topographical features, soils, terrains and types of animal and plant life can be found. Its **terrain**, while mainly mountainous, is extremely varied on account of shifting altitudes, and ranges from wet tropical forest to high peaks where the temperature can drop below freezing at night. According to the classification system devised by L.R. Holdridge (see Contexts), Amistad has at least seven (some say eight or nine) **life zones**, along with six transition zones. Even more important is Amistad's function as the last bastion of some of the species most in danger of **extinction** in both Costa Rica and the isthmus. Within its boundaries roam the jaguar and the puma, the ocelot and the tapir. Along with Corcovado on the Península de Osa, Amistad may also be the last holdout of the **harpy eagle**, feared extinct in Costa Rica.

The trails

Its rugged terrain limits access to much of the park, but there are two **trails** that depart from the Altamira ranger station (see below). If you're hiking solo, your only option is the **Gigantes del Bosque** trail, a 3km-long round-route that meanders through mostly primary rainforest. There are two towers along the way, the first of which is ideal for **birdwatching**, particularly just after daybreak which is the best time to see some of the 400 species that live in the park. The path is reasonably well marked, but not always maintained, and tall grass often grows over parts of the latter half of the trail: allow between 2–3hr to make the loop.

Much longer and far more exhausting is the **Valle del Silencio** trail, which is 20km long and provides an excellent introduction to the varied habitats found in La Amistad. The trail climbs steadily to a campsite on a flat ridge near the base of Cerro Kamuk, offering stunning vistas of the park and further afield en route. There's a good chance of spotting **wildlife** along the way, possibly including quetzals and Baird's tapirs, which are thought to have larger populations here than anywhere else in the country. The trail takes about eight to ten-hour round-trip and you cannot hike it without a guide; the park ranger at the Altamira station can make arrangements.

Park practicalities

The small hamlet of **Altamira**, 25km northeast of San Vito, functions as the park headquarters, with a ranger station (☎2200-5355) maintained by a full-time ranger who can provide **information**. You can **camp** here ($5) and there are shower and toilet facilities. You'll need a 4WD to get to the ranger station, whatever the season; there is no public transport.

Near Las Tablas, bordering the park, *La Amistad Eco-Lodge*, 3km from the hamlet of Las Mellizas on the way to Sabalito (☎2289-7667; ❻) has comfortable rustic rooms. It's on the Montero family farm, which also grows organic coffee and has a few kilometres of trails in its surrounding woods – the Monteros can provide transport if you ask in advance.

Sabalito and the Río Sereno border crossing into Panamá

About 15km east of San Vito, the tiny village of **Sabalito** is the nearest community of any size to the Río Sereno border crossing into Panamá. From here you can catch one of five buses daily that arrive from San Vito and continue on to the border (15min). Ask the driver to drop you off at the Costa Rican **migración** to avoid walking up a hill with your bags: after clearing customs, you can walk to Panamá's *migración*. Once in Río Sereno on the Panamanian side, walk down the main street to the station at the street's end. From here you can catch a bus that will take you onto David and La Concepción in Panamá.

Crossing into Panamá

To cross from Costa Rica into Panamá, most nationalities need a **tourist card**; UK citizens need only show their passport. Tourist cards should be collected in advance from the **Panamanian consulate**, or from the office of Copa, Panamá's national airline, in San José. Many people also need a **visa** – Canadians, Australians and New Zealanders among them. You may also need a return ticket back to Costa Rica (or an onward ticket out of Panamá to another country), but bear in mind that immigration requirements frequently change, seemingly at whim, so always check with the Panamanian consulate before setting off.

Ciudad Neily

If you're making your way south to the Paso Canoas border crossing, soporific **CIUDAD NEILY** makes a good spot to stock up on any last-minute supplies before you cross into Panamá (18km away). Though it is one of the largest towns in the southern third of the country and the point where the Interamericana and Hwy-237 converge, there's not much to detain you and chances are you'll pass through it quickly en route to Panamá.

Hwy-237 runs right down the middle of Ciudad Neily, before ending at the Interamericana; all the town's services are within a couple of blocks either side of it. **Buses** from San José (4 daily) and San Isidro El General (4 daily) arrive at the Terminal Tracopa, a couple of blocks uphill and east of Hwy-237 in the centre of town. There's a Banco Popular on Hwy-237 at the northern end of town and a Banco Nacional branch a couple of blocks south, with **internet cafés** adjacent to both banks. The biggest **supermarket** in Ciudad Neily (and surely all of southern Costa Rica) is the Loaiza, a block northeast of the Banco Nacional. If you need to **stay overnight**, make a beeline for the pretty *Hotel Andrea* (☎2783-3784; ❹), just west of the bus terminal, which has comfortable rooms with fans or air conditioning and an open-air restaurant that serves hearty and inexpensive *comida típica* meals.

Paso Canoas and the Panamanian border

South of Neily duty-free shops and stalls start to line the Interamericana announcing the approach to **PASO CANOAS**, about 17km beyond Neily. As you come into town, either driving or on the TRACOPA or international Ticabus service, you'll pass the Costa Rican customs checkpoint, where everybody gets a going-over. Foreigners don't attract much interest, however; customs officials are far more concerned with nabbing Ticos coming back over the border with unauthorized amounts of bargain consumer goods. Barring a build-up of buses, the Paso Canoas crossing is generally quicker than the Río Sereno crossing, if much less scenic.

The **migración** is on the Costa Rican side, next to the TRACOPA bus terminal. You'll have to wait in line, especially if a San José–David–Panamá City Ticabus comes through, as all international bus passengers are processed together. Arrive early to get through fastest. There's no problem **changing money**: there's a Banco Nacional on the Costa Rican side of the border and, beyond that, plenty of moneychangers. Note that Panamá has no paper currency of its own, and US dollars – called *balboas* – are used. It does have its own coins, however, which are equivalent to US coins and in wide circulation. Also beware that you cannot take any **fruit or vegetables** across the border, even if they're for your lunch; they will be confiscated.

If you absolutely have to bed down in Paso Canoas, there are about a dozen rock-bottom budget **cabinas** and *hospedajes*. These are all extremely basic, with cell-like rooms, private bath and cold water. They can also be full at weekends. One place a cut above the pack is *Cabinas Interamericano* (☎2732-2041; ❶), on a side road to the right after the TRACOPA bus terminal, heading towards the border: the rooms aren't bad, and there's a restaurant.

Buses run from the Panamanian border bus terminal (every hour or so until 5pm) to **DAVID**, the first city of any size in Panamá and about ninety minutes beyond the border. From David it's easy to pick up local services, including the Ticabus to Panamá City, which you can't get at the border.

Península de Osa

In the extreme south of the country, the **Península de Osa** is an area of immense biological diversity, somewhat separate from the mainland, and few will fail to be moved by its beauty. Whether you approach the peninsula by *lancha* from Sierpe or Golfito, on the Jiménez bus, driving in from the mainland, or – especially – by air, you'll see what looks like a floating island – an intricate mesh of blue and green, with tall canopy trees sailing high and flat like elaborate floral hats. A surfeit of natural wonder awaits, from the sweeping arc of **Bahía Drake** in the northwest and the world-class diving and snorkelling spots of nearby **Isla del Caño** to one of the planet's most biologically rich pockets, **Parque Nacional Corcovado**, which covers the bulk of the peninsula. In the early years of the twentieth century, Osa was something of a penal colony; a place to which men were either sent forcibly or went, machete in hand, to forget. Consequently, a violent, frontier-lands folklore permeates the whole peninsula, and old-time residents of **Puerto Jiménez** are only too happy to regale you with hosts of gory tales. Some may be apocryphal, but they certainly add colour to the place.

You could feasibly explore the whole peninsula in four days, but this would be rushing it, especially if you want to spend time walking the trails and wildlife-spotting at Corcovado. Most people allot five to seven days for the area, taking it at a relaxed pace, and more if they want to stay in and explore Bahía Drake. Hikers and walkers who come to Osa without their own car tend to base themselves in Puerto Jiménez – a place where it's easy to strike up a conversation, and people are relaxed, environmentally conscientious and not yet overwhelmed by tourism.

Some history

It was on the Península de Osa that the Diquis found **gold** in such abundant supply that they hardly had to pan or dig for it. Indeed, the precious metal can still be found today, as can the odd *orero* (goldminer/panner). When Parque Nacional Corcovado was established in the mid-1970s, substantial numbers of miners were panning within its boundaries, but the heaviest influx of *oreros* stemmed directly from the pull-out of the United Brands Company in 1985. Many were laid-off banana plantation workers with no other means of making a living. They resorted to panning for gold, an activity that posed a threat to the delicate ecosystem of the park – and a clear example of how the departure of a large-scale employer can lead to environmental destruction. In 1986 the *oreros* were forcibly deported from the park by the Costa Rican police. Today, several well-known international conservationist groups are involved in protecting and maintaining Osa's ecological integrity.

A revealing picture of *precarista* (squatter) life on the country's extreme geographical margins persists in the peninsula. Since the 1980s, when the road between Jiménez and Rincón was improved, many families have arrived here seeking land. Most have built simple shacks and cultivated a little roadside plot, burning away the forest to do so. They plant a few vegetables and a banana patch and may keep a few cattle. Soil here is classically tropical, with few nutrients, poor absorption and minimal regenerative capacity. In a few years it will have exhausted itself and the smallholders will have to cultivate new areas or move on.

Bahía Drake and around

BAHÍA DRAKE (pronounced "Dra-kay") is named after Sir Francis Drake, who anchored here in 1579. Today a favourite spot for sailors, the calm waters of the bay are dotted with flotillas of swish-looking yachts. This is one of the most stunning areas in Costa Rica, with the blue wedge of **Isla del Caño** floating just off the coast, and fiery-orange Pacific sunsets. The bay is rich in marine life, and a number of **boat trips** offer opportunities for spotting manta rays, marine turtles, porpoises and even whales. The bay's lone settlement of any size is the sprawling village of **Aguijitas**, which acts as the area's main transport hub.

Accommodation

Accommodation is clustered either in the tiny village of Agujitas itself, or on Punta Agujitas, the rocky point on the other side of Río Agujitas. It's worth noting that every lodge beyond *Aguila de Osa* is off the main electricity grid and therefore runs diesel generators, which, while hidden, are not always silent. Virtually all the eco-lodges listed below offer a range of **tours**, from guided excursions to Corcovado to boat trips around Bahía Drake and out to Isla del Caño. The larger lodges often bring visitors on packages from San José and can include transport from the capital, from Palmar, or from Sierpe. The packages usually include three meals a day – there are few eating options in Bahía Drake otherwise – and all the price codes given below include full-board. Although hoteliers say you can't **camp** in the Drake area, people do – if you want to join them, pitch your tent considerately and be sure to leave no litter.

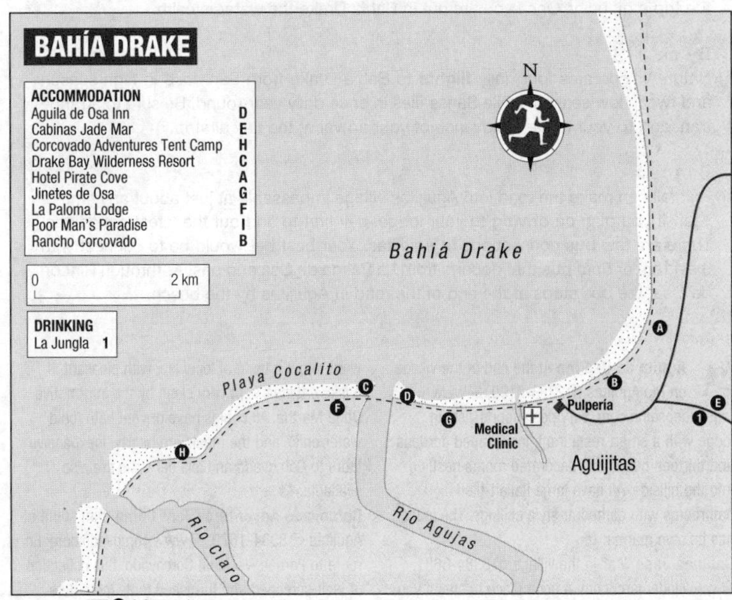

Getting to Bahía Drake

Like many other places in Zona Sur, **getting to Bahía Drake** requires some planning. There are four options: the really tough way, hiking in from Corcovado; the cheap way, by bus from San José and then by boat along the Río Sierpe; the bumpy way, by 4WD along the gravel and dirt road between Rincón and Aguijitas (which is impassible at various times of the year); and the luxury way, flying from San José to Drake, and taking one of the many **packages** offered by hotels in the area. If you do this, transport to your lodge is taken care of.

By boat from Sierpe

Travelling independently, you'll need to get a bus from San José to Palmar; depending on what time you get in, you can then either bed down in Palmar Norte for the night or get a local bus (see p.395) or taxi to **Sierpe** (about $12), where there are a few *cabinas*. If you're coming from San José and hoping to make it to Drake on the same day, you'll need to catch the 5am bus. In Sierpe, you must find a **boatman** to take you the 30km downriver to Bahía Drake, a journey of one hour. You'll need someone with experience, a motorized *lancha*, and lifejackets: ask Sonia Rojas at the Fenix *pulpería* to help you find someone or try the riverfront bar of the *Hotel Oleaje Sereno* or the *Bar Las Vegas*, both of which are popular hangouts for boat captains. The going rate for a one-way trip to Drake is about $20–30 per person or around $65–85 per boatload (maximum usually eight). Some hotel *lanchas* will take independent travellers if there's room, but be sure to arrive early; note that owing to fierce afternoon tides, the last *lancha* leaves at around 3.30pm.

The trip down the mangrove-lined Río Sierpe is calm enough (you can spot monkeys, sloths and sometimes kingfishers), until you see the Pacific rolling in at the mouth of the river. The Sierpe is very wide where it meets the sea, and huge breakers crash in from the ocean, making it a turbulent and treacherous crossing (sharks reportedly wait here for their dinner). If the tide is right and the boatman knows his water, you'll be fine. All the *lanchas* used by the lodges have powerful outboard motors, and there's little chance of an accident; all the same, some find this part of the trip a bit hairy. Once you are out in Bahía Drake the water is calm.

By air

NatureAir operates four daily **flights** to Bahía Drake from San José in high season and two in low season, while Sansa flies in once daily year-round. Be sure to arrange transport to your lodge in advance of your arrival at the tiny airstrip.

By road

Rainfall can make the road into Aguijitas village impassable at just about any time of year; if you plan on **driving** to your lodge, call first to find out the latest conditions. There are few **bus** connections to Aguijitas. Your best bet would be to connect with the 11am or 5pm **bus** that departs from La Palma de Osa and passes through Rincón de Osa; the bus stops at the end of the road in Aguijitas by the beach.

Aguila de Osa Inn At the end of the village on Río Agujitas ☎2296-2190, Ⓦwww.aguiladeosainn.com. Very posh sports-fishing lodge with a smart restaurant, landscaped gardens and thirteen beautifully decorated rooms nestling into the hillside. All have large Italian-tiled bathrooms with cathedral-style ceilings. The lodge has its own marina. ❽

Cabinas Jade Mar In the village ☎8384-6681, Ⓦwww.jademarcr.com. A good place to stay if you want to get a taste of local life, with pleasant, if basic, *cabinas*, kept very clean by the informative Doña Martha. All cabins have private bath (cold water only), and the meals are hearty. Inexpensive tours to Corcovado and Isla del Caño are also available. ❹

Corcovado Adventures Tent Camp 2km south of Agujitas ☎8384-1679, Ⓦwww.corcovado.com. En route to Parque Nacional Corcovado, this collection of well-screened and furnished tents (complete with beds and tables) sits on platforms on an isolated beach facing the sea. 6

Drake Bay Wilderness Resort Punta Agujitas ⓣ2775-1715, ⓦwww.drakebay.com. The most established lodge in the area, providing a buffer zone between tourist and wilderness with rustic, comfortable *cabinas* or, if you want to rough it a bit, well-appointed tents – both options are well screened. There's hearty local food available, and the camp also has its own solar-heated water supply, night-time electricity, plus excellent snorkelling and canoeing. It's pricey at about $695 for three nights, but this includes air transfers from San José (and free laundry). 8

Hotel Pirate Cove About 2km north of Agujitas ⓣ2234-6154, ⓦwww.piratecovecostarica.com. Seven en-suite tent-style *cabinas* (including three very large family *cabinas*) in a lush rainforest overlooking a pristine two-kilometre stretch of beach. The excellent restaurant serves Costa Rican and European cuisine. Tours of Parque Nacional Corcovado and Isla del Caño are offered. 6

Jinetes de Osa Between Punta Agujitas and Agujitas ⓣ2231-5806, ⓦwww.costaricadiving.com. Right on the main beach, this is one of the less expensive options in Bahía Drake. The accommodation is clean, simple and comfortable – you might even hear monkeys hanging out on the roof. There's an on-site PADI dive school run by two American brothers, as well as the only canopy tours in Drake Bay. 4

La Paloma Lodge Punta Agujitas ⓣ2293-7502, ⓦwww.lapalomalodge.com. Beautiful, rustic rooms in hilltop bungalows, with private bath, balconies and hammocks. The airy, two-storey bungalows are best, surrounded by forest and boasting spectacular views, particularly at sunset. Kayaks, boogie boards and snorkelling gear are available for guests to explore the Río Agujitas behind the lodge, and there's an attractively tiled swimming pool. Excellent service with friendly and helpful staff, but astoundingly expensive. Three-night packages start at $1195 and include return airfare from San José, all meals and guided tours to Isla del Caño and Corcovado.

Poor Man's Paradise Past Playa San Josecito, just beyond the San Pedrillo entrance on the way to Bahía Drake ⓣ2771-4582, ⓦwww.mypoormansparadise.com. One of the most secluded lodges in what is, after all, a pretty secluded area. The tent-style *cabinas* are set in pretty gardens and have ocean views. A mixture of private and shared bathrooms are available and you can also camp in the grounds for $8 per person. Meals are served in the lodge's lovely indigenous-style thatched-roof restaurant. 4

Proyecto Campanario Near Sierpe ⓣ2258-5778, ⓦwww.campanario.org. Established by ex-Peace Corps volunteers, this remote field station, reachable via a three-day hike or by boat from Sierpe, offers courses in tropical ecology and tour "packages" for hardy eco-tourists not fazed by its isolation. Tours consist of short walks, long hikes or all-day expeditions to the Reserva Biológica Campanario or Parque Nacional Corcovado as well as trips to deforested and impacted areas to talk to local communities. They also offer snorkelling and scuba-diving excursions to the Isla del Caño. Six-night "rainforest conservation camps" start at $724 and include accommodation, transportation, all meals and activities. 8

Rancho Corcovado On the beach in front of Agujitas ⓣ2241-7083, ⓦwww.ranchocorcovado.com. Set on the best part of the beach for swimming, this family-run hotel has beautiful views over the bay and 14 simple, clean en-suite rooms. You can camp in the grounds ($10 per person), or take one of their camping or horseriding tours. They also have three boats, and competitive rates for trips to Isla del Caño. 8

Agujitas and the bay

Bahía Drake and its tiny hamlet of **Agujitas** make a good base to explore the Parque Nacional Corcovado on the northwest of the Península de Osa – the park's San Pedrillo entrance is within a day's walk, and hikers can combine serious trekking with serious comfort by staying at one of the region's upmarket rainforest eco-lodge-type hotels. Other than the lodges and a couple of inexpensive, locally run hotels in Agujitas, there are very few facilities here, though the village does have a small *pulpería* with a radio phone and **medical clinic**, Hospital Clinica Biblica, on the beach. Nightlife options are limited to *La Jungla*, a cute bar in the village across the street from *Cabinas Jade Mar*.

Beyond trips to Corcovado and Isla del Caño, there is one activity not to be missed in Bahía Drake: the **evening insect tour** ($35 per person; reservations required; ⓦwww.thenighttour.com; 2hr 30min) led by an enthusiastic American biologist known as "Tracie the Bug Lady". The tour departs from a few of the bay's lodges and explores the fascinating world of nocturnal insects, arachnids and

Hiking to Corcovado from Agujitas

From Agujitas you can follow the 17km-long **beachside trail** via Marenco to the San Pedrillo entrance of Parque Nacional Corcovado (see p.413), a walk of around eight to twelve hours. You can **camp** at San Pedrillo, though you should inform the Fundación de Parques Nacionales in advance by contacting the Puerto Jiménez office (☎2735-5036). If you are staying at any of the Bahía Drake lodges, they should be able to contact the Puerto Jiménez office of Corcovado and make a reservation for you to stay and eat in San Pedrillo with the rangers.

other animals; with luck you might spot a trapdoor spider or a caecilian, an extremely rare and little-known amphibian.

Isla del Caño

The tiny **RESERVA BIOLÓGICA ISLA DEL CAÑO** ($10) sits placidly in the ocean some 20km due west of Bahía Drake. Just 3km long by 2km wide, the uninhabited island is the exposed part of an underwater mountain, thrown up by an ancient collision of the two tectonic plates on either side of Costa Rica. It's a pretty sight in the distance, and going there is even better – if you can afford it. You can't get there on your own, but a **tour** is usually included in the package price of the Bahía Drake lodges. Alternatively, tours are increasingly run by operators in Dominical (p.388).

The island is thought to have been a burial ground of the Diquis, who brought their famed **lithic spheres** here from the mainland in large, ocean-going canoes. Your guide can take you hiking into the thick rainforest interior to look for examples near the top of the 110-metre-high crest, and you'll probably see some en route too, as the trail passes a few groups of them. Caño is also a prime **snorkelling** and diving destination; there are six dive sites around the island. Underwater you'll see coral beds and a variety of **marine life**, including spiny lobsters and sea cucumber, snapper, sea urchins, manta rays, octopus and the occasional barracuda. On the surface, porpoises and olive ridley turtles are often spotted, along with less frequent sightings of humpback and even sperm whales.

Puerto Jiménez

The peninsula's biggest town, relaxed **PUERTO JIMÉNEZ** – known locally simply as Jiménez – has plenty of places to stay and eat and good public transport connections. It caters mainly to the budget end of the spectrum, its basic *cabinas* in a whole different class and price range from the luxury lodges (many American-owned) lining the road to Carate, 43km southwest (see p.408). From Jiménez, you can also take a *colectivo* truck, the local transport, to Carate from where it's possible to enter Corcovado.

Arrival and information

Three **buses** arrive daily from San José (C 12, Av 7/9), one of which is direct (noon; 8hr), while the other two arrive via San Isidro (11.30am & 5pm; 9hr). One daily bus leaves Jiménez for San Jose at noon from the **bus station** one block west of the football field where you can also buy tickets (open daily 7–11am & 1–5pm). A **lancha** departs Golfito for Puerto Jiménez daily at 11am (1hr 30min), returning to Golfito daily at 6am. You can **fly** in from San José with Sansa or NatureAir, or from Quepos with NatureAir.

The best source of **tourist information** is *CafeNet el Sol* (☎2735-5702, Ⓦwww.soldeosa.com), one block south of the football field on the main street.

Getting around

The main form of local public transport, the *colectivo*, departs one block south of the bus station in Jiménez to **Carate** ($10), twice daily (except Sundays in the dry season) at about 6am and 1.30pm. Note that it's an achingly bumpy drive and involves the careful negotiation of at least half a dozen small (and in the rainy season not so small) rivers. The *colectivo* will drop you off at any of the lodges between Jiménez and Carate, and will also pick you up on its way back to town if you arrange this in advance – ask the driver. If you don't get a place on the truck, a number of local taxi drivers have 4WDs. The *colectivo* also heads to **Bahía Drake** on Mondays and Fridays at noon (less frequently in the wet season) but confirm the times at *CafeNet el Sol* or at the El Tigre supermarket. Note that Puerto Jiménez has the only petrol station on the entire Península de Osa, so be sure to fill up before you leave.

Accommodation

Jiménez's **hotels** are reasonably priced, clean and basic. Though in the dry season it's best to reserve a bed in advance, this may not always be possible, as phone and fax lines sometimes go down. There are a few comfort-in-the-wilderness places **between Jiménez and Carate** around the lower hump of the peninsula, a couple of which make great retreats or honeymoon spots. These tend to be quite upmarket; backpackers usually stay in Jiménez.

In Puerto Jiménez

Cabinas Jiménez One block north of the football field, across from the Golfo Dulce ⓣ2735-5090, ⓦwww.cabinasjimenez.com. Quiet *cabinas* next to the waterfront, with simple, nicely furnished and spotlessly clean rooms. They're well screened, with bath and fan, though some can be dark – ask to see a few before you choose. ❹

Cabinas Oro Verde On the main street ⓣ2735-5241. Ten basic, clean rooms right in the middle of town, with restaurant, laundry service and friendly owners. Ask for one of the five front rooms with streetside terraces. ❷

Hotel Agua Luna On the waterfront near the *lancha* pier ⓣ2735-5393, ⓔagualu@racsa.co.cr. A range of comfortable waterfront accommodation, from basic rooms with fans (❷) to luxury lodgings with cable TV, a/c and fridge. ❺

The Palms On the waterfront, just east of the football field ⓣ2735-5012, ⓦwww.thepalmscostarica.com. This clean, bright backpacker complex overlooking the gulf offers a choice of dormitory-style rooms ($45) or slightly more comfortable double rooms. ❻

Outside town

Crocodile Bay Lodge 4km out of town towards Playa Platanares ⓣ2735-5631, ⓦwww.crocodilebay.com. Luxury sports-fishing resort with swimming pool, jacuzzi, landscaped gardens and a large pier. Very expensive package deals only. ❽

Iguana Lodge Follow the signs for 5km out of Jiménez to Playa Platanares ⓣ8848-0752, ⓦwww.iguanalodge.com. Wonderful hotel run by very friendly Americans Toby and Lauren, with luxurious club rooms and four two-storey *casitas* (❽) in lovely gardens right on the beach – all rooms face the sea and are attractively decorated. Breakfast is included in the club room rate, while breakfast and dinner is included in the *casita* rate. ❼

The Town

Despite its small size, lack of big city facilities and somewhat sleepy, down-at-heel appearance, Puerto Jiménez nonetheless has a distinctly cosmopolitan flavour to it, welcoming a constant flow of visitors by land, sea and air throughout the year. Most are backpackers looking for a cheaper route to Corcovado than that offered via Bahía Drake. It is, however, a transient cosmopolitanism. Puerto Jiménez has no permanent expat community in the manner of Dominical or Puerto Viejo. This is a place to pass through – not to linger. The **main street**, which runs for just a few hundred metres from the football field in the north to the petrol station in the south, represents the rather dusty heart of town.

Activities

Escondido Trex (ⓣ2735-5210, ⓦwww.escondidotrex.com), with an office in the *Restaurante Carolina*, offers a wide range of **tours**, including hikes into Corcovado. For a more unique excursion, biologist Andy Pruter of Everyday Adventures (ⓣ8353-8619, ⓦwww.psychotours.com) takes people on high adrenaline "psycho" tours that include climbing 45-metre fig trees, rappelling waterfalls and ocean kayaking ($55–75). They also lead short **hikes** into the rainforest ($45).

If you're planning a **trip to Corcovado**, the Oficina de Area de Conservación Osa (Mon–Fri 8am–noon & 1–4pm; ⓣ2735-5036), facing the airstrip, is staffed by friendly rangers who can answer questions and arrange accommodation and meals at Sirena (though you're advised to sort this out well before you arrive – see p.409 for details).

A good place to relax after a strenuous hike out of Corcovado is **Playa Platanares**, a pleasant beach with plenty of empty sand about 5km east of Puerto Jiménez.

Eating and drinking

Café la Onda Near the southern edge of town, one block west of the main road ⓣ2735-5312. Small café serving the best coffee in town as well as bagels and smoothies. Mon–Fri 7.30am–5pm, Sat 8am–3pm. Closed Oct & Nov.

Il Giardino On the waterfront road by the jetty. For the most refined dining in town check out this quaint Italian restaurant which, strangely enough, also boasts the only sushi bar in town. Daily 5–10pm.

Juanita's Around the corner from *CafeNet El Sol*. The most popular place in town (particularly with tourists), this funky little restaurant serves up reasonable Mexican food, including a very hot chilli. It's a great place to hang out with a cool drink even if you're not eating. Daily 6am–midnight.

Pearl of the Osa At the *Iguana Lodge*. Lively open-air restaurant and bar serving international fare and solid Costa Rican dishes. Their "Pasta Night", when a DJ sets up shop, speakers blare and locals arrive in droves, is well known throughout the area. Daily 11am–10pm.

Restaurante Carolina On the main road. A popular spot among locals, this no-frills open-air restaurant has an inexpensive *comida tipica* menu. Try to find a spot beneath one of the ceiling fans, as it can get sweltering inside. Daily 7am–10pm.

Sarpes On the main road. Very popular seafood restaurant and bar, heavy on the sailing motif, with garden seating available. While most of what's on the menu is unfailingly tasty, their specialties are dishes that feature locally sourced food, with ginger and mango sauces and rice. Mon–Sat 11am–11pm, Sun 5–11pm.

Listings

Airline tickets The helpful Osa Tropical (Ⓣ2735-5062, Ⓔosatropi@racsa.co.cr), on the main road 50m north of the petrol station, is the local NatureAir and Sansa agent.

Banks The Banco Nacional, just north of the petrol station on the southern edge of town, changes travellers' cheques and dollars.

Health centres The Red Cross (Ⓣ2735-5109) and medical clinic (Ⓣ2735-5203) are opposite each other on the road that leads to the bus station.

Internet At the post office and at *CafeNet el Sol* (Ⓣ2735-5702, Ⓦwww.soldeosa.com) one block south of the football field on the main street.

Post office Opposite the football field.

Supermarkets One block west of the main road.

Telephones At the post office; Osa Tropical (see above) also provides phone and fax services.

Tour information Osa Tropical (see above); *CafeNet el Sol* (see above) can also provide details about tours to Corcovado and Bahía Drake.

South of Puerto Jiménez

The area south of Puerto Jiménez is still largely undeveloped, with huge stretches of sand seeing very few visitors. The road to **Cabo Matapalo**, at the tip of the peninsula, and further on to sleepy **Carate**, the southeastern gateway to Corcovado, is a pretty one, with the jungle pressing against much of it. It's also one best suited for a 4WD, as the bumps are substantial for much of it and water levels can make passage tricky in places.

Cabo Matapalo

Occupying Osa's southern edge about 17km from Puerto Jiménez, **Cabo Matapalo** was for many years the exclusive domain of surfers, who still come here for some of the country's best breaks. Nowadays, it's become increasingly popular as a place to build holiday homes and for its excellent wilderness lodges hidden in the primary rainforest.

The first beach on the cape, **Pan Dulce** is the best one for swimming and has long breaks for surfers. The most southerly, **Playa Matapalo** provides the hardest tests for surfers and is a great spot to watch if your own skills aren't quite up to the challenge. Nearby is the largest **waterfall** in the area, 90-metre King Louis, which can be reached on a short hike from the trailhead off the Playa Matapalo road.

All the local lodges lead **tours** of the area. If you're planning to come to Cabo Matapalo for the day, Everyday Adventures in Puerto Jiménez (see opposite) runs several half- and full-day tours of the cape.

Accommodation

Bosque del Cabo Above Playa Matapalo, down a private road to the left off the Carate road Ⓣ2735-5206, Ⓦwww.bosquedelcabo.com. Run by a friendly American couple, this grand lodge has ten luxurious hardwood and stucco *cabinas* (several with magnificent ocean views) plus two even more luxurious houses that sleep up to six. The lodge sits in landscaped grounds with acres of rainforest and is very eco-friendly; all the electricity is supplied by solar and hydro power. There's also a very good restaurant and tours are available. ❽

Lapa Ríos 20km south of Puerto Jiménez ⓣ2735-5130, ⓦwww.laparios.com. One of the country's most comfortable and impressive jungle lodges, set in a large private nature reserve with excellent birdwatching. Rooms have big beds and mosquito nets, and, being built of locally sourced materials (bamboo furniture, hardwood floors, palm thatched roofs), blend nicely with the surrounding forest. There's also a huge thatched restaurant, complete with spiral staircase, and a swimming pool. ❽

Carate and around

About 25km west of Cabo Matapalo and 43km from Jiménez, **CARATE** is literally the end of the road – the beach is just steps away from the road with the Parque Nacional Corcovado to the west. There's nothing in the tiny hamlet to detain you, save for the **mini-grocery** (*pulpería*) just off the beach. You can pitch your **tent** right outside it (a minimal charge of $2 per tent per night covers the use of toilets and showers) and stock up on basic foodstuffs before entering the park, though it's not cheap. For those requiring more comfort, however, there are a few idyllic **lodges** and **tent camps** in the area that are well worth considering.

Accommodation

Corcovado Lodge Tent Camp About a 45min walk along the beach from Carate (book via Costa Rica Expeditions, ⓣ2257-1665, ⓦwww.costaricaexpeditions.com). Twenty self-contained and fully screened "tent-camps" elevated on short stilts in an amazing beachside location, with bedrooms and screened verandas, communal baths and good local cooking. Packages are available, some including flights right to Carate, and they also offer guided tours around Parque Nacional Corcovado ($45–75) and horseriding. ❻

La Leona Eco Lodge Tent Camp Just south of La Leona ranger station ⓣ2735-5705, ⓦwww.laleonaecolodge.com. Striking a balance between comfort and convenience, the *La Leona* complex of rustic-style tent *cabinas* is set right on the beach just a short walk from the entrance to Parque Nacional Corcovado. Though they can get uncomfortably hot, the tents are well equipped and there's a very good restaurant (the price includes three meals a day). The lodge also offers a range of tours including crocodile-spotting, night hikes and rappelling. ❼

Lookout Inn Just north of Carate ⓣ2735-5431, ⓦwww.lookout-inn.com. Kick off your shoes and relax – there's a barefoot policy and an informal, fun atmosphere at this beach house set on a rainforested hillside with six large rooms, swimming pool and beautiful ocean views. Birdlife is rife, with plenty of scarlet macaws and hummingbirds. It's remote – bring everything you think you might need with you. Several tours are offered, including kayaking, dolphin boat cruises and hiking on area trails. ❼

Luna Lodge Set in the hills above Carate ⓣ2206-5859, ⓦwww.lunalodge.com. Remote, tranquil and beautiful lodge with welcoming owners and staggering views over the surrounding virgin rainforest. The eight thatched-roof bungalows each have private gardens, large windows, high ceilings and are comfortably furnished. Yoga classes take place on a specially built platform overlooking the jungle and there's healthy home-grown food available. ❽

Parque Nacional Corcovado

Created in 1975, **PARQUE NACIONAL CORCOVADO** (daily 8am–4pm; $10) protects an undeniably beautiful and biologically complex area of land, with deserted beaches, some laced with waterfalls, high canopy trees and better-than-average wildlife-spotting opportunities. Many people come with the sole purpose of spotting a **margay**, **ocelot**, **tapir** and other rarely seen animals. Of course, it's all down to luck, but if you walk quietly and there aren't too many other humans around, you should have a better chance of seeing some of these creatures here than elsewhere.

Serious walking in Corcovado is not for the faint-hearted. Quite apart from the distances and the terrain, **hazards** include insects (*lots* of them, especially in the rainy season: take a mosquito net, tons of repellent and all the precautions you can

Local guides

In recent years, a programme to train local men and women between the ages of 18 and 35 as **naturalist guides** has been initiated at Rincón de Osa, a village about 35km northwest of Jiménez, snug in the curve of the Golfo Dulce. The programme is typical in Costa Rica – Rara Avis and Selva Verde in Sarapiquí, among others, have similar schemes – enabling people not only to make a living from their local knowledge, but also to appreciate the many ways in which a rainforest can be sustainable. Guides are taught to identify some of the 367 or more species of birds recorded in the area, the 177 amphibians and reptiles, nearly 6000 insects, 140 mammals and 1000 trees – Corcovado's biodiversity makes for a lot of homework. They are also given lectures in tourism and tutored by working professional guides. If you wish to hire a local guide, ask in Rincón or at the Fundación Neotrópica office in San José for details. This arrangement works best if you are planning to hike around the Los Patos–Sirena Trail, as this has the nearest entrances to Rincón.

think of), herds of peccaries – who have been known to menace hikers – rivers full of crocodiles (and, in one case, sharks) and nasty snakes, including the terciopelo and bushmaster, which can attack without provocation. That said, most of these are present elsewhere in the country anyway, and everybody seems to make it through Corcovado just fine. But you must at least be prepared to get wet, dirty and incredibly hot – bear in mind that the sea does contain **sharks**, though everyone swims in it and no attacks have ever been recorded.

The **terrain** in Corcovado (literally "hunchback") varies from beaches of packed or soft sand, riverways, mangroves and *holillo* (palm) swamps to dense forest, although most of it is at lowland elevations. Hikers can expect to spend most of their time on the beach trails that ring the outer perimeters of the peninsular section of the park. Inland, the broad, alluvial Corcovado plain contains the **Corcovado Lagoon**, and for the most part the cover constitutes the only sizeable chunk of tropical **premontane wet forest** (also called tropical humid forest) on the Pacific side of Central America. The Osa forest is as visually and biologically magnificent as any on the subcontinent: biologists often compare the tree heights and density here with that of the Amazon basin cover – practically the only place in the entire isthmus of which this can still be said.

The coastal areas of the peninsular section of the park receive at least 3800mm of **rain** a year, with precipitation rising to about 5000mm in the higher elevations of the interior. This intense wetness is ideal for the development of the intricate, densely matted cover associated with tropical wet forests; there's also a dry season (Dec–March). The inland lowland areas, especially those around the lagoon, can be amazingly **hot**, even for those accustomed to tropical temperatures.

Park practicalities

Unless you're coming to Corcovado with Costa Rica Expeditions and staying in their tent camp or the nearby *La Leona Tent Camp*, in the dry months, at least, you have to **reserve** in advance with the Fundación de Parques Nacionales (Ⓣ2735-5036, Ⓔpncorcovado@gmail.com). You'll have to specify in advance your group size and dates, plus any **meals** you require at Sirena (see p.411). In the rainy season or off-peak times (generally between Easter and Christmas), it's possible to do all this at the park's office in Jiménez (see p.406), but the Fundación prefers that you go through their San José office. Be warned that the park is one of Costa Rica's most popular, and you'll need to book at least six weeks in advance or risk not getting in.

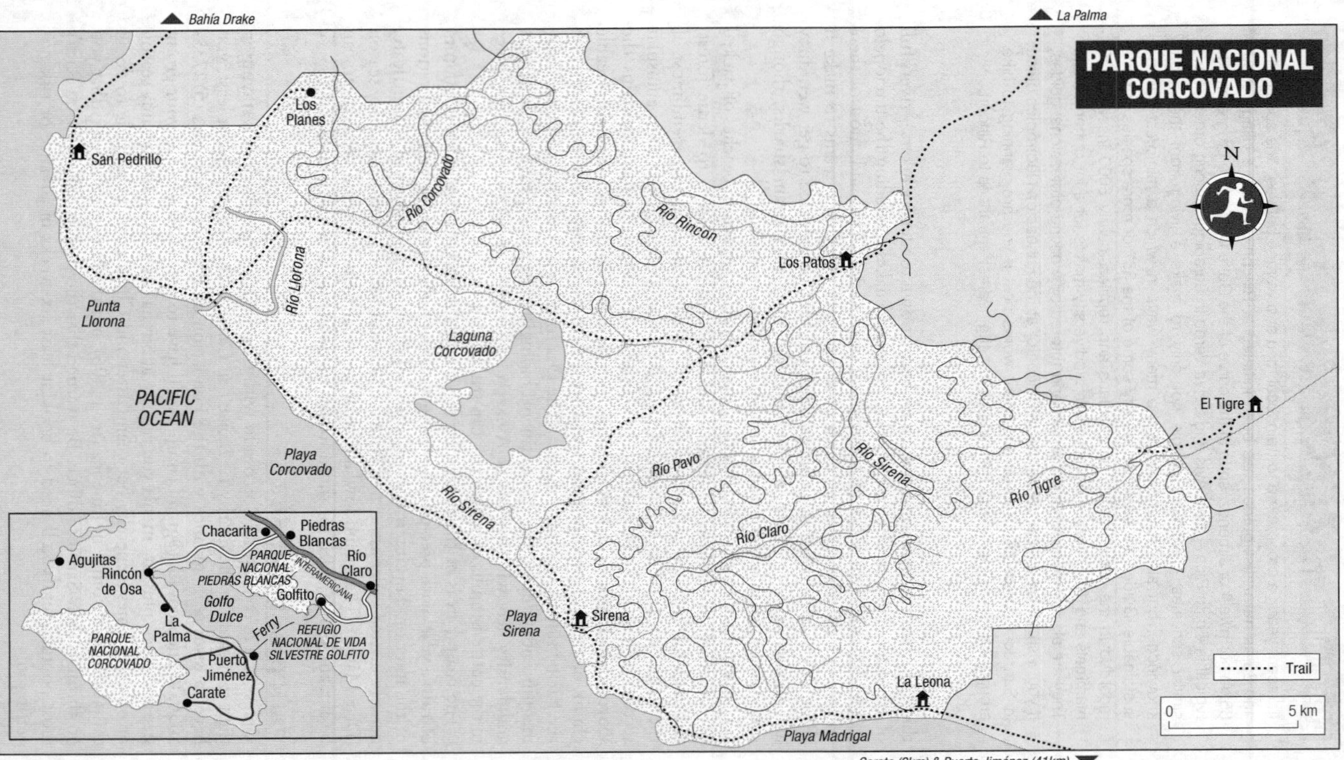
PARQUE NACIONAL CORCOVADO
N
Bahía Drake
La Palma
Carate (2km) & Puerto Jiménez (41km)
Los Planes
San Pedrillo
Río Corcovado
Río Rincon
Los Patos
Río Llorona
Punta Llorona
Laguna Corcovado
PACIFIC OCEAN
Playa Corcovado
Río Sirena
Río Pavo
Río Sirena
Río Claro
Río Tigre
El Tigre
Sirena
Playa Sirena
La Leona
Playa Madrigal
Trail
0
5 km
Chacarita
Piedras Blancas
Agujitas
Rincón de Osa
PARQUE NACIONAL PIEDRAS BLANCAS
INTERAMERICANA
Río Claro
Golfo Dulce
Golfito
La Palma
Ferry
REFUGIO NACIONAL DE VIDA SILVESTRE GOLFITO
PARQUE NACIONAL CORCOVADO
Puerto Jiménez
Carate

All the ranger stations have **camping areas**, drinking water, **information**, toilets and telephone or radio-telephone contact. It currently costs $4 per night to camp at the ranger stations, or $8 (plus a $2 reservation fee) to sleep in the comfortable **accommodation block** at Sirena ranger station. Breakfast at Sirena costs $15, while lunch and dinner costs $20. The biggest ranger station in the park, Sirena is also a research station, and often full of biologists. If you plan to bring your own food and utensils, the park rangers will allow you to use the stoves at all the ranger stations.

It's suggested that you come in a group of at least two people, that you bring your own mosquito net, sleeping bag, food and water – though you can fill up at the beachside waterfalls and at the ranger stations – and be more or less experienced in hiking in this kind of terrain. If you can afford it, your best option is to hire a **local guide**, particularly useful to spot the recalcitrant wildlife. Ask at the Puerto Jiménez office for advice; Ballardo Diaz (Ⓔjaguardman@hotmail.com) and Oscar Cortes Alfaro both come highly recommended.

You should plan to **hike** early in the day – though not before dawn, due to snakes – and take shelter at midday. Corcovado is set up so that the rangers at each station always know how many people are on a given trail, and how long they are expected to be. If you are late getting back, they will go looking for you. This gives a measure of security but, all the same, take **precautions**. There have been no mishaps (like people getting lost) in the park of late, but always check with the rangers or ask around in Jiménez regarding current conditions. A few years ago things were tense between the *oreros* who still mine, some of them illegally, in and around Corcovado, and the rangers, whose job it is to stop them. Though no tourist has been hurt, the *oreros* may well be suspicious of strangers, and it's best not to walk alone just in case.

When you enter the park, make sure you jot down the details of the **marea** (tides) which are posted in prominent positions at all the ranger stations. You'll need to cross most of the rivers at low tide – to do otherwise is dangerous. Rangers can advise on conditions. Incidentally, it's especially important when coming to Corcovado to brush up on your **Spanish**. You'll be asking the rangers for a lot of crucial information and few, if any, speak English. Bring a phrase book if you're not fluent.

The trails

The park's three longest **trails** all lead from the peripheral ranger stations **to Sirena**, where you can stay for a day or two in the simple lodge (see above), exploring the local trails around the Río Sirena. Though there is some overlap in the type of flora and fauna you might see along the way on the different trails, each offers a distinct hiking experience. For this reason, and if your schedule permits, it's a good idea to walk into Sirena on one trail and back out via another. If you plan to spend a few days in the park, consider hiking in from Los Patos, spend a night or two in Sirena and then back out to La Leona; it's much easier to move on from La Leona at the end of a hike than from Los Patos.

Los Patos to Sirena

The small hamlet of **La Palma**, 24km northwest of Puerto Jiménez, is the starting point for getting to the **LOS PATOS** ranger station. It's a twelve-kilometre walk to the park, much of it through hot lowland terrain. A much more sensible idea, however – given the hike that awaits you in the park – is to try and arrange for a taxi in La Palma to take you as far as water levels on the bumpy dirt track will allow. You'll want to start your hike from Los Patos to Sirena early, so plan on arriving at Los Patos soon after dawn or, preferably, the night before.

If you want to stay near La Palma and get up early, *Danta Lodge* (Ⓣ2735-1111, Ⓦwww.dantalodge.com; ④) is an outstanding choice, just 8km from Los Patos. A friendly, family-run lodge, *Danta* was built entirely from sustainable materials and the

What to see at Corcovado

Chances are you'll have read much about Corcovado's unparalleled **biodiversity** before your arrival, but that does little to prepare you for the sheer scope of it when you step into the park. Suffice it to say, there is much to feast your eyes on in Corcovado.

Plants and trees

Walking through Corcovado you'll see many lianas, vines, mosses and spectacularly tall trees – some of them 50 or 60m high, and a few more than 80m high. All in all, Corcovado's area is home to about a quarter of all the tree species in the country, including the **silkwood** (or *ceiba pentandra*), characterized by its height – thought to be the largest tree in Central America – and its smooth grey bark. One silkwood, near the Llorona–San Pedrillo section of the trail, is over 80m high and 3m in diameter. You'll also notice huge **buttresses**: above-ground roots shot out by the silkwoods and other tall canopy species. These are used to help anchor the massive tree in thin tropical soil, where drainage is particularly poor.

Mammals

Corcovado supports a higher volume of **large mammals** than most other areas of the country, except perhaps the wild and rugged Talamancas. **Jaguars** need more than 100 square kilometres each for their hunting; if you are a good tracker you may be able to spot their traces within the park, especially in the fresh mud along trails and riverbeds. Initially they look identical to those made by a large dog, but the four toes are of unequal size (the outermost one is the smallest) and the fore footprint should be wider than its length. You might, too, see the **margay**, a spotted wildcat about the size of a large domesticated house cat, which comes down from the forest to sun itself on rocks at midday. The **ocelot**, a larger spotted cat, is even shyer, rarely seen for more than a second, poking its head out of the dense cover and then melting away into the forest again immediately.

With a body shape somewhere between a large pig and a cow, the **Baird's tapir** is an odd-looking animal, most immediately recognizable for its funny-looking

woodwork and handmade furniture is stunning. Accommodation is in attractive rooms or bungalows, the latter 200m from the main lodge. Rates include breakfast; hearty lunches ($12) and dinners ($15) are served in the communal open-air dining area. They rent out horses for the 2hr trip to Los Patos and lead several well-run tours in the area including kayaking in Golfo Dulce and night walks on their 70 hectares.

The well-marked twenty-kilometre inland **trail from Los Patos to Sirena** is, for many, the holy grail of Corcovado hikes. From Los Patos the trail takes you steeply uphill for some 5km into high, wet and dense rainforest, after which the rest of the walk is flat, but extremely hot. This is a trail for experienced rainforest hikers and hopeful **mammal**-spotters, giving you a reasonable chance of coming across, for example, tapirs, peccaries, margay or the tracks of tapirs and jaguars. That said, some hikers come away very disappointed, having not seen a thing. It's a gruelling trek, especially with the hot inland temperatures (at least 26°C, with 100 percent humidity) and the lack of sea breezes, although there are crude shelters en route where you can rest in the shade (but not camp), but it is probably best avoided if you've not done much rainforest hiking before.

La Leona to Sirena

It's a ninety-minute walk along the beach from the village of **Carate** (see p.408) to enter Corcovado at the **LA LEONA** ranger station: refreshments are available en route at the *Corcovado* or *La Leona* tent camps (see p.408). Once at La Leona, a sixteen-kilometre trail runs **to Sirena** just inland from the beach, making it easy snout, a truncated elephant-type trunk. Tapirs are very shy – and have been made even more so through large-scale hunting – though you stand a reasonable chance of spotting one crossing the clearing at Sirena's airfield. More threatening are the packs of white-collared **peccaries**, a type of wild pig, who in Corcovado typically group themselves in packs of about thirty. They are often seen along the trails and should be treated with caution, since they can bite you. The accepted wisdom is to climb a tree if they come at you threateningly, clacking their jaws and growling, though this, of course, means you have to be good at climbing trees, some of which have painful spines.

More common mammals that you'll likely spot are the ubiquitous **agouti**, foraging in the underbrush. Essentially a large rodent with smooth, glossy hair, the agouti looks similar to a large squirrel. The **coati**, a member of the raccoon family, with a long ringed tail, is also sure to cross your path. Another mammal found in significant numbers in the park – and all over the peninsula – is the **tayra** (tolumuco), a small and swift mink-like creature. They will in most cases run from you, but should not be approached, as they have teeth and can be aggressive.

Birds

Among Corcovado's resident **birds** is the **scarlet macaw**, around 300 of which live in the park – more, in terms of birds per square kilometre, than anywhere else in the country. Macaws are highly prized as caged birds and, despite the efforts of the SPN, poaching is still a problem here, as their (relative) abundance makes them easy prey. Around the Río Sirena estuary, especially, keep an eye out for the **boat-billed heron**, whose wide bill gives it a lopsided quality. The big black **king vulture** can also be found in Corcovado; a forager rather than a hunter, it nevertheless looks quite ominous. There are many other smaller birds in Corcovado including, perhaps, the fluffy-headed **harpy eagle**. Though the harpy is thought to be extinct in Costa Rica, ornithologists reckon there's a chance that a few pairs still live in Corcovado, and in the Parque Internacional La Amistad on the Talamanca coast.

to keep your bearings. You can only walk its full length at low tide; if you do get stuck, the only thing to do is wait for the water to recede. If you can avoid problems with the tides, you should be able to do the walk in five to six hours, taking time to look out for birds. The walking can get a bit monotonous, but the beaches are uniformly lovely and deserted, and you may be lucky enough to spot a flock of **scarlet macaws** in the coastal trees – a rare sight. You will probably see (or hear) monkeys, too. Take lots of sunscreen, a big hat and at least five litres of water per person – the trail gets very hot, despite the sea breezes.

San Pedrillo to Sirena

Hikers and tour groups coming from the Bahía Drake area enter the park at the **SAN PEDRILLO** ranger station, from where there are a few well-marked and short trails leading into the forest. The ranger station itself can be a good spot to see foraging wildlife, as there are several fruit trees within close proximity to it.

Corcovado's most heroic walk, all 25km of it, is from **San Pedrillo to Sirena**, the stretch along which you'll see the most impressive trees. It's a two-day trek, so you need a tent, sleeping bag and mosquito net, and you mustn't be worried by having to set up camp in the jungle. Fording the **Río Sirena**, just 1km before the Sirena ranger station, is the biggest obstacle: this is the deepest of all the rivers on the peninsula, with the strongest out-tow current, and has to be crossed with care, and at low tide only – **sharks** come in and out in search of food at high tide. Be sure to get the latest information from the San Pedrillo rangers before you set out.

The first half of the walk – a seven-hour stint – is in the jungle, just inland from the coast. Much of the rest of the hike is spent slogging it out on the beach, where the sand is more tightly packed than along the La Leona–Sirena stretch. Some hikers do the beach section of the walk well before dawn or after dark; there are fewer dangers (like snakes) at night on the beach and as long as you have a good torch with lots of batteries and/or the moon is out, this is a reasonable option.

Around El Tigre

EL TIGRE ranger station, at the eastern inland entrance to the park, is a decent place to take breakfast or lunch with the ranger(s) before setting off on the local trails. To get there from Jiménez, drive 10km north and take the second left, a dirt track, signed to El Tigre and Dos Brazos. The short walking trails laid out around the ranger station provide an introduction to Corcovado without making you slog it out on the marathon trails, and can easily be covered in a morning or afternoon.

Golfito and around

The former banana port of **GOLFITO**, 33km north of the Panamanian border, straggles for 2.5km along the water of the same name (*golfito* means "little gulf"). The town's setting is spectacular, backed up against steep, thickly forested hills to the east, and with the glorious Golfo Dulce – one of the deepest gulfs of its size in the world – to the west. The low shadow of the Península de Osa shimmers in the distance, and everywhere the vegetation has the soft, muted look of the undisturbed tropics. It is also very **rainy**; even if you speak no Spanish, you'll certainly pick up the local expression *va a caer baldazos* – "it's gonna pour".

Golfito extends for ages without any clear centre, through stretches where the main road is hemmed in by hills on one side and the lapping waters of the *golfito* on

United Brands ("La Yunai")

Golfito's history is inextricably intertwined with the giant transnational **United Brands** – known locally as "La Yunai" – which first set up in the area in 1938, twenty years before the Interamericana hit town. The company built schools, recruited doctors and police and brought prosperity to the area, though "problems" with labour union organizers began soon afterwards, and came to characterize the relationship between company and town. What with fluctuating banana prices, a three-month strike by workers and local social unrest, the company eventually decided Golfito was too much trouble and pulled out in a hurry in 1985. The town declined and, in the public eye, became synonymous with rampant unemployment, alcoholism, abandoned children, prostitution and general unruliness.

Today, at the big old *muelle bananero* (banana dock) container ships are still loaded up with bananas to be processed further up towards Palmar. This residual traffic, along with tourism, has combined to help revive the local economy. Many visitors come to Golfito because it's a good base for getting to the Parque Nacional Corcovado by *lancha* or plane, and also a major **sports-fishing** centre. The real rescue, though, came from the Costa Rican government, who in the early 1990s established a **Depósito Libre** – or tax-free zone – in the town, where Costa Ricans can buy manufactured goods imported from Panamá without the 100 percent tax normally levied. Ticos who come to shop here have to buy their tickets for the Depósito 24 hours in advance, obliging them to spend at least one night, and therefore colones, in the town.

the other. The town is effectively split in two – by a division in wealth as well as architecture. In the north is the **Zona Americana**, where the banana company executives used to live and where better-off residents still reside in beautiful wooden houses shaded by dignified palms. Here you'll find the tax-free **Depósito Libre** (see box above), an unaesthetic outdoor mall ringed by a circular concrete

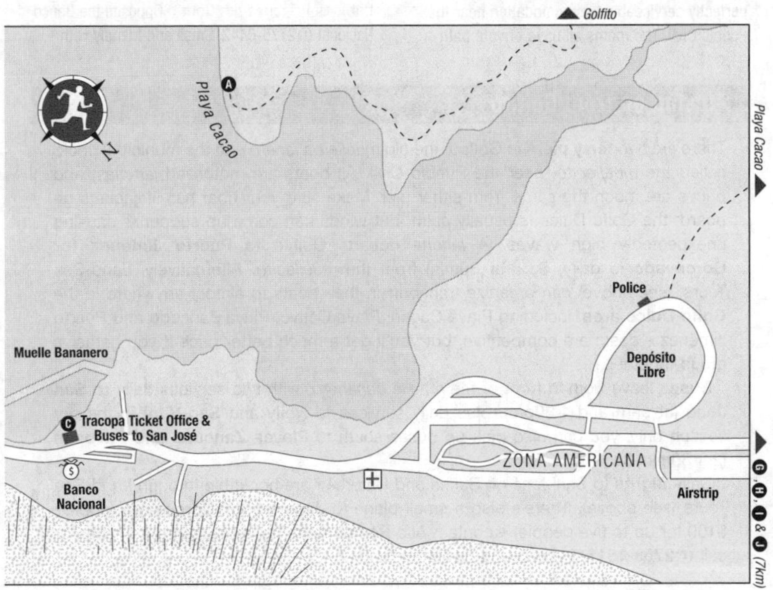

wall. Some two kilometres to the south of the Depósito, the **Pueblo Civil** (civilian town), is a very small, tight nest of streets – hotter, noisier and more crowded than the *zona*. It's here you'll find the *lancha* across the Golfo Dulce to Puerto Jiménez and the Península de Osa. Although the Pueblo Civil is perfectly civil in the daytime, be careful at night. Be wary of entering any bar with a sign positioned outside so that you can't see in – these are for professional transactions only.

Arrival and information

Buses to Golfito (8hr) currently leave San José's TRACOPA terminal daily at 7am and 3.30pm with an extra bus at 10.15pm on Friday. You should book your ticket in advance, particularly in December, when hordes of bargain hunters descend on the Depósito Libre to do their Christmas shopping. Buy your return ticket as soon as you disembark. You can also **fly** here with both Sansa and NatureAir; the airstrip is in the Zona Americana. There is no official **information** centre in town; Land-Sea Tours on the waterfront at the southern end of the *pueblo* (T 2775-1614, W www.marinaservices-yachtdelivery.com) is a capable stand-in for area information.

Accommodation

Much of Golfito's **accommodation** is basic and inexpensive, catering to Costa Ricans visiting the Depósito Libre, though there are a couple of slightly smarter hotels too. Be warned that the sheer number of people coming to Golfito to shop, especially at Christmas, means that rooms are often booked in advance – if you don't have reservations try to get to town as early in the day as possible. You'll find several luxurious accommodation options along the coast north of Golfito; options are fewer to the south.

In town

Cabinas II Tucán On the main road, 50m north of the *muellecito* T 2775-0553. Basic but perfectly serviceable accommodation near the Pueblo Civil. The rooms all have private bath and fans and the owner is a great source of local information (and stories). Free parking available. 2

Cabinas Princesa del Golfito Opposite the Banco Nacional T 2775-0442. Small and friendly with

Moving on from Golfito

There are two **ferry piers** in Golfito, the old *muelle bananero* and the municipal dock, called the *muellecito*, near the Pueblo Civil. All boats are motorized *lanchas*, and prices are much the same from either pier. Make sure your boat has lifejackets on board: the Golfo Dulce is usually calm, but winds can come up suddenly, causing unexpectedly high waves. A *lancha* departs Golfito to **Puerto Jiménez for Corcovado** (6 daily; $3; 1hr 30min) from the *muellecito*. Alternatively, Land-Sea Tours, (see above) can organize transport in their boats to almost anywhere in the **Golfo Dulce area**, including Playa Cacao, Playa Cativo, Playa Zancudo and Puerto Jiménez – costs are competitive, but you'll get a much better price if you gather a group together.

Buses leave from in front of the *muelle bananero*, with two services daily **to San José** (at 5am and 1.30pm), plus daily services to **Neily** and **San Vito**: in the dry season only, you can also pick up buses south to **Playas Zancudo** and **Pavones** (2hr 30min–3hr).

Daily **flights** to San José on Sansa and NatureAir are bookable through Land-Sea Tours (see above). There's also a small plane to **Jiménez for Corcovado** (approx $100 for up to five people) – contact Alfa Romeo Aero Taxi's office at the airstrip, or call T 2755-1515, E corcovadotaxi@racsa.co.cr.

pleasantly decorated, good-value rooms. Hearty Tico meals are served in the adjacent *soda*. ❷

Las Gaviotas At the southern entrance to town ⓣ2775-0062, ⓦwww.lasgaviotasmarinaresort.com. Well-equipped, if slightly shabby resort with nice views out over the gulf and the town's only swimming pool. The somewhat barrack-like (but very affordable) rooms all have private baths with hot water, a/c and cable TV. The waterside open-air restaurant serves great local seafood, and the weekend buffets are a veritable feast. ❺

Happy Daze In the Pueblo Civil ⓣ2775-0058. Basic but clean double rooms, owned by a friendly American surfer and sports-fisherman. ❷

Samoa del Sur On the main road between the Zona Americana and the Pueblo Civil ⓣ2775-0233, ⓦsamoadelsur.com. Fourteen spacious but slightly gloomy rooms on the waterfront, with a large and rather raucous boat-shaped bar-restaurant (it's the bar of choice for US marines on shore leave). ❹

Around Golfito

Cabinas Isabel (also known as *Cabinas Playa Cacao*) West of Golfito on Playa Cacao ⓣ2382-1593, ⓔsabel@racsa.co.cr. Indigenous-styled, thatched-roof *cabinas* right on the water. Though simply furnished, they're very comfortable with en-suite bathrooms and fans and there's a communal dining area. Jungle walks, no-frills fishing tours and trips out to the local mangrove swamps to see the crocodiles are also available. Be sure to check out nearby *Siete Mares*, a quality, reasonably priced seafood restaurant. ❹

Esquinas Rainforest Lodge La Gamba, about 7km from Km-37 on the Interamericana ⓣ2741-8001, ⓦwww.esquinaslodge.com. Friendly eco-lodge, originally funded by Austria's government as part of a project combining development aid, nature conservation and rainforest research – all profits go to the local community. It's set in primary rainforest, with resident wildlife and on-site hiking and horseriding trails leading into Parque Nacional Piedras Blancas. The fourteen pleasantly rustic rooms have ceiling fans and private bathrooms and are adorned with textiles crafted by local indigenous artisans. There's also a roomy jungle villa set off from the main lodge that can accommodate four (4-night minimum; from $650, not including meals). A wide range of packages are available, plus a variety of tours, including to Corcovado and the Wilson Botanical Gardens. Three fantastic meals a day are included in the room rate. ❼

La Purruja Lodge 4km south of Golfito towards the Interamericana ⓣ2775-5054, ⓦwww.purruja.com. Small family-run hotel set in lovely gardens, with spacious rooms, pool table and dart-board. Camping and tours are also available. Good choice if you have a car. ❸

Playa San Josecito

Dolphin Quest Playa San Josecito ⓣ8811-2099, ⓦwww.dolphinquestcostarica.com. This secluded eco-lodge has a range of accommodation, from spacious dormitory rooms (❷) to private *cabinas* (❹) to a small house that sleeps five (❻). The lodge's extensive grounds are wedged between the ocean and dense rainforest crisscrossed by a network of trials. Between periods of lazing about in a hammock, you'll find plenty of activities and tours to keep you occupied, from snorkelling and kayaking to horseriding and fishing. Book in advance and you'll be picked up by *lancha* from Golfito.

Golfo Dulce Lodge Playa San Josecito ⓣ8821-5398, ⓦwww.golfodulcelodge.com. Only accessible by a boat ride of about 30 minutes either from Golfito or Puerto Jiménez, this Swiss-run eco-lodge is surrounded by the undisturbed primary rainforest of Parque Nacional Piedras Blancas. Five detached wooden bungalows are named after local wildlife, each with private verandas with hammocks. There are also three standard rooms. A thatched restaurant, nearby observation platform and a small freshwater pool are also in the grounds. Three-night minimum stay; bungalows $345, rooms $285.

Playa Nicuesa Rainforest Lodge Playa San Josecito ⓣ2258-8250, ⓦwww.nicuesalodge.com. One part nature retreat, one part adventure camp, one part all-inclusive resort. Sustainability to the max: local lumber, recycled roof tiles and solar energy are just the beginning of the story here. Owners Michael and Donna go the distance to welcome guests to the jungle. Spectacular ocean and forest views from private verandas or the treetop bar. Hit the beach for kayaking, snorkelling, fishing, sailing or just go for a swim. A resident naturalist will guide you to a nearby waterfall. Access is by boat only. ❽

The Town

There's little to see in Golfito itself, other than the **old homes** of the banana company executives in the **ZONA AMERICANA** near the Depósito Libre. These are obvious from their grandeur: wide verandas, painted in jolly, if sun-bleached, colours, with huge screens and sun canopies. One row, just east of the main street in the centre of town (near the Banco Nacional) displays a particularly fine series of washed-out tropical hues – lime-green blends into faded oyster-yellow, followed by tired-pink and metallic-orange.

Immediately to the east of town, some **trails** lead up a steep hill, giving fantastic views across the Golfo Dulce in the tiny **REFUGIO NACIONAL DE VIDA SILVESTRE GOLFITO.** It isn't easily explored, however, since the trail entrances tend to be overgrown and difficult to find, so ask around locally; the most accessible trailhead is the one across from *Samoa del Sur*.

Less than a kilometre from town across the *golfito*, **PLAYA CACAO** has good swimming and a number of decent bars and restaurants nearby, although the beach itself is a little grimy. You can catch a water taxi there (around $4) from the *muellecito* (ferry dock) just north of the petrol station. In the dry season, you can drive there along a rough unfinished track from the turn-off right in front of the *guardia*, bearing left.

Activities

If you're in Golfito to **sports-fish**, the larger hotels can help arrange tours and tackle – the area is particularly rich in marlin and sailfish. **Swimming** is no good, however, as the bay is polluted, and you'll see oil in the water and various bits of floating refuse all around Golfito. Your best bet for a swim is to head across to Playa Cacao, or to move south towards the Península Burica (see opposite).

For activities out of town, the highly recommended Land-Sea Tours (see p.416) can arrange imaginative **tours** of the area, featuring jungle hikes, panning for gold and cave exploration, as well as *lanchas* to Playa Zancudo ($50 for up to six people; see opposite). They also maintain a "cruisers' clubhouse" with a book exchange, movie collection and a wealth of local information. Upstairs there is one bedroom, which if available, is a steal at $20 per night; there's free wi-fi too.

Eating and drinking

Golfito has plenty of **places to eat**. For *casados* and *platos del día* there are two groups of simple *sodas*: one near the Depósito Libre, catering to Ticos who have come to Golfito on shopping trips, and another, slightly better-value cluster on the main drag of the Pueblo Civil and in the surrounding streets.

Coconut Café Opposite the main dock. Both a nice place for a beer or a *refresco* and a great source of local information – the American owner seems to know just about everyone in Golfito.

Las Gaviotas See p.417. *Las Gaviotas* has an all-you-can-eat barbecue ($10–15) on Friday and Saturday evenings from 6pm, with good meat dishes and a reasonable wine list, though its best feature is the waterside location on the *golfito*.

Restaurante La Eurekita In the Pueblo Civil. Inexpensive spot serving solid *típico* food, very good burgers and with a nice breezy view of the water.

Restaurante Hong Kong In the Pueblo Civil. Renowned for its excellent (and cheap) chow mein dishes and a magnet for expat yachters: despite the completely forgettable interior, it serves up some of the best Chinese food to be found in the south.

Samoa del Sur See p.417. The beachside bar and restaurant at the *Samoa del Sur* hotel is a pleasant spot for an evening beer or meal, with a menu featuring seafood and pizza ($6–10).

Listings

Bank The Banco Nacional opposite the TRACOPA terminal changes travellers' cheques.

Post office Right in the centre of the Pueblo Civil (Mon–Fri 7.30am–5pm, Sat 8am–noon).

Internet café On the main street next to the petrol station.

Hospital In the Zona Americana (☎2775-0011).

Parque Nacional Piedras Blancas

Stretching inland from the Golfo Dulce and abutting La Gamba north of Golfito, **Parque Nacional Piedras Blancas** comprises land that was formerly part of Parque Nacional Corcovado as well as parcels purchased and donated by such disparate entities as the international hydroelectric behemoth Tenaska, the Austrian government and The Nature Conservancy. All told, almost 150 square kilometres of mountainous rainforest, beaches and portions of the Piedras Blancas and Esquinas rivers are protected, an area teeming with tropical flora and some of Costa Rica's signature mammals, including jaguars, pumas, two-toed sloths, kinkajous and squirrel and capuchin monkeys. The most prevalent mammals, though, are bats: over fifty species have been observed here, among them the vampire bat. The park is also one of the top spots in the country for birdwatching, mainly due to it being a favoured stopover for migrating birds. Poaching was a significant problem when the park was formed two decades ago, though efforts throughout the previous decade have been successful in greatly reducing illegal hunting.

The park has a few, somewhat difficult to reach **access points**; your best bet is to enter from *Esquinas Rainforest Lodge* (see p.417) in La Gamba, where you can make arrangements for a guide to lead you through the forest. As the park does not yet have any infrastructure for visitors, having a guide with you is a sensible way to explore the thick primary forest.

The Southern beaches

South of Golfito are a couple of very isolated **beaches** en route to the **Península Burica**, a thin, pristine finger of land that's shared with Panamá. You can reach both **Pavones** and **Zancudo** from Golfito by *lancha* (45min) or, in the dry season only (Jan–Sept), by bus (2hr 30min–3hr) from in front of the *muelle bananero*. Driving to the beaches takes two hours from Golfito and entails crossing the Río Coto Colorado on a tiny ferry. You need a 4WD, whatever time of year; during the wet season it's worth checking the levels of the creeks and fords that you'll have to pass before you set out.

Playa Zancudo

Ask anyone in town where you can swim, and they'll direct you to black-sand **PLAYA ZANCUDO**, 15km southeast of Golfito, facing the Golfo Dulce and bordered on one side by the Río Coto Colorado. On summer weekends from December to April, Playa Zancudo fills with Zona Sur Ticos taking a beach break, but otherwise it's fairly low-key, except for a small colony of mainly US expats. There are a couple of professional **sports-fishing** outfits, while other local activities include **surfing**, **river trips** and excursions (run by *Cabinas Los Cocos*, see below) across the bay to the beautiful **Casa Orchidea Botanical Gardens** ($20 per person), reachable only by boat.

It's a friendly place, perfect for unwinding, and there are several decent **places to stay**. *Cabinas Los Cocos* (ⓣ2776-0012, ⓦwww.loscocos.com; ❺) is the most upmarket with well-equipped *cabinas* – each with kitchen, fridge, screens, fans and hammocks – surrounded by dense tropical foliage. Bikes, kayaks, boogie boards and beach chairs are available for guests. Nearby *Sol y Mar* (ⓣ2276-0014, ⓦwww.zancudo.com; ❺) has four groovy screened cabins in a garden by the beach and they offer sports-fishing outings and boat trips through the mangrove swamps of the Río Coto. The centre of daytime activities as well as nightlife, *Maria's* (ⓣ2776-0131; ❶) has very basic but good-value rooms above a restaurant. For **food**, the usual array of *sodas* around town serve *casados* and other typical filling fare. Alternatively, *Estero Mar* serves tasty seafood, or you can dine on gourmet French cuisine at *Sol y Mar*, which has a lively **bar** and popular volleyball competitions on Saturday afternoons.

Playa Pavones and Punta Banco

About 12km further south is **PLAYA PAVONES**, famed among surfers for having the longest continuous wave in the world – exactly how long, they do not divulge. The waves are biggest and best from May to November. Needless to say, the water's too rough for anything else and the community here largely consists of avid surfers. There are few facilities in Pavones other than basic *cabinas* for rent and a couple of nondescript bars.

After another 10km or so south you come to **Punta Banco**, site of the beautiful *Tiskita Lodge* (T 2296-8125, W www.tiskita-lodge.co.cr; 7), a friendly, extremely comfortable rainforest lodge (that doubles as a biological research station) with 16 *cabinas* overlooking the beach and a swimming pool in the grounds. Trails weave through the surrounding forest and the birdwatching is good. You can also tour their fruit farm (the owner is an agronomist). They offer good-value packages ($475 for 3 nights, including two guided hikes and three high-quality meals a day).

Travel details

Buses

Ciudad Neily to: Puerto Jiménez (2 daily; 4hr).
Dominical to: Quepos (4 daily; 2hr); San Isidro (3 daily; 40min–1hr); San José (2 daily; 7hr); Uvita (7 daily; 20min).
Golfito to: Playas Pavones and Zancudo (dry season only, 1 daily; 2hr 30min); San José (2 daily; 8hr).
Palmar to: San José (7 daily; 5hr 30min); Sierpe (5 daily; 30min).
Paso Canoas to: San Isidro (2 daily; 6hr); San José (6 daily; 9hr).
Playas Pavones and Zancudo to: Golfito (dry season only, 1 daily; 2hr 30min).
Puerto Jiménez to: Ciudad Neily (2 daily; 4hr); San Isidro (2 daily; 5hr); San José (1 daily; 8–9hr).
Quepos to: Dominical (4 daily; 2hr).
San Gerardo de Rivas to: San Isidro (2 daily; 40min).
San Isidro to: Dominical (4 daily; 40min–1hr); Paso Canoas (2 daily; 6hr); Puerto Jiménez (3 daily; 5hr); Quepos (4 daily; 3hr 30min); San Gerardo de Rivas (2 daily; 1hr 40min); San José (16 daily; 3hr); Uvita (2 daily; 1hr 30min).
San José to: Dominical (2 daily; 7hr); Golfito (2–3 daily; 8hr); Palmar (7 daily; 5hr 30min); Paso Canoas (6 daily; 9hr); Puerto Jiménez (3 daily; 8–9hr); San Isidro (16 daily; 3hr).
Sierpe to: Palmar (5 daily; 30min).
Uvita to: Dominical (6 daily; 20min); San Isidro (2 daily; 1hr 30min).

Lancha

Golfito to: Puerto Jiménez (6 daily; 1hr 30min), returning from Jiménez 5 times daily.

Flights

Golfito to: Puerto Jiménez (1 daily; 5min); San José (4 daily; 55min).
Palmar Sur to: San José (3 daily; 1hr)
Puerto Jiménez to: Golfito (1 daily; 5min); San José (2–5 daily; 50min).
San José to: Golfito (5 daily; 55min); Palmar Sur (3 daily; 1hr); Puerto Jiménez (3 daily; 50min).

Contexts

Contexts

History

The peopling of Costa Rica probably took place sometime around 10,000 BC, about 25,000 years after the first *Homo sapiens* had crossed the Bering Strait into what is now the Americas (though the only thing to support this tentative date is a single flint arrowhead excavated in the 1890s in Guanacaste). Archeologists know almost nothing of the various people who inhabited modern-day Costa Rica until about 1000 BC. Certainly no written records were left, and what little knowledge we do have stems mostly from limited excavations of the Monumento Nacional Guayabo in the western Valle Central.

Costa Rica before the Spanish

Pre-Columbian Costa Rica was a contact zone – a corridor for merchants and trading expeditions – between the Mesoamerican empires to the north and the Inca Empire to the south. Excavations of pottery, jade and trade goods, and accounts of cultural traditions, have shown that the pre-Columbian peoples of Costa Rica adopted liberally from both areas.

When the Spaniards arrived in Costa Rica in the early sixteenth century, it was inhabited by as many as 27 different **indigenous groups** or clans. Most clans were assigned names by the invaders, which they took from the **cacique** (chief) with whom they dealt. The modern-day Zona Norte was home to the **Catapas**, the **Votos** and the **Suerres**; the extreme south of the Talamancas held the **Cabécars** and the **Guayamís**, whose influence spread to modern-day Zona Sur and the Osa Peninsula. In the nearby Valle de Diquis and Valle de El General were the **Térrabas** and their subgroup, the **Borucas**. The Valle Central contained the **Huetars**, while modern-day Guanacaste – the most heavily populated and farmed area in pre-Columbian Costa Rica – was home to the **Chorotegas** and the older Nicoyan peoples. The Chorotegas, in particular, showed signs of cultural inheritance from the Olmec peoples of southern Mexico, while those of the extreme south and the Osa Peninsula had affinities with peoples in Panamá and Colombia.

Most of these groups existed in a state of almost constant **warfare**. However, unlike in the Mesoamerican states and in the Inca Empire, where victorious campaigns had led to the establishment of complex, far-reaching empires, in Costa Rica no one group gained ascendancy, and the political position of the clans seemed to remain more or less constant throughout the ages. One reason could be that although these groups were only too willing to go to war, they did not do so in order to increase their territory – a perennially low-population density meant that there was plenty of land, and plenty of space into which persecuted or vanquished groups could escape. Like the forest-dwelling tribes in Amazonia to the south, these pre-Columbian peoples waged war to capture slaves, victims for potential sacrifice, marriage partners or simply for revenge.

As for **religion**, the clans were highly complex and specialized. Shamans were respected members of society, officiating at funerals, which were the most important rites of passage, especially in the Talamancan groups. Some clans had animal taboos that prevented them from hunting and killing certain beasts, and which neatly complemented each other – one group might not be able to hunt the tapir, for example, while the neighbouring clan would be prohibited from hunting the main prey of another group. This delicate balance played itself out on various levels, promoting harmony between man and nature. Like everywhere from southern Mexico to Brazil, the jaguar was much revered among all the groups, and only hunted to provide shamans with pelts, teeth and other ritualistic articles.

Gender divisions were, to an extent, along familiar lines: men made war and performed religious duties, while women were confined to domestic roles. However, women of the Boruca group in the southwest fought alongside men, and the Votos of the Zona Norte regularly had women chiefs. In many clans, the inheritance of names and objects was matrilineal.

People lived **communally** in stockaded villages, called **palenques** by the Spaniards. Whole groups, not necessarily related by kin, would live kibbutz-like in a village big-house. They organized work "gangs" who would tackle labour projects, usually agricultural. In most cases, land was held communally and harvests shared to ensure the survival of all. **Social hierarchy** was complex, with an ascending scale of *caciques* and shamans occupying the elite positions.

The Chorotegas in Guanacaste in particular developed a high level of **cultural expression**, possessing a written, symbol-based language, and harvesting and trading such diverse products as honey, natural dyes and cotton.

Costa Rica "discovered"

On September 18, 1502, on his fourth and last voyage to the Americas, **Columbus** sighted Costa Rica. Battered by a storm, he ordered his ships to drop anchor just off Isla Uvita, 1km offshore from present-day Puerto Limón. The group stayed seventeen days, making minor forays into the heavily forested coast and its few villages. The indigenous peoples that Columbus met – as he could not fail to notice – were liberally attired in gold headbands, mirrored breastplates, bracelets and the like, convincing him of potential riches. In fact, the **gold** worn by those first welcoming envoys would have been traded or come to the peoples of

Gold, land and souls

The first Spanish accounts of Costa Rican **indigenous peoples** were made in the sixteenth century by "**chroniclers**", the official scribes who accompanied mapping and evangelical expeditions. In general, these were either soldiers or missionaries who showed almost no talent for ethnography. Rather, they approached the pre-Columbian world as inventory-takers or suspicious accountants, writing terse and unimaginative reports liberally spiced with numbers and accounts of **gold** (although they found almost none). It was they who started the trend of portraying the cultures of the indigenous peoples of Costa Rica as "low" and underdeveloped; what they in fact meant was that there was little that could be expropriated for the Crown. Of the narratives that stand out is one by **Columbus** himself, who described the small welcoming party he received in 1502 in vivid and rather romanticized prose in his *lettera rarissima*, meant for the eyes of his sovereign.

Another, more important, account is by **Gonzalo Fernández de Oviedo**, whose comprehensive, nineteen-volume *Historía General de las Indias, Islas y Tierra Firme del Mar Oceano* was first published in 1535. Oviedo spent only ten or twelve days with the **Chorotega** peoples but he had a fine eye for detail, and recorded many aspects of the Chorotega diet, dress and social customs. He also noticed that they spoke a form of Nahua, the language of the Aztecs and the lingua franca of Mesoamerica, an observation that has since convinced most historians of a direct cultural link between the empires to the north and the peoples of pre-Columbian Costa Rica and Nicaragua.

One of the first things the Spanish chroniclers noticed was that the indigenous peoples in the **Talamancas** in the southeast and the **Greater Chiriquí** in the southwest practised **ritual sacrifice**. Every full moon, prisoners captured in the most recent raid would be ritually beheaded. The Spanish, of course, were repelled, and so began the systematic baptism campaigns, and the destruction of indigenous "idolatry".

the Caribbean coast through inter-tribal warfare. There was very little gold on this side of the country; rather, it came from the Valle de Diquis, in the southwest, the other side of the near-impenetrable hump of the Cordillera de Talamanca. With dreams of wealth, Columbus sailed on, charting the entire coastal region from Honduras to Panamá, and naming it **Veragua**.

In 1506, King Ferdinand of Spain despatched **Diego de Nicuesa** to govern what would become Costa Rica. From the start his mission was beset by hardship, beginning when their ship ran aground on the coast of Panamá, forcing the party to walk up the Caribbean shore. There they met native people who, unlike those who had welcomed Columbus tentatively but politely with their shows of gold, burned their crops rather than submit to the authority of the Spanish. This, together with the impenetrable jungles, the creatures that lived in them and tropical diseases, meant that the expedition had to be abandoned.

Next came **Gil González Davila**, in 1521–22, who concentrated on Costa Rica's Pacific coast, which offered safer anchorages. González and his men covered practically the entire length of Pacific Costa Rica on foot, baptizing as they went: the expedition priest later claimed that some 32,000 souls had been "saved" in the name of the King of Spain. The indigenous peoples, meanwhile, began a campaign of **resistance** that was to last nearly thirty years, employing guerrilla tactics, infanticide, attacks on colonist settlements and burning their own villages. There were massacres, defeats and submissions on both sides, but by 1540 Costa Rica was officially a **Royal Province of Spain**, and a decade later, the Conquest was more or less complete. Most of the key areas of the country had been charted or settled, with the exception of the Talamanca region, which remained largely unexplored for centuries.

Indigenous people in the colonial period

During the first years of the Spanish invasion, those indigenous Costa Ricans who grouped themselves in large settlements, like the Chorotegas, proved more easily subjected, and were carted off by the Spanish to work in the mines, build the first Costa Rican towns or co-opted to general slavery in the guise of farm work. The more scattered groups fared better, in the main exiling themselves to the rugged Talamancas. By then, however, the real conquerors of the New World had arrived: smallpox, influenza and measles. In the seventeenth and eighteenth centuries, huge pandemics swept the country, among them the so-called **Great Pandemic** of 1611–60, in which whole towns and villages disappeared virtually overnight; *caciques* as well as commoners died, leaving groups without leadership. Although colonial censuses are notoriously inaccurate, in 1563 it is reckoned that an estimated 80,000 indigenous peoples lived in Costa Rica; by 1714, the official count was 999. Today, in a country of 4.5 million, less than two percent, or around 65,000, are indigenous. For more on the current status of indigenous people in Costa Rica, see box, p.433.

In 1560, **Juan de Cavallon** and **Juan Vásquez de Coronado** – the first true conquistadors of Costa Rica – succeeded in penetrating the Valle Central, the area that would become most significant in the development of the nation. As Cortés had done in Mexico, the Spaniards of Costa Rica took advantage of existing rivalries among the native groups and played them off against each other; in this way, they managed to dominate the groups of the Pacific coast with the help of tribes from the Valle Central.

In the early years of the colony, the Spaniards quickly established the **encomienda**, a system widespread in the Spanish Crown's Central American possessions that gave the conquistadors and their descendants the right to demand tribute or labour from the indigenous population. The *encomienda* applied to all indigenous males in Costa Rica between the ages of 18 and 50, and to a lesser extent to women, with quotas set for the donation of foods such as cacao fruit, corn, chicken, honey and chilli peppers. From the Spanish point of view, the *encomienda* was compensation for the risks and hazards involved in coming to the New World, and its capacity to enrich the colonies was immense – as many people have said, no man came to America to be poorer than he was in Europe.

Costa Rica's indigenous peoples resisted servitude to the colonials quite fiercely, although (in the words of one *cacique*) they did get tired of "running around in the jungle and hiding all the time". Nor was there total acceptance of the way the native population was treated during this period. High-ranking clergymen protested to their Spanish overlords – as early as 1542, the **New Laws**, influenced by the passionate appeals of Fray Bartolomé de las Casas, decreed that colonizers had a duty to "protect" the indigenous peoples, and in 1711 the Bishop of Nicaragua, Fray Benito Garret y Arlovi, informed on the governor of Costa Rica for his brutal policies. These decrees assuaged the conscience of the Spanish Crown, but what happened on the ground in the colonies was, of course, quite a different matter.

The early settlers

It seems more appropriate to discuss the country's lack of colonial experience, rather than a bona fide colonization. In 1562, **Juan Vásquez de Coronado,** renowned for his favourable treatment of the indigenous peoples, became the second governor of Costa Rica. It was under his administration that the first settlement of any size or importance was established, and **Cartago**, in the heart of the Valle Central, was made capital of the colony. During the next century, settlers confined themselves more or less to the centre of the country. The Caribbean coast remained the haunt of buccaneers – mainly English – who put ashore and wintered here after plundering the lucrative Spanish Main, while the Pacific saw its share of pirate activity, too, most famously when Sir Francis Drake came ashore briefly in Bahía Drake in 1579.

This first epoch of the colony is remembered as one of unremitting **poverty**. Within a decade of its invasion Costa Rica was notorious throughout the Spanish Empire for its lack of gold. The settlers and their descendants, unlike those to the north and the south, who became wealthy on the gold of the Aztecs and Inca, never achieved their dreams of instant aristocracy. Instead, they were confronted with almost insuperable obstacles, including tropical fever, hunger and belligerent natives. The Valle Central was fertile, but there was uncertainty as to what crops to grow. Coffee had not yet been imported to Costa Rica, nor had tobacco, so it was to subsistence agriculture that most settlers turned, growing just enough to live on. There were no export crops and no national markets for foodstuffs. Spanish fabrics, manufactured goods and money itself became so scarce that by 1709 Valle Central settlers were forced to adopt cacao beans as currency. Goat's hair and bark were used as clothing fabrics, making your average eighteenth-century Costa Rican farmer look as wild and uncivilized as Romulus and Remus before the founding of Rome. In 1719, the governor of Costa Rica famously complained that he had to till his own land. With the emphasis on agriculture, and with little industry or trade, Costa Rica was unsurprisingly slow in founding urban settlements. In 1706, Cubujuquí (present-day Heredia) was established; in 1737, four years after Volcán Irazú blew its top, nearly destroying the capital, Villa Nueva de la Boca del Monte (later shortened, thankfully, to San José) was founded; and in 1782, it was the turn of Villa Hermosa (present-day Alajuela).

The tough yeoman **settler farmers** who survived in these conditions are the most distinct figures in Costa Rica's early colonial history, and their independent, though impoverished, state is widely believed to be the root of the country's modern-day egalitarianism. Recent historical works, however, concede that while everybody in the early days of the colony may have been equally poor, social distinctions still counted, and where they did not exist, were manufactured: indeed, there is evidence to show that, had economic conditions permitted, a system of indentureship would have been imposed on the local *mestizo* (mixed-race) population, as happened in the highlands of Nicaragua, El Salvador and Guatemala.

Two other crucial factors went into the making of the modern nation: one was **coffee**, eventually to become Costa Rica's main export, a crop that requires many smallholders rather than large hacienda systems; the other was **ethnic** as, quite simply, the vast majority of peasants in Costa Rica were descendants of the Spanish colonists, rather than **indigenos** or **mestizos**, and as such were treated as equals by the ruling elite, who saw them as **hermaniticos**, or "little brothers".

Independence and prosperity

The nineteenth century was the most significant era in the development of Costa Rica. Initially, after 1821, when Central America declared **independence** from Spain, freedom made little difference to Costa Ricans. Although granted on September 15, 1823, the news did not reach Costa Rica until a month later, when a mule messenger arrived from Nicaragua to tell the astonished citizens of Cartago the good news. Rather than rejoicing in being freed from the Spanish – Spain had not paid much attention to the poor and isolated province anyway – a **civil war** promptly broke out among the inhabitants of the Valle Central, dividing the citizens of Alajuela and San José from those of Heredia and Cartago. The Alajuela–San José faction triumphed, and **San José** became the capital city in 1823.

Costa Rica made remarkable progress in the latter half of the century, building roads, bridges and railways and filling San José with neo-Baroque, European-style edifices. Virtually all this activity was fuelled by the **coffee trade**, bringing wealth that the settlers just a century earlier could hardly have dreamed of. The coffee story begins as early as 1808, when beans from Cuba or Jamaica – depending on which sources you believe – were first planted in the Valle Central. The plants thrived in the highlands climate, and by 1820 citizens of Cartago were being encouraged – ordered, even – to plant coffee in their backyards. But most significant in its early history was the arrival in 1844 of English merchant **William Le Lacheur**. His ship, the *Monarch*, had emptied her hold of its cargo, and Le Lacheur arrived in the Pacific port of Puntarenas looking for ballast to take back to Liverpool. He travelled to the Valle Central, where he secured a cargo of coffee beans, which he bought on credit, promising to return and pay in two years' time.

Until that point, most of Costa Rica's coffee had made its way to Chile, where it was mixed with a lower-grade South American bean, packaged for export under the brand of **Café de Valparaíso** and sent to England, taking the long way around Cape Horn. With Le Lacheur's shipment, however, British taste buds were won round to the mellow, high-quality bean. A trading partnership began that saw the Costa Rican upper classes using Sheffield steel cutlery and Manchester linens for most of the eighteenth century.

The **coffee bourgeoisie** played a vital role in the cultural and political development of the country, and in 1848 the newly influential **cafetaleros** elected to the presidency their chosen candidate, Juan Rafael Mora. Extremely conservative and pro-trade, Mora came to distinguish himself in the battle against the American-backed filibuster William Walker in 1856, only to fall from grace and be executed in 1860 (see p.280).

Banana Republic: the United Fruit Company and race relations

The history of **banana growing** in Costa Rica is inextricably linked to the creation of the railroads. The San José–Puerto Limón railway – the "Jungle Train" – was designed by American capitalist **Minor Keith** to establish an easy route for Valle Central coffee to reach the Caribbean coast; previously the beans were transported via the Río Sarapiquí to Puntarenas then around Cape Horn. The railway took twenty years to build, its labour provided by an uneasy coalition of Highlanders, imported Chinese "coolie" labour, Italians and Jamaicans fleeing economic difficulties in their home country, and finally puffed its way out of the capital in 1890.

Minor had ingeniously planted bananas along the tracks in order to help pay for the route's construction, and as the fruit flourished and new markets opened up in Europe and the US, it became an exportable commodity: Costa Rica was the first Central American republic to grow bananas in bulk. In 1899, Keith and a colleague founded the **United Fruit Company**. The company, or **Yunai**, as it was called locally, came to transform the social, political and cultural face of Central America – and of all the countries in which it operated, it had the biggest dealings in Costa Rica. Opinions of Yunai oscillate between capitalist scourge and saviour of the nation. Almost from the beginning, the UFC – from 1970 known as the **United Brands Company** and since 1984 **Chiquita** – gained a reputation for **anti-union practices**, deserting entire areas once the workforce showed any signs of being organized. While the banana companies have always generally offered high salaries, workers would often spend their income – for many years given in redeemable scrip instead of cash – on drink and dissipation. To a degree, this was a deliberate plan by the company to have their labour force continuously in hock and therefore pliable.

As long as the UFC provided a steady flow of jobs, there was no real temptation for the **Jamaican population** (some 11,000 arrived in Costa Rica between 1874 and 1891) to leave the Caribbean coast, where they had effectively transported their own culture intact. In isolated Limón, they could retain their traditional food and religion and play West Indian games like cricket, preserving their culture in the face of a much larger Highlands majority. They could also use their ability to speak English to their advantage – often Afro-Caribbeans attained high-ranking positions in the *bananeros* because they could communicate with the American foremen in their own language.

When the plantations began to close down in Limón in 1925 as a result of the dreaded banana maladies Sigatoka and Panamá disease, their fortunes began to change. The UFC started to look for locations elsewhere in the country, acquiring land and planting bananas in the area around modern-day Quepos in the Central Pacific, and Golfito in the Zona Sur, and unbeknown to its Afro-Caribbean workers signed a contract with the government stipulating that **employment preference** be given to native Costa Ricans. It was not the first time the country's leaders had displayed such institutional racism – it is generally held that for the first half of the nineteenth century a law existed prohibiting the migration of Afro-Caribbeans to the Valle Central, while in 1933 the government had petitioned Congress to prohibit the

The early twentieth century

The first years of the **twentieth century** witnessed a difficult transition towards democracy in Costa Rica. Universal male suffrage had come into effect during the last years of the nineteenth century, but class and power conflicts still dogged the country, with several **caudillo** (authoritarian) leaders, familiar figures in other Latin American countries, hijacking power. In general, however, these characters ended up in exile, and neither the army nor the church gained much of a foothold in politics. A number of radical labour initiatives were created during the 1920s, inspired by the Russian Revolution, though for much of the twentieth entry of blacks into the country "because they are of a race inferior to ours" – and when the contract became public in September 1930, racial tensions rose to boiling point in Limón.

Afro-Caribbeans were caught, unable to afford the passage home to Jamaica on the one hand and prohibited from working elsewhere in the country on the other, and in 1934 the most virulent **strike** yet seen in the Costa Rican *bananeros* began. It was organized by **Carlos Luis Fallas**, labour activist and novelist, who had been exiled to Limón as a result of his militancy on behalf of labour organizations in the Valle Central. As historian Michael Seligson puts it, sending Fallas to the *bananeros* "was like throwing Brer Rabbit into the briar patch. For the judges Limón was the Siberia of Costa Rica; for Fallas, it was the Nirvana of union organizers". Fallas proved a brilliant organizer, though initially the proposals he put forward to the Company were quite mild, requesting things like malaria drugs, snakebite serum and payment in cash rather than scrip, which could easily be squandered. Nonetheless, the Company refused to recognize these proposals, and in August 1934 the strike began in earnest, tenaciously holding on in the face of physical harassment by the Company and police forces. For the next four years, strikes and worker opposition raged on, and in 1938 the Company pulled out of Limón Province for good, deserting it for the Pacific coast.

Left behind in the economic devastation and unable to migrate within the country in search of work, the Afro-Caribbean population either took up cacao cultivation, hacked out their own smallholdings or took to fishing or other subsistence activities. Overnight, the schools, bunkhouses, American dollars, scrip economy, liquor and cigarettes disappeared, as did the US foremen and the ample plantation-style homes they had occupied. From about 1934 to 1970, the region was virtually destitute, without much of a cash economy or any large-scale employers. It is only now beginning to recover in terms of banana production – under the aegis of the national banana-franchise operators **Standard Fruit Company** (now **Dole**) – and only at considerable cost to the environment, as more tropical forests are felled and more rivers polluted with the pesticides used on the fruit.

It is hard to appreciate the overwhelming presence that the Company wielded in communities until you see the schools and hospitals that it established, the accommodation it built for its managers and the rows upon rows of barrack-like houses it provided for its workers. You can get a flavour of this in the banana towns of Limón's Valle Estrella and on the road from Jacó to Quepos, where you pass through a long corridor of African palm-oil plantations, its only major remaining investment in Costa Rica. The Company also left its mark on the collective consciousness of the region – Carlos Luis Fallas's **novels** *Mamita Yunai* (see p.461) and *Gentes y gentecillas*, García Márquez's *One Hundred Years of Solitude* and Guatemalan Asturias's masterly *El Papa Verde* all document the power of the Company in the everyday life of the *pueblitos* of Central America.

century Costa Rica's successive administrations, whatever their political colour, have proved no friend of labour relations, beginning in 1924 when most **strikes** were outlawed. In 1931, the Communist Party was formed, followed quickly by the National Republican Party in 1932. The latter dominated the political scene for most of the 1940s, with the election in 1940 of the Republican (PRN) candidate **Rafael Calderón Guardia**, a doctor educated in part in Belgium and a devout Catholic.

It was Calderón who instigated the social reforms and state support for which Costa Rica is still almost unique in the region. In 1941, he established a new **Labour Code** that reinstated the right of workers to organize and strike, and a social security system providing free schooling for all. Calderón also paved the way for the establishment of the University of Costa Rica, health insurance, income security and assistance schemes, and thus won the support of the impoverished and the lower classes – and the suspicion of the governing elites. One of those less than convinced by his policies was the man who would come to be known as **"Don Pepe"**, the coffee farmer **José Figueres Ferrer**, who denounced Calderón and his expensive reforms in a radio broadcast in 1941 and was then abruptly forced into exile in Mexico, from where he plotted his return.

The "revolution" of 1948 and after

The **elections of 1948** heralded the most eventful year of the twentieth century for Costa Rica. Constitutionally, Costa Rican presidents could not serve consecutive terms, so the election battle that year was between **Teodorico Picado**, widely considered to be a Calderón puppet, and **Otilio Ulate Blanco**, an ally of Figueres, who during two years in exile had become a heroic figure in some circles, returning to Costa Rica to play a key part in the **Acción Democrática**, a loose group of anti-Calderonistas. Ulate won the presidency, but the PRN won the majority in Congress – a fact that effectively annulled the election results.

Figueres, back on the scene and intent upon overthrowing Picado, who had stepped in and declared himself president in the face of the annulment, soon formed an opposition party, ideologically opposed to the PRN, calling them, somewhat ironically in view of the "republican" in their name, "communists". In March, **fighting** around Cartago began, culminating in an attack by the Figueres rebels on San José. To a degree, the battles were fought to safeguard the system of democratic election in the face of corruption, and in order to stem the clannishness and personality cults that dogged all Costa Rican political parties and presidential campaigns.

While Figueres's rebel forces were well equipped with arms, some supplied through CIA contacts, the militia defending President Picado was not: the national army consisted of only about three hundred men at the time, and had to be supplemented by machete-wielding banana workers. Two thousand were dead by mid-April, when hostilities ceased. In May, the **Junta of the Second Republic** was formed, with Figueres as acting president, despite an after-the-fact attack from Nicaraguan Picado supporters in December.

Figueres wanted above all to engineer a complete break with the country's past, and especially the policies and legacies of the Calderonistas. Seeing himself as fighting both communism and corruption, he not only outlawed the PVP, the Popular Vanguard Party – formerly known as the Communist Party – but also nationalized the banks and devised a tax to hit the rich particularly hard, thus alienating the establishment. The new **constitution** drawn up in 1949 gave full citizenship to Afro-Caribbeans, full suffrage to women and abolished Costa Rica's army. In a way, the **abolition of the army** fitted with political precedents in Costa Rica. Nearly thirty years before, in 1922, former president Ricardo Jiménez Oreamuno had given a famous speech in which he said: "the school shall kill militarism, or militarism shall kill the Republic…we are a country with more teachers than soldiers…and a country that turns military headquarters into schools". Although the warming sentiment behind Jiménez's words is oft-repeated in Costa Rica, the truth is somewhat darker. Figueres's motives were not utopian but rather a pragmatic bid to limit the political instability that had been the scourge of so many Latin American countries, and an attempt to save valuable resources. Today, while the country still has no army, the police forces are powerful, highly specialized and, in some cases, heavily armed. Paramilitary organizations do exist, chief among them the Free Costa Rica Movement

(MCRL), formed in 1961 and active until the mid-1980s, which was allegedly involved in a number of deeds more reminiscent of the Guatemalan army's death squads than the spirit of a harmonious and army-free Costa Rica.

In 1951, Figueres formed the **National Liberation Party**, or PLN, in order to be legitimately elected. He was a genius in drawing together disparate strands of society: when the elections came around the following year, he got the agricultural smallholder vote, while winning the support of the urban working classes with his retention of the welfare state. At the same time, he appeased the right-of-centrists with his essentially free-marketeering and staunch anti-communist stance.

The **1960s** and **1970s** were a period of prosperity and stability in Costa Rica, when the welfare state was developed to reach nearly all sectors of society. In 1977, the **Indigenous Bill** established the right of aboriginal peoples to their own land reserves – a progressive measure at the time, although indigenous peoples today are not convinced the system has served them well (see box, p.433). At the end of the 1970s, regional conflicts deflected attention from the domestic agenda, with the Carazo (1978–82) administration announcing its support for the FSLN revolutionary movement in Nicaragua, who had finally managed to despatch the Somoza family into exile.

Storm in the isthmus: the 1980s

Against all odds, Costa Rica in the 1980s not only saw its way through the serious political conflicts of its neighbours, but also successfully managed predatory US interventionism, economic crisis and staggering debt. Like many Latin American countries, Costa Rica had taken out bank and government **loans** in the 1960s and 1970s to finance vital development. But in the early 1980s, the slump in international coffee and banana prices put the country's finances into the red. In September 1981, Costa Rica defaulted on its interest payments, becoming the first third-world country to do so and sparking off a chain of similar defaults in Latin America that threw the international banking community into crisis. Despite its defaults, Costa Rica's debt continued to accumulate and by 1989 had reached a staggering US $5 billion, one of the highest per capita debt loads in the world at the time.

To compound the economic crisis came the simultaneous escalation of the **Nicaraguan Civil War**. During the entire decade, Costa Rica's foreign policy – and to an extent its domestic agenda – would be overshadowed by tensions with Nicaragua and the US. Initially, the Monge PLN administration (1982–86) more or less capitulated to US demands that Costa Rica be used as a supply line for the Contra rebels, and Costa Rica also accepted military training for its police force from the US. At the same time, the country's first agreement for a structural adjustment loan with the IMF was signed. It seemed increasingly clear that Costa Rica was on the path to both violating its declared neutrality in the conflicts of its neighbours and condemning its population to wage freezes, price increases and other side effects associated with the IMF restructuring.

In May 1984, the situation escalated with the events at the **La Penca** press conference, given by the US-backed Contra leader Edén Pastora. Held in a simple hut on the banks of the Río San Juan, the conference had minimal security. A bomb was apparently carried into the hut by a "Danish" cameraman, concealed within an equipment case, and was intended to kill all. Miraculously, an aide of Pastora's accidentally kicked the case over, so that when it was detonated the force of the blast went up and down instead of sideways, thus saving the lives of most of those within, including Pastora himself. Although nobody is quite sure who was behind the bombing – both the CIA and freelance Argentinian terrorists have been implicated – it seems that the point of the carnage was to implicate Managua, thus cutting off international support and destabilizing the Sandinista government further. The immediate effect was to shock the Costa Rican government and the international community into paying more attention to the deadly conflicts of Nicaragua and, by association, El Salvador and Guatemala.

The Arias peace plan

In 1986, PLN candidate **Oscar Arias Sánchez** was elected to the presidency, and Costa Rica's relations with the US and Nicaragua took a different tack. The former political scientist began to play the role of peace broker in the conflicts of Nicaragua, El Salvador and, to a lesser extent, Honduras and Guatemala, mediating between these countries and also between domestic factions within them. In October 1987, just eighteen months after taking office, Arias was awarded the Nobel Prize for Peace, attracting worldwide attention.

Arias's **peace plan** focused on regional objectives, tying individual and domestic conflicts into the larger picture: the stability of the isthmus. It officially called for a ceasefire, the discontinuation of military aid to the Contra insurrectionists, amnesties for political prisoners and for guerrillas who voluntarily relinquished the fight, and, lastly and perhaps most importantly, intergovernmental negotiations leading to free and fair elections. The peace plan began, rather than ended, with the awarding of the Nobel Prize, dragging on throughout 1987 and 1988 and running into obstacles as, almost immediately, all nations involved charged one another with non-compliance or other violations. The situation deteriorated when the US stationed troops in southern Honduras, ready to attack Nicaragua. Meanwhile, Washington continued to undermine Costa Rica's declared neutrality, requesting in April 1988 that Arias approve Costa Rican territory as a corridor for "humanitarian aid" to the Contras. The same month, Arias met with US President George Bush in Washington, his diplomatic credibility enabling him to secure millions of dollars worth of American aid for Costa Rica without compromising the country politically. For its part, the last thing the US wanted was internal unrest in Costa Rica, its natural (if not entirely compliant) ally in the region.

However, while Arias had obviously stalled on the US using Costa Rica's northern border as a base from which to attack Nicaragua, he seemed to have fewer quibbles about what was happening in the south, in **Panamá**. In July 1989, CIA-supported anti-Noriega guerrilla forces (many of them ex-Contras) amassed along the Costa Rica–Panamá border in preparation for the US invasion of Panamá that would take place in December.

Though Arias had gained the admiration of statesmen around the world, he proved to be less than popular at home. Many Costa Ricans saw him as neglecting domestic affairs, while increasing prices caused by the IMF's economic demands meant that by the end of the decade conditions had not improved much in Costa Rica.

The 1990s

In 1990, the mantle of power fell to **Rafael Ángel Calderón Fournier** (son of Calderón Guardia), who, in the 1980s, had been instrumental in consolidating the opposition that became the free-marketeering Partido Unidad Social Cristiana, or PUSC. A year later, Costa Rica was rocked by its most powerful **earthquake** since the one that laid waste to most of Cartago in 1910. Centred in Limón Province, the quake killed 62 people and caused expensive structural damage. At the same time, nationals of El Salvador, Honduras, Guatemala and especially Nicaragua were looking to Costa Rica – the only stable country in the region – for asylum, and tension rose as the **refugees** poured in. In 1992, Costa Rica faced

Indigenous peoples in modern Costa Rica

You won't see much evidence of **native traditions** in Costa Rica today. Less than two percent of the country's population is of aboriginal extraction, and the dispersion of the various groups ensures that they frequently do not share the same concerns and agendas. Contact between them, apart from through bodies such as CONAI – the national indigenous affairs organization – is minimal.

Although a system of **indigenous reserves** was set up by the Costa Rican administration in 1977, giving aboriginal peoples the right to remain in self-governing communities, titles to the reserve lands were withheld, so that while the communities may live on the land, they do not actually own it. This has led to government contracts being handed out to, for example, mining operations in the Talamanca area, leading to infringements on the communities themselves, which are further hampered by the presence of missionaries in settlements like Amubrí and San José Cabécar. The 24 "Indian reserves" scattered around the country are viewed by their inhabitants with some ambivalence. As in North America, establishing a reservation system has led in many cases to a banishing of indigenous peoples to poor-quality land where enclaves of poverty soon develop.

In the last couple of decades, there has been a growing recognition of the importance of **preserving indigenous culture** and of providing reserves with increased services and self-sufficiency. In 1994, the first **indigenous bank** was set up in Suretka, Talamanca, by the Bribrí and Cabécar groups, to counter the fact that major banks have often refused indigenous business and initiatives credit; in the same year, indigenous people earned the **right to vote** in the country's elections for the first time. Political participation has been slow in coming, however, and basic rights such as control over their own land and its natural resources, and access to healthcare and an education that reflects their view of the world, are still wilfully disregarded; in 2008, in a direct violation of their **indigenous rights**, the government amended the Biodiversity Law without consulting the communities whose land it affected. A long-mooted law that will grant autonomy to indigenous communities should form part of President Chinchilla's **National Development Plan**, though whether it will bring them any real practical power remains to be seen.

more trouble as it was brought to law in US courts for its failure to abide by international labour laws, a continuing black mark on the country's copybook for most of the twentieth century.

Until 1994, elections in Costa Rica had been relatively genteel affairs, involving lots of flag-waving and displays of national pride in democratic traditions. The elections of that year, however, were probably the dirtiest to date. The campaign opened and closed with an unprecedented bout of mudslinging and attempts to smear the reputations of both candidates, tactics which shocked many Costa Ricans. The PLN candidate – the choice of the left, for his promises to maintain the role of the state in the economy – was none other than **José María Figueres**, the son of Don Pepe, who had died four years previously. During the campaign, Figueres was accused of shady investment rackets and influence peddling. His free-market PUSC opposition candidate, Dr Miguel Angel Rodríguez, fared no better, having admitted to being involved in a tainted-beef scandal in the 1980s. Figueres won, narrowly, though his term in office was plagued by a series of scandals. On a more positive note, in January 1995 a Free Trade agreement was signed with Mexico in order to try to redress the lack of preference given to Costa Rican goods in the US market by the signing of NAFTA. Costa Rica's economy received a further shot in the arm in 1996 when the communications giant INTEL chose the country for the site of their new factory in Latin America, creating thousands of jobs.

In February 1998, PUSC candidate **Dr Miguel Angel Rodríguez** was elected president, thus continuing the trend in Costa Rican politics for the past half-century, wherein power has been traded more or less evenly between the PLN and the PUSC. The new government committed itself to solving Costa Rica's most pressing problems, making improvements to the country's dreadful road system top priority, but financing this and other major public works by private (usually foreign) investment, a strategy that is still the order of the day.

The new millennium

Rodríguez was succeeded in April 2002 by Abel Pacheco de Espriella, a psychiatrist also from the PUSC; it was the first time that party had been re-elected. One of the key issues Pacheco faced was **CAFTA**, the Central American Free Trade Agreement (known in Spanish as the *Tratado de Libre Comercio* or **TLC**), a proposed trade agreement with the US that Costa Ricans feared would erode the country's advanced social system. Pacheco added Costa Rica's name to those of all the other Central American nations, but fierce debate within the country would continue to stall its ratification. Meanwhile, in 2004, Costa Rica's squeaky clean regional image was shattered by a series of **corruption** charges aimed at three of the country's former presidents: Rafael Angel Calderón Fournier, José María Figueres and Miguel Angel Rodríguez, all of whom were accused of accepting illegal financial kickbacks from foreign sources.

Promising to clamp down on government corruption, **Oscar Arias Sánchez** was elected president for the second time in February 2006, only narrowly beating rival Ottón Solís of the Citizens' Action Party. The main issue dividing the candidates was the ratification of CAFTA. Solís was against the accord, memorably stating, "The law of the jungle benefits the big beast. We are a very small beast". Arias was a strong advocate, claiming that lowering the trade barrier would bring much-needed investment and jobs to a nation with few natural resources. Post-election, CAFTA continued to split the country, sparking fiery nationwide protests and leading to a first national referendum in October 2007. Anti-CAFTA groups lobbied strongly, arguing that free-market policies would result in widespread job losses, that a flood of cheap food imports would undermine small-scale farmers and that the agreement would inevitably lead to international interference in the country's economic sovereignty. Despite this, the "*Sí*" vote scraped through with just over 51 percent of the vote, though continued opposition to the agreement meant that Arias spent the majority of his second term in office trying to push the deal through. Costa Rica finally **officially entered CAFTA** in January 2009 – the same month, perhaps portentously, that the most powerful **earthquake** in more than 150 years struck the Valle Central (see box, p.141) – though wrangling over the wording of individual bills meant that it wasn't until May 2010 that the final piece of legislation, a controversial copyright law, was approved.

Despite the divisive force of CAFTA, it was the PLN candidate, **Laura Chinchilla**, who triumphed in the February 2010 election, and in doing so became Costa Rica's **first female president**. A former vice president (she resigned from Arias' government the year before to concentrate on her campaign) and a consultant on Latin America for such organizations as the United Nations Development Program, Chinchilla had pledged to continue the free-market policies of her predecessor, claiming 47 percent of the vote ahead of regular rival Ottón Solís. More important, perhaps, were her promises to tackle **violent crime**, an escalating problem in a country better known for its peaceful disposition. This alarming rise has been linked with the growing presence of **drug-trafficking**, as Columbian and Mexican cartels increasingly use the country as a convenient pick-up point – Costa

Invasion by internet

On October 18, 2010, a group of Nicaraguan soldiers set up base on **Isla Calero**, an island on the south side of the Río San Juan, as part of an ongoing operation to dredge the river. With the centre of the San Juan serving as the historical border between Costa Rica and Nicaragua, the soldiers were technically occupying Costa Rican territory, but their commander had a simple, one-word justification for their apparent incursion: Google.

On their global mapping project, **Google Maps**, the internet giant had bestowed the island (some 1.7km of land at the river's eastern end) to Nicaragua – wrongly, according to Costa Rica, who believe that the border should follow the demarcation laid out in the **1897 Alexander Award**, but rightly according to Nicaragua, who feel that the **1858 Cañas-Jerüz Treaty**, which states that Isla Calero is in their territory, still holds true.

The "occupation" of Isla Calero is just the latest footnote in a dispute over the Río San Juan that stretches back over two hundred years, the arguments growing ever more intense as the river's delta dries out and the border shifts further northwards. At the time of writing, however, this most recent episode had involved the **Organization of American States** (**OAS**) and the **International Court of Justice**, as both sides sought to clarify once and for all just where one country ends and the other begins.

Rican police seized over ninety tonnes of cocaine between 2006 and 2009, nearly twice the amount they captured over the course of the previous decade. The fight against the cartels is a regional issue, and Chinchilla was quick to show her commitment to the Central American Integration System (or **SICA**) by touring Guatemala, El Salvador, Honduras and Nicaragua shortly after her victory.

The path to regional integration, however, remains a long one, and in October 2010 old hostilities were revived when Nicaraguan troops crossed into Costa Rica in the latest instalment of their protracted **border dispute** (see box above). This renewed round of mudslinging with their northern neighbours capped a difficult first six months in office for Chinchilla, who inherited several problems from her predecessor – soon after coming to power, she was forced to close part of the **Caldera Highway** (the new toll road linking San José with the Pacific that many believe was rushed through in time for Arias to put his name to it) after rock falls and mudslides made the section between Atenas and Orotina impassable – and faces a series of difficult decisions if she is to deliver on her electoral promises. Chief among these is raising the necessary resources to fulfill those campaign pledges, by **reforming the tax system**, exploring trade revenues with countries beyond the Americas (the signing of the Association Agreement with the European Union in May 2010 has given Costa Rica unprecedented access to European markets) and privatizing the state-run insurance and telecommunications industries, the latter a direct result of CAFTA. The opening of the country's **mobile-phone market** is already underway, and three new operators are expected to be providing services by September 2011.

Tourism continues to play a vital part in the nation's economy, and while the country bounced back well from the global recession to again break the two-million-visitor mark in 2010, the downturn was a timely reminder that summer visitors are notoriously fickle, and today's fashionable gated resort hotel can easily become tomorrow's five-star white elephant. Treading the fine line between preserving Costa Rica's social system and creating a more stable economic foundation, while developing the tourist sector in a sustainable and sensible way, seem to be the key challenges facing the nation in the early years of the third millennium.

Landscape and wildlife

New World animals are believed to have crossed from Asia via the Bering Strait land bridge and migrated steadily southward through North America, evolving on the way. Because of Costa Rica's own celebrated position as a land bridge between the temperate Nearctic zone to the north and the Neotropics to the south, its varied animal life features tropical forms like the jaguar, temperate-zone animals like the deer and some unusual, seemingly hybrid combinations such as the coati.

Habitats

Although roughly the size of West Virginia, Nova Scotia or Wales, Costa Rica has nearly as many **habitats** as the whole of the US, including forests, riverside mangroves, seasonal wetlands and offshore marine forms such as coral reefs. Within this relatively small area, there is a remarkably varied **terrain**, ranging from the plains of Guanacaste, where there is often no rain for five months of the year, to the Caribbean lowlands, thick-forested and deluged with a liberal 6000mm of precipitation annually. In terms of **elevation**, too, the country possesses great diversity: from the very hot and humid lowlands of Corcovado, the terrain rises within just 150km to the chilly heights of Cerro Chirripó, at 3819m.

Life zones

Because Costa Rica's territory is almost bewilderingly varied, with similar geographical features found in many different places, it makes sense to speak of **life zones**, a detailed system of categorization referring primarily to forest habitats, developed in 1947 by biologist L.R. Holdridge to describe particular characteristics of terrain, climate and the life they support. Although he conceived the system in Haiti, with temperature and rainfall being the main determinants, this system has been used to create ecological maps of various countries, including Costa Rica. To read more about the cloudforest, see box on p.330; for the dry forest, see box on p.267.

The most endangered of all the life zones in Costa Rica is the **tropical dry forest**, which needs about six dry months a year. Most trees here are deciduous or semi-deciduous; some lose their leaves near the end of the dry season, primarily to conserve water. They are less stratified than rainforests, with two layers rather than three or four, and appear far less dense. Orchids flower in the silver and brown branches, and bees, wasps and moths proliferate. Animal inhabitants include iguanas, white-tailed deer and some of the larger mammals, including the jaguar. The best examples are in the northwest, especially **Guanacaste** and **Santa Rosa national parks**.

The **tropical wet forest** is home, metre per metre, to the greatest number of species of flora and fauna, including the bushmaster snake and tapir, along with jaguar and other wild cats. Here the canopy trees can be very tall (up to 80m) and, true to its name, it receives an enormous amount of rain – typically 5000–6000mm per year. Found in lowland areas, tropical wet forest is now confined to large protected blocks, chiefly the **Sarapiquí–Tortuguero** area and the large chunk preserved as **Parque Nacional Corcovado** on the Osa Peninsula.

Anatomy of a rainforest

Rainforests can feature **primary forest**, which has not been disturbed for several hundreds, or even thousands, of years, and what's known as **secondary growth**, which is the vegetation that springs up in the wake of some disturbance, such as cutting, cultivation or habitation. A tropical rainforest is characterized by the presence of several **layers**, each interconnected by a mesh of horizontal lianas and climbers. At its most complex, it will be made up of four layers: the **canopy**, about 40 to 80m high, at the very top of which are emergent trees, often flat-topped; the **subcanopy**, beneath the emergent trees; the **understory** trees, typically 10 to 20m in height; and finally the **shrub**, or ground, layer.

Premontane wet forests are found upon many of Costa Rica's mountains. Some trees are evergreen and most are covered with a thick carpet of moss. These forests typically exist at a high altitude and receive a lot of rain: the cover in **Parque Nacional Tapantí-Macizo Cerro de la Muerte** in the southwest Valle Central is a good example, as is **Parque Nacional Braulio Carrillo**, which has all five of the montane life zones within its boundaries. Many of the same animals that exist in the tropical wet forest live here, along with brocket deer and peccaries.

Perhaps the most famous of Costa Rica's life zones are the tropical lower montane wet forests, or **cloudforests**, which occur in very isolated patches, mainly south of Cartago and on the Pacific slopes of the Cordillera de Tilarán. They're produced when the northeasterly trade winds from the Caribbean drift across to the high ridge of the Continental Divide, where they cool to become dense clouds that create a perennial near-one-hundred-percent humidity. The primeval-looking cloudforest hosts many bromeliads, including orchids, and has an understorey thick with vines, ferns and drooping lianas; its animal life includes tapirs, pumas and quetzals. Costa Rica's best known cloudforest is at **Monteverde**.

Tropical montane rainforest occurs at the highest altitudes; the tops of **Poás** and **Irazú** volcanoes are good examples. Although large mosses and ferns can be seen, much of the vegetation has a shrunken, or dwarfed aspect, due to the biting wind and lofty altitude. Animals that live here include the Poás squirrel (endemic to that volcano) and some of the larger birds, including raptors and vultures.

At the very top of the country near **Cerro Chirripó** is the only place you'll find **tropical subalpine rain paramo**, inhospitably cold, with almost no trees. Costa Rica is the northern frontier of this particular Andean type of paramo. Except for hardy hawks and vultures, birds tend to shun this cold milieu, although at lower elevations you may spot quetzals.

Mangroves, wetlands and rivers

The **mangrove** is an increasingly fragile and endangered ecosystem that occurs along tropical coastlines and is particularly vulnerable to dredging: among others, the *Hotel de Playa Tambor* in the Central Pacific (see box, p.340) has been accused of irresponsibly draining mangroves. With their extensive root system, mangrove trees are unique for their ability to adapt to the salinity of seaside or tidal waters, or to areas where freshwater rivers empty into the ocean. Because they absorb the thrust of waves and tides, they act as a buffer zone behind which species of aquatic and land-based life can flourish unmolested. Meanwhile, the beer-coloured mangrove swamp water is like a nutritious primordial soup where a range of species can grow, including crustaceans and shrimp as well as turtles, caimans and crocodiles, and their banks are home to a variety of bird life.

Birds and reptiles are especially abundant in the country's remaining **wetlands**, which are typically seasonal, caused by the flooding of rivers with the rains, only to shrink back to pleated mud flats in the dry season. The lagoons of the **Refugio Nacional de Vida Silvesetre Caño Negro** in the Zona Norte and the Río Tempisque, within the boundary of **Parque Nacional Palo Verde** in Guanacaste, are the prime wetlands in Costa Rica.

Despite increasing silting and pollution caused largely by banana plantations, Costa Rica's **rivers** support a variety of life, from fish, including snook and tarpon, to migratory birds, crocodiles, caimans and freshwater turtles. The waterways that yield the best wildlife-watching are the Tortuguero canals and the *ríos* San Juan, Frío and Sierpe, as well as the Río Tárcoles in Parque Nacional Carara on the central Pacific coast.

Marine habitats

Costa Rica's **coral reefs**, never as extensive as those in Belize, are under threat. Much of the **Caribbean coast** was seriously damaged by the 1991 earthquake, which heaved the reefs up above the water. The last remaining ones on this side of the country are at **Cahuita** and a smaller one further south at **Manzanillo** in the Refugio de Vida Silvestre Gandoca-Manzanillo. Though the Cahuita reef has been under siege for some time from silting caused by clearing of land for banana plantations, and pesticides used in banana cultivation, you can still see some fine – extremely localized – specimens of moose horn and deer horn coral. On the **Pacific coast**, the most pristine reef is at **Bahía Ballena**, protected within Costa Rica's first marine national park, and also the reef that fringes Isla del Caño, about 20km offshore from the north coast of the Osa Peninsula. Meanwhile, lying 535km southwest of Costa Rica's pacific coast, **Parque Nacional Isla del Coco** remains the country's marine treasure, a coveted destination for experienced divers whose surrounding waters are home to more than thirty species of coral.

Wildlife

It is a source of constant woe for guides in Costa Rica to have to deal with tourists who have paid their national park entrance fees and then expect to be reimbursed in kind by seeing a tapir, jaguar or ocelot. Many of the country's more exotic **mammals** are either nocturnal, endangered or made shy through years of hunting and human encroachment. Although encounters do occur, they are usually brief, with the animal in question dipping quietly back into the shadows from which it first emerged. That said, however, it's very possible you will come into (usually fleeting) contact with some of the smaller and more abundant mammals.

Despite its reputation, Costa Rica does not have Central America's most diverse vertebrate fauna – that honour goes to Guatemala. However, Costa Rican **insects** and **birds** are particularly numerous, with 850 species of birds (including migratory ones) – more than the US and Canada combined. Costa Rica is also home to a quarter of the world's known **butterflies** – more than in all Africa – thousands of moths, and scores of bees and wasps.

Many of the birds, mammals, reptiles and amphibians detailed below feature in the full-colour **wildlife guide** on pp.22–32.

Birds (*pájaros*, *aves*)

Bird life, both migratory and indigenous, is abundant in Costa Rica and includes some of the most colourful birds in the Americas: the **quetzal**, the **toucan** and the **scarlet macaw**. Many are best observed while feeding – guides often point out quetzals, for instance, when they are foraging from their favoured **aguacatillo** tree, and you might catch a glimpse of the hummingbird hovering over a bright flower as it sups on its nectar.

Cloudforest and rainforest birds

It's only fair that any discussion of birds in Costa Rica starts with the one that so many people come to see: the brilliant green and red **resplendent quetzal** (*quetzal*). With a range historically extending from southern Mexico to northern Panamá – more or less the delineations of Mesoamerica – the dazzling quetzal was highly prized by the Aztecs and the Maya. In the language of the Aztecs, *quetzali* means, roughly, "beautiful", and along with jade, the shimmering, jewel-coloured feathers were used as currency in Maya cities. The feathers were also worn by Maya nobles to signify religious qualities and social superiority, and formed the headdress of the plumed serpent Quetzalcoatl, the supreme Aztec god.

Hunting quetzals is particularly cruel, as it is well known that the bird cannot (or will not) live in captivity, a poignant characteristic that has made it a symbol of freedom throughout Mesoamerica. The male in particular – who possesses the distinctive feather train of up to 1.5m long – is still pursued by poachers, and the quetzal is further endangered due to the destruction of its favoured cloudforest habitat. These days the remaining cloudforests (particularly Monteverde and Los Quetzales) are among the best places to try to see the birds (March–May is most favourable), although they are always difficult to spot, in part due to shyness and in part because the vibrant green of their feathers, seemingly so eye-catchingly bright, actually means that they blend in well with the wet and shimmering cloudforest. Quetzals are officially protected in Costa Rica in Braulio Carrillo and Volcán Poás national parks in the Valle Central, in Parque Nacional Los Quetzales and Chirripó in the Zona Sur, and in Monteverde.

The rarer **scarlet macaw** (*lapa roja*), with its liberal splashes of red, yellow and blue, was once common on the Pacific coast of southern Mexico and Central America. The birds, which are monogamous, live in lowland forested areas, but these days your best chance of spotting them is in Parque Nacional Corcovado on the Osa Peninsula, though their numbers are on the increase in Parque Nacional Carara in the central Pacific, the Refugio Nacional de Vida Silvestre Curú on the southern Nicoya Peninsula, and in Parque Nacional Palo Verde and the Reserva Biológica Lomas Barbudal in Guanacaste. They are usually spotted in or near their nesting holes (they nest in tree trunks), in the upper branches, or while flying high in pairs and calling to one another with their distinctive raucous squawk.

Parakeets are still fairly numerous and are most often seen in the lowland forested areas of the Pacific coast. You're also likely to see the **chestnut-mandibled** and **keel-billed toucans** (*tucánes*), with their ridiculous but beautiful banana-shaped beaks. The chestnut-mandibled is the largest; their bills are two-tone brown and yellow. Keel-billed toucans have the more rainbow-coloured beaks and are smaller, which is sometimes taken advantage of by their larger cousins, who may drive them away from a cache of food or hound them out of a particular tree. At other times, though, both types seem to commune quite happily. Toucans can be found in both higher and lower elevations, but in Costa Rica you are most likely to see them in the Caribbean lowlands, particularly the Sarapiquí area. They are most often spotted at dawn and in the afternoon as early as 4 or 4.30pm – although dusk is best – sitting in the open upper branches of secondary forest.

Hardly anyone gets through a day or two in Monteverde or Santa Elena without at least hearing the distinctive, metallic call of the **three-wattled bellbird** (*pájaro campana*). If you catch a glimpse of them, you'll see that they look even stranger than their clunk-sounding clarion call, with three worm-like black sacks hanging off their beak. Monteverde is also a good place to watch the antics of the tiny thumb-sized **hummingbirds** (*colibrís*), who buzz about like particularly swift, engorged bees. Thanks to their wings' unusual round hinges, hummingbirds can feed on flower nectar while actually hovering – their wings can beat at up to eight times a second. They are numerous in Costa Rica (there are over fifty species), and some local types, like the purple-throated mountain gem, are particularly pretty.

Water birds

Most birds you'll see in the country's **waterways** and **wetlands** are **migratory** species from the north, including herons, gulls, sandpipers and plovers. Larger marine birds – pelicans and frigatebirds for example – come from much further afield, often making the journey from New Zealand or Cape Horn. Most migratory species are in residence between January and April, though a few arrive as early as November. The seasonal lagoons of the **Río Tempisque** basin in Guanacaste and **Caño Negro** in the Zona Norte are home to the largest diversity and number of freshwater birds, both migratory and resident, in Central America.

Permanent residents of Costa Rican river areas include **cormorants** and **anhingas** (sometimes called "snakebirds" in English, due to their sinuous necks), which impale their prey on the knife-point of their beaks before swallowing. The elegant, long-limbed **white ibis** (*ibis blanco*) often stands motionless on river-level branches and banks; harder to spot and more endangered is the giant **jabirú stork** (*cigüeña jabirú*).

Travelling the Tortuguero canals or on the Río Sierpe down to Bahía Drake on the Osa Peninsula you are likely to see a **kingfisher** (*martín pescador*); the green kingfisher, with its deep forest-green back and distinctive crown is particularly lovely. The world's largest colony of Nicaraguan **grackle** (*zanate*) makes regular appearances in Caño Negro, the only place in Costa Rica where these dark, crow-like birds nest. Other water birds include **brown pelicans** (*buchón*) and the pretty pink **roseate spoonbills** (*espátula rosada*) found mainly in the Río Tempisque basin, where you can also see huge clumps of nesting **night-herons** (*cuacu*). The most common bird, and the one you're likely to come across hiking or riding in cattle country, is the unprepossessing grey-white **egret** (*garza*).

Birds of prey

Of the raptors (hawks and eagles), the **laughing falcon** (*guaco*), found all over the country, probably has the most distinct call, which sounds exactly like its Spanish name – the "laughing" bit comes from a much lower-pitched variation, which resembles muted human laughter. The falcon preys on reptiles, including venomous snakes, biting off the head before bringing the body back to its eyrie, where it drapes it over a branch, sings a duet with its mate and proceeds to dine. The sharp-eyed, mottled brown **osprey** (*águila pescadora*) still has a reasonably good species count, despite the blows that deforestation has dealt to its rainforest habitat. You're most likely to see ospreys patrolling the skies of the canals between Barra del Colorado and Limón or in the Refugio de Vida Silvestre Gandoca-Manzanillo. **Harpy eagles** (*águila harpía*) have not fared so well, and are thought to be locally extinct, due to widespread destruction of their favoured upper-canopy habitat. There is a chance that some may still live and hunt in the interior of

Parque Nacional Corcovado on the Osa Peninsula, or within the rugged Parque Internacional La Amistad in the south of the country. Their bushy crowns give them a tousled look, rather than the usual fierce appearance of raptors, and they have a delicate, hooked beak.

The shrunken-shouldered **vulture** (*zópilote*) is not usually considered of interest to birders. That said, it is the one bird that almost everyone will see at some point – both the black and turkey varieties – hanging out opportunistically at the side of major highways waiting for rabbits and iguanas to be thumped beneath the wheels of a passing vehicle.

You're unlikely to see much of owls, as they are nocturnal, but the **tropical screech owl** (*sorococa*) is commonly heard, even in the suburbs of San José, with its distinctive whirring call that builds to a screech or laugh as it takes flight.

Mammals (*mamíferos*)

Costa Rica's **mammals** range from the fairly unexotic (at least for North Americans and Europeans) white-tailed deer and brocket deer, via the seemingly antediluvian, such as Baird's tapir or "mountain cow", to the preternatural or semi-sacred jaguar.

Cats

Now an endangered species, the **jaguar** (*tigre*) is endemic to the New World tropics and has a range from southern Mexico to northern Argentina. Once common throughout Central America, especially in the lowland forests and mangroves of coastal areas, the jaguar's main foe has long been man, who has hunted it for its valuable pelt and because of its reputation among farmers as a predator of calves and pigs. It is easily tracked, due to its distinctive footprint (which is as close as you're likely to get to seeing one), and incredibly, the hunting of jaguars for sport was allowed right up until the 1980s – although the trade was hampered by the fact that it is illegal to import the pelts into most countries, including the US. Considered sacred by the Maya, jaguars are a very striking mid-sized cat; nearly always golden with black spots, and much more rarely a sleek, beautiful black. They feed on smaller mammals such as agoutis, monkeys and peccaries, and may also eat fish and birds. Not to be confused with the jaguar, the **jaguarundi** (*león breñero*) is a small cat, also rarely seen, ranging in colour from reddish to black. Little studied, the jaguarundi has short legs and a low-slung body; they are swift and shy, and although they live in many lowland areas and forests, are very rarely encountered by walkers.

All Costa Rica's cats have been made extremely shy through centuries of hunting. The one exception, since its pelt isn't big enough to make it a worthwhile target, is the small, sinuous-necked **margay** (*tigrillo*), with its complex black-spotted markings and large, inquisitive eyes. It has been known to peek out of the shadows and even sun itself on rocks. The **ocelot** (*manigordo*) is similar, somewhere between the margay and jaguar in size, but is another animal you are very unlikely to see. Of all the cats, the sandstone-coloured **puma or mountain lion** (*puma*) is said to be the most forthcoming – it's a big animal, and although not usually aggressive towards humans, should be treated with respect.

Monkeys

Costa Rica is home to four species of monkey. Most people can expect to at least hear, if not see, the **mantled howler monkey** (*mono congo*), especially in the lowland forests: the male has a mechanism in its thick throat by which it can make sounds that resemble those of a gorilla. Their whoops are most often heard at dawn or dusk. The **white-faced capuchin monkey** (*mono carablanca*) is slighter than the howler, with a distinctly humanoid expression on its delicate face. This, combined with its intelligence, often consigns it to being a pet in a hotel or private zoo. In the wild, it's also the most curious of the monkeys, often descending to the lower branches of trees to get a better look at the strange pinkish creatures staring up at them. The **spider monkey** (*mono araña*) takes its name from its spider-like ability to move through the trees employing its five limbs – the fifth is its prehensile tail, which it uses to grip branches. A troupe of spider monkeys making their leaping, gymnastic way through the jungle (usually following a well-worn trail known as a "monkey highway") is a particularly impressive sight. The **squirrel monkey** (*mono tití*) is presently only found in and around Parque Nacional Manuel Antonio. Their delicate grey and white faces have long made them attractive to pet owners and zoos, and consequently they have been hunted to near extinction in Costa Rica. However, they are extremely gregarious – though they can be easily put off by too many people tramping through Manuel Antonio – and you may well catch sight of one.

Sloths

Two types of **sloth** live in Costa Rica: the **three-toed sloth** (*perezoso de tres dedos*), active by day, and the more nocturnal **two-toed sloth** (*perezoso de dos dedos*). True to their name, sloths ("*perezoso*" means "lazy" in Spanish) move very little during the day and have an extremely slow metabolism. They are excellently camouflaged from their main predators, eagles, by the algae that often covers their brown hair. In the first instance at least, they are very difficult to spot without the help of a guide; scan the V-intersections in trees, particularly the middle and upper elevations – from a distance, they resemble a ball of fur or a hornet's nest. Their sharp, taloned claws are best suited to the arboreal world, and outside the tree limbs they are a bit lost, exposing themselves to predators such as jaguars and other animals, yet once a week, risking life and limb, they descend to the forest floor to defecate. No one has yet come up with a solid hypothesis for this irrational behaviour.

Ungulates

Along with the jaguar, the tapir is perhaps the most fantastical form inhabiting the Neotropical rainforest, where it is called **Baird's tapir** (*danta*). A distant relative of the rhinoceros, the tapir also occurs in the tropics of Southeast Asia. Rather homely, with eyes set back on either side of its head, the tapir looks something between a horse and an overgrown pig, with a stout grey-skinned body and a head that suggests an elephant with a truncated trunk. Their antediluvian look comes from their prehensile snout, small ears and delicate cloven feet. Weighing as much as 300kg (and vegetarian), they are extremely shy in the wild, largely nocturnal, and stick to densely forested or rugged land: consequently, they are very rarely seen by casual rainforest walkers, though you may spot one in the inner reaches of Parque Nacional Corcovado. Like the jaguar, its main foe is man, who hunts it for its succulent meat, though it is protected to a degree in national parks and reserves. Unlike the jaguar, the tapir is certain to be unaggressive should you be lucky enough to come upon one.

The **peccary** (*saíno*), usually described as a wild pig or boar, comes in two little-differentiated species in Costa Rica: collared or white-lipped. While peccaries are not on the whole dangerous, they can be menacing when encountered in packs, and, if they get a whiff of you – their sight is poor, so they'll smell you before they see you – they may clack their teeth and growl. The usual advice, especially in Parque Nacional Corcovado, where they travel in groups as large as thirty, is to climb a tree.

Anteaters, rodents, weasels and raccoons

You may well see an **anteater** vacuuming an anthill at some point. Of the two species that inhabit Costa Rica (the giant anteater that was once found on both the Caribbean and Pacific slopes, is now thought to be extinct), you're much more likely to see the **northern tamandua** (*osa hormiguero*), although it is largely nocturnal. It hunts ants, occasionally bees, and termites, digging into nests using its sharp claws and inserting its proboscis-like snout into the mound to lick up its prey. Far rarer, the **silky anteater** (*serafín del platanar*) is arboreal, a lovely golden in colour, and hardly ever seen.

Some of the animals you are more likely to see – because of their abundance and diurnal activity – look like outsize versions or variations on temperate-zone mammals: the rabbit-like **agouti** (*guatusa*), for example, the **paca** (*tepezcuintle*), a large water-rodent, or the mink-like **tayra** (*tolumuco*), who may flash by you on its way up a tree; notable for its lustrous coat and snake-like sinuosity, the tayra can be fierce if cornered. The Neotropical **river otter** (*nutria*) is an altogether friendlier creature, although extremely shy. The **coati** (often mistakenly called *coatimundi*; *pizote* in Spanish) looks like a confused combination of a raccoon, domestic cat and an anteater and is regularly seen in packs of a dozen or more, on the scrounge for food. There are also two **raccoons**, the northern raccoon (*mapache norteño*) and the slightly larger crab-eating raccoon (*mapache cangrejero*), which lives only in southwest Costa Rica. Nearly all of these are foragers and forest-floor dwellers.

Bats

With 109 species in Costa Rica, **bats** (*murciélagos*) make up over half of the country's mammal species; most of them are spotted whizzing about at dusk,

Guises and disguises

Rainforest fauna and flora have an elaborate repertoire of ruses, poisons and camouflages that they put to a variety of uses, from self-protection to pollination. Many tropical animals are well known for their gaudy **colour**, which can mean one of two things: warning potential predators to keep away, or flaunting an invulnerable position at the top of the food chain. Particularly notable are the birds that inhabit the rainforest canopy: toucans, parakeets and scarlet macaws, not to mention the resplendent quetzal. Unfortunately, while showing off the fact that they have hardly any predators, these beautiful birds make themselves vulnerable to perhaps the most threatening adversary of them all: man.

Advertising **toxicity** is another ingenious evolutionary development. The amazingly colourful poison-dart frogs are a case in point, as is the venomous coral snake. These reptiles give the "keep away" signal loud and clear to potential predators, some of whom, after successive bad experiences, build up a species memory and cease preying upon them.

Some animals are **camouflage** experts, which again serves one of two purposes: to be able to hide in order to ensnare prey, or to avoid predators. The predatorial jaguar looks exactly like the mottled light of the ground floor of the rainforest, making it easier to both hide and hunt, while the clear-winged butterfly literally disappears into thin air. Sloths, too, hide from their attackers, with a greasy green alga growing on their fur, making them look even more like the clump of leaves that they already resemble.

Then there are the **mimics**, usually insects, which have an evolutionary ability to look like something that they are not. The asilidae family in particular features many copycats: flies impersonate wasps and wasps disguise themselves as bees, all in the pursuit of safety or predation.

though you can also see them hang out by day, sleeping on the underside of branches, where they look like rows of small grey triangles. In Tortuguero, you may see a **fishing bat** (*murcielago pescador*) skimming the water, casting its aural net in front in search of food: being blind, it fishes by sonar. For the best bat-viewing opportunities, head to Parque Nacional Barra Honda caves on the Nicoya Peninsula, where they roost in huge numbers.

Amphibians and reptiles (*anfíbios y reptiles*)

There are many, many **frogs** (*ranas*) and **toads** (*sapos*) in Costa Rica. Though they seem vulnerable – small, and with few defences – many tropical frogs look after themselves by secreting poison through their skin. Using some of the most powerful natural toxins known, the frog can directly target the heart muscle of the predator, paralysing it and causing immediate death; as these poisons are transmittable through skin contact, you should never touch a Costa Rican frog. Probably the best known, and most toxic, of the frogs, is the colourful **poison-dart frog** (*rana venenosa*), usually quite small, and found in various combinations of bright red and blue or green and black. Even the innocuous-looking **shore** or **beach frog** can shoot out a jet of toxins; while it may not be fatal to humans, it can kill heedless cats and dogs who try to pick it up in their mouths.

The more common ways in which tropical frogs defend themselves are through camouflage (usually mottled brown, green or variations thereon – they blend perfectly into the tropical cover) or by jumping, a good method of escape in thick ground cover. Jumping also throws snakes – who hunt by scent, and are probably their most prevalent predator – off track. You will most likely see frogs around dusk or at night; some of them make a regular and dignified procession down paths and trails, sitting motionless for long periods before hopping off again. The chief thing you'll notice about the more common frogs is their size: they're much stouter than temperate-zone frogs. Look out for the **red-eyed tree frog** (*rana calzonuda*), star of many a frog calendar: relatively large, it is an alarming bright green, with orange hands and feet and dark blue thighs; its sides are purple, and its eyes are pure red, to scare off potential predators.

Crocodiles, caiman and lizards

Travelling along or past Costa Rica's waterways, you may well see **caiman** (same in Spanish) and **crocodiles** (*cocodrilo*). Crocs hang out on muddy riverbanks, basking in the sun, while the smaller, shyer caiman will sometimes perch on submerged tree branches, scuttling away at your approach. Both are under constant threat from hunters, who sell their skin to make shoes and handbags. Your best chance of seeing either is in Tortuguero.

Pot-bellied **iguanas** (*gallina de palo*) are the most ubiquitous of Costa Rica's lizards, as common here as chickens are in Europe or the US (indeed, their Spanish name means "tree chicken", though this is a reference more to the taste of their meat). Masters of camouflage, they can occasionally be spotted on the middle and lower branches of trees and on the ground. Despite their dragon-like appearance, they are very shy, and when you do spot them, it's likely that they'll be scurrying away in an ungainly fashion. In wetlands and on rivers, watch out for a tiny form skittering across the water: this is the **basilisk** or **"Jesus Christ" lizard** (*basilisk*), so-called for its web-like foot and speed, which allows it to "walk" on water.

Snakes

Costa Rica is home to a vast array of **snakes** (*serpientes*, *culebras*). Many of them, both venomous and non-venomous, are amazingly beautiful: this can be appreciated more if you see them in captivity than if you come across one in the wild. That said, the chances of the latter happening – let alone getting bitten – are very slim. Snakes are largely nocturnal, and for the most part far more wary of you than you are of them.

Out of 162 species found in the country, only 22 are venomous. These are usually well camouflaged, but some advertise their danger with a flamboyance of colour. One such is the highly venomous **coral** (*coralillo*) snake, which, although retiring, is easily spotted – and avoided – with its bright rings of carmine red, yellow and black. The **false coral** snake (*coralillo falso*), which is not venomous, looks very similar; a guide or a ranger will be able to point out the subtle differences. Of all the Costa Rican snakes, the **bushmaster** (*matabuey*) is the one of which even *guardaparques* are afraid. With a range extending from southern Mexico to Brazil, it is the largest venomous snake in the Americas – in Costa Rica, it can reach a size of nearly 2m. The most aggressive of snakes, the bushmaster will actually chase people, if it is so inclined. The good news is that you are extremely unlikely to encounter one, as it prefers dense and mountainous territory – Braulio Carrillo, the Sarapiquí region and Corcovado, for example – and rarely emerges during the day.

Once the inhabitant of the rainforests, the **fer-de-lance** (*terciopelo*) has adapted quite well to cleared areas, grassy uplands and even some inhabited stretches, although you are far more likely to see them in places that have heavy rainfall (such as the Limón coast) and near streams or rivers at night. Though it can reach more than 2m in length, the *terciopelo* ("velvet") is well camouflaged and very difficult to spot, resembling a big pile of leaves with its grey-black skin with a light crisscross pattern. Along with the bushmaster, it is one of the few snakes that may attack without provocation. They are usually killed when encountered, due to their venom and fairly healthy species count – these are the ones you'll see coiled in jars of formaldehyde at rainforest lodges, often on display beside the supper table.

The very pretty **eyelash viper** (*bocaracá*) is usually tan or green, but sometimes brilliant yellow when inhabiting golden palm-fruit groves. Largely arboreal and generally well camouflaged, it takes its name from the raised scales around its eyes. They are quite venomous to humans and should be given a wide berth if seen hanging from a branch or negotiating a path through the groves.

Considering the competition, it's not hard to see why the **boa constrictor** (*boa*) wins the title of most congenial snake. Often with beautiful semi-triangular markings, largely retiring and shy of people, the boa is one of the few snakes you may see in the daytime. Although they are largely torpid, it is not a good idea to bother them. They have big teeth and can bite, though they are not venomous and are unlikely to stir unless startled. If you encounter one, either on the move or lying still, the best thing is to walk around it slowly, giving it a good 5m berth.

For more details on **precautions** when dealing with snakes, see p.55.

Turtles

Five species of **marine turtle** visit Costa Rica's shores. Nesting takes place mostly at night, when hundreds of turtles come ashore on the same beach at a certain time of year, laying hundreds of thousands of eggs. Greens, hawksbills and leatherbacks come ashore on both coasts, while the olive ridley only inhabits the Pacific. The strange blunt-nosed **loggerhead**, which seems not to nest in Costa Rica, can sometimes be seen in Caribbean coastal waters.

The **green turtle** (*verde*), long-prized for the delicacy of its flesh, has become nearly synonymous with its favoured nesting grounds in Parque Nacional Tortuguero. In the 1950s, it was classified as endangered, and, thanks in part to the protection offered by areas like Tortuguero, is making a comeback. Some greens make Herculean journeys of as much as 2000km to their breeding beaches at Tortuguero, returning to the same stretch year after year. *Arribadas* are most concentrated in June and October. Green turtles are careful nesters: if a female is disturbed by human presence she will go back to the ocean and return only when all is clear.

The **hawksbill** (*carey*), so-named for its distinctive down-curving "beak", is found all over the tropics, often preferring rocky shores and coral reefs. It used to be hunted extensively on the Caribbean coast for its meat and shell, but this is now banned. Poaching does still occur, however, and you should avoid buying any tortoiseshell that you see for sale. Hawksbills do not come ashore in *arribadas* to the extent that green turtles do, preferring to nest alone.

Capable of growing to a length of 5m, the **leatherback** (*baula*) is the largest reptile in the world. Its "shell" is actually a network of bones overlaid with a very tough leathery skin. Though it nests in most numbers at the Parque Nacional Las Baulas on the western Nicoya Peninsula, it also comes ashore elsewhere, including Tortuguero. The **olive ridley** (*lora*) turtle nests on just a few beaches, among them Playa Nancite in Parque Nacional Santa Rosa and Refugio Nacional de Vida Silvestre Ostional near Nosara on the Nicoya Peninsula. They come ashore in their thousands (known as *arribadas*), and, unusually, often nest during the day. Olive ridley eggs are as prized as any, but its species count seems to be fairly healthy.

Among the freshwater **turtles** (*tortugas*) in Costa Rica, the **yellow turtle** (*tortuga amarilla*) can be most often seen in Caño Negro. The **black river turtle** and the **snapping turtle**, about whom little is known (except that it snaps), also inhabit rivers and mangrove swamps, and may occasionally be spotted on the riverbanks.

Insects (*insectos, bichos*)

Costa Rica supports an enormous diversity of insects, of which the **butterflies** (*mariposas*) are the most flamboyant and sought after. Active during the day, they can be seen, especially from about 8am to noon, almost anywhere in the country. Most adult butterflies take their typical food of nectar – usually from red flowers – through a proboscis. Others feed on fungi, dung and rotting fruit. Best known, and quite often spotted, especially along forest trails, is the fast-flying **blue morpho**, whose titanium-bright wings seem to shimmer electrically. Like other garish butterflies, the morpho uses its colour to startle or shock potential predators. Far more difficult to spot, for obvious reasons, is the **clear-winged butterfly**.

Of the annoying insects, you'll surely get acquainted with **mosquitoes** (*zancudos*), a few of which along the southern Caribbean carry malaria and dengue fever (see p.55). In hot, slightly swampy lowland areas such as the coastal Osa or the southern Nicoya peninsulas, you may also come across **purrujas**, similar to blackflies or midges. They can inflict itchy bites, as can the **chiggers** (*colorados*) that inhabit scrub and secondary-growth areas, attaching themselves to the skin, leech-like, in order to feed. Though not really bothersome, the **lantern fly** (*machaca*) emits an amazingly strong mint-blue light, like a mini lightning streak – if you have one in your hotel room, you'll know it as soon as you turn out the light.

The ant kingdom is well represented in Costa Rica. Chief among the rainforest salarymen are the **leaf-cutter ants** (*zampopas*), who work in businesslike cadres, carrying bits of leaf to and fro to build their distinctive nests. The ones to watch out for are the big **bullet ants** that resemble moving blackberries (their colloquial name is **veinticuatro** – "24" – referring to the fact that if you get bitten by one it will hurt for 24 hours). Endemic to the Neotropics, carnivorous **army ants** (*ronchadores*) are often encountered in the forest, typically living in large colonies, some of more than a million individuals. They are most famous for their "dawn raids", when they pour out of a hideaway, typically a log, and divide into several columns to create a swarm. In this columnar formation they go off in search of prey – other ants and insects – which they carry back to the nest to consume.

Among the many **bees and wasps** (*abejas*, *avispas*) are aggressive **Africanized bees**, which migrated from Africa to Brazil and then north to Costa Rica, where they have colonized certain localities. Although you have to disturb their nests before they'll bother you, people sensitive or allergic to bee-stings should avoid Parque Nacional Palo Verde.

Marine mammals

Among Costa Rica's **marine mammals** is the sea cow or **manatee** (*manatí*), elephantine in size, lumbering, good-natured and well intentioned, not to mention endangered. Manatees all over the Caribbean are declining in number, due to the disappearance and pollution of the fresh- and saltwater riverways in which they live. In Costa Rica, your only reasonable chance of seeing one is in the Tortuguero canals in Limón Province, where they sometimes break the surface – though there are a few in the more recently protected lagoons of the Refugio de Vida Silvestre Mixto Maquenque, near the border with Nicaragua. At first, you might mistake it for a tarpon, but the manatee's overlapping snout and long whiskers are quite distinctive.

Though **dolphins** and **whales** thread themselves through the waters of the Pacific coast, it is rare to see them. While **dolphins** (*delfines*) can be sighted in the Gulf of Nicoya and the Manuel Antonio and Dominical areas, the best chance of spotting one is on a boat trip in the Parque Nacional Ballena. Getting to see a **whale** (*ballena*) is even harder, though you may have some luck around Dominical, Bahía Drake and Isla del Caño in April and May, when sperm and humpback whales migrate along this stretch of coast.

Fish (*pez*)

Costa Rica is one of the richest sports-fishing grounds in the Neotropics. The best-known big-game fish is the startlingly huge white **tarpon** (*sábalo*). Other fish prized for their fighting spirit are **snook** (*robalo*), **marlin** (*aguja*) and **wahoo** (same in Spanish) – all of which ply the waters of Barra del Colorado; Quepos and Golfito, on the Pacific coast; and Playa Flamingo in Guanacaste. More laidback are the **trout** (*trucha*) and **rainbow bass** (*guapote*) that live in the freshwater rivers and in Laguna de Arenal. Costa Rica also features a few oddities and evolutionary throwbacks, including the undeniably homely **garfish**, which inhabits Caño Negro and the canals of Limón Province.

Snorkellers will see a number of exotic fish, including enormous, plate-flat **manta rays** (same in Spanish) and the **parrotfish** (*vieja*), so-called less for its rich colouring than for its distinctive "beak" (actually a number of tiny teeth, welded together), which is used to munch coral; there's another set of teeth at the back of the mouth that then grinds the coral down in order to digest it. Many of the white-sand beaches throughout the Caribbean, including the one just south of Cahuita, are the result of aeons of coral excreted by these fish. Other sea creatures include stingrays, oysters, sponges, ugly moray eels, sea urchins, starfish, spiny lobsters and fat, slug-like **sea cucumbers** that lie half submerged in the sea bed, digesting and excreting sand and mud.

Sharks (*tiburón*) are generally found on beaches where turtles nest, especially along the northern Caribbean coast, on Playa Ostional in the Nicoya Peninsula –

although not as far south as Playa Nosara – and in the waters surrounding Corcovado; bull sharks, one of the few sharks that can live in both fresh water and sea water, have been known to enter the rivers here, as well as the Río San Juan on their way between Lago Nicaragua and the sea. The marine-life-rich waters surrounding the remote Parque Nacional Isla del Coco are considered one of the world's prime playgrounds for **hammerhead sharks** (*tiburón martillo*). Experienced scuba-divers brave the 36-hour boat journey to the UNESCO World Heritage-protected island in order to swim with schools of hundreds of these harmless beasts, with the rainy season (May–Nov) seeing the sharks out in full force. Hammerheads, however, face continual threats from the illicit trade in shark fins, which remain in high demand in Asia.

Conservation and tourism

Costa Rica is widely seen as being at the cutting edge of worldwide **conservation strategy**, an impressive feat for a tiny Central American nation. At the centre of Costa Rica's internationally applauded efforts is a complex system of **national parks** and **wildlife refuges**, which protect a full 25 percent of its territory, one of the largest percentages of protected land among Western-hemisphere nations. These statistics are used with great effect to attract tourists and, along with Belize, Costa Rica has become virtually synonymous with ecotourism in Central America.

On the other hand, the National Parks Service does not possess the funds to protect adequately more than half the boundaries of these areas, which are under constant pressure from logging and squatters, and to a lesser extent from mining interests. In addition, the question uppermost in the minds of conservationists and biologists is what, if any, damage is being caused by so many feet walking through the rainforests.

Conservation in the New World tropics

The **traditional view** of conservation is a European one of preserving, museum-like, pretty animals and flowers; an idea that was conceived and upheld by relatively wealthy Old World countries in which the majority of the forests have long-since disappeared. In the contemporary world, this definition of conservation no longer works, and certainly not in the New World tropics, besieged as they are by a lack of resources, huge income inequities, legislation that lacks bite and the continual appetite of the world market for tropical hardwoods, not to mention the Old World zeal for coffee and picture-perfect supermarket fruits.

There's a leftist perspective on conservation that sees an imperialistic, bourgeois and anti-*campesino* agenda among the large conservation organizations of the North. By this reckoning, saving the environment is all very well but does little for the day-to-day realities of the 21 percent or so of Costa Rica's population who live below the poverty line. These people have, in many cases, been made landless and impoverished by, for instance, absentee landowners speculating on land (in the Zona Norte and in Guanacaste) or by the pulling-out of major employers like Chiquita (in the Zona Sur near Golfito and on the Osa Peninsula). Many are left with simply no choice but to engage in the kind of activity – be it gold-panning, slash-and-burn agriculture or monobiotic fruit production – that is universally condemned by conservationists in the North.

Conservation in Costa Rica

Costa Rica has a long history of conservation-consciousness, although it has taken different forms and guises. As early as 1775, laws were passed to limit the destructive impact of *quemas*, or brush-burning, though the bulk of **preservation laws** were passed after 1845, concurrent with Costa Rica's period of greatest economic and cultural growth. That said, most of this legislation was directed at protecting resource extraction rather than the areas themselves – to guard fishing and hunting grounds and to conserve what were already seen as valuable timber supplies. In 1895, laws were passed protecting water supplies and establishing *guardabosques* (forest rangers) to fight the *quemas* caused by the regular burning of deforested land and pasture by cattle-ranchers. The forerunners of several institutions later to be important to the development of conservation in Costa Rica were founded by

The case of Tortuguero

National parks are now such an entrenched part of Costa Rica's landscape that they might be taken to have always been there. In fact, most have been established in the last forty years, and the process of creating them has not always been a smooth one...

Turtle Bogue (the old Miskito name for Tortuguero) has always been isolated. Even today, access is by boat or air only, and before the dredging of the main canal in the 1960s it was even more cut off from the rest of the country. Most of the local people were of Miskito or Afro-Caribbean extraction, hunting and fishing and living almost completely without consumer goods. There was virtually no cash economy in the village, with local trade and barter being sufficient for most people's needs.

In the 1940s, **lumbering** began in earnest in the area. A sawmill was built in the village, and during the next two decades the area experienced a boom. The local lumber exhausted itself by the 1960s, but in the twenty-year interim it brought outsiders and a dependence on cash-obtainable consumer goods. Simultaneously, the number of **green turtles** began to decline rapidly, due to overfishing and egg harvesting, and by the 1950s the once-numerous turtle was officially endangered. The alarm raised by biologists over their precipitous decline paved the way for the establishment, in 1970, of **Parque Nacional Tortuguero**, protecting 30 of the 35km of turtle-nesting beach and extending to more than two hundred square kilometres of surrounding forests, canals and waterways. The establishment of this protective area put former sources of income off-limits to local populations, and villagers who had benefited from the wood-and-turtle economy either reverted to the subsistence and agricultural life they had known before or left the area in search of a better one. Nowadays, however, many locals make a good living off the increasing amount of tourism the park brings, especially those with their own independent businesses.

The establishment of Parque Nacional Tortuguero effectively broke the **boom-and-bust cycle** so prevalent in the tropics, whereby local resources are used to extinction, leaving no viable alternatives after the storm has passed. In Tortuguero, the hardwoods have made a bit of a comeback, and the green turtle's numbers are up dramatically from their low point of the 1950s and 1960s. Considering the popularity of the national park and its lagoons and turtle tours, there's no doubt that conservation and protection of Tortuguero's wetlands can have lasting benefits to local folk, as well as local flora and fauna.

the end of the nineteenth century, including the Museo Nacional and the Instituto Físico Geográfico.

Much of the credit for helping establish Costa Rica's system of national parks has to go to **Olof Wessberg** and **Karen Mogensen**, long-time foreign residents who in 1963, largely through their own efforts, founded the Reserva Natural Absoluta Cabo Blanco near their home on the southwest tip of the Nicoya Peninsula. The couple helped raise national consciousness through an extensive campaign in the mid-1960s, so that by the end of the decade there was broad support for the founding of a national parks service. In 1969, the Parque y Monumento Nacional Santa Rosa was declared, and in 1970 the SPN (Servicio de Parques Nacionales) was officially inaugurated. Spearheaded by a recently graduated forester, Mario Boza, the system developed slowly at first, as the law that established Santa Rosa really existed only on paper: neighbouring farmers and ranchers continued to encroach on the land for pasture and brush-burning as before.

Although it remains a mystery, the murder of Olof Wessberg in 1975 on the Osa Peninsula is an illustration of the powerful interests that are thwarted by conservation. Wessberg was conducting a preliminary survey in Osa to assess the possibility of a national park there (the site of modern-day Parque Nacional Corcovado).

Although his assailant – the man who had offered to guide him – was caught, a motive was never discovered and the crime has not been satisfactorily solved.

Nonetheless, despite the pressures of vested interests, the Costa Rican conservation programme moved forward in the early 1980s with the founding of **MINAE** (Ministerio del Ambiente y Energía), the government body entrusted with the overall control of the country's ecological resources. In 1988, the Arias government drafted a national conservation strategy, and, soon after his election victory in 1994, president José María Figueres started the drive to bring together all the various conservation efforts taking place throughout the country under direct government control. For decades, much of the most important conservation work had been undertaken by privately (often foreign) funded initiatives, and so, in 1996, the **Red Costarricense de Reservas Naturales** was founded, bringing the country's disparate patchwork of privately owned reserves and refuges (of which there are more than one hundred) under the control of a single administrative body subject to the same rules and regulations as state-owned parks. Privately funded conservation programmes are still vital, as they help to remove some of the financial burden from the beleaguered state coffers, which struggle to raise the revenue necessary to maintain the increasingly overstretched national parks. Indeed, private investment accounted for over a third of the $56 million the Costa Rican government received in October 2010 as it sought to triple the size of its protected marine areas – around Isla Cocos and Corcovado national parks, Barra del Colorado and Gandoca-Manzanillo – by 2015, and in doing so boost its total protected areas to 26 percent of the country.

Eco-paradise lost: pesticides and pollution

There are, however, flaws in this Garden of Eden. Chief among them is the importance of the **agro-export** economy. The growth of the large-scale agro-industries depends on a continual supply of cheap labour and land, and the **pollution** wreaked by the pesticides used in banana plantations – the country's major agro-export – is becoming an increasing threat. Foreign consumers attach an amazing level of importance to the appearance of supermarket bananas and pineapples, and about twenty percent of potentially dangerous **pesticides** used in the cultivation of bananas serve only to improve the look of the fruit and not, as it is often thought, to control pestilence. Travellers who pass through banana plantations in Costa Rica or who take river trips, especially along the Río Sarapiquí, can't fail to notice the ubiquitous blue plastic bags. The pristine appearance of Costa Rican bananas is due largely to the fact that they grow inside these pesticide-lined bags, which make their way into waterways where they are fatally consumed by fish, mammals (such as the manatee) or iguanas. In the Río Tempisque basin, armadillos and crocodiles are thought to have been virtually exterminated by agricultural pesticides.

Animals are not alone in being at risk from pesticides. In 1987, a hundred Costa Rican plantation workers sued the Standard Fruit Company, Dow Chemical and Shell Oil for producing a pesticide that is a known cause of **sterility** in banana-plantation workers. Since then, several harmful pesticides have been banned, although Costa Rican plantation workers were involved in the multi-country lawsuit that was brought against Dole and Chiquita in 2007.

Conservation initiatives

In recent years, Mario Boza, a prominent conservationist who was heavily involved in the founding of the national parks system, has been advocating a

Conservation organizations in Costa Rica

The following list represents just a sample of the large number of **conservation organizations** working in Costa Rica, and there are many more local operations as well. For details of voluntary conservation opportunities, see p.72.

Fundación Neotrópica Aptdo 236-1002, Paseo de los Estudiantes, Curridabat, San José (ⓣ2253-2130, ⓦwww.neotropica.org). Well-established organization that works with several small-scale and (typically) local conservation initiatives in Costa Rica. Their Curridabat office (opposite the Colegio de Ingenieros y Arquitectos) sells posters, books and T-shirts in aid of funds. Accepts donations.

Fundación Amigos de la Isla del Coco Aptdo 276-1005, Barrio Corazón de Jesús, San José (ⓣ2257-9257, ⓦwww.cocosisland.org). Organization set up in 1994 to raise funds to preserve the unique flora and fauna of the remote Parque Nacional Isla del Coco (see box, p.337), a UNESCO World Heritage Site.

World Wide Fund for Nature (ⓦwww.wwfca.org) 1250 24th St NW, Washington DC, 20037 USA (ⓣ202/293-4800); 245 Eglinton Ave E, Suite 410, Toronto, Ontario (ⓣ416/489-8800); Panda House, Weyside Park, Godalming, Surrey GU7 1XR (ⓣ01483/426444). The fund is a major donor to wildlife preservation schemes throughout Central America, including projects in Monteverde and Tortuguero. The organization's Costa Rican contact details are Aptdo Postal 629-2350, San Francisco de Dos Ríos, San José (ⓣ2234-8434).

strategy of **macro-conservation**. By uniting concerns and "joining up" chunks of protected land, he argued, the macro-areas will allow larger protected areas for animals that need room to hunt, like jaguars and pumas, or require sizeable migratory areas, such as the great green macaw. Most of all, they will allow countries to make more effective joint conservation policies and decisions. Macro-conservation projects currently include El Proyecto Paseo Pantera ("Path of the Panther", the idea being to create an unbroken stretch of jungle throughout all of Mesoamerica), El Mundo Maya (Belize, El Salvador, Guatemala, Honduras and Mexico) and the Parque Internacional La Amistad (Costa Rica and Panamá).

Arguably, however, the most revolutionary change in conservation management, and the one likely to have the biggest pay-off in the long term, is the shift toward **local initiatives**. Some projects are truly local, such as the tiny grassroots organization TUVA and its selective logging of naturally felled rainforest trees on the Osa Peninsula, or the ecotourism co-operative of Las Delicias in Parque Nacional Barra Honda on the Nicoya Peninsula.

Another initiative, even more promising in terms of how it affects the lives of many rural-based Costa Ricans, is the creation of "**buffer zones**" around some national parks. In these zones, *campesinos* and other smallholders can do part-time farming, are allowed restricted hunting rights and receive education about the ecological and economic value of the forest. Locals may be trained as nature guides, and *campesinos* may be given incentives to enter into non-traditional forms of agriculture and ways of making a living that are less environmentally destructive.

In the past, Costa Rica's **waste-disposal problems** have given the country a garbage nightmare, culminating in a scandal in 1995 with the overflowing of the Río Azul site, San José's main dump. The government fully recognizes the irony of this – rubbish lining the streets of a country with such a high conservation profile – and in an admirable, typically Tico grassroots initiative, legions of schoolchildren are now sent on rubbish-collecting after-school projects and weekend brigades. Even more ingenious is the national movement that sends Costa Rican schoolchildren to national parks and other preserves as **volunteers** to work on conservation projects during school holidays, thus planting the seeds for a future generation of dedicated – or at least aware – conservationists.

Tourism

Around two million tourists a year come to Costa Rica – mostly from the US, Canada and Europe – an incredible number, considering that its population is just 4.5 million. Along with the charms of the country itself, Costa Rica's popularity is linked with the growing trend toward **eco-tourism** – for the most part, tourists with a genuine concern and interest in the country's flora, fauna and cultural life can choose from a variety of places to spend their money constructively, including top-notch rainforest lodges that have worked hard to integrate themselves with their surroundings (and those who want to rough it can still do so heroically in places like Corcovado and Chirripó). If managed properly, low-impact **eco-tourism** is one of the best ways in which forests, beaches, rivers, mangroves, volcanoes and other natural formations can pay their way – in *dólares* – while remaining pristine and intact. However, eco-tourism is a difficult term to define. It was often seen in relation to what it was not: package tourism, wherein visitors have limited contact with nature and with the day-to-day lives of local people. Although the Tourist Board's clever creation of the Certificate for Sustainable Tourism (see box, p.454) had made it harder for organizations and businesses to hijack the "eco" prefix for dubious uses, the authentic ecotourism experience is still difficult to pin down. One of the best attempts at a **definition** has been put forward by ATEC, the Asociación Talamanqueña de Ecoturismo y Conservación, which seeks to promote, as it says, "socially responsible tourism", by integrating local Bribrí and Afro-Caribbean culture into tourists' experience of the area, as well as giving residents pride in their unique cultural heritage and natural environment. Their view of ecotourism is:

> **Eco-tourism means more than bird books and binoculars. Eco-tourism means more than native art hanging on hotel walls or ethnic dishes on the restaurant menu. Eco-tourism is not mass tourism behind a green mask.**
>
> **Eco-tourism means a constant struggle to defend the earth and to protect and sustain traditional communities. Eco-tourism is a cooperative relationship between the non-wealthy local community and those sincere, open-minded tourists who want to enjoy themselves in a Third World setting and, at the same time, enrich their consciousness by means of significant educational and cultural experience.**

Several pioneering projects in Costa Rica have set out to combine tourism with sustainable methods of farming, rainforest preservation and scientific research. Some of these, like the **Rainforest Aerial Tram** and the **Reserva Biológica Bosque Nuboso Monteverde**, are the most advanced of their kind in the Americas, if not the world. Not only does the Aerial Tram provide a fascinating glimpse of the tropical canopy – normally completely inaccessible to human eyes – but it also offers a rare safe and stable method for biologists to investigate this little-known habitat. Income from visitors is funnelled into maintaining and augmenting the surrounding reserve. Monteverde, meanwhile, preserves a large piece of complex tropical forest, giving scientists a valuable stomping ground for taxonomic study. Tourism is just one of the activities in the reserve, which has been a research ground for tropical biologists from all over the world, and provides revenue for maintenance and, more importantly, continued expansion.

The success of the country's eco-tourism initiatives have brought their own problems, however. The huge growth of tourism worries many Costa Ricans, even those who make their living from it, and many, as yet unanswered, questions

Turning over a new leaf: the ICT and the CST

Criticized in the past for prioritizing capacity over credentials when it comes to the country's accommodation, the **ICT**, Costa Rica's tourist board, deserves full credit for its groundbreaking new initiative, the **Certificate for Sustainable Tourism** (Ⓦwww.turismo-sostenible.co.cr) or **CST**. In an area that has traditionally been hard to quantify, the scheme helps shed light on the murky issue of just how eco an eco-lodge or tour company really is, by measuring how much they comply with the ICT's **model of sustainable best practice**. The scheme rates companies up to five levels (or "leaves"), according to the following criteria:

- physical impact on its surroundings;
- eco-friendly initiatives such as energy-saving technology and waste-disposal policies (for lodges only);
- representation of the areas in which it works and, to a lesser extent, Costa Rica itself (for tour operators only);
- ability to enable customers to contribute to its sustainability;
- involvement with local communities and its positive effect on the wider region as a whole.

As well as providing greater transparency for the paying customer, the carrot for the companies themselves is a considerable one: in addition to the kudos the scheme generates, as a company's rating increases, so do its benefits, which include publicity and promotion from the ICT, training and the like. So far, eleven **lodges** – including *Villa Blanca Cloudforest Hotel & Nature Reserve* (see p.139), *Finca Rosa Blanca Coffee Plantation & Inn* (see p.145), *Arenas del Mar* (see p.369) and *Lapa Rios* (see p.408) – and six **tour operators** – including ACTUAR (see p.46) and Simbiosis Tours (see p.47) – have been awarded the maximum five leaves.

remain. Is it just a fad that will fade away, only to be replaced by another unprepared country-of-the-moment? What, if any, are the advantages of having an economy led by tourism instead of the traditional exports of bananas and coffee? Furthermore, how do you reconcile the need to attract enough visitors to make tourism economically viable while ensuring that this tourism remains low-impact? It is a problem made all the more difficult by ongoing arguments between two of the main organizations charged with managing the country's ecotourism industry: **MINAE**, the government body that directly controls the country's network of national parks, and the **Costa Rican Tourist Board** (Instituto Costarricense de Turismo or **ICT**). Whereas MINAE is, despite severe underfunding, widely seen as having done a reasonably good job in ensuring that tourism doesn't overwhelm the parks' fragile ecosystems, the ICT is often regarded as putting commercial interests above environmental ones. In contrast to the somewhat impoverished state of MINAE, the ICT makes a lot of money out of tourism, much of it derived from the three percent tax collected on every occupied hotel room. This has led some to accuse the ICT of being more concerned with generating new accommodation (and thus money) than with the possible impact the increase in visitors could have on the environment and local communities. The ICT has, however, taken an admirable step in the right direction with their development of the **Certificate for Sustainable Tourism** (see box above), which encourages sustainable practices in the hotel industry and among tour operators.

The question of who pays for Costa Rica's environmental well-being, though, is one that continues to provoke fierce debate. While the government actively welcomes contributions from **foreign sources**, many Costa Ricans are alarmed by what they see as the virtual purchase of their country by foreigners. Though many hotels and businesses are still Costa Rican-owned and managed, North American and European ownership is on the rise, relegating many Costa Ricans to low-paid jobs in the service sector. Gated "**gringo" communities** are springing up along the Pacific coast, and across the country, **rising property prices** are having a drastic effect on Costa Ricans, with many being priced out of their own communities.

At times, the government seems bent on turning the country into a **high-income tourist enclave**. North Americans and Europeans will still consider many things quite cheap, but Costa Rica is already the most expensive country to visit in the region, and the government has admitted that they have no qualms about discouraging "backpackers" (meaning budget tourists) from coming to Costa Rica. Better-heeled tourists, the thinking goes, not only make a more significant investment in the country dollar for dollar, but are more easily controlled, choosing in the main to travel in tour groups or to stay in big holiday resorts such as the *Hotel de Playa Tambor* on the southern Nicoya Peninsula.

Ironically, such holiday resorts are often dogged by **environmental scandal**. In early 2008, during the height of the tourist season, the three hundred-room *Hotel de Occidental Allegro Papagayo* in Playa Manzanillo was closed down following almost a year's worth of complaints that it had been dumping sewage in illegal disposal sites in local communities. The trigger that led authorities to finally shut it down was the discovery of pipes depositing waste in a nearby estuary: the Spanish-owned hotel lacked something as fundamental as a functioning sewage treatment plant.

Another flipside to Costa Rica's tourism success story is its ascendancy to one of the world's top **sex tourism** destinations. Prostitution with women over the age of eighteen is legal, and it is estimated that approximately ten percent of foreign visitors are sex tourists. Disturbingly, paedophiles also come to Costa Rica, and they find no shortage of desperate underage prostitutes stricken by poverty and drug addiction. In 1999, Costa Rica's parliament passed a law against the sexual exploitation of minors, and while penalties are harsh and initiatives in place to educate taxi drivers, police officers, tour guides and hotel receptionists about the illegality of profiteering from promoting child prostitution, the problem is still prevalent.

Books

The most comprehensive volumes written on Costa Rica tend to be about **natural history** – many make better introductions to what you'll see in the country than the glossy literature pumped out by the government tourist board and most guidebooks. Frustratingly, many of the most informative works on both natural and cultural history are out of date or out of print (designated "o/p" in the list below). You'll find a number of the titles listed below in San José bookshops, but don't expect to see them elsewhere in the country.

Those interested in **Costa Rican fiction** (which is alive and well, although not extensively translated or known abroad) will have much richer and varied reading with some knowledge of Spanish. Costa Rica has no single internationally recognized towering figure in its national literature, and in sharp contrast to other countries in the region the most sophisticated and best-known writers in the country are women. Carmen Naranjo is the most widely translated, with a number of novels, poems and short-story collections (plus some of the country's most prestigious literary awards) to her name, but there are a number of lesser-read writers, including the brilliant Yolanda Oreamuno, and an upsurge of younger women, tackling contemporary social issues like domestic violence and alcoholism in their fiction and poetry. The publication in 1940 of Carlos Luis Fallas's seminal novel *Mamita Yunai*, about labour conditions in the United Fruit Company banana plantations of Limón Province, sparked a wave of "proletarian" novels, which became the dominant form in Costa Rican fiction until well into the 1970s. Until recently, Costa Rican fiction also leant heavily on picturesque stories of rural life with some writers – usually men – drawing on the country's wealth of fauna. There are a number of *cuentos* (stories), fable-like in their simplicity and not a little ponderous in their symbolism, featuring turtles, fish and rabbits as characters.

Travel narrative

Peter Ford *Tekkin a Waalk: Along the Miskito Coast* (o/p). Journalist Ford was based in Managua for most of the terrible 1980s. After that, his idea of a holiday seems to have been to "tek a waalk" (as it's called in the local patois) along the eastern coast of the isthmus. In the very short part of the book that deals with Costa Rica, Ford's boatmen overshoot the river entrance to Greytown, Nicaragua, and end up in the northeastern Costa Rican village of Barra del Colorado, much to the chagrin of the *migración* – Ford must be one of the few people ever to be deported from Costa Rica.

Paul Theroux *The Old Patagonian Express: By Train Through the Americas.* Somewhat out of date (Theroux went through over thirty years ago), but a great read nonetheless. Laced with the author's usual tetchy black humour and general misanthropy, the descriptions of his two Costa Rican train journeys (neither of which still runs) to Limón and Puntarenas remain apt – as is the account of passing through San José, where he meets American men on sex-and-booze vacations.

Culture and folk traditions

Roberto Cabrera *Santa Cruz Guanacaste: Una Aproximación a la Historia y la Cultura Populares*. The best cultural history of Guanacaste, written by a respected Guanacastecan sociologist. Verbal snapshots of nineteenth- and twentieth-century hacienda life, accounts of bull riding and details of micro-regional dances such as the *punto guanacasteco* (adopted as the national dance), *el torito* and the veiled dance.

Paula Palmer *What Happen: A Folk-History of Costa Rica's Talamanca Coast*. The definitive – although now dated – folk history of the Afro-Caribbean community on Limón Province's Talamancan coast. Palmer first went to Cahuita in the early 1970s as a Peace Corps volunteer, serving as Director of the Cahuita English School for three years, later to return as a sociologist, collecting oral histories from older members of the local communities. Great stories and atmospheric testimonies of pirate treasure, ghosts and the like; complemented by photos and accounts of local agriculture, foods and traditional remedies.

Paula Palmer, Juanita Sánchez and Gloria Mayorga *Taking Care of Sibá's Gifts*. Manifesto for the future of Bribrí culture, ecological survival of the *talamanqueña* ecosystems and a concise explication of differing views of the land and people's relationship to it held by the *ladinos* and Bribrí on the KéköLdi indigenous reserve.

Conservation

Catherine Caulfield *In the Rainforest: Report from a Strange, Beautiful World*. Thirty years old, but still one of the best introductions to the rainforest, dealing in an accessible fashion with many of the issues covered in the more specialized titles. Her chapter on Costa Rica is a wary elucidation of the destruction that cattle-ranching in particular wreaks, as well as an interesting profile of the farming methods used by the Monteverde community.

Luis Fournier Origgi *Desarrollo y Perspectivas del Movimiento Conservacionista Costarricense*. Seminal, if dry, survey of conservation policy from the dawn of the nation until the early 1990s, by one of Costa Rica's most eminent scientists and conservationists. In Spanish only.

Gordon W. Frankie, Alfonso Mata and S. Bradleigh Vinson (eds) *Biodiversity in Costa Rica: Learning the Lessons in a Seasonal Dry Forest*. The first in-depth study of Guanacaste's endangered dry forest paints a detailed picture – biologically, environmentally, socially and politically – of this fragile ecosystem and its vital link to the country's other ecosystems.

Susanna Hecht and Alexander Cockburn *The Fate of the Forest: Developers, Destroyers and Defenders of the Amazon*. The best single book readily available on rainforest destruction, this exhaustive volume is written with a sound knowledge of Amazonian history. The beautiful prose dissects some of the more pervasive myths about rainforest destruction, and it's comprehensive enough to be applicable to any forested areas under threat in the New World tropics.

Bill Weinberg *War on the Land: Ecology and Politics in Central America*. Just one chapter, but a good one, devoted to Costa Rica. While not failing to congratulate the country for its conservation achievements, the author also reveals the internal wranglings of conservationist policy.

History and current affairs

Suzane Abel *Between Continents, Between Seas: Precolumbian Art of Costa Rica* (o/p). Produced as a catalogue to accompany the exhibition that toured the US in 1982, this is the best single volume on pre-Conquest history and craftsmanship, with illuminating accounts of the lives, beliefs and customs of Costa Rica's pre-Columbian peoples as interpreted through artefacts and excavations. The photographs, whether of jade pendants, Chorotega pottery or the more diabolical of the Diquis's gold pieces, are uniformly wonderful.

Elías Zamora Acosta *Ethnografía Histórica de Costa Rica (1561–1615)*. Hugely impressive archival research that reconstructs the economic, political and social life in the province in the years immediately following the Spanish invasion. A masterwork, distressingly difficult to get hold of. In Spanish only.

Tony Avirgan and Martha Honey *La Penca: On Trial in Costa Rica: the CIA vs the Press*. Avirgan, a journalist and long-time resident of San José, was wounded at the La Penca news conference bombing in 1984. After this, he and Honey sunk their teeth into the dark underbelly of US/CIA politics and operations in the area during the years of the Nicaraguan Civil War. In contrast to her more recent and more definitive book (see below), Honey concludes here that the attack was carried out by the CIA.

Richard Biesanz, Mavis Hiltunen Biesanz, Karen Zubris Biesanz *The Ticos: Culture and Social Change in Costa Rica*. An intriguing blend of quantitative and qualitative research, supported by personal interviews with many Costa Ricans, this book seeks to get under the skin of Costa Rican society, examining (among other things) government, class and ethnic relations, the family, health and sport, and managing to be rigorous and anecdotal at the same time.

Richard Biesanz, Mavis Hiltunen Biesanz and Karen Zubris Biesanz *The Costa Ricans*. Rather outdated generalizations and idealizations about the Costa Rican "character". However, though descriptive rather than analytical, many of the authors' observations and conclusions, especially about sexual conduct, inequality and marriage, ring true.

Omar Hernandez, Eugenia Ibarra and Juan Rafael Quesada (eds) *Discriminación y Racismo en la Historia Costarricense*. Most of these essays are written in the language and form of legal case studies but nonetheless provide a history of the racial bias of legal discrimination in Costa Rica, and that of ethnicity in human rights abuses. Interesting counterpoint to Costa Rica's reputation for harmonious social relations, although probably only of use to specialists and those with a particular interest in race issues. In Spanish only.

Martha Honey *Hostile Acts: US Policy in Costa Rica in the 1980s*. Those sceptical of elaborate conspiracy theories may have their minds changed by this exhaustively researched, weighty tome detailing the US's "dual diplomacy" against Costa Rica in the 1980s. In this heroic volume, Honey concludes that the La Penca bomber was a leftist Argentinian terrorist with connections to Nicaragua's Sandinista government.

Steven Palmer and Iván Molina (eds) *The Costa Rica Reader: History, Culture, Politics*. One of the best introductions to the country for the general reader, this book features more than fifty texts by Costa Ricans, from essays and memoirs to histories and poems, interspersed with photographs, maps, cartoons and fliers.

Mitchell A. Seligson *Peasants of Costa Rica and the Development of Agrarian Capitalism* (o/p). The best single history available in English, although only a university or specialist library will have it. Much wider in scope than the title suggests, this is an excellent intermeshing of ethnic and racial issues, economics and sociology along with hard-core analysis of the rise and fall of the Costa Rican peasant.

Wildlife, natural history and field guides

Paul H. Allen *The Rainforests of the Golfo Dulce*. Obviously a labour of love, this is the best descriptive book on the lush rainforest cover found in the southwest of the country. It's a scientific work, with complete taxonomic accounts, although still very readable and with interesting photographs.

Les Beletsky *Travellers' Wildlife Guides: Costa Rica*. This readable wildlife and natural history handbook, written by a professional wildlife biologist, is a good compromise between a guidebook and a heavy field guide. The well-illustrated plates are accompanied by contextual discussions of ecotourism and ecology in Costa Rica. Includes concise information on around 220 bird, 50 mammal and 80 amphibian and reptile species.

Mario A. Boza *Costa Rica's National Parks (Parques Nacionales)*. Essentially a coffee-table book, this informed volume is a great taster for what you'll find in the national parks. The text is in Spanish and English, and there are uniformly stunning photographs.

A.S. and P.P. Calvert *A Year of Costa Rican Natural History*. Although now very old – the year in question is 1910 – this is a brilliant, insightful and charmingly enthusiastic travelogue/natural history/autobiography by American biologist and zoologist husband-and-wife team. It features much, much more than natural history, with sections such as "Blood Sucking Flies", "Fiestas in Santa Cruz" and "Earthquakes". The best single title ever written on Costa Rica – the only problem is finding it. Try good libraries and specialist bookstores.

Philip J. DeVries *The Butterflies of Costa Rica and their Natural History: Volume I* (o/p). Much-admired volume (Volume II, written ten years later in 1997, is smaller in breadth), really for serious butterfly enthusiasts or scientists only, but illustrated with beautiful colour plates so you can marvel at the incremental differences between various butterflies.

Joseph Franke *Costa Rica's National Parks and Preserves*. A park-by-park discussion of the system of national parks and wildlife refuges, with detailed information on hiking and trails, as well as a topographical and environmental profile of each park. Useful if you're intending to spend any time hiking in more than one or two parks.

Richard Garrigues *The Birds of Costa Rica*. This excellent, all-encompassing field guide to the country's myriad birdlife is fast threatening Stiles and Skutch's tour de force (see p.460) as the birdwatchers' bible – succinct and portable, it makes the ideal handbook for everyday use in the field.

Daniel H. Janzen (ed) *Costa Rican Natural History*. The definitive reference source, with accessible, continuously fascinating species-by-species accounts, written by a highly influential figure – Janzen was involved on a policy level in the governing of the national parks system. The introduction is especially worth reading, dealing in a cursory but lively fashion with tectonics, meteorology, history and archeology. Illustrated throughout with gripping photographs. Available in paperback, but still doorstep-thick.

Sam Mitchell *Pura Vida: The Waterfalls and Hot Springs of Costa Rica*. Jolly, personably written concise guide to the many little-known waterholes, cascades and waterfalls of Costa Rica. Complete with detailed directions and accounts of surrounding trails. Available in English in San José.

Donald Perry *Life Above the Jungle Floor: A Biologist Explores a Strange and Hidden Treetop World*. Nicely poised, lyrical account of biologist Perry's trials and tribulations in conceiving and mounting his Rainforest Aerial Tram (see p.149). Most of the book deals with his time at Rara Avis, where he conceived and tested his tram prototype, the Automated Web for Canopy Exploration.

Fiona A. Reid, Twan Leenders, Jim Zook & Robert Dean *The Wildlife of Costa Rica*. This handy introduction to the main species you're likely to encounter, from mammals and birds to reptiles and amphibians, works well as a non-specialist field guide. The illustrations, particularly of the birds and mammals, are good and the species accounts detailed and informative – there's even a small section on insects, including butterflies, bullet ants and the extremely strange-looking tailless whip scorpion.

F. Gary Stiles and Alexander F. Skutch *A Guide to the Birds of Costa Rica*. All over Costa Rica you'll see guides clutching well-thumbed copies of this seminal tome, illustrated with colour plates to aid identification. Hefty, even in paperback, and too pricey for the amateur, but you may be able to pick up good secondhand copies in Costa Rica.

Mark Wainwright *The Mammals of Costa Rica*. The most comprehensive guide to the country's mammal species, including the oft-overlooked bats, is an amalgamation of hundreds of field researchers' work and features detailed but accessible information on natural history, conservation and, interestingly, mythology. The animal tracks are useful, though there are better illustrations in other books of this ilk.

Allen M. Young *Sarapiquí Chronicle: A Naturalist in Costa Rica* (o/p). Lavishly produced book based on entomologist Allen M. Young's twenty years' work in the Sarapiquí area and featuring a well-written combination of autobiography, travelogue and natural science, centring on the insect life he encounters.

Fiction

Miguel Benavides *The Children of Mariplata: Stories from Costa Rica*. A short collection of short stories, most of which are good examples of fable-like or allegorical Costa Rican tales. Many are written in the anthropomorphized voice of an animal; others, like *The Twilight Which Lost its Colour* describe searing slices of poverty-stricken life.

Carlos Cortés *Cruz de Olvido*. Told in the macho, exhausted and regretful tone of a disillusioned revolutionary, this novel charts the return of a Costa Rican Sandinista supporter from Nicaragua to his home country, where "nothing has happened since the big bang". The narrative marries the storyteller's humorous disaffection with boring old Costa Rica and his investigation into the bizarre, excessively symbolic death of his son.

Fabián Dobles *Ese Que Llaman Pueblo*. Born in 1918, Dobles is Costa Rica's elder statesman of letters. Set in the countryside among *campesinos*, this is a typical "proletarian" novel. In Spanish only. *Years Like Brief Days* is the first novel by Dobles to be translated into English, this epistolary story is told in the form of a letter written by an old man to his mother, describing the village he grew up in and his eventful life.

Carlos Luis Fallas *Mamita Yunai: El Infierno de las Bananeras*. Exuberant, full of local colour, culture and diction: this entertaining, leftist novel depicting life in the hell of the banana plantations is a great read. It's set in La Estrella valley in Limón Province, where Fallas, a pioneering labour organizer in the 1930s and 1940s, was instrumental in forcing the United Fruit Company to take workers' welfare into account. In Spanish only.

Joaquín Gutiérrez *Puerto Limón*. One of the best of the "proletarian" genre, by one of the nation's foremost literary figures, who was also a prominent journalist. While very much focused on the gritty realism of labour conditions in mid-twentieth-century Costa Rica, the writing is lyrical and beautifully simple.

Amanda Hopkinson (ed) *Lovers and Comrades: Women's Resistance Poetry from Central America* (o/p). Heartfelt contributions by Costa Rican poets Janina Fernandez, Eulalia Bernard and Lilly Guardia. Poems such as Bernard's *We are the Nation of Threes* shows that Costa Rican poetry is no less political and no less felt than the more numerous contributions from the countries torn by war in the 1980s.

Enrique Jaramillo Levi (ed) *When New Flowers Bloomed: Short Stories by Women Writers from Costa Rica and Panamá*. Collection of the best-known Costa Rican women writers, including Rima de Vallbona, Carmen Naranjo, Carmen Lyra and Yolanda Oreamuno. Most of the stories are from the late 1980s, with shared themes of domestic violence – a persistent problem in Costa Rica – sexual and economic inequality, and the tyrannies of female anatomy and desire. Look out especially for Emilia Macaya, a younger writer.

Tatiana Lobo *Assault on Paradise*. Costa Rica's first great historical novel tells the story of the arrival of the Spaniards in Costa Rica and, as the title indicates, their destruction of the land and life of the indigenous peoples they encountered.

Carmen Naranjo *Los Perros no Ladraron* (1966), *Responso por el Niño Juan Manuel* (1968), *Ondina* (1982) and *Sobrepunto* (1985). In keeping with a tradition in Latin American letters but unusually for a woman, Naranjo has occupied several public posts, including Secretary of Culture, director of the publishing house EDUCA and Ambassador to Israel. She is widely considered to be an experimentalist, and her novels can be found throughout Costa Rica in Spanish only: her collection of stories *There Never Was Once Upon a Time*, however, is available in English.

Yolanda Oreamuno *La Ruta de su Evasión*. Oreamuno had a short life, dying at the age of 40 in 1956. By the time she was 24, however, she had distinguished herself as the most promising writer of her generation with her novel *Por Tierra Firme*. *La Ruta* – concerning a child sent to look for his father, who has disappeared, possibly on a drinking binge – displays her continually surprising lyrical style. The search is both actual and spiritual, the novel a complex weave of themes. In Spanish only.

Barbara Ras *Costa Rica: A Traveller's Literary Companion*. This anthology is probably the most accessible starting point for readers interested in Costa Rican literature, with flowing and well-translated stories arranged by geographical zone. The best stories are also the most heartrending – read *The Girl Who Came from the Moon* and *The Carbonero* for a glimpse of real life beyond the tourist-brochure images.

Yasmin Ross *La Flota Negra*. Originally a journalist from Mexico, Ross has made Costa Rica her home and in *La Flota Negra* wrote one of the best-received novels set in Costa Rican in recent years. It takes as its starting point the story of the Black Star Line, the shipping company that brought so many of the Caribbean immigrants whose descendants now make up the population of Limón, along with the Pan-Africanist Marcus Garvey's visit to the province. In Spanish only.

Anacristina Rossi *La Loca de Gandoca* (*The Madwoman of Gandoca*). Rossi's popular novel is really "faction", documenting in businesslike prose and with tongue firmly in cheek the bizarre and Byzantine wranglings over the Refugio de Vida Silvestre Gandoca-Manzanillo, including the surveying of the indigenous Bribrí on the KéköLdi reserve. In Spanish only.

Rosario Santos (ed) *And We Sold the Rain: Contemporary Fiction from Central America*. Put together in the late 1980s, this collection attempts to show the faces of real people behind the newspaper headlines about guerrillas and militaries during the political conflicts of that decade. Including Costa Rican stories by Samuel Rovinski, Carmen Naranjo and Fabián Dobles.

Rima de Vallbona *Flowering Inferno: Tales of Sinking Hearts*. Slim volume of affecting short stories by one of Costa Rica's most respected (and widely translated) writers on social life, customs and – most poignantly, in the case of *Flowering Inferno* – the position of women.

Language

Language

Spanish

Although it is commonly said that everyone speaks **English** in Costa Rica, it is not really the case. Certainly, many who work in the tourist trade speak some English, and there are a number of expats who speak anything from English to German to Dutch, but the people you'll meet day to day are likely to speak only Spanish. The one area where you will hear English widely spoken is on the Caribbean coast, where many of the Afro-Caribbean inhabitants are of Jamaican descent, and speak a distinctive regional **Creole**.

If you want to get to know Costa Ricans, then it makes sense to acquire some **Spanish** before you arrive. Ticos are polite, patient and forgiving interlocutors, and will not only tolerate but appreciate any attempts you make to speak their language. The rules of **pronunciation** are pretty straightforward. Unless there's an accent, all words ending in "l", "r" and "z" are stressed on the last syllable, all others on the second last. Unlike in the rest of Latin America, in Costa Rica the final "d" in many words sometimes gets dropped; thus you'll hear "*usté*" for "*usted*" or "*¿verdá?*" for "*¿verdad?*" Other Costa Rican peculiarities are the "ll" and "r" sounds. All vowels are pure and short.

A somewhere between the A sound in "b**a**ck" and that in "f**a**ther".

E as in "g**e**t".

I as in "pol**i**ce".

O as in "h**o**t".

U as in "r**u**le".

C is soft before E and I, hard otherwise: *cerca* is pronounced "serka".

G works the same way: a guttural H sound (like the ch in "loch") before E or I, a hard G elsewhere: *gigante* becomes "higante".

H is always silent.

J the same sound as a guttural G: *jamón* is pronounced "hamon".

LL may be pronounced as a soft J (as in parts of Chile and Argentina) instead of Y: *ballena* (whale) becomes "bajzhena" instead of "bayena".

N is as in English, unless it has a tilde (accent) over it, when it becomes NY: *mañana* sounds like "manyana".

QU is pronounced like the English K.

R is not rolled Scottish burr-like as much as in other Spanish-speaking countries: *carro* is said "cahro", with a soft rather than a rolled R.

V sounds more like B: *vino* becomes "beano".

Z is the same as a soft C: *cerveza* is thus "servesa".

A Costa Rican dictionary

Miguel Ángel Quesada Pacheco **Nuevo diccionario de Costarriqueñismos**. An entertaining, illustrated dictionary of slang and *dichos* (sayings) for Spanish-speakers interested in understanding heavily argot-spiced spoken Costa Rican Spanish. It's a fascinating compendium, giving the regional location of word usage and sayings, what age group uses them and some etymology. It also reveals a wealth of localisms developed to describe local phenomena – witness, for example the number of different words for "wasp".

Useful expressions and vocabulary

Basics

Yes, No	Sí, No	**Open, Closed**	Abierto/a, Cerrado/a
Please	Por favor	**With, Without**	Con, Sin
Thank you	Gracias	**Good, Bad**	Buen(o)/a, Mal(o)/a
Where, When?	¿Dónde, Cuando?	**Big, Small**	Gran(de), Pequeño/a
What, How much?	¿Qué, Cuánto?	**More, Less**	Más, Menos
Here, There	Aquí, Allí	**Today, Tomorrow**	Hoy, Mañana
This, That	Este, Eso	**Yesterday**	Ayer
Now, Later	Ahora, Más tarde		

Greetings and responses

Hello, Goodbye	Hola, Adiós	**Do you speak English?**	¿Habla (usted) inglés?
Good morning	Buenos días	**I don't speak Spanish**	(No) Hablo español
Good afternoon/night	Buenas tardes/noches	**My name is...**	Me llamo...
See you later	Hasta luego	**What's your name?**	¿Como se llama usted?
Sorry	Lo siento/discúlpame	**I am American/English/Australian/New Zealander/South African**	Soy estadoudinense/inglés(a)/australiano(a)/nuevo(a) zelanda/africano del sur
Excuse me	Con permiso/perdón		
How are you?	¿Cómo está (usted)?		
I (don't) understand	(No) Entiendo		
What did you say?	¿Cómo?		
Not at all/You're welcome	De nada		

Needs and directions

I want	Quiero	**It's too expensive**	Es demasiado caro
I'd like	Quisiera	**Don't you have anything cheaper?**	¿No tiene algo más barato?
Do you know...?	¿Sabe...?	**Can one...?**	¿Se puede...?
I don't know	No sé	**...camp (near) here?**	¿...acampar (cerca de) aquí?
There is (is there?)	(¿)Hay(?)	**Is there a hotel near here?**	¿Hay un hotel cerca de aquí?
Give me...	Deme...	**How do I get to...?**	¿Como llega a...?
(one like that)	(uno así)	**Left, right, straight on**	Izquierda, derecha, derecho
Do you have...?	¿Tiene...?	**Where is...?**	¿Dónde está...?
...the time	...la hora	**...the bus station**	...el estación autobuses
...a room	...un cuarto	**...the nearest bank**	...el banco más cercano
...with two beds/	...con dos camas/	**...the post office**	...el correo
...double bed	...cama matrimonial	**...the toilet**	...el baño/servicio
It's for one person (two people)	Es para una persona (dos personas)		
...for one night	...para una noche		
(one week)	(una semana)		
It's fine, how much is it?	¿Está bien, cuánto es?		

Where does the bus to...leave from?	¿De dónde sale el autobus para...?
I'd like a (return) ticket to...	Quisiera un tiquete (de ida y vuelta) para...
What time does it leave (arrive in...)?	¿A qué hora sale (llega en...)?
What is there to eat?	¿Qué hay para comer?
What's that?	¿Qué es eso?
What's this called in Spanish?	¿Como se llama éste en español?

Useful accommodation terms

Ceiling fan	Abanico
Hot water	Agua caliente
Cold water	Agua fría
Air conditioned	Aire-acondicionado
Shared bath	Baño colectivo/ compartido
Double bed	Cama matrimonial
Single bed	Cama sencillo
Check-out time (usually 2pm)	Hora de salida
Taxes	Impuestos
Desk fan	Ventilador

Numbers, days and months

1	un/uno/una
2	dos
3	tres
4	cuatro
5	cinco
6	seis
7	siete
8	ocho
9	nueve
10	diez
11	once
12	doce
13	trece
14	catorce
15	quince
16	diez y seis
20	veinte
21	veintiuno
30	treinta
40	cuarenta
50	cincuenta
60	sesenta
70	setenta
80	ochenta
90	noventa
100	cien(to)
101	ciento uno
200	doscientos
201	doscientos uno
500	quinientos
1000	mil
2000	dos mil
1990	mil novocientos noventa
1991	...y uno
first	primero/a
second	segundo/a
third	tercero/a
Monday	lunes
Tuesday	martes
Wednesday	miércoles
Thursday	jueves
Friday	viernes
Saturday	sábado
Sunday	domingo
January	enero
February	febrero
March	marzo
April	abril
May	mayo
June	junio
July	julio
August	agosto
September	septiembre
October	octubre
November	noviembre
December	diciembre

A Costa Rican menu reader

Basics

Aceite Oil
Aceitunas Olives
Ajo ("al ajillo") Garlic (in garlic sauce)
Cebolla Onion
Cilantro Coriander
Frijoles Beans
Huevos Eggs
Leche Milk
Queso Cheese
Salsa Sauce

Meat (carne), fish (pescado) and seafood/shellfish (mariscos)

Atún Tuna
Bistec Steak
Cerdo Pork
Corvina Sea bass
Jamón Ham
Langosta Lobster
Lomito Cut of beef (filet mignon)
Pargo Red snapper
Trucha Trout

Fruits

Anona Custard fruit; sweet, thick ripe taste: one of the best fruits in the country
Carambola Starfruit
Cas Pale-flesh fruit with sweet-sour taste
Chinos Usually used for *refrescos*
Fresas Strawberries
Guanábana Soursop; very large green mottled fruit, with sweet white flesh tasting like a cross between a mango and a pear; mostly found on the Caribbean coast
Guayaba Guava; very sweet fruit, usually used for making spreads and jams
Limón Lemon
Mamones chinos Spiny-covered red or yellow fruits that look diabolical but reveal gently flavoured lychee-type fruit inside; somewhat like peeled green grapes, but sweeter and more fragrant. Usually sold in small bags of a dozen on street corners or buses
Maracuyá Passion fruit; small yellow fruits, sharp and sweet
Moras Blackberries
Naranja Orange
Papaya Papaya/pawpaw; large, round or oblong fruit with sweet orange flesh. Best eaten with fresh lime juice, and very good for stomach bugs
Pejibaye A Costa Rican speciality, you'll find this small green-orange fruit (known as the peach palm fruit) almost nowhere

else. Like its relative, the coconut, it grows in bunches on palm trees: the texture is unusual, as is the nutty flavour

Piña	Pineapple
Sandía	Watermelon
Tamarindo	A large pod of seeds, covered in a sticky, light-brown flesh; the unique taste – at once tart and sweet – is best first sampled in a *refresco*
Zapote	Large sweet orange fruit, with a dark-brown outer casing

Vegetables

Aguacate	Avocado
Chayote	Resembling a light-green avocado, this vegetable is tender and delicate when cooked, and excellent in stews and with meat and rice dishes
Fruta de pan	Breadfruit; eaten more as a starch substitute than a fruit
Hongos	Mushrooms
Palmito	Heart-of-palm; the inner core of palm trees, usually eaten in salads, with a somewhat bitter taste and fibrous texture
Plátanos	Plantains; eaten sweet
Zanahorias	Carrots

Typical dishes (platos)

Arreglados	Meat and mayonnaise sandwiches on greasy bread buns
Arroz…	Rice…
…con pollo	…with chicken
…con carne	…with meat
…con pescado	…with fish
…con mariscos	…with seafood
…con camarones	…with shrimps/ prawns
Bocas	Small snacks, usually eaten as an accompaniment to a beer
Casado	Plate of meat or fish, rice and salad, sometimes served with fried plantains
Ceviche	Raw fish, usually sea bass, "marinated" in lime juice, onions, chillies and coriander
Chicarrones	Fried pork rinds
Chilasquilas	Tortillas and beef with spices and battered eggs
Empanadas	Meat or vegetable patties
Frijoles molidos	Mashed black beans with onions, chilli peppers, coriander and thyme
Gallo pinto	"Painted rooster"; breakfast dish of rice and beans
Gallos	Small sandwiches
Pan de maíz	Corn bread; white rather than yellow
Picadillo	Potatoes cooked with beef and beans
Sopa negra	Black-bean soup with egg and vegetables
Tacos	Tortilla filled with beef or chicken, cabbage, tomatoes and mild chillies

Tamal	One of the best local specialities, usually consisting of maize flour, chicken or pork, olives, chillies and raisins all wrapped in a plantain leaf	**Tortilla**	Thin, small and bland bread, served as an accompaniment to meals and, especially in Guanacaste, breakfast

Desserts

Cajeta	Dessert made of milk, sugar, vanilla and sometimes coconut	**Queque seco**	Pound cake
Helado	Ice cream	**Tamal asado**	Cake made of corn flour, cream, eggs, sugar and butter
Milanes	Delicate chocolate fingers	**Tres leches**	Boiled milk and syrup-drenched cake
Queque	Cake		

Regional dishes

Caribbean		Guanacaste	
Pan bon	Sweet glazed bread with fruit and cheese	**Chorreados**	Corn pancakes
Patacones	Plantain chips, often served with frijoles molidos (see p.469)	**Horchata**	Hot drink made with corn or rice and flavoured with cinnamon
Rice and beans	Rice and beans cooked in coconut milk	**Natilla**	Sour cream
		Olla de carne	Rich, hearty meat stew
Rundown	Meat and vegetables stewed in coconut milk	**Pinolillo**	Milky corn drink
		Rosquillas	Corn doughnuts
		Tanelas	Scone-like corn snack

Idioms and slang

Costa Rican Spanish is a living language full of flux and argot. Local slang and usage are often referred to as **tiquismos** (from *Costarriqueñismos*, or Costa Ricanisms) or, as Costa Ricans will say when enlightening the foreigner as to their meaning, "*palabras muy ticas*". Some of the expressions and terms discussed below may be heard in other countries in the region, especially in Nicaragua and El Salvador, but still they are highly regional. Others are purely endemic, including *barbarismos* (bastardizations) and *provincialismos* (words particular to specific regions of Costa Rica).

The noun "Tico" used as a short form for Costa Rican comes less from a desire to shorten "Costarriquense" than from the traditional trend toward **diminution**, which is supposed to signal classlessness, eagerness to band together and desire not to cause offence. In Costa Rica, the common Spanish diminution of "ito" – applied as a suffix at the end of the word, as in "herman*ito*" ("little brother")

– often becomes "itico" ("herman*itico*"). That said, you hear the -ito or -itico endings less and less nowadays.

Costa Rican Spanish often displays an astounding **formality** that borders on servility. Instead of "*de nada*" ("you're welcome"), many Costa Ricans will say, "*para servirle*", which means, literally, "I'm here to serve you". When they meet you, Costa Ricans will say "*con mucho gusto*", "it's a pleasure", and you should do the same. Even when you leave people you do not know well, you will be told "*que le vaya bien*" ("may all go well with you").

Nicknames and a delight in the informal mix with a quite proper formal tone used in spoken Costa Rican Spanish. Nicknames centre on your most obvious physical characteristic: popular ones include *flaco/a* (thin); *gordo/a* (fat), and *macho/a* (light-skinned). Terms of endearment are also very current in popular speech; along with the ubiquitous *mi amor*, you may also get called *joven*, young one.

Intimate address

It's difficult to get your head round forms of **second-person address** in Costa Rica. Children are often spoken to in the "*usted*" form, which is technically formal and reserved for showing respect (in other Spanish-speaking countries, children are generally addressed as "*tu*"). Even friends who have known each other for years in Costa Rica will address each other as "*usted*". But the single most confounding irregularity of Costa Rican speech for those who already speak Spanish is the use of "**vos**" as personal intimate address – generally between friends of the same age. Many people on a short trip to the country never quite get to grips with it.

Now archaic, "vos" is only used widely in the New World in Argentina and Costa Rica. It has an interesting rhythm and sound, with verbs ending on a kind of diphthong-ized stress: *vos sabés*, *vos queres* (you know, you want), as opposed to *tu sabes/usted sabe* or *tu quieres/usted quiere*. If you are addressed in the "*vos*" form, it is a sign of friendship, and you should try to use it back if you can. It is an affront to use "*vos*" improperly, with someone you don't know well, when it can be seen as being patronizing. Again, Costa Ricans are good-hearted in this respect, however, and put errors down to the fact that you are a foreigner.

Everyday expressions

Here are some everyday **peculiarities** that most visitors to Costa Rica will become familiar with pretty quickly:

¡achará! expression of regret: "what a pity", like "*¡qué lástima!*"

adiós "hi", used primarily in the *campo* (country) when greeting someone on the road or street. Confusingly, as in the rest of Latin America, *adiós* is also "goodbye", but only if you are going away for a long time.

¿diay? slightly melancholic interjection in the vein of "ah, but what can you expect?"

fatal reserved for the absolutely worst possible eventuality: "*esta carretera para Golfito es fatal*" means "the road to Golfito is the very worst".

feo literally "ugly", but can also mean rotten or lousy, as in "*Todos los caminos en Costa Rica están muy feos*" ("All the roads in Costa Rica are in really bad shape").

maje literally "dummy", used between young men as an affirmation of their friendship/maleness: it's used like "buddy, pal" (US) or "mate" (UK). There is no equivalent for women, unfortunately.

pura vida perhaps the best-known *tiquismo*, meaning "great", "OK" or "cool".

que mala/buena nota expression of disapproval/approval – "how uncool/great".

Luck and God

Both **luck** and **God** come into conversation often in Costa Rica. Thus, you get the pattern:

"¿Cómo amaneció?"	"How did you sleep?" (Literally, "how did you wake up?")
"Muy bien, por dicha, ¿y usted?"	"Very well, fortunately, and you?"
"Muy bien, gracias a Dios."	"Very well, thank God."

Also, you will hear *dicha* and *Dios* used in situations that seem to have not much to do with luck or divine intervention: "*¡Qué dicha que usted llegó!*" ("What luck that you arrived!"), along with such phrases as "*Vamos a la playa esta fin de semana, si Dios quiere*" ("We'll go to the beach this weekend, God willing"). Even a shrug of the shoulders elicits a "*¡Dios sabe!*" "God only knows." And the usual forms "*hasta luego*" or "*hasta la vista*" become in Costa Rica the much more God-fearing "*Que Dios le acompañe*" ("may God go with you").

"Where is your boyfriend?"

"*¿Dónde está su novio?/padres?*" ("Where is your boyfriend/family?") is a query women, especially those travelling alone, will hear often. **Family** is very important in explaining to many Costa Ricans who you are and where you come from, and people will place you by asking how many brothers and sisters you have, where your family (*padres*) lives, whether your grandmother (*abuela*) is still alive… It's a good idea to get to grips with the following:

madre/padre	mother/father
abuelo/abuela	grandfather/grandmother
hijo/hija	son/daughter
hermano/hermana	brother/sister
tío/tía	uncle/aunt
primo/prima	cousin

Glossary

abastecedor a general store, usually in a rural area or *barrio* (neighbourhood) that keeps a stock of groceries and basic toiletries.

agringarse (verb) to adopt the ways of the gringos.

agua potable drinking water.

aguacero downpour.

ahorita "right now" (any time within the coming hour).

area de acampar camping area.

area restringido restricted area.

bárbaro fantastic, cool (literally "barbaric").

barrio neighbourhood (usually urban).

bomba petrol station.

botica pharmacy.

burro can refer to the animal (donkey), but is usually an adjective denoting "really big", as in "*vea este bicho sí burro*": "come see this really big insect".

campesino peasant farmer, smallholder.

campo literally countryside, but more often in Costa Rica "space", as in "seat" when travelling. Thus, "*¿Hay un campo en este autobus?*": "is there a (free) seat on this bus?"

cantina bar, usually patronized by the working class or rural labouring class.

capa rain gear, poncho.

carro car (not *coche*, as in Spain).

cazadora literally, huntress; a beaten-up old schoolbus that serves as public transport in rural areas.

chance widely used Anglicism to denote chance, or opportunity; like *oportunidad*.

chiquillos kids; also *chiquititos, chiquiticos*.

chivo cute.

chorreador sack-and-metal coffee-filter contraption, still widely used.

choteo quick-witted sarcasm, something Costa Ricans admire, provided it's not too sharp-tongued.

colectivo An open-back truck used as a form of public transport in some rural, remote areas such as the Osa Peninsula.

conchos yokels, hicks from the sticks.

cordillera mountain range.

correo post office.

dando cuerda colloquial expression meaning, roughly, to "make eyes at", in an approximation of sexual interest (men to women, hardly ever the other way around).

entrada entrance.

evangélico usually refers to anyone who is of a religion other than Catholic, but particularly Protestant even if they are not evangelical. Such religions are also called *cultos*, belying a general wariness and disapproval for anything other than Catholicism.

finca farm or plantation.

finquero coffee grower.

foco flashlight/torch.

galletas biscuits.

gambas buttresses, the giant above-ground roots that some rainforest trees put out.

gaseosa fizzy drink.

gasolina petrol.

gringo not-at-all pejorative term for a North American. A European is usually *europeo*.

guaca pre-Columbian burial ground or tomb.

güila child.

güisqui whisky (usually bad unless imported, and astronomically expensive).

hacienda big farm, usually a ranch.

hospedaje very basic *pensión*.

humilde humble, simple; an appearance and quality that is widely respected.

ICE Instituto Costarricense de Electricidad, the country's principal telecommunications provider.

ICT Instituto Costarricense de Turismo, the national tourist board.

indígena an indigenous person; preferred term among indigenous groups in Costa Rica, rather than the less polite *índio* (Indian).

invierno winter (May–Nov).

jornaleros day labourers, usually landless peasants who are paid by the day, for instance to pick coffee in season.

mal educado literally, badly educated; a gentle if effective insult, especially useful for women harassed by hissing, leering men.

malecón seaside promenade.

marimba type of large xylophone played mainly in Guanacaste. Also refers to the style of music.

mestizo person of mixed race indigenous/Spanish; not usually pejorative.

metate pre-Columbian stone table used for grinding corn, especially by the Chorotega people of Guanacaste. Many of the archeological finds in Costa Rica are metates.

MINAE the ministry in charge of the national parks system.

mirador lookout or viewing platform.

morenos offensive term for Afro-Caribbeans. The best term to use is *negros* or *Limonenses*.

muelle dock.

Neotrópicos Neotropics: tropics of the New World.

Nica Nicaraguan, from *Nicaragüense*.

palenque a thatched-roofed longhouse inhabited by indigenous people; more or less equivalent to the Native American longhouse.

pasear to be on vacation/holiday; literally, to be passing through.

peón farm labourer, usually landless.

personaje someone of importance, a VIP, although usually used pejoratively to indicate someone who is putting on airs.

PLA National Liberation Party, the dominant political party.

precarista squatter.

puesto post (ranger post or ranger station).

pulpería general store or corner store. Also sometimes serves cooked food and drinks.

purrujas spectacularly annoying, tiny biting insects encountered in lowland areas.

PUSC Social Christian Unity Party, the opposition party-of-the-moment.

rancho palm-thatched roof, also smallholding.

redondel de toros bullring, not used for bullfighting but for local rodeos.

refresco drink, usually made with fresh fruit or water; sometimes a fizzy drink, although this is most often called *gaseosa*.

regalar (verb) usually to give, as in to give a present, but in Costa Rica the usual command or request of "*deme uno de estos*" ("give me one of those"), becomes "*regáleme*". Thus "*¿regáleme un cafecito, por favor?*": "could you give me a coffee?".

rejas security grille, popularly known in English as The Cage: the iron grille you see around all but the most humble dwellings in an effort to discourage burglary.

sabanero Costa Rican cowboy.

salida exit.

sendero trail.

soda cafeteria or diner; in the rest of Central America, it's usually called a *comedor*.

temporada season: *la temporada de lluvia* is the rainy season.

temporales early-morning rains in the wet season (mainly in the Valle Central).

terreno land, small farm.

UCR Universidad de Costa Rica (in San Pedro, San José).

UNA Universidad Nacional (in Heredia).

verano summer (Dec–April).

Travel store

NOTES

Small print and

Index

A Rough Guide to Rough Guides

Published in 1982, the first Rough Guide – to Greece – was a student scheme that became a publishing phenomenon. Mark Ellingham, a recent graduate in English from Bristol University, had been travelling in Greece the previous summer and couldn't find the right guidebook. With a small group of friends he wrote his own guide, combining a highly contemporary, journalistic style with a thoroughly practical approach to travellers' needs.

The immediate success of the book spawned a series that rapidly covered dozens of destinations. And, in addition to impecunious backpackers, Rough Guides soon acquired a much broader and older readership that relished the guides' wit and inquisitiveness as much as their enthusiastic, critical approach and value-for-money ethos.

These days, Rough Guides include recommendations from shoestring to luxury and cover more than 200 destinations around the globe, including almost every country in the Americas and Europe, more than half of Africa and most of Asia and Australasia. Our ever-growing team of authors and photographers is spread all over the world, particularly in Europe, the US and Australia.

In the early 1990s, Rough Guides branched out of travel, with the publication of Rough Guides to World Music, Classical Music and the Internet. All three have become benchmark titles in their fields, spearheading the publication of a wide range of books under the Rough Guide name.

Including the travel series, Rough Guides now number more than 350 titles, covering: phrasebooks, waterproof maps, music guides from Opera to Heavy Metal, reference works as diverse as Conspiracy Theories and Shakespeare, and popular culture books from iPods to Poker. Rough Guides also produce a series of more than 120 World Music CDs in partnership with World Music Network.

Visit www.roughguides.com to see our latest publications.

Rough Guide credits

Text editor: Mandy Tomlin
Layout: Anita Singh
Cartography: Jasbir Sandhu
Picture editor: Rhiannon Furbear
Production: Rebecca Short
Proofreader: Karen Parker
Cover design: Nicole Newman, Dan May, Sarah Cummins
Photographer: Greg Roden
Editorial: **London** Andy Turner, Keith Drew, Edward Aves, Alice Park, Lucy White, Jo Kirby, James Smart, Natasha Foges, James Rice, Emma Beatson, Emma Gibbs, Kathryn Lane, Monica Woods, Mani Ramaswamy, Harry Wilson, Lucy Cowie, Alison Roberts, Lara Kavanagh, Eleanor Aldridge, Ian Blenkinsop, Charlotte Melville, Joe Staines, Matthew Milton, Tracy Hopkins; **Delhi** Madhavi Singh, Jalpreen Kaur Chhatwal
Design & Pictures: **London** Scott Stickland, Dan May, Diana Jarvis, Mark Thomas, Nicole Newman, Sarah Cummins; **Delhi** Umesh Aggarwal, Ajay Verma, Jessica Subramanian, Ankur Guha, Pradeep Thapliyal, Sachin Tanwar, Nikhil Agarwal, Sachin Gupta
Production: Liz Cherry, Louise Minihane, Erika Pepe
Cartography: **London** Ed Wright, Katie Lloyd-Jones; **Delhi** Rajesh Chhibber, Ashutosh Bharti, Rajesh Mishra, Animesh Pathak, Swati Handoo, Deshpal Dabas, Lokamata Sahu
Marketing, Publicity & roughguides.com: Liz Statham
Digital Travel Publisher: Peter Buckley
Reference Director: Andrew Lockett
Operations Coordinator: Becky Doyle
Operations Assistant: Johanna Wurm
Publishing Director (Travel): Clare Currie
Commercial Manager: Gino Magnotta
Managing Director: John Duhigg

Publishing information

This sixth edition published September 2011 by

Rough Guides Ltd,
80 Strand, London WC2R 0RL
11, Community Centre, Panchsheel Park, New Delhi 110017, India

Distributed by the Penguin Group

Penguin Books Ltd,
80 Strand, London WC2R 0RL

Penguin Group (USA)
375 Hudson Street, NY 10014, USA

Penguin Group (Australia)
250 Camberwell Road, Camberwell, Victoria 3124, Australia

Penguin Group (NZ)
67 Apollo Drive, Mairangi Bay, Auckland 1310, New Zealand

Rough Guides is represented in Canada by Tourmaline Editions Inc. 662 King Street West, Suite 304, Toronto, Ontario M5V 1M7

Cover concept by Peter Dyer.

Typeset in Bembo and Helvetica to an original design by Henry Iles.

Printed in Singapore

496pp includes index
A catalogue record for this book is available from the British Library
ISBN: 978-1-84836-906-1

1 3 5 7 9 8 6 4 2

Help us update

We've gone to a lot of effort to ensure that the sixth edition of **The Rough Guide to Costa Rica** is accurate and up-to-date. However, things change – places get "discovered", opening hours are notoriously fickle, restaurants and rooms raise prices or lower standards. If you feel we've got it wrong or left something out, we'd like to know, and if you can remember the address, the price, the hours, the phone number, so much the better.

Please send your comments with the subject line "**Rough Guide Costa Rica Update**" to ⓔmail@uk.roughguides.com. We'll credit all contributions and send a copy of the next edition (or any other Rough Guide if you prefer) for the very best emails.

Find more travel information, connect with fellow travellers and book your trip on ⓦwww.roughguides.com

Acknowledgements

Keith would like to send a grateful *muchas gracias* to: Sarah Wilson; George Schwarzenbach; Sherill Broudy and Marcela Arias; Jonathan Saborio; Andrew, Emma and Elisa; Rebecca Zúñiga; Diana Salas; Andy and Connie; Alejandro Solano; Jana Daigle; Teri Jampol; Beatriz and Leo; Luis Carlos Ulloa and Kenneth Alfaro; Andrea and Giovanna Holbrook; Helen Rodríguez; Gabriela Elizondo; Geovanny Soto Ruiz; Melania López Herrera; Juan Sostheim; Dan Siegel; Natalie Ewing and Valentin Corral; Mia Roberts; Alexandra Espinosa; Moraya Iacono; Bruce Smith; Jonny Alvarado; Hans Pfister and Danny Porras; Chris Paul; Richard Lemire; Claudio Morris; and the countless other Ticos who pitched in with words of wisdom and advice along the way. Thanks, too, to Steve, for trading tips and his continued commitment; the excellent team at Rough Guides, especially to Mani, for backing me; Anita, for tight typesetting; Jasbir and Katie, for map magic; Rhiannon, for sourcing some superb images; and to Mandy, for considerate editing and unflappable problem-solving. Most of all, though, a huge and heartfelt squeezy hug to Family Drew: to Kate, for her love, courage and unwavering support; to Maisie, for charming everyone she met and for embracing Costa Rican life like only a two-year-old can; and to Joe, who was there in spirit and who I look forward to sharing many jungle adventures with over the coming years.

Steven would like to thank Amanda for her adroit editing and for steering the project so steadily. Thanks as well to Keith for his enthusiasm and support along the way. In Costa Rica thanks to all those who provided invaluable information and assistance, including Offi, Ballardo Diaz, Mariana, Rocio López, Mayra Güell, Rick Vogel, Terry Lillian Newton, Chris and Charlie Foerster, Nichole DuPont, Terri and Mark Lovis, and the guides of Jinetes de Osa. Lastly, thank you to the Rough Guides crew in the Delhi and London offices whose skill and hard work made this edition possible.

ROUGH GUIDES

SMALL PRINT

Readers' letters

Thanks to all the readers who have taken the time to write in with comments and suggestions (and apologies if we've inadvertently omitted or misspelt anyone's name):

Kristin Adams; Brenna Aileo; Pamela Arroyo; Lisette Beljon; Cedric Brown; Emma Bunning; Ana and Pablo Céspedes; Heather Curran; Ruth Deiseroth-Kweton; John L. M. Denham; Elissa Dennis; Nicol M. Diamond; Alana Duggan and Geoff Polci; Rosemary Emmett; Frances Figart; Arnold Flather; Jessica Forte; Viviana Gutierrez; Barbara H. and Theresa McCarthy; Carlos Lopez; Rika Manzur; Johanna Marin; Kyra Cruz Meyer; Tra and Penny McPeak; Paul Moll; Luis Alberto Sanchez Montero; Pablo Padrutt; Marc Roegiers; Gabriela Sanchéz; Roberta Ward Smiley and Daniel Spreen Wilson; Kirsten Smith; Chris Starr; Razia Tajuddin; and Larissa Veldhorst.

Photo credits

All photos © Rough Guides except the following:

Introduction

Surfers perched on a fallen trunk © Bruno Ehrs/Corbis
Hanging Bridges Trail, Arenal © John Coletti/AWL
Keel-billed toucan © Tom Ulrich/Getty
Clearwing butterfly © Gail Shumway/Getty
Arenal volcano © Oliver Gerhard/Superstock
White-faced capuchin monkeys © Wolfgang Kaehler/Superstock

Things not to miss

01 Hiker, Corcovado National Park © Michael Robertson/Alamy
02 Santa Rosa National Park © Nick Turner/Alamy
03 Green turtle hatchling © Kevin Schafer/Getty
04 Arenal Volcano erupting at night © Schafer & Hill/Getty
08 Community tourism © ACTUAR
09 Caño Negro © Keith Drew/Rough Guides
10 Sport-fishing in Drake Bay © CarverMostardi/Alamy
11 Volunteering © Rancho Margot
14 *El Silencio* eco-lodge © El Silencio Lodge
15 Scarlet macaws arguing © Marco Simoni/Getty
19 Carnival, Puerto Limón © Axiom Photographic Limited/Superstock
21 Poás Volcano © Radius Images/Getty
22 Surfing at Santa Teresa, Nicoya Peninsula © Yadid Levy/Alamy
23 Cafe Britt © Stefano Paterna/Alamy
24 Mudpots © Costa Rica Photos - www.costaricaphotos.com
25 Local house, Tortuguero © Martin Bache/Alamy

The wildlife of Costa Rica colour section

Spider monkey © Kevin Schafer/Corbis
White-faced capuchin monkey © Kevin Schafer/Getty
Squirrel monkey © Lars-Olof Johansson/Naturbild/Corbis
Hoffman's two-toed sloth © Tom Brakefield/Getty
Brown-throated sloth © DEA/C. DANI-I. JESKE/Getty
Kinkajou © Tom Brakefield/Corbis
Tamandua © Michael & Patricia Fogden/Corbis
White-nosed coati © David W. Middleton/SuperStock
Agouti © Mary Ann McDonald/Corbis
Baird's tapir © Thomas Marent,/Visuals Unlimited/Corbis
Leatherback turtle © Kennan Ward/Corbis
Hawksbill turtle © Visuals Unlimited/Corbis
Olive ridley turtle © age fotostock/SuperStock
Spectacled caiman © Schafer & Hill/Getty
Green iguana © Tony Waltham/Getty
Spiny-tailed iguana © Adrian Hepworth/Nhpa/Photoshot
Emerald basilisk © Costa Rica Photos - www.costaricaphotos.com
Fer-de-lance snake © Michael & Patricia Fogden/Corbis
Bushmaster © Michael & Patricia Fogden/Corbis
Red-eyed tree frog © Paul Souders/Corbis
Fleischmann's glass frog © Michael & Patricia Fogden/Corbis
Strawberry poison-dart frog © Paul Souders/Corbis
Boat-billed heron © Rick & Nora Bowers /Alamy
Roseate spoonbill © John Cornell/Visuals Unlimited/Corbis
Black vulture © Adrian Hepworth/Nhpa
Northern jacana © Costa Rica Photos - www.costaricaphotos.com
Scarlet macaw © Marco Simoni/Getty
Violet sabrewing © Juan Carlos Ulate/Reuters/Corbis
Green hermit © imagebroker.net/SuperStock
Violaceous trogon © James Carmichael Jr/Nhpa/Photoshot
Resplendent quetzal © Panoramic Images/Getty
Blue-crowned motmot © Eric and David Hosking/Corbis
Chestnut-mandibled toucan © Reed Kaestner/Corbis
Great kiskadee © Glenn Bartley/All Canada Photos/Corbis
Three-wattled bellbird © Oyvind Martinsen/Alamy
Red-capped manakin © Marie Read/Nhpa

Adventure travel colour section

Man surfing on Playa Santa Teresa © Christian Aslund/Getty
Man rappelling © Randy Faris/Corbis
White-water rafting, Pacuare River © Marco Simoni/Robert Harding World Imagery/Getty
Bungee jumper © Marco Simoni/Getty
Woman climbing waterfall © Flirt/Superstock
Shoal of Moorish idols, Cocos Island © Norbert Probst/Superstock
Hammerhead shark © Jeremy Stafford-Deitsch/Oceans Image/Photoshot
Tourists at Cerro Chirripó © Adrian Hepworth/Nhpa

Black and white

p.122 Orosí Church © Costa Rica Photos - www.costaricaphotos.com
p.214 Volcán Arenal © Costa Rica Photos - www.costaricaphotos.com
p.256 Leatherback turtle © Photoshot
p.376 Cerro Chirripó © Costa Rica Photos - www.costaricaphotos.com

Index

Map entries are in colour.

H

I

J

K

L

M

N

INDEX

T

U

V

W

Y

Z

Map symbols

maps are listed in the full index using coloured text

- International boundary
- Chapter division boundary
- Carretera
- Major road
- Minor road
- Unpaved road
- Footpath
- Wall
- Railway
- Coastline/river
- Ferry route
- Point of interest
- Peak
- Viewpoint
- Rocks
- Ranger station
- Domestic airport
- International airport
- Waterfall
- Volcano
- Springs
- Ruins/archeological site
- Hills
- Gardens
- Museum
- Campsite
- Gate
- Accommodation
- Bus stop
- Internet cafe
- Parking
- Toilets
- Tourist office
- Post office
- Hospital
- Bank
- Fuel station
- Bridge
- Market
- Stadium
- Building
- Church
- Cemetery
- Park
- Swamp
- Beach